Merriam-Webster's Rhyming Dictionary

Merriam-Webster's
Rhyming Dictionary

MERRIAM-WEBSTER, INCORPORATED
Springfield, Massachusetts, U.S.A.

A GENUINE MERRIAM-WEBSTER

The name *Webster* alone is no guarantee of excellence. It is used by a number of publishers and may serve mainly to mislead an unwary buyer.

Merriam-Webster™ is the name you should look for when you consider the purchase of dictionaries or other fine reference books. It carries the reputation of a company that has been publishing since 1831 and is your assurance of quality and authority.

ISBN 0-87779-913-X

MADE IN THE UNITED STATES OF AMERICA

11QP/B02

PREFACE

Merriam-Webster's Rhyming Dictionary is a listing of words grouped according to the way they rhyme. All of the words are drawn from *Merriam-Webster's Collegiate Dictionary, Tenth Edition*, and decisions about what constitutes a rhyming group are based on pronunciations given in that dictionary. In selecting words for entry, the editors have focused on words that are most likely to be used in poetry; highly technical or otherwise obscure words are generally not included. However, some words that are restricted in their applications (such as slang words and words that carry a stigmatizing usage label or usage note in *Merriam-Webster's Collegiate Dictionary*) as well as words that are likely to be unfamiliar to many users have been included. Thus, not every word listed in this book will be appropriate in every context and *it is essential that the rhyming dictionary be used in conjunction with an adequate dictionary.*

The editors have assigned words to rhyming groups on the basis of pronunciations that are in standard and widespread use. However, many words have more than one standard pronunciation, and these variants often produce alternate rhyming sounds. Thus, some words may appear in more than one list, and not every word on every list will rhyme for every person.

Users of this book who are uncertain about any aspect of meaning, usage status, or pronunciation of any word listed here should consult the entry for that word in *Merriam-Webster's Collegiate Dictionary, Tenth Edition*.

The rhyming sound Words in this book are gathered into entries on the basis of their rhyming sound. The rhyming sound is the terminal part of the word — from the vowel sound in the last stressed syllable to the end of the word. In this book, the rhyming sound may have one, two, or three syllables. One-syllable rhyming sounds are found in one-syllable words and in words in which primary or secondary stress falls on the final syllable. For example, **wide** \ˈwīd\, **appeal** \ə-ˈpēl\, **mongoose** \ˈmän-ˌgüs\, and **undergrad** \ˈən-dər-ˌgrad\ all have one-syllable rhyming sounds. For *wide*, the rhyming sound is \īd\, as in *bedside* and *qualified*. For *appeal*, it is \ēl\, as in *heal* and *cockatiel*. For *mongoose*, it is \üs\, as in *juice* and *introduce*. For *undergrad*, it is \ad\, as in *plaid* and *comrade*.

Two-syllable rhyming sounds are found in words in which the last syllable with primary or secondary stress is the next-to-last syllable in the word (often called the penultimate syllable or penult). For example, *cola* \ˈkō-lə\ and *remover* \rē-ˈmü-vər\ have two-syllable rhyming sounds. For *cola*, the rhyming sound is \ō-lə\, as in *granola* and *Gorgonzola*. For *remover*, it is \ü-vər\, as in *louver* and *maneuver*.

Three-syllable rhyming sounds are found in words in which the syllable before the penult (the antepenultimate syllable or antepenult) carries primary or secondary stress. For example, *mutable* \ˈmüt-ə-bəl\ and *frivolity* \friv-ˈäl-ət-ē\ have three-syllable rhyming sounds. For *mutable*, it is \üt-ə-bəl\, as in *suitable* and *unscrutable*. For *frivolity*, it is \äl-ət-ē\, as in *jollity* and *equality*.

Using this book *Merriam-Webster's Rhyming Dictionary* is designed to be used with a minimum of instruction. In order to use this book successfully, the reader needs to understand the following four points:

1. All of the words in this book are gathered into main entries on the basis of their rhyming sounds.
2. All of the main entries are arranged according to the way the rhyming sound is most often spelled, represented by the boldface form that begins each main entry.
3. Alternate spellings of the rhyming sound are entered as cross-reference entries that direct the user to the appropriate main entry. The alternate spelling is the boldface form that begins each cross-reference entry.
4. All main entries and cross-reference entries, whether for one-, two-, or three-syllable rhyming sounds, are alphabetized by the boldface form in a single sequence.

To find a rhyme for a given word, then, you need to know only the spelling of the word and its rhyming sound. If, for instance, you wanted to find a word to rhyme with *deep*, you would look up *eep*, because that is the way the rhyming sound is spelled. When you look up *eep*, you will find the following entry:

> **eep** \ēp\ beep, bleep, cheap, cheep,
> clepe, creep, deep, heap, jeep,
> Jeep, keep, . . .

If the word you wanted to find a rhyme for had been *cheap*, you might have looked up *eap*, because that is how the rhyming sound is spelled in that word. If you had done so, you would have found the following cross-reference entry:

eap \ēp\ see EEP

In some cases (explained in more detail later in this Preface), you may find two entries for the same spelling. If, for instance, you wanted a rhyme for *give*, you would have found the following entries at *ive*:

[1]**ive** \īv\ chive, dive, drive, five,
gyve, hive, I've, jive, . . .
[2]**ive** \iv\give, live, sheave, shiv,
sieve, spiv, forgive, . . .
[3]**ive** \ēv\ see [1]EAVE

In cases like this, you would look at the pronunciation given in the entry. The rhyming sound in *give* is \iv\, and the pronunciation given at [2]*ive* is \iv\; therefore the entry [2]*ive* is the appropriate one.

The following sections of this Preface discuss in detail the major features of this book. A careful reading of these sections will ensure that the user gets the maximum benefit from this book.

Main entries Main entries consist of three principal elements: an entry form, a pronunciation, and a list of words that rhyme:

arten \ärt-ᵊn\ Barton, carton,
hearten, marten, martin, Martin,
smarten, Spartan, tartan, baum
marten, dishearten, Dumbarton,
freemartin, Saint Martin, Sint
Maarten, kindergarten

The main entry form in this entry is **arten**. It represents the way the rhyming sound is most often spelled. When two or more spellings are used with virtually equal frequency, the editors have chosen one arbitrarily to be the main entry form.

The rhyming sound itself is \ärt-ᵊn\, as shown in pronunciation symbols which appear within reversed virgules following the entry word. These symbols are listed and explained beginning on page xii. The pronunciations include no stress marks; the reader is meant to understand that the first syllable in the pronunciation is the last stressed syllable in the word. The pronunciation is given for identification purposes only; that is, it is meant to help the user confirm that the entry includes words with the desired rhyming sound. Each entry includes only one pronunciation even though there may be more than one way to pronounce the main entry form. Users who wish to find alternate pronunciations of a word in the list can consult the entry for that word in *Merriam-Webster's Collegiate Dictionary, Tenth Edition.* Following the pronunciation is the list of words that share the rhyming sound. The words are arranged by the number of syllables: the words with the fewest syllables are listed first, followed by groups of words with successively more syllables. Groups of words having the same number of syllables are arranged alphabetically. In the list in the sample entry shown above, *Barton, carton, hearten, marten, martin, Martin, smarten, Spartan*, and *tartan*, each with two syllables, come first. They are followed by *baum marten, dishearten, Dumbarton, freemartin, Saint Martin*, and *Sint Maarten*, with three syllables, and *kindergarten*, with four syllables.

Cross-reference entries Main entries in this book are supplemented by cross-reference entries. Like main entries, cross-reference entries have an entry form and a pronunciation, but in place of a list of rhyming words, cross-reference entries provide a note that directs the user to a main entry where the list of rhyming words can be found. The following cross-reference entries, for instance, send the reader to the entry **arten** shown as a sample earlier:

> **artin** \ärt-ᵊn\ see ARTEN
> **aarten** \ärt-ᵊn\ see ARTEN

The entry form in a cross-reference entry represents an alternate spelling of the rhyming sound. In the sample entries above, the cross-reference entries **artin** and **aarten** have been included because the spellings *-artin* and *-aarten* are represented by the words *freemartin* and *Sint Maarten*, respectively. A cross-reference entry has been included for every alternate spelling of a rhyming sound that is represented by one or more words in the list at the main entry.

The pronunciation in the cross-reference entry matches the pronunciation shown at the main entry. The pronunciation is provided to help the user confirm that the cross-reference leads to the desired main entry, which is shown in small capital letters.

Identification numbers In some cases, the same spelling has been used to represent more than one rhyme and therefore appears as a main entry form more than once.

[1]**age** \äj\ dodge, lodge, raj, stodge, wodge, barrage, collage, corsage, dislodge, garage, hodgepodge, Karaj, massage, swaraj, camouflage, espionage, counterespionage
[2]**age** \äzh\ plage, assuage, barrage, collage, corsage, dressage, frottage, gavage, lavage, massage, ménage, mirage, montage, moulage, . . .
[3]**age** \āj\ age, cage, gage, Gage, gauge, mage, page, rage, sage, stage, swage, wage, assuage, backstage, birdcage, broad-gauge, downstage, . . .
[4]**age** \āg\ see [1]EG
[5]**age** \āzh\ see [1]EIGE
[6]**age** \äg-ə\ see [1]AGA

In order to alert users whenever this situation occurs, identification numbers (in the form of small raised numerals that precede the entry form) have been added to all identically spelled entry forms. In order to assist readers in following cross-references, identification numbers also appear as part of the cross-reference when necessary.

aj \äj\ see [1]AGE
itey \īt-ē\ see [2]ITE

Inflected and derived forms In order to save space, most regular inflected forms of words have not been included in the lists of rhymes. For example, there is no entry **eaks** to cover words such as *beaks, cheeks, cliques*, and *antiques*. In order to find a rhyme for these words, the user needs to go to the entry for the base word (in this case [1]**eak** \ēk\) and look for words on the list that will take the inflection that creates the desired rhyming sound.

In some cases, both inflected and noninflected forms share the same rhyming sounds. For example, the uninflected forms *lox* and *paradox* share the same rhyming sound with the inflected forms *docks* and *socks*. In such cases, all of the uninflected forms are listed at the entry for the rhyming sound. At the end of the list, an italicized note appears telling the user that additional rhymes exist and giving directions to the entry where the base words can be found:

> **ox** \äks\ box, cox, fox, . . . *—also plurals and possessives of nouns and third person singular presents of verbs listed at* ¹OCK

Such notes have been added whenever two or more rhyming words could be created by adding inflections to the base words at the entry. If only one such rhyme could be created, it has simply been added to the list.

The particular inflected forms that are covered by these notes are plurals and possessives of nouns, comparatives and superlatives of adjectives, and past tense and third person singular present tense forms of verbs. In addition, present participles of verbs are covered at entries where the spelling of the entry form (after the *-ing* ending has been removed and any elided *e* or doubled consonant has been taken into account) does not match the spelling of the entry for the base words:

> **aining** \ā-niŋ\veining, complaining, sustaining, . . . *—also present participles of verbs listed at* ¹ANE

The treatment of words derived by adding a suffix to another word is somewhat similar. There is no entry for a rhyming sound if all of the words that would be on the list are regular derived words formed by adding a suffix to words drawn from another list. This treatment applies mostly to adverbs ending in *-ly*, nouns ending in *-ness* or *-ment*, and adjectives ending in *-less*. For instance, there is no entry for **arkly** \ärk-lē\, because the only words on the list would be *darkly* and *starkly*, and they are both formed by adding an *-ly* ending to the adjectives found at the entry **ark** \ärk\. If, however, any of the words on the list are not derived forms, a complete list is entered. There is an entry at **¹eanly** \ēn-lē\, for instance, because among the adverbs at the entry there is also the adjective *queenly*; and, for the purposes of this book, adjectives ending in *-ly* are not treated as regular derived forms.

Editorial acknowledgements Like all Merriam-Webster publications, *Merriam-Webster's Rhyming Dictionary* is the product of a collective effort. It draws much of its material from *Webster's Compact Rhyming Dictionary*, and as such, is based on work done by the editors of that book. The updating and expanding of that earlier work was done by Dr. Mary Wood Cornog. Copyediting of the text was the responsibility of Katherine Chapekis Sietsema, Assistant Editor. Cross-reference of the book was done by Adrienne M. Scholz, Editorial Assistant. Data-entry work was accomplished by Florence A. Fowler. Jennifer N. Cislo and Peter D. Haraty, both Assistant Editors, were responsible for proofreading. Robert D. Copeland, Senior Editor, managed the book through its typesetting stages. Overall project coordination was provided by John M. Morse, Vice President and Executive Editor.

PRONUNCIATION SYMBOLS

ə . . . . . banana, collide, abut

ᵊ . . . . . immediately preceding \l\ and \n\, as in battle, mitten, and eaten; immediately following \l\, \m\, \r\, as often in French table, prisme, titre

ər . . . . . further, merger, bird

a . . . . . mat, map, mad, gag, snap, patch

ā . . . . . day, fade, date, aorta, drape, cape

ä . . . . . bother, cot

au̇ . . . . . now, loud, out

b . . . . . baby, rib

ch . . . . . chin, nature \ˈnā-chər\ (actually, this sound is \t\ + \sh\)

d . . . . . did, adder

e . . . . . bet, bed, peck

ē . . . . . fee, easy

f . . . . . fifty, cuff

g . . . . . go, big, gift

h . . . . . hat, ahead

i . . . . . tip, banish, active

ī . . . . . site, side, buy, tripe (actually, this sound is \ä\ + \i\)

j . . . . . job, gem, edge, join, judge (actually, this sound is \d\ + \zh\)

k . . . . . kin, cook, ache

k̲ . . . . . German ich, Buch; one pronunciation of loch

l . . . . . lily, pool

m . . . . . murmur, dim, nymph

n . . . . . no, own

ⁿ . . . . . indicates that a preceding vowel or diphthong is pronounced with the nasal passages open, as in French *un bon vin blanc* \œⁿ-bōⁿ-vaⁿ-bläⁿ\

ŋ . . . . . sing \ˈsiŋ\, singer \ˈsiŋ-ər\, finger \ˈfiŋ-gər\, ink \ˈiŋk\

ō . . . . . bone, know, beau

ȯ . . . . . . saw, all, gnaw, caught

ȯi . . . . . . coin, destroy

p . . . . . . pepper, lip

r . . . . . . red, car, rarity

s . . . . . . source, less

sh . . . . . . as in shy, mission, machine, special (actually, this is a single sound, not two); with a hyphen between, two sounds as in *grasshopper* \ˈgras-ˌhäp-ər\

t . . . . . . tie, attack, late, latter

th . . . . . . as in thin, ether (actually, this is a single sound, not two); with a hyphen between, two sounds as in *knighthood* \ˈnīt-ˌhu̇d\

t͟h . . . . . . then, either, this (actually, this is a single sound, not two)

ü . . . . . . rule, youth, union \ˈyün-yən\, few \ˈfyü\

u̇ . . . . . . pull, wood, book, curable \ˈkyu̇r-ə-bəl\, fury \ˈfyu̇(ə)r-ē\

v . . . . . . vivid, give

w . . . . . . we, away

y . . . . . . yard, young, cue \ˈkyü\, mute \ˈmyüt\, union \ˈyün-yən\

z . . . . . . zone, raise

zh . . . . . . as in vision, azure \ˈazhər\ (actually, this is a single sound, not two); with a hyphen between, two sounds as in *hogshead* \ˈhȯgz-ˌhed, ˈhägz-\

**** . . . . . . slant line used in pairs to mark the beginning and end of a transcription: \ˈpen\

ˈ . . . . . . mark preceding a syllable with primary (strongest) stress: \ˈpen-mən-ˌship\

ˌ . . . . . . mark preceding a syllable with secondary (medium) stress: \ˈpen-mən-ˌship\

- . . . . . . mark of syllable division

a

[1]a \ä\ aah, ah, baa, bah, blah, bra, dah, droit, fa, Fra, ha, Jah, Kwa, la, ma, na, nah, pa, pas, qua, Ra, rah, schwa, shah, ska, spa, à bas, aba, Accra, aha, Allah, Armagh, blah-blah, Borgia, bourgeois, brava, Casbah, chamois, Chang-sha, Chita, Degas, Dumas, éclat, fa la, faux pas, fellah, fetah, foie gras, gaga, galah, Galois, grandma, grandpa, ha-ha, halvah, Hama, hoo-ha, hoopla, Hsia, hurrah, huzzah, isba, Issa, Luda, Marat, markka, mudra, Oita, opah, orgeat, Oujda, quinoa, pai-hua, paisa, Para, pasha, patois, pooh-bah, prutah, pya, San'a, sangfroid, selah, Shema, sola, supra, tola, Tonghua, Ufa, Utah, Valois, Vaudois, viva, voilà, whoopla, abaca, Adana, agora, ahimsa, Akita, aloha, assignat, Aymara, baccarat, baklava, Bogotá, brouhaha, cervelat, Chippewa, coup d'état, Cumanà, Delacroix, entrechat, feria, habdalah, haftarah, haniwa, Kashiwa, koruna, Kostroma, la-di-da, Libera, ma-and-pa, Machida, Malinois, Mardi Gras, Modena, moussaka, Omaha, Oshawa, Ottawa, padishah, pakeha, panama, Panama, Paraná, parashah, pas de trois, persona, picara, pietà, podesta, polenta, polynya, port de bras, Quebecois, reseda, rufiyaa, Shangri-la, tempura, ulema, usquebaugh, Ahvenanmaa, Alma-Ata, ayatollah, Baha' Allah, caracara, con anima, coureur de bois, hispanidad, hors de combat, je ne sais quoi, Karaganda, ménage à trois, phenomena, res publica, sursum corda, tamandua, Alto Paraná, Haleakala, Katharevusa, Makhachkala, mousseline de soie, Nishinomiya, Isthmus of Panama, pâté de foie gras, Utsunomiya, Afars and the Isas, exempli gratia, Novaya Zemlya, Tokorozawa

[2]a \ā\ see [1]AY

[3]a \ȯ\ see [1]AW

[1]aa \a\ see [3]AH

[2]aa \ä\ see [1]A

aachen \ä-k̲ən\ Aachen, lochan

aag \äg\ see [1]OG

[1]aal \āl\ see AIL

[2]aal \ȯl\ see ALL

[3]aal \äl\ see [1]AL

aam \äm\ see [1]OM

aan \an\ see [5]AN

[1]aans \äns\ see [2]ANCE

[2]aans \änz\ see ONZE

aard \ärd\ see [1]ARD
aari \är-ē\ see [1]ARI
aaron \ar-ən\ see [2]ARON
aarten \ärt-ᵊn\ see ARTEN
aas \äs\ see [1]OS
aatz \ätz\ see OTS
[1]**ab** \äb\ see [1]OB
[2]**ab** \äv\ see [2]OLVE
[3]**ab** \ab\ blab, cab, crab, dab, drab, flab, gab, grab, jab, lab, Lab, Mab, nab, scab, slab, stab, tab, Ahab, Moab, baobab, Cantab, confab, prefab, Rajab, rehab, smack-dab, astrolabe, minilab, pedicab, taxicab
aba \äb-ə\ Kaaba, Labe, PABA, Saba, Sabah, casaba, djellaba, indaba, Ali Baba, Orizaba, Sorocaba, jaboticaba, Pico de Orizaba
abah \äb-ə\ see ABA
abala \ab-ə-lə\ cabala, cabbalah, parabola
abalist \ab-ə-ləst\ cabalist, diabolist
abard \ab-ərd\ clapboard, scabbard, tabard—*also pasts of verbs listed at* [2]ABBER
abatis \ab-ət-əs\ abatis, habitus
abbalah \ab-ə-lə\ see ABALA
abbard \ab-ərd\ see ABARD
abbas \ab-əs\ see ABBESS
abbat \ab-ət\ see ABIT
[1]**abbed** \ab-əd\ crabbed, rabid
[2]**abbed** \abd\ blabbed, stabbed—*also pasts of verbs listed at* [3]AB
[1]**abber** \äb-ər\ see OBBER
[2]**abber** \ab-ər\ blabber, clabber, crabber, dabber, drabber, gabber, grabber, jabber, slabber, stabber, yabber, rehabber, bonnyclabber
abbess \ab-əs\ abbess, Barabbas
abbet \ab-ət\ see ABIT
abbey \ab-ē\ see ABBY
[1]**abbie** \äb-ē\ see OBBY
[2]**abbie** \ab-ē\ see ABBY
abbin \ab-ən\ see ABIN
abbit \ab-ət\ see ABIT
abbitry \ab-ə-trē\ see ABBITTRY
abbitt \ab-ət\ see ABIT
abbittry \ab-ə-trē\ Babbittry, rabbitry
[1]**abble** \äb-əl\ bauble, bobble, cobble, gobble, hobble, Kabul, nobble, obol, squabble, wabble, wobble
[2]**abble** \ab-əl\ Babel, babble, brabble, dabble, drabble, gabble, grabble, habile, rabble, scrabble, bedabble, hardscrabble, psychobabble, technobabble
abblement \ab-əl-mənt\ babblement, rabblement
abbler \ab-lər\ babbler, dabbler, gabbler, grabbler, rabbler, scrabbler
abbly \ab-lē\ see ABLY
abbot \ab-ət\ see ABIT
abby \ab-ē\ abbey, Abby, blabby, cabbie, crabby, flabby, gabby, grabby, scabby, shabby, tabby, kohlrabi, Panjabi, Punjabi
[1]**abe** \āb\ babe, mabe, nabe, astrolabe
[2]**abe** \ab\ see AB
[3]**abe** \ä-bə\ see ABA
abel \ā-bəl\ see ABLE
aben \äb-ən\ see OBIN
[1]**aber** \ā-bər\ see ABOR

²aber \äb-ər\ see OBBER
abes \ā-bēz\ see ABIES
¹abi \äb-ē\ see OBBY
²abi \əb-ē\ see UBBY
³abi \ab-ē\ see ABBY
abia \ā-bē-ə\ Arabia, labia, Swabia, Bessarabia, Saudi Arabia
abian \ā-bē-ən\ Fabian, gabion, Arabian, Bessarabian
abid \ab-əd\ see ABBED
abies \ā-bēz\ rabies, scabies, tabes—*also plurals and possessives of nouns listed at* ABY
abile \ab-əl\ see ²ABBLE
abilis \äb-ə-ləs\ obelus, annus mirabilis
abin \ab-ən\ cabin, rabbin
abion \ā-bē-ən\ see ABIAN
abit \ab-ət\ abbot, babbitt, Babbitt, Cabot, habit, rabbet, rabbit, sabbat, cohabit, inhabit, jackrabbit
abitant \ab-ət-ənt\ habitant, cohabitant, inhabitant
abitus \ab-ət-əs\ see ABATIS
able \ā-bəl\ Abel, able, Babel, cable, fable, Froebel, gable, label, Mabel, sable, stable, table, disable, enable, instable, pin-table, retable, round table, timetable, turntable, unable, unstable, worktable
abled \ā-bəld\ fabled, gabled—*also pasts of verbs listed at* ABLE
ablis \ab-lē\ see ABLY
ably \ab-lē\ chablis, drably, scrabbly
abo \ab-ō\ abo, sabot
abola \ab-ə-lə\ see ABALA
abolist \ab-ə-ləst\ see ABALIST
abor \ā-bər\ caber, labor, neighbor, saber, tabor, belabor, von Weber, zeitgeber
aborer \ā-bər-ər\ laborer, taborer
¹abot \ab-ō\ see ABO
²abot \ab-ət\ see ABIT
abra \äb-rə\ sabra, Sabra, candelabra
abre \äb\ see ¹OB
abul \äb-əl\ see ¹ABBLE
abular \ab-yə-lər\ fabular, tabular, vocabular, acetabular
abulous \ab-yə-ləs\ fabulous, fantabulous
abulum \ab-yə-ləm\ pabulum, acetabulum, incunabulum
aby \ā-bē\ baby, gaby, maybe, crybaby, grandbaby
¹ac \ak\ see ²ACK
²ac \äk\ see ¹OCK
³ac \ȯ\ see ¹AW
¹aca \äk-ə\ see ¹AKA
²aca \ak-ə\ Dacca, Dhaka, paca, alpaca, malacca, Malacca, sifaka, portulaca, Strait of Malacca
acable \ak-ə-bəl\ see ACKABLE
acao \ō-kō\ see OCO
acas \ak-əs\ Bacchus, fracas, Gracchus, Caracas
¹acca \ak-ə\ see ACA
²acca \äk-ə\ see ¹AKA
accent \ak-sənt\ accent, relaxant
acchanal \ak-ən-ᵊl\ see ACONAL
acchic \ak-ik\ bacchic, halakic, stomachic, tribrachic, amphibrachic
acchus \ak-əs\ see ACAS
accid \as-əd\ see ACID

accio \ä-chē-ō\ bocaccio, Bocaccio, carpaccio
[1]**acco** \ak-ə\ see ACA
[2]**acco** \ak-ō\ see [2]AKO
acculus \ak-yə-ləs\ sacculus, miraculous
[1]**ace** \ās\ ace, base, bass, brace, case, chase, dace, face, grace, Grace, lace, mace, Mace, pace, place, plaice, prase, race, res, space, Thrace, trace, vase, abase, airspace, Alsace, ambsace, apace, backspace, best-case, biface, birthplace, blackface, boldface, bookcase, bootlace, braincase, briefcase, crankcase, debase, deface, disgrace, displace, dogface, doughface, efface, embrace, emplace, encase, enchase, enlace, erase, firebase, fireplace, footpace, footrace, foreface, gyrase, half-space, hard case, headspace, Jerez, lightface, manes, millrace, milreis, misplace, notecase, null-space, outface, outpace, outrace, paleface, postface, Quilmes, replace, retrace, scapegrace, shoelace, showcase, showplace, slipcase, smearcase, someplace, staircase, subbase, subspace, suitcase, surbase, tailrace, tenace, typeface, ukase, unbrace, unlace, watchcase, wheelbase, wheyface, whiteface, workplace, worst-case, about-face, aerospace, anyplace, boniface, bouillabaisse, carapace, commonplace, contrabass, double-space, everyplace, interface, interlace, kilobase, lemures, lowercase, marketplace, pillowcase, Samothrace, single-space, steeplechase, thoroughbass, thoroughbrace, triple-space, uppercase, rarae aves, betalactamase, in medias res, Aguascalientes, Goya y Lucientes, superoxide dismutase, litterae humaniores
[2]**ace** \ā-sē\ see ACY
[3]**ace** \äs\ see [1]OS
[4]**ace** \as\ see [3]ASS
[5]**ace** \äch-ē\ see OTCHY
[6]**ace** \äs-ə\ see [1]ASA
aceable \ā-sə-bəl\ placeable, traceable, displaceable, effaceable, embraceable, erasable, persuasible, replaceable, ineffaceable, irreplaceable
acean \ā-shən\ see [1]ATION
aced \āst\ based, baste, chaste, faced, geest, haste, laced, mayest, paste, taste, waist, waste, bald-faced, barefaced, bold-faced, distaste, dough-faced, foretaste, impaste, lambaste, lightfaced, moonfaced, pie-faced, po-faced, posthaste, rad waste, self-paced, shamefaced, shirtwaist, snail-paced, slipcased, stone-faced, straight-faced, straitlaced, toothpaste, two-faced, unchaste, unplaced, white-faced, aftertaste, brazen-faced, double-faced, Janus-faced, hatchet-faced, pantywaist,

poker-faced, thorough-paced—*also pasts of verbs listed at* [1]ACE

aceless \ā-sləs\ baseless, faceless, graceless, laceless, placeless, spaceless, traceless

aceman \ā-smən\ baseman, placeman, spaceman

acement \ā-smənt\ basement, casement, placement, abasement, debasement, defacement, displacement, effacement, embracement, emplacement, encasement, enlacement, misplacement, outplacement, replacement, self-effacement

acence \ās-ᵊns\ see [1]ASCENCE

acency \ās-ᵊn-sē\ adjacency, complacency, subjacency

acent \ās-ᵊnt\ nascent, adjacent, complacent, complaisant, subjacent, circumjacent, superjacent

aceor \ā-sər\ see [1]ACER

aceous \ā-shəs\ see ACIOUS

[1]acer \ā-sər\ baser, bracer, chaser, facer, pacer, placer, racer, spacer, tracer, defacer, disgracer, effacer, embraceor, embracer, eraser, replacer, subchaser, steeplechaser

[2]acer \as-ər\ see ASSER

acery \ās-rē\ tracery, embracery

[1]acet \ā-sət\ hic jacet, nonplacet

[2]acet \as-ət\ asset, facet, tacet, tacit

acewalking \ās-wȯ-kiŋ\ racewalking, spacewalking

acey \ā-sē\ see ACY

[1]ach \äk̲\ Bach, saugh, Pesach, pibroch, Offenbach, Mönchengladbach

[2]ach \äk\ see [1]OCK

[3]ach \ak\ see [2]ACK

[4]ach \ach\ see [4]ATCH

acha \äch-ə\ cha-cha, dacha, kwacha, viscacha

achary \ak-ə-r-ē\ see [2]ACKERY

[1]ache \āk\ see [1]AKE

[2]ache \ash\ see [3]ASH

[3]ache \äch-ē\ see OTCHY

[4]ache \ach-ē\ see ATCHY

acheal \ā-kē-əl\ brachial, tracheal

ached \acht\ attached, detached, unattached, semidetached—*also pasts of verbs listed at* [4]ATCH

acher \ā-kər\ see [1]AKER

achet \ach-ət\ see ATCHET

achi \äch-ē\ see OTCHY

achial \ā-kē-əl\ see ACHEAL

achian \ā-shən\ see [1]ATION

achic \ak-ik\ see ACCHIC

aching \ā-kiŋ\ see [1]AKING

[1]achio \ash-ō\ mustachio, pistachio

[2]achio \ash-ē-ō\ mustachio, pistachio

achm \am\ see [2]AM

achment \ach-mənt\ see ATCHMENT

achne \ak-nē\ see ACNE

acho \äch-ō\ muchacho, quebracho

achou \a-shü\ see ASHEW

achsen \äk-sən\ see OXEN

acht \ät\ see [1]OT

achtsman \ät-smən\ see OTSMAN

achy \ā-kē\ see AKY

acia \ā-shə\ Dacia, fascia,

geisha, acacia, Croatia, Dalmatia, ex gratia, Galatia, prima facie, exempli gratia

acial \ā-shəl\ facial, glacial, racial, spatial, abbatial, bifacial, biracial, englacial, palatial, primatial, subglacial, interfacial, interglacial, interracial, multiracial

acian \ā-shən\ see [1]ATION

acias \ā-shəs\ see ACIOUS

acid \as-əd\ acid, Chasid, flaccid, Hasid, jassid, placid, Abbasid, antacid

acie \ā-shə\ see ACIA

acient \ā-shənt\ see ATIENT

[1]**acier** \ā-shər\ see [1]ASURE

[2]**acier** \ā-zhər\ see AZIER

acile \as-əl\ see [2]ASSEL

acing \ā-siŋ\ bracing, casing, facing, lacing, racing, spacing, tracing, catfacing, effacing, all-embracing, interfacing, letterspacing, self-effacing

acious \ā-shəs\ gracious, spacious, audacious, bodacious, capacious, ceraceous, cretaceous, crustaceous, curvaceous, edacious, fallacious, flirtatious, fugacious, herbaceous, Horatius, Ignatius, loquacious, mendacious, mordacious, pomaceous, predaceous, pugnacious, rapacious, sagacious, salacious, sebaceous, sequacious, setaceous, tenacious, testaceous, ungracious, veracious, vexacious, vinaceous, vivacious, voracious, alliaceous, arenaceous, argillaceous, carbonaceous, contumacious, coriaceous, disputatious, efficacious, farinaceous, foliaceous, ostentatious, pectinaceous, perspicacious, pertinacious, saponaceous, scire facias, stercoraceous, violaceous, inefficacious, fieri facias

acis \as-ē\ see ASSY

acist \ā-səst\ see ASSIST

acit \as-ət\ see [2]ACET

[1]**acity** \as-tē\ see [2]ASTY

[2]**acity** \as-ət-ē\ audacity, capacity, fugacity, loquacity, mendacity, opacity, rapacity, sagacity, tenacity, veracity, vivacity, voracity, efficacity, incapacity, overcapacity

acive \ā-siv\ see ASIVE

[1]**ack** \äk\ see [1]OCK

[2]**ack** \ak\ back, black, clack, claque, crack, flack, flak, hack, jack, Jack, knack, lac, lack, mac, Mac, Mack, pack, plaque, quack, rack, sac, Sac, sack, sacque, shack, slack, smack, snack, stack, tach, tack, thwack, track, Wac, whack, wrack, yak, aback, ack-ack, alack, amtrac, Anzac, Arak, attack, backpack, backtrack, Balzac, bareback, blackjack, blue-black, bootblack, bootjack, brushback, bushwhack, buyback, callback, calpac, champac, cheapjack, Coalsack, coatrack, cognac,

come back, comeback, cookshack, cossack, crackback, crookback, cut back, cutback, Dayak, dieback, draw back, drawback, fall back, fallback, fastback, fast-track, fatback, feedback, finback, fireback, flapjack, flareback, flashback, fullback, gimcrack, graywacke, greenback, gripsack, guaiac, halfback, half-track, hardback, hardhack, hardtack, hatchback, hayrack, haystack, hijack, hogback, hold back, holdback, hopsack, horseback, humpback, hunchback, Iraq, jam-pack, jet-black, kayak, Kazak, Kazakh, kickback, knapsack, knickknack, Kodak, kulak, kyack, laid-back, lampblack, leaseback, linac, macaque, man jack, manpack, Micmac, mossback, muntjac, Muzak, notchback, offtrack, outback, packsack, payback, pitch-black, play back, playback, plow back, plowback, Polack, pullback, quillback, racetrack, ransack, rickrack, roll back, rollback, roorback, rucksack, runback, scatback, serac, set back, setback, shellac, shellback, shoeblack, shoepac, sidetrack, six-pack, skewback, skipjack, skyjack, slapjack, slotback, Slovak, smokejack, smokestack, snap back, snapback, snowpack, softback, sumac, swayback, sweepback, swept-back, switchback, tailback, tarmac, thornback, throw back, throwback, thumbtack, ticktack, tieback, tie tack, tombac, touchback, tow sack, trictrac, tripack, unpack, Welsbach, wetback, whaleback, wingback, wisecrack, woolpack, woolsack, yashmak, Yurak, zwieback, almanac, amberjack, anorak, antiblack, applejack, Arawak, Armagnac, birdyback, bivouac, bric-a-brac, camelback, canvasback, cardiac, carryback, celiac, coeliac, cornerback, Cousin Jack, crackerjack, cul-de-sac, diamondback, fiddleback, fishyback, Frontenac, gunnysack, hackmatack, haversack, high-low-jack, huckaback, hydrocrack, iliac, ipecac, Kodiak, ladder-back, leatherback, lumberjack, maniac, medevac, minitrack, moneyback, nunatak, otomac, paperback, Pasternak, pickaback, piggyback, Pontiac, portapak, quarterback, razorback, retropack, running back, sandarac, Sarawak, Sazerac, silverback, single-track, Skaggerak, snapper-back, solonchak, steeplejack, stickleback, supplejack, Syriac, tamarack, tenure-track, theriac, tokamak, turtleback, umiak, zodiac, Adirondack, ammoniac, amnesiac, Aniakchak, biofeedback, celeriac, counterattack, demoniac, elegiac, insomniac, Monterey Jack, paranoiac, simoniac, tacamahac, aphrodisiac, coprophiliac, Dionysiac, dipsomaniac, egomaniac, hemophiliac, hypochondriac, intracardiac, kleptomaniac, melancholiac, monomaniac, mythomaniac, necrophiliac, neophiliac, nymphomaniac, pedophiliac, pyromaniac, Rhodesian Ridgeback, sacroiliac, sal ammoniac, megalomaniac, Cyrano de Bergerac

ackable \ak-ə-bəl\ packable, placable, stackable, implacable

ackage \ak-ij\ package, trackage, prepackage, repackage

ackal \ak-əl\ see ACKLE

acked \akt\ see ACT

acken \ak-ən\ blacken, bracken, flacon, slacken, Arawakan

ackened \ak-ənd\ blackened—*also pasts of verbs listed at* ACKEN

acker \ak-ər\ backer, clacker, cracker, hacker, jacker, knacker, lacquer, packer, sacker, slacker, smacker, stacker, tacker, tracker, whacker, attacker, backpacker, bushwacker, firecracker, hijacker, kayaker, linebacker, nutcracker, racetracker, ransacker, safecracker, shellcracker, skyjacker, unpacker, wisecracker, simulacre, counterattacker

ackeray \ak-ə-rē\ see ACKERY

ackerel \ak-rəl\ see ACRAL

ackery \ak-ə-rē\ flackery, quackery, Thackeray, Zachary, gimcrackery

acket \ak-ət\ bracket, jacket, packet, placket, racket, bluejacket, straitjacket, yellowjacket

ackey \ak-ē\ see ACKY

ackguard \ag-ərd\ see AGGARD

ackie \ak-ē\ see ACKY

acking \ak-iŋ\ backing, blacking, cracking, packing, sacking, smacking, tracking, whacking, bushwacking, kayaking, linebacking, meatpacking, nerve-racking, nerve-wracking, safecracking, skyjacking

ackish \ak-ish\ blackish, brackish, quackish

ackle \ak-əl\ cackle, crackle, grackle, hackle, jackal, macle, rackle, shackle, spackle, tackle, debacle, gang-tackle, ramshackle, unshackle, tabernacle

ackly \ak-lē\ blackly, crackly, hackly, abstractly, compactly, exactly, inexactly

ackman \ak-mən\ hackman, packman, trackman

ackney \ak-nē\ see ACNE

ackneyed \ak-nēd\ see ACNED

acko \ak-ō\ see ²AKO

acksman \ak-smən\ see AXMAN

ackson \ak-sən\ see AXON

acky \ak-ē\ hackie, Jackie,

Jacky, khaki, lackey, Paki, tacky, wacky, ticky-tacky
[1]acle \ik-əl\ see ICKLE
[2]acle \äk\ see [1]OCK
[3]acle \äk-əl\ see OCKLE
[4]acle \ak-əl\ see ACKLE
acne \ak-nē\ acne, hackney, Hackney, Arachne
acned \ak-nēd\ acned, hackneyed
aco \äk-ō\ see OCCO
[1]acon \ā-kən\ see [1]AKEN
[2]acon \ak-ən\ see ACKEN
aconal \ak-ən-ᵊl\ bacchanal, diaconal, archidiaconal
[1]acque \ak\ see [2]ACK
[2]acque \äk\ see [1]OCK
acquer \ak-ər\ see ACKER
acques \äk\ see [1]OCK
acral \ak-rəl\ mackerel, sacral
[1]acre \ā-kər\ see [1]AKER
[2]acre \ak-ər\ see ACKER
acrum \ak-rəm\ sacrum, simulacrum
act \akt\ act, backed, bract, cracked, fact, packed, pact, stacked, tact, tracked, tract, abstract, attract, coact, compact, contact, contract, crookbacked, detract, didact, diffract, distract, enact, entr'acte, epact, exact, extract, half-tracked, humpbacked, hunchbacked, impact, infract, intact, mossbacked, playact, protract, react, redact, refract, subtract, swaybacked, transact, unbacked, abreact, artifact, cataract, chain-react, counteract, cross-react, inexact, interact, overact, paperbacked, precontact, razor-backed, reenact, subcompact, subcontract, underact, vacuum-packed, ventifact, autodidact, matter-of-fact, overreact, semiabstract, underreact—*also pasts of verbs listed at* [2]ACK
actable \ak-tə-bəl\ actable, tractable, abstractable, attractable, compactible, contractible, distractable, extractable, intractable
actance \ak-təns\ attractance, reactance
actant \ak-tənt\ attractant, reactant, surfactant, interactant
[1]acte \äkt\ see OCKED
[2]acte \akt\ see ACT
acted \ak-təd\ fracted, abstracted, impacted—*also pasts of verbs listed at* ACT
acter \ak-tər\ see ACTOR
actery \ak-trē\ see ACTORY
actible \ak-tə-bəl\ see ACTABLE
actic \ak-tik\ lactic, tactic, atactic, climactic, didactic, galactic, syntactic, ataractic, chiropractic, parallactic, paratactic, prophylactic, anaphylactic, anticlimactic, autodidactic, extragalactic, intergalactic, intragalactic, stereotactic
actical \ak-ti-kəl\ practical, tactical, didactical, impractical, syntactical
actice \ak-təs\ cactus, practice, malpractice, cataractous
actics \ak-tiks\ tactics, didactics, syntactics,

phonotactics—*also plurals and possessives of nouns listed at* ACTIC
actile \ak-tᵊl\ dactyl, tactile, contractile, protractile, refractile, retractile, polydactyl, pterodactyl
acting \ak-tiŋ\ acting, exacting, self-acting—*also present participles of verbs listed at* ACT
action \ak-shən\ action, faction, fraction, taction, traction, abstraction, attraction, bolt-action, coaction, compaction, contraction, detraction, diffraction, distraction, exaction, extraction, impaction, inaction, infraction, olfaction, protraction, reaction, redaction, refraction, retraction, subtraction, transaction, benefaction, counteraction, interaction, liquefaction, malefaction, overaction, petrifaction, putrefaction, rarefaction, retroaction, satisfaction, single-action, stupefaction, tumefaction, dissatisfaction, photoreaction, self-satisfaction
actional \ak-shnəl\ factional, fractional, tractional, abstractional, contractional, redactional, transactional, interactional, rarefactional
actious \ak-shəs\ factious, fractious
active \ak-tiv\ active, tractive, abstractive, attractive, coactive, contractive, detractive, distractive, extractive, impactive, inactive, proactive, reactive, refractive, subtractive, bioactive, counteractive, hyperactive, interactive, overactive, psychoactive, putrefactive, retroactive, unattractive, radioactive
actly \ak-lē\ see ACKLY
actor \ak-tər\ actor, factor, tractor, abstractor, attractor, cofactor, compactor, contractor, detractor, enactor, exactor, extractor, g-factor, impactor, infractor, protractor, reactor, redactor, refractor, retractor, subtracter, transactor, benefactor, chiropractor, malefactor, subcontractor, bioreactor, campylobacter
actory \ak-trē\ factory, olfactory, phylactery, refractory, calefactory, manufactory, satisfactory, dissatisfactory, unsatisfactory
actous \ak-təs\ see ACTICE
actress \ak-trəs\ actress, benefactress
actual \ak-chəl\ actual, factual, tactual, artifactual, counterfactual
acture \ak-chər\ facture, fracture, contracture, manufacture, remanufacture
actus \ak-təs\ see ACTICE
actyl \ak-tᵊl\ see ACTILE
acular \ak-yə-lər\ macular, oracular, spectacular, spiracular, tentacular, vernacular, tabernacular

aculate \ak-yə-lət\ maculate, ejaculate, immaculate
aculous \ak-yə-ləs\ see ACCULUS
acy \ā-sē\ Basie, lacy, pace, précis, racy, spacey, Stacey, Stacy, Tracey, Tracy, O'Casey, prima facie, Sulawesi, Veronese
acyl \as-əl\ see [2]ASSEL
[1]ad \ä\ see [1]A
[2]ad \äd\ see [1]OD
[3]ad \ad\ ad, add, bad, bade, brad, cad, chad, Chad, clad, dad, fad, gad, Gad, glad, grad, had, lad, mad, pad, plaid, rad, sad, scad, shad, tad, Thad, trad, Akkad, aoudad, Baghdad, Belgrade, Carlsbad, caudad, comrade, Conrad, crawdad, doodad, dorsad, dryad, dyad, egad, farad, footpad, forbade, gonad, granddad, heptad, hexad, horn-mad, ironclad, keypad, launchpad, maenad, Mashad, monad, naiad, nicad, nomad, notepad, pentad, pleiad, Sinbad, Sindbad, tetrad, thinclad, triad, triclad, Troad, armor-clad, Ashkhabad, cephalad, chiliad, ennead, Galahad, hebdomad, helipad, Hyderabad, laterad, mediad, oread, overplaid, Pythiad, undergrad, Volgograd, superadd, Trinidad, Allahabad, bromeliad, gesneriad, hamadryad, hispanidad, Kaliningrad, Kirovograd, olympiad, seminomad, Upanishad, Voroshilovgrad
[1]ada \äd-ä\ Dada, Dhu'l-Qa'dah, aficionada
[2]ada \äd-ə\ nada, sadhe, tsade, Agada, Agade, Aggada, armada, cicada, gelada, Granada, Haggadah, Jumada, Nevada, panada, posada, tostada, autostrada, empanada, enchilada, Ensenada, Theravada, aficionada, Ponta Delgada, Vijayawada, cascara sagrada, Sierra Nevada
[3]ada \ād-ə\ Ada, Veda, armada, cicada, Grenada, alameda, Avellaneda
adable \ād-ə-bəl\ gradable, tradable, wadable, abradable, degradable, evadable, persuadable, biodegradable
a'dah \äd-ä\ see [1]ADA
adah \äd-ə\ see [2]ADA
adal \ad-ᵊl\ see ADDLE
adam \ad-əm\ Adam, madam, macadam, tarmacadam
adams \ad-əmz\ Adams—*also possessives and plurals of nouns listed at* ADAM
[1]adan \ad-n\ see ADDEN
[2]adan \äd-n\ see ODDEN
adant \ād-ᵊnt\ cadent, abradant
add \ad\ see [3]AD
adden \ad-ᵊn\ gladden, madden, sadden, Aladdin, Ibadan
adder \ad-ər\ adder, bladder, gadder, ladder, madder, stepladder—*also comparatives of adjectives listed at* [3]AD
addie \ad-ē\ see ADDY
addik \äd-ik\ see ODIC

addin \ad-ᵊn\ see ADDEN
adding \ad-iŋ\ cladding, madding, padding
[1]addish \äd-ish\ see ODDISH
[2]addish \ad-ish\ see ADISH
addison \ad-ə-sən\ Addison, Madison
addle \ad-ᵊl\ addle, paddle, raddle, saddle, staddle, straddle, astraddle, foresaddle, gonadal, packsaddle, sidesaddle, skedaddle, unsaddle, fiddle-faddle
[1]addler \äd-lər\ see ODDLER
[2]addler \ad-lər\ saddler, paddler, straddler, skedaddler
addo \ad-ō\ see ADOW
[1]addock \ad-ik\ see [2]ADIC
[2]addock \ad-ək\ haddock, paddock, shaddock
[1]addy \ad-ē\ baddie, caddie, caddy, daddy, faddy, laddie, paddy, Paddy, forecaddie, granddaddy, finnan haddie
[2]addy \äd-ē\ see [1]ODY
[1]ade \ād\ aid, aide, bade, blade, braid, cade, clade, fade, glade, grade, jade, lade, laid, made, maid, paid, raid, rayed, shade, spade, stade, staid, suede, they'd, trade, wade, Wade, abrade, afraid, aggrade, arcade, Band-Aid, barmaid, Belgrade, blockade, bondmaid, bridesmaid, brigade, brocade, cascade, Cascade, charade, clichéd, cockade, corrade, cross-trade, crusade, decade, degrade, dissuade, downgrade, evade, eyeshade, fair-trade, forebade, gainsaid, glissade, grenade, handmade, handmaid, homemade, housemaid, inlaid, invade, limeade, low-grade, man-made, mermaid, milkmaid, navaid, nightshade, nursemaid, outlaid, parade, persuade, pervade, plain-laid, pomade, postpaid, repaid, sacheted, scalade, sea-maid, self-made, shroud-laid, souffléed, stockade, sunshade, switchblade, tirade, torsade, twayblade, twice-laid, unbraid, unlade, unmade, unpaid, upbraid, upgrade, waylaid, accolade, Adelaide, ambuscade, aquacade, autocade, balustrade, barricade, bastinade, cable-laid, cannonade, carronade, cavalcade, centigrade, chambermaid, chiffonade, colonnade, countertrade, custom-made, dairymaid, defilade, enfilade, escalade, escapade, esplanade, everglade, fusillade, gallopade, gasconade, grant-in-aid, hawser-laid, intergrade, lemonade, marinade, marmalade, masquerade, medicaid, motorcade, orangeade, orthograde, overtrade, palisade, pasquinade, plantigrade, promenade, ready-made, renegade, retrograde, serenade, stock-in-trade, tailor-made, underlaid, fanfaronade, harlequinade, overpersuade, rodomontade
[2]ade \äd\ see [1]OD

[3]ade \ad\ see [3]AD
[4]ade \äd-ə\ see [2]ADA
aded \ād-əd\ bladed, arcaded, brocaded, cockaded, colonnaded—*also pasts of verbs listed at* [1]ADE
adeless \ād-ləs\ fadeless, gradeless, shadeless
adely \ad-lē\ see ADLY
[1]aden \ād-ᵊn\ Aden, laden, maiden, handmaiden, menhaden
[2]aden \äd-ən\ Aden, Wiesbaden
adent \ād-ᵊnt\ see ADANT
ader \ād-ər\ aider, braider, cheder, fader, grader, heder, nadir, raider, seder, shader, spader, trader, wader, blockader, crusader, dissuader, evader, persuader, masquerader, serenader
[1]ades \ād-ēz\ ladies, Hades, quaker-ladies
[2]ades \ādz\ AIDS, Glades, Cascades, antitrades, Everglades, jack-of-all-trades—*also plurals and possessives of nouns and third singular presents of verbs listed at* [1]ADE
adge \aj\ badge, cadge, Madge, hajj
adger \aj-ər\ badger, cadger
adh \äd\ see [1]OD
[1]adhe \äd-ə\ see [2]ADA
[2]adhe \äd-ē\ see [1]ODY
adia \ād-ē-ə\ stadia, Acadia, arcadia, Arcadia, palladia
adial \ād-ē-əl\ radial, biradial, interstadial
adian \ād-ē-ən\ Acadian, Akkadian, arcadian, Arcadian, Barbadian, Canadian, circadian, Orcadian, Palladian
adiant \ād-ē-ənt\ gradient, radiant
[1]adic \ād-ik\ Vedic, tornadic
[2]adic \ad-ik\ Braddock, haddock, paddock, balladic, dyadic, faradic, haggadic, hexadic, maenadic, monadic, nomadic, sporadic, tetradic, tornadic, triadic, Iliadic, seminomadic
adie \ād-ē\ see ADY
adient \ād-ē-ənt\ see ADIANT
adies \ād-ēz\ see [1]ADES
ading \ād-iŋ\ braiding, lading, shading, arcading, degrading, downgrading, unfading
adir \ād-ər\ see ADER
adish \ad-ish\ caddish, faddish, radish, horseradish
adison \ad-ə-sən\ see ADDISON
[1]adist \ȯd-əst\ broadest, sawdust, haggadist
[2]adist \äd-əst\ see ODEST
adium \ād-ē-əm\ radium, stadium, caladium, palladium, vanadium
adle \ād-ᵊl\ cradle, dreidel, ladle, wedel
adley \ad-lē\ see ADLY
adly \ad-lē\ badly, Bradley, gladly, madly, sadly, comradely
adness \ad-nəs\ badness, gladness, madness, sadness
[1]ado \äd-ō\ bravado, camisado, carbonado, cruzado, Manado, mikado, passado, stoccado, strappado, avocado, bastinado, Colorado, Coronado, desperado, El

Dorado, hacendado, amontillado, zapateado, aficionado, incommunicado, Llano Estacado

[2]**ado** \ād-ō\ dado, credo, crusado, gambado, strappado, teredo, tornado, barricado, bastinado, camisado, carbonado, desperado, El Dorado, fettuccine Alfredo

ados \ā-dəs\ see ADUS

adow \ad-ō\ Caddo, shadow, foreshadow, overshadow

adrate \äd-rət\ see ODERATE

adre \ad-rē\ see ADERY

adrian \ā-drē-ən\ Adrian, Adrienne, Hadrian

adrienne \ā-drē-ən\ see ADRIAN

adt \ät\ see [1]OT

adual \aj-əl\ see AGILE

adus \ā-dəs\ Padus, Barbados—*also possessives and plurals of nouns listed at* [3]ADA

ady \ād-ē\ cedi, glady, lady, Sadie, shady, forelady, landlady, milady, saleslady

[1]**ae** \ā\ see [1]AY

[2]**ae** \ē\ see [1]EE

[3]**ae** \ī\ see [1]Y

aea \ē-ə\ see [1]IA

aean \ē-ən\ see [1]EAN

aedal \ēd-^{ə}l\ see EEDLE

aedile \ēd-^{ə}l\ see EEDLE

aedra \ē-drə\ see EDRA

[1]**aegis** \ā-jəs\ see AGEOUS

[2]**aegis** \ē-jəs\ see EGIS

ael \āl\ see AIL

aeli \ā-lē\ see AILY

[1]**aelic** \äl-ik\ see [1]OLIC

[2]**aelic** \al-ik\ see ALLIC

aemon \ē-mən\ see [1]EMON

aen \ä^{n}\ see [1]ANT

[1]**aena** \ā-nä\ scena, faena

[2]**aena** \ē-nə\ see [2]INA

[1]**aenia** \ē-nē-ə\ see [1]ENIA

[2]**aenia** \ē-nyə\ see [2]ENIA

aens \ä^{n}s\ see [1]ANCE

aeon \ē-ən\ see [1]EAN

aera \ir-ə\ see [2]ERA

[1]**aere** \er-ē\ see [1]ARY

[2]**aere** \ir-ē\ see EARY

[1]**aerial** \er-ē-əl\ see ARIAL

[2]**aerial** \ir-ē-əl\ see ERIAL

[1]**aerie** \ā-rē\ aerie, aery, faerie, fairy

[2]**aerie** \er-ē\ see [1]ARY

[3]**aerie** \ir-ē\ see EARY

[1]**aero** \er-ō\ see [2]ERO

[2]**aero** \ar-ō\ see [2]ARROW

[1]**aeroe** \ar-ō\ see [2]ARROW

[2]**aeroe** \er-ō\ see [2]ERO

[1]**aery** \ā-rē\ see [1]AERIE

[2]**aery** \er-ē\ see [1]ARY

aesar \ē-zər\ see [2]EASER

aese \ā-zə\ see [2]ESA

aestor \ē-stər\ see EASTER

aestus \es-təs\ see ESTIS

aet \āt\ see [1]ATE

aetor \ēt-ər\ see [1]EATER

aeum \ē-əm\ see [1]EUM

aeus \ē-əs\ see [1]EUS

af \af\ see APH

[1]**afe** \āf\ chafe, safe, strafe, waif, fail-safe, vouchsafe, bathyscaphe

[2]**afe** \af\ see APH

afel \äf-əl\ offal, waffle, falafel, pantofle, rijsttafel

afer \ā-fər\ chafer, safer, strafer, wafer, cockchafer

aff \af\ see APH

affable \af-ə-bəl\ affable, laughable

affe \af\ see APH

affed \aft\ see ²AFT
¹affer \äf-ər\ see ¹OFFER
²affer \af-ər\ chaffer, gaffer, Kaffir, kafir, Kafir, laugher, staffer, zaffer, paragrapher, polygrapher
affia \af-ē-ə\ raffia, agraphia
affic \af-ik\ see APHIC
affick \af-ik\ see APHIC
affir \af-ər\ see ²AFFER
affish \af-ish\ raffish, giraffish
¹affle \äf-əl\ see AFEL
²affle \af-əl\ baffle, raffle, snaffle
affron \af-rən\ saffron, Biafran
affy \af-ē\ chaffy, daffy, taffy
afic \af-ik\ see APHIC
afir \af-ər\ see ²AFFER
afran \af-rən\ see AFFRON
¹aft \äft\ toft, waft, gemeinschaft, gesellschaft—*also pasts of verbs listed at* ¹OFF
²aft \aft\ aft, craft, daft, draft, graft, haft, kraft, raft, shaft, Taft, waft, abaft, aircraft, campcraft, camshaft, crankshaft, engraft, handcraft, indraft, kingcraft, rockshaft, scoutcraft, seacraft, spacecraft, stagecraft, statecraft, updraft, witchcraft, woodcraft, countershaft, fore-and-aft, handicraft, Hovercraft, overdraft, rotorcraft, turboshaft, understaffed, watercraft, antiaircraft
aftage \af-tij\ graftage, waftage
after \af-tər\ after, dafter, drafter, grafter, laughter, rafter, hereafter, thereafter, fore-and-after, handicrafter, hereinafter, thereinafter
aftness \af-nəs\ daftness, Daphnis, halfness
aftsman \af-smən\ craftsman, draftsman, raftsman, handcraftsman, handicraftsman
afty \af-tē\ crafty, drafty
ag \ag\ bag, brag, crag, dag, drag, fag, flag, gag, hag, jag, lag, mag, nag, quag, rag, sag, scag, scrag, shag, slag, snag, sprag, stag, swag, tag, wag, YAG, zag, beanbag, black-flag, chin-wag, dirtbag, dishrag, fleabag, gasbag, greylag, handbag, hangtag, mailbag, postbag, ragbag, ragtag, ratbag, sandbag, schoolbag, scumbag, seabag, sleazebag, washrag, wigwag, windbag, workbag, zigzag, ballyrag, bullyrag, carpetbag, litterbag, lollygag, saddlebag, scalawag, tucker-bag
¹aga \äg-ə\ quagga, raga, saga, anlage, vorlage's gravenhage
²aga \ā-gə\ Vega, bodega, omega, rutabaga
³aga \eg-ə\ see ¹EGA
⁴aga \ȯ-gə\ see AUGA
agan \ā-gən\ see AGIN
¹agar \ā-gər\ Hagar, jaeger
²agar \äg-ər\ see ¹OGGER
³agar \əg-ər\ see ¹UGGER
agary \ag-ə-rē\ see AGGERY
agate \ag-ət\ see AGGOT
¹age \äj\ dodge, lodge, raj, stodge, wodge, barrage, collage, corsage, dislodge, garage, hodgepodge, Karaj,

massage, swaraj, camouflage, espionage, counterespionage

[2]**age** \äzh\ plage, assuage, barrage, collage, corsage, dressage, frottage, gavage, lavage, massage, ménage, mirage, montage, moulage, portage, potage, treillage, triage, arbitrage, assemblage, badinage, bon voyage, bricolage, cabotage, camouflage, colportage, curettage, decoupage, empennage, enfleurage, entourage, fuselage, Hermitage, maquillage, persiflage, repechage, sabotage, vernissage, décolletage, espionage, photomontage, rite de passage, counterespionage

[3]**age** \āj\ age, cage, gage, Gage, gauge, mage, page, rage, sage, stage, swage, wage, assuage, backstage, birdcage, broad-gauge, downstage, encage, engage, enrage, forestage, front-page, greengage, offstage, onstage, Osage, outrage, presage, rampage, restage, soundstage, space-age, substage, teenage, uncage, upstage, disengage, multistage, ossifrage, overage, saxifrage, underage

[4]**age** \āg\ see [1]EG

[5]**age** \āzh\ see [1]EIGE

[6]**age** \äg-ə\ see [1]AGA

ageable \ā-jə-bəl\ gaugeable, stageable, unassuageable

aged \ājd\ aged, gauged, broad-gauged, engaged, unpaged, middle-aged—*also pasts of verbs listed at* [3]AGE

agel \ā-gəl\ bagel, Hegel, plagal, finagle, inveigle, wallydraigle

ageless \āj-ləs\ ageless, wageless

[1]**agen** \ā-gən\ see AGIN

[2]**agen** \ä-gən\ see OGGIN

agenous \aj-ə-nəs\ see AGINOUS

ageous \ā-jəs\ aegis, ambagious, courageous, contagious, outrageous, rampageous, umbrageous, advantageous, disadvantageous

[1]**ager** \ā-jər\ gauger, major, Major, pager, stager, wager, teenager, Canis Major, golden-ager, middle-ager, Ursa Major

[2]**ager** \äg-ər\ see [1]OGGER

agey \ā-jē\ see AGY

agga \äg-ə\ see [1]AGA

aggar \äg-ər\ see [1]OGGER

aggard \ag-ərd\ blackguard, haggard, laggard

agged \ag-əd\ cragged, jagged, ragged

agger \ag-ər\ bagger, bragger, dagger, dragger, gagger, jagger, lagger, nagger, sagger, stagger, swagger, wagger, foot dragger, four-bagger, one-bagger, sandbagger, three-bagger, two-bagger, carpetbagger

aggery \ag-ə-rē\ jaggery, staggery, vagary, waggery, carpetbaggery

aggie \ag-ē\ see [2]AGGY

agging \ag-iŋ\ bagging,

flagging, lagging, nagging, brown bagging, foot-dragging, unflagging, carpetbagging
aggish \ag-ish\ haggish, waggish
aggle \ag-əl\ draggle, gaggle, haggle, raggle, straggle, waggle, bedraggle, raggle-taggle
aggly \ag-lē\ scraggly, straggly, waggly
aggot \ag-ət\ agate, faggot, fagot, maggot
[1]aggy \äg-ē\ see [1]OGGY
[2]aggy \ag-ē\ aggie, baggy, braggy, craggy, draggy, jaggy, quaggy, ragi, scraggy, shaggy, snaggy, staggy, swaggy
agh \ä\ see [1]A
[1]agi \äg-ē\ see [1]OGGY
[2]agi \ag-ē\ see [2]AGGY
agian \ā-jən\ see AJUN
agic \aj-ik\ magic, tragic, choragic, pelagic
agile \aj-əl\ agile, fragile, gradual, vagile
agin \ā-gən\ fagin, pagan, Reagan, Copenhagen
aginal \aj-ən-ᵊl\ paginal, vaginal, imaginal
aging \ā-jiŋ\ aging, raging, staging, unaging
aginous \aj-ə-nəs\ collagenous, farraginous, plumbaginous, viraginous, cartilaginous, mucilaginous, oleaginous
agion \ā-jən\ see AJUN
agious \ā-jəs\ see AGEOUS
[1]aglia \äl-yə\ see [1]AHLIA
[2]aglia \al-yə\ see ALUE
aglio \al-yō\ intaglio, seraglio
agm \am\ see [2]AM
agma \ag-mə\ magma, syntagma
agman \ag-mən\ bagman, flagman, swagman
agna \än-yə\ see [1]ANIA
agne \ān\ see [1]ANE
agnes \ag-nəs\ Agnes, Albertas Magnus
agnum \ag-nəm\ magnum, sphagnum
agnus \ag-nəs\ see AGNES
[1]ago \äg-ō\ lago, Chicago, farrago, galago, virago, Asiago, Calinago, Santiago, solidago
[2]ago \ā-gō\ dago, sago, farrago, galago, imago, lumbago, plumbago, sapsago, Tobago, virago, solidago, San Diego, Tierra del Fuego
ago \äŋ-gō\ see ONGO
agon \ag-ən\ dragon, flagon, lagan, wagon, bandwagon, jolt-wagon, Pendragon, snapdragon, battlewagon
agonal \ag-ən-ᵊl\ agonal, diagonal, heptagonal, hexagonal, octagonal, pentagonal, tetragonal
agora \ag-ə-rə\ agora, mandragora
agoras \ag-ə-rəs\ Protagoras, Pythagoras
agot \ag-ət\ see AGGOT
agrance \ā-grəns\ flagrance, fragrance
agrancy \ā-grən-sē\ flagrancy, fragrancy, vagrancy
agrant \ā-grənt\ flagrant, fragrant, vagrant, conflagrant

agster \ag-stər\ dragster, gagster
agua \äg-wə\ majagua, Managua, piragua, Aconcagua, Nicaragua
[1]ague \āg\ see [1]EG
[2]ague \äg\ see [1]OG
aguey \eg-ē\ see EGGY
agus \ā-gəs\ magus, Tagus, choragus, Las Vegas, Simon Magus
agy \ā-jē\ cagey, Meiji, stagy
[1]ah \ä\ see [1]A
[2]ah \ȯ\ see [1]AW
[3]ah \a\ baa, nah, pas de chat
aha \ä-hä\ Baja, Naha, Praha
aham \ā-əm\ see AHUM
ahd \äd\ see [1]OD
ahdi \äd-ē\ see [1]ODY
ahdom \äd-əm\ see ODOM
ahib \äb\ see [1]OB
ahl \äl\ see [1]AL
ahler \äl-ər\ see OLLAR
[1]ahlia \äl-yə\ dahlia, passacaglia
[2]ahlia \al-yə\ see ALUE
[3]ahlia \ā-lē-ə\ see [1]ALIA
[1]ahma \ā-mə\ see [3]AMA
[2]ahma \äm-ə\ see [2]AMA
[3]ahma \am-ə\ see [4]AMA
[1]ahman \äm-ən\ see OMMON
[2]ahman \am-ən\ see AMMON
ahn \än\ see [1]ON
ahms \ämz\ see ALMS
ahnda \än-də\ see ONDA
ahr \är\ see [3]AR
ahru \ä-rü\ see ARU
aht \ät\ see [1]OT
ahua \ä-wə\ see [1]AWA
ahum \ā-əm\ Graham, mayhem, Nahum, Te Deum
ahveh \ä-vā\ see [1]AVE
[1]ai \ā\ see [1]AY
[2]ai \ē\ see [1]EE
[3]ai \ī\ see [1]Y
[4]ai \ȯi\ see OY
[5]ai \ä-ē\ see AII
a'i \ī\ see [1]Y
[1]aia \ā-ə\ Freya, Aglaia, cattleya, Hosea, Isaiah, Nouméa, Himalaya, Kilauea, Mauna Kea, Meghalaya
[2]aia \ī-ə\ see [1]IAH
[1]aiad \ā-əd\ naiad, pleiad
[2]aiad \ī-əd\ see YAD
aiah \ā-ə\ see AIA
aias \ā-əs\ see [1]AIS
aic \ā-ik\ laic, alcaic, Altaic, archaic, Chaldaic, deltaic, Hebraic, Incaic, Judaic, Mishnaic, Mithraic, mosaic, Mosaic, prosaic, Romaic, spondaic, stanzaic, trochaic, voltaic, algebraic, Aramaic, Cyrenaic, faradaic, formulaic, pharisaic, Ptolemaic, apotropaic, paradisaic, photomosaic, Ural-Altaic
aica \ā-ə-k-ə\ Judaica, Cyrenaica
aical \ā-ə-kəl\ laical, pharisaical, paradisaical
aice \ās\ see [1]ACE
aich \āk̲\ see AIGH
aiche \esh\ see [1]ESH
aicos \ā-kəs\ see ECAS
[1]aid \ād\ see [1]ADE
[2]aid \ed\ see [1]EAD
[3]aid \ad\ see [3]AD
aida \ī-də\ see [2]IDA
[1]aide \ād\ see [1]ADE
[2]aide \īd-ē\ see IDAY
aiden \ād-ᵊn\ see ADEN
aider \ād-ər\ see ADER

aiding \ād-iŋ\ see ADING
aido \ī-dō\ see [1]IDO
aids \ādz\ see [2]ADES
aiety \ā-ət-ē\ see AITY
aif \āf\ see [1]AFE
aig \āg\ see [1]EG
aiga \ī-gə\ taiga, Auriga
aigh \āk\ laigh, quaich
aight \āt\ see [1]ATE
aighten \āt-ən\ see [1]ATEN
aightly \āt-lē\ see [1]ATELY
aign \ān\ see [1]ANE
aigne \ān\ see [1]ANE
aignment \ān-mənt\ see AINMENT
aii \ä-ē\ Hawaii, Tubuai
aiian \ä-yən\ zayin, Hawaiian
aijin \ī-jēn\ gaijin, hygiene
aik \īk\ see [2]IKE
aika \ī-kə\ see [1]ICA
ail \āl\ ail, ale, baal, bail, bale, brail, braille, Braille, dale, Dale, drail, fail, flail, frail, Gael, gale, Gale, Gayle, grail, hail, hale, Hale, jail, kale, mail, male, nail, pail, pale, quail, Quayle, rail, sail, sale, scale, shale, snail, stale, swale, tael, tail, taille, tale, they'll, trail, vail, vale, veil, wail, wale, whale, Yale, abseil, airmail, assail, avail, bangtail, bewail, blackmail, blacktail, bobtail, broadscale, broadtail, bucktail, canaille, cattail, Clydesdale, coattail, cocktail, contrail, curtail, derail, detail, doornail, dovetail, downscale, ducktail, E-mail, entail, exhale, fantail, female, fishtail, folktale, foresail, foxtail, full-scale, Glendale, greenmail, guardrail, Hallel, handrail, hangnail, headsail, hightail, hobnail, horntail, horsetail, impale, inhale, Longueuil, lugsail, mainsail, oxtail, pass-fail, percale, pigtail, pintail, pinwale, portrayal, prevail, rattail, regale, resale, rescale, retail, ringtail, Sangreal, sei whale, shavetail, shirttail, skysail, small-scale, springtail, spritsail, staysail, surveil, swordtail, taffrail, telltale, thumbnail, timescale, toenail, topsail, travail, treenail, trysail, unnail, unveil, upscale, ventail, wagtail, wassail, whitetail, wholesale, abigail, Abigail, aventail, betrayal, bristletail, Chippendale, Corriedale, cottontail, countervail, defrayal, disentail, draggle-tail, farthingale, fingernail, flickertail, forestaysail, gaff-topsail, galingale, martingale, monorail, montadale, nightingale, Nightingale, overscale, ponytail, romeldale, scissortail, swallowtail, tattletale, tripletail, trundle-tail, yellowtail, self-betrayal, Fort Lauderdale, Oregon Trail, Santa Fe Trail
ailable \ā-lə-bəl\ bailable, mailable, sailable, salable, scalable, assailable, available, resalable, unassailable
ailand \ī-lənd\ see IGHLAND
ailant \ā-lənt\ see ALANT

aile \ī-lē\ see YLY
ailed \āld\ mailed, nailed, sailed, scaled, tailed, veiled, detailed, engrailed, hobnailed, pigtailed, ring-tailed, unveiled, ponytailed, swallow-tailed—*also pasts of verbs listed at* AIL
ailer \ā-lər\ alar, bailer, bailor, baler, hailer, jailer, mailer, malar, nailer, sailer, sailor, scalar, scaler, tailer, tailor, Taylor, trailer, wailer, waler, whaler, blackmailer, curtailer, derailleur, detailer, entailer, inhaler, loud-haler, retailer, wassailer, wholesaler, semitrailer—*also comparatives of adjectives listed at* AIL
ailey \ā-lē\ see AILY
ailful \āl-fəl\ see ALEFUL
ailie \ā-lē\ see AILY
ailiff \ā-ləf\ bailiff, caliph
ailing \ā-liŋ\ failing, grayling, mailing, paling, railing, sailing, tailing, veiling, whaling, boardsailing, prevailing, retailing, self-mailing, unfailing, parasailing, unavailing
1aille \āl\ see AIL
2aille \ī\ see 1Y
3aille \īl\ see 1ILE
4aille \ä-yə\ see 1AYA
ailles \ī\ see 1Y
ailleur \ā-lər\ see AILER
ailment \āl-mənt\ ailment, bailment, curtailment, derailment, entailment, impalement
ailor \ā-lər\ see AILER
ails \ālz\ see ALES
ailsman \ālz-mən\ see ALESMAN
aily \ā-lē\ bailey, Bailey, bailie, daily, gaily, grayly, paly, scaly, shaley, wally, Bareilly, Bareli, Disraeli, Israeli, shillelagh, triticale, ukulele
aim \ām\ see 1AME
aima \ī-mə\ see YMA
aimable \ā-mə-bəl\ see AMABLE
aiman \ā-mən\ see 1AMEN
aimant \ā-mənt\ see AYMENT
aiment \ā-mənt\ see AYMENT
aimer \ā-mər\ blamer, claimer, framer, gamer, tamer, declaimer, defamer, disclaimer, exclaimer—*also comparatives of adjectives listed at* 1AME
aimless \ām-ləs\ see AMELESS
1ain \ā-ən\ see 1AYAN
2ain \ān\ see 1ANE
3ain \en\ see 1EN
4ain \in\ see 1IN
5ain \īn\ see 1INE
6ain \a^n\ see 4IN
aina \ī-nə\ see 1INA
ainable \ā-nə-bəl\ stainable, trainable, attainable, containable, explainable, maintainable, restrainable, retrainable, sustainable, inexplainable
ainder \ān-dər\ attainder, remainder
1aine \ān\ see 1ANE
2aine \en\ see 1EN
ained \ānd\ brained, caned, craned, drained, grained, maned, pained, paned, stained, strained, vaned,

veined, birdbrained, bloodstained, close-grained, coarse-grained, crackbrained, cross-grained, edge-grained, harebrained, ingrained, lamebrained, mad-brained, membraned, restrained, tearstained, unfeigned, featherbrained, rattlebrained, scatterbrained, self-contained, unrestrained—*also pasts of verbs listed at* [1]ANE

ainer \ā-nər\ caner, drainer, feigner, gainer, planar, planer, seiner, stainer, strainer, trainer, veiner, campaigner, complainer, container, coplanar, cordwainer, detainer, lupanar, maintainer, ordainer, profaner, restrainer, retainer, sustainer, Trakehner, entertainer—*also comparatives of adjectives listed at* [1]ANE

ainful \ān-fəl\ baneful, gainful, painful, disdainful

aininess \ā-nē-nəs\ braininess, graininess

aining \ā-niŋ\ veining, complaining, sustaining, self-sustaining, uncomplaining—*also present participles of verbs listed at* [1]ANE

ainish \ā-nish\ brainish, Danish, swainish

ainless \ān-ləs\ brainless, painless, stainless

ainly \ān-lē\ mainly, plainly, thegnly, vainly, humanely, insanely, profanely, ungainly, inhumanely

ainment \ān-mənt\ arraignment, attainment, containment, detainment, detrainment, enchainment, entrainment, ordainment, refrainment, entertainment, preordainment, self-containment

aino \ī-nō\ see [1]INO

ains \ānz\ Keynes, reins, cremains, Great Plains, Mains Plains, remains—*also plurals and possessives of nouns and third person singular presents of verbs listed at* [1]ANE

ainsman \ānz-mən\ plainsman, reinsman

aint \ānt\ ain't, faint, feint, mayn't, paint, plaint, quaint, saint, taint, 'tain't, acquaint, attaint, bepaint, complaint, constraint, distraint, greasepaint, impaint, restraint, unconstraint, unrestraint

ain't \ānt\ see AINT

ainting \ān-tiŋ\ underpainting—*also present participles of verbs listed at* AINT

aintly \ānt-lē\ faintly, quaintly, saintly

ainy \ā-nē\ brainy, grainy, meiny, rainy, veiny, zany, Allegheny

ainz \īnz\ see [3]INES

aipse \āps\ see APES

[1]**air** \er\ see [4]ARE

[2]**air** \īr\ see [1]IRE

aira \ī-rə\ see YRA

aird \erd\ see AIRED

[1]**aire** \er\ see [4]ARE

[2]**aire** \ir\ see [2]EER

[3]**aire** \īr\ see [1]IRE

aired \ard\ caird, haired, laird, merde, fair-haired, impaired, long-haired, misleared, prepared, shorthaired, unpaired, wirehaired, multilayered, underprepared, unimpaired—*also pasts of verbs listed at* [4]ARE

airer \er-ər\ see [3]EARER

[1]**aires** \er\ see [4]ARE

[2]**aires** \ar-ēs\ see [2]ARES

[1]**airess** \er-əs\ see ERROUS

[2]**airess** \ar-əs\ see [2]ARIS

airie \er-ē\ see [1]ARY

airing \ar-iŋ\ see [1]ARING

airish \er-ish\ see [1]ARISH

airist \er-əst\ see ARIST

airly \er-lē\ fairly, ferlie, rarely, squarely

airn \ern\ see [1]ERN

airo \ī-rō\ see [1]YRO

airs \erz\ theirs, backstairs, downstairs, nowheres, somewheres, upstairs, unawares—*also plurals and possessives of verbs listed at* [4]ARE

[1]**airy** \ẹr-ē\ see [1]ARY

[2]**airy** \ā-rē\ see [1]AERIE

[1]**ais** \ā-əs\ dais, Laius, Isaias, Menelaus

[2]**ais** \ā\ see [1]AY

[1]**aisal** \ā-zəl\ see [2]ASAL

[2]**aisal** \ī-səl\ see [1]ISAL

aisance \ās-^{ə}ns\ see [1]ASCENCE

aisant \ās-^{ə}nt\ see ACENT

[1]**aise** \āz\ see [1]AZE

[2]**aise** \ez\ see [1]AYS

aisement \āz-mənt\ see AZEMENT

[1]**aiser** \ā-zər\ see AZER

[2]**aiser** \ī-zər\ see IZER

aisian \ā-zhən\ see ASION

aisin \āz-^{ə}n\ see AZON

aising \ā-ziŋ\ braising, glazing, hazing, phrasing, appraising, fund-raising, hair-raising, hell-raising, house-raising, stargazing, trailblazing—*also present participles of verbs listed at* [1]AZE

aisle \īl\ see [1]ILE

aisley \āz-lē\ paisley, nasally

aisne \ān\ see [1]ANE

aisse \ās\ see [1]ACE

aisson \ās-^{ə}n\ see [1]ASON

[1]**aist** \ā-əst\ see AYEST

[2]**aist** \āst\ see ACED

[3]**aist** \äst\ see [1]OST

aisy \ā-zē\ see AZY

[1]**ait** \ā\ see [1]AY

[2]**ait** \āt\ see [1]ATE

[3]**ait** \īt\ see [1]ITE

[4]**ait** \at\ see [5]AT

aite \īt\ see [1]ITE

aited \āt-əd\ see ATED

aiten \āt-^{ə}n\ see [1]ATEN

aiter \āt-ər\ see ATOR

aith \āth\ eighth, faith, Faith, saithe, scathe, wraith, unfaith, interfaith

aithe \āth\ see AITH

aithless \āth-ləs\ faithless, natheless

aiti \āt-ē\ see ATY

aitian \ā-shən\ see [1]ATION

aiting \āt-iŋ\ see ATING

aitly \āt-lē\ see [1]ATELY

aitor \āt-ər\ see ATOR

aitorous \āt-ə-rəs\ see ATERESS

aitour \āt-ər\ see ATOR

aitress \ā-trəs\ traitress, waitress, aviatress

aity \ā-ət-ē\ deity, gaiety, laity, corporeity, spontaneity, synchroneity, diaphaneity,

contemporaneity, extemporaneity
[1]**aius** \ā-əs\ see [1]AIS
[2]**aius** \ī-əs\ see [1]IAS
aiva \ī-və\ see [1]IVA
aive \āv\ see [2]AVE
aix \ā\ see [1]AY
aize \āz\ see [1]AZE
aj \äj\ see [1]AGE
[1]**aja** \ä-hä\ see AHA
[2]**aja** \ī-ə\ see [1]IAH
ajan \ā-jən\ see AJUN
ajj \aj\ see ADGE
ajor \ā-jər\ see [1]AGER
ajos \ā-əs\ see [1]AIS
ajun \ā-jən\ Cajun, Trajan, contagion, Pelagian, reagin
[1]**ak** \äk\ see [1]OCK
[2]**ak** \ak\ see [2]ACK
[1]**aka** \äk-ə\ Dacca, Dhaka, kaka, paca, taka, Lusaka, maraca, medaka, Oaxaca, Osaka, pataca, Mbandaka, saltimbocca, Toyonaka, Lake Titicaca, Higashiosaka
[2]**aka** \ak-ə\ see [2]ACA
akable \ā-kə-bəl\ breakable, makable, shakable, mistakable, unslakable, unmistakable
[1]**akan** \äk-ən\ see [2]AKEN
[2]**akan** \ak-ən\ see ACKEN
akar \äk-ər\ see OCKER
[1]**ake** \āk\ ache, bake, Blake, brake, break, cake, crake, drake, Drake, fake, flake, hake, jake, Jake, lake, make, quake, rake, sake, shake, sheikh, slake, snake, spake, stake, steak, strake, take, wake, Wake, awake, backache, beefcake, beefsteak, betake, blacksnake, canebrake, caretake, cheesecake, clambake, corncrake, cupcake, daybreak, earache, earthquake, firebreak, firedrake, forsake, friedcake, fruitcake, grubstake, handshake, headache, heartache, heartbreak, hoecake, hotcake, housebreak, intake, jailbreak, keepsake, lapstrake, mandrake, Marsquake, mistake, moonquake, muckrake, namesake, newsbreak, oatcake, opaque, outbreak, outtake, Pan-Cake, pancake, partake, remake, retake, rewake, seaquake, seedcake, sheldrake, shortcake, snowflake, sweepstake, toothache, unmake, uptake, windbreak, youthquake, bellyache, give-and-take, halterbreak, johnnycake, kittiwake, make-or-break, microquake, overtake, pat-a-cake, patty-cake, put-and-take, rattlesnake, stomachache, undertake, wapentake, wideawake, semiopaque
[2]**ake** \ak\ see [2]ACK
[3]**ake** \äk-ē\ see OCKY
aked \ākt\ awaked, half-baked, ringstraked, sunbaked—*also pasts of verbs listed at* [1]AKE
akeless \ā-kləs\ brakeless, wakeless
[1]**aken** \ā-kən\ bacon, Bacon, Macon, waken, shaken, taken, awaken, partaken, retaken, betaken, forsaken, mistaken,

rewaken, well-taken, godforsaken, overtaken, undertaken

[2]**aken** \äk-ən\ kraken, Arawakan

[1]**aker** \ā-kər\ acre, baker, breaker, faker, laker, maker, nacre, quaker, Quaker, raker, saker, shaker, taker, waker, backbreaker, bookmaker, caretaker, carmaker, comaker, dressmaker, drugmaker, earthshaker, filmmaker, glassmaker, groundbreaker, grubstaker, hatmaker, haymaker, heartbreaker, homemaker, housebreaker, icebreaker, jawbreaker, kingmaker, lawbreaker, lawmaker, mapmaker, matchmaker, mistaker, muckraker, mythmaker, noisemaker, oddsmaker, pacemaker, peacemaker, phrasemaker, platemaker, playmaker, printmaker, rainmaker, saltshaker, shirtmaker, shoemaker, snowmaker, stavesacre, steelmaker, strikebreaker, tastemaker, tiebreaker, toolmaker, trailbreaker, watchmaker, windbreaker, wiseacre, automaker, bellyacher, boilermaker, merrymaker, moneymaker, moviemaker, papermaker, simulacre, troublemaker, undertaker, cabinetmaker, holidaymaker, policymaker

[2]**aker** \ak-ər\ see ACKER

akery \ā-krē\ bakery, fakery

akes \āks\ jakes, cornflakes, Great Lakes, sweepstakes—*also plurals and possessives of nouns and third person singular presents of verbs listed at* [1]AKE

ake-up \ā-kəp\ break-up, breakup, make-up, makeup, shake-up, shakeup, take-up, wake-up

akey \ā-kē\ see AKY

[1]**akh** \äk\ see [1]OCK

[2]**akh** \ak\ see [2]ACK

[1]**aki** \äk-ē\ see OCKY

[2]**aki** \ak-ē\ see ACKY

akian \äk-ē-ən\ see OCKIAN

akic \ak-ik\ see ACCHIC

[1]**aking** \ā-kiŋ\ aching, making, waking, bookmaking, breathtaking, caretaking, dressmaking, earthshaking, filmmaking, glassmaking, groundbreaking, heartbreaking, housebreaking, lawbreaking, lawmaking, leave-taking, lovemaking, mapmaking, matchmaking, mythmaking, noisemaking, pacemaking, painstaking, pathbreaking, peacemaking, phrasemaking, printmaking, rainmaking, snowmaking, stocktaking, strikebreaking, toolmaking, watchmaking, world-shaking, merrymaking, moneymaking, moviemaking, papermaking, undertaking, cabinetmaking, policymaking

[2]**aking** \ak-iŋ\ see ACKING

[1]**ako** \äk-ō\ see OCCO

[2]**ako** \ak-ō\ shako, wacko, tobacco

aku \äk-ü\ Bunraku, gagaku, nunchaku
akum \ā-kəm\ vade mecum, shalom aleichem
aky \ā-kē\ achy, braky, cakey, flaky, laky, shaky, snaky, headachy
[1]**al** \äl\ Bâle, col, dahl, dal, doll, loll, moll, nal, pol, sol, Sol, Taal, toile, Algol, atoll, austral, Baikal, Bhopal, cabal, Chagall, chorale, grand mal, gun moll, hamal, jacal, mistral, narwhal, Natal, nopal, Pascal, petrol, quetzal, real, rial, riyal, Shawwal, tical, timbale, Transvaal, à cheval, aerosol, Emmenthal, falderal, femme fatale, folderol, Heyerdahl, parasol, pastoral, pastorale, protocol, Provençal, Simmental, urial, Wuppertal, entente cordiale, Neanderthal, procès-verbal, sublittoral, succès de scandale
[2]**al** \el\ see [1]EL
[3]**al** \ȯl\ see ALL
[4]**al** \al\ Al, gal, Hal, pal, rale, sal, Val, banal, cabal, canal, Chagall, chorale, copal, corral, decal, fal-lal, grand mal, joual, La Salle, Laval, locale, mescal, moral, morale, nopal, pall-mall, pascal, percale, quetzal, salal, serval, vinal, bacchanal, caracal, chaparral, femme fatale, musicale, pastoral, pastorale, pedocal, rationale, retinal, Seconal, Guadalcanal, kilopascal, sublittoral
[1]**ala** \äl-ä\ à la, Allah, gala
[2]**ala** \äl-ə\ Allah, olla, tala, wallah, cabala, cantala, Chapala, chuckwalla, cicala, corolla, Douala, halala, Kampala, koala, Lingala, marsala, nyala, tambala, Tlaxcala, Valhalla, Walhalla, ayotollah, Guatemala, Gujranwala
[3]**ala** \ā-lə\ ala, gala, Venezuela, zarzuela
[4]**ala** \al-ə\ see ALLOW
alaam \ā-ləm\ Balaam, golem, Salem, Winston-Salem
alable \ā-lə-bəl\ see AILABLE
alace \al-əs\ see [2]ALIS
alad \al-əd\ see [2]ALID
alam \äl-əm\ see OLUMN
alamine \al-ə-mən\ allemande, calamine
alan \al-ən\ see ALLON
alance \al-əns\ balance, valance, imbalance, outbalance, unbalance, counterbalance, overbalance
alant \ā-lənt\ assailant, bivalent, covalent, exhalent, inhalant, multivalent, pentavalent, quadrivalent, surveillant, tetravalent, trivalent, univalent
alap \al-əp\ see [2]ALLOP
alar \ā-lər\ see AILER
[1]**alary** \al-rē\ see ALLERY
[2]**alary** \al-ə-rē\ calorie, gallery, Mallory, Malory, salary, Valerie, Valery, kilocalorie
alas \al-əs\ see [2]ALIS
alate \al-ət\ see [2]ALLET
[1]**alcon** \ȯ-kən\ see [1]ALKIN
[2]**alcon** \al-kən\ falcon, gyrfalcon, grimalkin
[1]**ald** \ȯld\ bald, scald, skald,

walled, close-hauled, keelhauled, kobold, piebald, ribald, skewbald, so-called, sunscald, Archibald, coveralled, overalled—*also pasts of verbs listed at* ALL

[2]**ald** \ȯlt\ see ALT

alder \ȯl-dər\ alder, balder, Balder

aldi \ȯl-dē\ Bartholdi, Vivaldi, Garibaldi

aldron \ȯl-drən\ aldron, caldron, cauldron, chaldron

[1]**ale** \ā-lē\ see AILY

[2]**ale** \āl\ see AIL

[3]**ale** \äl\ see [1]AL

[4]**ale** \al\ see [4]AL

[5]**ale** \äl-ē\ see [1]OLLY

[6]**ale** \al-ē\ see [4]ALLY

alea \ā-lē-ə\ see [1]ALIA

[1]**aleck** \el-ik\ see [2]ELIC

[2]**aleck** \al-ik\ see ALLIC

aled \āld\ see AILED

aleful \āl-fəl\ baleful, wailful

[1]**aleigh** \äl-ē\ see [1]OLLY

[2]**aleigh** \ȯl-ē\ see AWLY

alem \ā-ləm\ see ALAAM

alement \āl-mənt\ see AILMENT

alen \ä-lən\ see [5]OLLEN

alence \ā-ləns\ valence, surveillance

alends \al-ənz\ see ALLANS

[1]**alent** \al-ənt\ see ALLANT

[2]**alent** \ā-lənt\ see ALANT

alep \al-əp\ see [2]ALLOP

[1]**aler** \ā-lər\ see AILER

[2]**aler** \äl-ər\ see OLLAR

alerie \al-ə-re\ see [2]ALARY

alery \al-ə-rē\ see [2]ALARY

[1]**ales** \ālz\ sales, Wales, entrails, Marseilles, New South Wales, Prince of Wales, cat-o'-nine-tails—*also plurals and possessives of nouns listed at* AIL

[2]**ales** \äl-əs\ see OLIS

alesman \ālz-mən\ bailsman, dalesman, salesman, talesman

alet \al-ət\ see [2]ALLET

alette \al-ət\ see [2]ALLET

aley \ā-lē\ see AILY

alf \af\ see APH

alfa \al-fə\ see ALPHA

alfness \af-nəs\ see AFTNESS

algia \al-jə\ neuralgia, nostalgia

[1]**ali** \äl-ē\ see [1]OLLY

[2]**ali** \al-ē\ see [4]ALLY

[3]**ali** \ȯ-lē\ see AWLY

[4]**ali** \ā-lē\ see AILY

[1]**alia** \ā-lē-ə\ dahlia, Australia, azalea, battalia, realia, regalia, vedalia, Westphalia, bacchanalia, genitalia, glossolalia, inter alia, Lupercalia, marginalia, Orientalia, paraphernalia, penetralia, saturnalia

[2]**alia** \al-yə\ dahlia, battalia, et alia, passacaglia

[1]**alian** \ā-lē-ən\ alien, Australian, Daedalian, Deucalion, Hegelian, mammalian, Pygmalion, Uralian, bacchanalian, Lupercalian, saturnalian, Episcopalian, sesquipedalian, tatterdemalion

[2]**alian** \al-yən\ see ALLION

alic \al-ik\ see ALLIC

alice \al-əs\ see [2]ALIS

[1]**alid** \äl-əd\ see OLID

[2]**alid** \al-əd\ ballad, pallid, salad, valid, invalid

alie \äl-yə\ see [1]AHLIA

alien \ā-lē-ən\ see [1]ALIAN
aling \ā-liŋ\ see AILING
alinist \äl-ə-nəst\ see OLONIST
alinn \al-ən\ see ALLON
[1]**alion** \ā-lē-ən\ see [1]ALIAN
[2]**alion** \al-yən\ see ALLION
aliph \ā-ləf\ see AILIFF
[1]**alis** \ā-ləs\ see AYLESS
[2]**alis** \al-əs\ Alice, balas, callous, callus, chalice, Dallas, gallus, malice, palace, Pallas, phallus, talus, thallous, thallus, oxalis, digitalis, hemerocallis, aurora borealis, Corona Borealis
alist \al-əst\ ballast, callused, gallused, cabalist, sodalist
[1]**ality** \äl-ət-ē\ jollity, polity, quality, equality, frivolity, coequality, inequality
[2]**ality** \al-ət-ē\ anality, banality, brutality, carnality, causality, centrality, duality, extrality, fatality, feudality, finality, formality, frontality, frugality, legality, locality, mentality, modality, morality, mortality, nasality, natality, neutrality, nodality, orality, plurality, primality, rascality, reality, regality, rurality, sodality, tonality, totality, venality, vitality, vocality, abnormality, actuality, amorality, animality, atonality, axiality, bestiality, bimodality, bipedality, cardinality, classicality, coevality, comicality, commonality, communality, conjugality, cordiality, corporality, criminality, criticality, ethicality, externality, factuality, farcicality, fictionality, functionality, generality, geniality, hospitality, ideality, illegality, immorality, immortality, informality, integrality, internality, irreality, lexicality, liberality, lineality, literality, logicality, musicality, mutuality, nationality, notionality, nuptiality, optimality, partiality, personality, physicality, principality, punctuality, rationality, seasonality, sexuality, sociality, spaciality, speciality, subnormality, technicality, temporality, topicality, triviality, unmorality, unreality, verticality, virtuality, whimsicality, asexuality, atypicality, bisexuality, collaterality, collegiality, colloquiality, commerciality, conceptuality, conditionality, congeniality, connaturality, conventionality, conviviality, corporeality, dimensionality, directionality, effectuality, emotionality, ephemerality, equivocality, essentiality, ethereality, eventuality, exceptionality, extensionality, fantasticality, grammaticality, illiberality, illogicality, impersonality, impracticality, inhospitality, instrumentality, irrationality, materiality, microtonality, monumentality, municipality, originality,

orthogonality, pansexuality, paranormality, polytonality, potentiality, provinciality, self-partiality, sentimentality, spirituality, substantiality, theatricality, transexuality, triaxiality, universality, veridicality, ambisexuality, artificiality, circumstantiality, confidentiality, consequentiality, constitutionality, homosexuality, hypersexuality, immateriality, individuality, ineffectuality, insubstantiality, intellectuality, internationality, intersexuality, paradoxicality, psychosexuality, referentiality, superficiality, supranationality, territoriality, tridimensionality, two-dimensionality, uncongeniality, unconventionality, ungrammaticality, unisexuality, unsubstantiality, exterritoriality, heterosexuality, inconsequentiality, unconstitutionality, unidimensionality, extraterritoriality

alium \al-ē-əm\ see ALLIUM

alius \ā-lē-əs\ alius, Sibelius

alk \ȯk\ auk, balk, calk, caulk, chalk, gawk, hawk, Koch, Salk, Sauk, squawk, stalk, talk, walk, Bartok, Black Hawk, bemock, boardwalk, cakewalk, catwalk, chalktalk, cornstalk, crosswalk, duckwalk, eyestalk, fast-talk, goshawk, jaywalk, langue d'oc, leafstalk, Mohawk, nighthawk, Norfolk, outtalk, ropewalk, shoptalk, sidewalk, skywalk, sleepwalk, Suffolk, sweet-talk, belle epoque, catafalque, double-talk, Swainson's hawk, tomahawk

alkan \ȯl-kən\ see [1]ALKIN

alker \ȯ-kər\ balker, caulker, gawker, hawker, squawker, stalker, walker, cakewalker, deerstalker, floorwalker, jayhawker, jaywalker, nightwalker, ropewalker, sleepwalker, spacewalker, streetwalker, trackwalker, double-talker

alkie \ȯ-kē\ balky, chalky, gawky, gnocchi, pawky, stalky, talkie, talky, Milwaukee, Handie-Talkie, walkie-talkie, Winnipesaukee

[1]**alkin** \ȯ-kən\ Balkan, falcon, malkin, grimalkin, gyrfalcon

[2]**alkin** \al-kən\ see [2]ALCON

alking \ȯ-kiŋ\ caulking, walking, racewalking, spacewalking, streetwalking

alkland \ȯk-lənd\ see AUCKLAND

alky \ȯ-kē\ see ALKIE

[1]**all** \ȯl\ all, awl, ball, bawl, brawl, call, caul, crawl, doll, drawl, fall, Gall, Gaul, hall, Hall, haul, kraal, mall, maul, moll, pall, Paul, pawl, Saul, scall, scrawl, shawl, small, Sol, spall, sprawl, squall, stall, tall, thrall, trawl, wall,

y'all, yauld, yawl, Algol, ALGOL, appall, argol, air ball, ashfall, at all, atoll, AWOL, baseball, Baikal, beanball, befall, Bengal, best-ball, birdcall, blackball, Bokmål, bookstall, boxhaul, bradawl, broomball, catcall, catchall, COBOL, cornball, Cornwall, cure-all, curveball, deadfall, de Gaulle, dewfall, dodgeball, downfall, downhaul, drywall, enthrall, eyeball, fastball, fireball, floodwall, football, footfall, footstall, footwall, forestall, forkball, four-ball, free-fall, gadwall, goofball, googol, grease ball, guildhall, hair ball, handball, hardball, headstall, heelball, highball, holdall, icefall, install, keelhaul, know-all, landfall, Landsmål, line-haul, lowball, meatball, menthol, Metol, miscall, mothball, naphthol, Nepal, nightfall, nutgall, oddball, outfall, outhaul, pitfall, plimsoll, pratfall, pub-crawl, puffball, punchball, pushball, rainfall, rainsquall, recall, rial, Riksmål, riyal, rockfall, rorqual, Saint Paul, save-all, screwball, seawall, short-haul, shortfall, sidewall, sleazeball, slimeball, snowball, snowfall, softball, speedball, spitball, Stendhal, stickball, stonewall, stoopball, T-ball, tell-all, three-ball, trackball, Tyrol, Walsall, waterfall, what all, Whitehall, whitewall, windfall, windgall, withal, withdrawal, you-all, aerosol, alcohol, barbital, basketball, bucky ball, butterball, buttonball, cannonball, carryall, caterwaul, cover-all, coverall, Demerol, disenthrol, Donegal, entresol, evenfall, free-for-all, gasohol, girasole, Grand Guignol, haute école, know-it-all, knuckleball, Komsomol, methanol, minié ball, Montreal, Nembutal, overall, overcall, overhaul, paddleball, parasol, Parsifal, Pentothal, protocol, racquetball, Seconal, Senegal, superball, tattersall, tetherball, therewithal, timolol, volleyball, wherewithal, cholesterol, Costa del Sol, Mariupol, Massif Central, Neanderthal, Sevastopol, Transalpine Gaul, Vincent de Paul, be-all and end-all

[2]**all** \äl\ see [1]AL

[3]**all** \al\ see [4]AL

[1]**alla** \äl-ə\ see [2]ALA

[2]**alla** \al-ə\ see [4]ALLOW

allable \ò-lə-bəl\ callable, spallable

allace \äl-əs\ see OLIS

allacy \al-ə-sē\ fallacy, jalousie

allad \al-əd\ see [2]ALID

allage \al-ə-jē\ see [2]ALOGY

[1]**allah** \äl-ä\ see [1]ALA

[2]**allah** \äl-ə\ see [2]ALA

[3]**allah** \al-ə\ see [4]ALLOW

allan \al-ən\ see ALLON

allans \al-ənz\ calends, Lallans—*also plurals and*

possessives of nouns listed at ALLON

allant \al-ənt\ callant, gallant, talent, topgallant, fore-topgallant

allas \al-əs\ see [2]ALIS

allasey \äl-ə-sē\ see OLICY

allast \al-əst\ see ALIST

[1]**alle** \al\ see [4]AL

[2]**alle** \al-ē\ see [4]ALLY

[3]**alle** \äl-ē\ see OLLY

alled \ȯld\ see ALD

allee \al-ē\ see [4]ALLY

allemande \al-ə-mən\ see ALAMINE

[1]**allen** \ȯ-lən\ fallen, stollen, befallen, chapfallen, chopfallen, crestfallen, downfallen, tarpaulin, unfallen

[2]**allen** \al-ən\ see ALLON

[1]**aller** \ȯ-lər\ bawler, brawler, caller, drawler, faller, hauler, mauler, scrawler, squaller, trawler, fireballer, footballer, forestaller, installer, stonewaller, knuckleballer

[2]**aller** \al-ər\ caller, pallor, valor, high yaller

alles \ī-əs\ see [1]IAS

[1]**allet** \äl-ət\ see OLLET

[2]**allet** \al-ət\ ballot, callet, mallet, palate, palette, pallet, sallet, shallot, valet

alley \al-ē\ see [4]ALLY

alli \al-ē\ see [4]ALLY

alliard \al-yərd\ galliard, halyard

allic \al-ik\ Gaelic, Gallic, malic, phallic, salic, Salic, thallic, cephalic, italic, mandalic, medallic, metallic, smart aleck, Uralic, Vandalic, vocalic, genitalic, intervallic, ithyphallic, nonmetallic, postvocalic, prevocalic, intervocalic

allid \al-əd\ see [2]ALID

allie \al-ē\ see [4]ALLY

alling \ȯ-liŋ\ balling, calling, drawling, falling, galling, hauling, infalling, mauling, name-calling, Pauling, stalling

alinn \al-ən\ see ALLON

allion \al-yən\ scallion, stallion, battalion, Italian, medallion, rapscallion, tatterdemalion

[1]**allis** \al-əs\ see [2]ALIS

[2]**allis** \al-ē\ see [4]ALLY

[3]**allis** \äl-əs\ see OLIS

allish \ȯ-lish\ Gaulish, smallish, tallish

allit \ä-lət\ see OLLET

[1]**allith** \äl-əs\ see OLIS

[2]**allith** \äl-ət\ see OLLET

allium \al-ē-əm\ allium, gallium, pallium, thallium, Valium

allment \ȯl-mənt\ enthrallment, forestallment, installment

allo \äl-ō\ see [1]OLLOW

allon \al-ən\ Alan, Allan, Allen, Allyn, gallon, lallan, Talinn, talon

[1]**allop** \äl-əp\ see OLLOP

[2]**allop** \al-əp\ gallop, galop, jalap, salep, Salop, scallop, shallop, escallop

allor \al-ər\ see [2]ALLER

[1]**allory** \al-re\ see ALLERY

[2]**allory** \al-ə-rē\ see [2]ALARY

allot \al-ət\ see [2]ALLET

allous \al-əs\ see [2]ALIS

[1]**allow** \el-ō\ see ELLO

²allow \äl-ə\ see ²ALA
³allow \äl-ō\ see ¹OLLOW
⁴allow \al-ə\ Allah, callow, fallow, gala, Galla, hallow, sallow, shallow, tallow, cavalla, impala, unhallow, Valhalla
⁵allow \al-ō\ aloe, callow, fallow, hallow, mallow, sallow, shallow, tallow, unhallow
allowed \al-ōd\ hallowed, unhallowed
allows \al-ōz\ gallows, Allhallows—*also plurals and possessives of nouns listed at* ⁴ALLOW
alls \ȯlz\ Angel Falls, Niagara Falls—*also possessives and plurals of nouns, third person singular presents of verbs listed at* ALL
allsy \ȯl-zē\ see ALSY
allus \al-əs\ see ²ALIS
allused \al-əst\ see ALIST
¹ally \ā-lē\ see AILY
²ally \äl-ē\ see ¹OLLY
³ally \ȯ-lē\ see AWLY
⁴ally \al-ē\ alley, bally, challis, dally, galley, gally, mallee, pally, rally, sallie, sally, Sally, tally, valley, Aunt Sally, bialy, crevalle, Death Valley, finale, Nepali, tomalley, dillydally, Mexicali, shilly-shally, teocalli, Great Rift Valley
allyn \al-ən\ see ALLON
alm \äm\ see ¹OM
alma \al-mə\ Alma, halma
almar \äm-ər\ see ¹OMBER
almer \äm-ər\ see ¹OMBER
almily \äm-ə-lē\ see OMALY
almish \äm-ish\ see ¹AMISH
almist \äm-əst\ palmist, psalmist, Islamist
almody \äm-əd-ē\ see OMEDY
almon \am-ən\ see AMMON
almoner \äm-ə-nər\ see OMMONER
alms \ämz\ alms, Brahms, Psalms—*also plurals and possessives of nouns and third singular presents of verbs listed at* ¹OM
almy \äm-ē\ see ¹AMI
alo \äl-ō\ see ¹OLLOW
aloe \al-ō\ see ⁵ALLOW
¹alogist \äl-ə-jəst\ see OLOGIST
²alogist \al-ə-jəst\ analogist, dialogist, mammalogist, genealogist
¹alogy \äl-ə-jē\ see OLOGY
²alogy \al-ə-jē\ analogy, hypallage, mammalogy, tetralogy, mineralogy
alom \äl-əm\ see OLUMN
alon \al-ən\ see ALLON
alop \al-əp\ see ²ALLOP
¹alor \äl-ər\ see OLLAR
²alor \al-ər\ see ²ALLER
¹alorie \al-rē\ see ¹ALLERY
²alorie \al-ə-rē\ see ²ALARY
¹alory \al-rē\ see ALLERY
²alory \al-ə-rē\ see ²ALARY
alousie \al-ə-sē\ see ALLACY
alp \alp\ alp, salp, scalp
alpa \al-pə\ salpa, catalpa, Tegucigalpa
alpal \al-pəl\ palpal, scalpel
alpel \al-pəl\ see ALPAL
alpha \al-fə\ alpha, alfalfa
¹alque \ȯk\ see ALK

²alque \alk\ calque, talc, catafalque
als \älz\ see OLS
alsa \ȯl-sə\ balsa, salsa
alse \ȯls\ false, waltz
alsey \ȯl-zē\ see ALSY
alsy \ȯl-zē\ ballsy, Halsey, palsy
alt \ȯlt\ fault, gault, halt, malt, salt, smalt, vault, volt, Walt, asphalt, assault, basalt, cobalt, default, desalt, exalt, footfault, gestalt, Great Salt, Schwarzwald, stringhalt, double-fault, somersault, pepper-and-salt
alta \äl-tə\ Malta, Salta, Volta, Yalta
altar \ȯl-tər\ see ALTER
alter \ȯl-tər\ altar, alter, falter, halter, palter, Psalter, salter, vaulter, Walter, defaulter, desalter, exalter, Gibraltar, pole-vaulter
altery \ȯl-trē\ see ALTRY
¹alti \əl-tē\ Balti, difficulty
²alti \ȯl-tē\ see ALTY
altic \ȯl-tik\ Baltic, asphaltic, cobaltic, systaltic, peristaltic
alting \ȯl-tiŋ\ halting, salting, vaulting
altless \ȯlt-ləs\ faultless, saltless
alto \al-tō\ alto, contralto, rialto
alton \ȯlt-ᵊn\ Alton, dalton, Dalton, Walton
altry \ȯl-trē\ paltry, psaltery, psaltry
alty \ȯl-tē\ Balti, faulty, malty, salty, vaulty
altz \ȯls\ see ALSE
alu \äl-ü\ Yalu, Tuvalu
alue \al-yü\ value, devalue, disvalue, misvalue, revalue, transvalue, overvalue, undervalue
¹alus \ā-ləs\ see AYLESS
²alus \al-əs\ see ²ALIS
¹alve \äv\ see ²OLVE
²alve \alv\ salve, valve, bivalve, univalve, inequivalve
³alve \av\ calve, halve, have, salve
alver \al-vər\ salver, salvor, quacksalver
alvin \al-vən\ Alvin, Calvin
alvor \al-vər\ see ALVER
aly \al-ē\ see ⁴ALLY
alyard \al-yərd\ see ALLIARD
alysis \al-ə-səs\ analysis, dialysis, paralysis, cryptanalysis, metanalysis, self-analysis
¹am \äm\ see ¹OM
²am \am\ am, cam, cham, clam, cram, dam, damn, damned, drachm, dram, DRAM, flam, gam, Graham, gram, ham, Ham, jam, jamb, lam, lamb, Lamb, ma'am, Pam, pram, ram, RAM, Sam, SAM, scam, scram, sham, slam, swam, tam, tram, wham, yam, Annam, ashram, Assam, dirham, Edam, ngram, exam, flimflam, goddamn, grandam, iamb, logjam, madame, mailgram, milldam, nizam, Priam, program, quondam, tam-tam, thiram, trigram, whim-wham, ziram, Abraham, aerogram, Amsterdam, anagram, Birmingham, Boulder Dam, cablegram, centigram,

Christogram, chronogram, cofferdam, cryptogram, decagram, deprogram, diagram, diaphragm, dithyramb, epigram, fluid dram, hexagram, histogram, Hohokam, hologram, Hoover Dam, kilogram, logogram, mammogram, milligram, Minicam, monogram, nomogram, oriflamme, pentagram, phonogram, pictogram, reprogram, Rotterdam, scattergram, skiagram, Smithfield ham, sonogram, subprogram, Surinam, telegram, tetradrachm, thank-you-ma'am, Uncle Sam, ad nauseam, cardiogram, heliogram, ideogram, in personam, microprogram, New Amsterdam, Omar Khayyam, parallelogram

[1]**ama** \äm-ə\ Brahma, comma, drama, Kama, lama, llama, mama, momma, squama, Rama, Bahama, pajama, Toyama, Atacama, cyclorama, Dalai Lama, diorama, docudrama, Fujiyama, Fukuyama, Matsuyama, melodrama, monodrama, Mount Mazama, Okayama, panorama, photodrama, psychodrama, Suriname, Wakayama, Yokohama, Fujinoyamia, Puna de Atacama

[2]**ama** \am-ə\ Brahma, drama, gamma, grama, mamma, da Gama, Manama, Miami, pajama, Alabama, anadama, cyclorama, diorama, docudrama, melodrama, monodrama, panorama, photodrama, psychodrama

amable \ā-mə-bəl\ blamable, claimable, framable, nameable, tamable, irreclaimable

amah \äm-ä\ see [1]AMA

[1]**aman** \ā-mən\ see [1]AMEN

[2]**aman** \äm-ən\ see OMMON

[1]**amant** \ā-mənt\ see AYMENT

[2]**amant** \am-ənt\ see [2]AMENT

amas \am-əs\ see AMICE

amash \äm-ish\ see [1]AMISH

amateur \am-ət-ər\ see AMETER

amatist \am-ət-əst\ dramatist, epigrammatist, melodramatist

amba \äm-bə\ gamba, mamba, samba, Zomba, Cochabamba, viola da gamba

[1]**ambar** \äm-bər\ see [2]OMBER

[2]**ambar** \am-bər\ amber, Amber, camber, sambar, timbre, liquidambar

ambe \am-bē\ see AMBY

ambeau \am-bō\ see AMBO

[1]**amber** \am-bər\ see [2]AMBAR

[2]**amber** \am-ər\ see AMMER

ambia \am-bē-ə\ Gambia, Zambia

ambit \am-bət\ ambit, gambit

[1]**amble** \äm-bəl\ see [1]EMBLE

[2]**amble** \am-bəl\ amble, bramble, gamble, gambol, ramble, scramble, shamble, preamble, unscramble, skimble-skamble

ambler \am-blər\ ambler, gambler, rambler, scrambler, unscrambler

ambo \am-bō\ crambo, jambeau, sambo, Ovambo
ambol \am-bəl\ see [2]AMBLE
ambray \am-brē\ see AMBRY
ambry \am-brē\ ambry, chambray
ambulant \am-byə-lənt\ ambulant, somnambulant
amby \am-bē\ crambe, Dushanbe, namby-pamby
[1]ame \ām\ aim, blame, came, claim, dame, fame, flame, frame, game, hame, kame, lame, maim, name, same, shame, tame, wame, A-frame, acclaim, aflame, airframe, became, byname, cross-claim, declaim, defame, disclaim, endgame, enframe, exclaim, forename, freeze-frame, grandame, inflame, mainframe, misname, nickname, place-name, prename, proclaim, quitclaim, reclaim, selfsame, surname, counterclaim, overcame, Niflheim
[2]ame \äm\ see [1]OM
[3]ame \am\ see [2]AM
[4]ame \äm-ə\ see [1]AMA
ameable \ā-mə-bəl\ see AMABLE
amed \āmd\ famed, named, ashamed, forenamed, unashamed—*also pasts of verbs listed at* [1]AME
ameful \ām-fəl\ blameful, shameful
amel \am-əl\ see AMMEL
ameless \ām-ləs\ aimless, blameless, nameless, shameless, tameless
amely \ām-lē\ gamely, lamely, namely, tamely
[1]amen \ā-mən\ bayman, Bremen, caiman, Cayman, Damon, drayman, flamen, Haman, layman, shaman, stamen, Yemen, examen, gravamen, highwayman
[2]amen \äm-ən\ see OMMON
ameness \ām-nəs\ gameness, lameness, sameness, tameness
[1]ament \ā-mənt\ see AYMENT
[2]ament \am-ənt\ ament, clamant
amer \ā-mər\ see AIMER
ames \āmz\ James—*also possessives and plurals of nouns, third person singular presents of verbs listed at* [1]AME
ameter \am-ət-ər\ amateur, decameter, diameter, heptameter, hexameter, octameter, parameter, pentameter, tetrameter
[1]amfer \am-pər\ see [2]AMPER
[2]amfer \am-fər\ camphor, chamfer
[1]ami \äm-ē\ balmy, commie, mommy, palmy, pommy, qualmy, swami, Tommy, gourami, pastrami, Sagami, salami, tatami, tsunami, origami
[2]ami \am-ə\ see [4]AMA
[3]ami \am-ē\ see AMMY
amia \ā-mē-ə\ lamia, zamia, Mesopotamia
[1]amic \ō-mik\ see [2]OMIC
[2]amic \am-ik\ gamic, Adamic, agamic, balsamic, ceramic, dynamic, adynamic, cleistogamic, cryptogrammic,

cycloramic, dioramic, exogamic, panoramic, phonogrammic, polygamic, aerodynamic, biodynamic, hydrodynamic, hypothalamic, ideogramic, thermodynamic, magnetodynamic
amice \am-əs\ amice, camas, chlamys, Lammas
amics \äm-iks\ see OMICS
[1]amie \ā-mē\ Amy, Jamie, Mamie, ramie, cockamamie, cockamamy
[2]amie \am-ē\ see AMMY
[1]amil \äm-əl\ see [1]OMMEL
[2]amil \am-əl\ see AMMEL
amily \am-lē\ family, profamily, stepfamily
amin \am-ən\ see AMMON
amina \am-ə-nə\ lamina, stamina
aminal \am-ən-ᵊl\ laminal, foraminal
aminant \am-ə-nənt\ contaminant, examinant
aminar \am-ə-nər\ see [2]AMINER
amine \am-ən\ see AMMON
[1]aminer \äm-ə-nər\ see OMMONER
[2]aminer \am-ə-nər\ laminar, gewurztraminer
aming \ā-miŋ\ flaming, framing, gaming
[1]amish \äm-ish\ Amish, qualmish, quamash, schoolmarmish
[2]amish \am-ish\ Amish, famish
amist \äm-əst\ see ALMIST
amity \am-ət-ē\ amity, calamity
amlet \am-lət\ camlet, hamlet, Hamlet, samlet
amlets \am-ləts\ Tower Hamlets—*also possessives and plurals of nouns listed at* AMLET
amma \am-ə\ see [4]AMA
ammable \am-ə-bəl\ flammable, programmable, diagrammable
ammal \am-əl\ see AMMEL
ammany \am-ə-nē\ see AMMONY
ammar \am-ər\ see AMMER
ammas \am-əs\ see AMICE
ammatist \am-ət-əst\ see AMATIST
amme \am\ see [2]AM
ammel \am-əl\ camel, mammal, stammel, Tamil, trammel, enamel
ammer \am-ər\ clamber, clammer, clamor, clamour, crammer, dammar, gammer, glamour, grammar, hammer, jammer, lamber, rammer, shammer, slammer, stammer, yammer, clawhammer, enamor, flimflammer, jackhammer, programmer, sledgehammer, trip-hammer, windjammer, katzenjammer, monogrammer, ninnyhammer, yellowhammer
ammes \äm-əs\ see OMISE
ammie \am-ē\ see AMMY
ammies \am-ēz\ jammies—*also possessives and plurals of nouns listed at* AMMY
amming \am-iŋ\ damning, programming
ammock \am-ək\ drammock, hammock, mammock
ammon \am-ən\ Brahman, famine, gamin, gammon,

mammon, salmon, backgammon, examine, cross-examine

ammony \am-ə-nē\ scammony, Tammany

ammy \am-ē\ chamois, clammy, gammy, Grammy, hammy, mammy, ramie, Sammie, Sammy, shammy, whammy, Miami

amn \am\ see 2AM

amned \am\ see 2AM

amning \am-iŋ\ see AMMING

amois \am-ē\ see AMMY

1amon \ā-mən\ see 1AMEN

2amon \äm-ən\ see OMMON

amor \am-ər\ see AMMER

amorous \am-rəs\ amorous, clamorous, glamorous

amos \ā-məs\ see AMOUS

amour \am-ər\ see AMMER

amous \ā-məs\ Amos, famous, shamus, squamous, biramous, mandamus, ignoramus, Nostradamus

1amp \ämp\ see 1OMP

2amp \ä^{n}\ see 1ANT

3amp \amp\ amp, camp, champ, clamp, cramp, damp, gamp, gramp, guimpe, lamp, ramp, samp, scamp, stamp, tamp, tramp, vamp, blackdamp, C-clamp, chokedamp, decamp, encamp, firedamp, headlamp, off-ramp, on-ramp, preamp, revamp, sunlamp, unclamp, afterdamp, aide-de-camp, minicamp

1ampean \äm-pē-ən\ pampean, tampion

2ampean \am-pē-ən\ see 2AMPION

1amper \äm-pər\ see OMPER

2amper \am-pər\ camper, chamfer, damper, hamper, pamper, scamper, stamper, tamper

amphor \am-fər\ see 2AMFER

1ampi \äm-pē\ see OMPY

2ampi \am-pē\ see AMPY

ampian \am-pē-ən\ see 2AMPION

1ampion \äm-pē-ən\ see 1AMPEAN

2ampion \am-pē-ən\ campion, champion, Grampian, pampean, rampion, tampion

ample \am-pəl\ ample, sample, trample, ensample, example, subsample, counterexample

ampler \am-plər\ sampler, trampler

ampo \äm-pō\ see OMPO

ampos \am-pəs\ see AMPUS

ampsia \am(p)-sē-ə\ eclampsia, preeclampsia

ampton \am-tən\ Hampton, Easthampton, Northampton, Southampton, Wolverhampton

ampus \am-pəs\ Campos, campus, grampus, hippocampus

ampy \am-pē\ campy, scampi

ams \amz\ Jams—*also possessives and plurals of nouns and third person singular presents of verbs listed at* 2AM

amson \am-sən\ damson, Samson

amster \am-stər\ hamster, lamster

amsun \äm-sən\ Hamsun, Thompson
amulus \am-yə-ləs\ famulus, hamulus
[1]amus \ā-məs\ see AMOUS
[2]amus \äm-əs\ see OMISE
amy \ā-mē\ see [1]AMIE
amys \am-əs\ see AMICE
[1]an \ä^{n}\ see [1]ANT
[2]an \än\ see [1]ON
[3]an \ən\ see UN
[4]an \aŋ\ see [2]ANG
[5]an \an\ an, Ann, Anne, ban, bran, can, clan, crayon, Dan, fan, Fan, flan, Jan, Klan, man, Mann, nan, Nan, pan, Pan, panne, plan, ran, scan, San, Shan, span, Stan, tan, van, Van, adman, Afghan, aidman, ape-man, ashcan, Bataan, bedpan, began, Bhutan, birdman, boardman, brainpan, brogan, caftan, caiman, cancan, capstan, captan, caveman, Cayman, Cèzanne, chessman, Cheyenne, chlordan, Chopin, claypan, clubman, Cohan, cooncan, corban, cowman, Cruzan, cyan, deadpan, deskman, Dian, Diane, Diann, Dianne, dishpan, divan, doorman, dustpan, fancy-dan, fan-tan, fibranne, flyman, foreran, FORTRAN, freedman, freeman, frogman, G-man, gagman, Georgeann, glucan, Gosplan, hardpan, he-man, iceman, inspan, Iran, japan, Japan, jazzman, Joann, Joanne, Kazan, kneepan, Koran, Kurgan, leadman, Leanne, legman, liftman, loran, Luanne, madman, Mandan, Marfan, mailman, merman, Milan, milkman, newsman, oilcan, oilman, outran, pavane, pecan, plowman, postman, preman, pressman, propman, Queen Anne, Qur'an, ragman, rattan, reedman, reman, rodman, Roseanne, routeman, Roxanne, Ruthann, Saipan, sampan, sandman, Saran, saucepan, scalepan, schoolman, sedan, sideman, snowman, soundman, soutane, spaceman, Spokane, stewpan, stickman, stockman, strongman, stuntman, Sudan, suntan, Susanne, Suzanne, T-man, TACAN, taipan, Tarzan, tisane, toucan, trainman, trashman, trepan, Tristan, unman, vegan, Walkman, wingspan, yardman, yes-man, Alcoran, allemande, also-ran, Ameslan, anchorman, Andaman, astrakhan, Astrakhan, ataman, Athelstan, attackman, automan, balmacaan, Baluchistan, Bantustan, bartizan, Belmopan, black-and-tan, bogeyman, boogeyman, businessman, Caliban, cameraman, caravan, catalan, cattleman, Civitan, colorman, cornerman, counterman, counterplan, countryman, courtesan, dairyman, defenseman, everyman, exciseman, expressman,

fellowman, funnyman, gamelan, garageman, garbageman, Hamadan, handyman, harmattan, Hindustan, hotelman, Isle of Man, jerrican, Juliann, Julianne, Kazakhstan, Ku Klux Klan, Kurdistan, Kyrgyzstan, man-for-man, man-to-man, Marianne, Maryann, Maryanne, middleman, minuteman, Monaghan, moneyman, Occitan, ombudsman, Omdurman, overman, overran, Pakistan, Parmesan, partisan, pattypan, Peter Pan, pivotman, plainclothesman, Port Sudan, Powhatan, Ramadan, repairman, rewrite man, Ryazan, safetyman, selectman, serviceman, shandrydan, Shantyman, shovelman, signalman, spick-and-span, superman, tallyman, tamarin, Teheran, teleman, teleran, triggerman, trimaran, turbofan, weatherman, workingman, yataghan, Yucatan, Afghanistan, arrière-ban, bipartisan, catamaran, catch-as-catch-can, cavalryman, committeeman, deliveryman, Kalimantan, newspaperman, orangutan, radioman, salary man, Tajikistan, Turkmenistan, Uzbekistan

[6]**an** \än-yə\ see [1]ANIA

[7]**an** \äng\ see [1]ONG

[8]**an** \änt\ see [2]ANT

[1]**ana** \än-ə\ ana, anna, Anna, bwana, Dona, donna, Donna, fauna, Ghana, Kana, Lana, Lonna, mana, Botswana, chicana, gymkhana, iguana, jacana, lantana, liana, Madonna, mañana, nagana, nirvana, piranha, Purana, ruana, Tijuana, Tirane, Toscana, zenana, Africana, belladonna, epifauna, French Guiana, Guadiana, Haryana, Hinayana, hiragana, ikebana, Ludhiana, Mahayana, marijuana, parmigiana, pozzolana, prima donna, Rajputana, Rosh Hashanah, Tatiana, Americana, fata morgana, Lincolniana, Ljubljana, nicotiana, Shakespeareana, Victoriana, Ciuda Guyana

[2]**ana** \ā-nə\ ana, Dana, Lana, Africana, cantilena, Cartagena, nicotiana, Shakespeareana

[3]**ana** \an-ə\ ana, Anna, canna, manna, Ghana, Hannah, Lana, nana, banana, bandanna, cabana, Deanna, Diana, Dianna, Fermanagh, goanna, Guiana, Guyana, gymkhana, Havana, hosanna, Joanna, Johanna, Montana, savanna, Savannah, sultana, Susanna, Susannah, Africana, Indiana, Juliana, Mariana, Marianna, poinciana, Pollyanna, Santa Ana, Americana, fata morgana, Louisiana, nicotiana, Shakespeareana, Victoriana

aña \än-yə\ see [1]ANIA

anacle \an-i-kəl\ see ANICAL
anage \an-ij\ manage, tannage, stage-manage, micro manage
anagh \an-ə\ see [3]ANA
[1]anah \ō-nə\ see [1]ONA
[2]anah \än-ə\ see [1]ANA
anal \ān-^{ə}l\ anal, banal
analyst \an-^{ə}l-əst\ analyst, annalist, panelist, cryptanalyst, psychoanalyst
anan \an-ən\ see ANNON
anape \an-ə-pē\ see ANOPY
[1]anary \ān-rē\ see ANERY
[2]anary \an-rē\ see [2]ANNERY
anate \an-ət\ see ANNET
anative \an-ət-iv\ sanative, explanative
anbe \am-bē\ see AMBY
[1]anc \a^{n}\ see [1]ANT
[2]anc \aŋ\ see [2]ANG
[3]anc \aŋk\ see ANK
anca \aŋ-kə\ barranca, Kanka, Casablanca, lingua franca, Salamanca
[1]ance \ä^{n}s\ Reims, nuance, outrance, séance, à outrance, Provence, Saint-Saëns, diligence, Fort-de-France, ordonnance, renaissance, mésalliance, par excellence, concours d'elegance, pièce de résistance
[2]ance \äns\ Hans, nonce, ponce, sconce, brisance, ensconce, faience, nuance, response, seance, Afrikaans, complaisance, fer-de-lance, nonchalance, provenance, renaissance, pièce de résistance
[3]ance \ans\ chance, dance, France, glance, lance, Lance, manse, nance, Nantes, prance, stance, trance, trans, Vance, advance, askance, bechance, enhance, entrance, expanse, finance, mischance, perchance, romance, Romance, side-glance, sweatpants, circumstance, complaisance, contredanse, country-dance, fer-de-lance, happenchance, happenstance, Liederkranz, Port-au-Prince, refinance, smarty-pants, underpants—*also plurals and possessives of verbs listed at* [5]ANT
anceable \an-sə-bəl\ see ANSIBLE
anced \anst\ canst, circumstanced, underfinanced—*also pasts of verbs listed at* [3]ANCE
ancel \an-səl\ cancel, chancel, handsel, expansile, precancel
anceler \an-slər\ canceler, chancellor, vice-chancellor
ancellor \an-slər\ see ANCELER
ancement \an-smənt\ advancement, enhancement
ancer \an-sər\ answer, cancer, dancer, glancer, lancer, prancer, advancer, enhancer, free-lancer, merganser, romancer, ropedancer, anticancer, geomancer, necromancer, rhabdomancer
ances \an(t)-səs\ see ANCIS
ancet \an-sət\ lancet, Narragansett
[1]anch \änch\ see [1]AUNCH
[2]anch \ònch\ see [2]AUNCH
[3]anch \anch\ blanch, Blanche,

branch, ranch, rebranch, avalanche
1anche \ä^{n}sh\ tranche, carte blanche, revanche
2anche \anch\ see 3ANCH
3anche \an-chē\ see ANCHY
1ancher \ȯn-chər\ see AUNCHER
2ancher \an-chər\ ceinture, rancher
anchi \an-chē\ see ANCHY
anchion \an-chən\ see ANSION
anchor \aŋ-kər\ see ANKER
anchoress \aŋ-krəs\ see ANKEROUS
anchy \an-chē\ branchy, Ranchi, Comanche
ancial \an-chəl\ see ANTIAL
ancis \an(t)-səs\ Frances, Francis, Aransas—*also third person singular presents of verbs and plurals of nouns listed at* ANCE
anck \änk\ see 1ONK
anco \äŋ-kō\ see ONCO
ancolin \aŋ-klən\ see ANKLIN
ancor \aŋ-kər\ see ANKER
ancorous \aŋ-krəs\ see ANKEROUS
ancre \aŋ-kər\ see ANKER
ancrous \aŋ-krəs\ see ANKEROUS
anct \aŋt\ see ANKED
ancy \an-sē\ chancy, fancy, Nancy, unchancy, chiromancy, geomancy, hydromancy, necromancy, pyromancy, rhabdomancy, sycophancy, oneiromancy
1and \ä^{n}\ see 1ANT
2and \änd\ see 1OND
3and \and\ and, band, bland, brand, canned, gland, grand, hand, land, manned, NAND, rand, Rand, sand, Sand, stand, strand, armband, backhand, backland, badland, bandstand, benchland, blackland, broadband, brushland, bushland, cabstand, cloudland, coastland, command, cowhand, crash-land, cropland, deckhand, demand, disband, dockhand, dockland, downland, dreamland, dryland, duneland, expand, farmhand, farmland, fenland, filmland, firebrand, firsthand, flatland, forehand, four-hand, free hand, freehand, gangland, glad-hand, Gotland, grandstand, grassland, handstand, hardstand, hatband, headband, headstand, heartland, heathland, homeland, Iceland, inkstand, inland, Inland, kickstand, Kokand, Lapland, left-hand, longhand, mainland, marshland, misbrand, newsstand, nightstand, northland, noseband, offhand, outland, outstand, parkland, pineland, playland, proband, Queensland, quicksand, rangeland, remand, repand, Rheinland, Rhineland, ribband, right-hand, rimland, roband, Saarland, scabland, screenland, scrubland, seastrand, shorthand, sideband, softland, southland, spaceband, stagehand, summand, swampland,

sweatband, Thailand, thirdhand, tideland, trainband, unhand, unmanned, waistband, washstand, wasteland, watchband, wetland, wildland, withstand, wristband, ampersand, beforehand, behindhand, bellyband, belly-land, borderland, bottomland, confirmand, contraband, countermand, Damavand, Dixieland, fairyland, fatherland, Ferdinand, forestland, four-in-hand, graduand, hand-to-hand, hand to hand, hinterland, Krugerrand, lotusland, meadowland, motherland, Nagaland, narrowband, no-man's-land, operand, ordinand, overhand, overland, pastureland, reprimand, Rio Grande, Samarkand, saraband, secondhand, Swaziland, tableland, Talleyrand, timberland, Togoland, underhand, undermanned, understand, wonderland, Zululand, analysand, Bechuanaland, cloud-cuckoo-land, fantasyland, misunderstand, multiplicand, Prince Rupert's Land, Somaliland, Sudetenland, vacationland, videoland, Witwatersrand, Matabeleland, Alice-in-Wonderland—*also pasts of verbs listed at* [5]AN

[4]**and** \än\ see [1]ON

[5]**and** \änt\ see [2]ANT

[1]**anda** \an-də\ Ganda, panda, Amanda, Luanda, Luganda, Miranda, Uganda, veranda, jacaranda, memoranda, nomina conservanda, propaganda

[2]**anda** \än-də\ see ONDA

andable \an-də-bəl\ mandible, commandable, demandable, expandable, understandable

andaed \an-dəd\ see ANDED

andal \an-dᵊl\ see ANDLE

andaled \an-dᵊld\ handled, sandaled, well-handled—*also pasts of verbs listed at* ANDLE

andall \an-dᵊl\ see ANDLE

andalous \an-dləs\ see [2]ANDLESS

andam \an-dəm\ seeANDUM

andant \an-dənt\ see ANDENT

andar \ənd-ər\ see UNDER

andarin \an-drən\ mandarin, alexandrine, salamandrine

[1]**ande** \ən\ see UN

[2]**ande** \an\ see [5]AN

[3]**ande** \an-dē\ see ANDY

[4]**ande** \and\ see [3]AND

[5]**ande** \än-də\ see ONDA

anded \an-dəd\ banded, branded, candid, handed, landed, stranded, backhanded, bare-handed, cleanhanded, forehanded, four-handed, freehanded, ham-handed, hardhanded, high-handed, ironhanded, left-handed, light-handed, offhanded, one-handed, red-handed, right-handed, shorthanded, sure-handed, three-handed, two-handed, unbranded, verandaed, empty-handed, evenhanded, heavy-handed, openhanded, overhanded, singlehanded, underhanded—*also pasts of verbs listed at* ³AND

andel \an-dᵊl\ see ANDLE

andem \an-dəm\ see ANDUM

andent \an-dənt\ candent, scandent, demandant

¹ander \en-dər\ see ENDER

²ander \än-dər\ see ¹ONDER

³ander \an-dər\ bander, brander, candor, dander, gander, grandeur, lander, pander, sander, slander, strander, zander, auslander, backhander, blackhander, bystander, commander, demander, expander, flatlander, germander, gladhander, goosander, grandstander, inlander, Leander, left-hander, mainlander, meander, outlander, philander, pomander, right-hander, scrimshander, soft-lander, Uitlander, Africander, alexander, Alexander, calamander, coriander, gerrymander, oleander, salamander, single-hander—*also comparatives of adjectives listed at* ³AND

anderous \an-drəs\ see ANDROUS

anders \an-dərz\ Flanders, Bouvier des Flandres, golden alexanders—*also plurals and possessives of verbs listed at* ³ANDER

andery \an-drē\ see ANDRY

andes \an-dēz\ Andes—*also possessives and plurals of nouns and third person singular presents of verbs listed at* ANDY

¹andeur \an-dər\ see ³ANDER

²andeur \an-jər\ see ⁴ANGER

andhi \an-dē\ see ANDY

andi \an-dē\ see ANDY

andible \an-də-bəl\ see ANDABLE

andid \an-dəd\ see ANDED

anding \an-diŋ\ standing, commanding, crossbanding, freestanding, hardstanding, long-standing, outstanding, upstanding, mind-expanding, notwithstanding, understanding

andish \an-dish\ blandish, brandish, standish, Standish, outlandish

andist \an-dəst\ contrabandist, propagandist—*also superlatives of adjectives listed at* ³AND

andit \an-dət\ bandit, pandit

andle \an-dᵊl\ candle, dandle, Handel, handle, Randall, sandal, scandal, vandal, footcandle, manhandle, mishandle, panhandle, stickhandle, coromandel, Coromandel

andled \an-dᵊl\ see ANDALED

andler \an-lər\ candler, chandler, handler, panhandler, stickhandler

andless \an-ləs\ see ANLESS

andly \an-lē\ see ²ANLY

andment \an-mənt\ commandment, disbandment

ando \an-dō\ Fernando, Orlando

andom \an-dəm\ see ANDUM
andor \an-dər\ see [3]ANDER
andra \an-drə\ Sandra, Cassandra, Alexandra, pachysandra
andrea \an-drē-ə\ see ANDRIA
andrel \an-drəl\ mandrel, mandrill, spandrel
andres \an-dərz\ see ANDERS
andria \an-drē-ə\ Andrea, Alexandria
andrill \an-drəl\ see ANDREL
andrine \an-drən\ see ANDARIN
andros \an-drəs\ see ANDROUS
androus \an-drəs\ Andros, slanderous, gynandrous, meandrous, polyandrous
andry \an-drē\ commandery, monandry, polyandry
ands \anz\ Badlands, Lowlands, Canyonlands
andsel \an-səl\ see ANCEL
andsman \anz-mən\ bandsman, clansman, Klansman, landsman
andsome \an-səm\ see ANSOM
andum \an-dəm\ fandom, grandam, random, tandem, memorandum, nomen conservandum, subpoena ad testificandum
andy \an-dē\ Andy, bandy, brandy, Brandy, candy, dandy, handy, Handy, pandy, randy, Randy, sandhi, sandy, Sandy, shandy, jim-dandy, unhandy, Rio Grande, modus operandi
[1]**ane** \ān\ ain, Aisne, ane, bane, blain, Blaine, brain, Cain, cane, chain, crane, Crane, Dane, deign, drain, Duane, Dwain, Dwayne, fain, fane, feign, gain, grain, Jane, Jayne. lane, Lane, main, Maine, mane, pain, Paine, pane, plain, plane, quean, rain, reign, rein, sain, sane, seine, Seine, skein, slain, Spain, sprain, stain, stane, strain, swain, thane, thegn, train, twain, Twain, vain, vane, vein, wain, wane, Wayne, Zane, abstain, again, airplane, amain, arcane, arraign, attain, Bahrain, Bassein, Beltane, biplane, birdbrain, Biscayne, bloodstain, bugbane, campaign, champagne, champaign, Champlain, checkrein, chicane, chilblain, chow mein, cinquain, cocaine, Cockaigne, coxswain, complain, constrain, contain, cordwain, cowbane, crackbrain, demesne, deplane, destain, detain, detrain, devein, disdain, distain, distrain, dogbane, domain, drivetrain, Duane, dumbcane, edge-grain, Elaine, emplane, enchain, engrain, enplane, entrain, explain, eyestrain, fleabane, floatplane, floodplain, Fort Wayne, Gawain, germane, grosgrain, Helaine, Helene, henbane, house-train, humane, Hussein Igraine, immane, inane, ingrain, insane, lamebrain, lightplane, lo mein, Loraine, Lorraine, maintain, marchpane, membrane migraine, Montaigne,

montane, moraine, mortmain, Moulmein, mundane, neckrein, obtain, octane, ordain, pertain, plain-Jane, profane, ptomaine, purslane, quatrain, refrain, remain, restrain, retain, retrain, romaine, sailplane, sea-lane, seaplane, seatrain, sustain, tearstain, terrain, terrane, triplane, Touraine, Ukraine, unchain, urbane, vervain, vicereine, villein, volplane, warplane, wolfsbane, aeroplane, appertain, aquaplane, Aquitaine, ascertain, avellane, Bloemfontain, cellophane, Charlemagne, Charles's Wain, chatelain, chatelaine, counterpane, de Montaigne, entertain, featherbrain, foreordain, frangipane, gyroplane, hurricane, hydroplane, hyperplane, inhumane, Kwajalein, La Fontaine, marocain, Mary Jane, mise-en-scène, monoplane, Novocain, neutercane, novocaine, overlain, paravane, papertrain, peneplain, Port of Spain, port-wine stain, preordain, rattlebrain, scatterbrain, shaggymane, Spanish Main, sugarcane, suzerain, Tamburlaine, Tamerlane, terreplein, tramontane, transmontane, windowpane, Alsace-Lorraine, auf Wiedersehen, balletomane, convertiplane, demimondaine, elecampane, extramundane, intermontane, Lake Pontchartraine, legerdemain, ultramontane, trichalomethane

[2]ane \an\ see [5]AN

[3]ane \än-ə\ see [1]ANA

[4]ane \än\ see [1]ON

anea \ā-nē-ə\ see [2]ANIA

anean \ā-nē-ən\ see [2]ANIAN

aned \ānd\ see AINED

anee \an-ē\ see ANNY

aneful \ān-fəl\ see AINFUL

anel \an-əl\ see ANNEL

anelist \an-əl-əst\ see ANALYST

aneous \ā-nē-əs\ cutaneous, extraneous, spontaneous, coetaneous, consentaneous, instantaneous, miscellaneous, porcelaneous, simultaneous, succedaneous, contemporaneous, extemporaneous

[1]aner \ā-nər\ see AINER

[2]aner \än-ər\ see [1]ONOR

anery \ān-rē\ granary, chicanery

anet \an-ət\ see ANNET

aneum \ā-nē-əm\ see ANIUM

aney \ȯ-nē\ see [1]AWNY

anford \an-fərd\ Sanford, Stanford

[1]ang \äŋ\ see [1]ONG

[2]ang \aŋ\ bang, bhang, clang, dang, fang, Fang, gang, gangue, hang, pang, prang, rang, sang, slang, spang, sprang, stang, tang, twang, whang, yang, cliff-hang, defang, ginseng, harangue, linsang, meringue, mustang, orang, parang, Pinang, pressgang, probang, shebang, slambang, straphang, trepang,

whizbang, boomerang, charabanc, overhang, parasang, siamang, interrobang, orangutan
[3]**ang** \ȯŋ\ see [2]ONG
anga \äŋ-gə\ see ONGA
angar \aŋ-ər\ see [2]ANGER
[1]**ange** \äⁿzh\ blancmange, mélange
[2]**ange** \ānj\ change, grange, mange, range, strange, arrange, derange, downrange, estrange, exchange, free-range, gearchange, long-range, outrange, short-range, shortchange, counterchange, disarrange, interchange, omnirange, Great Dividing Range
[3]**ange** \anj\ flange, phalange
angel \aŋ-gəl\ see ANGLE
angell \aŋ-gəl\ see ANGLE
angement \ānj-mənt\ arrangement, derangement, estrangement, disarrangement
angency \an-jən-sē\ plangency, tangency
angent \an-jənt\ plangent, tangent
[1]**anger** \ān-jər\ changer, danger, granger, manger, ranger, stranger, bushranger, endanger, estranger, exchanger, shortchanger, interchanger
[2]**anger** \aŋ-ər\ banger, clanger, clangor, clangour, ganger, hangar, hanger, languor, Sanger, twanger, cliff-hanger, straphanger, haranguer, paperhanger
[3]**anger** \aŋ-gər\ anger, clangor
[4]**anger** \an-jər\ flanger, grandeur, phalanger
angi \aŋ-ē\ see [2]ANGY
angible \an-jə-bəl\ frangible, tangible, infrangible, intangible, refrangible
angie \aŋ-ē\ see [2]ANGY
[1]**anging** \ān-jiŋ\ bushranging, unchanging, wide-ranging
[2]**anging** \aŋ-iŋ\ hanging, cliff-hanging, paperhanging
angle \aŋ-gəl\ angle, bangle, dangle, jangle, mangel, mangle, spangle, strangle, tangle, wangle, wrangle, embrangle, entangle, Mount Wrangell, pentangle, quadrangle, rectangle, triangle, untangle, wide-angle, disentangle
angled \aŋ-gəld\ angled, tangled, newfangled, oldfangled, right-angled, star-spangled—*also pasts of verbs listed at* ANGLE
anglement \aŋ-gəl-mənt\ tanglement, embranglement, entanglement, disentanglement
angler \aŋ-glər\ angler, dangler, jangler, mangler, strangler, wangler, wrangler, entangler
angles \aŋ-gəlz\ Angles, strangles—*also plurals and possessives of nouns and third singular presents of verbs listed at* ANGLE
anglian \aŋ-glē-ən\ Anglian, ganglion
angling \aŋ-gliŋ\ angling, gangling

anglion \aŋ-glē-ən\ see ANGLIAN
angly \aŋ-glē\ gangly, jangly, tangly
ango \aŋ-gō\ mango, tango, Durango, fandango
[1]**angor** \aŋ-ər\ see [2]ANGER
[2]**angor** \aŋ-gər\ see [3]ANGER
angorous \aŋ-ə-rəs\ clangorous, languorous
angour \aŋ-ər\ see [2]ANGER
angster \aŋ-stər\ gangster, prankster
anguage \aŋ-gwij\ language, slanguage, metalanguage, paralanguage, protolanguage
angue \aŋ\ see [2]ANG
anguer \aŋ-ər\ see [2]ANGER
anguish \aŋ-gwish\ anguish, languish
anguor \aŋ-ər\ see [2]ANGER
anguorous \aŋ-ə-rəs\ see ANGOROUS
angus \aŋ-gəs\ Angus, Brangus
[1]**angy** \ān-jē\ mangy, rangy
[2]**angy** \aŋ-ē\ tangy, twangy, Ubangi, collieshangie
anha \än-ə\ see [1]ANA
anhope \an-əp\ see ANNUP
[1]**ani** \än-ē\ Bonnie, bonny, Connie, Donnie, fawny, johnny, Ronnie, tawny, afghani, Fulani, chalcedony, Kisangani, maharani, Nuristani, quadriphony, Rajasthani, mulligatawny
[2]**ani** \an-ē\ see ANNY
[1]**ania** \än-yə\ Agana, España, lasagna, Titania, Emilia-Romagna
[2]**ania** \ā-nē-ə\ mania, titania, Titania, Urania, Acarnania, Anglomania, Aquitania, collectanea, dipsomania, egomania, hypomania, kleptomania, Lithuania, Mauretania, Mauritania, miscellanea, monomania, mythomania, nymphomania, Oceania, Pennsylvania, Pomerania, pyromania, Transylvania, balletomania, bibliomania, decalcomania, megalomania—*see also* [3]ANIA
[3]**ania** \ān-yə\ Campania, Catania, Hispania, Titania, Aquitania, malaguena, Tripolitania—*also words listed at* [2]ANIA
[1]**anian** \än-ē-ən\ Kiwanian, Araucanian, Turanian
[2]**anian** \ā-nē-ən\ Albanian, Dardanian, Iranian, Romanian, Rumanian, Sassanian, Turanian, Ukrainian, Uranian, vulcanian, Lithuanian, Pennsylvanian, Pomeranian, Ruritanian, subterranean, Indo-Iranian, Mediterranean
aniard \an-yərd\ lanyard, Spaniard
anic \an-ik\ manic, panic, tannic, Brahmanic, Britannic, cyanic, firemanic, galvanic, Germanic, Hispanic, Koranic, mechanic, melanic, organic, Romanic, satanic, shamanic, Sudanic, titanic, tympanic, volcanic, aldermanic, Alemannic, councilmanic, epiphanic, inorganic, messianic, oceanic, Ossianic, pre-Hispanic, talismanic,

theophanic, Indo-Germanic, megalomanic, Rhaeto-Romanic, suboceanic, transoceanic
anical \an-i-kəl\ manacle, panicle, sanicle, botanical, mechanical, tyrannical, puritanical
anice \an-əs\ see ANISE
anicle \an-i-kəl\ see ANICAL
anics \an-iks\ annex, mechanics—*also plurals and possessives of nouns listed at* ANIC
[1]**anid** \ā-nəd\ ranid, tabanid
[2]**anid** \an-əd\ canid, ranid, Sassanid
[1]**aniel** \an-ᵊl\ see ANNEL
[2]**aniel** \an-yəl\ see ANUAL
anigan \an-i-gən\ see ANNIGAN
anikin \an-i-kən\ see ANNIKIN
animous \an-ə-məs\ animus, magnanimous, unanimous, pusillanimous
animus \an-ə-məs\ see ANIMOUS
[1]**anion** \än-yən\ see [1]ONYON
[2]**anion** \an-yən\ banyan, canon, canyon, fanion, companion, Grand Canyon, Hells Canyon
anis \an-əs\ see ANISE
anise \an-əs\ anise, Janice, Janis, stannous, johannes, Johnannes, pandanus, titanous, Scipio Africanus
[1]**anish** \ā-nish\ see AINISH
[2]**anish** \an-ish\ banish, clannish, mannish, planish, Spanish, tannish, vanish, Pollyannish, Judeo-Spanish
anist \än-əst\ see ONEST
anister \an-ə-stər\ canister, ganister
anite \an-ət\ see ANNET
anity \an-ət-ē\ sanity, vanity, humanity, inanity, insanity, profanity, urbanity, Christianity, churchianity, inhumanity, superhumanity
anium \ā-nē-əm\ cranium, geranium, uranium, succedaneum
ank \aŋk\ bank, blank, brank, clank, crank, dank, drank, flank, franc, frank, Frank, hank, lank, plank, prank, rank, sank, shank, shrank, spank, stank, swank, tank, thank, yank, Yank, Burbank, claybank, embank, foreshank, gangplank, greenshank, nonbank, outflank, outrank, pickthank, point-blank, redshank, sandbank, sheepshank, snowbank, mountebank, riverbank, clinkety-clank
[1]**anka** \äŋ-kə\ concha, tanka, Sri Lanka
[2]**anka** \aŋ-kə\ see ANCA
ankable \aŋ-kə-bəl\ bankable, frankable
anked \aŋt\ shanked, tanked, spindle-shanked, sacrosanct—*also pasts of verbs listed at* ANK
ankee \an-kē\ see ANKY
anken \aŋ-kən\ flanken, Rankine
anker \aŋ-kər\ anchor, banker, canker, chancre, flanker, franker, hanker, rancor, ranker, spanker, tanker,

thanker, co-anchor, unanchor—*also comparatives of adjectives listed at* ANK
ankerous \aŋ-krəs\ anchoress, cankerous, chancrous, rancorous, cantankerous
ankh \äŋk\ see [1]ONK
ankie \an-kē\ see ANKY
ankine \aŋ-kən\ see ANKEN
ankish \aŋ-kish\ Frankish, prankish
ankle \aŋ-kəl\ ankle, crankle, rankle
ankly \aŋ-klē\ blankly, dankly, frankly
anks \aŋs\ see ANX
ankster \aŋ-stər\ see ANGSTER
anky \aŋ-kē\ cranky, hankie, lanky, swanky, Yankee, hanky-panky
anless \an-ləs\ handless, manless, planless
anley \an-lē\ see [2]ANLY
anli \an-lē\ see [2]ANLY
[1]anly \än-lē\ fondly, thrawnly, wanly
[2]anly \an-lē\ blandly, grandly, manly, Stanley, Osmanli, unmanly
[1]ann \an\ see [5]AN
[2]ann \än\ see [1]ON
[1]anna \än-ə\ see [1]ANA
[2]anna \an-ə\ see [3]ANA
annage \an-ij\ see ANAGE
annah \an-ə\ see [3]ANA
annalist \an-ᵊl-əst\ see ANALYST
annan \an-ən\ see ANNON
anne \an\ see [5]AN
anned \and\ see [3]AND
annel \an-ᵊl\ channel, Channel, Daniel, flannel, panel, scrannel, spaniel, impanel, English Channel
annequin \an-i-kən\ see ANNIKIN
anner \an-ər\ banner, canner, fanner, lanner, manner, manor, planner, scanner, spanner, tanner, vanner, deadpanner, japanner, caravanner
[1]annery \än-rē\ ornery, swannery
[2]annery \an-rē\ cannery, granary, tannery
annes \an-əs\ see ANISE
anness \än-nəs\ fondness, wanness
annet \an-ət\ gannet, granite, Janet, planet, pomegranate
annexe \an-iks\ see ANICS
annibal \an-ə-bəl\ cannibal, Hannibal
annic \an-ik\ see ANIC
annie \an-ē\ see ANNY
annigan \an-i-gən\ brannigan. shenanigan
annikin \an-i-kən\ cannikin, manikin, mannequin, pannikin
annin \an-ən\ see ANNON
annish \an-ish\ see [2]ANISH
annon \an-ən\ cannon, canon, Shannon, tannin, Buchanan, Clackmannan, colcannon
annous \an-əs\ see ANISE
anns \anz\ see [4]ANS
annual \an-yəl\ see ANUAL
annular \an-yə-lər\ annular, cannular, granular
annulate \an-yə-lət\ annulate, annulet, campanulate
annulet \an-yə-lət\ see ANNULATE

annum \an-əm\ see [2]ANUM

annup \an-əp\ sannup, stanhope

anny \an-ē\ Annie, canny, cranny, Danny, fanny, granny, Lanny, nanny, afghani, ca'canny, kokanee, uncanny, frangipani, Hindustani, hootenanny

[1]ano \än-ō\ guano, Kano, llano, mano, mono, Chicano, Marrano, Nagano, piano, Romano, Serrano, soprano, altiplano, boliviano, forte-piano, mezzo piano, mezzo-soprano, Cittá del Vaticano

[2]ano \ā-nō\ ripieno, volcano

[3]ano \an-ō\ Hispano, piano, soprano, fortepiano, mezzo-soprano

[1]anon \an-ən\ see ANNON

[2]anon \an-yən\ see [2]ANION

anopy \an-ə-pē\ canape, canopy

anor \an-ər\ see ANNER

anous \an-əs\ see ANISE

anqui \än-kē\ see ONKY

[1]ans \äns\ see [2]ANCE

[2]ans \änz\ see ONZE

[3]ans \ans\ see [3]ANCE

[4]ans \anz\ banns, Hans, sans, trans, Sextans—*also plurals and possessives of nouns and third singular presents of verbs listed at* [5]AN

[5]ans \a^{n}\ see [1]ANT

ansard \an-sərd\ see ANSWERED

[1]ansas \an(t)-səs\ see ANCIS

[2]ansas \an-zəs\ Kansas, Arkansas

anse \ans\ see [3]ANCE

ansea \än-zē\ see ANZY

anser \an-sər\ see ANCER

anset \an-sət\ see ANCET

ansett \an-sət\ see ANCET

ansible \an-sə-bəl\ danceable, expansible

ansile \an-səl\ see ANCEL

ansing \an-siŋ\ Lansing—*also present participles of verbs listed at* [3]ANCE

ansion \an-chən\ mansion, scansion, stanchion, expansion

ansk \änsk\ Bryansk, Gdansk, Murmansk, Saransk

ansman \anz-mən\ see ANDSMAN

ansom \an-səm\ handsome, hansom, ransom, transom, unhandsome

anst \anst\ see ANCED

answer \an-sər\ see ANCER

answered \an-sərd\ answered, mansard, unanswered

ansy \an-zē\ pansy, tansy, chimpanzee

[1]ant \ä^{n}\ Caen, Gant, arpent, beurre blanc, croissant, en banc, Mont Blanc, riant, roman, Rouen, Tátouan, savant, versant, accouchement, aide-de-camp, au courant, battement, cidevant, contretemps, debridement, denouement, en passant, Maupassant, Mitterand, Orléans, Perpignan, rapprochement, revenant, se tenant, soi-disant, vol-au-vent, arrondissement, chateaubriand, Chateaubriand, Clermont-Ferrand, de Maupassant, idiot savant, ressentiment, sauvignon blanc

[2]ant \änt\ aunt, can't, daunt,

flaunt, font, fount, gaunt, taunt, vaunt, want, wont, avant, avaunt, bacchant, bacchante, Balante, Beaumont, bouffant, brisant, courante, détente, entente, Fremont, gallant, grandaunt, piedmont, Piedmont, piquant, romaunt, Rostand, savant, sirvente, Vermont, bon vivant, commandant, complaisant, confidant, debridement, debutant, debutante, dilettante, John of Gaunt, intrigant, nonchalant, poste restante, restaurant, symbiont, dicynodont, subdebutante, Montcalm de Saint Veran, sinfonia concertante

[3]**ant** \ənt\ see [1]ONT

[4]**ant** \ȯnt\ see [1]AUNT

[5]**ant** \ant\ ant, aunt, brant, cant, can't, chant, grant, Grant, hant, Kant, pant, plant, rant, scant, shan't, slant, aslant, bacchant, bacchante, bezant, courante, decant, descant, discant, displant, eggplant, enceinte, enchant, explant, extant, formant, gallant, grandaunt, houseplant, implant, incant, leadplant, levant, Levant, pieplant, pissant, plainchant, pourpoint, preplant, rampant, recant, replant, savant, supplant, transplant, adamant, commandant, complaisant, confidant, cormorant, corposant, Corybant, covenant, demipointe, dilettante, disenchant, gallivant, hierophant, interplant, sycophant

anta \ant-ə\ anta, manta, Atlanta, infanta, vedanta, Atalanta

antage \ant-ij\ vantage, advantage, coign of vantage, disadvantage

antain \ant-ᵊn\ see [2]ANTON

[1]**antal** \änt-ᵊl\ see [1]ONTAL

[2]**antal** \ant-ᵊl\ see ANTLE

antam \ant-əm\ bantam, phantom

antar \ant-ər\ see [2]ANTER

antasist \ant-ə-səst\ see ANTICIST

[1]**ante** \än-tā\ Brontë, Dante, andante, Asante, volante, Belo Horizonte

[2]**ante** \änt\ see [2]ANT

[3]**ante** \ant\ see [5]ANT

[4]**ante** \änt-ē\ see [1]ANTI

[5]**ante** \ant-ē\ ante, canty, chantey, pantie, scanty, shanty, slanty, andanti, Asante, Ashanti, Chianti, infante, non obstante, penny-ante, vigilante, pococurante, status quo ante

antean \ant-ē-ən\ Dantean, Atlantean, post-Kantian

anteau \an-tō\ see [2]ANTO

anted \an-təd\ disenchanted—*also pasts of verbs listed at* [5]ANT

antel \ant-ᵊl\ see ANTLE

antelet \ant-lət\ mantelet, plantlet

[1]**anter** \änt-ər\ see [1]AUNTER

[2]**anter** \ant-ər\ antre, banter, canter, cantor, chanter, granter, grantor, plantar,

planter, ranter, scanter, decanter, implanter, instanter, levanter, transplanter, trochanter, covenanter, covenantor, disenchanter

[1]**antes** \an-tēz\ Cervantes—*also possessives and plurals of nouns and third person singular presents of verbs listed at* [5]ANTE

[2]**antes** \ans\ see [3]ANCE

antey \ant-ē\ see [5]ANTE

anth \anth\ amaranth, coelacanth, perianth, tragacanth

antha \an-thə\ Samantha, polyantha, pyracantha

anthemum \an-thə-məm\ chrysanthemum, mesembryanthemum

anther \an-thər\ anther, panther

anthropy \an-thrə-pē\ lycanthropy, misanthropy, philanthropy

anthus \an-thəs\ acanthus, ailanthus, dianthus, agapanthus, amianthus, polyanthus, Rhadamanthus

[1]**anti** \änt-ē\ Brontë, jaunty, monte, Monte, Monty, vaunty, andante, Asante, Ashanti, Chianti

[2]**anti** \ant-ē\ see [5]ANTE

antial \an-chəl\ financial, substantial, circumstantial, consubstantial, insubstantial, transsubstantial, unsubstantial, supersubstantial

[1]**antian** \änt-ē-ən\ see ONTIAN

[2]**antian** \ant-ē-ən\ see ANTEAN

[1]**antic** \änt-ik\ see ONTIC

[2]**antic** \ant-ik\ antic, frantic, mantic, Atlantic, bacchantic, gigantic, pedantic, romantic, semantic, Vedantic, corybantic, geomantic, hierophantic, necromantic, sycophantic, transatlantic

anticist \ant-ə-səst\ fantasist, Atlanticist, romanticist, semanticist

antid \ant-əd\ mantid, Quadrantid—*also pasts of verbs listed at* [5]ANT

antie \ant-ē\ see [5]ANTE

antine \ant-ᵊn\ see [2]ANTON

[1]**anting** \ant-iŋ\ anting, canting, disenchanting

[2]**anting** \ənt-iŋ\ see UNTING

antis \ant-əs\ cantus, mantis, Santos, Atlantis

antish \ant-ish\ dilettantish, sycophantish

antle \ant-ᵊl\ cantle, mantel, mantle, quintal, dismantle, quadrantal, consonantal, covenantal, overmantel, determinantal

antlet \ant-lət\ see ANTELET

antling \ant-liŋ\ bantling, scantling

[1]**anto** \än-tō\ Squanto, Toronto, Esperanto, bel canto

[2]**anto** \an-tō\ canto, panto, coranto, Otranto, portmanteau, Esperanto, Strait of Otranto

antom \ant-əm\ see ANTAM

[1]**anton** \änt-ᵊn\ see ONTON

[2]**anton** \ant-ᵊn\ Anton, canton, Canton, plantain, Scranton, Stanton, adamantine

antor \ant-ər\ see [2]ANTER

[1]**antos** \an-təs\ see ANTIS

[2]**antos** \än-təs\ Santos, Propontis
antra \ən-trə\ tantra, yantra
antre \ant-ər\ see [2]ANTER
antry \an-trē\ chantry, gantry, pantry
ants \ans\ see [3]ANCE
antua \anch-wə\ mantua, Gargantua
antus \ant-əs\ see ANTIS
anty \ant-ē\ see [5]ANTE
[1]**anual** \an-yəl\ Daniel, spaniel, Nathaniel
[2]**anual** \an-yə-wəl\ annual, manual, Manuel, biannual, bimanual, Emanuel, Emmanuel, Immanuel, semiannual, Victor Emmanuel
anuel \an-yəl\ see [2]ANUAL
anular \an-yə-lər\ see ANNULAR
anulate \an-yə-lət\ see ANNULATE
[1]**anum** \ā-nəm\ paynim, arcanum
[2]**anum** \an-əm\ per annum, solanum
[1]**anus** \ā-nəs\ see AYNESS
[2]**anus** \an-əs\ see ANISE
anx \aŋs\ Manx, thanks, Grand Banks, phalanx—*also plurals and possessives of nouns and third singular presents of verbs listed at* ANK
[1]**any** \ā-nē\ see AINY
[2]**any** \en-ē\ see ENNY
anyan \an-yən\ see [2]ANION
anyard \an-yərd\ see ANIARD
anyon \an-yən\ see [2]ANION
anz \ans\ see [3]ANCE
[1]**anza** \än-zə\ kwanza, Kwanza, Kwanzaa, Sancho Panza
[2]**anza** \an-zə\ stanza, zanza, bonanza, organza, Sancho Panza, extravaganza
anzaa \än-zə\ see [1]ANZA
anzee \an-zē\ see ANSY
anzer \än-sər\ see ONSOR
anzo \än-zō\ gonzo, garbanzo
anzy \än-zē\ bronzy, Ponzi, Swansea
[1]**ao** \ā-ō\ see [1]EO
[2]**ao** \ō\ see [1]OW
[3]**ao** \au̇\ see [2]OW
[4]**ao** \ä-ō\ Caliao, Mindanao
aoedic \ēd-ik\ see [1]EDIC
aoighis \āsh\ see [1]ECHE
aole \au̇-lē\ see [2]OWLY
aône \ōn\ see [1]ONE
aori \au̇r-ē\ see OWERY
[1]**aos** \au̇s\ see [2]OUSE
[2]**aos** \ā-äs\ chaos, Laos
aotian \ō-shən\ see OTION
aow \au̇\ see [2]OW
[1]**ap** \äp\ see [1]OP
[2]**ap** \əp\ see UP
[3]**ap** \ap\ cap, chap, clap, crap, flap, frap, gap, gape, hap, Jap, JAP, knap, lap, Lapp, map, nap, nape, nappe, pap, rap, sap, scrap, slap, snap, strap, tap, trap, wrap, yap, Yap, zap, backslap, backwrap, blackcap, bootstrap, burlap, catnap, claptrap, dewlap, dognap, earflap, entrap, enwrap, firetrap, flatcap, foolscap, giddap, heeltap, hubcap, jockstrap, kidnap, kneecap, lagniappe, livetrap, madcap, mantrap, mayhap, mishap, mobcap, mousetrap, nightcap, pinesap, rattrap, recap, redcap, remap, riprap, satrap, shiplap,

shrink-wrap, skullcap, skycap, snowcap, steel-trap, stopgap, unsnap, unstrap, unwrap, verb sap, whitecap, wiretap, afterclap, gingersnap, handicap, overlap, rattletrap, thunderclap, verbum sap, wentletrap, Venus's-flytrap

[1]**apa** \äp-ə\ grappa, Joppa, papa, poppa, tapa, Jalapa, jipijapa

[2]**apa** \ap-ə\ kappa, tapa, Phi Beta Kappa

apable \ā-pə-bəl\ capable, drapable, shapable, escapable, incapable, inescapable

apal \ā-pəl\ see APLE

apas \äp-əs\ Chiapas—*also possessives and plurals of nouns listed at* [1]APA

apboard \ab-ərd\ see ABARD

[1]**ape** \āp\ ape, cape, chape, crape, crepe, drape, gape, grape, jape, nape, rape, scape, scrape, shape, tape, agape, broomrape, cloudscape, duct tape, escape, landscape, moonscape, North Cape, reshape, seascape, shipshape, snowscape, streetscape, townscape, transshape, undrape, waveshape, cityscape, masking tape, waterscape, Xeriscape, audiotape, stereotape, videotape

[2]**ape** \ap\ see [3]AP

[3]**ape** \äp-ē\ see OPPY

[4]**ape** \ap-ē\ see APPY

aped \āpt\ bell-shaped—*also pasts of verbs listed at* [1]APE

apel \ap-əl\ see APPLE

apelin \ap-lən\ see APLAIN

apen \ā-pən\ capon, shapen, unshapen

aper \ā-pər\ caper, draper, gaper, paper, scraper, shaper, taper, tapir, vapor, vapour, curlpaper, endpaper, flypaper, glasspaper, landscaper, newspaper, notepaper, sandpaper, skyscraper, wallpaper, wastepaper, run-of-paper

aperer \ā-pər-ər\ paperer, taperer, vaporer

apery \ā-prē\ drapery, japery, napery, papery, vapory, sandpapery

apes \āps\ traipse, jackanapes—*also plurals and possessives of nouns and third singular presents of verbs listed at* [1]APE

apey \ā-pē\ crepey, drapy, grapey, grapy, kepi, scrapie

aph \af\ caff, calf, chaff, daff, gaff, gaffe, graph, half, laugh, quaff, raff, sclaff, staff, staph, Waf, waff, agrafe, behalf, carafe, chiffchaff, cowlstaff, digraph, distaff, Falstaff, flagstaff, giraffe, half-staff, horselaugh, kenaf, mooncalf, paraph, pikestaff, riffraff, tipstaff, autograph, barograph, bathyscaphe, cenotaph, chronograph, cryptograph, epigraph, epitaph, half-and-half, hectograph, holograph, homograph, hygrograph, kymograph, lithograph, logograph, micrograph, monograph, pantograph, paragraph, phonograph, photograph, pictograph, polygraph, quarterstaff, seismograph, serigraph, shadowgraph, shandygaff, spectrograph, sphygmograph, telegraph, thermograph, typograph, understaff, cardiograph, choreograph, heliograph, ideograph, mimeograph, oscillograph, pseudepigraph, radiograph, chromolithograph, cinematograph, encephalograph, photomicrograph, radiotelegraph, electrocardiograph, electroencephalograph

aphael \af-ē-əl\ see APHIAL

[1]aphe \āf\ see [1]AFE

[2]aphe \af\ see APH

apher \af-ər\ see [2]AFFER

aphia \af-ē-ə\ see AFFIA

aphial \af-ē-əl\ Raphael, epitaphial

aphic \af-ik\ graphic, maffick, sapphic, traffic, digraphic, edaphic, serafic, triaphic, allographic, autographic, barographic, biographic, calligraphic, cartographic, cosmographic, cryptographic, demographic, epigraphic, epitaphic, ethnographic, geographic, hectographic, homographic, hydrographic, lithographic, logographic, mammographic, monographic, orthographic, pantographic, paragraphic, petrographic, phonographic, photographic, pictographic, polygraphic, pornographic, reprographic, stenographic, stratigraphic, telegraphic, tomographic, topographic, typographic, xerographic, bibliographic, choreographic, crystallographic, hagiographic, homolographic, iconographic, ideographic, lexicographic, oceanographic, stereographic, autobiographic, cinematographic, echocardiographic, historiographic, electroencephalographic

aphical \af-i-kəl\ graphical, biographical, cartographical, cosmographical, cryptographical, epigraphical, ethnographical, geographical, orthographical, petrographical, topographical, typographical, bibliographical, choreographical, hagiographical, iconographical, lexicographical, oceanographical, autobiographical, historiographical

aphics \af-iks\ graphics, demographics, micrographics, supergraphics

aphnis \af-nəs\ see AFTNESS

aphora \a-fə-rə\ anaphora, cataphora

api \äp-ē\ see OPPY

apid \ap-əd\ rapid, sapid, vapid

apie \ā-pē\ see APEY

apin \ap-ən\ see APPEN

apine \ap-ən\ see APPEN

apir \ā-pər\ see APER

apis \ā-pəs\ Apis, Priapus, Serapis

apist \ā-pəst\ papist, rapist, escapist, landscapist

aplain \ap-lən\ capelin, chaplain, chaplin, sapling

aple \ā-pəl\ maple, papal, staple

aples \ā-pəlz\ Naples—*also plurals and possessives of nouns and third person singular presents of verbs listed at* APLE

apless \ap-ləs\ hapless, napless, sapless, strapless

aplin \ap-lə-n\ see APLAIN

aply \ap-lē\ see APTLY

apnel \ap-n^{ə}l\ grapnel, shrapnel

apo \äp-ō\ capo, da capo, gestapo, Mount Apo

apolis \ap-ə-ləs\ Annapolis, Minneapolis, Indianapolis

apon \ā-pən\ see APEN

apor \ā-pər\ see APER

aporer \ā-pər-ər\ see APERER

apory \ā-prē\ see APERY

apour \ā-pər\ see APER

app \ap\ see [3]AP

[1]appa \äp-ə\ see [1]APA

[2]appa \ap-ə\ see [2]APA

appable \ap-ə-bəl\ flappable, mappable, recappable, unflappable

appalli \äp-ə-lē\ see OPOLY

appe \ap\ see [3]AP

apped \apt\ see APT

appen \ap-ən\ happen, lapin, rapine

[1]apper \äp-ər\ see OPPER

[2]apper \ap-ər\ capper, clapper, crapper, dapper, flapper, knapper, rapper, sapper, scrapper, snapper, strapper, tapper, wrapper, zapper, backslapper, catnapper, didapper, kidnapper, kneeslapper, petnapper, wiretapper, handicapper, snippersnapper, understrapper, whippersnapper

appet \ap-ət\ lappet, tappet

apphic \af-ik\ see APHIC

appie \äp-ē\ see OPPY

appily \ap-ə-lē\ happily, scrappily, snappily, unhappily

appiness \ap-ē-nəs\ happiness, sappiness, scrappiness, snappiness, unhappiness

apping \ap-iŋ\ capping, mapping, strapping, trapping, wrapping, kneecapping, petnapping

apple \ap-əl\ apple, chapel, dapple, grapple, scrapple, antechapel, mayapple, pineapple

apps \aps\ see APSE

appy \ap-ē\ crappy, flappy, gappy, happy, nappy, pappy, sappy, scrappy, snappy, zappy, satrapy, serape, slaphappy, unhappy, triggerhappy

aps \aps\ see APSE

apse \aps\ apse, chaps, craps, lapse, schnapps, taps, traps, collapse, elapse, perhaps, prolapse, relapse, synapse, time-lapse—*also plurals and possessives of nouns and third singular presents of verbs listed at* [3]AP

apt \apt\ apt, napped, rapt, adapt, black-capped, coapt, dewlapped, enrapt, inapt,

snowcapped, unapt, untapped, periapt—*also pasts of verbs listed at* [3]AP
apter \ap-tər\ captor, chapter, raptor, adapter
aption \ap-shən\ caption, adaption, contraption
aptive \ap-tiv\ captive, adaptive, maladaptive, preadaptive
aptly \ap-lē\ aptly, haply, raptly, inaptly, unaptly
aptor \ap-tər\ see APTER
apture \ap-chər\ rapture, enrapture, recapture
apular \ap-yə-lər\ papular, scapular
apus \ā-pəs\ see APIS
[1]**apy** \ā-pē\ see APEY
[2]**apy** \ap-ē\ see APPY
[1]**aq** \äk\ see [1]OCK
[2]**aq** \ak\ see [2]ACK
aqi \äk-ē\ see OCKY
[1]**aque** \āk\ see [1]AKE
[2]**aque** \ak\ see [2]ACK
aqui \äk-ē\ see OCKY
[1]**ar** \er\ see [4]ARE
[2]**ar** \ȯr\ see [1]OR
[3]**ar** \är\ ar, are, bar, barre, car, carr, char, charr, czar, far, gar, gnar, guar, jar, Lar, mar, moire, noir, our, par, parr, R, quare, Saar, scar, spar, SPAR, star, tar, tahr, Thar, tsar, tzar, yare, Adar, afar, ajar, all-star, armoire, attar, bazaar, beaux arts, Bihar, bizarre, boudoir, boxcar, boyar, briard, bulbar, Bulgar, bursar, canard, catarrh, Cathar, chukar, cigar, clochard, cougar, couloir, crossbar, crowbar, Dakar, daystar, debar, decare, devoir, dinar, disbar, drawbar, Dunbar, durbar, earthstar, Elgar, eschar, eyebar, feldspar, five-star, flatcar, four-star, fulmar, gazar, guitar, Gunnar, Hagar, handcar, Hoggar, horsecar, hussar, Invar, Ishtar, Kolar, Loire, Iyar, jack-tar, jowar, Khowar, lahar, Lamar, lekvar, lodestar, Magyar, memoir, Mizar, Mylar, Navarre, nightjar, paillard, peignoir, petard, Pindar, pissoir, planar, plantar, polestar, pourboire, pulsar, qintar, quasar, radar, railcar, rebar, Renoir, Safar, Samar, sandbar, scalar, shikar, shofar, sidebar, sidecar, sirdar, sitar, sofar, solar, sonar, streetcar, Svalbard, tramcar, trocar, unbar, volar, voussoir, Weimar, abattoir, acinar, Ahaggar, Aligarh, aide-memoire, au revoir, avatar, bete noire, beurre noir, bolivar, Bolivar, café noir, caviar, cinnabar, commissar, communard, coplanar, Côte d'Ivoire, cultivar, deciare, deodar, Dreyfusard, escolar, escritoire, exemplar, fluorspar, handlebar, insofar, isobar, Issachar, jacamar, jaguar, Kandahar, Kashgar, kilobar, Krasnodar, Malabar, megabar, megastar, millibar, minicar, montagnard, motorcar, Mudejar, muscle car, Myanmar, Nicobar, objet d'art, pinot noir, Qiqihar,

registrar, rent-a-car, repertoire, reservoir, ricercar, samovar, scimitar, seminar, simular, steak tartare, subahdar, superstar, tutelar, turbocar, VCR, Veadar, zamindar, Zanzibar, budgerigar, conservatoire, Gulf of Mannar, Hubli-Dharwar, kala-azar, Kathiawar, proseminar

[1]**ara** \är-ə\ Kara, Laura, Mara, Nara, para, vara, Asmara, Bambara, begorra, Bukhara, Camorra, Ferrara, Gomorrah, saguaro, Samara, samsara, tantara, tiara, capybara, carbonara, Connemara, deodara, Gemarara, Guadalajara, Guanabara, solfatara, tuatara, Ogasawara, Sagamihara, Tarahumara, Timisoara

[2]**ara** \er-ə\ see [1]ERA

[3]**ara** \ar-ə\ Clara, jarrah, Kara, Sara, Sarah, Tara, Bukhara, cascara, mascara, Sahara, Samara, Tamara, tantara, tiara, capybara, caracara, marinara, Santa Clara

[4]**ara** \ȯr-ə\ see [2]ORA

arab \ar-əb\ Arab, Carib, carob, scarab, shatt-al-Arabk

arable \ar-ə-bəl\ arable, bearable, parable, shareable, spareable, wearable, declarable, unbearable, inenarrable

aracen \ar-ə-sən\ see ARISON

aracin \ar-ə-sən\ see ARISON

arad \ar-əd\ see ARID

araday \ar-əd-ē\ faraday, parody

arage \ar-ij\ see ARRIAGE

aragon \ar-ə-gən\ paragon, tarragon

[1]**arah** \er-ə\ see [1]ERA

[2]**arah** \ar-ə\ see [1]ARROW

[1]**aral** \ar-əl\ see [2]ARREL

[2]**aral** \ər-əl\ see ERRAL

[1]**aralee** \ar-ə-lē\ Marilee, Saralee

[2]**aralee** \er-ə-lē\ see ARILY

[1]**aran** \er-ən\ see [1]ARON

[2]**aran** \ar-ən\ see [2]ARON

[1]**arant** \er-ənt\ see [1]ARENT

[2]**arant** \ar-ənt\ see [2]ARENT

[1]**araoh** \er-ō\ see [2]ERO

[2]**araoh** \ar-ō\ see [2]ARROW

araph \ar-əf\ see ARIFF

aras \är-əs\ see [1]ORRIS

arass \ar-əs\ see [2]ARIS

arat \ar-ət\ Barrett, carat, caret, carrot, claret, garret, Garrett, karat, parrot, disparate

arate \ar-ət\ see ARAT

[1]**arative** \er-ət-iv\ declarative, imperative

[2]**arative** \ar-ət-iv\ narrative, comparative, declarative, preparative, reparative

arator \ar-ət-ər\ barrator, apparitor, comparator, preparator

arb \ärb\ barb, barbe, carb, darb, garb, bicarb, rhubarb

arbel \är-bəl\ see [1]ARBLE

arber \är-bər\ see ARBOR

arbered \är-bərd\ see ARBOARD

arbin \är-bən\ see ARBON

[1]**arble** \är-bəl\ barbel, garble, marble

[2]**arble** \ȯr-bəl\ see ORBEL

arboard \är-bərd\ barbered, larboard, starboard, astarboard, unbarbered
arbon \är-bən\ carbon, Harbin
arbor \är-bər\ arbor, barber, harbor, Pearl Harbor
[1]arc \äk\ see [1]OCK
[2]arc \ärk\ see [1]ARK
arca \är-kə\ see [1]ARKA
[1]arce \ers\ scarce, Nez Percé
[2]arce \ärs\ see [1]ARSE
arcel \är-səl\ see ARSAL
arcener \ärs-nər\ larcener, parcener, coparcener
arch \ärch\ arch, larch, march, March, parch, starch, cornstarch, frog-march, countermarch
archal \är-kəl\ darkle, sparkle, exarchal, monarchal, hierarchal, matriarchal, patriarchal
archate \är-kət\ see ARKET
arche \ärsh\ see ARSH
arched \ärcht\ arched, parched—*also pasts of verbs listed at* ARCH
archer \är-chər\ archer, marcher, departure
arches \är-chəz\ Arches, Marches
archic \är-kik\ anarchic, autarchic, autarkic, monarchic, tetrarchic, hierarchic, oligarchic
archical \är-ki-kəl\ autarchical, autarkical, monarchical, oligarchical
archon \är-kən\ see ARKEN
archy \är-kē\ barky, charqui, darky, larky, snarky, anarchy, autarchy, autarky, dyarchy, eparchy, exarchy, heptarchy, malarkey, menarche, monarchy, pentarchy, squirearchy, tetrarchy, triarchy, trierarchy, hierarchy, matriarchy, patriarchy, oligarchy
arck \ärk\ see [1]ARK
arco \är-kō\ arco, narco
arct \ärkt\ see ARKED
[1]arctic \ärk-tik\ arctic, Arctic, antarctic, Antarctic, Holarctic, Nearctic, subarctic, Palearctic, subantarctic
[2]arctic \ärt-ik\ see [1]ARTIC
arcy \är-sē\ farcy, Parsi
[1]ard \ärd\ bard, barred, card, chard, Dard, fard, guard, hard, lard, nard, pard, sard, shard, yard, Asgard, backyard, bankcard, barnyard, Bernard, blackguard, blowhard, boatyard, bombard, boneyard, brassard, brickyard, canard, churchyard, courtyard, deeryard, die-hard, diehard, discard, dockyard, dooryard, farmyard, filmcard, fireguard, foreyard, foulard, Gerard, graveyard, ill-starred, jacquard, junkyard, lifeguard, Lombard, mansard, Midgard, milliard, mudguard, noseguard, petard, placard, postcard, poularde, rear guard, rearguard, regard, retard, ritard, safeguard, scorecard, shipyard, spikenard, steelyard, stockyard, switchyard, tabard, tanyard, tiltyard, unbarred, unguard, vanguard, vizard, avant-garde, Beauregard,

bodyguard, boulevard, disregard, goliard, Hildegard, interlard, Kierkegaard, Langobard, leotard, Longobard, no-holds-barred, lumberyard, Saint Bernard, Savoyard, Scotland Yard, self-regard, undercard, unitard, camelopard—*also pasts of verbs listed at* [3]AR
[2]**ard** \är\ see [3]AR
[3]**ard** \ōrd\ see OARD
ardant \ärd-^{ə}nt\ ardent, guardant, regardant, retardant
arde \ärd\ see [1]ARD
[1]**arded** \ärd-əd\ guarded, mansarded, retarded, unguarded—*also pasts of verbs listed at* [1]ARD
[2]**arded** \ȯrd-əd\ corded, sordid, swarded, warded—*also pasts of verbs listed at* [2]OARD
ardee \ȯrd-ē\ see [1]ORDY
[1]**arden** \ärd-^{ə}n\ Arden, Dardan, garden, harden, pardon, bombardon, caseharden, face-harden, Kincardine
[2]**arden** \ȯrd-^{ə}n\ cordon, Gordon, Jordan, warden, churchwarden
ardener \ärd-nər\ gardener, hardener, pardner, pardoner, partner
ardent \ärd-^{ə}nt\ see ARDANT
[1]**arder** \ärd-ər\ ardor, carder, guarder, harder, larder, discarder, green-carder
[2]**arder** \ȯrd-ər\ see ORDER
ardi \ärd-ē\ see ARDY
[1]**ardian** \ärd-ē-ən\ guardian, Edwardian, Lombardian
[2]**ardian** \ȯrd-ē-ən\ see ORDION
ardic \ärd-ik\ bardic, Dardic, Lombardic, Sephardic, goliardic, Longobardic
ardine \ärd-^{n}\ see [1]ARDEN
arding \ȯrd-iŋ\ see [1]ORDING
ardingly \ȯrd-iŋ-lē\ see ORDINGLY
ardom \ärd-əm\ czardom, stardom, superstardom
ardon \ärd-^{ə}n\ see [1]ARDEN
ardoner \ärd-nər\ see ARDENER
ardor \ärd-ər\ see [1]ARDER
ardy \ärd-ē\ hardy, Hardy, lardy, tardy, foolhardy, Lombardy, Sephardi
[1]**are** \er-ē\ see [1]ARY
[2]**are** \är\ see [3]AR
[3]**are** \är-ē\ see [1]ARI
[4]**are** \er\ air, Ayr, bare, bear, Blair, blare, chair, chare, Claire, Clare, dare, Dare, e'er, ere, err, eyre, fair, fare, flair, flare, glair, glare, hair, hare, Herr, heir, lair, mare, ne'er, pair, pare, pear, prayer, quare, rare, rear, scare, share, snare, spare, square, stair, stare, swear, tare, tear, their, there, they're, vair, ware, wear, weir, where, yare, affair, aglare, airfare, Ajmer, Altair, armchair, au pair, aware, barware, Basseterre, Baudelaire, beachwear, beware, bricklayer, bugbear, caneware, carfare, clayware, cochair, coheir, compare, compere, confrere, cookware, corsair, courseware, creamware, cudbear, day-care, daymare, decare, declare, delftware, despair, dishware, éclair, elsewhere, enclair,

ensnare, eyewear, fanfare, fieldfare, firmware, flatware, Flaubert, footwear, forbear, forebear, forswear, foursquare, funfair, galère, giftware, glassware, Great Bear, Gruyère, hardware, hectare, horsehair, impair, infare, Khmer, Kildare, knitwear, Lake Eyre, life-care, longhair, loungewear, menswear, meunière, midair, mohair, Molière, neckwear, nightmare, outstare, outwear, Pierre, playwear, plein air, plowshare, Poor Clare, portiere, premiere, prepare, pushchair, rainwear, redware, repair, Saint Pierre, Sancerre, shorthair, skiwear, sleepwear, slipware, software, somewhere, spongeware, sportswear, stemware, stoneware, swimwear, threadbare, tinware, torchère, tracklayer, trouvère, tuyere, unfair, unhair, unswear, Voltaire, warfare, welfare, wheelchair, wirehair, workfare, aftercare, air-to-air, antiair, anywhere, bayadere, bêche-de-mer, billionaire, boutonniere, Camembert, chinaware, crackleware, cultivar, debonair, deciare, de la Mare, Delaware, derriere, dinnerware, disrepair, doctrinaire, earthenware, étagère, everywhere, Cape Finisterre, fourragère, Frigidaire, graniteware, hollowware, ironware, jasperware, kitchenware, laissez-faire, Lake Saint Clair, laquerware, legionnaire, luminaire, lusterware, maidenhair, mal de mer, medicare, metalware, millionaire, minaudière, minelayer, Mon-Khmer, Mousquetaire, nom de guerre, otherwhere, outerwear, overbear, overwear, potty-chair, porte cochere, questionnaire, rivière, Robespierre, Santander, savoir faire, self-aware, self-despair, silverware, solitaire, tableware, thoroughfare, unaware, underwear, vaporware, Venushair, vivandière, willowware, woodenware, yellowware, zillionaire, chargé d'affaires, chemin de fer, commissionaire, concessionaire, couturiere, Croix de guerre, devil-may-care, enamelware, memoriter, pied-à-terre, ready-to-wear, son et lumière, vin ordinaire, cordon sanitaire

area \er-ē-ə\ see ARIA

[1]**areable** \er-ə-bəl\ see [1]EARABLE

[2]**areable** \ar-ə-bəl\ see ARABLE

areal \er-ē-əl\ see ARIAL

[1]**arean** \er-ē-ən\ see [1]ARIAN

[2]**arean** \ar-ē-ən\ see [2]ARIAN

ared \erd\ see AIRED

aredness \ar-əd-nəs\ see ARIDNESS

arel \ar-əl\ see [2]ARREL

[1]**arely** \er-lē\ see AIRLY

[2]**arely** \är-lē\ see ARLIE
arem \er-əm\ see [2]ARUM
[1]**arence** \er-əns\ clarence, Clarence, Terence, Terrance, Terrence, forbearance, transparence
[2]**arence** \ar-ən(ts)\ see ARENTS
[1]**arent** \er-ənt\ daren't, errant, parent, aberrant, afferent, apparent, declarant, deferent, efferent, godparent, grandparent, inapparent, inerrant, knight-errant, sederunt, stepparent, transparent, semitransparent
[2]**arent** \ar-ənt\ arrant, daren't, parent, apparent, declarant, godparent, grandparent, stepparent, transparent, inapparent, semitransparent
[1]**aren't** \er-ənt\ see [1]ARENT
[2]**aren't** \ar-ənt\ see [2]ARENT
arents \ar-ən(t)s\ Barents, Clarence—*also plurals of nouns listed at* [2]ARENT
[1]**arer** \er-ər\ see [1]EARER
[2]**arer** \ar-ər\ see [3]EARER
[1]**ares** \erz\ see AIRS
[2]**ares** \ar-ēz\ Ares, caries, nares, Antares, Buenos Aires, primus inter pares—*also plurals and possessives of nouns and third singular presents of verbs listed at* [3]ARRY
[3]**ares** \är-əs\ see [1]ORRIS
aret \ar-ət\ see ARAT
areve \är-və\ see ARVA
[1]**arey** \ar-ē\ see [3]ARRY
[2]**arey** \er-ē\ see [1]ARY
arez \är-əs\ see [1]ORRIS
[1]**arf** \ärf\ barf, scarf
[2]**arf** \ȯrf\ see ORPH
arfarin \ȯr-fə-rən\ warfarin, hematoporphyrin
argain \är-gən\ bargain, jargon, plea-bargain
arge \ärj\ barge, charge, large, marge, Marge, parge, sarge, sparge, targe, discharge, enlarge, litharge, recharge, surcharge, take-charge, uncharge, by and large, hypercharge, overcharge, supercharge, undercharge
argent \är-jənt\ argent, margent, sargent, sergeant
arger \är-jər\ charger, discharger, enlarger, recharger, supercharger, turbocharger, turbosupercharger
arget \är-gət\ argot, garget, target, nontarget
argle \är-gəl\ gargle, argle-bargle
argo \är-gō\ Argo, argot, cargo, Fargo, largo, Margo, Margot, embargo, supercargo
argon \är-gən\ see ARGAIN
[1]**argot** \är-gət\ see ARGET
[2]**argot** \är-gō\ see ARGO
arh \är\ see [3]AR
[1]**ari** \är-ē\ Bari, gharry, laari, sari, scarry, sorry, starry, Bihari, curare, Imari, safari, scalare, shikari, tamari, calamari, cheboksary, Kalahari, Stradivari, zamindari, certiorari
[2]**ari** \er-ē\ see [1]ARY
[3]**ari** \ar-ē\ see [3]ARRY
aria \er-ē-ə\ area, Beria, feria, kerria, varia, Bavaria,

Bulgaria, hysteria, malaria, planaria, Samaria, adularia, Carpentaria, cineraria, fritillaria, laminaria, luminaria, militaria, sanguinaria, calceolaria, opera seria, acetabularia

arial \er-ē-əl\ aerial, areal, Ariel, burial, gharial, glossarial, notarial, subaerial, vicarial, actuarial, adversarial, estuarial, secretarial, prothonotarial

[1]arian \er-ē-ən\ Arian, Aryan, Carian, Marian, Marion, parian, Parian, agrarian, Aquarian, barbarian, Bavarian, Bulgarian, Cancerian, cesarean, Caesarian, cnidarian, frutarian, grammarian, Hungarian, Khymorian, librarian, Maid Marian, ovarian, Pierian, riparian, rosarian, Rotarian, sectarian, Sumerian, Tartarean, Tartarian, Tocharian, Tractarian, Vulgarian, Wagnerian, antiquarian, apiarian, centenarian, culinarian, Indo-Aryan, jubilarian, lapidarian, libertarian, millenarian, nonsectarian, postlapsarian, prelapsarian, Presbyterian, proletarian, Rastafarian, Ripuarian, Sabbatarian, Sagittarian, sanitarian, seminarian, trinitarian, Trinitarian, unitarian, Unitarian, vegetarian, zoantharian, abecedarian, Austro-Hungarian, authoritarian, communitarian, disciplinarian, documentarian, egalitarian, equalitarian, futilitarian, hereditarian, humanitarian, majoritarian, necessitarian, nonagenarian, octogenarian, parliamentarian, postmillinarian, premillinarian, predestinarian, radiolarian, Sacramentarian, sexagenarian, totalitarian, utilitarian, veterinarian, establishmentarian, inegalitarian, latitudinarian, platitudinarian, septuagenarian, solitudinarian, uniformitarian, valetudinarian, disestablishmentarian

[2]arian \ar-ē-ən\ Arian, Aryan, carrion, clarion, Marian, Marion, parian, Parian, agrarian, Aquarian, barbarian, Bavarian, Bulgarian, caesarean, Caesarian, cesarean, contrarian, Hungarian, Megarian, ovarian, rosarian, Tartarean, Tartarian, Tocharian, vulgarian, Indo-Aryan, Rastafarian, Austro-Hungarian

ariance \ar-ē-əns\ tarriance, variance, covariance, vicariance

ariant \ar-ē-ənt\ variant, vicariant

[1]ariat \er-ē-ət\ heriot, lariat, variate, bivariate, salariat, vicariate, commissariat, multivariate, proletariat, secretariat, undersecretariat

[2]ariat \är-ē-ət\ see [1]AUREATE

[3]**ariat** \ar-ē-ət\ chariot, lariat, bivariate, salariat, commissariat, proletariat, Judas Iscariot
ariate \er-ē-ət\ see [1]ARIAT
arib \ar-əb\ see ARAB
aric \ar-ik\ barrack, carrack, Amharic, barbaric, Dinaric, Megaric, Pindaric, isobaric, Balearic
arice \ar-əs\ see [2]ARIS
aricide \ar-ə-sīd\ see ARRICIDE
arid \ar-əd\ arid, farad, semiarid
aridin \ar-ə-dᵊn\ see ARRIDAN
aridness \ar-əd-nəs\ aridness, preparedness
[1]**aried** \er-ēd\ see ERRIED
[2]**aried** \ar-ēd\ see ARRIED
ariel \er-ē-əl\ see ARIAL
[1]**arier** \er-ē-ər\ see ERRIER
[2]**arier** \ar-ē-ər\ see [2]ARRIER
aries \ar-ēz\ see [2]ARES
ariff \ar-əf\ paraph, tariff
aril \ar-əl\ see [2]ARREL
[1]**arilee** \ar-ə-lē\ see ARALEE
[2]**arilee** \er-ə-lē\ see ARILY
arily \er-ə-lē\ Marilee, merrily, Merrily, Saralee, scarily, sterily, verily, contrarily, primarily, arbitrarily, customarily, dietarily, exemplarily, fragmentarily, honorarily, literarily, mercenarily, militarily, momentarily, necessarily, salutarily, sanguinarily, sanitarily, secondarily, temporarily, unitarily, voluntarily, contemporarily, elementarily, extemporarily, extraordinarily, hereditarily, imaginarily, involuntarily, preliminarily, rudimentarily, subsidiarily, unnecessarily, documentarily, evolutionarily, revolutionarily
arin \är-ən\ see [1]ORIN
arinate \ar-ə-nət\ see ARONET
arinet \ar-ə-nət\ see ARONET
[1]**aring** \ar-iŋ\ airing, Bering, fairing, flaring, glaring, herring, paring, raring, sparing, tearing, wearing, cheeseparing, childbearing, seafaring, time-sharing, unerring, unsparing, wayfaring
[2]**aring** \er-ən\ see [1]ARON
ario \er-ē-ō\ stereo, Ontario
[1]**arion** \ar-ē-ən\ see [2]ARIAN
[2]**arion** \er-ē-ən\ see [1]ARIAN
ariot \ar-ē-ət\ see [3]ARIAT
arious \ar-ē-əs\ Arius, carious, Darious, scarious, various, Aquarius, burglarious, calcareous, contrarious, denarius, gregarious, guarnerius, hilarious, nefarious, precarious, senarius, vagarious, vicarious, multifarious, omnifarious, septenarius, Stradivarius, Sagittarius, temerarious
[1]**aris** \är-əs\ see [1]ORRIS
[2]**aris** \ar-əs\ arras, arris, Clarice, harass, Harris, heiress, Paris, parous, varus, coheiress, embarrass, Polaris, disembarrass, millionairess, Lewis with Harris, plaster of paris
[1]**arish** \er-ish\ bearish, cherish,

fairish, garish, perish, squarish, nightmarish
[2]**arish** \ar-ish\ garish, marish, parish
arison \ar-ə-sən\ characin, garrison, Garrison, Harrison, Saracen, warison, caparison, comparison
arist \er-əst\ Marist, querist, aquarist, pleinairist, scenarist, apiarist—*also superlatives of adjectives listed at* [4]ARE
aritan \er-ət-ᵊn\ see ERATIN
aritor \ar-ət-ər\ see ARATOR
[1]**arity** \er-ət-ē\ see ERITY
[2]**arity** \ar-ət-ē\ carroty, charity, clarity, parity, rarity, barbarity, disparity, hilarity, imparity, polarity, unclarity, vulgarity, angularity, familiarity, insularity, peculiarity, popularity, regularity, similarity, singularity, solidarity, complementarity, dissimilarity, irregularity, particularity, unfamiliarity, unpopularity
arium \er-ē-əm\ barium, aquarium, herbarium, sacrarium, samarium, solarium, terrarium, velarium, vivarium, cinerarium, columbarium, honorarium, leprosarium, oceanarium, planetarium, sanitarium, syllabarium, termitarium, armamentarium
arius \er-ē-əs\ see ARIOUS
[1]**ark** \ärk\ arc, ark, bark, Clark, Clarke, dark, hark, lark, marc, Marc, mark, Mark, marque, narc, nark, park, Park, quark, sark, shark, spark, stark, aardvark, airpark, anarch, ballpark, birchbark, birthmark, Bismarck, bookmark, debark, demark, Denmark, earmark, embark, endarch, exarch, footmark, futhark, Graustark, hallmark, ironbark, landmark, Lake Clark, Lamarck, monarch, ostmark, Ozark, Petrarch, pitch-dark, Plutarch, pockmark, postmark, pressmark, pugmark, reichsmark, remark, remarque, Remarque, ringbark, seamark, shagbark, sitzmark, skylark, soapbark, tanbark, tetrarch, tidemark, titlark, touchmark, trademark, acritarch, cutty sark, deutsche mark, disembark, double-park, hierarch, Joan of Arc, matriarch, meadowlark, metalmark, minipark, oligarch, patriarch, stringybark, telemark, trierarch, watermark, heresiarch, symposiarch
[2]**ark** \ȯrk\ see [2]ORK
[3]**ark** \ərk\ see [1]ORK
[1]**arka** \är-kə\ charka, parka, anasarca, Hamilcar Barca
[2]**arka** \ər-kə\ see [1]URKA
arke \ärk\ see [1]ARK
arked \ärkt\ marked, chop-marked, infarct, ripple-marked, unremarked—*also pasts of verbs listed at* [1]ARK
arken \är-kən\ darken, hearken
arker \är-kər\ barker, larker,

marker, parker, Parker, sparker, bookmarker, skylarker, nosey parker—*also comparatives of adjectives listed at* [1]ARK

arket \är-kət\ market, downmarket, mass-market, newmarket, test-market, upmarket, aftermarket, hypermarket, matriarchate, patriarchate, supermarket

arkey \är-kē\ see ARCHY

arkian \är-kē-ən\ Graustarkian, Lamarckian, Monarchian

arkic \är-kik\ see ARCHIC

arking \är-kiŋ\ barking, Barking, carking, parking, loan-sharking

arkle \är-kəl\ see ARCHAL

arks \ärks\ Marks, parks—*also plurals of nouns and third person singular presents of verbs listed at* ARK

arky \är-kē\ see ARCHY

arl \ärl\ carl, Carl, farl, gnarl, jarl, Karl, marl, parle, quarrel, snarl, ensnarl, housecarl, unsnarl, Albemarle

arla \är-lə\ Carla, Darla, Karla, Marla

arlan \ä-lən\ see ARLINE

arland \är-lənd\ garland, Garland, Harland

arlatan \är-lət-ᵊn\ charlatan, tarlatan

arlay \är-lē\ see ARLIE

arle \ärl\ see ARL

arlen \är-lən\ see ARLINE

arler \är-lər\ see ARLOR

arless \är-ləs\ Carlos, parlous, scarless, starless

arlet \är-lət\ charlotte, Charlotte, harlot, scarlet, starlet, varlet

arley \är-lē\ see ARLIE

arlic \är-lik\ garlic, pilgarlic

arlie \är-lē\ barley, charlie, Charlie, gnarly, Harley, marly, parlay, parley, snarly, yarely, bizarrely, Mr. Charlie

arlin \är-lən\ see ARLINE

arline \är-lən\ Arlen, carline, Harlan, marlin, Marlin, marline, Marlyn

arling \är-liŋ\ carling, darling, Darling, starling

arlor \är-lər\ parlor, quarreler, snarler

arlos \är-ləs\ see ARLESS

arlot \är-lət\ see ARLET

arlotte \är-lət\ see ARLET

arlous \är-ləs\ see ARLESS

arlow \är-lō\ Barlow, Harlow

arly \är-lē\ see ARLIE

arlyn \ä-lən\ see ARLINE

[1]**arm** \ärm\ arm, barm, charm, farm, harm, smarm, alarm, disarm, firearm, forearm, gendarme, gisarme, poor farm, rearm, sidearm, stiff-arm, straight-arm, strong-arm, tonearm, unarm, yardarm, overarm, underarm

[2]**arm** \äm\ see [1]OM

[3]**arm** \ȯrm\ see [2]ORM

[1]**arma** \är-mə\ dharma, karma, Parma

[2]**arma** \ər-mə\ see ERMA

arman \är-mən\ barman, Carmen, carmine, Harmon

armed \ärmd\ armed, charmed, unarmed—*also pasts of verbs listed at* [1]ARM

armen \är-mən\ see ARMAN

arment \är-mənt\ garment, varmint, debarment, disbarment, undergarment, overgarment
[1]**armer** \är-mər\ armor, charmer, farmer, harmer, disarmer
[2]**armer** \ȯr-mər\ see [1]ORMER
armic \ər-mik\ see ERMIC
armine \är-mən\ see ARMAN
[1]**arming** \är-miŋ\ charming, farming, alarming, disarming
[2]**arming** \ȯr-miŋ\ see ORMING
armint \är-mənt\ see ARMENT
armless \ärm-ləs\ armless, charmless, harmless
armoir \är-mər\ see [1]ARMER
armon \är-mən\ see ARMAN
army \är-mē\ army, barmy, smarmy
[1]**arn** \ärn\ Arne, barn, darn, Marne, tarn, yarn, carbarn, lucarne
[2]**arn** \ȯrn\ see [2]ORN
arna \ər-nə\ see ERNA
arnal \ärn-[ə]l\ see ARNEL
arnate \är-nət\ Barnet, garnet, discarnate, incarnate
[1]**arne** \ärn\ see [1]ARN
[2]**arne** \är-nē\ see ARNY
arnel \ärn-[ə]l\ carnal, charnel, darnel
[1]**arner** \är-nər\ darner, garner, yarner
[2]**arner** \ȯr-nər\ see ORNER
arness \är-nəs\ harness, bizarreness
arnet \är-nət\ see ARNATE
arney \är-nē\ see ARNY
arnhem \är-nəm\ see ARNUM
arning \ȯr-niŋ\ see ORNING
arnish \är-nish\ garnish, tarnish, varnish
arnum \är-nəm\ Arnhem, Barnum
arny \är-nē\ Barney, barny, blarney, carny, Killarney, chili con carne
[1]**aro** \er-ō\ see [2]ERO
[2]**aro** \ar-ō\ see [2]ARROW
[3]**aro** \är-ə\ see [1]ARA
[4]**aro** \är-ō\ see [1]ORROW
arob \ar-əb\ see ARAB
arody \ar-əd-ē\ see ARADAY
[1]**aroe** \ar-ō\ see [2]ARROW
[2]**aroe** \er-ō\ see [2]ERO
arol \ar-əl\ see [2]ARREL
[1]**arold** \ar-əld\ Darold, Harold
[2]**arold** \er-əld\ see ERALD
arole \ar-əl\ see [2]ARREL
arom \er-əm\ see [2]ARUM
[1]**aron** \er-ən\ Aaron, Charon, Erin, garron, heron, perron, raring, Sharon, Sharron, sierran, rose of Sharon, sub-Saharan
[2]**aron** \ar-ən\ Aaron, baron, barren, Charon, garron, Sharon, Sharron, rose of Sharon, sub-Saharan
aronet \ar-ə-nət\ baronet, carinate, clarinet
[1]**arous** \er-əs\ see ERROUS
[2]**arous** \ar-əs\ see [2]ARIS
[1]**arp** \ärp\ carp, harp, scarp, sharp, tarp, cardsharp, escarp, Jews harp, Autoharp, vibraharp
[2]**arp** \ȯrp\ see ORP
arpen \är-pən\ sharpen, tarpon
arper \är-pər\ carper, harper, scarper, sharper, cardsharper
arpie \är-pē\ see ARPY

arpon \är-pən\ see ARPEN
arpy \är-pē\ harpy, sharpie
arque \ärk\ see [1]ARK
arquetry \är-kə-trē\ marquetry, parquetry
arqui \är-kē\ see ARCHY
arrable \ar-ə-bəl\ see ARABLE
[1]**arrack** \ar-ik\ see ARIC
[2]**arrack** \ar-ək\ arrack, barrack, carrack
arragon \ar-ə-gən\ see ARAGON
arral \ar-əl\ see [2]ARREL
arram \ar-əm\ see [2]ARUM
[1]**arrant** \ar-ənt\ see [2]ARENT
[2]**arrant** \ȯr-ənt\ see ORRENT
arras \ar-əs\ see [2]ARIS
arrass \ar-əs\ see [2]ARIS
arrative \ar-ət-iv\ see [2]ARATIVE
arrator \ar-ət-ər\ see ARATOR
arre \är\ see [3]AR
arred \ärd\ see [1]ARD
[1]**arrel** \ȯrl\ see [3]ORAL
[2]**arrel** \ar-əl\ Aral, aril, barrel, Beryl, carol, Carol, Carole, Caryl, carrel, Carroll, Darrel, Darrell, Darryl, Daryl, Errol, Karol, parol, parral, parrel, apparel, cracker-barrel, double-barrel
arreler \är-lər\ see ARLOR
arrell \ar-əl\ see [2]ARREL
arrely \är-lē\ see ARLIE
[1]**arren** \ar-ən\ see [2]ARON
[2]**arren** \ȯr-ən\ see [2]ORIN
[3]**arren** \är-ən\ see [1]ORIN
arrener \ȯr-ə-nər\ see ORONER
arreness \är-nəs\ see ARNESS
arret \ar-ət\ see ARAT
arrett \ar-ət\ see ARAT
arrh \är\ see [3]AR
arriage \ar-ij\ carriage, marriage, disparage, miscarriage, intermarriage, undercarriage
arriance \ar-ē-əns\ see ARIANCE
arricide \ar-ə-sīd\ parricide, acaricide
arridan \ar-ə-d^{ə}n\ harridan, cantharidin
arrie \ar-ē\ see [3]ARRY
arried \ar-ēd\ harried, married, varied, unmarried
[1]**arrier** \ȯr-ē-ər\ see ARRIOR
[2]**arrier** \ar-ē-ər\ barrier, carrier, farrier, harrier, varier, ballcarrier, spear-carrier
arrion \ar-ē-ən\ see [2]ARIAN
arrior \ȯr-ē-ər\ quarrier, sorrier, warrior
arris \ar-əs\ see [2]ARIS
arrison \ar-ə-sən\ see ARISON
arro \är-ō\ see [1]ORROW
arroll \ar-əl\ see [2]ARREL
arron \ar-ən\ see [2]ARON
arrot \ar-ət\ see ARAT
arroty \ar-ət-ē\ see [2]ARITY
arrow \ar-ō\ aero, arrow, barrow, Darrow, Faeroe, faro, Faroe, farrow, harrow, Harrow, marrow, narrow, pharaoh, sparrow, taro, tarot, yarrow, handbarrow, Point Barrow, wheelbarrow
arrowy \ar-ə-wē\ arrowy, marrowy
[1]**arry** \är-ē\ see [1]ARI
[2]**arry** \ȯr-ē\ see ORY
[3]**arry** \ar-ē\ Barrie, Barry, Carey, Carrie, carry, Cary, chary, Gary, Garry, gharry, harry, Harry, Larry, marry, nary, parry, Shari, tarry, glengarry, miscarry, safari, shikari, cash-and-carry, hari-

kari, intermarry, Stradivari; Tom, Dick, and Harry
arryl \ar-əl\ see [2]ARREL
ars \ärz\ Lars, Mars, ours—*also plurals and possessives of nouns and third person singular presents of verbs listed at* [3]AR
arsal \är-səl\ parcel, versal, tarsal, metatarsal
[1]arse \ärs\ arse, farce, marse, parse, sparse
[2]arse \ärz\ see ARS
arsh \ärsh\ harsh, marsh, demarche
arshal \är-shəl\ see ARTIAL
arshall \är-shəl\ see ARTIAL
arshen \är-shən\ harshen, martian
arsi \är-sē\ see ARCY
arsis \är-səs\ see ARSUS
arsle \äs-əl\ see OSSAL
arson \ärs-ᵊn\ arson, Carson, parson
arsus \är-səs\ arsis, tarsus, Tarsus, catharsis, metatarsus
[1]art \ärt\ art, Art, Bart, cart, chart, Chartres, dart, hart, Harte, heart, kart, mart, part, Sartre, scart, smart, start, tart, apart, blackheart, compart, depart, Descartes, dispart, dogcart, Earhart, flowchart, forepart, go-cart, greenheart, handcart, Hobart, impart, jump-start, Mozart, mouthpart, outsmart, oxcart, oxheart, pushcart, rampart, redstart, restart, street-smart, Stuttgart, sweetheart, tipcart, upstart, à la carte, anti-art, applecart, Bonaparte, counterpart, heart-to-heart, purpleheart, underpart, upperpart
[2]art \ȯrt\ see [1]ORT
arta \är-tə\ Marta, Sparta, Djarkarta, Magna Carta, Santa Marta, Surakarta, yogyakarta
artable \ärt-ə-bəl\ see ARTIBLE
[1]artan \ärt-ᵊn\ see ARTEN
[2]artan \ȯrt-ᵊn\ see ORTEN
artar \ärt-ər\ see [1]ARTER
[1]arte \ärt-ē\ see [1]ARTY
[2]arte \ärt\ see [1]ART
[1]arted \ärt-əd\ see EARTED
[2]arted \ȯrt-əd\ see ORTED
arten \ärt-ᵊn\ Barton, carton, hearten, marten, martin, Martin, smarten, Spartan, tartan, baum marten, dishearten, Dumbarton, freemartin, Saint Martin, Sint Maarten, kindergarten
[1]arter \ärt-ər\ barter, carter, Carter, charter, darter, garter, martyr, starter, tartar, nonstarter, self-starter, protomartyr—*also comparatives of adjectives listed at* [1]ART
[2]arter \ȯt-ər\ see [1]ATER
[3]arter \ȯrt-ər\ see ORTER
artern \ȯt-ərn\ see AUTERNE
artery \ärt-ə-rē\ artery, martyry
artes \ärt\ see [1]ART
artford \ärt-fərd\ Hartford, Hertford
arth \ärth\ garth, Garth, hearth, Hogarth
arti \ärt-ē\ see [1]ARTY
artial \är-shəl\ marshal, Marshal, Marshall, martial,

Martial, partial, court-martial, impartial
artian \är-shən\ see ARSHEN
artible \ärt-ə-bəl\ partible, startable, impartible, restartable
[1]**artic** \ärt-ik\ arctic, Arctic, antarctic, Antarctic, cathartic, Nearctic, Palearctic
[2]**artic** \ȯrt-ik\ quartic, aortic
article \ärt-i-kəl\ article, particle, microparticle
artile \ȯrt-ᵊl\ see ORTAL
artily \ärt-ᵊl-ē\ artily, heartily
artin \ärt-ᵊn\ see ARTEN
arting \ärt-iŋ\ carting, charting, karting, parting, starting, flowcharting, self-starting
artisan \ärt-ə-zən\ artisan, bartizan, partisan, bipartisan, nonpartisan
artist \ärt-əst\ artist, chartist, Chartist, Bonapartist
artizan \ärt-ə-zən\ see ARTISAN
artless \ärt-ləs\ artless, heartless
artlet \ärt-lət\ martlet, partlet, tartlet
[1]**artly** \ärt-lē\ partly, smartly, tartly
[2]**artly** \ȯrt-lē\ see [2]ORTLY
artment \ärt-mənt\ apartment, compartment, department
artner \ärt-nər\ partner, kindergartner
[1]**arton** \ȯrt-ᵊn\ see ORTON
[2]**arton** \ärt-ᵊn\ see ARTEN
artre \ärt\ see [1]ART
artres \ärt\ see [1]ART
artridge \är-trij\ cartridge, partridge
[1]**arts** \är\ see [3]AR
[2]**arts** \ärts\ Hartz—*also plurals and possessives of nouns and third person singular presents of verbs listed at* [1]ART
arture \är-chər\ see ARCHER
[1]**arty** \ärt-ē\ arty, hearty, party, smarty, tarty, Astarte, ex parte, Havarti, Buonaparte, commedia del l'arte
[2]**arty** \ȯrt-ē\ see ORTY
artyr \ärt-ər\ see [1]ARTER
artyry \ärt-ə-rē\ see ARTERY
[1]**artz** \ȯrts\ see ORTS
[2]**artz** \ärts\ see [2]ARTS
aru \ä-rü\ Bukaru, Johore Bahru, Pakan Baru
[1]**arum** \är-əm\ larum, alarum
[2]**arum** \er-əm\ arum, carom, harem, Sarum, Muharram, harum-scarum, arbiter elegantiarum
arus \ar-əs\ see [2]ARIS
arva \är-və\ larva, Marva, parve, pareve
arval \är-vəl\ see ARVEL
[1]**arve** \ärv\ carve, starve, varve
[2]**arve** \är-və\ see ARVA
arvel \är-vəl\ carvel, larval, marvel
arven \är-vən\ carven, Marvin, Caernarvon
arvin \är-vən\ see ARVEN
arvon \är-vən\ see ARVEN
[1]**ary** \er-ē\ aerie, aery, airy, berry, bury, Carey, Cary, Cherie, cherry, Cherry, chary, clary, dairy, Derry, faerie, fairy, ferry, Gary, Garry, Gerry, glairy, glary, hairy, Jere, Jeri, Jerrie, Jerry, kerry, Kerry, Mary, marry, merry, Merry, nary, perry, Perry, prairie, quaere, query, scary,

serry, Shari, Sheri, Sherrie, sherry, Sherry, skerry, terry, Terry, vary, very, wary, wherry, baneberry, barberry, bayberry, bearberry, bilberry, blackberry, blaeberry, blueberry, Bradbury, bunchberry, Burberry, canary, Canary, chokeberry, chokecherry, cloudberry, contrary, coralberry, costmary, cowberry, cranberry, crowberry, deerberry, dewberry, equerry, gooseberry, ground-cherry, hackberry, hegari, inkberry, Juneberry, knobkerrie, library, mulberry, nondairy, pokeberry, primary, raspberry, rosemary, Rosemary, scalare, shadberry, sheepberry, snowberry, soapberry, strawberry, summary, teaberry, tilbury, twinberry, unwary, vagary, wolfberry, youngberry, actuary, adversary, airy-fairy, ancillary, antiquary, apiary, arbitrary, aviary, axillary, beriberi, bestiary, biliary, boysenberry, breviary, budgetary, calamari, calamary, candleberry, Canterbury, capillary, cartulary, cassowary, catenary, cautionary, cavitary, cemetery, centenary, certiorari, chartulary, checkerberry, chinaberry, ciliary, cinerary, cometary, commentary, commissary, condottiere, corollary, coronary, culinary, customary, dictionary, dietary, dignitary, dingleberry, dromedary, dysentery, elderberry, emissary, estuary, farkleberry, February, formicary, formulary, fragmentary, fritillary, functionary, funerary, honorary, huckleberry, intermarry, janissary, January, lamasery, lapidary, lectionary, legendary, legionary, limitary, lingonberry, literary, loganberry, luminary, mammillary, mandatary, maxillary, medullary, mercenary, miliary, military, millenary, milliary, millinery, miserere, missionary, momentary, monastery, monetary, mortuary, necessary, ordinary, ossuary, papillary, parcenary, partridgeberry, pensionary, phalanstery, pigmentary, plagiary, planetary, Pondicherry, prebendary, presbytery, pulmonary, pupillary, quaternary, questionary, reliquary, rowanberry, salivary, salmonberry, salutary, sanctuary, sanguinary, sanitary, secondary, secretary, sedentary, seminary, serviceberry, silverberry, solitary, stationary, stationery, statuary, Stradivari, subcontrary, sublunary, sugarberry, sumptuary, syllabary, temporary, termitary, tertiary, textuary, thimbleberry, Tipperary, Tom and Jerry, topiary, tributary, tutelary, unitary, urinary, vestiary, visionary, voluntary, vulnerary, Waterbury, whortleberry, winterberry, ablutionary, accretionary, antiphonary, apothecary, bicentenary, bilmillenary, concessionary, conclusionary, concretionary, confectionary, confectionery, consigliere, constabulary, contemporary, convulsionary, coparcenary, depositary, delusionary, digressionary, disciplinary, discretionary, distributary, diversionary, electuary, epistolary, exclusionary, expansionary, expeditionary, extemporary, extortionary, extraordinary, fiduciary, hereditary, illusionary, imaginary, incendiary, inflationary, insanitary, intercalary, involuntary, itinerary, judiciary, libationary, obituary, officiary, pecuniary, petitionary, precautionary, preliminary, presidiary, previsionary, probationary, proprietary, provisionary, reactionary, recessionary, reflationary, residuary, reversionary, revisionary, stagflationary, stipendiary, subliterary, subsidiary, subversionary, tercentenary, traditionary, tumultuary, unnecessary, veterinary, vocabulary, voluptuary, abolitionary, beneficiary, consuetudinary, deflationary, devolutionary, disinflationary, domiciliary, eleemosynary, elocutionary, evidentiary, evolutionary, extraliterary, intermediary, paramilitary, penitentiary, quatercentenary, revolutionary, semicentenary, semilegendary, sesquicentenary, superciliary, supernumerary, tintinnabulary, transdisciplinary, usufructuary, valetudinary, interdisciplinary, plenipotentiary, counterrevolutionary

[2]**ary** \ar-ē\ see [3]ARRY

[3]**ary** \är-ē\ see [1]ARI

[1]**aryan** \er-ē-ən\ see [1]ARIAN

[2]**aryan** \ar-ē-ən\ see [2]ARIAN

aryl \ar-əl\ see [2]ARREL

[1]**as** \ash\ see [3]ASH

[2]**as** \as\ see [3]ASS

[3]**as** \az\ see AZZ

[4]**as** \ä\ see [1]A

[5]**as** \äsh\ see [1]ASH

[6]**as** \äz\ see [1]OISE

[7]**as** \əz\ see [1]EUSE

[8]**as** \äs\ see [1]OS

[9]**as** \ȯ\ see [1]AW

[1]**asa** \äs-ə\ casa, fossa, glossa, Lhasa, Ossa, kielbasa, Kinshasa, Landrace, Mombasa, tabula rasa

[2]**asa** \äz-ə\ see [1]AZA

[3]**asa** \as-ə\ see ASSA

[1]**asable** \ā-zə-bəl\ grazeable, persuasible, paraphrasable

[2]**asable** \ā-sə-bəl\ see ACEABLE

[1]**asal** \ā-səl\ basal, Basil, stay sail, forestay sail
[2]**asal** \ā-zəl\ basal, Basil, hazel, Hazel, nasal, phrasal, appraisal, Azazel
asally \āz-lē\ see AISLEY
asca \as-kə\ see ASKA
ascal \as-kəl\ paschal, rascal
ascan \as-kən\ see ASKIN
ascar \as-kər\ see ASKER
[1]**ascence** \ās-ᵊns\ nascence, complacence, complaisance, renascence
[2]**ascence** \as-ᵊns\ nascence, renascence
[1]**ascent** \as-ᵊnt\ nascent, passant, renascent
[2]**ascent** \ās-ᵊnt\ see ACENT
[1]**asch** \ask\ see ASK
[2]**asch** \äsh\ see [1]ASH
[3]**asch** \ȯsh\ see [2]ASH
aschal \as-kəl\ see ASCAL
[1]**ascia** \ā-shə\ see ACIA
[2]**ascia** \ash-ə\ see [2]ASHA
ascible \as-ə-bəl\ see ASSABLE
ascicle \as-i-kəl\ see ASSICAL
[1]**asco** \äs-kō\ see OSCOE
[2]**asco** \as-kō\ fiasco, Tabasco
ascon \as-kən\ see ASKIN
ascot \as-kət\ see ASKET
ascus \as-kəs\ Damascus, Velazquez
[1]**ase** \ās\ see [1]ACE
[2]**ase** \āz\ see [1]AZE
[3]**ase** \äz\ see [1]OISE
asel \äz-əl\ see OZZLE
ased \āst\ see ACED
aseless \ā-sləs\ see ACELESS
aseman \ā-smən\ see ACEMAN
asement \ās-mənt\ basement, casement, debasement, bargain-basement

[1]**aser** \ā-sər\ see [1]ACER
[2]**aser** \ā-zər\ see AZER
asey \ā-sē\ see ACY
[1]**ash** \äsh\ bosh, cosh, Fosh, frosh, gosh, gouache, josh, Mâche, nosh, posh, quash, slosh, squash, swash, tosh, wash, awash, backwash, blackwash, cohosh, czardas, Dias, Diaz, downwash, eyewash, galosh, ganache, goulash, kibosh, midrash, mishmash, mouthwash, musquash, panache, rainwash, Siwash, whitewash, wish-wash, hamantasch, mackintosh, McIntosh
[2]**ash** \ȯsh\ Bosch, Foch, gosh, grosz, quash, slosh, squash, swash, wash, awash, backwash, Balkhash, blackwash, brainwash, brioche, Bydgoszcz, downwash, eyewash, hogwash, Iasi, mouthwash, outwash, rainwash, Siwash, whitewash, wish-wash, hamantasch
[3]**ash** \ash\ ash, bash, brash, cache, cash, clash, crash, dash, fash, flash, gash, gnash, hash, lash, mash, pash, plash, rash, sash, slash, smash, splash, stash, thrash, thresh, trash, abash, backlash, backsplash, Balkhash, calash, Chumash, czardas, encash, eyelash, goulash, mishmash, moustache, mustache, panache, potash, rehash, slapdash, soutache, stramash, tongue-lash, unlash, whiplash,

balderdash, calabash, succotash
[1]**asha** \äsh-ə\ kasha, pasha, quassia, Falasha
[2]**asha** \ash-ə\ cassia, fascia, pasha
ashan \ash-ən\ see ASSION
[1]**ashed** \ȯsht\ sloshed, stonewashed, unwashed—*also pasts of verbs listed at* [2]ASH
[2]**ashed** \asht\ dashed, Rasht, smashed, unabashed—*also pasts of verbs listed at* [3]ASH
ashen \ash-ən\ see ASSION
[1]**asher** \äsh-ər\ josher, nosher, squasher, swasher, washer, dishwasher
[2]**asher** \ȯsh-ər\ swasher, washer, brainwasher, dishwasher, whitewasher
[3]**asher** \ash-ər\ Asher, basher, brasher, clasher, crasher, dasher, flasher, masher, rasher, slasher, smasher, splasher, thrasher, gate-crasher, haberdasher
ashew \a-shü\ cachou, cashew
[1]**ashi** \äsh-ē\ see [1]ASHY
[2]**ashi** \ash-ē\ see [2]ASHY
ashing \ash-iŋ\ crashing, dashing, flashing, mashing, slashing, smashing
ashion \ash-ən\ see ASSION
asht \asht\ see [2]ASHED
[1]**ashy** \äsh-ē\ dashi, Iasi, Kashi, squashy, washy, Funabashi, Lubumbashi, Toyohashi, wishy-washy
[2]**ashy** \ash-ē\ ashy, flashy, Kashi, splashy, trashy
[1]**asi** \äs-ē\ see [1]OSSY
[2]**asi** \äz-ē\ see [1]AZI
[3]**asi** \ȯsh\ see [2]ASH
[4]**asi** \äsh-ē\ see [1]ASHY
asia \ā-zhə\ Asia, aphasia, Eurasia, fantasia, Malaysia, Anastasia, Australasia, euthanasia, antonomasia
[1]**asian** \ā-shən\ see [1]ATION
[2]**asian** \ā-zhən\ see ASION
asible \ā-zə-bəl\ see [1]ASABLE
asic \ā-zik\ basic, phasic, biphasic, diphasic, multiphasic, polyphasic
asid \as-əd\ see ACID
asie \ā-sē\ see ACY
[1]**asil** \as-əl\ see [2]ASSEL
[2]**asil** \az-əl\ see AZZLE
[3]**asil** \ās-əl\ see [1]ASAL
[4]**asil** \āz-əl\ see [2]ASAL
[5]**asil** \äz-əl\ see OZZLE
asin \ās-ᵊn\ see [1]ASON
[1]**asing** \ā-siŋ\ see ACING
[2]**asing** \ā-ziŋ\ see AISING
asion \ā-zhən\ Asian, suasion, abrasion, Caucasian, corrasion, dissuasion, equation, Eurasian, evasion, invasion, occasion, persuasion, pervasion, Amerasian, Athanasian, dermabrasion, Rabelaisian, overpersuasion
asional \āzh-nəl\ equational, occasional
[1]**asis** \ā-səs\ basis, stasis, oasis
[2]**asis** \as-əs\ see [2]ASSIS
asium \ā-zē-əm\ dichasium, gymnasium
asive \ā-siv\ suasive, abrasive, assuasive, corrasive, dissuasive, embracive, evasive, invasive, persuasive, pervasive, noninvasive

ask \ask\ ask, bask, Basque, cask, casque, flask, mask, masque, Pasch, task, unmask, photomask
aska \as-kə\ Alaska, Itasca, Nebraska, Athabaska
askan \as-kən\ see ASKIN
asked \ast\ see ²AST
asker \as-kər\ lascar, masker, masquer, Madagascar
asket \as-kət\ ascot, basket, casket, gasket, breadbasket, handbasket, wastebasket, workbasket
askin \as-kən\ gascon, gaskin, Alaskan, Tarascan, Athapaskan
asking \as-kiŋ\ multitasking—*also present participles of verbs listed at* ASK
asm \az-əm\ chasm, plasm, spasm, chiasm, orgasm, phantasm, sarcasm, chiliasm, ectoplasm, pleonasm, enthusiasm, blepharospasm, iconoclasm
asma \az-mə\ asthma, plasma, chiasma, miasma, phantasma
asman \az-mən\ see ASMINE
asmine \az-mən\ jasmine, Tasman
asn't \əz-ənt\ doesn't, wasn't
¹**aso** \as-ō\ see ¹ASSO
²**aso** \äs-ō\ see ²ASSO
¹**ason** \ās-ən\ basin, caisson, chasten, hasten, Jason, mason, Mason, Foxe Basin, Freemason, Great Basin, stonemason, washbasin, diapason, Donets Basin
²**ason** \āz-ən\ see AZON
asp \asp\ asp, clasp, gasp, grasp, hasp, rasp, enclasp, handclasp, last-gasp, unclasp
asper \as-pər\ clasper, jasper, Jasper
asperate \as-prət\ aspirate, exasperate
aspirate \as-prət\ see ASPERATE
asque \ask\ see ASK
asquer \as-kər\ see ASKER
¹**ass** \ās\ see ¹ACE
²**ass** \äs\ see ¹OS
³**ass** \as\ as, bass, Bass, brass, class, crass, frass, gas, glass, grass, has, lass, mass, pass, sass, sauce, strass, tace, tasse, trass, vas, wrasse, admass, alas, Alsace, amass, avgas, bagasse, band-pass, bluegrass, bromegrass, bunchgrass, bypass, cordgrass, crabgrass, crevasse, cuirass, cut-grass, declass, degas, Donbas, Drygas, eelgrass, en masse, eyeglass, first-class, groundmass, harass, high-class, hourglass, impasse, knotgrass, Kuzbass, landmass, Madras, morass, outclass, outgas, palliasse, Petras, plateglass, repass, ribgrass, rubasse, ryegrass, sandglass, shortgrass, spyglass, subclass, sunglass, surpass, switchgrass, tallgrass, teargas, trespass, Troas, wineglass, wiseass, witchgrass, biogas, biomass, demiglace, demitasse, fiberglass, gallowglass, gravitas, Hallowmas, hardinggrass, hippocras, isinglass, Kiribati, lemongrass, lower-class,

middle-class, overpass, pampas grass, peppergrass, Plexiglas, sassafras, superclass, underclass, underpass, upper-class, weatherglass
assa \as-ə\ massa, Lake Nyasa, Manasseh
assable \as-ə-bəl\ chasuble, passable, passible, impassable, impassible, irascible
assail \äs-əl\ see OSSAL
assailer \äs-ə-lər\ see OSSULAR
assal \as-əl\ see [2]ASSEL
assant \as-ᵊnt\ see [1]ASCENT
assar \as-ər\ see ASSER
[1]**asse** \as\ see [3]ASS
[2]**asse** \äs\ see [1]OS
assed \ast\ see [2]AST
assee \as-ē\ see ASSY
asseh \as-ə\ see ASSA
[1]**assel** \äs-əl\ see OSSAL
[2]**assel** \as-əl\ acyl, basil, castle, facile, gracile, hassle, Kassel, passel, tassel, vassal, wrestle, forecastle, Newcastle
asser \as-ər\ crasser, gasser, Nasser, placer, harasser, antimacassar
asset \as-ət\ see [2]ACET
[1]**assia** \ash-ə\ see [2]ASHA
[2]**assia** \äsh-ə\ see [1]ASHA
assian \ash-ən\ see ASSION
assible \as-ə-bəl\ see ASSABLE
assic \as-ik\ classic, Jurassic, Liassic, thalassic, Triassic, neoclassic, pseudoclassic, semiclassic
assical \as-i-kəl\ classical, fascicle, postclassical, unclassical, semiclassical
assid \as-əd\ see ACID
[1]**assie** \as-ē\ see ASSY
[2]**assie** \äs-ē\ see [1]OSSY
[1]**assim** \äs-əm\ see OSSUM
[2]**assim** \as-əm\ passim, sargassum
assin \as-ᵊn\ see [2]ASTEN
assion \ash-ən\ ashen, fashion, passion, ration, Circassian, compassion, dispassion, impassion, refashion, Wakashan
assional \ash-nəl\ see [3]ATIONAL
[1]**assis** \as-ē\ see ASSY
[2]**assis** \as-əs\ classis, stasis, Parnassus, Halicarnassus
assist \ā-səst\ bassist, racist, contrabassist
assive \as-iv\ massive, passive, impassive
assle \as-əl\ see [2]ASSEL
assless \as-ləs\ classless, glassless, massless
assment \as-mənt\ blastment, amassment, harassment
assness \as-nəs\ see ASTNESS
[1]**asso** \as-ō\ basso, lasso, El Paso, Picasso, sargasso, Sargasso, Bobo-Dioulasso
[2]**asso** \äs-ō\ Campo Basso, Burkina Faso
assock \as-ək\ cassock, hassock
assum \as-əm\ see [2]ASSIM
assus \as-əs\ see ASSIS
assy \as-ē\ brassy, chassis, classy, gassy, glacis, glassie, glassy, grassy, lassie, massy, sassy, saucy, Malagasy, Tallahassee, Haile Salassie
[1]**ast** \əst\ see [1]UST
[2]**ast** \ast\ bast, blast, cast, caste, clast, fast, gast, ghast, hast,

last, mast, past, vast, aghast, avast, bedfast, Belfast, bombast, broadcast, bypast, contrast, dicast, dismast, downcast, dynast, fantast, flypast, forecast, foremast, forepassed, gymnast, half-caste, half-mast, handfast, holdfast, lightfast, mainmast, makefast, march-past, miscast, newscast, oblast, offcast, outcast, outcaste, precast, recast, repast, roughcast, sandblast, sand-cast, shamefast, soothfast, sportscast, steadfast, sunfast, topmast, trade-last, typecast, unasked, upcast, windblast, acid-fast, chiliast, cineast, colorcast, colorfast, flabbergast, fore-topmast, hard-and-fast, main-topmast, mizzenmast, narrowcast, opencast, overcast, pederast, rebroadcast, scholiast, simulcast, telecast, weathercast, ecdysiast, encomiast, enthusiast, iconoclast, radiocast, symposiast, radiobroadcast—*also pasts of verbs listed at* [3]ASS

[1]**asta** \äs-tə\ see OSTA

[2]**asta** \as-tə\ Rasta, canasta, Jocasta, Mount Shasta

astable \at-ə-bəl\ see ATIBLE

astard \as-tərd\ bastard, dastard, mastered, plastered

[1]**aste** \āst\ see ACED

[2]**aste** \ast\ see [2]AST

asted \as-təd\ blasted, masted, plastid—*also pasts of verbs listed at* [2]AST

asteful \āst-fəl\ tasteful, wasteful, distasteful

[1]**asten** \ās-^{ə}n\ see [1]ASON

[2]**asten** \as-^{ə}n\ fasten, assassin, unfasten

[1]**aster** \ā-stər\ taster, waster

[2]**aster** \as-tər\ aster, Astor, caster, castor, Castor, faster, gaster, master, pastor, plaster, raster, bandmaster, bushmaster, cadastre, choirmaster, disaster, drillmaster, headmaster, linecaster, loadmaster, paymaster, piaster, pilaster, postmaster, quizmaster, remaster, ringmaster, schoolmaster, scoutmaster, shinplaster, shipmaster, spymaster, taskmaster, three-master, toastmaster, truckmaster, wharfmaster, whoremaster, yardmaster, alabaster, burgomaster, concertmaster, criticaster, ironmaster, oleaster, overmaster, poetaster, quartermaster, rallymaster, stationmaster, weathercaster, Zoroaster, cotoneaster

astered \as-tərd\ see ASTARD

astering \as-tə-riŋ\ overmastering—*also present participles of verbs listed at* ASTER

astes \as-tēz\ cerastes, Ecclesiastes—*also plurals and possessives of nouns listed at* [2]ASTY

asthma \az-mə\ see ASMA

astian \as-chən\ see ASTION
astic \as-tik\ drastic, mastic, plastic, spastic, bombastic, dynastic, elastic, fantastic, gymnastic, monastic, sarcastic, scholastic, stochastic, anelastic, Hudibrastic, inelastic, onomastic, orgiastic, paraphrastic, pederastic, periphrastic, superplastic, ecclesiastic, enthusiastic, iconoclastic, interscholastic, semimonastic
astics \as-tiks\ gymnastics, slimnastics
astid \as-təd\ see ASTED
astie \as-tē\ see [2]ASTY
astiness \ā-stē-nəs\ hastiness, pastiness
[1]**asting** \ā-stiŋ\ basting, wasting—*also present participles of verbs listed at* ACED
[2]**asting** \as-tiŋ\ typecasting, everlasting, narrowcasting, overcasting
astion \as-chən\ bastion, Erastian
astle \as-əl\ see [2]ASSEL
astly \ast-lē\ ghastly, lastly
astment \as-mənt\ see ASSMENT
astness \as-nəs\ crassness, fastness, gastness, pastness
asto \as-tō\ impasto, antipasto
astor \as-tər\ see [2]ASTER
astoral \as-trəl\ see ASTRAL
astral \as-trəl\ astral, gastral, pastoral, plastral, cadastral
astre \as-tər\ see [2]ASTER
astric \as-trik\ gastric, nasogastric
astrophe \as-trə-fē\ anastrophe, catastrophe
[1]**asty** \ā-stē\ hasty, pasty, tasty
[2]**asty** \as-tē\ blastie, nasty, pasty, vasty, capacity, contrasty, pederasty, angioplasty, bepharoplasty, osteoplasty, overcapacity
asuble \as-ə-bəl\ see ASSABLE
[1]**asure** \ā-shər\ glacier, Glacier, rasure, erasure
[2]**asure** \ā-zhər\ see AZIER
asy \as-ē\ see ASSY
[1]**at** \ä\ see [1]A
[2]**at** \ät\ see [1]OT
[3]**at** \ət\ see [1]UT
[4]**at** \ȯt\ see [1]OUGHT
[5]**at** \at\ bat, batt, blat, brat, cat, Cat, chat, chert, drat, fat, flat, frat, gat, gnat, hat, mat, matt, Matt, matte, pat, Pat, plait, plat, rat, Rat, sat, scat, scatt, skat, slat, spat, splat, sprat, stat, tat, that, vat, all that, at bat, backchat, begat, bobcat, brickbat, bullbat, Cassatt, chitchat, combat, comsat, cowpat, cravat, Croat, defat, dingbat, doormat, expat, fiat, firebrat, format, Hallstatt, hellcat, hepcat, high-hat, jurat, meerkat, muscat, Muscat, muskrat, nonfat, polecat, Sadat, savate, Sno-Cat, stand pat, standpat, stonechat, strawhat, Surat, thereat, tipcat, tomcat, whereat, whinchat, wildcat, wombat, acrobat, apparat, Ararat, assignat, autocrat, Automat, bureaucrat, butterfat, caveat, cervelat, concordat, copycat, democrat,

diplomat, Dixiecrat, Eurocrat, habitat, Kattegat, Laundromat, marrowfat, mobocrat, monocrat, Montserrat, ochlocrat, pas de quatre, photostat, pit-a-pat, plutocrat, pussycat, rat-a-tat, scaredy-cat, semimatte, technocrat, theocrat, thermostat, tit for tat, Uniate, ziggurat, aristocrat, gerontocrat, heliostat, Jehoshaphat, magnificat, meritocrat, Physiocrat, requiescat, thalassocrat, proletoriat, professoriat, secretariat

[6]**at** \a\ see [3]AH

[1]**ata** \ät-ə\ cotta, kata, balata, cantata, Carlotta, data, errata, fermata, frittata, La Plata, Maratha, Niigata, non grata, piñata, pro rata, reata, riata, regatta, sonata, Sorata, toccata, caponata, Hirakata, Mar del Plata, serenata, terracotta, Uspallata, Basilicata, desiderata, inamorata, medulla oblongata, missa cantata, persona grata, res judicata, persona non grata, res adjudicata, Rio de la Plata

[2]**ata** \āt-ə\ beta, data, eta, strata, theta, zeta, muleta, peseta, potato, pro rata, substrata, tomato, viewdata, corona radiata

[3]**ata** \at-ə\ data, errata, mulatto, non grata, pro rata, reata, regatta, riata, viewdata, paramatta, Paramatta, persona grata, persona non grata

[1]**atable** \āt-ə-bəl\ datable, ratable, statable, debatable, dilatable, inflatable, locatable, rotatable, translatable, allocatable, circulatable, confiscatable, correlatable, detonatable, undebatable

[2]**atable** \at-ə-bəl\ see ATIBLE

atal \āt-ᵊl\ fatal, natal, ratel, shtetl, hiatal, postnatal, prenatal, antenatal, neonatal, perinatal

atalie \at-ᵊl-ē\ see ATTILY

atally \āt-ᵊl-ē\ fatally, natally, postnatally, prenatally, antenatally, neonatally, perinatally

atalyst \at-ᵊl-əst\ catalyst, philatelist

[1]**atan** \āt-ən\ see [1]ATEN

[2]**atan** \at-ᵊn\ see [2]ATIN

atancy \āt-ᵊn-sē\ blatancy, latency, dilatancy

[1]**atant** \āt-ᵊnt\ blatant, latent, natant, patent, statant

[2]**atant** \at-ᵊnt\ patent, combatant, noncombatant

atany \at-ᵊn-ē\ atony, rhatany

atar \ät-ər\ see OTTER

atary \ät-ə-rē\ see OTTERY

[1]**atch** \ech\ see ETCH

[2]**atch** \äch\ see OTCH

[3]**atch** \ȯch\ see [1]AUCH

[4]**atch** \ach\ bach, batch, catch, cratch, hatch, klatch, latch, match, natch, patch, ratch, scratch, snatch, thatch, attach, book-match, crosshatch, crosspatch, despatch, detach, dispatch, nuthatch, outmatch, potlatch, rematch, Sasquatch, throatlatch, unlatch, Wasatch,

coffee klatch, kaffeeklatsch, overmatch

[1]**atcher** \äch-ər\ botcher, watcher, bird-watcher, clock-watcher, debaucher, topnotcher

[2]**atcher** \ach-ər\ batcher, catcher, hatcher, matcher, scratcher, stature, thatcher, cowcatcher, dispatcher, dogcatcher, eye-catcher, flycatcher, gnatcatcher, oyster catcher

atchet \ach-ət\ hatchet, latchet, rachet, ratchet

atchily \ach-ə-lē\ patchily, patchouli

atching \ach-iŋ\ back-scratching, cross-hatching, eye-catching, nonmatching

atchman \äch-mən\ see OTCHMAN

atchment \ach-mənt\ catchment, hatchment, attachment, detachment

atchouli \ach-ə-lē\ see ATCHILY

atchy \ach-ē\ catchy, patchy, scratchy, Apache

[1]**ate** \āt\ ait, ate, bait, bate, blate, cate, Cate, crate, date, eight, fate, fete, freight, gait, gate, grate, great, haet, hate, Kate, late, mate, pate, plait, plate, prate, quoit, rate, sate, skate, slate, spate, state, straight, strait, teth, trait, wait, weight, abate, ablate, adnate, aerate, age-mate, agnate, airdate, airfreight, alate, arête, await, backdate, baldpate, bedmate, bedplate, berate, birthrate, bistate, bookplate, breastplate, casemate, castrate, caudate, cerate, cheapskate, checkmate, chordate, classmate, clavate, cognate, collate, comate, conflate, connate, cordate, create, cremate, crenate, curate, cut-rate, deadweight, debate, deflate, delate, dentate, derate, dictate, dilate, disrate, donate, doorplate, downstate, drawplate, elate, equate, estate, faceplate, falcate, fellate, filtrate, first-rate, fishplate, fixate, flatmate, floodgate, flyweight, formate, frustrate, gelate, gestate, gyrate, hamate, hastate, headgate, helpmate, housemate, hydrate, ice-skate, inflate, ingrate, inmate, innate, instate, irate, jailbait, jugate, khanate, Kuwait, lactate, legate, liftgate, ligate, lightweight, liquate, lobate, locate, lunate, lustrate, lych-gate, lyrate, magnate, makebate, makeweight, mandate, messmate, migrate, misstate, mutate, nameplate, narrate, negate, Newgate, nitrate, notate, nutate, oblate, orate, ornate, ovate, palmate, palpate, peltate, phonate, pinnate, placate, playmate, plicate, portrait, postdate, predate, primate, probate, prolate, prorate, prostate, prostrate, pulsate, punctate, pupate, quadrate, ramate, rebate, red-bait, relate, restate, roommate, rostrate, rotate,

saccate, schoolmate, seatmate, sedate, sensate, septate, serrate, shipmate, short weight, soleplate, spectate, spicate, squamate, stagnate, stalemate, stellate, striate, sublate, substrate, sulcate, summate, tailgate, teammate, Tebet, tenth-rate, ternate, terneplate, testate, third-rate, tinplate, toeplate, tollgate, tractate, translate, tristate, truncate, unweight, update, uprate, upstate, V-8, vacate, vallate, valvate, vibrate, virgate, vulgate, whitebait, workmate, zonate, abdicate, abnegate, abrogate, absorbate, acclimate, acerbate, acetate, activate, actuate, acylate, adsorbate, advocate, adulate, adumbrate, aggravate, aggregate, agitate, allocate, altercate, alternate, ambulate, amputate, animate, annotate, annulate, antedate, antiquate, apartheid, apostate, approbate, approximate, arbitrate, arcuate, arrogate, aspirate, automate, aviate, bantamweight, bifurcate, billingsgate, bipinnate, boilerplate, bombinate, brachiate, cachinnate, calculate, calibrate, caliphate, candidate, cantillate, capitate, captivate, carbonate, carbon-date, carinate, castigate, catenate, cavitate, celebrate, cerebrate, circinate, circulate, city-state, cogitate, collimate, collocate, commentate, commutate, compensate, complicate, concentrate, condensate, confiscate, conglobate, conjugate, consecrate, constellate, consternate, constipate, consummate, contemplate, copperplate, copulate, coronate, correlate, corrugate, coruscate, counterweight, crenulate, crepitate, criminate, cruciate, cucullate, culminate, cultivate, cumulate, cuneate, cupulate, cuspidate, cyclamate, decimate, decollate, decorate, decussate, dedicate, defalcate, defecate, delegate, demarcate, demonstrate, denigrate, deviate, deprecate, depredate, derivate, derogate, desecrate, desiccate, designate, desolate, detonate, devastate, deviate, digitate, diplomate, discarnate, dislocate, dissertate, dissipate, distillate, divagate, dominate, duplicate, edentate, educate, elevate, elongate, eluate, emanate, emigrate, emirate, emulate, enervate, ephorate, escalate, estimate, estivate, excavate, exculpate, execrate, expiate, explicate, expurgate, exsiccate, extirpate, extricate, exudate, fabricate, fascinate, featherweight, fecundate, federate, fenestrate, festinate, fibrillate, flabellate, flagellate, flocculate, fluctuate, fluoridate, foliate, formulate, fornicate, fractionate, fragmentate, fulminate, fumigate, fustigate, geminate, generate, germinate, glaciate, Golden Gate, graduate, granulate, gratulate, gravitate, heavyweight, hebetate, herniate, hesitate, hibernate, hundredweight, hyphenate, ideate, illustrate, imamate, imbricate, imitate, immigrate, immolate, impetrate, implicate, imprecate, impregnate, incarnate, increate, incubate, inculcate, inculpate, incurvate, indagate, indicate, indurate, infiltrate, innervate, innovate, insensate, insolate, inspissate, instigate, insulate, interstate, intestate, intimate, intonate, intraplate, inundate, invocate, iodate, irrigate, irritate, isolate, iterate, jubilate, juniorate, lacerate, laminate, Latinate, laureate, legislate, levigate, levitate, liberate, liquidate, litigate, littermate, lubricate, macerate, machinate, magistrate, marginate, margravate, marinate, masticate, masturbate, maturate, mediate, medicate, meditate, meliorate, menstruate, microstate, micturate, middleweight, militate, ministrate, miscreate, mithridate, mitigate, moderate, modulate, motivate, multistate, mutilate, nation-state, nauseate, navigate, neonate, nictitate, niobate, nominate, numerate, obfuscate, objurgate, obligate, obovate, obviate, operate, opiate, orchestrate, ordinate, oscillate, osculate, out-of-date, overstate, overweight, ovulate, paginate, palliate, palpitate, paperweight, patinate, peculate, penetrate, pennyweight, percolate, perennate, perforate, permeate, perorate, perpetrate, personate, pollinate, populate, postulate, potentate, predicate, procreate, profligate, promulgate, propagate, prorogate, pullulate, pulmonate, punctuate, quantitate, rabbinate, radiate, re-create, reclinate, recreate, regulate, reinstate, relegate, relocate, reluctate, remonstrate, renovate, replicate, reprobate, resonate, retardate, retranslate, roseate, rubricate, ruminate, runagate, rusticate, sagittate, salivate, sanitate, satiate, saturate, scintillate, second-rate, segregate, separate, sequestrate, seriate, sibilate, simulate, sinuate, situate, speculate, spoliate, stablemate, stimulate, stipulate, strangulate, stridulate, stylobate, subjugate, sublimate, subrogate, subulate, suffocate, sultanate, supplicate, surrogate, syncopate, syndicate, tablemate, tabulate, terminate, tessellate, tête-à-tête, thirty-eight, titillate, titivate, tolerate, transmigrate, transudate, tribulate, tribunate, trifurcate, trilobate, tripinnate, triplicate, tunicate, turbinate, ulcerate, ululate, umbellate, uncinate, underrate, understate, underweight, undulate, ungulate, urinate, vaccinate, vacillate, validate, valuate, variate, vaticinate, vegetate, venerate, ventilate, vertebrate, vicarate, vindicate, violate, vitiate, Watergate, welterweight, abbreviate, abominate, accelerate, accentuate, accommodate, acculturate, accumulate, acidulate, adjudicate, administrate, adulterate, affiliate, agglomerate, agglutinate, alienate, alleviate, alliterate, amalgamate, ameliorate, annihilate, annunciate, anticipate, apostolate, appreciate, appropriate, articulate, asphyxiate, assassinate, asseverate, assimilate, associate, attenuate, authenticate, barbiturate, bicarbonate, calumniate, campanulate, capacitate, capitulate, catholicate, certificate, circumvallate, coagulate, coelenterate, collaborate, commemorate, commiserate, communicate, compassionate, concatenate, concelebrate, conciliate, confabulate, confederate, conglomerate, congratulate, consociate, consolidate, contaminate, cooperate, coordinate, corroborate, de-escalate, deaerate, debilitate, decapitate, decerebrate, deconcentrate, deconsecrate, decrepitate, defibrinate, defribrillate, degenerate, deliberate, delineate, demodulate, denominate, depopulate, depreciate, deregulate, desegregate, desiderate, devaluate, diaconate, dilapidate, discriminate, disintegrate, disseminate, dissimilate, dissimulate, dissociate, divaricate, domesticate, edulcorate, effectuate, ejaculate, elaborate, electroplate, eliminate, elucidate, elucubrate, elutriate, emaciate, emancipate, emarginate, emasculate, encapsulate, enumerate, enunciate, episcopate, equilibrate, equivocate, eradicate, etiolate, evacuate, evaluate, evaporate, eventuate, eviscerate, exacerbate, exaggerate, exasperate, excogitate, excoriate, excruciate, exfoliate, exhilarate, exonerate, expatiate, expatriate, expectorate, expostulate, expropriate, extenuate, exterminate, extrapolate, extravagate, exuberate, facilitate, fantasticate, felicitate, gesticulate, habilitate, habituate, hallucinate, homologate, humiliate, hypothecate, illuminate, impersonate, inactivate, inaugurate, incarcerate, incinerate, incorporate, incriminate, indoctrinate, inebriate, infatuate, infuriate, ingratiate, ingurgitate, initiate, inoculate, inosculate, inseminate, insinuate, instantiate, intenerate, intercalate, interpellate, interpolate, interrelate, interrogate, intimidate, intoxicate, invaginate, invalidate, investigate, invigilate, invigorate, irradiate, italianate, itinerate, lanceolate, legitimate, luxuriate, machicolate, mandarinate, manipulate, matriarchate, matriculate, Merthiolate, necessitate, negotiate, noncandidate, obliterate, obnubilate, officiate, orientate, originate, oxygenate, participate, particulate, patriarchate, patriciate, penicillate, perambulate, peregrinate, perpetuate, pontificate, potentiate, precipitate, predestinate, predominate, prefabricate, premeditate, prenominate, preponderate, prevaricate, procrastinate, prognosticate, proliferate, propitiate, proportionate, quadruplicate, quintuplicate, reciprocate, recriminate, recuperate, redecorate, redintegrate, reduplicate, reeducate, refrigerate, regenerate, regurgitate, reincarnate, reintegrate, reiterate, rejuvenate, remunerate, renominate, repatriate, repristinate, repudiate, resupinate, resuscitate, retaliate, reticulate, revaluate, revegetate, reverberate, scholasticate, self-portrait, seventy-eight, sextuplicate, somnambulate, sophisticate, stereobate, subordinate, substantiate, syllabicate, tergiversate, transliterate, transvaluate, triangulate, variegate, vituperate, vociferate, beneficiate, circumambulate, circumnavigate, circumstantiate, contraindicate, decontaminate, deteriorate, differentiate, disaffiliate, disambiguate, disarticulate, disassociate, discombobulate, disintoxicate, disorientate, disproportionate, domiciliate, excommunicate, free-associate, hyperventilate, incapacitate, individuate, intermediate, interpenetrate, lithium niobate, superheavyweight, microencapsulate, misappropriate, multivariate, ratiocinate, recapitulate, rehabilitate, renegotiate, superannuate, superelevate, superordinate, supersaturate, transilluminate, transubstantiate, underestimate, intercommunicate, diammonium phosphate, phosphoenolpyruvate, peroxyacetyl nitrate

[2]ate \at\ see [5]AT

[3]ate \ät\ see [1]OT

[4]ate \ät-ē\ see ATI

[5]ate \ət\ see [1]UT

ated \āt-əd\ gaited, lated, pated, stated, belated, ill-fated, outdated, pustulated, related, striated, three-gaited, truncated, unbated, X-rated, aberrated, addlepated, animated, asteriated, calculated, capsulated, carbonated, carburated, castellated, complicated, crenellated, disrelated, elevated, fenestrated, fimbriated, floriated, foliated, inspissated, intoxicated, laminated, marginated, mentholated, perforated, pileated, pixilated, saturated, tessellated, trabeated, unabated, uncreated, understated, variegated, affiliated, configurated, coordinated, decaffeinated, domesticated, incorporated, inebriated, interrelated, intoxicated, opinionated, sophisticated, uncalculated, uncelebrated, uncomplicated, underinflated, unmediated, unmitigated, unsaturated, unsegregated, unadulterated, unanticipated, unarticulated, unconsolidated, undereducated, underpopulated, undissociated, unsophisticated, polyunsaturated, underappreciated—*also pasts of verbs listed at* [1]ATE

ateful \āt-fəl\ fateful, grateful, hateful, ungrateful

[1]atel \ət-ᵊl\ see OTTLE

[2]atel \āt-ᵊl\ see ATAL

ateless \āt-ləs\ dateless, stateless, weightless

atelist \at-ᵊl-əst\ see ATALYST

[1]ately \āt-lē\ greatly, lately, stately, straightly, straitly, innately, irately, ornately, up-to-dately, Johnny-come-lately

[2]ately \at-ᵊl-ē\ see ATTILY

atem \ät-əm\ see [1]ATUM

atement \āt-mənt\ statement, abatement, debatement, misstatement, restatement, overstatement, reinstatement, understatement

[1]aten \āt-ᵊn\ greaten, laten, Satan, straighten, straiten, Keewatin

[2]aten \at-ᵊn\ see [2]ATIN

[3]aten \ät-ᵊn\ see OTTEN

[1]atent \āt-ᵊnt\ see [1]ATANT

[2]atent \at-ᵊnt\ see [2]ATANT

[1]ater \ȯt-ər\ daughter, slaughter, tauter, water, backwater, bathwater, blackwater, breakwater, cutwater, dewater, deepwater, dishwater, firewater, floodwater, forequarter, freshwater, goddaughter, granddaughter, groundwater, headwater, hindquarter, jerkwater, limewater, manslaughter, meltwater, rainwater, rosewater, saltwater, seawater, self-slaughter, shearwater, springwater, stepdaughter, tailwater, tidewater, wastewater, milk-and-water, polywater, underwater

[2]**ater** \āt-ər\ see ATOR

ateral \at-ə-rəl\ lateral, bilateral, collateral, trilateral, contralateral, dorsolateral, equilateral, ipsilateral, multilateral, quadrilateral, unilateral, ventrolateral, posterolateral

aterer \ȯt-ər-ər\ slaughterer, waterer, dewaterer

ateress \āt-ə-rəs\ cateress, traitorous

atering \ȯt-ə-riŋ\ mouth-watering—*also present participles of verbs listed at* [1]ATER

[1]**atery** \ät-ə-rē\ see OTTERY

[2]**atery** \ȯt-ə-rē\ cautery, watery

[1]**ates** \āts\ Yeats, Gulf States, Papal States, Persian Gulf States, United States, Federated Malay States, United Arab Emirates—*also plurals and possessives of nouns and third person singular presents of verbs listed at* ATE

[2]**ates** \āt-ēz\ Achates, nates, Euphrates, Penates—*also plurals and possessives of nouns listed at* ATY

atest \āt-əst\ latest, statist—*also superlatives of adjectives listed at* [1]ATE

atey \āt-ē\ see ATY

[1]**ath** \äth\ see [1]OTH

[2]**ath** \ȯth\ see [2]OTH

[3]**ath** \ath\ bath, hath, lath, math, path, rathe, snath, strath, wrath, birdbath, bloodbath, bypath, footbath, footpath, sunbath, towpath, warpath, aftermath, polymath, psychopath, telepath, naturopath, osteopath, sociopath

atha \ät-ə\ see [1]ATA

[1]**athe** \ät͟h\ swathe, enswathe, unswathe

[2]**athe** \āt͟h\ bathe, lathe, rathe, saithe, scathe, spathe, swathe, sunbathe, unswathe

[3]**athe** \ath\ see [3]ATH

atheless \āth-ləs\ see AITHLESS

[1]**ather** \ät͟h-ər\ bother, father, pother, rather, forefather, godfather, grandfather, housefather, stepfather

[2]**ather** \ət͟h-ər\ see [1]OTHER

[3]**ather** \at͟h-ər\ blather, Cather, gather, lather, Mather, rather, slather, forgather, ingather, wool-gather

athering \at͟h-riŋ\ ingathering, woolgathering

athi \ät-ē\ see ATI

athic \ath-ik\ empathic, amphipathic, psychopathic, telepathic, homeopathic, idiopathic, sociopathic

athlon \ath-lən\ biathlon, decathlon, pentathlon, triathlon

athy \ath-ē\ Cathie, Cathy, Kathie, Kathy, wrathy, allelopathy

[1]**ati** \ät-ē\ Ate, Dottie, dotty, Dotty, grotty, knotty, naughty,

plotty, potty, Scottie, Scotty, snotty, spotty, squatty, Amati, basmati, chapati, coati, flokati, karate, Marathi, metate, Scarlatti, Tol'yati, glitterati, Gujarati, Hakodate, literati, manicotti, illuminati

[2]**ati** \atē\ see ATTY

[3]**ati** \äts\ see OTS

[4]**ati** \as\ see [3]ASS

atia \ā-shə\ see ACIA

atial \ā-shəl\ see ACIAL

atian \ā-shən\ see [1]ATION

atians \ā-shənz\ see ATIONS

atible \at-ə-bəl\ compatible, getatable, incompatible, self-compatible, biocompatible, self-incompatible

[1]**atic** \ät-ik\ see [1]OTIC

[2]**atic** \at-ik\ attic, Attic, batik, phatic, static, vatic, agnatic, aquatic, astatic, asthmatic, chromatic, climatic, comatic, dalmatic, dogmatic, dramatic, ecstatic, emphatic, erratic, fanatic, hepatic, judgmatic, komatik, lymphatic, magmatic, neumatic, phlegmatic, plasmatic, pneumatic, pragmatic, prismatic, protatic, quadratic, rheumatic, schematic, schismatic, sciatic, sematic, Socratic, somatic, spermatic, stigmatic, sylvatic, thematic, traumatic, villatic, achromatic, acrobatic, Adriatic, aerobatic, anabatic, antistatic, aromatic, Asiatic, astigmatic, autocratic, automatic, bureaucratic, charismatic, cinematic, democratic, dilemmatic, diplomatic, Dixiecratic, Eleatic, emblematic, enigmatic, enzymatic, fungistatic, Hanseatic, hieratic, Hippocratic, kerygmatic, leviratic, melismatic, miasmatic, mobocratic, monocratic, morganatic, numismatic, ochlocratic, operatic, phonematic, plutocratic, pre-Socratic, problematic, programmatic, symptomatic, syntagmatic, systematic, technocratic, theocratic, timocratic, undogmatic, undramatic, anagrammatic, apothegmatic, aristocratic, asymptomatic, axiomatic, conglomeratic, diagrammatic, diaphragmatic, epigrammatic, gerontocratic, gynecocratic, homeostatic, idiomatic, logogrammatic, melodramatic, meritocratic, monochromatic, monodramatic, monogrammatic, pantisocratic, paradigmatic, physiocratic, psychodramatic, psychosomatic, semiaquatic, theorematic, undemocratic, undiplomatic, antidemocratic, Austroasiatic, biosystematic, ideogrammatic, semiautomatic

atica \at-i-kə\ Attica, hepatica, sciatica, viatica

atical \at-i-kəl\ statical, dogmatical, erratical, fanatical, grammatical, piratical, pragmatical, sabbatical, schismatical, autocratical, emblematical, enigmatical, magistratical, mathematical, ochlocratical, problematical, systematical, theocratical, timocratical, ungrammatical, anagrammatical, diagrammatical, epigrammatical, pantisocratical

atics \at-iks\ statics, chromatics, dogmatics, dramatics, pneumatics, pragmatics, acrobatics, informatics, mathematics, numismatics, systematics, melodramatics, psychosomatics—*also plurals and possessives of nouns listed at* [2]ATIC

atie \āt-ē\ see ATY

atiens \ā-shənz\ see ATIONS

atient \ā-shənt\ patient, impatient, inpatient, outpatient, rubefacient, somnifacient, abortifacient

atik \at-ik\ see [2]ATIC

atile \at-ᵊl-ē\ see ATTILY

atim \āt-əm\ see [2]ATUM

[1]atin \ät-ᵊn\ see OTTEN

[2]atin \at-ᵊn\ batten, fatten, flatten, gratin, Latin, latten, matin, paten, patten, Patton, platan, platen, ratton, satin, cisplatin, manhattan, Manhattan, Powhatan, lovastatin, Neo-Latin

[3]atin \āt-ᵊn\ see [1]ATEN

atinate \at-ᵊn-ət\ concatenate, Palatinate, Rhineland-Palatinate

ating \āt-iŋ\ bating, grating, plating, rating, skating, slating, abating, bearbaiting, bullbaiting, frustrating, self-rating, calculating, lancinating, maid-in-waiting, nauseating, operating, titillating, humiliating, lady-in-waiting, nonterminating, self-liquidating, self-regulating, self-replicating, subordinating, uncalculating, undeviating, unhesitating, indiscriminating, self-incriminating

atinous \at-nəs\ see ATNESS

[1]ation \ā-shən\ Asian, Haitian, nation, Nation, ration, station, Thracian, ablation, agnation, Alsatian, carnation, castration, causation, cessation, cetacean, chrismation, citation, cognation, collation, conation, conflation, creation, cremation, crenation, Croatian, crustacean, cunctation, dalmatian, damnation, deflation, dictation, dilation, donation, duration, elation, enation, equation, Eurasian, filtration, fixation, flotation, formation, foundation, frustration, furcation, gestation, gradation, gustation, gyration, hydration, illation, inflation, lactation, laudation, lavation, legation, libation, libration, ligation, location, lustration, mentation, migration, mutation, narration, natation, negation, nitration, notation, novation, nutation, oblation, oration, outstation, ovation, phonation, planation, plantation, plication, potation, predation, privation, probation, pronation, proration, prostration, pulsation, purgation, quotation, reflation, relation, rogation, rotation, saltation, salvation, sedation, sensation, serration, slumpflation, squamation, stagflation, stagnation, starvation, striation, stylization, sublation, substation, summation, tarnation, taxation, temptation, translation, truncation, vacation, venation, vexation, vibration, vocation, workstation, zonation, abdication, aberration, abjuration, abnegation, acceptation, acclamation, acclimation, accusation, activation, actuation, adaptation, adjuration, admiration, adoration, adulation, adumbration, advocation, affectation, affirmation, aggravation, aggregation, allegation, allocation, amputation, alteration, altercation, alternation, Amerasian, angulation, animation, annexation, annotation, annulation, antiquation, Appalachian, appellation, application, approbation, arbitration, aspiration, assentation, assignation, attestation, augmentation, Aurignacian, automation, aviation, avocation, blaxploitation, botheration, brachiation, cachinnation, calculation, calibration, cancellation, capitation, captivation, carbonation, carburation, castigation, celebration, cementation, cerebration, circulation, claudication, cogitation, collocation, coloration, combination, commendation, commination, commutation, compellation, compensation, compilation, complication, compurgation, computation, concentration, condemnation, condensation, condonation, confirmation, confiscation, conflagration, conformation, confrontation, confutation, congelation, congregation, conjugation, conjuration, connotation, consecration, conservation, consolation, conspiration, constellation, consternation, constipation, consultation, consummation, contemplation, contestation, conurbation, conversation, convocation, copulation, coronation, corporation, correlation, corrugation, coruscation, crenellation, culmination, cupellation, cuspidation, cybernation, decimation, declamation, declaration, declination, decoration, dedication, defalcation, defamation, defecation, defloration, deformation, degradation, degustation, dehydration, delectation, delegation, demarcation, demonstration, denegation, denigration, denotation, depilation, deportation, depravation, depredation, deprivation, deputation, derivation, derogation, desecration, desiccation, designation, desolation, desperation, destination, detestation, detonation, devastation, deviation, dilatation, disclamation, disinflation, dislocation, dispensation, disputation, disrelation, dissertation, dissipation, distillation, divination, domination, dubitation, duplication, education, elevation, elongation, emanation, embarkation, embrocation, emendation, emigration, emulation, encrustation, enervation, epilation, equitation, eructation, escalation, estimation, estivation, evocation, exaltation, excavation, excitation, exclamation, exculpation, execration, exhalation, exhortation, expectation, expiation, expiration, explanation, explication, exploitation, exploration, exportation, expurgation, extirpation, extrication, exudation, exultation, fabrication, fascination, federation, fenestration, fermentation, fibrillation, figuration, filiation, flagellation, fluoridation, fluctuation, foliation, fomentation, formulation, fornication, fragmentation, fulguration, fulmination, fumigation, gemination, généeration, germination, glaciation, graduation, granulation, gravitation, habitation, hesitation, hibernation, hyphenation, ideation, illustration, imbrication, imitation, immigration, immolation, implantation, implication, importation, imprecation, imputation, incantation, incarnation, incitation, inclination, incrustation, incubation, inculcation, indentation, indexation, indication, indignation, induration, infestation, infiltration, inflammation, information, inhalation, innovation, insolation, inspiration, installation, instauration, insufflation, insulation, intonation, inundation, invitation, invocation, irrigation, irritation, isolation, iteration, jactitation, jubilation, laceration, lacrimation, lamentation, lamination, legislation, levitation, liberation, limitation, lineation, liquidation, literation, litigation, lubrication, lucubration, maceration, machination,

maculation, malformation,
malversation, margination,
mastication, masturbation,
maturation, mediation,
medication, meditation,
melioration, menstruation,
mensuration, metrication,
ministration, moderation,
modulation, molestation,
motivation, navigation,
nomination, numeration,
obfuscation, objurgation,
obligation, observation,
obturation, occultation,
occupation, operation,
orchestration, ordination,
oscillation, osculation,
ostentation, ovulation,
oxidation, ozonation,
pagination, palliation,
palpitation, patination,
penetration, perforation,
permeation, permutation,
peroration, perpetration,
perspiration, perturbation,
pigmentation, pixilation,
pollination, population,
postulation, predication,
preformation, prelibation,
preparation, presentation,
proclamation, procreation,
procuration, profanation,
prolongation, propagation,
prorogation, protestation,
provocation, publication,
punctuation, radiation,
recitation, reclamation,
recordation, re-creation,
recreation, reformation,
refutation, registration,
regulation, relaxation,
relocation, reparation,
replantation, replication,
reprobation, reputation,
reservation, resignation,
respiration, restoration,
retardation, revelation,
revocation, ruination,
salivation, salutation,
sanitation, satiation,
saturation, scatteration,
scintillation, segmentation,
segregation, separation,
sequestration, sexploitation,
simulation, situation,
solmization, speciation,
speculation, spoliation,
sternutation, stimulation,
stipulation, strangulation,
structuration, subjugation,
sublimation, subrogation,
suffocation, suspiration,
susurration, sustentation,
syncopation, syndication,
tabulation, termination,
tessellation, titillation,
titivation, toleration,
transformation, translocation,
transmigration, transmutation,
transpiration, transplantation,
transportation, trepidation,
tribulation, trituration,
ulceration, ululation,
undulation, urination,
usurpation, vaccination,
vacillation, validation,
valuation, variation,
vegetation, veneration,
ventilation, vindication,
violation, visitation,
abbreviation, abomination,
acceleration, accentuation,
accommodation, accreditation,
acculturation, accumulation,

actualization, adjudication, administration, adulteration, affiliation, afforestation, agglomeration, agglutination, alienation, alleviation, alliteration, amalgamation, amelioration, amortization, amplification, analyzation, anglicization, annihilation, annunciation, anticipation, appreciation, appropriation, approximation, argumentation, articulation, asphyxiation, assassination, asseveration, assimilation, association, attenuation, authorization, autoxidation, barbarization, bastardization, beautification, bowdlerization, brutalization, canalization, canonization, capacitation, capitulation, carbonylation, centralization, certification, cicatrization, civilization, clarification, classification, coagulation, coeducation, cohabitation, colonization, collaboration, columniation, commemoration, commiseration, communication, communization, compartmentation, complementation, concatenation, conciliation, confabulation, confederation, configuration, conglomeration, congratulation, consideration, consociation, consolidation, contamination, continuation, cooperation, coordination, corroboration, crustification, crystallization, deactivation, debilitation, decapitation, decompensation, defenestration, deforestation, degeneration, deglaciation, deification, deliberation, delineation, denomination, denunciation, depopulation, depreciation, deregulation, desegregation, despoliation, determination, devaluation, dilapidation, diphthongization, disapprobation, discoloration, discrimination, disembarkation, disinclination, disinformation, disintegration, dissemination, dissimilation, dissimulation, dissociation, divarication, documentation, domestication, dramatization, echolocation, edification, ejaculation, elaboration, elicitation, elimination, elucidation, emaciation, emancipation, emasculation, enumeration, enunciation, epoxidation, equalization, equivocation, eradication, evacuation, evagination, evaluation, evaporation, evisceration, exacerbation, exaggeration, examination, exasperation, excoriation, excruciation, exercitation, exhilaration, exoneration, expostulation, expropriation, extenuation, extermination, extrapolation, facilitation, factorization, falsification, fantastication, feminization, fertilization,

Finlandization, formalization, formulization, fortification, fossilization, fructification, gasification, gentrification, gesticulation, glamorization, globalization, glorification, glycosylation, gratification, habituation, hallucination, harmonization, haruspication, hellenization, humanization, hyperinflation, idolization, illumination, imagination, immunization, impersonation, implementation, improvisation, inauguration, incarceration, incardination, incineration, incorporation, incrimination, indoctrination, inebriation, infatuation, ingratiation, inhabitation, initiation, inoculation, insemination, insinuation, instrumentation, internalization, interpretation, interrelation, intimidation, intoxication, invagination, investigation, invigoration, irradiation, itemization, jollification, justification, labanotation, laicization, latinization, legalization, lionization, localization, machicolation, magnetization, magnification, maladaptation, manifestation, masculinization, matriculation, maximization, mechanization, miscegenation, mobilization, modernization, modification, mollification, mongrelization, monopolization, moralization, mortification, multiplication, mystification, nationalization, naturalization, necessitation, negotiation, neutralization, normalization, notarization, notification, novelization, nullification, optimization, organization, orientation, ornamentation, ossification, pacification, paralyzation, participation, pasteurization, patronization, penalization, perambulation, perpetuation, perseveration, personalization, plasticization, pluralization, petrification, polarization, pontification, preadaptation, precipitation, predestination, prefiguration, premeditation, preoccupation, preregistration, prettification, procrastination, prognostication, proliferation, pronunciation, propitiation, pulverization, purification, qualification, quantification, ramification, randomization, ratification, ratiocination, realization, reciprocation, recombination, recommendation, recrimination, recuperation, redecoration, reduplication, reforestation, refrigeration, regeneration, regimentation, regurgitation, reification, reincarnation, reintegration, remediation, remuneration, renunciation, representation, republication, repudiation, reticulation, retrogradation, reverberation, robotization, romanization, sanctification, sanitization, scarification, secularization, sedimentation, sensitization, Serbo-Croatian, signification, simplification, socialization, solemnization, solicitation, solidification, sophistication, specialization, specification, stabilization, standardization, sterilization, stratification, stultification, subalternation, subinfeudation, subordination, subpopulation, subsidization, summarization, supplementation, syllabication, symbolization, synchronization, systemization, teleportation, tergiversation, terrorization, theorization, transfiguration, transliteration, transvaluation, traumatization, triangulation, trivialization, uglification, unification, unionization, urbanization, vandalization, vaporization, variegation, vaticination, velarization, verbalization, verification, versification, victimization, vilification, vinification, vitalization, vituperation, vocalization, vociferation, vulgarization, westernization, x-radiation, acclimatization, allegorization, alphabetization, autocorrelation, automatization, beneficiation, capitalization, characterization, circumnavigation, codetermination, commercialization, conceptualization, consubstantiation, containerization, counterreformation, criminalization, cross-examination, cryopreservation, decarboxylation, decimilization, de-Stalinization, decasualization, decentralization, declassification, decontamination, dehumanization, dehydrogenation, delegitimation, demystification, derealization, derivitization, desulfurization, deterioration, differentiation, disassociation, discombobulation, disorientation, disorganization, disproportionation, disqualification, diversification, dolomitization, electrification, excommunication, exemplification, experimentation, extemporization, externalization, familiarization, federalization, generalization, homogenization, hospitalization, hyperventilation, idealization, identification, immobilization, immortalization, incapacitation, inconsideration, incoordination, indemnification, indetermination, indiscrimination, individuation, institutionalization, insubordination, intensification, intermediation, intermodulation, intrapopulation, italicization, legitimization, lexicalization, maladministration, mathematization, megacorporation, militarization, miniaturization, misappropriation, miscommunication, misinterpretation, mispronunciation, misrepresentation, noncooperation, nonproliferation, overcompensation, overpopulation, palatalization, periodization, personification, photoduplication, photoexcitation, popularization, predetermination, prestidigitation, proselytization, radicalization, ratiocination, rationalization, reafforestation, recapitulation, reconciliation, reconsideration, rehabilitation, reinterpretation, renegotiation, reorganization, revitalization, ritualization, Schrödinger equation, subvocalization, supererogation, syllabification, tintinnabulation, transubstantiation, unappreciation, underestimation, undervaluation, unsophistication, visualization, Americanization, automanipulation, decriminalization, depersonalization, electrodesiccation, intercommunication, industrialization, materialization, oversimplification, particularization, pictorialization, photointerpretation, pseudosophistication, recapitalization, spiritualization, telecommunication, universalization, biodeterioration, deindustrialization, intellectualization, reindustrialization, internationalization, deinstitutionalization

[2]**ation** \ā-zhən\ see ASION

[3]**ation** \ash-ən\ see ASSION

[1]**ational** \ā-shnəl\ stational, citational, formational, gestational, gradational, migrational, narrational, notational, relational, sensational, vocational, aberrational, adaptational, avocational, compensational, computational, conformational, confrontational,

congregational, conjugational, connotational, conservational, conversational, convocational, derivational, educational, fluctuational, generational, gravitational, ideational, informational, innovational, inspirational, invitational, irrotational, limitational, navigational, observational, operational, orchestrational, postranslational, prevocational, progestational, recreational, reformational, situational, transformational, communicational, coeducational, denominational, improvisational, interpretational, investigational, organizational, representational, nonrepresentational, reorganizational, interdenominational

²ational \āzh-nəl\ see ASIONAL

³ational \ash-nəl\ national, passional, rational, binational, cross-national, irrational, transnational, international, multinational, supranational, suprarational

ationist \ā-shnəst\ salvationist, vacationist, annexationist, confrontationist, conservationist, educationist, integrationist, isolationist, liberationist, operationist, preservationist, recreationist, segregationist, separationist, preservationist, accomodationist, administrationist, assimilationist, associationist, collaborationist, emancipationist

ations \ā-shənz\ Galatians, impatiens, relations, Lamentations, Revelations, United Nations, Rhode Island and Providence Plantations

atious \ā-shəs\ see ACIOUS

¹atis \at-əs\ see ³ATUS

²atis \ät-əs\ see OTTIS

atist \āt-əst\ see ATEST

atitude \at-ə-tüd\ see ATTITUDE

atium \ā-shē-əm\ Latium, pancratium, solatium

atius \ā-shəs\ see ACIOUS

ative \āt-iv\ dative, native, stative, ablative, constative, creative, dilative, mutative, rotative, summative, translative, aggregative, agitative, alterative, applicative, carminative, cogitative, combinative, commutative, connotative, consecrative, consultative, contemplative, copulative, corporative, cumulative, decorative, denotative, dissipative, educative, explicative, facultative, federative, generative, germinative, imitative, implicative, innovative, integrative, irritative, iterative, legislative, limitative, meditative, meliorative, motivative, nominative, nuncupative, operative, palliative, pejorative, penetrative, procreative, propagative, qualitative, quantitative, recreative, regulative, replicative, separative, speculative, terminative, vegetative, accelerative, accumulative, administrative, agglutinative, alliterative, appreciative, assimilative, associative, authoritative, collaborative, commemorative, commiserative, communicative, contaminative, continuative, cooperative, corroborative, degenerative, deliberative, delineative, determinative, discriminative, evaporative, exhilarative, exonerative, illuminative, interpretative, investigative, justificative, multiplicative, obliterative, opinionative, originative, postoperative, premeditative, preoperative, proliferative, reciprocative, recuperative, regenerative, remunerative, reverberative, significative, vituperative, excommunicative, incommunicative, noncooperative, quasi-legislative, semiquantitative, uncommunicative

atl \ät-ᵊl\ see OTTLE

atlas \at-ləs\ atlas, Atlas, hatless

atless \at-ləs\ see ATLAS

atli \ät-lē\ see OTLY

atling \at-liŋ\ fatling, flatling, rattling

atly \at-lē\ flatly, rattly

atnam \ət-nəm\ Machilipatnam, Vishakhapatnam

atness \at-nəs\ fatness, flatness, platinous, gelatinous

[1]ato \ät-ō\ auto, blotto, grotto, lotto, motto, otto, Otto, potto, annatto, castrato, legato, marcato, mulatto, rabato, rebato, ridotto, rubato, sfumato, spiccato, staccato, agitato, animato, ben trovato, Guanajuato, moderato, obbligato, ostinato, pizzicato

[2]ato \āt-ō\ Cato, Plato, Orvieto, potato, tomato, Barquisimeto

atomist \at-ə-məst\ atomist, anatomist

atomy \at-ə-mē\ atomy, anatomy

aton \at-ᵊn\ see [2]ATIN

atony \at-ᵊn-ē\ see ATANY

ator \āt-ər\ baiter, cater, crater, Crater, dater, faitour, freighter, gaiter, gator, grater, hater, krater, later, mater, plater, rater, satyr, skater, slater, stater, stator, tater, traitor, waiter, aerator, collator, Bay Stater, creator, curator, debater, Decatur, dictator, donator, dumbwaiter, equator, first-rater, glossator, headwaiter, levator, locator, mandator, Mercator, narrator, pronator, pulsator, rotator, spectator, tailgater, testator, theater, third-rater, translator, upstater, vibrator, actuator, abdicator, activator, adulator, advocator, agitator, alligator, allocator, alternator, animator, annotator, applicator, arbitrator, aspirator, aviator, buccinator, calculator, captivator, carburetor, celebrator, circulator, commentator, commutator, compensator, compurgator, concentrator, confiscator, congregator, consecrator, consummator, contemplator, corporator, correlator, depredator, desecrater, desecrator, designator, cultivator, decorator, delegator, demonstrator, detonator, deviator, dissipater, dominator, duplicator, dura mater, educator, elevator, emulator, escalator, estimator, excavator, explicator, expurgator, extirpator, fascinator, formulator, fornicator, generator, gladiator, hibernator, illustrator, incubator, indicator, infiltrator, innovator, inhalator, inspirator, insulator, integrator, lacrimator, liquidator, literator, mediator, moderator, motivator, navigator, nomenclator, nominator, numerator, obturator, operator, orchestrator, oscillator, percolator, perpetrator, pia mater, pollinator, postulator, procreator, procurator, propagator, radiator, regulator, resonator, respirator, revelator, second-rater, selling-plater, separator, simulator, subjugator, syndicator, tabulator, terminator, valuator, ventilator, violator, accelerator, accommodator, accumulator, administrator, adulterator, alienator, alleviator, annihilator, annunciator, anticipator, appreciator, appropriator, assassinator, attenuator, continuator, calumniator, collaborator, commemorator, communicator, conciliator, congratulator, consolidator, contaminator, cooperator, coordinator, corroborator, defibrillator, delineator, denominator, depreciator, determinator, discriminator, disseminator, dissimulator, ejaculator, eliminator, emancipator, enumerator, equivocator, eradicator, evaluator, evaporator, exterminator, extrapolator, impersonator, improvisator, incinerator, inseminator, interrogator, intimidator, investigator, negotiator, oxygenator, pacificator, perambulator, predestinator, procrastinator, purificator, redecorator, refrigerator, regenerator, resuscitator, totalizator, subordinator, excommunicator, rehabilitator, turbogenerator, immunomodulator—*also comparatives of adjectives listed at* [1]ATE

atra \ä-trə\ Tatra, Sumatra

[1]**atre** \ätrᵊ\ coup de theatre, pas de quatre
[2]**atre** \at\ see [5]AT
atric \a-trik\ Patrick, sympatric, theatric, allopatric, geriatric, pediatric, podiatric, psychiatric
atrick \a-trik\ see ATRIC
atrics \a-triks\ theatrics, pediatrics
atrist \a-trəst\ geriatrist, physiatrist
atrix \ā-triks\ matrix, cicatrix, testatrix, aviatrix, dominatrix, executrix, mediatrix, administratrix
atron \ā-trən\ matron, natron, patron
[1]**ats** \äts\ see OTS
[2]**ats** \ats\ bats, rats, ersatz—*also plurals and possessives of nouns and third singular presents of verbs listed at* [5]AT
atsa \ät-sə\ see [1]ATZO
atsch \ach\ see [4]ATCH
atsk \ätsk\ Bratsk, Okhotsk, Petrozavodsk
atsu \ät-sü\ Hamamatsu, shiatsu, shiatzu, Takamatsu
atsy \at-sē\ see [3]AZI
[1]**att** \at\ see [5]AT
[2]**att** \ät\ see [1]OT
atta \ät-ə\ see [1]ATA
attage \ät-ij\ see OTTAGE
attan \at-ᵊn\ see [2]ATIN
atte \at\ see [5]AT
atted \a-təd\ superfatted—*also pasts of verbs listed at* [5]AT
attel \at-ᵊl\ see ATTLE
atten \at-ᵊn\ see [2]ATIN
atter \at-ər\ attar, batter, blatter, chatter, clatter, fatter, flatter, hatter, latter, matter, natter, patter, platter, ratter, satyr, scatter, shatter, smatter, spatter, splatter, tatter, backscatter, bespatter, flat-hatter, standpatter, wildcatter, antimatter, pitter-patter
attering \at-ə-riŋ\ nattering, smattering, backscattering, earth-shattering, self-flattering, unflattering, Rayleigh scattering
attern \at-ərn\ pattern, Saturn, slattern
attery \at-ə-rē\ battery, cattery, clattery, flattery, mattery, Cape Flattery, self-flattery
[1]**atti** \ät-ē\ see [1]ATI
[2]**atti** \at-ē\ see ATTY
attic \at-ik\ see [2]ATIC
attica \at-i-kə\ see ATICA
[1]**attice** \at-əs\ see [3]ATUS
[2]**attice** \at-ish\ see ATTISH
attie \at-ē\ see ATTY
attily \at-ᵊl-ē\ cattily, chattily, Natalie, Nathalie, nattily, rattly, philately, sal volatile
atting \at-iŋ\ batting, matting, tatting
attish \at-ish\ brattish, fattish, flattish
attitude \at-ə-tüd\ attitude, latitude
attle \at-ᵊl\ battle, brattle, cattle, chattel, prattle, rattle, tattle, embattle, Seattle, tittle-tattle
attler \at-lər\ battler, prattler, rattler, tattler
attling \at-liŋ\ see ATLING
[1]**attly** \at-ᵊl-ē\ see ATTILY
[2]**attly** \at-lē\ see ATLY
[1]**atto** \at-ə\ see [3]ATA

[2]atto \ät-ō\ see [1]ATO
atton \at-^{ə}n\ see [2]ATIN
atty \at-ē\ batty, catty, bratty, chatty, fatty, Hattie, natty, Patti, Pattie, patty, Patty, platy, ratty, scatty, tattie, tatty, Cincinnati
[1]atum \ät-əm\ bottom, datum, satem, erratum, pomatum, desideratum
[2]atum \āt-əm\ datum, pomatum, substratum, verbatim, ageratum, literatim, seriatim, ultimatum, corpus allatum, corpus striatum, desideratum
[3]atum \at-əm\ atom, datum, erratum, substratum, seriatim
atuous \ach-wəs\ fatuous, ignis fatuus
atur \āt-ər\ see ATOR
atural \ach-rəl\ natural, connatural, transnatural, unnatural, preternatural, seminatural, supernatural
[1]ature \ā-chər\ nature, denature, 4-H'er, magistrature, nomenclature, supernature
[2]ature \ach-ər\ see [2]ATCHER
aturn \at-ərn\ see ATTERN
[1]atus \āt-əs\ flatus, gratis, status, stratus, afflatus, hiatus, meatus, apparatus, coitus reservatus
[2]atus \ät-əs\ see OTTIS
[3]atus \at-əs\ brattice, gratis, lattice, status, stratus, clematis, altostratus, apparatus, cirrostratus, nimbostratus
atute \ach-ət\ see ATCHET
atuus \ach-wəs\ see ATUOUS
aty \āt-ē\ eighty, Haiti, Katie, Katy, Leyte, matey, platy, slaty, weighty, yeti, 1080, Papeete
atyr \āt-ər\ see ATOR
[1]atz \ats\ see [2]ATS
[2]atz \äts\ see OTS
[1]atzo \ät-sə\ matzo, tazza, Hidatsa, piazza
[2]atzo \ät-sō\ see [1]AZZO
atzu \ät-sü\ see ATSU
[1]au \ō\ see [1]OW
[2]au \ü\ see [1]EW
[3]au \au̇\ see [2]OW
[4]au \ȯ\ see [1]AW
aub \äb\ see [1]OB
auba \ȯ-bə\ carnauba, Catawba
aube \ōb\ see [1]OBE
auber \ȯb-ər\ dauber, Micawber
auble \äb-əl\ see [1]ABBLE
[1]auce \as\ see [3]ASS
[2]auce \ȯs\ see [1]OSS
aucer \ȯ-sər\ see OSSER
aucet \äs-ət\ see OSSET
[1]auch \ȯch\ nautch, watch, debauch
[2]auch \äch\ see OTCH
auche \ōsh\ see [2]OCHE
auchely \ōsh-lē\ see OCIALLY
auckland \ȯk-lənd\ Auckland, Falkland
aucous \ȯ-kəs\ caucus, glaucous, raucous
aucus \ȯ-kəs\ see AUCOUS
aucy \as-ē\ see ASSY
[1]aud \ȯd\ awed, baud, bawd, broad, Claud, Claude, clawed, fraud, gaud, god, jawed, laud, Maud, Maude, yod, abroad, applaud, belaud, defraud, dewclawed, maraud, whipsawed, eisteddfod, lantern-jawed, quartersawed—

also pasts of verbs listed at [1]AW
[2]**aud** \äd\ see [1]OD
audable \ȯd-ə-bəl\ audible, laudable, applaudable, illaudable, inaudible
audal \ȯd-ᵊl\ caudal, caudle, dawdle
audative \ȯd-ət-iv\ see AUDITIVE
[1]**aude** \au̇d-ē\ see OWDY
[2]**aude** \ȯd-ē\ see AWDY
[3]**aude** \au̇d-ə\ howdah, cum laude, magna cum laude, summa cum laude
[4]**aude** \ȯd\ see [1]AUD
audible \ȯd-ə-bəl\ see AUDABLE
auding \ȯd-iŋ\ auding, applauding, self-applauding
audit \ȯd-ət\ audit, plaudit
auditive \ȯd-ət-iv\ auditive, laudative
audle \ȯd-ᵊl\ see AUDAL
[1]**audy** \äd-ē\ see [1]ODY
[2]**audy** \ȯd-ē\ see AWDY
auer \au̇r\ see [2]OWER
auf \au̇f\ see OWFF
auffeur \ō-fər\ see OFER
auga \ȯ-gə\ massasauga, Mississauga, Onondaga
auge \āj\ see [3]AGE
augeable \ā-jə-bəl\ see AGEABLE
auged \ājd\ see AGED
[1]**auger** \ȯ-gər\ see [2]OGGER
[2]**auger** \ā-jər\ see [1]AGER
[1]**augh** \af\ see APH
[2]**augh** \ä\ see [1]A
[3]**augh** \äk\ see [1]ACH
[4]**augh** \ȯ\ see [1]AW
aughable \af-ə-bəl\ see AFFABLE
augham \ȯm\ see [1]AUM
[1]**aughn** \än\ see [1]ON
[2]**aughn** \ȯn\ see [3]ON
[1]**aught** \ät\ see [1]OT
[2]**aught** \ȯt\ see [1]OUGHT
[1]**aughter** \af-tər\ see AFTER
[2]**aughter** \ȯt-ər\ see [1]ATER
aughterer \ȯt-ər-ər\ see ATERER
[1]**aughty** \ȯt-ē\ haughty, naughty, zloty, Michelangelo Buonarroti
[2]**aughty** \ät-ē\ see ATI
augre \ȯg-ər\ see [2]OGGER
augur \ȯg-ər\ see [2]OGGER
augury \ȯ-gə-rē\ see [2]OGGERY
aui \au̇-ē\ see OWIE
auk \ȯk\ see ALK
aukee \ȯ-kē\ see ALKIE
aul \ȯl\ see ALL
aulay \ȯ-lē\ see AWLY
[1]**auld** \ȯl\ see ALL
[2]**auld** \ō\ see [1]OW
auldron \ȯl-drən\ see ALDRON
auled \ȯld\ see ALD
auler \ȯ-lər\ see [1]ALLER
aulin \ȯ-lən\ see ALLEN
auling \ȯ-liŋ\ see ALLING
aulish \ȯ-lish\ see ALLISH
aulk \ȯk\ see ALK
aulker \ȯ-kər\ see ALKER
aulking \ȯ-kiŋ\ see ALKING
aulle \ȯl\ see [1]ALL
aulm \ȯm\ see [1]AUM
[1]**ault** \ȯlt\ see ALT
[2]**ault** \ō\ see [1]OW
aulter \ȯl-tər\ see ALTER
aulting \ȯl-tiŋ\ see ALTING
aultless \ȯlt-ləs\ see ALTLESS
aulty \ȯl-tē\ see ALTY
[1]**aum** \ȯm\ gaum, haulm, Maugham, poem, qualm, shawm, meerschaum, Radom

[2]**aum** \äm\ see [1]OM
[1]**aun** \än\ see [1]ON
[2]**aun** \ən\ see UN
[3]**aun** \ȯn\ see [3]ON
[4]**aun** \au̇n\ see [2]OWN
[1]**auna** \än-ə\ see [1]ANA
[2]**auna** \ȯn-ə\ see [1]ONNA
aunce \ȯns\ jaunce, launce
[1]**aunch** \änch\ conch, cranch, craunch, paunch, raunch, stanch, Romansh
[2]**aunch** \ȯnch\ craunch, haunch, launch, paunch, raunch, stanch, staunch
auncher \ȯn-chər\ launcher, stancher, stauncher
aunchy \ȯn-chē\ paunchy, raunchy
aund \ȯnd\ awned, maund—*also pasts of verbs listed at* [3]ON
[1]**aunder** \ȯn-dər\ launder, maunder
[2]**aunder** \än-dər\ see [1]ONDER
aunish \än-ish\ see ONISH
[1]**aunt** \ȯnt\ daunt, flaunt, gaunt, haunt, jaunt, taunt, vaunt, want, wont, avant, avaunt, keeshond, romaunt, John of Gaunt
[2]**aunt** \ant\ see [5]ANT
[3]**aunt** \änt\ see [2]ANT
aunted \ȯnt-əd\ see ONTED
[1]**aunter** \änt-ər\ saunter, mishanter, rencontre
[2]**aunter** \ȯnt-ər\ gaunter, haunter, saunter
[1]**aunty** \ȯnt-ē\ flaunty, jaunty, vaunty
[2]**aunty** \änt-ē\ see [1]ANTI
aunus \än-əs\ see [1]ONUS
aup \ȯp\ gawp, scaup, whaup, yawp
aupe \ōp\ see OPE
auphin \ȯ-fən\ see OFFIN
[1]**aur** \au̇r\ see [2]OWER
[2]**aur** \ȯr\ see [1]OR
[1]**aura** \ȯr-ə\ see [2]ORA
[2]**aura** \är-ə\ see [1]ARA
aural \ȯr-əl\ see [2]ORAL
[1]**aure** \ōr\ see [1]ORE
[2]**aure** \ȯr\ see [1]OR
aurea \ȯr-ē-ə\ see ORIA
aurean \ȯr-ē-ən\ see ORIAN
[1]**aureate** \är-ē-ət\ baccalaureate, commisariat
[2]**aureate** \ȯr-ē-ət\ aureate, laureate, baccalaureate, professoriat
aurel \ȯr-əl\ see [2]ORAL
[1]**auren** \är-ən\ see [1]ORIN
[2]**auren** \ȯr-ən\ see [2]ORIN
aurence \ȯr-ən(t)s\ see AWRENCE
aureus \ȯr-ē-əs\ see ORIOUS
auri \au̇r-ē\ see OWERY
aurian \ȯr-ē-ən\ see ORIAN
auric \ȯr-ik\ see ORIC
[1]**aurice** \är-əs\ see [1]ORRIS
[2]**aurice** \ȯr-əs\ see AURUS
auricle \ȯr-i-kəl\ see ORICAL
[1]**aurie** \ȯr-ē\ see ORY
[2]**aurie** \är-ē\ see ARI
aurous \ȯr-əs\ see AURUS
aurus \ȯr-əs\ aurous, Boris, chorus, Doris, Flores, Horace, Maurice, morris, Morris, Norris, orris, porous, sorus, Taurus, Torres, torus, canorous, Centaurus, clitoris, decorous, Delores, Dolores, pelorus, phosphorous, sonorous, thesaurus,

allosaurus, brontosaurus, stegosaurus, apatosaurus, tyrannosaurus
aury \ȯr-ē\ see ORY
[1]**aus** \ā-əs\ see [1]AIS
[2]**aus** \au̇s\ see [2]OUSE
[3]**aus** \ȯz\ see [1]AUSE
ausal \ȯ-zəl\ causal, clausal, menopausal, postmenopausal
[1]**ause** \ȯz\ Broz, cause, clause, gauze, hawse, pause, tawse, yaws, applause, because, kolkhoz, sovkhoz, aeropause, diapause, menopause, Santa Claus—*also plurals and possessives of nouns and third person singular presents of verbs listed at* [1]AW
[2]**ause** \əz\ see [1]EUSE
auseous \ȯ-shəs\ see AUTIOUS
auser \ȯ-zər\ causer, hawser
ausey \ȯ-zē\ causey, gauzy
auss \au̇s\ see [1]OUSE
[1]**aussie** \äs-ē\ see [1]OSSY
[2]**aussie** \ȯ-sē\ see [2]OSSY
[1]**aust** \au̇st\ see OUST
[2]**aust** \ȯst\ see [3]OST
austen \ȯs-tən\ see OSTON
austin \ȯs-tən\ see OSTON
austless \ȯst-ləs\ costless, exhaustless
[1]**austral** \äs-trəl\ see OSTREL
[2]**austral** \ȯs-trəl\ see [1]OSTRAL
[1]**aut** \ō\ see [1]OW
[2]**aut** \au̇t\ see [3]OUT
[3]**aut** \ät\ see [1]OT
[4]**aut** \ȯt\ see [1]OUGHT
autch \ȯch\ see [1]AUCH
aute \ōt\ see OAT
auten \ȯt-ᵊn\ boughten, tauten
auterne \ȯt-ərn\ quartern, sauterne, sauternes
auternes \ȯt-ərn\ see AUTERNE
autery \ȯt-ə-rē\ see ATERY
autic \ȯt-ik\ orthotic, aeronautic, astronautic
autical \ȯt-i-kəl\ nautical, aeronautical, astronautical
autics \ät-iks\ see OTICS
aution \ȯ-shən\ caution, groschen, incaution, precaution
autious \ȯ-shəs\ cautious, nauseous, incautious
[1]**auto** \ȯt-ō\ auto, Giotto, risotto
[2]**auto** \ät-ō\ see [1]ATO
auve \ōv\ see [2]OVE
auze \ȯz\ see [1]AUSE
auzer \au̇-zər\ see OUSER
auzy \ȯ-zē\ see AUSEY
[1]**av** \äv\ see [2]OLVE
[2]**av** \av\ see [2]ALVE
[1]**ava** \äv-ə\ brava, fava, guava, java, Java, kava, lava, baklava, cassava, ottava, balaclava, Bratislava, Costa Brava, lavalava, piassava, Warszawa
[2]**ava** \av-ə\ java, Ungava, balaclava
avage \av-ij\ ravage, savage
avan \ā-vən\ see [1]AVEN
avant \av-ənt\ haven't, savant
avarice \av-rəs\ see AVEROUS
[1]**ave** \äv-ā\ ave, clave, grave, Jahveh, soave
[2]**ave** \āv\ brave, clave, cave, crave, Dave, fave, gave, glaive, grave, knave, lave, nave, pave, rave, save, shave, slave, stave, they've, trave, waive, wave, Wave, airwave, behave, concave, conclave, deprave, dissave, drawshave,

enclave, engrave, enslave, exclave, forgave, Great Slave, margrave, octave, outbrave, p-wave, palsgrave, shortwave, spokeshave, after-shave, architrave, biconcave, microwave, contraoctave, photoengrave

[3]**ave** \av\ see [3]ALVE

[4]**ave** \äv\ see [2]OLVE

aved \āvd\ waved, depraved, unsaved—*also pasts of verbs listed at* [2]AVE

avel \av-əl\ cavil, gavel, gravel, ravel, travel, unravel

aveless \āv-ləs\ graveless, waveless

aveling \av-liŋ\ raveling, traveling

avement \āv-mənt\ pavement, depravement, enslavement

[1]**aven** \ā-vən\ Avon, Cavan, craven, graven, haven, maven, raven, shaven, New Haven, riboflavin, Stratford-upon-Avon

[2]**aven** \av-ən\ see AVIN

aven't \av-ənt\ see AVANT

[1]**aver** \äv-ər\ slaver, palaver, windhover

[2]**aver** \ā-vər\ caver, claver, favor, flavor, graver, haver, laver, quaver, raver, saver, savor, shaver, slaver, waiver, waver, disfavor, enslaver, face-saver, flag-waver, lifesaver, semiquaver, demisemiquaver, hemidemisemiquaver—*also comparatives of adjectives listed at* [2]AVE

[3]**aver** \av-ər\ slaver, cadaver, palaver

avern \av-ərn\ cavern, klavern, tavern

averous \av-rəs\ avarice, cadaverous

avery \āv-rē\ bravery, knavery, quavery, savory, slavery, wavery, unsavory

avey \ā-vē\ see AVY

avia \ā-vē-ə\ Moldavia, Moravia, Scandinavia

avial \ā-vē-əl\ gavial, margravial

avian \ā-vē-ən\ avian, Shavian, Moravian, Scandinavian

avid \av-əd\ avid, gravid, pavid

avie \ā-vē\ see AVY

avil \av-əl\ see AVEL

avin \av-ən\ Avon, raven, ravin, savin, spavin

aving \ā-viŋ\ caving, craving, paving, raving, saving, shaving, flagwaving, lifesaving, timesaving, laborsaving

avis \ā-vəs\ Davis, favus, mavis, Mavis, rara avis

[1]**avish** \ā-vish\ knavish, slavish

[2]**avish** \av-ish\ lavish, ravish

avist \äv-əst\ Slavist, suavest, Pan-Slavist

avity \av-ət-ē\ cavity, gravity, concavity, depravity, antigravity, microgravity, supergravity

avl \äv-əl\ see [1]OVEL

[1]**avo** \äv-ō\ bravo, Bravo, centavo, octavo

[2]**avo** \ā-vō\ octavo, relievo, mezzo relievo

[1]**avon** \ā-vən\ see [1]AVEN

[2]**avon** \a-vən\ see AVIN
avor \ā-vər\ see [2]AVER
avored \ā-vərd\ favored, flavored, ill-favored, well-favored—*also pasts of verbs listed at* [2]AVER
avory \āv-rē\ see AVERY
avus \ā-vəs\ see AVIS
avvy \av-ē\ navvy, savvy
avy \ā-vē\ cavy, Davey, Davy, gravy, navy, shavie, slavey, wavy
[1]**aw** \ȯ\ aw, awe, blaw, braw, ca, caw, chaw, claw, craw, daw, draw, faugh, flaw, gnaw, haugh, haw, jaw, la, law, maw, pa, paw, pshaw, Ra, rah, raw, saw, shah, shaw, Shaw, slaw, spa, squaw, straw, tau, taw, thaw, yaw, backsaw, bashaw, bedstraw, bucksaw, bylaw, catclaw, cat's-paw, coleslaw, cumshaw, cushaw, Danelaw, declaw, dewclaw, Esau, forepaw, fretsaw, grandma, grandpa, guffaw, hacksaw, handsaw, hawkshaw, hee-haw, hurrah, in-law, jackdaw, jackstraw, jigsaw, kickshaw, lockjaw, macaw, Nassau, old-squaw, outdraw, outlaw, pasha, pooh-bah, ricksha, rickshaw, ringtaw, ripsaw, scofflaw, scrimshaw, seesaw, southpaw, trishaw, tussah, undraw, Utah, vizsla, Warsaw, whipsaw, windflaw, wiredraw, withdraw, Arkansas, Chickasaw, Chippewa, clapperclaw, decree-law, foofaraw, jinrikisha, Kiowa, Mackinac, mackinaw, Omaha, Ottawa, overawe, overdraw, oversaw, overslaugh, padishah, panama, son-in-law, usquebaugh, Wichita, williwaw, windlestraw, Yakima, brother-in-law, daughter-in-law, father-in-law, mother-in-law, pipsissewa, serjeant-at-law, sister-in-law, Straits of Mackinac
[2]**aw** \äv\ see [2]OLVE
[3]**aw** \ȯf\ see [2]OFF
[4]**aw** \äf\ see [1]OFF
[1]**awa** \ä-wə\ Chihuahua, Tarawa, Urawa, Fujisawa, Ichikawa, Kanzawa, Okinawa, Ahashikawa
[2]**awa** \ä-və\ see [1]AVA
awain \au̇-ən\ see [2]OWAN
awan \au̇-ən\ see [2]OWAN
awar \au̇r\ see [2]OWER
awba \ȯ-bə\ see AUBA
[1]**awber** \äb-ər\ see OBBER
[2]**awber** \ȯb-ər\ see AUBER
awd \ȯd\ see [1]AUD
awddle \äd-ᵊl\ see ODDLE
awdle \ȯd-ᵊl\ see AUDAL
awdry \ȯ-drē\ Audrey, tawdry
awdust \ȯd-əst\ see [1]ADIST
awdy \ȯd-ē\ bawdy, gaudy, summa cum laude
awe \ȯ\ see [1]AW
awed \ȯd\ see [1]AUD
aweless \ȯ-ləs\ see AWLESS
awer \ȯr\ see [1]OR
awers \ōrz\ see OORS
awful \ȯ-fəl\ awful, coffle, lawful, offal, god-awful, unlawful

awfully \ȯf-ə-lē\ awfully, lawfully, offaly, unlawfully
awing \ȯiŋ\ cloying, drawing, wappenschawing
awk \ȯk\ see ALK
awker \ȯ-kər\ see ALKER
awkes \ȯks\ Fawkes—*also possessives and plurals of nouns, third person singular presents of verbs listed at* ALK
awkish \ȯ-kish\ gawkish, hawkish, mawkish
awky \ȯ-kē\ see ALKIE
awl \ȯl\ see ALL
awler \ȯ-lər\ see [1]ALLER
awless \ȯ-ləs\ aweless, flawless, lawless
awling \ȯ-liŋ\ see ALLING
awly \ȯ-lē\ brawly, crawly, dolly, drawly, Raleigh, scrawly, squally, Bengali, Macaulay
awm \ȯm\ see [1]AUM
[1]**awn** \än\ see [1]ON
[2]**awn** \ȯn\ see [3]ON
awned \ȯnd\ see AUND
[1]**awner** \ȯn-ər\ fawner, goner, pawner, prawner, spawner
[2]**awner** \än-ər\ see [1]ONOR
awney \ȯ-nē\ see [1]AWNY
awning \än-iŋ\ see [1]ONING
awnly \än-lē\ see [1]ANLY
[1]**awny** \ȯ-nē\ brawny, fawny, lawny, sawney, scrawny, Taney, tawny, mulligatawny
[2]**awny** \än-ē\ see [1]ANI
awp \ȯp\ see AUP
awrence \ȯr-ən(t)s\ Florence, Laurence, Lawrence, Torrence, abhorrence, Saint Lawrence—*also possessives and plurals of nouns listed at* ORRENT
awry \ȯr-ē\ see ORY
aws \ȯz\ see [1]AUSE
awse \ȯz\ see [1]AUSE
awser \ȯ-zər\ see AUSER
awsi \au̇-sē\ see [2]OUSY
awy \ȯi\ see OY
awyer \ȯ-yər\ lawyer, sawyer
[1]**ax** \äks\ see OX
[2]**ax** \aks\ ax, fax, flax, lax, max, Max, pax, rax, sax, tax, wax, addax, Ajax, anthrax, banjax, beeswax, borax, broadax, climax, coax, earwax, galax, gravlax, hyrax, meat-ax, panchax, pickax, poleax, pretax, relax, smilax, storax, styrax, surtax, syntax, thorax, toadflax, aftertax, battle-ax, Halifax, minimax, overtax, parallax, supertax, anticlimax, Astyanax—*also plurals and possessives of nouns and third person singular presents of verbs listed at* [2]ACK
axant \ak-sənt\ see ACCENT
axen \ak-sən\ see AXON
axi \ak-sē\ see AXY
axic \ak-sik\ ataraxic, stereotaxic
axis \ak-səs\ axis, Naxos, praxis
axman \ak-smən\ axman, cracksman
axon \ak-sən\ flaxen, Jackson, Klaxon, Saxon, waxen, Port Jackson, Anglo-Saxon
axos \ak-səs\ see AXIS
axy \ak-sē\ flaxy, maxi, taxi, waxy
[1]**ay** \ā\ a , ae, aye, bay, bey, blae, brae, bray, chez, clay,

Clay, day, dey, dray, eh, fay, Fay, Faye, fey, flay, fley, frae, fray, Frey, gay, Gay, gey, gley, gray, Gray, greige, Grey, hae, hay, he, hey, Hue, j, jay, Jay, Jaye, k, kay, Kay, Kaye, lay, lei, may, May, nay, né, née, neigh, pay, pe, play, pray, prey, qua, quai, quay, Rae, ray, Ray, re, say, sei, shay, slay, sleigh, spae, spay, splay, spray, stay, stray, sway, they, tray, trey, way, weigh, whey, yea, abbé, affray, agley, airplay, airway, all-day, allay, allée, Angers, Anhui, Anhwei, archway, array, ashtray, assay, astray, Augier, away, aweigh, backstay, ballet, beignet, belay, beltway, benday, Benet, beret, betray, bewray, bidet, bikeway, birthday, Biscay, Bizet, blasé, bobstay, Bombay, bombe, bouchée, bouclé, boule, bouquet, bourrée, breezeway, Broadway, buffet, byplay, byway, cachet, café, cahier, Cambay, Cape May, Cartier, Cathay, causeway, chaîné, chalet, chambray, chassé, ciré, cliché, cloqué, congé, convey, corvée, coudé, coupé, crawlway, crochet, croquet, crossway, cube, curé, cy pres, DA, daresay, decay, deejay, defray, delay, dengue, dismay, display, distrait, DJ, donnée, doomsday, doorway, dossier, downplay, dragée, driveway, duvet, embay, entrée, épée, essay, estray, Ewe, fairway, filé, filet, fillet, fireclay, fishway, flambé, floodway, flyway, folkway, footway, foray, forebay, foreplay, forestay, formée, forte, fouetté, four-way, fourchée, foyer, franglais, frappé, freeway, frieze, frisé, fumet, gainsay, Galway, gamay, gangway, Gaspé, gateway, gelée, glacé, godet, gourmet, Green Bay, greenway, guideway, gunplay, halfway, hallway, hatchway, headway, hearsay, Hebei, Hefei, heyday, highway, homestay, hooray, horseplay, Hubei, in re, inlay, inveigh, issei, jackstay, jeté, keyway, Kobe, koine, kouprey, lamé, laneway, leeway, lifeway, Lomé, Lough Neagh, lwei, lycée, M-day, maguey, mainstay, Malay, malgré, man-day, Mande, Manet, manqué, margay, Marseilles, massé, maté, May Day, Mayday, melee, metier, meze, midday, Midway, Millay, Millet, mislay, misplay, moiré, Monet, moray, nevé, Niamey, nisei, noonday, Norway, nosegay, obey, ofay, OK, olé, ombré, osprey, outlay, outré, outstay, outweigh, oyez, PA, parfait, parkway, parlay, parquet, partway, passé, pâté, pathway, pavé, payday, per se, pince-nez, piqué, piquet, PK, plié, plissé, pommée, Pompeii,

, Saguenay, San Jose,
é, Santa Fe, São
semplice, sobriquet,
lier, steerageway,
way, stowaway,
taway, Table Bay,
t, take-away, tarsier,
ay, tearaway, teleplay,
ere, Tenebrae, thataway,
vaway, Thunder Bay,
e, underlay, underpay,
rplay, underway,
guay, velouté, Venite,
té, vertebra, virelay,
kaway, waterway,
laway, Whitsunday,
rkaday, Yenisey, Zuider
e, Agnus Dei, areaway,
to-da-fé, bichon frisé,
ulevardier, cabriolet, café
lait, cantabile, cDNA,
communiqué, costumier,
couturier, décolleté, diamanté,
Dies Irae, eglomisé, felo-de-
se, Fiesole, garde-manger,
habitué, Jubilate, laissez-
passer, Lavoisier, marrons
glacé, mezzo forte, Morgan le
y, objet trouvé, out-of-the-
y, papier collé, papier-
ché, pas de bourrée, photo-
ay, Port Philip Bay,
illy-fuissé, Pouilly-Fumé,
-à-porter, roche
tonnée, roman à clef,
ier, sine die, sub judice,
rhighway, ukiyo-e, Ulan-
yerba maté, Alto Adige,
e pensée, Guanabara
lettre de cachet,
gue raisonné, cinema
, Dumfries and
Galloway, vers de société, video verité, sinfonia concertante, Trentino-Alto Adige

[2]**ay** \ē\ see [1]EE

[3]**ay** \ī\ see [1]Y

[1]**aya** \ä-yə\ ayah, maya, taille, Malaya, Koshigaya

[2]**aya** \ī-ə\ see [1]IAH

[3]**aya** \ā-ə\ see [1]AIA

ayable \ā-ə-bəl\ payable, playable, sayable, defrayable, displayable, unsayable

ayah \ī-ə\ see [1]IAH

ayal \āl\ see AIL

[1]**ayan** \ā-ən\ crayon, Chilean, Malayan, ouabain, papain, Pompeian, Pompeiian, Galilean, Himalayan

[2]**ayan** \ī-ən\ see [1]ION

[1]**aybe** \ā-bē\ see ABY

[2]**aybe** \eb-ē\ see EBBY

ayday \ā-dā\ Ede, Mayday, May Day

ayden \ī-dᵊn\ see IDEN

[1]**aye** \ā\ see [1]AY

[2]**aye** \ī\ see [1]Y

ayed \ād\ see [1]ADE

[1]**ayer** \ā-ər\ brayer, layer, mayor, payer, player, prayer, preyer, sayer, sprayer, stayer, strayer, ballplayer, betrayer, bilayer, bricklayer, cardplayer, conveyer, crocheter, decayer, delayer, doomsayer, doomsdayer, gainsayer, horseplayer, inlayer, essayer, forayer, inveigher, obeyer, manslayer, minelayer, portrayer, purveyor, ratepayer, soothsayer, swordplayer, surveyor, taxpayer, tracklayer,

portray, prepay, projet, pulque, puree, purvey, quale, raceway, railway, rappee, relay, Rene, Renee, repay, replay, risqué, roadway, role-play, ropeway, rosé, rosebay, Roubaix, roué, routeway, runway, sachet, Salé, sansei, sashay, sauté, screenplay, seaway, semé, shar-pei, shipway, short-day, sideway, Skopje, skyway, slideway, slipway, sluiceway, soigné, soiree, someday, someway, soothsay, soufflé, speedway, spillway, stairway, sternway, stingray, straightway, strathspey, subway, survey, swordplay, Taipei, tempeh, thoughtway, three-way, thruway, tideway, Tigré, today, Tokay, tollway, Torbay, touché, toupee, trackway, tramway, unlay, unsay, valet, V-day, veejay, vide, visé, Vouvray, walkway, waylay, weekday, windway, wireway, wordplay, workday, X ray, x-ray, Yaoundé, Adige, A-OK, alleyway, anyway, appliqué, arrivé, atelier, attaché, ballonet, Beaujolais, beurre manié, BHA, botonée, braciole, breakaway, bustier, cabaret, cableway, Camagüey, canapé, cap-a-pie, caraway, carriageway, Cartier, cassoulet, castaway, champlevé, chansonnier, chardonnay, Charolais, chevalier, Chippewa, cloisonné, consommé,

coryph
cutawa
debauc
degree-c
disarray,
divorcé, c
émigré, en
entremets,
etoufée, eve
expressway,
fallaway, far
faraway, fian
flageolet, flya
Galloway, Geo
getaway, givea
gratinée, guillen
haulageway, Her
hereaway, hideaw
Hogmanay, holida
Capet, IgA, inter s
intraday, IPA, IRA,
Kootenay, Kutenai,
lackaday, latter-day, layaway, lingerie, macramé, Mandalay, Massenet, matinee, MIA, Molise, Monterrey, motorway, muscadet, negligee, overlay,
overstay, overweig
Paraguay, passage
patissier, Petare,
pikake, piolet, pi
by-play, poly (A
popinjay, pourp
café, present-da
protégée, Rabe
rambouillet, ra
rechauffé, rec
reconvey, rep
résumé, retro
right-of-way
rondelet, ro

runawa
San Jos
Tomé,
somme
standa
straig
tabore
taxiw
Tem
thro
Udi
und
Uru
véri
wa
we
wo
Ze
au
b

F
w
m
ess
po
prê
mo
rot
sup
Ude
arriè
Bay,
catal
verité

portray, prepay, projet, pulque, puree, purvey, quale, raceway, railway, rappee, relay, Rene, Renee, repay, replay, risqué, roadway, role-play, ropeway, rosé, rosebay, Roubaix, roué, routeway, runway, sachet, Salé, sansei, sashay, sauté, screenplay, seaway, semé, shar-pei, shipway, short-day, sideway, Skopje, skyway, slideway, slipway, sluiceway, soigné, soiree, someday, someway, soothsay, soufflé, speedway, spillway, stairway, sternway, stingray, straightway, strathspey, subway, survey, swordplay, Taipei, tempeh, thoughtway, three-way, thruway, tideway, Tigré, today, Tokay, tollway, Torbay, touché, toupee, trackway, tramway, unlay, unsay, valet, V-day, veejay, vide, visé, Vouvray, walkway, waylay, weekday, windway, wireway, wordplay, workday, X ray, x-ray, Yaoundé, Adige, A-OK, alleyway, anyway, appliqué, arrivé, atelier, attaché, ballonet, Beaujolais, beurre manié, BHA, botonée, braciole, breakaway, bustier, cabaret, cableway, Camagüey, canapé, cap-a-pie, caraway, carriageway, Cartier, cassoulet, castaway, champlevé, chansonnier, chardonnay, Charolais, chevalier, Chippewa, cloisonné, consommé, coryphée, croupier, crudités, cutaway, day-to-day, debauchee, déclassé, dégagé, degree-day, démodé, devotee, disarray, disobey, distingué, divorcé, divorcée, DNA, émigré, engagé, entranceway, entremets, entryway, espalier, etoufée, everyday, exposé, expressway, fadeaway, fallaway, faraday, Faraday, faraway, fiancé, fiancée, flageolet, flyaway, foldaway, Galloway, Georgian Bay, getaway, giveaway, gratiné, gratinée, guillemet, Harare, haulageway, Hemingway, hereaway, hideaway, HLA, Hogmanay, holiday, Hugh Capet, IgA, inter se, interplay, intraday, IPA, IRA, Joliet, Kootenay, Kutenai, kyrie, lackaday, latter-day, layaway, lingerie, macramé, Mandalay, Massenet, matinee, MIA, Molise, Monterrey, motorway, muscadet, negligee, overlay, overplay, overstay, overweigh, Paraguay, passageway, patissier, Petare, photoplay, pikake, piolet, pis aller, play-by-play, poly (A), Ponape, popinjay, pourparler, pousse-café, present-day, protégé, protégée, Rabelais, rambouillet, ratiné, recamier, rechauffé, recherché, reconvey, repartee, repoussé, résumé, retroussé, ricochet, right-of-way, rockaway, rondelet, roundelay, RNA, runaway, Saguenay, San Jose, San José, Santa Fe, São Tomé, semplice, sobriquet, sommelier, steerageway, standaway, stowaway, straightaway, Table Bay, taboret, take-away, tarsier, taxiway, tearaway, teleplay, Tempere, Tenebrae, thataway, throwaway, Thunder Bay, Udine, underlay, underpay, underplay, underway, Uruguay, velouté, Venite, vérité, vertebra, virelay, walkaway, waterway, wellaway, Whitsunday, workaday, Yenisey, Zuider Zee, Agnus Dei, areaway, auto-da-fé, bichon frisé, boulevardier, cabriolet, café au lait, cantabile, cDNA, communiqué, costumier, couturier, décolleté, diamanté, Dies Irae, eglomisé, felo-de-se, Fiesole, garde-manger, habitué, Jubilate, laissez-passer, Lavoisier, marrons glacé, mezzo forte, Morgan le Fay, objet trouvé, out-of-the-way, papier collé, papier-mâché, pas de bourrée, photo-essay, Port Philip Bay, pouilly-fuissé, Pouilly-Fumé, prêt-à-porter, roche moutonnée, roman à clef, roturier, sine die, sub judice, superhighway, ukiyo-e, Ulan-Ude, yerba maté, Alto Adige, arrière pensée, Guanabara Bay, lettre de cachet, catalogue raisonné, cinema verité, Dumfries and Galloway, vers de société, video verité, sinfonia concertante, Trentino-Alto Adige

[2]**ay** \ē\ see [1]EE

[3]**ay** \ī\ see [1]Y

[1]**aya** \ä-yə\ ayah, maya, taille, Malaya, Koshigaya

[2]**aya** \ī-ə\ see [1]IAH

[3]**aya** \ā-ə\ see [1]AIA

ayable \ā-ə-bəl\ payable, playable, sayable, defrayable, displayable, unsayable

ayah \ī-ə\ see [1]IAH

ayal \āl\ see AIL

[1]**ayan** \ā-ən\ crayon, Chilean, Malayan, ouabain, papain, Pompeian, Pompeiian, Galilean, Himalayan

[2]**ayan** \ī-ən\ see [1]ION

[1]**aybe** \ā-bē\ see ABY

[2]**aybe** \eb-ē\ see EBBY

ayday \ā-dā\ Ede, Mayday, May Day

ayden \ī-dᵊn\ see IDEN

[1]**aye** \ā\ see [1]AY

[2]**aye** \ī\ see [1]Y

ayed \ād\ see [1]ADE

[1]**ayer** \ā-ər\ brayer, layer, mayor, payer, player, prayer, preyer, sayer, sprayer, stayer, strayer, ballplayer, betrayer, bilayer, bricklayer, cardplayer, conveyer, crocheter, decayer, delayer, doomsayer, doomsdayer, gainsayer, horseplayer, inlayer, essayer, forayer, inveigher, obeyer, manslayer, minelayer, portrayer, purveyor, ratepayer, soothsayer, swordplayer, surveyor, taxpayer, tracklayer,

yea-sayer, disobeyer, holidayer—*also comparatives of adjectives listed at* [1]AY
[2]**ayer** \er\ see [4]ARE
ayered \erd\ see AIRED
ayest \ā-əst\ mayest, sayest, épéeist, essayist, fideist, Hebraist, Mithraist—*also superlatives of adjectives listed at* [1]AY
[1]**ayin** \ī-ən\ see [1]ION
[2]**ayin** \īn\ see [1]INE
[3]**ayin** \ä-yən\ see AIIAN
aying \ā-iŋ\ gleying, maying, playing, saying, bricklaying, delaying, long-playing, soothsaying, surveying, taxpaying, tracklaying
ayish \ā-ish\ clayish, grayish
ayist \ā-əst\ see AYEST
ayle \āl\ see AIL
ayless \ā-ləs\ rayless, talus, wayless, Morelos, aurora australis, Corona Australis
ayling \ā-liŋ\ see AILING
aylor \ā-lər\ see AILER
ayly \ā-lē\ see AILY
ayman \ā-mən\ see [1]AMEN
ayment \ā-mənt\ ament, claimant, clamant, payment, raiment, co-payment, embayment, prepayment, underlayment, underpayment
ayne \ān\ see [1]ANE
ayness \ā-nəs\ anus, feyness, gayness, grayness, heinous, Janus, manus, awayness, uranous, Uranus, everydayness
aynim \ā-nəm\ see [1]ANUM
ayn't \ā-ənt\ see EYANT
[1]**ayo** \ā-ō\ see [1]EO
[2]**ayo** \ī-ō\ see [1]IO
[1]**ayon** \an\ see [5]AN
[2]**ayon** \ā-ən\ see [1]AYAN
ayor \ā-ər\ see [1]AYER
[1]**ayou** \ī-ə\ see [1]IAH
[2]**ayou** \ī-ō\ see [1]IO
ayr \er\ see [4]ARE
[1]**ays** \ez\ fez, Fez, Geez, prez, says, Cortez, gainsays, Inez, Suez, unsays, crème anglaise, Louis Seize, Louis Treize, Isthmus of Suez, Vincente López
[2]**ays** \āz\ see [1]AZE
aysia \ā-zhə\ see ASIA
ay-so \ā-sō\ see [1]ESO
ayton \āt-ᵊn\ Clayton, Dayton, Layton
[1]**ayyid** \ī-əd\ see YAD
[2]**ayyid** \ēd-ē\ see EEDY
[1]**az** \az\ see AZZ
[2]**az** \äz\ see [1]OISE
[3]**az** \äts\ see OTS
[1]**aza** \äz-ə\ Gaza, plaza, piazza, tabula rasa
[2]**aza** \az-ə\ plaza, piazza
[1]**azar** \äz-ər\ see OZZER
[2]**azar** \az-ər\ lazar, alcazar, Belshazzar
azard \az-ərd\ hazard, mazard, mazzard, haphazard
[1]**aze** \āz\ baize, blaze, braise, braze, chaise, craze, days, daze, Draize, faze, feaze, fraise, gaze, glaze, graze, Hays, haze, lase, laze, maize, maze, phase, phrase, praise, raise, rase, raze, smaze, vase, ways, ablaze, agaze, amaze, appraise, breadthways, catchphrase, crossways, deglaze, dispraise, edgeways,

emblaze, endways, flatways, foodways, gainsays, hereways, leastways, lengthways, liaise, malaise, mores, pj's, sideways, slantways, stargaze, ukase, upraise, weekdays, anyways, chrysoprase, cornerways, crème anglaise, holidays, Louis Seize, Louis Treize, lyonnaise, mayonnaise, metaphrase, multiphase, nowadays, overglaze, overgraze, paraphrase, polonaise, polyphase, single-phase, underglaze—*also plurals and possessives of nouns and third person singular presents of verbs listed at* 1AY

2aze \äz\ see 1OISE

3aze \äz-ē\ see 1AZI

azeable \ā-zə-bəl\ see 1ASABLE

azed \āzd\ unfazed—*pasts of verbs listed at* 1AZE

azel \ā-zəl\ see 2ASAL

azement \āz-mənt\ amazement, appraisement

azen \āz-ᵊn\ see AZON

azer \ā-zər\ blazer, brazer, Fraser, gazer, glazer, grazer, hazer, laser, maser, mazer, praiser, razer, razor, appraiser, fund-raiser, hair-raiser, hell-raiser, stargazer, trailblazer, paraphraser, free-electron laser

1azi \äz-ē\ quasi, Swazi, Benghazi, Anasazi, kamikaze

2azi \az-ē\ see AZZY

3azi \at-sē\ Nazi, patsy, Patsy, neo-Nazi

4azi \ät-sē\ Nazi, neo-Nazi

azier \ā-zhər\ brazier, Frasier, glacier, glazier, grazier, leisure, measure, pleasure, rasure, treasure, admeasure, embrasure, erasure

azing \ā-ziŋ\ see AISING

azo \az-ō\ diazo, terrazzo

azon \āz-ᵊn\ blazon, brazen, raisin, emblazon, Marquesan, diapason, hexenbesen

azor \ā-zər\ see AZER

azquez \as-kəs\ see ASCUS

azy \ā-zē\ crazy, daisy, Daisy, hazy, lazy, mazy, stir-crazy, witch of Agnesi

azz \az\ as, has, jazz, razz, spaz, Hejaz, La Paz, pizzazz, topaz, whenas, whereas, razzmatazz

1azza \az-ə\ see 2AZA

2azza \äz-ə\ see 1AZA

3azza \ät-sə\ see 1ATZO

azzar \az-ər\ see 2AZAR

azzard \az-ərd\ see AZARD

azzle \az-əl\ basil, Basil, dazzle, frazzle, bedazzle, razzle-dazzle

1azzo \ät-sō\ matzo, palazzo, terrazzo, paparazzo

2azzo \az-ō\ see AZO

azzy \az-ē\ jazzy, snazzy, Ashkenazi

e

[1]e \ā\ see [1]AY
[2]e \ē\ see [1]EE
[3]e \ə\ see [3]U
é \ā\ see [1]AY
[1]ea \ā\ see [1]AY
[2]ea \ā-ə\ see [1]AIA
[3]ea \ē\ see [1]EE
[4]ea \ē-ə\ see [1]IA
eabee \ē-bē\ see [1]EBE
eace \ēs\ see IECE
eaceable \ē-sə-bəl\ see [1]EASABLE
each \ēch\ beach, beech, bleach, breach, breech, each, fleech, leach, leech, peach, pleach, preach, reach, screech, speech, teach, beseech, forereach, impeach, Long Beach, outreach, unteach, overreach, practice-teach, Huntington Beach
eachable \ē-chə-bəl\ bleachable, leachable, reachable, teachable, impeachable, unimpeachable
eacher \ē-chər\ bleacher, creature, feature, leacher, preacher, reacher, screecher, teacher, defeature, disfeature, schoolteacher
eacherous \ech-rəs\ see ECHEROUS
eachery \ech-rē\ see ECHERY
eaching \ē-chiŋ\ see EECHING
eachment \ēch-mənt\ preachment, impeachment
eachy \ē-chē\ beachy, chichi, Nietzsche, peachy, preachy, screechy, caliche, Campeche
eacle \ē-kəl\ see [1]ECAL
eacly \ē-klē\ see EEKLY
eacon \ē-kən\ beacon, deacon, sleeken, weaken, archdeacon, Mohican, subdeacon, Neorican
[1]**ead** \ed\ bed, bled, bread, bred, dead, dread, ed, Ed, fed, fled, Fred, head, Jed, lead, led, med, Ned, ped, pled, read, red, Red, redd, said, shed, shred, sled, sped, spread, stead, ted, Ted, thread, tread, wed, zed, abed, afraid, ahead, airhead, baldhead, beachhead, bedspread, bedstead, beebread, behead, bestead, bighead, biped, blackhead, blockhead, bloodred, bloodshed, bobsled, bonehead, bridgehead, brown bread, bulkhead, bullhead, cathead, childbed, coed, cokehead, corn-fed, cowshed, crispbread, crossbred, crosshead, daybed, deadhead, death's-head, deathbed, dispread, dogsled, dopehead, drophead, drumhead, dumbhead, egghead, embed, far-red, farmstead, fathead, flatbed, forehead, foresaid, gainsaid, Gateshead, godhead,

green-head, half-bred, hardhead, highbred, hogshead, homebred, homestead, hophead, hotbed, hothead, ill-bred, inbred, instead, jarhead, juicehead, lamed, light bread, longhead, lowbred, lunkhead, masthead, meathead, misled, misread, moped, naled, nonsked, outsped, outspread, packthread, phys ed, pinhead, pithead, pothead, premed, printhead, purebred, railhead, re-tread, redhead, retread, riverbed, roadbed, roadstead, Roundhead, saphead, scarehead, seabed, seedbed, sheep ked, sheepshead, sheetfed, shewbread, shortbread, sickbed, skinhead, snowshed, softhead, sorehead, spearhead, springhead, steelhead, straightbred, streambed, subhead, sweetbread, swellhead, thickhead, thunderhead, toolhead, toolshed, towhead, trailhead, unbred, undead, unread, unsaid, unthread, untread, warhead, webfed, well-bred, well-read, wellhead, white-bread, whitehead, widespread, wingspread, woodshed, woolshed, acidhead, aforesaid, arrowhead, barrelhead, Birkenhead, bubblehead, bufflehead, chowderhead, chucklehead, colorbred, copperhead, dragonhead, dunderhead, featherbed, featherhead, fiddlehead, figurehead, fire-engine red, fountainhead, gingerbread, go-ahead, hammerhead, infrared, interbred, knucklehead, letterhead, loggerhead, lowlihead, maidenhead, newlywed, overhead, overspread, pinniped, pointy-head, poppyhead, quadruped, saddlebred, Saint John's bread, Samoyed, showerhead, sleepyhead, slugabed, standardbred, straight-ahead, timberhead, thoroughbred, underbred, underfed, watershed, woodenhead, far-infrared, near-infrared, West Quoddy Head, parallelepiped

[2]**ead** \ēd\ see EED

[3]**ead** \əd\ see [1]UD

[1]**eadable** \ēd-ə-bəl\ kneadable, pleadable, readable

[2]**eadable** \ed-ə-bəl\ see EDIBLE

[1]**eaded** \ed-əd\ bedded, headed, bareheaded, bigheaded, bullheaded, clearheaded, coolheaded, eggheaded, embedded, fatheaded, hardheaded, hotheaded, light-headed, longheaded, lunkheaded, pigheaded, pinheaded, roundheaded, sapheaded, softheaded, soreheaded, swelled-headed, swellheaded, thickheaded, towheaded, bubbleheaded, chowderheaded, chuckleheaded, dunderheaded, featherheaded, unleaded, white-headed, empty-headed, hydra-headed, knuckleheaded,

levelheaded, muddleheaded, pointy-headed, puzzleheaded, woodenheaded, woolly-headed

[2]**eaded** \ē-dəd\ see EEDED

eaden \ed-ᵊn\ deaden, leaden, redden, steading, Armageddon

[1]**eader** \ēd-ər\ cedar, ceder, feeder, kneader, leader, pleader, reader, seeder, speeder, weeder, bandleader, cheerleader, conceder, lip-reader, newsreader, nonreader, proofreader, repleader, ringleader, seceder, stampeder, stockbreeder, succeeder, copyreader, interpleader

[2]**eader** \ed-ər\ bedder, cheddar, chedar, header, shedder, shredder, sledder, spreader, tedder, threader, wedder, homesteader, doubleheader, triple-header

eadily \ed-ᵊl-ē\ headily, readily, unsteadily

[1]**eading** \ed-iŋ\ bedding, heading, Reading, steading, wedding, bobsledding, farmsteading, subheading, wide-spreading

[2]**eading** \ed-ᵊn\ see EADEN

[3]**eading** \ēd-ᵊn\ see EDON

[4]**eading** \ēd-iŋ\ see [1]EEDING

[1]**eadle** \ed-ᵊl\ see [1]EDAL

[2]**eadle** \ēd-ᵊl\ see EEDLE

eadly \ed-lē\ see EDLEY

eadow \ed-ə\ see EDDA

[1]**eadsman** \edz-mən\ headsman, leadsman

[2]**eadsman** \ēdz-mən\ see EEDSMAN

[1]**eady** \ed-ē\ Eddie, eddy, Eddy, Freddie, heady, leady, ready, steady, Teddie, teddy, Teddy, thready, already, makeready, unsteady, gingerbready, rough-and-ready

[2]**eady** \ēd-ē\ see EEDY

[1]**eaf** \ef\ see [1]EF

[2]**eaf** \ēf\ see [1]IEF

eafless \ē-fləs\ see IEFLESS

eafy \ē-fē\ see EEFY

eag \ēg\ see IGUE

eagan \ā-gən\ see AGIN

eager \ē-gər\ eager, leaguer, meager, beleaguer, intriguer, Xinjiang Uygur

eagh \ā\ see [1]AY

eagle \ē-gəl\ see EGAL

eague \ēg\ see IGUE

eaguer \ē-gər\ see EAGER

eah \ē-ə\ see [1]IA

[1]**eak** \ēk\ beak, bleak, cheek, chic, cleek, clique, creak, creek, Creek, eke, flic, freak, geek, gleek, Greek, keek, leak, leek, meek, peak, peek, peke, pic, pique, reek, screak, seek, sheik, sheikh, shriek, sic, Sikh, sleek, sneak, speak, squeak, steek, streak, streek, teak, tweak, weak, week, wreak, antique, apeak, batik, Belgique, Belleek, bespeak, bezique, boutique, cacique, caique, critique, debeak, forepeak, forespeak, grosbeak, hairstreak, halfbeak, houseleek, misspeak, muzhik, mystique, newspeak, nonpeak, oblique, off-peak, outspeak, perique, physique, Pikes Peak, pip-squeak, pratique, relique,

technic, technique, Tajik, unique, unspeak, workweek, biunique, Bolshevik, Chesapeake, dominique, doublespeak, ecofreak, fenugreek, hide-and-seek, Lassen Peak, Martinique, Menshevik, Mozambique, semi-antique, verd antique, Veronique, electroweak, opéra comique, realpolitik

[2]**eak** \ā k\ see [1]AKE

[3]**eak** \ek\ see ECK

eakable \ā-kə-bəl\ see AKABLE

eake \ēk\ see [1]EAK

[1]**eaked** \ē-kəd\ peaked, streaked

[2]**eaked** \ēkt\ beaked, freaked, peaked, streaked, apple-cheeked—*also pasts of verbs listed at* [1]EAK

[3]**eaked** \ik-əd\ see [1]ICKED

eaken \ē-kən\ see EACON

[1]**eaker** \ē-kər\ beaker, leaker, reeker, seeker, sneaker, speaker, squeaker, loudspeaker, self-seeker, sunseeker, doublespeaker—*also comparatives of adjectives listed at* [1]EAK

[2]**eaker** \ā-kər\ see [1]AKER

[1]**eaking** \ē-kiŋ\ freaking, sneaking, speaking, streaking, heat-seeking, self-seeking

[2]**eaking** \ā-kiŋ\ see [1]AKING

eakish \ē-kish\ bleakish, cliquish, freakish, weakish

eakly \ē-klē\ see EEKLY

eaky \ē-kē\ cheeky, cliquey, creaky, freaky, leaky, piki, reeky, sneaky, screaky, squeaky, streaky, tiki, daishiki, dashiki, Tajiki, cock-a-leekie, Kurashiki, Manihiki

[1]**eal** \ē-əl\ empyreal, hymeneal, laryngeal, apophyseal, pharmacopeial

[2]**eal** \ēl\ ceil, chiel, creel, deal, deil, eel, feel, heal, heel, he'll, keel, Kiel, kneel, leal, meal, Neal, Neil, peal, peel, real, reel, seal, seel, she'll, shiel, speel, spiel, squeal, steal, steel, Steele, Streel, teal, tuille, veal, weal, we'll, wheal, wheel, zeal, aiguille, allheal, anneal, appeal, Arbil, bastille, Bastille, bonemeal, bonspiel, Camille, Castile, cartwheel, Cecile, chainwheel, chenille, cogwheel, conceal, congeal, cornmeal, enwheel, Erbil, flywheel, forefeel, four-wheel, freewheel, genteel, handwheel, ideal, inchmeal, Irbil, irreal, Kuril, Lucille, misdeal, mobile, Mobile, newsreel, nosewheel, oatmeal, O'Neill, ordeal, pastille, piecemeal, pinwheel, repeal, reveal, schlemiel, self-heal, side-wheel, singspiel, somedeal, stabile, surreal, tahsil, Tarheel, thumbwheel, unreal, unreel, unseal, acetyl, airmobile, Ardabil, bidonville, beau ideal, blastocoel, bloodmobile, Bogomil, bookmobile, campanile, chamomile, cochineal, cockatiel, commonweal, difficile, dishabille, down-at-heel, glockenspiel, goldenseal, Guayaquil, manchineel,

megadeal, mercantile, pimpmobile, skimobile, snowmobile, thunderpeal, waterwheel, automobile, Solomon's seal, varicocele
[3]**eal** \āl\ see AIL
[4]**eal** \il\ see ILL
ealable \ē-lə-bəl\ peelable, reelable, stealable, appealable, concealable, revealable, repealable, irrepealable, unappealable
ealand \ē-lənd\ see ELAND
eald \ēld\ see IELD
ealed \ēld\ see IELD
ealer \ē-lər\ dealer, feeler, healer, heeler, kneeler, peeler, reeler, sealer, spieler, squealer, stealer, stelar, vealer, velar, wheeler, appealer, concealer, four-wheeler, freewheeler, newsdealer, repealer, revealer, scene-stealer, side-wheeler, stern-wheeler, three-wheeler, two-wheeler, double-dealer, eighteen-wheeler, 18-wheeler, snowmobiler, wheeler-dealer
ealie \ē-lē\ see EELY
ealing \ē-liŋ\ see EELING
[1]**eally** \ē-ə-lē\ leally, ideally, hymeneally, industrially
[2]**eally** \il-ē\ see [1]ILLY
[3]**eally** \ē-lē\ see EELY
ealm \elm\ see ELM
ealment \ēl-mənt\ concealment, congealment, revealment
ealot \el-ət\ see ELLATE
ealotry \el-ə-trē\ see ELOTRY
ealous \el-əs\ Ellis, Hellas, jealous, trellis, zealous, cancellous, ocellus
ealousy \el-ə-sē\ see ELACY
ealth \elth\ health, stealth, wealth, commonwealth
ealthy \el-thē\ healthy, stealthy, wealthy, unhealthy
ealty \ēl-tē\ fealty, realty
[1]**eam** \ēm\ beam, bream, cream, deem, deme, dream, gleam, mime, neem, Nîmes, ream, scheme, scream, seam, seem, seme, steam, stream, team, teem, theme, abeam, agleam, airstream, berseem, beseem, bireme, blaspheme, bloodstream, centime, daydream, downstream, esteem, extreme, grapheme, Gulf Stream, hakim, headstream, hornbeam, ice cream, inseam, kilim, lexeme, mainstream, midstream, millime, millstream, moonbeam, morpheme, onstream, phoneme, redeem, regime, sememe, sidestream, slipstream, sunbeam, supreme, Tarim, taxeme, toneme, trireme, unseam, upstream, academe, disesteem, double-team, enthymeme, misesteem, monotreme, self-esteem, succès d'estime, treponeme
[2]**eam** \im\ see [1]IM
eaman \ē-mən\ see [1]EMON
[1]**eamed** \emt\ see EMPT
[2]**eamed** \ēmd\ beamed, steamed, teamed—*also pasts of verbs listed at* [1]EAM
eamer \ē-mər\ creamer, dreamer, femur, lemur, reamer, schemer, screamer,

seamer, steamer, streamer, blasphemer, daydreamer, redeemer

eaming \ē-miŋ\ see EEMING

eamish \ē-mish\ beamish, squeamish

eamless \ēm-ləs\ dreamless, seamless

eamon \ē-mən\ see [1]EMON

eamster \ēm-stər\ seamster, teamster

eamy \ē-mē\ beamy, creamy, dreamy, gleamy, preemie, seamy, steamy, polysemy

[1]**ean** \ē-ən\ aeon, eon, Ian, Leon, paean, peon, paeon, zein, Achaean, Actaeon, Aegean, Antaean, Archean, Augean, Chaldean, Chilean, Fijian, Korean, Kuchean, Linnaean, Mandaean, Matthean, pampean, plebeian, protean, pygmaean, Tupi-Guaranian, Tupian, apogean, Aramaean, Atlantean, Caribbean, Cerberean, circadian, cyclopean, Clytherean, Damoclean, empyrean, epigean, European, Galilean, Hasmonaean, Herculean, Jacobean, kallikrein, Maccabean, Manichaean, Mycenaean, Odyssean, panacean, perigean, Sadducean, Sisyphean, Typhoean, Tyrolean, antipodean, epicurean, Laodicean, Ponce de Leon, proboscidean, Pythagorean, terpsichorean, un-European, epithalamion, Indo-European

[2]**ean** \ēn\ see [3]INE

[3]**ean** \ȯn\ see [3]ON

[4]**ean** \ā-ən\ see [1]AYAN

eane \ēn\ see [3]INE

eaner \ē-nər\ cleaner, gleaner, keener, meaner, preener, teener, weaner, weiner, wiener, congener, demeanor, fourteener, carabiner, intervenor, misdemeanor, submariner, trampoliner

eanery \ēn-rē\ beanery, deanery, greenery, scenery, machinery, turbomachinery

eanid \ē-ə-nəd\ Leonid, Oceanid

eanie \ē-nē\ see [1]INI

eaning \ē-niŋ\ greening, leaning, meaning, screening, housecleaning, spring-cleaning, sunscreening, unmeaning, well-meaning, overweening—*also present participles of verbs listed at* [3]INE

[1]**eanist** \ē-nəst\ see [2]INIST

[2]**eanist** \ē-ə-nist\ see IANIST

eanliness \en-lē-nəs\ see ENDLINESS

eanling \ēn-liŋ\ greenling, weanling, yeanling

[1]**eanly** \ēn-lē\ cleanly, greenly, leanly, meanly, queenly, pristinely, routinely, serpentinely, uncleanly

[2]**eanly** \en-lē\ see ENDLY

eanne \ēn\ see [3]INE

eanness \ēn-nəs\ cleanness, greenness, meanness, betweenness, uncleanness

eannie \ē-nē\ see [1]INI

eano \ē-nō\ see [2]INO

eanor \ē-nər\ see EANER
eanse \enz\ see [1]ENS
eant \ent\ see [1]ENT
eany \ē-nē\ see [1]INI
eap \ēp\ see EEP
eapen \ē-pən\ see EEPEN
eaper \ē-pər\ see EEPER
eapie \ē-pē\ see EEPY
eapish \ē-pish\ see EEPISH
eapo \ē-pō\ see EPOT
[1]ear \er\ see [4]ARE
[2]ear \ir\ see [2]EER
[1]earable \er-ə-bəl\ bearable, shareable, terrible, wearable, unbearable, unwearable
[2]earable \ar-ə-bəl\ see ARABLE
earage \ir-ij\ see EERAGE
[1]earance \ir-əns\ see [1]ERENCE
[2]earance \er-əns\ see ARENCE
earch \ərch\ see URCH
[1]eard \ird\ beard, eared, tiered, weird, afeard, bat-eared, bluebeard, crop-eared, dog-eared, graybeard, lop-eared, misleared, whitebeard, chandeliered, engineered, pre-engineered—*also pasts of verbs listed at* [2]EER
[2]eard \ərd\ see IRD
eare \ir\ see [2]EER
earean \ir-ē-ən\ see [1]ERIAN
[1]eared \erd\ see AIRED
[2]eared \ird\ see [1]EARD
[1]earer \er-ər\ airer, bearer, carer, error, sharer, terror, casebearer, crossbearer, cupbearer, declarer, furbearer, pallbearer, seafarer, talebearer, torchbearer, trainbearer, wayfarer, color-bearer, standard-bearer, stretcher-bearer—*also comparatives of adjectives listed at* [4]ARE
[2]earer \ir-ər\ cheerer, clearer, fearer, hearer, mirror, shearer, smearer, coherer, sheepshearer, veneerer, electioneerer—*also comparatives of adjectives listed at* [2]EER
[3]earer \ar-ər\ airer, bearer, casebearer, crossbearer, cupbearer, declarer, furbearer, live-bearer, pallbearer, seafarer, talebearer, torchbearer, trainbearer, wayfarer, color-bearer, standard-bearer, stretcher-bearer
earful \ir-fəl\ cheerful, earful, fearful, tearful
earies \ir-ēz\ see ERIES
[1]earing \ir-iŋ\ clearing, earing, earring, gearing, God-fearing, sheepshearing, fictioneering, hard-of-hearing, orienteering—*also present participles of verbs listed at* [2]EER
[2]earing \er-iŋ\ see [1]ARING
earish \er-ish\ see [1]ARISH
earl \ərl\ see [1]IRL
earle \irl\ see [1]IRL
earler \ər-lər\ see IRLER
earless \ir-ləs\ cheerless, fearless, gearless, peerless, tearless
[1]earling \ir-liŋ\ shearling, yearling
[2]earling \ər-lən\ see ERLIN
[1]early \ir-lē\ clearly, dearly, merely, nearly, queerly, yearly, austerely, biyearly,

severely, sincerely, cavalierly, semiyearly, insincerely

[2]early \ər-lē\ see URLY

earn \ərn\ see URN

earned \ərnd\ see URNED

earner \ər-nər\ see URNER

earnist \ər-nəst\ see ERNIST

earnt \ərnt\ burnt, learnt, weren't

earring \ir-iŋ\ see [1]EARING

earsal \ər-səl\ see [1]ERSAL

earse \ərs\ see ERSE

earser \ər-sər\ see URSOR

earst \ərst\ see URST

eart \ärt\ see [1]ART

earted \ärt-əd\ hearted, parted, bighearted, coldhearted, downhearted, fainthearted, freehearted, good-hearted, greathearted, halfhearted, hard-hearted, kindhearted, largehearted, lighthearted, proudhearted, softhearted, stouthearted, truehearted, uncharted, warmhearted, weakhearted, wholehearted, brokenhearted, chickenhearted, heavyhearted, ironhearted, lionhearted, openhearted, single-hearted, stonyhearted, tenderhearted—*also pasts of verbs listed at* [1]ART

[1]earth \ärth\ see ARTH

[2]earth \ərth\ see IRTH

eartha \ər-thə\ see ERTHA

earthen \ər-th̲ən\ see URTHEN

earthy \ər-th̲ē\ see ORTHY

eartily \ärt-ᵊl-ē\ see ARTILY

eartless \ärt-ləs\ see ARTLESS

earty \ärt-ē\ see [1]ARTY

eary \ir-ē\ aerie, beery, bleary, cheery, dreary, eerie, Erie, leery, Peary, peri, quaere, query, smeary, sphery, teary, veery, weary, aweary, Kashmiri, Lake Erie, Valkyrie, world-weary, hara-kiri, miserere, overweary, whigmaleerie, Mount Dhaulagiri

eas \ē-əs\ see [1]EUS

[1]easable \ē-sə-bəl\ peaceable, increasable

[2]easable \ē-zə-bəl\ see EASIBLE

[1]easand \iz-ᵊn\ see [2]ISON

[2]easand \ēz-ᵊnd\ see EASONED

[1]ease \ēs\ see IECE

[2]ease \ēz\ see EZE

[1]eased \ēzd\ pleased, diseased—*also pasts of verbs listed at* EZE

[2]eased \ēst\ see [1]EAST

easel \ē-zəl\ bezel, deasil, diesel, easel, measle, teasel, weasel

easeless \ē-sləs\ ceaseless, creaseless, greaseless

easelly \ē-zlē\ see EASLY

easement \ēz-mənt\ easement, appeasement

[1]easer \ē-sər\ creaser, greaser, piecer, increaser, one-piecer, releaser, two-piecer

[2]easer \ē-zər\ Caesar, freezer, geezer, greaser, pleaser, sneezer, squeezer, teaser, tweezer, appeaser, brainteaser, crowd-pleaser, misfeasor, stripteaser, timepleaser

eash \ēsh\ see [2]ICHE

easible \ē-zə-bəl\ feasible, squeezable, appeasable, defeasible, infeasible,

inappeasable, indefeasible, unappeasable
easil \ē-zəl\ see EASEL
easily \ēz-lē\ see EASLY
[1]**easing** \ē-siŋ\ leasing, unceasing—*also present participles of verbs listed at* IECE
[2]**easing** \ē-ziŋ\ pleasing, subfreezing—*also present participles of verbs listed at* EZE
easingly \ē-siŋ-lē\ decreasingly, increasingly, unceasingly
easle \ē-zəl\ see EASEL
easly \ēz-ə-lē\ easily, measly, weaselly
eason \ēz-ᵊn\ reason, season, seisin, treason, disseisin, off-season, unreason, diocesan
easonable \ēz-nə-bəl\ reasonable, seasonable, treasonable, unreasonable, unseasonable
easoned \ēz-ᵊnd\ weasand, unreasoned—*also pasts of verbs listed at* EASON
easoning \ēz-niŋ\ seasoning, unreasoning
easonless \ēz-ᵊn-ləs\ reasonless, seasonless
easor \ē-zər\ see [2]EASER
[1]**east** \ēst\ beast, east, East, feast, fleeced, geest, least, piste, priest, reest, triste, yeast, archpriest, artiste, batiste, deceased, Far East, hartebeest, modiste, Near East, northeast, southeast, tachiste, arriviste, dirigiste, hartebeest, Middle East, north-northeast, pointillist, wildebeest—*also pasts of verbs listed at* IECE
[2]**east** \est\ see EST
easted \es-təd\ see ESTED
easter \ē-stər\ Dniester, Easter, keister, leister, quaestor, down-easter, northeaster, southeaster
eastie \ē-stē\ see EASTY
eastly \ēst-lē\ beastly, Priestley, priestly
easty \ē-stē\ beastie, yeasty
easurable \ezh-rə-bəl\ pleasurable, treasurable, immeasurable
[1]**easure** \ezh-ər\ leisure, measure, pleasure, treasure, admeasure, displeasure, countermeasure
[2]**easure** \ā-zhər\ see AZIER
easurer \ezh-ər-ər\ measurer, treasurer
[1]**easy** \ē-zē\ breezy, cheesy, easy, greasy, queasy, sleazy, sneezy, wheezy, pachisi, Parcheesi, speakeasy, uneasy, Zambezi
[2]**easy** \ē-sē\ see EECY
[1]**eat** \ēt\ beat, beet, bleat, cheat, cleat, Crete, deet, eat, feat, fleet, Geat, gleet, greet, heat, keet, lied, meat, meet, mete, neat, peat, Pete, pleat, seat, sheet, skeet, sleet, street, suite, sweet, teat, treat, tweet, weet, wheat, accrete, aesthete, afreet, athlete, backbeat, backseat, backstreet, bedsheet, bolete, Bradstreet, broadsheet, browbeat, buckwheat, bystreet, clipsheet, compete, compleat, complete, conceit,

concrete, crabmeat, deadbeat, deceit, defeat, delete, deplete, discreet, discrete, disseat, downbeat, drumbeat, effete, elite, en suite, entreat, escheat, esthete, excrete, facete, forcemeat, foresheet, groundsheet, heartbeat, heat-treat, helpmeet, hoofbeat, ill-treat, mainsheet, maltreat, mesquite, mincemeat, mistreat, offbeat, petite, preheat, receipt, recheat, regreet, repeat, replete, retreat, secrete, slip-sheet, sweetmeat, terete, unmeet, unseat, upbeat, vegete, volkslied, zizith, aquavit, biathlete, bittersweet, cellulite, corps d'elite, countryseat, decathlete, exegete, incomplete, indiscreet, indiscrete, lorikeet, marguerite, Marguerite, Masorete, meadowsweet, Nayarit, obsolete, overeat, overheat, Paraclete, parakeet, pentathlete, plebiscite, polychaete, progamete, self-conceit, semisweet, tête-à-tête, superheat, triathlete, winding-sheet

[2]eat \āt\ see [1]ATE

[3]eat \et\ see [1]ET

[4]eat \it\ see [1]IT

eatable \ēt-ə-bəl\ eatable, heatable, treatable, depletable, escheatable, repeatable, unbeatable

[1]eated \ēt-əd\ heated, pleated, conceited, deep-seated, repeated, overheated, superheated—*also pasts of verbs listed at* [1]EAT

[2]eated \et-əd\ see ETID

[3]eated \it-əd\ see ITTED

[1]eaten \ēt-ᵊn\ eaten, beaten, Cretan, cretin, Eaton, Eton, neaten, sweeten, wheaten, browbeaten, moth-eaten, secretin, unbeaten, worm-eaten, overeaten, weather-beaten

[2]eaten \āt-ᵊn\ see [1]ATEN

[1]eater \ēt-ər\ beater, bleater, cheater, eater, fetor, greeter, heater, liter, meter, peter, Peter, pleater, praetor, rhetor, seater, sheeter, skeeter, teeter, treater, tweeter, anteater, beefeater, blue peter, Demeter, drumbeater, eggbeater, excreter, fire-eater, flowmeter, man-eater, Main Streeter, maltreater, preheater, propraetor, repeater, saltpeter, secretor, seedeater, toadeater, Wall Streeter, windcheater, world-beater, altimeter, centiliter, centimeter, deciliter, decimeter, drunkometer, lotus-eater, milliliter, millimeter, overeater, taximeter—*also comparatives of adjectives listed at* [1]EAT

[2]eater \et-ər\ see ETTER

eatery \ēt-ə-rē\ see ETORY

[1]eath \ēth\ eath, heath, Keith, Meath, neath, sheath, wreath, beneath, bequeath, hadith, monteith, underneath

[2]eath \ē<u>th</u>\ see EATHE

eathe \ē<u>th</u>\ breathe, Meath, seethe, sheathe, teethe,

wreathe, bequeath, ensheathe, enwreathe, inbreathe, unsheathe, unwreathe, Westmeath
eathean \ē-thē-ən\ lethean, Promethean
[1]**eather** \eth-ər\ see [1]ETHER
[2]**eather** \ē-thər\ see EITHER
eathern \eth-ərn\ see ETHERN
eathery \eth-rē\ feathery, heathery, leathery
eathing \ē-thiŋ\ breathing, sheathing, teething, firebreathing
eathless \eth-ləs\ breathless, deathless
eathy \ē-thē\ heathy, lethe, wreathy
eating \ēt-iŋ\ beating, eating, meeting, seating, sheeting, sweeting, breast-beating, drumbeating, fire-eating, man-eating, unweeting, Sunday-go-to-meeting
eatise \ēt-əs\ see ETUS
[1]**eatly** \āt-lē\ see [1]ATELY
[2]**eatly** \ēt-lē\ see EETLY
eaton \ēt-ᵊn\ see [1]EATEN
[1]**eats** \ēts\ Keats—*also possessives and plurals of nouns and third person singular presents of verbs listed at* EAT
[2]**eats** \āts\ see [1]ATES
eature \ē-chər\ see EACHER
eaty \ēt-ē\ meaty, peaty, sleety, sweetie, treaty, ziti, entreaty, Tahiti, Dolomiti, spermaceti
eau \ō\ see [1]OW
eaucracy \äk-rə-sē\ see OCRACY
eauteous \üt-ē-əs\ see UTEOUS
eautiful \üt-i-fəl\ see UTIFUL
eauty \üt-ē\ see [1]OOTY
eaux \ō\ see [1]OW
eavable \ē-və-bəl\ see EIVABLE
eaval \ē-vəl\ see IEVAL
[1]**eave** \ēv\ breve, cleave, eve, Eve, greave, grieve, heave, leave, lief, peeve, reave, reeve, reive, scrieve, sheave, shrieve, sleave, sleeve, steeve, Steve, thieve, weave, weve, Abib, achieve, aggrieve, believe, bereave, conceive, deceive, inweave, khedive, Maldive, motive, naive, perceive, qui vive, receive, relieve, reprieve, retrieve, shirtsleeve, unreeve, unweave, upheave, apperceive, by-your-leave, disbelieve, Genevieve, interleave, interweave, Laccadive, make-believe, misbelieve, misconceive, preconceive, semibreve, Tel Aviv, undeceive, adam-and-eve, recitative, ticket-of-leave, underachieve, Saint Agnes' Eve
[2]**eave** \iv\ see [2]IVE
eaved \ēvd\ leaved, sleeved, aggrieved, bereaved, relieved—*also pasts of verbs listed at* [1]EAVE
eavement \ēv-mənt\ see EVEMENT
eaven \ev-ən\ devon, Devon, Evan, heaven, Kevin, leaven, levin, Nevin, seven, Sevin, sweven, eleven, replevin, South Devon
eaver \ē-vər\ see IEVER
eavers \ē-vərz\ cleavers, vivers

eaves \ēvz\ eaves, Treves, shirtsleeves

eavey \ē-vē\ peavey, divi-divi

eaward \ē-wərd\ see EEWARD

[1]**eaze** \ēz\ see EZE

[2]**eaze** \āz\ see [1]AZE

eazo \ē-zō\ see [1]IZO

eazy \ē-zē\ see [1]EASY

eb \eb\ bleb, deb, ebb, neb, pleb, reb, Reb, web, ardeb, celeb, cobweb, cubeb, Deneb, Horeb, subdeb, Zagreb, zineb, cause célèbre, Johnny Reb, spiderweb

eba \ē-bə\ Chiba, Reba, Sheba, amoeba, zareba, copaiba, Curitiba

ebate \ab-ət\ see ABIT

ebb \eb\ see EB

ebbie \eb-ē\ see EBBY

ebble \eb-əl\ pebble, rebel, treble

ebbuck \eb-ək\ kebbuck, rebec

ebby \eb-ē\ blebby, Debbie, Debby, maybe, webby, cobwebby

[1]**ebe** \ē-bē\ BB, freebie, Hebe, phoebe, Phoebe, Seabee, caribe, Galibi

[2]**ebe** \ēb\ glebe, grebe, hebe, plebe, ephebe, sahib

ebec \eb-ək\ see EBBUCK

ebel \eb-əl\ see EBBLE

eber \ā-bər\ see ABOR

ebes \ēbz\ Thebes—*also possessives and plurals of nouns listed at* EBE

eble \eb-əl\ see EBBLE

ebo \ē-bō\ see IBO

ebral \ē-brəl\ cerebral, palpebral, vertebral

ebrity \eb-rət-ē\ celebrity, muliebrity

[1]**ebs** \eps\ see EPS

[2]**ebs** \ebz\ Debs—*also possessives and plurals of nouns, third person singular presents of verbs listed at* EB

ebt \et\ see [1]ET

ebted \et-əd\ see ETID

ebtor \et-ər\ see ETTER

ebus \ē-bəs\ Phoebus, rebus, ephebus

[1]**ec** \ek\ see ECK

[2]**ec** \ets\ see ETS

eca \ē-kə\ see [1]IKA

ecal \ē-kəl\ cecal, fecal, meikle, treacle, intrathecal, bibliothecal

ecan \ek-ən\ see ECKON

ecant \ē-kənt\ piquant, secant

ecas \ā-kəs\ Turksand Caicos, Zacatecas

ecca \ek-ə\ Decca, mecca, Mecca, weka, Rebecca, Rebekah, Rijeka

eccable \ek-ə-bəl\ see ECKABLE

eccan \ek-ən\ see ECKON

ecce \ek-ē\ see ECKY

ecco \ek-ō\ see ECHO

ecency \ēs-ᵊn-sē\ decency, recency, indecency

ecent \ēs-ᵊnt\ decent, recent, indecent, obeisant

eces \ē-sēz\ see ECIES

[1]**ech** \ek\ see ECK

[2]**ech** \ək\ see UCK

[3]**ech** \esh\ see [1]ESH

[1]**eche** \āsh\ crèche, flèche, Laoighis, Leix, resh, seiche, bobeche, Bangladesh, tête-bêche, Andhra Pradesh, Madhya Pradesh, Uttar

Pradesh, Himadral Pradesh, Arunachal Pradesh
[2]eche \esh\ see [1]ESH
eche \ē-chē\ see EACHY
êche \esh\ see [1]ESH
èche \esh\ see [1]ESH
eched \echt\ see ETCHED
echerous \ech-rəs\ lecherous, treacherous
echery \ech-rē\ lechery, treachery
echie \ek-ē\ see ECKY
echin \ek-ən\ see ECKON
echo \ek-ō\ deco, echo, gecko, secco, el Greco, reecho
echnical \ek-ni-kəl\ technical, biotechnical, geotechnical
echt \ekt\ see ECT
ecia \ē-shə\ see [1]ESIA
ecially \esh-lē\ see ESHLY
ecian \ē-shən\ see [1]ETION
ecibel \es-ə-bəl\ see ESSIBLE
[1]**ecie** \ē-sē\ see EECY
[2]**ecie** \ē-shē\ see ISHI
ecies \ē-sēz\ feces, species, theses, prostheses, subspecies, exegeses
[1]**ecil** \ē-səl\ Cecil, diesel
[2]**ecil** \es-əl\ see [1]ESTLE
ecile \es-əl\ see [1]ESTLE
ecily \es-ə-lē\ see ESSALY
ecimal \es-ə-məl\ see ESIMAL
eciman \es-mən\ see ESSMAN
ecious \ē-shəs\ specious, capricious, facetious, Lucretius
ecium \ē-shē-əm\ aecium, lutecium, technetium, zoecium, androecium, apothecium, gynoecium, paramecium, perithecium
eck \ek\ beck, check, cheque, Czech, deck, dreck, fleck, heck, lek, neck, pec, peck, reck, sec, sneck, spec, speck, trek, wreak, wreck, Aztec, Baalbek, backcheck, bedeck, breakneck, Capek, cromlech, crookneck, cross-check, cusec, ewe-neck, exec, flyspeck, fore-check, foredeck, gooseneck, haček, hatcheck, henpeck, high tech, kopeck, limbeck, low-tech, Lubeck, Mixtec, paycheck, pinchbeck, Quebec, rebec, redneck, ringneck, roll-neck, roughneck, samekh, shipwreck, spot-check, Steinbeck, tenrec, Toltec, Uzbek, wryneck, xebec, afterdeck, à la grecque, Aquidneck, biotech, bodycheck, bottleneck, Chiang Kai-shek, countercheck, demi-sec, discotheque, double-check, double-deck, hunt-and-peck, leatherneck, littleneck, Pont l'évêque, quarterdeck, rubberneck, triple sec, turtleneck, Yucatec, Zapotec, cinematheque, Melchizedek, de Toulouse-Lautrec
eckable \ek-ə-bəl\ checkable, impeccable
ecked \ekt\ see ECT
ecker \ek-ər\ checker, chequer, decker, pecker, trekker, wrecker, exchequer, three-decker, woodpecker, dominicker, double-decker, rubbernecker, triple-decker
ecking \ek-iŋ\ decking, necking

ecklace \ek-ləs\ see ECKLESS

eckle \ek-əl\ deckle, freckle, heckle, shekel, speckle, kenspeckle

eckless \ek-ləs\ feckless, checkless, necklace, reckless, affectless

ecko \ek-ō\ see ECHO

eckon \ek-ən\ beckon, Brecon, Deccan, reckon, zechin, Aztecan, misreckon, Toltecan, Yucatecan

ecks \ecks\ eks\ see EX

ecky \ek-ē\ Becky, recce, techie, shimonoseki

econ \ek-ən\ see ECKON

[1]**econd** \ek-ənd\ see ECUND

[2]**econd** \ek-ənt\ see ECCANT

ecque \ek\ see ECK

ecs \eks\ see EX

ect \ekt\ necked, sect, specked, abject, affect, aspect, bisect, cathect, collect, confect, connect, convect, correct, defect, deflect, deject, detect, direct, dissect, effect, eject, elect, erect, ewe-necked, expect, goosenecked, infect, inflect, inject, insect, inspect, neglect, object, pandect, perfect, porrect, prefect, prelect, project, prospect, protect, rednecked, refect, reflect, reject, resect, respect, ring-necked, select, stiff-necked, subject, suspect, traject, transect, trisect, Utrecht, V-necked, acrolect, architect, circumspect, deselect, dialect, disaffect, disconnect, disinfect, disrespect, double-decked, genuflect, grapholect, incorrect, indirect, intellect, interject, intersect, introject, introspect, misdirect, preselect, re-collect, recollect, redirect, reelect, resurrect, retrospect, self-respect, turtlenecked, vivisect, aftereffect, hypercorrect, idiolect, interconnect, megaproject, semierect, semi-indirect—*also pasts of verbs listed at* ECK

ecta \ek-tə\ dejecta, ejecta, perfecta, trifecta

ectable \ek-tə-bəl\ affectable, collectible, correctable, deflectable, delectable, detectable, ejectable, erectable, expectable, inflectable, injectable, electable, indefectible, perfectible, projectable, respectable, disrespectable, indefectible

ectacle \ek-ti-kəl\ see ECTICAL

ectal \ek-tᵊl\ see ECTILE

ectance \ek-təns\ expectance, reflectance

ectant \ek-tənt\ expectant, humectant, injectant, protectant, disinfectant

ectar \ek-tər\ see ECTOR

ectarous \ek-trəs\ see ECTRESS

ectary \ek-tə-rē\ sectary, insectary

ected \ek-təd\ affected, collected, complected, dejected, recollected, self-affected, self-collected, self-elected, self-selected, unaffected, undirected, unexpected, unselected, inner-directed, other-directed—*also pasts of verbs listed at* ECT

ecten \ek-tən\ nekton, pecten, pectin, fibronectin, ivermectin

ecter \ek-tər\ see ECTOR

ectible \ek-tə-bəl\ see ECTABLE

ectic \ek-tik\ hectic, pectic, cathectic, eclectic, synectic, anorectic, apoplectic, catalectic, dialectic

ectical \ek-ti-kəl\ spectacle, dialectical

ectile \ek-tᵊl\ sectile, erectile, insectile, projectile, colorectal, dialectal

ectin \ek-tən\ see ECTEN

ecting \ek-tiŋ\ affecting, self-respecting, self-correcting

ection \ek-shən\ flexion, lection, section, abjection, advection, affection, bisection, collection, complexion, confection, connection, connexion, convection, correction, C-section, defection, deflection, dejection, detection, direction, dissection, ejection, election, erection, evection, infection, inflection, injection, inspection, midsection, objection, perfection, prelection, projection, protection, refection, reflection, rejection, resection, selection, subjection, subsection, trajection, transection, trisection, by-election, circumspection, disaffection, disconnection, disinfection, genuflection, imperfection, indirection, introjection, introspection, insurrection, intellection, interjection, intersection, misdirection, predilection, preselection, recollection, redirection, reelection, reinfection, resurrection, retroflexion, retrospection, vivisection, antirejection, hypercorrection, interconnection, Cesarean section

ectional \ek-shnəl\ sectional, affectional, bisectional, complexional, connectional, convectional, correctional, cross-sectional, directional, inflectional, projectional, reflectional, bidirectional, introspectional, interjectional, resurrectional, vivisectional, omnidirectional, unidirectional

ectionist \ek-shə-nəst\ perfectionist, projectionist, protectionist, selectionist, introspectionist, resurrectionist, vivisectionist

ective \ek-tiv\ advective, affective, adjective, bijective, collective, connective, convective, corrective, defective, deflective, detective, directive, effective, elective, ejective, infective, inflective, injective, invective, objective, perfective, perspective, projective, prospective, reflective, respective, selective, subjective, cost-effective,

imperfective, ineffective, intellective, introspective, nondirective, nonobjective, retrospective, cryoprotective, intersubjective
ectless \ek-ləs\ see ECKLESS
ectly \ekt-lē\ abjectly, correctly, directly, erectly, incorrectly, indirectly
ectness \ekt-nəs\ abjectness, correctness, directness, erectness, selectness, incorrectness, indirectness, hypercorrectness
ecto \ek-tō\ recto, perfecto
ectomy \ek-tə-mē\ mastectomy, vasectomy, appendectomy, hysterectomy, tonsillectomy, clitoridectomy
ector \ek-tər\ hector, Hector, lector, nectar, rector, sector, specter, vector, bisector, collector, convector, corrector, defector, deflector, detector, director, dissector, effector, ejector, elector, erector, infector, injector, inspector, neglecter, objector, perfecter, projector, prospector, protector, reflector, selector, trisector, vivisector
ectoral \ek-trəl\ spectral, pectoral, electoral, protectoral, multispectral
ectorate \ek-tə-rət\ rectorate, directorate, electorate, inspectorate, protectorate
ectory \ek-tə-rē\ rectory, directory, protectory, refectory, trajectory, ex-directory
ectral \ek-trəl\ see ECTORAL
ectress \ek-trəs\ nectarous, directress, electress, protectress
ectrix \ek-triks\ rectrix, directrix
ectrum \ek-trəm\ plectrum, spectrum, electrum
[1]**ectual** \ek-chə-wəl\ effectual, ineffectual, intellectual, anti-intellectual
[2]**ectual** \eksh-wəl\ see EXUAL
ectually \ek-chə-lē\ effectually, ineffectually, intellectually
[1]**ectural** \ek-chə-rəl\ conjectural, prefectural, architectural
[2]**ectural** \ek-shrəl\ flexural, conjectural, architectural
ecture \ek-chər\ lecture, conjecture, prefecture, architecture
ectus \ek-təs\ conspectus, prospectus
ecular \ek-yə-lər\ secular, specular, molecular
ecum \ē-kəm\ vade mecum, subpoena duces tecum
ecund \ek-ənd\ fecund, second, femtosecond, microsecond, millisecond, nanosecond—*also pasts of verbs listed at* ECKON
ecutive \ek-ət-iv\ consecutive, executive, inconsecutive
ed \ed\ see [1]EAD
e'd \ēd\ see EED
[1]**eda** \ēd-ə\ Freda, Frieda, Leda, Vida, Machida, alameda, olla podrida
[2]**eda** \ād-ə\ see [3]ADA
[1]**edal** \ed-[ə]l\ heddle, medal, meddle, pedal, peddle,

treadle, backpedal, bipedal, soft-pedal, intermeddle
[2]edal \ēd-ᵊl\ see EEDLE
edance \ēd-ᵊns\ see EDENCE
[1]edar \ed-ər\ see [2]EADER
[2]edar \ēd-ər\ see [1]EADER
edator \ed-ət-ər\ see EDITOR
edd \ed\ see [1]EAD
edda \ed-ə\ Jedda, Vedda
eddar \ed-ər\ see [2]EADER
edded \ed-əd\ see EADED
edden \ed-ᵊn\ see EADEN
edder \ed-ər\ see [2]EADER
eddie \ed-ē\ see [1]EADY
edding \ed-iŋ\ see [1]EADING
eddle \ed-ᵊl\ see [1]EDAL
eddler \ed-lər\ meddler, medlar, peddler
eddon \ed-ᵊn\ see EADEN
eddy \ed-ē\ see [1]EADY
[1]ede \ād\ see [1]ADE
[2]ede \ēd\ see EED
[3]ede \ā-dā\ see AYDAY
edeas \ēd-ē-əs\ see [1]EDIOUS
eded \ē-dəd\ see EEDED
edel \ād-əl\ see ADLE
eden \ēd-ᵊn\ Eden, Sweden, Dunedin
edence \ēd-ᵊns\ credence, impedance, precedence, antecedence
edent \ēd-ᵊnt\ credent, needn't, decedent, precedent, succedent, antecedent
[1]eder \ād-ər\ see ADER
[2]eder \ ēd-ər\ see [1]EADER
edes \ē-dēz\ Diomedes, Archimedes
edge \ej\ dredge, edge, fledge, hedge, kedge, ledge, pledge, sedge, sledge, veg, wedge, allege, frankpledge, gilt-edge, two-edged, hard-edge, knife-edge, nutsedge, straightedge, featheredge, sortilege
edged \ejd\ edged, wedged, alleged, full-fledged, gilt-edged, two-edged, unfledged, deckle-edged, double-edged—*also pasts of verbs listed at* EDGE
edger \ej-ər\ dredger, edger, hedger, ledger, leger, pledger
edgie \ej-ē\ see EDGY
edgy \ej-ē\ edgy, ledgy, Reggie, sedgy, veggie, wedgie, wedgy, Himeji
edi \ād-ē\ see ADY
edia \ēd-ē-ə\ media, Media, acedia, cyclopedia, via media, encyclopedia
edial \ēd-ē-əl\ medial, predial, remedial
edian \ēd-ē-ən\ median, comedian, tragedian
ediant \ēd-ē-ənt\ see EDIENT
edible \ed-ə-bəl\ credible, edible, spreadable, incredible, inedible
[1]edic \ēd-ik\ comedic, cyclopedic, logaoedic, orthopedic, encyclopedic
[2]edic \ed-ik\ Eddic, medic, comedic, paramedic, samoyedic
[3]edic \ād-ik\ see [1]ADIC
edicable \ed-i-kə-bəl\ medicable, predicable, immedicable
edical \ed-i-kəl\ medical, pedicle, premedical, biomedical, paramedical
edicate \ed-i-kət\ dedicate, predicate

edicle \ed-i-kəl\ see EDICAL
edience \ēd-ē-əns\ expedience, obedience, disobedience, inexpedience
edient \ēd-ē-ənt\ mediant, expedient, ingredient, obedient, submediant, disobedient, inespedient
ediment \ed-ə-mənt\ pediment, sediment, impediment
edin \ēd-ᵊn\ see EDEN
eding \ēd-iŋ\ see [1]EEDING
[1]**edious** \ēd-ē-əs\ tedious, supersedeas
[2]**edious** \ē-jəs\ see EGIS
edist \ēd-əst\ orthopedist, encyclopedist
edit \ed-ət\ credit, edit, accredit, coedit, discredit, noncredit, reedit, subedit, copyedit
editor \ed-ət-ər\ creditor, editor, predator, coeditor, subeditor
edium \ēd-ē-əm\ medium, tedium, cypripedium
edlar \ed-lər\ see EDDLER
edley \ed-lē\ deadly, medley, redly, chance-medley
edly \ed-lē\ see EDLEY
[1]**edo** \ēd-ō\ credo, lido, Lido, speedo, aikido, libido, Toledo, torpedo, tuxedo
[2]**edo** \ād-ō\ see [2]ADO
[3]**edo** \ēd-ə\ see [1]EDA
[4]**edo** \e-dō\ Edo, meadow, Yedo
edom \ēd-əm\ see EDUM
edon \ēd-ᵊn\ bleeding, Eden, steading, Sarpedon, boustrophedon
edouin \ed-wən\ see EDWIN
edra \ē-drə\ Phaedra, cathedra
edral \ē-drəl\ cathedral, dihedral, trihedral, hemihedral, holohedral, octahedral, pentahedral, polyhedral, procathedral, tetrahedral, dodecahedral, icosahedral, tetartohedral
edro \ā-drō\ Pedro, Murviedro
edulous \ej-ə-ləs\ credulous, sedulous, incredulous
edum \ēd-əm\ Edam, Edom, freedom, sedum
edure \ē-jər\ besieger, procedure, supersedure
edwin \ed-wən\ Edwin, bedouin
[1]**ee** \ē\ b, be, bee, Brie, c, cay, cee, Cree, d, dee, Dee, dree, e, fee, flea, flee, free, g, gee, ghee, gie, glee, gree, he, key, Key, Klee, knee, lea, lee, Lee, Leigh, li, me, mi, p, pea, plea, pree, quay, re, scree, sea, see, she, shri, si, ski, spree, sri, t, tea, tee, the, thee, three, ti, tree, Tshi, twee, Twi, v, vee, we, wee, whee, ye, z, zee, agley, aiguille, agree, alee, ani, Bacchae, bailee, Bangui, banshee, bargee, bawbee, Belgae, Black Sea, bohea, bootee, bougie, buckshee, bungee, burgee, Bt, Capri, carefree, Castries, CB, CD, Chablis, Chaldee, chick-pea, Chi-li, chili, confit, cowpea, croquis, curie, Curie, Dead Sea, debris, decree, deep-sea, degree, Denis, donee, DP, draftee, drawee, Dundee, emcee, ennui, esprit, etui, farci, feoffee, foresee, fusee, GB, germfree, glacis, goatee, grand prix, grandee, grantee, GT, heart-free, he/she, HIV,

Horae, IC, IV, Jaycee, jaygee, jayvee, knock-knee, KP, latchkey, lessee, look-see, low-key, LP, mame, maquis, Marie, marquee, MC, métis, Midi, mille-feuille, muggee, must-see, Nancy, ngwee, OD, off-key, ogee, Osee, Parcae, pardie, passkey, Pawnee, payee, PC, perdie, per se, PG, pledgee, pongee, post-free, précis, puree, puttee, qt, raki, rani, razee, rooftree, rupee, rushee, RV, sati, scotfree, settee, Shaanxi, Shanxi, Shawnee, s/he, sightsee, signee, sirree, spadille, spahi, spondee, squeegee, squilgee, standee, strophe, suttee, sycee, T_3, T-3, TB, testee, 3-D, titi, to-be, topee, towhee, townee, trainee, trustee, trusty, Tupi, turfski, turnkey, tutee, Tutsi, tutti, TV, unbe, vendee, vestee, Volsci, vouchee, whangee, whoopee, would-be, Yang-Tze, yen-shee, abatis, ABC, ABD, absentee, addressee, adoptee, advisee, alienee, allottee, ambergris, AMP, amputee, appellee, appointee, après-ski, arrestee, assignee, attendee, B.V.D., Bahai, barley-bree, batterie, billi-bi, bonhomie, booboisie, bourgeoisie, brasserie, brusquerie, bumblebee, camporee, cap-a-pie, causerie, CCD, chickaree, chimpanzee, coati, Coligny, committee, conferee, consignee, counselee, context-free, counterplea, Danae, DDD, Debussy, departee, DDT, debauchee, DDE, deportee, dernier cri, deshabille, designee, detainee, devisee, devotee, diploe, disagree, discharge, dishabille, divorce, divorcee, DME, DMT, dungaree, duty-free, eau-de-vie, employee, endorsee, enlistee, enrollee, epopee, escadrille, escapee, ESP, evictee, expellee, FAD, fancy-free, fantasie, fantasy, fedayee, filigree, fleur-de-lis, formulae, franchisee, fricassee, galilee, Galilee, garnishee, gaucherie, Gemini, GTP, guarani, guarantee, Hawaii, honeybee, honoree, humble-bee, hydro-ski, IgE, IgG, inductee, internee, invitee, IUD, jacquerie, jamboree, Jiangxi, jus soli, Kayseri, kidnappee, LCD, LED, legatee, libelee, licensee, LSD, maître d', manatee, Medici, millidegree, murderee, NAD, nominee, obligee, oversea, oversee, parolee, parti pris, patentee, pedigree, peppertree, picotee, piroshki, point d'appui, potpourri, praecipe, presentee, promisee, rapparee, referee, refugee, rejectee, renminbi, repartee, retiree, retrainee, returnee, Rosemarie, RPV, saddletree, Sadducee, San Luis, sangaree, Savaii, selectee, Semele, shivaree, snickersnee, SOB, SST, STD,

Tenebrae, Tennessee, thirty-three, TNT, toile de Jouy, torii, transferee, undersea, Urümqi, vaccinee, value-free, verdigris, VIP, vis-à-vis, warrantee, Adar Sheni, Agri Dagi, alienee, biographee, bouquet garni, casus belli, charcuterie, charivari, chincherinchee, chinoiserie, covenantee, DBCP, dedicatee, de Medici, delegatee, distributee, ESOP, evacuee, examinee, exuviae, facetiae, fait accompli, felo-de-se, fortunately, Galilei, HTLV, interrogee, interviewee, jaborandi, Jiamusi, minutiae, Omega-3, Pasiphae, patisserie, prima facie, reliquiae, relocatee, Sargasso Sea, Simon Legree, Sault Sainte Marie, Southend on Sea, communicatee, HTLV-III, taedium vitae, Tupi-Guarani, ignoratio elenchi, petitio principii

[2]ee \ā\ see [1]AY

ée \ā\ see [1]AY

eeable \ē-ə-bəl\ seeable, skiable, agreeable, foreseeable, disagreeable

eebie \ē-bē\ see [1]EBE

eece \ēs\ see IECE

eeced \ēst\ see [1]EAST

eech \ēch\ see EACH

eecher \ē-chər\ see EACHER

eeches \ich-əz\ see ITCHES

eeching \ē-chiŋ\ breeching, far-reaching—*also present participles of verbs listed at* EACH

eechy \ē-chē\ see EACHY

eecy \ē-sē\ fleecy, greasy, specie, Tbilisi, AC/DC

eed \ēd\ bead, Bede, bleed, brede, breed, cede, creed, deed, feed, Gide, glede, gleed, greed, he'd, heed, keyed, knead, kneed, lead, mead, Mead, Mede, meed, need, plead, read, rede, reed, Reed, Reid, screed, seed, she'd, speed, steed, swede, Swede, treed, tweed, Tweed, we'd, weed, accede, airspeed, allseed, bindweed, birdseed, blueweed, bourride, breast-feed, bugseed, burweed, cheerlead, chickweed, concede, crossbreed, cudweed, debride, degreed, duckweed, exceed, fairlead, fireweed, flaxseed, Godspeed, gulfweed, half-breed, hand-feed, hawkweed, hayseed, high-speed, horseweed, impede, implead, inbreed, indeed, ironweed, Jamshid, jetbead, knapweed, knotweed, Lake Mead, linseed, lip-read, milkweed, misdeed, mislead, misread, moonseed, nosebleed, off-speed, oilseed, pigweed, pinweed, pokeweed, pondweed, Port Said, precede, proceed, proofread, ragweed, rapeseed, recede, reseed, rockweed, seaweed, secede, self-feed, Siegfried, sight-read, silkweed, smartweed, snakeweed, sneezeweed, speed-read, spoon-feed, stall-feed, stampede, stickseed, stickweed, stinkweed, succeed, ten-speed, tickseed, weak-kneed, witchweed, wormseed, aniseed, antecede, beggarweed, bitterweed, bottle-feed, bugleweed, butterweed, carpetweed, centipede, copyread, cottonseed, cottonweed, crazyweed, Ganymede, interbreed, intercede, interplead, jewelweed, jimsonweed, locoweed, millipede, overfeed, pedigreed, pickerelweed, pumpkinseed, retrocede, riverweed, rosinweed, Runnymede, silverweed, supersede, thimbleweed, tumbleweed, underfeed, waterweed, velocipede

eedal \ēd-ᵊl\ see EEDLE

eeded \ē-dəd\ beaded, deeded, kneaded, receded—*also pasts of verbs listed at* EED

eeder \ēd-ər\ see [1]EADER

eedful \ēd-fəl\ heedful, needful

[1]**eeding** \ēd-iŋ\ bleeding, breeding, leading, reading, reeding, inbreeding, linebreeding, lipreading, outbreeding, preceding, speed-reading

[2]**eeding** \ēd-ᵊn\ see EDON

eedle \ēd-ᵊl\ aedile, beadle, credal, creedal, daedal, needle, wheedle

eedless \ēd-ləs\ deedless, heedless, needless, seedless

eedn't \ēd-ᵊnt\ see EDENT

eedo \ēd-ō\ see [1]EDO

eedom \ēd-əm\ see EDUM

eeds \ēdz\ Leeds, needs, Beskids, proceeds—*also plurals and possessives of nouns and third person singular presents of verbs listed at* EED

eedsman \ēdz-mən\ beadsman, seedsman

eedy \ēd-ē\ beady, deedy, greedy, needy, reedy, seedy, speedy, tweedy, weedy

eef \ēf\ see [1]IEF

eefe \ēf\ see [1]IEF

eefy \ē-fē\ beefy, leafy, reefy

eegee \ē-jē\ see IJI

eeing \ē-iŋ\ seeing, skiing, farseeing, ill-being, sight-seeing, turfskiing, well-being, heli-skiing, waterskiing

[1]**eek** \ik\ see ICK

[2]**eek** \ēk\ see [1]EAK

eeked \ēkt\ see [2]EAKED

eeken \ē-kən\ see EACON

eeker \ē-kər\ see [1]EAKER

eekie \ē-kē\ see EAKY

eeking \ē-kiŋ\ see [1]EAKING

eekly \ē-klē\ bleakly, chicly, sleekly, weakly, weekly, treacly, biweekly, midweekly, newsweekly, triweekly, semiweekly

eeks \ēks\ see [1]IXE

eeky \ē-kē\ see EAKY

eel \ēl\ see [2]EAL

eelable \ē-lə-bəl\ see EALABLE

eele \ēl\ see [2]EAL

eeled \ēld\ see IELD

eeler \ē-lər\ see EALER

eeley \ē-lē\ see EELY

eelie \ē-lē\ see EELY

eelin \ē-lən\ see ELIN

eeling \ē-liŋ\ ceiling, dealing,

Ealing, feeling, peeling, shieling, wheeling, appealing, Darjeeling, freewheeling, self-dealing, self-feeling, self-sealing, unfeeling, double-dealing, self-revealing, snowmobiling, unappealing—*also present participles of verbs listed at* [2]EAL

eelson \el-sən\ see ELSON

eely \ē-lē\ Chi-li, dele, eely, Ely, freely, Greeley, mealie, mealy, really, seely, steelie, steely, stele, surreally, syli, vealy, wheelie, scungilli, Swahili, campanile, contumely, Isle of Ely, monostele, touchy-feely

eem \ēm\ see [1]EAM

eeman \ē-mən\ see [1]EMON

eemer \ē-mər\ see EAMER

eemie \ē-mē\ see EAMY

eeming \ē-miŋ\ seeming, streaming, redeeming, unbeseeming—*also present participles of verbs listed at* [1]EAM

eemly \ēm-lē\ seemly, supremely, unseemly

[1]een \in\ see [1]IN

[2]een \ēn\ see [3]INE

e'en \ēn\ see [3]INE

eena \ē-nə\ see [2]INA

eene \ēn\ see [3]INE

eener \ē-nər\ see EANER

eenery \ēn-rē\ see EANERY

eening \ē-niŋ\ see EANING

eenling \ēn-liŋ\ see EANLING

eenly \ēn-lē\ see [1]EANLY

eenness \ēn-nəs\ see EANNESS

eens \ēnz\ Queens, teens, Grenadines, Philippines, smithereens

eenwich \in-ich\ see INACH

eeny \ē-nē\ see [1]INI

eep \ēp\ beep, bleep, cheap, cheep, clepe, creep, deep, heap, jeep, Jeep, keep, leap, neap, neep, peep, reap, seep, sheep, sleep, sneap, steep, sweep, threap, veep, weep, asleep, barkeep, bopeep, dustheap, housekeep, knee-deep, skin-deep, upkeep, upsweep, overleap, oversleep, Lakshadweep, Louis Philippe

eepage \ē-pij\ creepage, seepage

eepen \ē-pən\ cheapen, deepen, steepen

eepence \əp-əns\ see UPPANCE

eepenny \əp-nē\ see OPENNY

eeper \ē-pər\ beeper, creeper, keeper, leaper, Dnieper, peeper, reaper, sleeper, sweeper, weeper, barkeeper, beekeeper, bookkeeper, crowkeeper, doorkeeper, gamekeeper, gatekeeper, goalkeeper, greenkeeper, groundskeeper, housekeeper, innkeeper, lockkeeper, minesweeper, peacekeeper, scorekeeper, shopkeeper, stockkeeper, storekeeper, timekeeper, zookeeper, honeycreeper—*also comparatives of adjectives listed at* EEP

eepie \ē-pē\ see EEPY

eeping \ē-piŋ\ creeping, keeping, weeping, beekeeping, bookkeeping, gatekeeping, housekeeping, minesweeping, peacekeeping, safekeeping, timekeeping

eepish \ē-pish\ cheapish, sheepish

eeple \ē-pəl\ see EOPLE

eepy \ē-pē\ cheapie, creepy, seepy, sleepy, sweepy, tepee, tipi, weepie, weepy

[1]eer \ē-ər\ freer, seer, skier, we're, CBer, decreer, foreseer, sightseer, overseer, water-skier

[2]eer \ir\ beer, bier, blear, cere, cheer, clear, dear, deer, drear, ear, fear, fere, fleer, gear, hear, here, jeer, Lear, leer, mere, mir, near, peer, pier, Pierre, queer, rear, schmear, sear, seer, sere, shear, sheer, skirr, smear, sneer, spear, speer, sphere, spier, steer, tear, tier, Trier, Tyr, veer, were, year, adhere, Aesir, Ajmer, ambeer, appear, arrear, Asir, austere, Ayrshire, Berkshire, besmear, brassiere, Cape Fear, career, cashier, cashmere, Cheshire, chimere, clavier, cohere, compeer, destrier, dog-ear, Ellesmere, emir, Empire, endear, ensphere, eyrir, Fafnir, Fifeshire, Flintshire, footgear, frontier, gambier, Goodyear, haltere, Hampshire, headgear, inhere, Izmir, Kashmir, kefir, killdeer, laveer, light-year, man-year, menhir, mishear, monsieur, mouse-ear, nadir, Nairnshire, out-year, Pamir, Perthshire, pickeer, portiere, premier, premiere, redear, rehear, reindeer, revere, Revere, Robespierre, revers, Saint Pierre, santir, severe, Shakespeare, Shropshire, sincere, slick-ear, tapir, uprear, Vanir, veneer, vizier, voir dire, wheatear, Wiltshire, Ymir, Yorkshire, zaire, Zaire, atmosphere, auctioneer, balladeer, bandolier, bayadere, Bedfordshire, Bedivere, belvedere, biosphere, black-tailed deer, bombardier, boutonniere, brigadier, buccaneer, budgeteer, Cambridgeshire, cameleer, cannoneer, cassimere, cavalier, chandelier, chanticleer, chevalier, chiffonier, chocolatier, commandeer, corsetiere, cuirassier, Denbighshire, Derbyshire, diapir, disappear, domineer, Dumfriesshire, ecosphere, Elzevir, engineer, fictioneer, financier, fourdrinier, fusilier, gadgeteer, gasolier, gazetteer, Gloucestershire, gondolier, grenadier, Guinevere, halberdier, hemisphere, Herefordshire, Hertfordshire, IJsselmere, insincere, interfere, jardiniere, junketeer, kerseymere, Lanarkshire, Lancashire, lavaliere, leafleteer, marketeer, Meyerbeer, missileer, Monmouthshire, Morayshire, mountaineer, Mount Ranier, muleteer, musketeer, mutineer, Oxfordshire, overhear, overseer, oversteer, pamphleteer, Pembrokeshire, persevere, pioneer, pistoleer, pontonier, privateer, profiteer, puppeteer, racketeer, Radnorshire, rocketeer, Rutlandshire, scrutineer, Selkirkshire, sloganeer, sonneteer, souvenir, Staffordshire, stratosphere, summiteer, Tyne and Wear, understeer, volunteer, Warwickshire, white-tailed deer, Windermere, Worcestershire, yesteryear, acyclovir, animalier, black marketeer, Buckinghamshire, Clackmannanshire, carabineer, Caernarvonshire, Cardiganshire, Carmarthenshire, charioteer, conventioneer, Dunbartonshire, electioneer, Eskisehir, Glamorganshire, free-marketeer, harquebusier, Huntingdonshire, Invernessshire, Kincardineshire, Montgomeryshire, Northamptonshire, Nottinghamshire, Merionethshire

e'er \er\ see [4]ARE

eerage \ir-ij\ peerage, steerage, arrearage

eered \ird\ see [1]EARD

eerer \ir-ər\ see [2]EARER

eeress \ir-əs\ see EROUS

eerful \ir-fəl\ see EARFUL

[1]**eerie** \ir-ē\ see EARY

[2]**eerie** \ē-rē\ see EIRIE

eering \ir-iŋ\ see [1]EARING

eerist \ir-əst\ see [1]ERIST

eerless \ir-ləs\ see EARLESS

eerly \ir-lē\ see [1]EARLY

eersman \irz-mən\ steersman, frontiersman

eerut \ir-ət\ see IRIT

eery \ir-ē\ see EARY

ees \ēz\ see EZE

eese \ēz\ see EZE

eesh \ēsh\ see [2]ICHE

eesi \ē-zē\ see [1]EASY

eesia \ē-zhə\ see [2]ESIA

eesome \ē-səm\ gleesome, threesome

[1]**eest** \āst\ see ACED

[2]**eest** \ēst\ see [1]EAST

eesy \ē-zē\ see [1]EASY

eet \ēt\ see [1]EAT

eetah \ēt-ə\ see [2]ITA

eete \āt-ē\ see ATY

eeten \ēt-ᵊn\ see [1]EATEN

eeter \ēt-ər\ see [1]EATER

eethe \ēth\ see EATHE

eether \ē-thər\ see EITHER

eething \ē-thiŋ\ see EATHING

eetie \ēt-ē\ see EATY

eeting \ēt-iŋ\ see EATING

eetle \ēt-ᵊl\ see ETAL

eetly \ēt-lē\ featly, fleetly, neatly, sweetly, completely, concretely, discreetly, discretely, effetely, bittersweetly, incompletely, indiscreetly

eety \ēt-ē\ see EATY

ee-um \ē-əm\ see [1]EUM

eeve \ēv\ see [1]EAVE

eeved \ēvd\ see EAVED

eeves \ēvz\ see EAVES

eevil \ē-vəl\ see IEVAL

eevish \ē-vish\ peevish, thievish

eeward \ē-wərd\ leeward, Leeward, seaward
eewee \ē-wē\ kiwi, peewee, pewee
eewit \ü-ət\ see UET
eez \ēz\ see EZE
eezable \ē-zə-bəl\ see EASIBLE
eeze \ēz\ see EZE
eezer \ē-zər\ see [2]EASER
eezing \ē-ziŋ\ see [2]EASING
eezy \ē-zē\ see [1]EASY
[1]**ef** \ef\ chef, clef, deaf, ef, f, lev, ref, teff, aleph, Brezhnev, enfeoff, H-F, Kiev, Lwiw, stone-deaf, tone-deaf, emf, Kishinev
[2]**ef** \ā\ see [1]AY
[3]**ef** \ēf\ see [1]IEF
efanie \ef-ə-nē\ see EPHONY
efany \ef-ə-nē\ see EPHONY
efe \ef-ē\ see EFFIE
eferable \ef-rə-bəl\ preferable, referable
eference \ef-rəns\ deference, preference, reference, cross-reference
eferent \ef-rənt\ deferent, referent
eff \ef\ see [1]EF
effer \ef-ər\ see EPHOR
efic \ef-ik\ Efik, benefic, malefic
eficence \ef-ə-səns\ beneficence, maleficence
efik \e-fik\ see EFIC
efsk \efsk\ Izhefsk, Profopyevsk
eft \eft\ cleft, deft, eft, heft, klepht, left, theft, weft, bereft
efty \ef-tē\ hefty, lefty
[1]**eg** \āg\ Craig, plague, vague, stravage, The Hague
[2]**eg** \eg\ beg, Craig, dreg, egg, gleg, Greg, Gregg, keg, leg, peg, reg, skeg, squeg, yegg, blackleg, bootleg, bowleg, dogleg, foreleg, jackleg, jake leg, muskeg, nutmeg, redleg, renege, roughleg, Tuareg, unpeg, Winnipeg, mumblety-peg
[3]**eg** \ej\ see EDGE
[1]**ega** \eg-ə\ omega, rutabaga
[2]**ega** \ā-gə\ see [2]AGA
[3]**ega** \ē-gə\ see [1]IGA
egal \ē-gəl\ beagle, eagle, egal, legal, regal, illegal, porbeagle, spread-eagle, viceregal, extralegal, paralegal, medicolegal
egan \ē-gən\ Megan, vegan, Mohegan
egas \ā-gəs\ see AGUS
[1]**ege** \ezh\ barege, cortege, Liège, manege, solfege
[2]**ege** \eg\ see [2]EG
[3]**ege** \ej\ see EDGE
[4]**ege** \ēg\ see IGUE
[5]**ege** \ig\ see IG
eged \ejd\ see EDGED
egel \āgəl\ see AGEL
egent \ē-jənt\ regent, sejant, allegiant, vice-regent
eger \ej-ər\ see EDGER
egg \eg\ see [2]EG
eggar \eg-ər\ see EGGER
eggary \eg-ə-rē\ beggary, Gregory
egger \eg-ər\ beggar, bootlegger, Heidegger, thousand-legger
eggie \ej-ē\ see EDGY
eggio \ej-ē-ō\ Reggio, arpeggio, solfeggio
eggs \egz\ see EGS

eggy \eg-ē\ dreggy, eggy, leggy, Peggy, plaguey, Carnegie
egia \ē-jə\ Ouija, aqua regia, aquilegia, paraplegia, quadriplegia
egian \ē-jən\ see EGION
egiant \ē-jənt\ see EGENT
egiate \ē-jət\ collegiate, elegit, intercollegiate
egic \ē-jik\ strategic, paraplegic, quadriplegic
egie \eg-ē\ see EGGY
egion \ē-jən\ legion, region, Norwegian, subregion, collegian
egious \ē-jəs\ see EGIS
egis \ē-jəs\ aegis, egis, Regis, tedious, egregious
egit \ē-jət\ see EGIATE
egm \em\ see [1]EM
egn \ān\ see [1]ANE
egnant \eg-nənt\ pregnant, regnant, impregnant, unpregnant
egnly \ān-lē\ see AINLY
egno \ān-yō\ see [1]ENO
[1]**ego** \ē-gō\ chigoe, ego, Vigo, amigo, alter ego, impetigo, superego
[2]**ego** \ā-gō\ see [2]AGO
egory \eg-ə-rē\ see EGGARY
egro \ē-grō\ Negro, Montenegro
egs \egz\ sheerlegs, yellowlegs, butter-and-eggs, daddy longlegs—*also plurals and possessives of nouns and third person singular presents of verbs listed at* [2]EG
egular \eg-lər\ see EGLER
[1]**eh** \ā\ see [1]AY
[2]**eh** \a\ see [3]AH
ehen \ān\ see [1]ANE
ehner \ā-nər\ see AINER
[1]**ei** \ēk\ dreich, skeigh
[2]**ei** \ā\ see [1]AY
[3]**ei** \ī\ see [1]Y
[1]**eia** \ē-ə\ see [1]IA
[2]**eia** \ī-ə\ see [1]IAH
eial \ē-əl\ see [1]EAL
[1]**eian** \ē-ən\ see [1]EAN
[2]**eian** \ā-ən\ see [1]AYAN
eic \ē-ik\ oleic, epigeic, logorrheic, mythopoeic, onomatopoeic
eich \ēk\ see [1]EI
eiche \āsh\ see [1]ECHE
eickel \ī-kəl\ see YCLE
[1]**eid** \āt\ see [1]ATE
[2]**eid** \īt\ see [1]ITE
[3]**eid** \ēd\ see EED
[1]**eidel** \ād-əl\ see ADLE
[2]**eidel** \īd-əl\ see IDAL
eidi \īd-ē\ see IDAY
eidon \īd-ən\ see IDEN
eier \īr\ see [1]IRE
eifer \ef-ər\ see EPHOR
[1]**eige** \āzh\ beige, assuage
[2]**eige** \ā\ see [1]AY
eiger \ī-gər\ see IGER
[1]**eigh** \ā\ see [1]AY
[2]**eigh** \ē\ see [1]EE
eighbor \ā-bər\ see ABOR
[1]**eight** \āt\ see [1]ATE
[2]**eight** \īt\ see [1]ITE
eighter \āt-ər\ see ATOR
eightless \āt-ləs\ see ATELESS
eights \īts\ see IGHTS
eighty \āt-ē\ see ATY
eign \ān\ see [1]ANE
eigner \ā-nər\ see AINER
eii \ā\ see [1]AY
eiian \ā-ən\ see [1]AYAN
eiji \ā-jē\ see AGY
eik \ēk\ see [1]EAK

eikh \ēk\ see [1]EAK
eikle \ē-kəl\ see ECAL
[1]**eil** \āl\ see AIL
[2]**eil** \el\ see [1]EL
[3]**eil** \ēl\ see [2]EAL
[4]**eil** \īl\ see [1]ILE
eila \ē-lə\ see [1]ELA
eiled \āld\ see AILED
eiler \ī-lər\ see ILAR
[1]**eiling** \ā-liŋ\ see AILING
[2]**eiling** \ē-liŋ\ see EELING
eill \ēl\ see [2]EAL
eillance \ā-ləns\ see ALENCE
eillant \ā-lənt\ see ALANT
[1]**eilles** \ā\ see [1]AY
[2]**eilles** \ālz\ see ALES
eilly \ā-lē\ see AILY
[1]**eim** \ām\ see [1]AME
[2]**eim** \īm\ see [1]IME
eimer \ī-mər\ see [1]IMER
[1]**eims** \ä^{n}s\ see [1]ANCE
[2]**eims** \ēmz\ Reims, Rheims—*also possessives and plurals of nouns and third person singular presents of verbs listed at* [1]EAM
[1]**ein** \ān\ see [1]ANE
[2]**ein** \ē-ən\ see [1]EAN
[3]**ein** \ēn\ see [3]INE
[4]**ein** \īn\ see [1]INE
[1]**eine** \ān\ see [1]ANE
[2]**eine** \ēn\ see [3]INE
[3]**eine** \ī-nə\ see [1]INA
[4]**eine** \en\ see [1]EN
eined \ānd\ see AINED
[1]**einer** \ā-nər\ see AINER
[2]**einer** \ē-nər\ see EANER
eing \ē-iŋ\ see EEING
einie \ī-nē\ see [1]INY
eining \ā-niŋ\ see AINING
einous \ā-nəs\ see AYNESS
eins \ānz\ see AINS
einsman \ānz-mən\ see AINSMAN
eint \ānt\ see AINT
einte \ant\ see [5]ANT
einture \an-chər\ see [2]ANCHER
einy \ā-nē\ see AINY
eipt \ēt\ see [1]EAT
eir \er\ see [4]ARE
eira \ir-ə\ see [2]ERA
eird \ird\ see [1]EARD
eiress \ar-əs\ see [2]ARIS
eiric \ī-rik\ see YRIC
eiro \er-ō\ see [2]ERO
eirs \erz\ see AIRS
[1]**eis** \ās\ see [1]ACE
[2]**eis** \ē-əs\ see [1]EUS
[3]**eis** \īs\ see [1]ICE
eisant \ēs-^{ə}nt\ see ECENT
eise \ēz\ see EZE
eisel \ī-zəl\ see [2]ISAL
eisen \īz-^{ə}n\ see [1]IZEN
[1]**eiser** \ī-sər\ see ICER
[2]**eiser** \ī-zər\ see IZER
[1]**eisha** \ā-shə\ see ACIA
[2]**elsha** \ē-shə\ see [1]ESIA
eisin \ēz-^{ə}n\ see EASON
eiss \īs\ see [1]ICE
eissen \īs-^{ə}n\ see [1]ISON
[1]**eist** \ā-əst\ see AYEST
[2]**eist** \īst\ see [1]IST
[1]**eister** \ī-stər\ shyster, concertmeister, kapellmeister
[2]**eister** \ē-stər\ see EASTER
eisure \ē-zhər\ see EIZURE
[1]**eit** \ē-ət\ fiat, albeit, howbeit
[2]**eit** \it\ see [1]IT
[3]**eit** \ēt\ see [1]EAT
[4]**eit** \īt\ see [1]ITE
eited \ēt-əd\ see [1]EATED
[1]**eiter** \it-ər\ see ITTER
[2]**eiter** \ī-tər\ see [1]ITER
eith \ēth\ see [1]EATH

either \ē-th̲ər\ breather, either, neither, teether

eitus \īt-əs\ see ITIS

eity \ē-ət-ē\ deity, velleity, corporeity, spontaneity, synchroneity, diaphaneity, homogeneity, incorporeity, instantaneity, contemporaneity, extemporaneity, heterogeneity, inhomogeneity

eivable \ē-və-bəl\ cleavable, achievable, believable, conceivable, deceivable, perceivable, receivable, relievable, retrievable, imperceivable, inconceivable, irretrievable, unbelievable, unconceivable

eive \ēv\ see [1]EAVE

eiver \ē-vər\ see IEVER

eix \āsh\ see [1]ECHE

[1]**eize** \āz\ see [1]AZE

[2]**eize** \ēz\ see EZE

eizure \ē-zhər\ leisure, seizure

ejant \ē-jənt\ see EGENT

eji \ej-ē\ see EDGY

ejo \ā-ō\ see [1]EO

ek \ek\ see ECK

[1]**eka** \ek-ə\ see ECCA

[2]**eka** \ē-kə\ see [1]IKA

ekah \ek-ə\ see ECCA

eke \ēk\ see [1]EAK

ekel \ek-əl\ see ECKLE

ekh \ek\ see ECK

eki \ek-ē\ see ECKY

ekker \ek-ər\ see ECKER

ekoe \ē-kō\ see ICOT

ekton \ek-tən\ see ECTEN

[1]**el** \el\ bel, bell, Bell, belle, cel, cell, dell, dwell, el, ell, fell, gel, Hel, hell, jell, knell, l, mell, quell, sel, sell, shell, smell, snell, spell, swell, tell, they'll, well, yell, Adele, Ardell, artel, barbell, befell, Blackwell, bluebell, boatel, bombshell, Boswell, botel, bridewell, cadelle, cartel, carvel, chandelle, clamshell, compel, cormel, cornel, corral, cowbell, Cromwell, cupel, Danielle, diel, dispel, doorbell, dumbbell, duxelles, echelle, eggshell, Estelle, excel, expel, farewell, fjeld, foretell, gabelle, gazelle, Giselle, gromwell, handbell, hard-shell, harebell, hotel, impel, indwell, inkwell, jurel, lampshell, lapel, marcel, maxwell, Maxwell, micelle, Michele, Michelle, misspell, morel, Moselle, motel, nacelle, Nobel, noel, nouvelle, nutshell, oat-cell, Orel, Orwell, outsell, pall-mall, Parnell, pastel, pell-mell, pixel, pointelle, presell, propel, quenelle, rakehell, rappel, Ravel, rebel, refel, repel, respell, retell, riel, Rochelle, rondel, saurel, scalpel, seashell, sequel, Seychelles, soft-shell, solgel, speedwell, spinel, stairwell, unsell, unwell, upwell, Weddell, wind-bell, Annabelle, APL, aquarelle, asphodel, Azazel, bagatelle, BAL, barbicel, bechamel, brocatelle, Camberwell, caramel, caravel, carousel, cascabel, chanterelle,

chaparral, Charles Martel, citadel, clientele, cockleshell, Cozumel, damozel, decibel, demoiselle, fare-thee-well, fontanel, immortelle, Isabel, Isabelle, Jezebel, kiss-and-tell, lenticel, mangonel, muscatel, ne'er-do-well, Neufchatel, nonpareil, organelle, oversell, parallel, pedicel, pennoncel, personnel, petronel, Philomel, pimpernel, show-and-tell, tortoiseshell, undersell, T4 cell, villanelle, William Tell, zinfandel, Aix-la-Chapelle, au naturel, crème caramel, mademoiselle, maître d'hôtel, matériel, Mont-Saint-Michel, spirituel, T-helper cell, Thompson's gazelle, VLDL, antiparallel, antipersonnel, AWOL

[2]**el** \āl\ see AIL

[1]**ela** \ē-lə\ Gila, Leila, Lela, selah, sheila, Sheila, stela, Vila, Braila, candela, tequila, weigela, sheila, Coahuila, Philomela, sinsemilla, Tutuila

[2]**ela** \ā-lə\ see [3]ALA

[3]**ela** \el-ə\ see ELLA

elable \el-ə-bəl\ see ELLABLE

elacy \el-ə-sē\ jealousy, prelacy

elagh \ā-lē\ see AILY

elah \ē-lə\ see [1]ELA

eland \ē-lənd\ eland, Leland, Zealand, New Zealand

elanie \el-ə-nē\ see ELONY

elar \ē-lər\ see EALER

elate \el-ət\ see ELLATE

elatin \el-ət-ᵊn\ see ELETON

elative \el-ət-iv\ relative, appellative, correlative, irrelative

elba \el-bə\ Elba, Elbe, Melba

elbe \el-bə\ see ELBA

elbert \el-bərt\ Delbert, Elbert, Mount Elbert

elch \elch\ belch, squelch, welch, Welch, Welsh

[1]**eld** \eld\ eld, geld, held, meld, shelled, weld, beheld, danegeld, handheld, hard-shelled, upheld, withheld, jet-propelled, self-propelled, unparalleled—*also pasts of verbs listed at* [1]EL

[2]**eld** \el\ see [1]EL

[3]**eld** \elt\ see ELT

elda \el-də\ Zelda, Dar el Belda

eldam \el-dəm\ see ELDOM

elder \el-dər\ elder, welder

eldom \el-dəm\ beldam, seldom, hoteldom

eldon \el-dən\ Sheldon, Weldon

eldt \elt\ see ELT

[1]**ele** \ā-lē\ see AILY

[2]**ele** \el\ see [1]EL

[3]**ele** \el-ē\ see ELLY

[4]**ele** \ē-lē\ see EELY

[1]**eled** \eld\ see [1]ELD

[2]**eled** \ēld\ see IELD

elen \el-ən\ see ELON

elena \el-ə-nə\ Elena, Helena

elens \el-ənz\ Saint Helens, Mount Saint Helens—*also plurals and possessives of nouns at* ELON

eleon \ēl-yən\ see [2]ELIAN

eletal \el-ət-ᵊl\ pelletal, skeletal

eleton \el-ət-ᵊn\ gelatin, skeleton

eleus \ē-lē-əs\ see ELIOUS

elf \elf\ elf, Guelf, pelf, self,

shelf, bookshelf, herself, hisself, himself, itself, meself, myself, nonself, oneself, ourself, top-shelf, thyself, yourself, mantelshelf, do-it-yourself

elfer \el-fər\ telpher, do-it-yourselfer

elfish \el-fish\ elfish, selfish, unselfish

elhi \el-ē\ see ELLY

eli \el-ē\ see ELLY

[1]**elia** \ēl-yə\ Delia, Lelia, Shelia, Amelia, camellia, Camellia, Cecilia, Cornelia, Karelia, lobelia, obelia, Ophelia, Rumelia, sedilia, stapelia, psychedelia, seguidilla

[2]**elia** \il-ē-ə\ see [1]ILIA

elial \ē-lē-əl\ Belial, epithelial

[1]**elian** \ē-lē-ən\ Melian, Pelion, abelian, Karelian, Mendelian

[2]**elian** \ēl-yən\ anthelion, aphelion, carnelian, chameleon, cornelian, Mendelian, parhelion, perihelion, Aristotelian, Mephistophelian

[3]**elian** \el-ē-ən\ see ELLIAN

elible \el-ə-bəl\ see ELLABLE

[1]**elic** \ē-lik\ parhelic, autotelic

[2]**elic** \el-ik\ melic, relic, telic, angelic, Goidelic, smart aleck, archangelic, autotelic, philatelic, psychedelic

elical \el-i-kəl\ helical, pellicle, angelical, double-helical, evangelical

elier \el-yer\ see ELURE

elin \ē-lən\ shieling, theelin

[1]**elion** \el-ē-ən\ see ELLIAN

[2]**elion** \ēl-yən\ see [2]ELIAN

[3]**elion** \ēl-ē-ən\ see [1]ELIAN

elios \ē-lē-əs\ see ELIOUS

elious \ē-lē-əs\ Helios, Peleus, Cornelius, contumelious

elish \el-ish\ see ELLISH

elist \el-əst\ trellised, cellist, Nobelist, pastelist

[1]**elius** \ā-lē-əs\ see ALIUS

[2]**elius** \ē-lē-əs\ see ELIOUS

elix \ē-liks\ Felix, helix, double helix

[1]**elk** \elk\ elk, whelk

[2]**elk** \ilk\ see ILK

ell \el\ see [1]EL

e'll \ēl\ see [2]EAL

ella \el-ə\ Celle, Della, Ella, fella, fellah, stella, Stella, Benguela, candela, Capella, Estella, favela, Gisela, glabella, lamella, Luella, Marcella, Mandela, novella, paella, patella, prunella, quiniela, rubella, sequela, umbrella, vanilla, a cappella, Cinderella, citronella, columella, fraxinella, Isabella, mortadella, mozzarella, panatela, salmonella, sarsaparilla, subumbrella, tarantella, villanella, valpolicella

ellable \el-ə-bəl\ fellable, gelable, compellable, expellable, indelible

ellah \el-ə\ see ELLA

ellan \el-ən\ see ELON

ellant \el-ənt\ gellant, appellant, flagellant, propellant, repellent, water-repellent

ellar \el-ər\ see ELLER

ellas \el-əs\ see EALOUS

ellate \el-ət\ helot, pellet,

prelate, zealot, appellate, flagellate, haustellate, lamellate, scutellate

ellative \el-ət-iv\ see ELATIVE

[1]elle \el\ see [1]EL

[2]elle \el-ə\ see ELLA

ellean \el-ē-ən\ see ELLIAN

elled \eld\ see [1]ELD

ellen \el-ən\ see ELON

ellent \el-ənt\ see ELLANT

eller \el-ər\ cellar, dweller, feller, heller, Keller, seller, sheller, smeller, speller, stellar, teller, yeller, best-seller, bookseller, compeller, expeller, foreteller, glabellar, impeller, indweller, lamellar, ocellar, patellar, propeller, rathskeller, repeller, rostellar, saltcellar, tale-teller, cereballar, circumstellar, columellar, fortune-teller, interstellar, Rockefeller, storyteller

[1]elles \el\ see [1]EL

[2]elles \elz\ see ELLS

ellet \el-ət\ see ELLATE

elletal \el-ət-ᵊl\ see ELETAL

elley \el-ē\ see ELLY

elli \el-ē\ see ELLY

ellia \ēl-yə\ see ELIA

ellian \el-ē-ən\ Chellean, Boswellian, pre-Chellean, Sabellian, triskelion, Pantagruelian, Machiavellian

ellicle \el-i-kəl\ see ELICAL

ellie \el-ē\ see ELLY

elline \el-ən\ see ELON

elling \el-iŋ\ belling, selling, spelling, swelling, telling, bookselling, compelling, indwelling, misspelling, tale-telling, upwelling, fortune-telling, self-propelling—*also present participles of verbs listed at* [1]EL

ellington \el-iŋ-tən\ Ellington, Wellington, beef Wellington

ellion \el-yən\ hellion, rebellion

ellis \el-əs\ see EALOUS

ellised \el-əst\ see ELIST

ellish \el-ish\ hellish, relish, disrelish, embellish

ellist \el-əst\ see ELIST

ello \el-ō\ bellow, Bellow, cello, fellow, Jell-O, mellow, yellow, Yellow, bargello, bedfellow, bordello, duello, hail-fellow, Longfellow, marshmallow, morello, niello, Othello, playfellow, schoolfellow, yokefellow, Pirandello, punchinello, ritornello, saltarello, Robin Goodfellow, violoncello

ell-o \el-ō\ see ELLO

ellous \el-əs\ see EALOUS

[1]ellow \el-ə\ see ELLA

[2]ellow \el-ō\ see ELLO

ells \elz\ Welles, Dardanelles—*also plurals and possessives of nouns and third person singular presents of verbs listed at*[1]EL

ellum \el-əm\ blellum, skellum, vellum, postbellum, rostellum, antebellum, cerebellum

ellus \el-əs\ see EALOUS

elly \el-ē\ belly, Delhi, deli, felly, jelly, Kellie, Kelly, Nellie, shelly, Shelley, Shelly, smelly, tele, telly, wellie, New Delhi, nice-nelly, potbelly, rakehelly, sowbelly,

Boticelli, nervous Nellie, underbelly, vermicelli, Machiavelli, Dadra and Nagar Haveli

ellyn \el-ən\ see ELON

elm \elm\ elm, helm, realm, whelm, overwhelm, underwhelm

elma \el-mə\ Selma, Velma

elmar \el-mər\ see ELMER

elmer \el-mər\ Delmar, Delmer, Elmer

elmet \el-mət\ helmet, Helmut, pelmet

elmut \el-mət\ see ELMET

elo \ē-lō\ see [2]ILO

elon \el-ən\ Ellen, Ellyn, felon, Helen, melon, avellan, Magellan, McClellan, muskmelon, Snellen, vitelline, Mary Ellen, watermelon, Strait of Magellan

elony \el-ə-nē\ felony, Melanie

elop \el-əp\ develop, envelop, redevelop, overdevelop

elopment \el-əp-mənt\ development, envelopment, redevelopment, overdevelopment

elos \ā-ləs\ see AYLESS

elot \el-ət\ see ELLATE

elotry \el-ə-trē\ helotry, zealotry

elp \elp\ help, kelp, skelp, whelp, yelp

elpher \el-fər\ see ELFER

elsea \el-sē\ see ELSIE

elsh \elch\ see ELCH

elsie \el-sē\ Chelsea, Elsie, Kensington and Chelsea

elson \el-sən\ keelson, nelson, Nelson

elt \elt\ belt, celt, Celt, dealt, delt, dwelt, felt, gelt, melt, pelt, Scheldt, smelt, spelt, svelte, veld, welt, black belt, flybelt, forefelt, greenbelt, heartfelt, hot-melt, jacksmelt, Krefeld, self-belt, snowbelt, snowmelt, Sunbelt, Bielefeld, Roosevelt, shelterbelt

elte \elt\ see ELT

elted \el-təd\ bias-belted—*also pasts of verbs listed at* ELT

elter \el-tər\ melter, pelter, shelter, skelter, smelter, spelter, swelter, welter, helter-skelter

eltered \el-tərd\ earth-sheltered—*also pasts of verbs listed at* ELTER

elting \el-tiŋ\ belting, felting, melting, pelting

elure \el-yər\ velure, hotelier

elve \elv\ delve, helve, shelve, twelve

elves \elvz\ elves, ourselves, theirselves, themselves, yourselves—*also plurals and possessives of nouns and third person singular present of verbs at* ELVE

elvin \el-vən\ Elvin, Kelvin, Melvin, Melvyn

elvyn \el-vən\ see ELVIN

ely \ē-lē\ see EELY

[1]**em** \em\ Clem, crème, em, femme, gem, hem, m, mem, phlegm, REM, Shem, stem, them, ad rem, ahem, AM, Arnhem, Belem, bluestem, condemn, contemn, FM, idem, in rem, item, mayhem, millieme, modem, poem,

problem, pro tem, proem, Shechem, ABM, anadem, apothegm, apothem, Bethlehem, diadem, exanthem, ibidem, IgM, meristem, OEM, SAM, stratagem, ad hominem, carpe diem, crème de la crème, ICBM, post meridiem, star-of-Bethlehem, terminus ad quem

[2]**em** \əm\ see [1]UM

ema \ē-mə\ bema, Lima, Pima, schema, Colima, eczema, edema, diastema, emphysema, Hiroshima, Iwo Jima, Kagoshima, Matsushima, terza rima, Tokushima, ottava rima

emacist \em-ə-səst\ see EMICIST

[1]**eman** \em-ən\ see [2]EMON

[2]**eman** \ē-mən\ see [1]EMON

emane \em-ə-nē\ see EMONY

emanence \em-ə-nəns\ see EMINENCE

emanent \em-ə-nənt\ see EMINENT

ematis \em-ət-əs\ see EMITUS

ematist \em-ət-əst\ see EMITIST

ematous \em-ət-əs\ see EMITUS

ember \em-bər\ ember, member, December, dismember, November, remember, September, disremember

[1]**emble** \äm-bəl\ wamble, ensemble

[2]**emble** \em-bəl\ tremble, assemble, atremble, dissemble, resemble, disassemble

embler \em-blər\ temblor, trembler, assembler, dissembler

emblor \em-blər\ see EMBLER

embly \em-blē\ trembly, assembly, disassembly, self-assembly, subassembly

[1]**eme** \em\ see [1]EM

[2]**eme** \ēm\ see [1]EAM

emel \ā-məl\ see EMILE

emely \ēm-lē\ see EEMLY

[1]**emen** \ē-mən\ see [1]EMON

[2]**emen** \em-ən\ see [2]EMON

[3]**emen** \ā-mən\ see [1]AMEN

emer \ē-mər\ see EAMER

emeral \em-rəl\ femoral, ephemeral

emery \em-rē\ emery, Emery, Emory, memory

emesis \em-ə-səs\ emesis, nemesis

emi \em-ē\ see EMMY

emia \ē-mē-ə\ anemia, bohemia, Bohemia, leukemia, toxemia, academia, septicemia, thalassemia, hypoglycemia, hypokalemia, beta-thalassemia

emian \ē-mē-ən\ anthemion, Bohemian

[1]**emic** \ē-mik\ emic, anemic, graphemic, morphemic, lexemic, phonemic, taxemic, tonemic, epistemic

[2]**emic** \em-ik\ chemic, alchemic, endemic, pandemic, polemic, sachemic, systemic, totemic, academic, epidemic, epistemic

emical \em-i-kəl\ chemical, alchemical, polemical, academical, biochemical, epidemical, petrochemical, biogeochemical

emicist \em-ə-səst\ polemicist, supremacist
emics \ē-miks\ graphemics, morphemics, phonemics, proxemics
emile \ā-məl\ Emile, Memel
eminal \em-ən-^{ə}l\ geminal, seminal
eminate \em-ə-nət\ geminate, effeminate
eminence \em-ə-nəns\ eminence, remanence, preeminence
eminent \em-ə-nənt\ eminent, remanent, preeminent
eming \em-iŋ\ Fleming, Heminge, lemming
eminge \em-iŋ\ see EMING
emini \em-ə-nē\ see EMONY
eminy \em-ə-nē\ see EMONY
emion \ē-mē-ən\ see EMIAN
emis \ē-məs\ see EMUS
emish \em-ish\ blemish, Flemish
emist \em-əst\ chemist, polemist, biochemist
emitist \em-ət-əst\ Semitist, systematist
emitus \em-ət-əs\ clematis, fremitus, edematous
emlin \em-lən\ gremlin, kremlin
emma \em-ə\ Emma, gemma, lemma, stemma, dilemma
emme \em\ see [1]EM
emmer \em-ər\ emmer, hemmer, stemmer, tremor, condemner, contemner
emming \em-iŋ\ see EMING
emmy \em-ē\ Emmy, gemmy, jemmy, phlegmy, semi, stemmy
emn \em\ see [1]EM
emner \em-ər\ see EMMER
emnity \em-nət-ē\ indemnity, solemnity
emo \em-ō\ demo, memo
[1]**emon** \ē-mən\ demon, freeman, Freeman, gleeman, Piman, seaman, semen, Lake Leman, pentstemon, Philemon, cacodemon, Lacedaemon
[2]**emon** \em-ən\ Bremen, leman, lemon, Yemen
emone \em-ə-nē\ see EMONY
emony \em-ə-nē\ Gemini, lemony, anemone, bigeminy, Gethsemane, hegemony
emor \em-ər\ see EMMER
emoral \em-rəl\ see EMERAL
emory \em-rē\ see EMERY
emous \ē-məs\ see EMUS
emp \emp\ hemp, kemp, temp
emperer \em-pər-ər\ emperor, temperer
emperor \em-pər-ər\ see EMPERER
emplar \em-plər\ Templar, exemplar
emple \em-pəl\ semple, temple
emps \ä^{n}\ see [1]ANT
empt \emt\ dreamt, kempt, tempt, attempt, contempt, exempt, preempt, undreamed, unkempt, tax-exempt
emptable \em-tə-bəl\ attemptable, contemptible
emptible \em-tə-bəl\ see EMPTABLE
emption \em-shən\ exemption, preemption, redemption
emptive \em-tiv\ preemptive, redemptive
emptor \em-tər\ tempter, preemptor, caveat emptor

e \en-rə-bəl\ generable,
able, regenerable
\en-rə-sē\ degeneracy,
eracy
\en-rət\ degenerate,
rate, unregenerate
e \en-rət-iv\ generative,
rative, regenerative,
egenerative
-ə-rəs\ mons veneris,
eris
-ə-rē\ see [2]ENARY
-rē\ see EANERY
ət\ see ENNET
t\ see EANUT
ee [2]ANG
ee [1]UNG
venge, avenge,
Stonehenge
\ dengue, sengi
glish\ English,
\ marengo,
o
length, strength,
half-length,
, understrength,
rength
see ENTH
ən\ lengthen,
see ENGI
N
aenia, Slovenia,
hizophrenia
rmenia,
genia, gardenia,
rinya
enial, menial,
ial
Fenian,
enian, Icenian,

sirenian, Slovenian, Tyrrhenian, Achaemenian, Magdalenian

[1]**enic** \ēn-ik\ genic, scenic

[2]**enic** \en-ik\ fennec, pfennig, phrenic, splenic, sthenic, arsenic, asthenic, Edenic, Essenic, eugenic, Hellenic, hygienic, irenic, transgenic, allergenic, androgenic, autogenic, calisthenic, chromogenic, cryogenic, cryptogenic, hygienic, mutagenic, Panhellenic, pathogenic, photogenic, Saracenic, schizophrenic, telegenic, carcinogenic, cariogenic, hallucinogenic, hypoallergenic

enical \en-i-kəl\ cenacle, arsenical, galenical, ecumenical

enice \en-əs\ see [1]ENIS

enicist \en-ə-səst\ eugenicist, ecumenicist

enics \en-iks\ eugenics, euphenics, euthenics, hygienics, calisthenics, cryogenics—*also plurals and possessives of nouns listed at* [2]ENIC

[1]**enie** \en-ē\ see ENNY

[2]**enie** \ē-nē\ see [1]INI

enience \ē-nyəns\ lenience, convenience, provenience, inconvenience

enient \ēn-yənt\ convenient, prevenient

enim \en-əm\ see ENOM

enin \en-ən\ see ENNON

enior \ē-nyər\ senior, monsignor

emptory \em-trē\ peremptory, redemptory

emulous \em-yə-ləs\ emulous, tremulous

emur \ē-mər\ see EAMER

emus \ē-məs\ Remus, in extremis, Polyphemus, polysemous

emy \ē-mē\ see EAMY

[1]**en** \en\ ben, Ben, den, en, fen, gen, glen, Glen, Glenn, Gwen, hen, ken, Ken, Len, men, n, pen, Penn, Rennes, Seine, sen, Sten, ten, then, wen, when, wren, Wren, yen, Zen, again, amen, Ardennes, Big Ben, Cayenne, Cevennes, Cheyenne, Chosen, Dairen, doyen, doyenne, Duchenne, Fulcien, hapten, hymen, Karen, La Tène, moorhen, peahen, pigpen, Phnom Penh, playpen, RN, Touraine, Tynmen, somewhen, Adrienne, Debrecen, DPN, five-and-ten, FMN, julienne, Kerguelen, La Fontaine, LPN, madrilene, mise-en-scène, samisen, Sun Yat-sen, TPN, carcinogen, comedienne, equestrienne, tamoxifen, tragedienne, Valenciennes

[2]**en** \ēn\ see [3]INE

[3]**en** \a^{n}\ see [4]IN

[4]**en** \ən\ see UN

[5]**en** \ä^{n}\ see [1]ANT

[1]**ena** \ā-nä\ see [1]AENA

[2]**ena** \ā-nə\ see [2]ANA

[3]**ena** \ān-yə\ see [3]ANIA

[4]**ena** \ē-nə\ see [2]INA

enable \en-ə-bəl\ tenable, amenable, untenable

enace \en-əs\ see [1]ENIS

enacle \en-i-kəl\ see ENICAL

enae \e-nē\ see [1]INI

enal \ēn-^{ə}l\ penal, renal, venal, adrenal, vaccinal, duodenal

enancy \en-ən-sē\ tenancy, lieutenancy, subtenancy

enant \en-ənt\ pennant, tenant, lieutenant, se tenant, subtenant, sublieutenant, undertenant

enary \en-ə-rē\ hennery, plenary, senary, venery, centenary, millenary, bicentenary, bimillenary, quincentenary, tercentenary, quatercentenary, semicentenary, sesquicentenary

enas \ē-nəs\ see [1]ENUS

enate \en-ət\ see ENNET

enator \en-ət-ər\ see ENITOR

ençal \en-səl\ see ENCIL

[1]**ence** \ens\ see ENSE

[2]**ence** \ä^{n}s\ see [1]ANCE

[3]**ence** \äns\ see [2]ANCE

encel \en-səl\ see ENCIL

enceless \en-sləs\ see ENSELESS

encer \en-sər\ see ENSOR

ench \ench\ bench, blench, clench, drench, french, French, mensch, quench, stench, tench, trench, wench, wrench, entrench, luftmensch, retrench, unclench, workbench, Anglo-French, Mariana Trench

enchant \en-chənt\ see ENTIENT

enched \encht\ trenched, unblenched—*also pasts of verbs listed at* ENCH

encher \en-chər\ see ENTURE

enchman \ench-mən\ Frenchman, henchman
encia \en-chə\ see ENTIA
encil \en-səl\ mensal, pencel, pencil, stencil, tensile, blue-pencil, commensal, extensile, Provençal, prehensile, red-pencil, utensil, intercensal
ençon \en-sən\ see ENSIGN
ency \en-sē\ Montmorency, residency, nonresidency
end \end\ bend, blend, blende, end, fend, friend, lend, mend, rend, scend, send, shend, spend, tend, trend, vend, wend, Wend, addend, amend, append, ascend, attend, augend, befriend, Big Bend, bookend, boyfriend, closed-end, commend, compend, contend, dead end, dead-end, defend, depend, descend, distend, downtrend, emend, expend, extend, forfend, girlfriend, godsend, hornblende, impend, intend, Land's End, low-end, missend, misspend, offend, outspend, perpend, pitchblende, portend, pretend, propend, protend, rear-end, resend, South Bend, stipend, subtend, suspend, transcend, unbend, unkenned, upend, uptrend, weekend, year-end, adherend, apprehend, bitter end, comprehend, condescend, Damavend, discommend, dividend, minuend, overspend, recommend, repetend, reprehend, subtrahend, vilipend, hyperextend, misapprehend, overextend, superintend—*also pasts of verbs listed at* [1]EN
enda \en-də\ Brenda, Glenda, Venda, agenda, hacienda—*also plurals of nouns listed at* ENDUM
endable \en-də-bəl\ lendable, mendable, spendable, vendible, amendable, ascendable, commendable, defendable, dependable, descendible, expendable, extendable, unbendable, comprehendable, recommendable
endal \en-d^{ə}l\ Grendel, Kendall, Mendel, Wendell, prebendal, pudendal
endall \en-d^{ə}l\ see ENDAL
endance \en-dəns\ see ENDENCE
endancy \en-dən-sē\ see ENDENCY
endant \en-dənt\ see ENDENT
[1]ende \end\ see END
[2]ende \en-dē\ see ENDI
ended \en-dəd\ ended, splendid, befriended, unfriended, double-ended, open-ended, undescended—*also pasts of verbs listed at* END
endel \en-d^{ə}l\ see ENDAL
endell \en-d^{ə}l\ see ENDAL
endence \en-dəns\ tendance, ascendance, attendance, intendance, resplendence, transcendence, condescendence, independence, Independence, superintendence
endency \en-dən-sē\ pendency,

tendency, ascendancy, dependency, resplendency, transcendency, superintendency, independency
endent \en-dənt\ pendant, pendent, splendent, appendant, ascendant, attendant, defendant, dependent, descendant, impendent, intendant, respendent, transcendent, independent, superintendant, semi-independent
ender \en-dər\ bender, blender, fender, gender, lender, render, mender, slender, spender, sender, splendor, tender, vendor, amender, ascender, attender, auslander, bartender, commender, contender, defender, descender, emender, engender, expender, extender, fork-tender, goaltender, hellbender, intender, offender, pretender, surrender, suspender, tailender, weekender, double-ender, moneylender, over-spender, self-surrender
endi \en-dē\ bendy, Mende, trendy, Wendy, effendi, modus vivendi
endible \en-də-bəl\ see ENDABLE
endid \en-dəd\ see ENDED
ending \en-diŋ\ bending, ending, pending, sending, ascending, attending, fenc- mending, goaltending, heartrending, mind-bendi- unbending, unending,

[1]**enis** \en-əs\ Denis, Dennis, Denys, genus, menace, tenace, tennis, Venice, frontenis, summum genus
[2]**enis** \ē-nəs\ see [1]ENUS
[1]**enison** \en-ə-sən\ benison, Tennyson, venison
[2]**enison** \en-ə-zən\ benison, denizen, venison
enist \en-əst\ tennist, euthenist
enitive \en-ət-iv\ genitive, lenitive, philoprogenitive, polyphiloprogenitive
enitor \en-ət-ər\ senator, progenitor, primogenitor
enity \en-ət-ē\ see ENTITY
enium \ē-nē-əm\ hymenium, proscenium
enius \ē-nē-əs\ see ENEOUS
enizen \en-ə-zən\ see [2]ENISON
enn \en\ see [1]EN
enna \en-ə\ Glenna, henna, senna, antenna, duenna, Gehenna, sienna, Vienna
ennae \en-ē\ see ENNY
ennant \en-ənt\ see ENANT
[1]**enne** \en\ see [1]EN
[2]**enne** \en-ē\ see ENNY
[3]**enne** \an\ see [5]AN
ennec \en-ik\ see [2]ENIC
enned \end\ see END
ennel \en-əl\ crenel, fennel, kennel, unkennel
enner \en-ər\ see [1]ENOR
ennery \en-ə-rē\ see [2]ENARY
ennes \en\ see [1]EN
ennet \en-ət\ Bennett, genet, jennet, rennet, senate, sennet, sennit, tenet
ennett \en-ət\ see ENNET
enney \en-ē\ see ENNY
enni \en-ē\ see ENNY
ennial \en-ē-əl\ biennial, centennial, decennial, millennial, perennial, quadrennial, quinquennial, septennial, triennial, vicennial, bicentennial, bimillennial, postmillennial, premillennial, quincentennial, tercentennial, semicentennial, sesquicentennial, quadricentennial
ennies \en-ēz\ tennies—*also possessives and plurals of nouns listed at* ENNY
ennig \en-ik\ see [2]ENIC
ennin \en-ən\ see ENNON
ennis \en-əs\ see [1]ENIS
ennist \en-əst\ see ENIST
ennit \en-ət\ see ENNET
ennium \en-ē-əm\ biennium, decennium, millennium, quadrennium, quinquennium, triennium
ennon \en-ən\ Lenin, pennon, rennin, tenon, antivenin
enny \en-ē\ any, benne, benny, Benny, blenney, Dene, Denny, fenny, genie, Jennie, jenny, Jenny, many, penni, penny, Penny, antennae, catchpenny, halfpenny, Kilkenny, Na-dene, pinchpenny, sixpenny, tenpenny, threepenny, truepenny, twopenny, lilangeni, spinning jenny
ennyson \en-ə-sən\ see [1]ENISON
[1]**eno** \ān-yō\ segno, dal segno, jalapeño
[2]**eno** \en-ō\ steno, ripieno
[3]**eno** \ā-nō\ see [2]ANO
enoch \ē-nik\ see [1]INIC

enom \en-əm\ denim, plenum, venom, envenom
enon \en-ən\ see ENNON
[1]**enor** \en-ər\ Brenner, Jenner, tenner, tenor, tenour, countertenor, heldentenor
[2]**enor** \ē-nər\ see EANER
enour \en-ər\ see [1]ENOR
enous \ē-nəs\ see [1]ENUS
[1]**ens** \enz\ cleanse, gens, lens, amends, beam-ends, weekends, sapiens, definiens, locum tenens—*also plurals and possessives of nouns and third person singular presents of verbs listed at* [1]EN
[2]**ens** \ens\ see ENSE
ensable \en-sə-bəl\ see ENSIBLE
ensal \en-səl\ see ENCIL
ensary \ens-rē\ see ENSORY
ensch \ench\ see ENCH
ense \ens\ cense, dense, fence, flense, gens, hence, mense, pence, sense, spence, tense, thence, whence, commence, condense, defense, dispense, expense, immense, incense, intense, missense, nonsense, offense, prepense, pretense, propense, sequence, sixpence, subsequence, suspense, twopence, accidence, antisense, commonsense, confidence, consequence, diffidence, evidence, frankincense, multisense, nondefense, providence, Providence, recompense, residence, self-defense, subsequence, coincidence, ego-defense, inconsequence, New Providence, nonresidence, self-confidence, self-evidence
enseful \ens-fəl\ menseful, senseful, suspenseful
enseless \en-sləs\ fenceless, senseless, defenseless, offenseless
ensem \en-səm\ see ENSUM
enser \en-sər\ see ENSOR
ensian \en-chən\ see ENSION
ensible \en-sə-bəl\ sensible, compensable, condensable, defensible, dispensable, distensible, extensible, insensible, ostensible, apprehensible, commonsensible, comprehensible, incondensable, indefensible, indispensable, reprehensible, supersensible, incomprehensible
ensign \en-sən\ ensign, alençon
ensil \en-səl\ see ENCIL
ensile \en-səl\ see ENCIL
ension \en-chən\ gentian, mention, pension, tension, abstention, ascension, attention, contention, convention, declension, descension, detention, dimension, dissension, distension, extension, indention, intension, intention, invention, Laurentian, low tension, posttension, prehension, pretension, prevention, recension, retention, subvention, suspension, sustention, Vincentian, Waldensian, Albigensian, apprehension

circumvention, comprehension, condescension, contravention, hypertension, hypotension, inattention, reinvention, reprehension, salientian, incomprehension, misapprehension, nonintervention, overextension, Premonstratensian

ensional \ench-nəl\ tensional, ascensional, attentional, conventional, declensional, dimensional, extensional, intensional, intentional, unconventional, tridimensional, unidimensional

ensioner \ench-nər\ see ENTIONER

ensis \en-səs\ see ENSUS

ensitive \en-sət-iv\ sensitive, insensitive, photosensitive, hypersensitive, oversensitive, photosensitive, supersensitive

ensity \en-sət-ē\ density, tensity, extensity, immensity, intensity, propensity

ensive \en-siv\ pensive, tensive, ascensive, defensive, expensive, extensive, intensive, offensive, ostensive, protensive, suspensive, apprehensive, coextensive, comprehensive, hypertensive, hypotensive, inexpensive, inoffensive, reprehensive, self-defensive, counteroffensive, labor-intensive

ensor \en-sər\ censer, censor, fencer, sensor, spencer, Spencer, Spenser, tensor, commencer, condenser, dispenser, extensor, precensor, sequencer, suspensor, biosensor—*also comparatives of adjectives listed at* ENSE

ensory \ens-rē\ sensory, dispensary, suspensory, extrasensory, multisensory, supersensory

[1]**ensual** \en-chəl\ see ENTIAL

[2]**ensual** \ench-wəl\ see [1]ENTUAL

ensum \en-səm\ sensum, per mensem

ensurable \ens-rə-bəl\ censurable, mensurable, commensurable, immensurable, incommensurable

ensure \en-chər\ see ENTURE

ensus \en-səs\ census, consensus, dissensus, amanuensis

[1]**ent** \ent\ bent, Brent, cent, dent, gent, Ghent, Gwent, hent, Kent, leant, lent, Lent, meant, pent, rent, scent, sent, sklent, spent, sprent, tent, Trent, vent, went, absent, accent, Advent, anent, ascent, assent, augment, besprent, cement, chimkent, comment, concent, consent, content, convent, descent, detent, dissent, docent, event, extent, ferment, foment, forewent, forspent, fragment, frequent, hell-bent, indent, intent, invent, lament, loment, low-rent, mordent, outspent,

outwent, percent, pigment, portent, present, prevent, quitrent, relent, repent, resent, segment, Tashkent, torment, unbent, well-meant, wisent, accident, aliment, argument, circumvent, compartment, complement, compliment, confident, devilment, diffident, discontent, document, evident, heaven-sent, implement, instrument, Jack-a-Lent, malcontent, nonevent, Occident, ornament, orient, president, provident, regiment, reinvent, represent, re-present, resident, sediment, self-content, Stoke on Trent, subsequent, underwent, supplement, coincident, disorient, experiment, ferro-cement, inconsequent, misrepresent, nonresident, privatdocent, self-evident

[2]ent \änt\ see [2]ANT

[3]ent \ä^{n}\ see [1]ANT

enta \ent-ə\ menta, yenta, magenta, momenta, placenta, polenta, tegmenta, tomenta, irredenta, impedimenta

entable \ent-ə-bəl\ presentable, documentable, fermentable, preventable, representable, sedimentable

entacle \ent-i-kəl\ see ENTICAL

entage \ent-ij\ tentage, ventage, percentage

ental \ent-^{ə}l\ cental, dental, dentil, gentle, lentil, mental, rental, cliental, fragmental, judgmental, parental, placental, segmental, accidental, adjustmental, apartmental, biparental, compartmental, complemental, condimental, continental, departmental, deterimental, developmental, documental, excremental, elemental, environmental, firmamental, fundamental, governmental, grandparental, incidental, incremental, instrumental, managemental, monumental, nonjudgmental, occidental, oriental, ornamental, regimental, rudimental, sacramental, sentimental, supplemental, temperamental, transcendental, vestamental, coincidental, developmental, experimental, presentimental, subcontinental, transcontinental, uniparental, intercontinental, interdepartmental, intergovernmental, semigovernmental

entalist \ent-^{ə}l-əst\ gentlest, mentalist, documentalist, fundamentalist, governmentalist, incrementalist, instrumentalist, orientalist, sacramentalist, sentimentalist, transcendentalist, environmentalist, experimentalist

entalness \ent-^{ə}l-nəs\ see ENTLENESS

entance \ent-^{ə}ns\ see ENTENCE

entary \en-trē\ gentry, sentry,

passementerie, reentry, subentry, alimentary, complementary, complimentary, documentary, elementary, filamentary, integumentary, parliamentary, rudimentary, sedimentary, supplementary, tenementary, testamentary, uncomplimentary, unparliamentary, semidocumentary

entative \ent-ət-iv\ tentative, augmentative, fermentative, frequentative, presentative, preventative, argumentative, representative, misrepresentative

[1]**ente** \en-tā\ al dente, lentamente

[2]**ente** \ent-ē\ see ENTY

[3]**ente** \änt\ see [2]ANT

ented \ent-əd\ tented, augmented, contented, demented, lamented, segmented, untented, battlemented, malcontented, oriented, self-contented, unfrequented, unprecedented, overrepresented, underrepresented—*also pasts of verbs listed at* [1]ENT

enten \ent-ᵊn\ Benton, dentin, Denton, Kenton, Lenten, Quentin, Trenton

entence \ent-ᵊns\ sentence, repentance

enter \ent-ər\ center, enter, mentor, renter, stentor, tenter, venter, assenter, augmentor, cementer, concenter, consentor, dissenter, incenter, indenter, fermenter, frequenter, inventor, precentor, preventer, rack-renter, reenter, repenter, subcenter, tormentor, documenter, epicenter, representer, supplementer, hypocenter, metacenter, experimenter, hundred-percenter

entered \en-tərd\ centered, face-centered, self-centered, body-centered—*also pasts of verbs listed at* ENTER

enterie \en-trē\ see ENTARY

entful \ent-fəl\ eventful, resentful, uneventful

enth \enth\ nth, strength, tenth, crème de menthe

enthe \enth\ see ENTH

enthesis \en-thə-səs\ epenthesis, parenthesis

enti \ent-ē\ see ENTY

entia \en-chə\ dementia, Florentia, sententia, Valencia, differentia, in absentia

ential \en-chəl\ cadential, consensual, credential, demential, essential, eventual, potential, prudential, sciential, sentential, sequential, tangential, torrential, componential, conferential, confidential, consequential, deferential, differential, evidential, existential, expedential, exponential, inessential, inferential, influential, nonessential, penitential, pestilential, preferential, presidential, providential, referential, residential, reverential, transferential, unessential, circumferential, equipotential, experiential, inconsequential, intelligential, interferential, jurisprudential, multipotential, reminiscential

entialist \en-chə-ləst\ essentialist, existentialist

entian \en-chən\ see ENSION

entiary \ench-rē\ century, penitentiary, plenipotentiary

entic \ent-ik\ lentic, argentic, authentic, crescentic, identic, inauthentic

entical \ent-i-kəl\ denticle, pentacle, tentacle, conventicle, identical, nonidentical, self-identical

entice \ent-əs\ see ENTOUS

enticle \ent-i-kəl\ see ENTICAL

entient \en-chənt\ penchant, sentient, trenchant, dissentient, insentient, presentient

entil \ent-ᵊl\ see ENTAL

entin \ent-ᵊn\ see ENTEN

enting \ent-iŋ\ dissenting, unrelenting

ention \en-chən\ see ENSION

entionable \ench-nə-bəl\ mentionable, pensionable, unmentionable

entional \ench- nəl\ see ENSIONAL

entioned \en-chənd\ aforementioned, well-intentioned—*also pasts of verbs listed at* ENSION

entioner \ench-nər\ mentioner, pensioner, tensioner

entious \en-chəs\ abstentious, contentious, dissentious, licentious, pretentious, sententious, tendentious, conscientious, unpretentious

entis \ent-əs\ see ENTOUS

entist \ent-əst\ dentist, cinquecentist, irredentist

entity \en-ət-ē\ entity, lenity, amenity, identity, nonentity, obscenity, serenity, coidentity, self-identity

entium \ent-ē-əm\ jus gentium, unnilpentium

entive \ent-iv\ adventive, attentive, incentive, inventive, pendentive, preventive, retentive, argumentive, disincentive, inattentive

entle \ent-ᵊl\ see ENTAL

entleness \ent-ᵊl-nəs\ gentleness, accidentalness

entment \ent-mənt\ contentment, presentment, resentment, discontentment, self-contentment

ento \en-tō\ cento, lento, Trento, memento, pimento, pimiento, seicento, trecento, cinquecento, papiamento, portamento, quatrocento, Sacramento, aggiornamento, divertimento, pronunciamento, risorgimento

enton \ent-ᵊn\ see ENTEN

entor \ent-ər\ see ENTER

entous \ent-əs\ prentice, apprentice, argentous, momentous, portentous, compos mentis, filamentous, ligamentous, non compos mentis, in loco parentis

entral \en-trəl\ central, ventral, subcentral, dorsiventral
entress \en-trəs\ gentrice, inventress
entric \en-trik\ centric, acentric, concentric, dicentric, eccentric, acrocentric, androcentric, Christocentric, egocentric, ethnocentric, Eurocentric, geocentric, phallocentric, polycentric, theocentric, topocentric, anthropocentric, areocentric, Europocentric, heliocentric, selenocentric
entrice \en-trəs\ see ENTRESS
entry \en-trē\ see ENTARY
ents \ents\ gents, events, dollars-and-cents—*also plurals of nouns listed at* [1]ENT
[1]**entual** \en-chə-wəl\ sensual, accentual, consensual, conventual, eventual
[2]**entual** \en-chəl\ see ENTIAL
entum \ent-əm\ centum, mentum, cementum, momentum, per centum, tegmentum, tomentum, argumentum
enture \en-chər\ bencher, censure, denture, drencher, trencher, venture, wencher, adventure, backbencher, debenture, front-bencher, indenture, misventure, misadventure, peradventure
enturer \ench-rər\ venturer, adventurer
enturess \ench-rəs\ see ENTUROUS
enturous \ench-rəs\ venturous, adventuress, adventurous
entury \ench-rē\ see ENTIARY
enty \ent-ē\ plenty, sente, senti, tenty, twenty, aplenty, licente, cognoscente, twenty-twenty, Deo volente, dolce far niente
enuis \en-yə-wəs\ see ENUOUS
enum \en-əm\ see ENOM
enuous \en-yə-wəs\ strenuous, tenuis, tenuous, ingenuous, disingenuous
[1]**enus** \ē-nəs\ genus, lenis, penis, venous, Venus, Campinas, Delphinus, Maecenas, Quirinus, silenus, intravenous
[2]**enus** \en-əs\ see [1]ENIS
eny \ā-nē\ see AINY
enys \en-əs\ see [1]ENIS
[1]**enza** \en-zə\ Penza, cadenza, credenza, influenza
[2]**enza** \en-sə\ Polenza, Vicenza, Piacenza
[1]**eo** \ā-ō\ mayo, Mayo, cacao, paseo, rodeo, aparejo, Bulawayo, cicisbeo, zapateo, Montevideo
[2]**eo** \ē-ō\ see [2]IO
[1]**eoff** \ef\ see [1]EF
[2]**eoff** \ēf\ see [1]IEF
eoffor \ef-ər\ see EPHOR
eolate \ē-ə-lət\ triolet, alveolate, areolate, urceolate
eoman \ō-mən\ see OMAN
[1]**eon** \ē-ən\ see [1]EAN
[2]**eon** \ē-än\ eon, freon, neon, prion
eonid \ē-ə-nəd\ see EANID
eopard \ep-ərd\ jeopard, leopard, peppered, shepard, shepherd
eopardess \ep-ərd-əs\ shepherdess, leopardess

eople \ē-pəl\ people, pipal, steeple, craftspeople, dispeople, laypeople, newspeople, salespeople, spokespeople, townspeople, tradespeople, tribespeople, unpeople, workpeople, anchorpeople, businesspeople, congresspeople

eopled \ē-pəld\ unpeopled—*also pasts of verbs listed at* EOPLE

eordie \ȯrd-ē\ see [1]ORDY

eorem \ir-əm\ see ERUM

eorge \ȯrj\ see ORGE

eorgian \ȯr-jən\ see ORGIAN

eorist \ir-əst\ see [1]ERIST

eoul \ōl\ see [1]OLE

eous \ē-əs\ see [1]EUS

ep \ep\ hep, pep, prep, rep, schlepp, skep, step, steppe, strep, yep, Alep, crowstep, doorstep, footstep, goose-step, instep, lockstep, misstep, one-step, quickstep, salep, sidestep, two-step, unstep, corbiestep, demirep, overstep, step-by-step, Gaziantep

eparable \ep-rə-bəl\ reparable, separable, inseparable, irreparable

epard \ep-ərd\ see EOPARD

epe \āp\ see [1]APE

epee \ē-pē\ see EEPY

eper \ep-ər\ see EPPER

eperous \ep-rəs\ leprous, obstreperous

epey \ā-pē\ see APEY

eph \ef\ see [1]EF

epha \ē-fə\ ephah, Recife, synalepha, synaloepha

ephalin \ef-ə-lən\ cephalin, encephalon, enkephalin, acanthocephalan

ephaly \ef-ə-lē\ anencephaly, brachycephaly, microcephaly

ephen \ē-vən\ see EVEN

epherd \ep-ərd\ see EOPARD

epherdess \ep-ərd-əs\ see EOPARDESS

ephone \ef-ə-nē\ see EPHONY

ephony \ef-ə-nē\ Stefanie, Stefany, Persephone, telephony

ephor \ef-ər\ deafer, ephor, feoffor, heifer, zephyr, hasenpfeffer

ephrine \ef-rən\ epinephrine, norepinephrine

epht \eft\ see EFT

ephyr \ef-ər\ see EPHOR

epi \ā-pē\ see APEY

epid \ep-əd\ tepid, trepid, intrepid

epo \ēp-ō\ see EPOT

epot \ēp-ō\ depot, Ipo, pepo, el cheapo

epp \ep\ see EP

eppe \ep\ see EP

epped \ept\ see EPT

epper \ep-ər\ hepper, leper, pepper, stepper, Colepeper, Culpeper, sidestepper

eppy \ep-ē\ peppy, preppy, orthoepy

eprous \ep-rəs\ see EPEROUS

eps \eps\ biceps, forceps, triceps, quadriceps, editio princeps—*also plurals and possessives of nouns and third person singular presents of verbs listed at* EP

epsis \ep-səs\ skepsis, prolepsis, syllepsis, omphaloskepsis

epsy \ep-sē\ catalepsy, epilepsy, narcolepsy, nympholepsy
ept \ept\ crept, kept, sept, slept, stepped, swept, wept, accept, adept, backswept, concept, except, incept, inept, percept, precept, transept, upswept, windswept, yclept, high-concept, intercept, nympholept, overslept, self-concept—*also pasts of verbs listed at* EP
eptable \ep-tə-bəl\ see EPTIBLE
eptacle \ep-ti-kəl\ skeptical, conceptacle, receptacle
epter \ep-tər\ see EPTOR
eptible \ep-tə-bəl\ acceptable, perceptible, susceptible, imperceptible, insusceptible, unacceptable
eptic \ep-tik\ peptic, septic, skeptic, aseptic, dyspeptic, eupeptic, proleptic, sylleptic, antiseptic, cataleptic, epileptic, narcoleptic, nympholeptic
eptical \ep-ti-kəl\ see EPTACLE
eptile \ep-tᵊl\ see EPTAL
eption \ep-shən\ conception, deception, exception, inception, perception, reception, subreption, apperception, contraception, interception, misconception, preconception, self-conception, self-perception
eptional \ep-shnəl\ conceptional, deceptional, exceptional, unexceptional
eptive \ep-tiv\ acceptive, conceptive, deceptive, exceptive, inceptive, perceptive, preceptive, receptive, susceptive, apperceptive, contraceptive, imperceptive
eptor \ep-tər\ scepter, accepter, acceptor, inceptor, preceptor, receptor, intercepter, interceptor
eptual \ep-chəl\ conceptual, perceptual
eptus \ep-təs\ conceptus, textus receptus
epy \ep-ē\ see EPPY
epys \ēps\ Pepys—*also possessives and plurals of nouns and third person singular presents of verbs listed at* EEP
equal \ē-kwəl\ equal, prequel, sequel, coequal, unequal
eque \ek\ see ECK
equel \ē-kwəl\ see EQUAL
equence \ē-kwəns\ frequence, sequence, infrequence, subsequence
equency \ē-kwən-sē\ frequency, sequency, infrequency
equent \ē-kwənt\ frequent, sequent, infrequent
equer \ek-ər\ see ECKER
[1]**er** \ā\ see [1]AY
[2]**er** \er\ see [4]ARE
[3]**er** \ər\ see [1]EUR
[4]**er** \ir\ see [2]EER
[1]**era** \er-ə\ era, Sara, Sarah, sclera, terra, caldera, Rivera, sierra, tiara, aloe vera, ciguatera, cordillera, guayabera, habanera, Halmahera, riviera, Riviera, Santa Clara
[2]**era** \ir-ə\ era, gerah, Hera, lira,

Pyrrha, sera, sirrah, Vera, wirra, chimaera, chimera, hetaera, lempira, Madeira, mbira, Altamira
erable \ər-ə-bəl\ thurible, conferrable, deferrable, deterrable, inferable, preferable, transferable
erah \ir-ə\ see [2]ERA
[1]eral \ir-əl\ Cyril, feral, seral, spheral, virile
[2]eral \er-əl\ see ERIL
[3]eral \ər-əl\ see ERRAL
erald \er-əld\ Gerald, Harold, herald, Jerald, Jerold, Jerrold, Fitzgerald, FitzGerald
eraph \er-əf\ see ERIF
erapy \er-əld\ therapy, chemotherapy, chronotherapy, aromatherapy
eratin \er-ət-ᵊn\ keratin, Sheraton, Samaritan
erative \er-ət-iv\ see [1]ARATIVE
eraton \er-ət-ᵊn\ see ERATIN
erb \ərb\ blurb, curb, herb, kerb, Serb, verb, acerb, adverb, disturb, exurb, perturb, potherb, pro-verb, proverb, reverb, suburb, superb
erbal \ər-bəl\ burble, gerbil, herbal, verbal, deverbal, nonverbal, preverbal
erbalist \ər-bə-ləst\ herbalist, verbalist, hyperbolist
erbally \ər-bə-lē\ verbally, hyperbole, nonverbally
erber \ər-bər\ see URBER
erberis \ər-bər-əs\ berberis, Cerberus
erberus \ər-bər-əs\ see ERBERIS
erbet \ər-bət\ see URBIT
erbia \ər-bē-ə\ see URBIA
erbial \ər-bē-əl\ adverbial, proverbial
erbid \ər-bəd\ see URBID
erbil \ər-bəl\ see ERBAL
erbium \ər-bē-əm\ erbium, terbium, ytterbium
erbole \ər-bə-lē\ see ERBALLY
erbolist \ər-bə-ləst\ see ERBALIST
erby \ər-bē\ derby, Derby, herby, Kirby
ercal \ər-kəl\ see IRCLE
erce \ərs\ see ERSE
ercé \ers\ see [1]ARCE
ercel \ər-səl\ see [1]ERSAL
ercement \ər-smənt\ amercement, disbursement, reimbursement
ercer \ər-sər\ see URSOR
ercery \ərs-rē\ see URSARY
erch \ərch\ see URCH
ercia \ər-shə\ see ERTIA
ercial \ər-shəl\ Herschel, Hershel, commercial, inertial, controversial, uncommercial, semicommercial
ercian \ər-shən\ see ERTIAN
ercible \ər-sə-bəl\ see ERSIBLE
ercion \ər-zhən\ see [1]ERSION
ercis \ər-səs\ see ERSUS
ercive \ər-siv\ see ERSIVE
ercular \ər-kyə-lər\ see IRCULAR
ercy \ər-sē\ Circe, mercy, Percy, pursy, gramercy, controversy
erd \ərd\ see IRD
[1]erde \erd\ see AIRED
[2]erde \ərd\ see IRD
[3]erde \ərd-ē\ see URDY

erder \ərd-ər\ birder, girder, herder, murder, self-murder, sheepherder
erderer \ərd-ər-ər\ see URDERER
[1]**erdi** \ər-dē\ see URDY
[2]**erdi** \er-dē\ Verdi, Monteverdi
erdin \ərd-ᵊn\ see URDEN
erding \ərd-iŋ\ wording, sheepherding
erdu \ər-dü\ perdu, perdue, Urdu
erdue \ər-dü\ see ERDU
erdure \ər-jər\ see ERGER
[1]**ere** \er\ see [4]ARE
[2]**ere** \er-ē\ see [1]ARY
[3]**ere** \ir\ see [2]EER
[4]**ere** \ir-ē\ see EARY
[5]**ere** \ər\ see [1]EUR
e're \ē-ər\ see [1]EER
ère \er\ see [4]ARE
ereal \ir-ē-əl\ see ERIAL
ereid \ir-ē-əd\ see ERIOD
erek \erik\ see [1]ERIC
erely \ir-lē\ see [1]EARLY
erement \er-ə-mənt\ see ERIMENT
[1]**erence** \ir-əns\ clearance, adherence, appearance, coherence, inherence, incoherence, interference, perseverance
[2]**erence** \ər-əns\ see URRENCE
[3]**erence** \er-ᵊns\ see ARENCE
[1]**erency** \ir-ən-sē\ coherency, vicegerency
[2]**erency** \er-ən-sē\ see ERRANCY
[1]**erent** \ir-ənt\ gerent, adherent, coherent, inherent, sederunt, vicegerent, incoherent
[2]**erent** \er-ənt\ see [1]ARENT
[1]**eren't** \ərnt\ see EARNT
[2]**eren't** \ər-ənt\ see URRENT
ereo \er-ē-ō\ see ARIO
ereous \ir-ē-əs\ see ERIOUS
erer \ir-ər\ see [2]EARER
[1]**eres** \erz\ see AIRS
[2]**eres** \ir-ēz\ see ERIES
[3]**eres** \ərs\ see ERS
eresy \er-ə-sē\ clerisy, heresy
ereth \er-ət\ see ERIT
ereus \ir-ē-əs\ see ERIOUS
erf \ərf\ see URF
erg \ərg\ berg, burg, erg, Augsburg, Boksburg, exergue, hamburg, Hamburg, Hapsburg, homburg, iceberg, Lemberg, Limburg, Lindbergh, Newburg, Pittsburgh, Salzburg, Sandburg, Strasbourg, svedberg, Tilburg, Drakensberg, Gutenberg, Harrisburg, Inselberg, Königsberg, Luxembourg, Magdeburg, Nuremberg, Toggenburg, Venusberg, Wallenberg, Würtemberg, Rube Goldberg, Johannesburg, St. Petersburg, von Hindenberg, Baden-Wurtenberg, Pietermaritzburg, Yekaterinburg, Roodepoort-Maraisburg
ergative \ər-gə-tir\ ergative, purgative
erge \ərj\ see URGE
ergeant \är-jənt\ see ARGENT
ergen \ər-gən\ Bergen, Spitzbergen
ergence \ər-jəns\ convergence, divergence, emergence, immergence, insurgence, resurgence, submergence

ergency \ər-jən-sē\ urgency, convergency, detergency, divergency, emergency, insurgency, counterinsurgency
ergent \ər-jənt\ see URGENT
ergeon \ər-jin\ see URGEON
erger \ər-jər\ merger, perjure, purger, scourger, urger, verdure, verger, deterger
ergh \ərg\ see ERG
ergic \ər-jik\ allergic, synergic, theurgic, demiurgic, dramaturgic, thaumaturgic, alpha-adrenergic, beta-adrenergic
ergid \ər-jid\ see URGID
[1]**ergne** \ərn\ see URN
[2]**ergne** \ern\ see [1]ERN
ergo \ər-gō\ ergo, Virgo
ergue \ərg\ see ERG
ergy \ər-jē\ see URGY
[1]**eri** \er-ē\ see [1]ARY
[2]**eri** \ir-ē\ see EARY
[1]**eria** \ir-ē-ə\ feria, Styria, Syria, Algeria, Assyria, asteria, bacteria, collyria, criteria, diphtheria, Egeria, franseria, Illyria, Liberia, Nigeria, plumeria, porphyria, Siberia, wisteria, cafeteria, cryptomeria, latimeria, sansevieria, washateria, opera seria
[2]**eria** \er-ē-ə\ see ARIA
erial \ir-ē-əl\ aerial, cereal, ferial, serial, arterial, bacterial, empyreal, ethereal, funereal, imperial, material, sidereal, venereal, vizierial, immaterial, magisterial, managerial, ministerial, presbyterial
[1]**erian** \ir-ē-ən\ Adlerian, Assyrian, Aterian, Cimmerian, criterion, Hesperian, Hutterian, Hyperion, Iberian, Illyrian, Mousterian, Mullerian, Pierian, Shakespearean, Spencerian, Spenglerian, Sumerian, valerian, Valerian, Wagnerian, Hanoverian, Presbyterian, Thraco-Illyrian
[2]**erian** \er-ē-ən\ see [1]ARIAN
[1]**eric** \er-ik\ Berwick, cleric, Derek, derrick, Eric, Erich, Erik, ferric, Herrick, xeric, aspheric, chimeric, choleric, cholesteric, entheric, generic, Homeric, mesmeric, numeric, alphanumeric, atmospheric, climacteric, congeneric, dysenteric, esoteric
[2]**eric** \ir-ik\ lyric, pyric, pyrrhic, spheric, xeric, aspheric, chimeric, empiric, satiric, satyric, atmospheric, hemispheric, stratospheric, panegyric
erica \er-i-kə\ erica, Erica, Erika, America, esoterica, North America, South America, Latin America
[1]**erical** \er-i-kəl\ clerical, chimerical, numerical, anticlerical
[2]**erical** \ir-i-kəl\ lyrical, miracle, spherical, spiracle, empirical, hemispherical
erich \erik\ see [1]ERIC
erics \er-iks\ sferics, hysterics—*also plurals and possessives of nouns listed at* [1]ERIC
eried \ir-ē-əd\ see ERIOD

eries \ir-ēz\ Ceres, series, dundrearies, miniseries—*also plurals and possessives of nouns and third person singular presents of verbs listed at* EARY
erif \er-əf\ seraph, serif, sheriff, teraph, sans serif
eriff \er-əf\ see ERIF
erik \erik\ see [1]ERIC
erika \er-i-kə\ see ERICA
eril \er-əl\ beryl, Beryl, Cheryl, Errol, feral, ferrule, ferule, Merrill, peril, Sherrill, Sheryl, sterile, Terrell, Terrill, imperil, chrysoberyl
erilant \er-ə-lənt\ see ERULENT
erile \er-əl\ see ERIL
erilous \er-ə-ləs\ perilous, querulous, glomerulus
eriment \er-ə-mənt\ cerement, experiment, gedankenexperiment
erin \er-ən\ see [1]ARON
ering \ar-iŋ\ see [1]ARING
eriod \ir-ē-əd\ myriad, nereid, Nereid, period, photoperiod
erion \ir-ē-ən\ see [1]ERIAN
erior \ir-ē-ər\ anterior, exterior, inferior, interior, posterior, superior, ulterior, Lake Superior—*also comparatives of adjectives listed at* EARY
eriot \er-ē-ət\ see [1]ARIAT
erious \ir-ē-əs\ cereus, Nereus, serious, Sirius, cinereous, delirious, Guarnerius, imperious, mysterious, Tiberius, deleterious
[1]**eris** \ir-əs\ see EROUS
[2]**eris** \er-əs\ see ERROUS
[1]**erist** \ir-əst\ querist, theorist, verist, careerist, panegyrist—*also superlatives of adjectives listed at* [2]EER
[2]**erist** \er-əst\ see ARIST
erisy \er-ə-sē\ see ERESY
erit \er-ət\ ferret, merit, terret, demerit, inherit, disinherit, Shemini Atzereth
eritable \er-ət-ə-bəl\ heritable, veritable, inheritable
eritor \er-ət-ər\ ferreter, heritor, inheritor
erity \er-ət-ē\ ferity, ferrety, rarity, verity, asperity, celerity, dexterity, legerity, posterity, prosperity, severity, sincerity, temerity, insincerity, ambidexterity, subsidiarity
erium \ir-ē-əm\ Miriam, criterium, bacterium, collyrium, delirium, imperium, psalterium, atmospherium, magisterium, archaeobacterium
[1]**erius** \er-ē-əs\ see ARIOUS
[2]**erius** \ir-ē-əs\ see ERIOUS
erjure \ər-jər\ see ERGER
erjury \ərj-rē\ perjury, surgery, microsurgery, neurosurgery
erk \ərk\ see [1]ORK
erker \ər-kər\ see [1]ORKER
erkin \ər-kən\ see IRKIN
erking \ər-kiŋ\ see ORKING
erkly \ər-klē\ clerkly, berserkly
erky \ər-kē\ birkie, jerky, murky, perky, smirky, turkey, Turkey, Turki, Albuquerque, herky-jerky
erle \ərl\ see [1]IRL
erlie \er-lē\ see AIRLY
erlin \ər-lən\ merlin, Merlin,

merlon, Merlyn, purlin, yearling
erling \ər-liŋ\ see URLING
erlon \ər-lən\ see ERLIN
erlyn \ər-lən\ see ERLIN
erm \ərm\ see [1]ORM
erma \ər-mə\ dharma, Erma, herma, Irma, scleroderma, terra firma
ermal \ər-məl\ dermal, thermal, nonthermal, subdermal, transdermal, ectodermal, endothermal, epidermal, exothermal, hydrothermal, hypodermal, hypothermal
erman \ər-mən\ ermine, german, German, germen, Herman, Hermann, merman, sermon, Sherman, Thurman, vermin, determine, extermine, Mount Hermon, predetermine, cousin-german, Tibeto-Burman
ermanent \ər-mə-nənt\ permanent, determinant, impermanent, semipermanent
ermann \ər-mən\ see ERMAN
ermary \ərm-rē\ see IRMARY
erment \ər-mənt\ averment, conferment, deferment, determent, interment, preferment, disinterment
ermer \ər-mər\ see URMUR
ermes \ər-mēz\ Hermes, kermes
ermi \ər-mē\ see ERMY
ermic \ər-mik\ dharmic, thermic, geothermic, hypodermic, taxidermic, electrothermic
ermin \ər-mən\ see ERMAN
erminable \ərm-nə-bəl\ terminable, determinable, interminable, indeterminable
erminal \ərm-nəl\ germinal, terminal, preterminal, subterminal
erminant \ər-mə-nənt\ see ERMANENT
ermine \ər-mən\ see ERMAN
ermined \ər-mənd\ ermined, determined, self-determined, overdetermined
erminous \ər-mə-nəs\ terminus, verminous, conterminous, coterminous
erminus \ər-mə-nəs\ see ERMINOUS
ermis \ər-məs\ dermis, kermis, kirmess, thermos, endodermis, epidermis, exodermis
ermit \ər-mət\ hermit, Kermit, Thermit
ermon \ər-mən\ see ERMAN
ermos \ər-məs\ see ERMIS
ermy \ər-mē\ fermi, germy, squirmy, wormy, diathermy, endothermy, taxidermy
[1]**ern** \ern\ bairn, Bern, cairn, hern, Nairn, Auvergne, moderne, Pitcairn, Sauternes, Ygerne, art moderne
[2]**ern** \ərn\ see URN
erna \ər-nə\ dharna, Myrna, sterna, Verna, cisterna
ernal \ərn-ᵊl\ colonel, journal, kernel, sternal, vernal, diurnal, eternal, external, fraternal, hibernal, infernal, internal, maternal, nocturnal, paternal, supernal, coeternal, sempiternal, semidiurnal
ernary \ər-nə-rē\ fernery, ternary, turnery, quaternary

[1]erne \ern\ see [1]ERN

[2]erne \ərn\ see URN

erned \ərnd\ see URNED

ernel \ərn-ᵊl\ see ERNAL

erner \ər-nər\ see URNER

[1]ernes \ern\ see [1]ERN

[2]ernes \ərn\ see URN

ernest \ər-nəst\ see ERNIST

ernia \ər-ne-ə\ hernia, Ibernia

ernian \ər-nē-ən\ Hibernian, quaternion, Saturnian

ernible \ər-nə-bəl\ see URNABLE

ernie \ər-nē\ see [1]OURNEY

ernier \ər-nē-ər\ see OURNEYER

ernion \ər-nē-ən\ see ERNIAN

ernist \ər-nəst\ earnest, Earnest, Ernest, internist

ernity \ər-nət-ē\ eternity, fraternity, maternity, modernity, paternity, quaternity, coeternity, confraternity, sempiternity

ernment \ərn-mənt\ adjournment, attornment, concernment, discernment, internment

ernum \ər-nəm\ see URNUM

erny \ər-nē\ see [1]OURNEY

[1]ero \ē-rō\ giro, gyro, hero, Hero, Nero, zero, subzero, antihero, superhero

[2]ero \er-ō\ aero, cero, Duero, Faeroe, faro, Faroe, pharaoh, taro, tarot, bolero, bracero, cruzeiro, Guerrero, Herero, Madero, montero, pampero, primero, ranchero, sombrero, torero, vaquero, burladero, caballero, Mescalero, novillero, banderillero, carabinero, embarcadero, Rio de Janeiro

[3]ero \ir-ō\ giro, guiro, gyro, hero, zero, primero

erod \er-əd\ Herod, out-Herod, viverrid

erold \er-əld\ see ERALD

eron \er-ən\ see [1]ARON

erous \ir-əs\ cerous, cirrous, cirrus, Eris, peeress, Pyrrhus, scirrhous, scirrhus, seeress, serous

erp \ərp\ see URP

erpe \ər-pē\ see IRPY

erque \ər-kē\ see ERKY

[1]err \er\ see [4]ARE

[2]err \ər\ see [1]EUR

erra \er-ə\ see [1]ERA

errable \ər-ə-bəl\ see ERABLE

errace \er-əs\ see ERROUS

erral \ər-əl\ bharal, scurrile, squirrel, conferral, deferral, demurral, referral, transferal

errance \er-əns\ see ARENCE

errancy \er-ən-sē\ errancy, aberrancy, coherency, inerrancy

errand \er-ənd\ errand, gerund

errant \er-ənt\ see [1]ARENT

erre \er\ see [4]ARE

errell \er-əl\ see ERIL

[1]errence \ər-əns\ see URRENCE

[2]errence \er-əns\ see ARENCE

errent \ər-ənt\ see URRENT

errer \ər-ər\ burrer, stirrer, conferrer, deferrer, demurer, demurrer, deterrer, inferrer, preferrer, referrer, transferrer

erret \er-ət\ see ERIT

erreter \er-ət-ər\ see ERITOR

erria \er-ē-ə\ see ARIA

errible \er-ə-bəl\ see [1]EARABLE

erric \er-ik\ see [1]ERIC
errick \er-ik\ see [1]ERIC
errid \er-əd\ see EROD
errie \er-ē\ see [1]ARY
erried \er-ēd\ berried, serried, varied—*also pasts of verbs listed at* [1]ARY
errier \er-ē-ər\ burier, terrier, varier, bullterrier—*also comparatives of adjectives listed at* [1]ARY
errill \er-əl\ see ERIL
errily \er-ə-lē\ see ARILY
[1]**erring** \ar-iŋ\ see [1]ARING
[2]**erring** \ər-iŋ\ see URRING
erris \er-əs\ see ERROUS
errol \er-əl\ see ERIL
errold \er-əld\ see ERALD
erron \er-ən\ see [1]ARON
error \er-ər\ see [1]EARER
errous \er-əs\ derris, Eris, ferrous, parous, terrace, nonferrous, millionairess
errule \er-əl\ see ERIL
erry \er-ē\ see [1]ARY
[1]**ers** \ərz\ furze, hers, somewheres, Voyageurs—*also plurals and possessives of nouns and third person singular presents of verbs listed at* [1]EUR
[2]**ers** \ā\ see [1]AY
ersa \ər-sə\ bursa, Bursa, vice versa
ersable \ər-sə-bəl\ see ERSIBLE
[1]**ersal** \ər-səl\ bursal, tercel, versal, dispersal, rehearsal, reversal, transversal, traversal, universal
[2]**ersal** \är-səl\ see ARSAL
ersant \ərs-ᵊnt\ versant, conversant
ersary \ərs-rē\ see URSARY
erse \ərs\ birse, burse, curse, Erse, hearse, nurse, perse, purse, terce, terse, thyrse, verse, worse, adverse, amerce, asperse, averse, coerce, commerce, converse, cutpurse, disburse, disperse, diverse, immerse, inverse, Nez Perce, obverse, perverse, rehearse, reverse, sesterce, stress-verse, submerse, transverse, traverse, intersperse, reimburse, universe
ersed \ərst\ see URST
erser \ər-sər\ see URSOR
ersey \ər-zē\ furzy, jersey, Jersey, kersey, Mersey, New Jersey
erschel \ər-shəl\ see ERCIAL
ershel \ər-shəl\ see ERCIAL
ersial \ər-shəl\ see ERCIAL
ersian \ər-zhən\ see [1]ERSION
ersible \ər-sə-bəl\ coercible, conversable, dispersible, eversible, immersible, reversible, submersible, traversable, incoercible, irreversible, semisubmersible
[1]**ersion** \ər-zhən\ Persian, version, aspersion, aversion, coercion, conversion, dispersion, diversion, emersion, eversion, excursion, immersion, incursion, inversion, perversion, recursion, reversion, submersion, subversion, ambiversion, extroversion, interspersion, introversion, reconversion, retroversion,

animadversion, seroconversion
[2]**ersion** \ər-shən\ see ERTIAN
ersional \ər-zhə-nəl\ versional, conversional, reversional
ersionist \ər-zhə-nəst\ diversionist, excursionist
[1]**ersity** \ər-sət-ē\ adversity, diversity, multiversity, university, biodiversity
[2]**ersity** \ər-stē\ see IRSTY
ersive \ər-siv\ cursive, ambersive, aversive, coercive, detersive, discursive, dispersive, excursive, inversive, perversive, recursive, subversive, extroversive, introversive
erson \ərs-ᵊn\ person, worsen, chairperson, craftsperson, draftsperson, houseperson, MacPherson, newsperson, nonperson, salesperson, spokesperson, unperson, anchorperson, businessperson, gentleperson, weatherperson
erst \ərst\ see URST
ersted \ər-stəd\ oersted, worsted, kilooersted
ersus \ər-səs\ cercis, thyrsus, versus, excursus
ersy \ər-sē\ see ERCY
[1]**ert** \ərt\ Bert, blurt, Burt, chert, curt, dirt, flirt, girt, hurt, Kurt, pert, quirt, shirt, skirt, spurt, squirt, sturt, vert, wert, wort, advert, alert, assert, avert, bellwort, birthwort, Blackshirt, brownshirt, Cape Vert, colewort, concert, convert, covert, desert, dessert, dissert, divert, evert, exert, expert, exsert, figwort, fleawort, frankfurt, glasswort, hoopskirt, hornwort, inert, insert, invert, lousewort, lungwort, madwort, milkwort, nightshirt, outskirt, overt, pervert, pilewort, ragwort, redshirt, revert, ribwort, saltwort, sandwort, seagirt, Shubert, soapwort, spearwort, spleenwort, stitchwort, stonewort, subvert, sweatshirt, toothwort, T-shirt, ungirt, ambivert, bladderwort, butterwort, controvert, disconcert, extrovert, feverwort, inexpert, introvert, liverwort, malapert, miniskirt, mitrewort, moneywort, overshirt, overskirt, pennywort, pettiskirt, preconcert, reconvert, Saint-John's-wort, spiderwort, swallowwort, thoroughwort, undershirt, underskirt, animadvert, interconvert
[2]**ert** \er\ see [4]ARE
[3]**ert** \at\ see [5]AT
erta \ərt-ə\ Gerta, Alberta, Roberta
ertain \ərt-ᵊn\ burton, Burton, certain, curtain, Merton, uncertain
ertant \ərt-ᵊnt\ see ERTENT
erted \ərt-əd\ skirted, concerted, perverted, T-shirted, extroverted, miniskirted, undershirted—*also pasts of verbs listed at* [1]ERT
ertedly \ərt-əd-lē\ assertedly, concertedly, pervertedly

ertence \ərt-ᵊns\ advertence, inadvertence
ertent \ərt-ᵊnt\ advertent, revertant, inadvertent
erter \ərt-ər\ blurter, skirter, squirter, stertor, converter, inverter, subverter, controverter—*also comparatives of adjectives listed at* [1]ERT
[1]**ertes** \ərt-ēz\ certes, Laertes
[2]**ertes** \ərts\ see ERTS
ertford \ärt-fərd\ see ARTFORD
erth \ərth\ see IRTH
ertha \ər-thə\ Bertha, Eartha
ertia \ər-shə\ Mercia, Murcia, inertia
ertial \ər-shəl\ see ERCIAL
ertian \ər-shən\ tertian, assertion, Cistercian, desertion, exertion, insertion, Mercian, self-assertion
ertible \ərt-ə-bəl\ convertible, invertible, controvertible, inconvertible, incontrovertible, interconvertible
ertile \ərt-ᵊl\ curtal, fertile, hurtle, kirtle, myrtle, Myrtle, spurtle, turtle, cross-fertile, exsertile, infertile, interfertile
ertinence \ərt-ᵊn-əns\ pertinence, purtenance, appurtenance, impertinence
[1]**ertinent** \ərt-ᵊn-ənt\ pertinent, appurtentant, impertinent
[2]**ertinent** \ərt-nənt\ see IRTINENT
erting \ərt-iŋ\ shirting, skirting, disconcerting, self-asserting—*also present participles of verbs listed at* [1]ERT
ertion \ər-shən\ see ERTIAN
ertisement \ərt-əs-mənt\ advertisement, divertissement
ertium \ər-shəm\ see URTIUM
ertive \ərt-iv\ furtive, assertive, self-assertive, unassertive
erton \ərt-n\ see ERTAIN
ertor \ərt-ər\ see ERTER
erts \ərts\ certes, hertz, nerts, weltschmerz, gigahertz, kilohertz, megahertz—*also plurals and possessives of nouns and third person singular presents of verbs listed at* [1]ERT
erty \ər-tē\ see IRTY
ertz \ərts\ see ERTS
erule \er-əl\ see ERIL
erulent \er-ə-lənt\ sterilant, puberulent, pulverulent
erulous \er-ə-ləs\ see ERILOUS
erum \ir-əm\ theorem, serum
erund \er-ənd\ see ERRAND
erunt \er-ənt\ see [1]ARENT
erval \ər-vəl\ see ERVIL
ervancy \ər-vən-sē\ see ERVENCY
ervant \ər-vənt\ fervent, servant, maidservant, manservant, observant
ervative \ər-vət-iv\ conservative, preservative, archconservative, neoconservative, semiconservative
ervator \ər-vət-ər\ see ERVITOR
erve \ərv\ curve, MIRV, nerve, serve, swerve, verve, conserve, deserve, disserve, hors d'oeuvre, incurve, innerve, observe, preserve,

reserve, self-serve, subserve, unnerve, unreserve
erved \ərvd\ nerved, decurved, deserved, recurved, reserved, underserved, unreserved—*also pasts of verbs listed at* ERVE
ervency \ər-vən-sē\ fervency, conservancy
ervent \ər-vənt\ see ERVANT
erver \ər-vər\ fervor, server, deserver, observer, timeserver
ervice \ər-vəs\ nervous, service, disservice, full-service, in-service, self-service, interservice
ervil \ər-vəl\ chervil, serval, servile
ervile \ər-vəl\ see ERVIL
erviness \ər-vē-nəs\ nerviness, topsy-turviness
erving \ər-viŋ\ Irving, serving, deserving, self-serving, timeserving, unswerving
ervitor \ər-vət-ər\ servitor, conservator
ervor \ər-vər\ see ERVER
ervous \ər-vəs\ see ERVICE
ervy \ər-vē\ see URVY
erwick \er-ik\ see [1]ERIC
erwin \ər-wən\ Irwin, Sherwin
[1]**ery** \er-ē\ see [1]ARY
[2]**ery** \ir-ē\ see EARY
eryl \er-əl\ see ERIL
erz \erts\ see [1]ERTZ
[1]**es** \ā\ see [1]AY
[2]**es** \ās\ see [1]ACE
[3]**es** \āz\ see [1]AZE
[4]**es** \es\ see ESS
[5]**es** \ēz\ see EZE
e's \ēz\ see EZE
[1]**esa** \ā-sə\ mesa, Mesa, presa, omasa, Teresa, Theresa
[2]**esa** \ā-zə\ presa, impresa, marchesa, Bel Paese, Maria Theresa
esage \es-ij\ see ESSAGE
[1]**esan** \āz-ᵊn\ see AZON
[2]**esan** \ēz-ᵊn\ see EASON
esant \ez-ᵊnt\ bezant, peasant, pheasant, pleasant, present, unpleasant, omnipresent
esas \ā-zəs\ Marquesas—*also plurals and possessives of nouns listed at* [2]ESA
esce \es\ see ESS
escence \es-ᵊns\ essence, candescence, concrescence, excrescence, florescence, fluorescence, pearlescence, pubescence, putrescence, quiescence, quintessence, senescence, tumescence, turgescence, virescence, acquiescence, adolescence, arborescence, coalescence, convalescence, decalescence, defervescence, deliquescence, detumescence, effervescence, efflorescence, evanescence, incandescence, inflorescence, iridescence, juvenescence, luminescence, obsolescence, opalescence, prepubescence, preadolescence
escency \es-ᵊn-sē\ excrescency, incessancy
escent \es-ᵊnt\ crescent, Crescent, candescent, canescent, concrescent, decrescent, depressant, excrescent, fluorescent, frutescent, incessant,

increscent, liquescent, pearlescent, pubescent, putrescent, quiescent, rufescent, senescent, suppressant, tumescent, turgescent, virescent, acaulescent, acquiescent, adolescent, coalescent, convalescent, detumescent, effervescent, efflorescent, arborescent, evanescent, incandescent, inflorescent, intumescent, irridescent, juvenescent, luminescent, opalescent, phosphorescent, prepubescent, recrudescent, viridescent, antidepressant, preadolescent

escible \es-ə-bəl\ see ESSIBLE

escience \ēsh-əns\ nescience, prescience

escive \es-iv\ see ESSIVE

esco \es-kō\ alfresco, barbaresco

escue \es-kyü\ fescue, rescue

[1]**ese** \ēs\ see IECE

[2]**ese** \ēz\ see EZE

[3]**ese** \ā-sē\ see ACY

esence \ez-ᵊns\ pleasance, presence, omnipresence

eseus \ē-sē-əs\ Theseus, Tiresias

[1]**esh** \esh\ crèche, flèche, flesh, fresh, mesh, thresh, afresh, bobeche, calèche, crème fraîche, enmesh, gooseflesh, horseflesh, immesh, parfleche, refresh, tête-bêche, Bangladesh, Gilgamesh, intermesh, Marrakech, Andhra Pradesh, Madhya Pradesh, Uttar Pradesh, Himachral Pradesh, Arunachal Pradesh

[2]**esh** \āsh\ see [1]ECHE

[3]**esh** \ash\ see [3]ASH

eshed \esht\ fleshed, meshed—*also pasts of verbs listed at* [1]ESH

eshen \esh-ən\ see ESSION

eshener \esh-ə-nər\ see ESSIONER

esher \esh-ər\ see ESSURE

eshly \esh-lē\ fleshly, freshly, specially, especially

eshment \esh-mənt\ fleshment, enmeshment, refreshment

[1]**esi** \ā-zē\ see AZY

[2]**esi** \ā-sē\ see ACY

[1]**esia** \ē-shə\ geisha, Moesia, Letitia, Lucretia, Magnesia, Phoenicia, alpoecia

[2]**esia** \ē-zhə\ freesia, amnesia, esthesia, frambesia, magnesia, rafflesia, Silesia, Tunisia, analgesia, anesthesia, Austronesia, Indonesia, Melanesia, Micronesia, Polynesia, synesthesia

esial \ē-zē-əl\ mesial, ecclesial

[1]**esian** \ē-zhən\ Friesian, Frisian, lesion, adhesion, Cartesian, cohesion, etesian, Salesian, Austronesian, holstein-friesian, Indonesian, Melanesian, Micronesian, Polynesian

[2]**esian** \ē-shən\ see [1]ETION

esias \ē-sē-əs\ see ESEUS

esicant \es-i-kənt\ see ESICCANT

esiccant \es-i-kənt\ desiccant, vesicant

esidency \ez-əd-ən-sē\ presidency, residency, nonresidency, vice-presidency

esident \ez-əd-ənt\ president,

resident, nonresident, vice-president
esima \es-ə-mə\ Quinquagesima, Sexagesima, Septuagesima
esimal \es-ə-məl\ centesimal, millesimal, vigesimal, duodecimal, planetesimal, sexagesimal, infinitesimal
esin \ez-ᵊn\ resin, muezzin, oleoresin
esion \ē-zhən\ see [1]ESIAN
esis \ē-səs\ Croesus, thesis, tmesis, ascesis, askesis, esthesis, mimesis, prosthesis, anamnesis, catachresis, catechesis, Dionysus, exegesis, hyperkinesis, Peloponnesus, psychokinesis, telekinesis, amniocentesis
esium \ē-zē-əm\ see EZIUM
esive \ē-siv\ adhesive, cohesive, self-adhesive
esk \esk\ see ESQUE
esley \es-lē\ see ESSLY
eslie \es-lē\ see ESSLY
esne \ēn\ see [3]INE
[1]eso \ā-sō\ peso, say-so
[2]eso \es-ō\ see ESSO
espass \es-pəs\ Thespis, trespass
espis \es-pəs\ see ESPASS
espite \es-pət\ see ESPOT
espot \es-pət\ despot, respite
esque \esk\ desk, burlesque, grotesque, moresque, arabesque, Bunyanesque, copydesk, gigantesque, humoresque, Junoesque, Kafkaesque, picaresque, picturesque, plateresque, Rubenesque, Romanesque, sculpturesque, statuesque, churrigueresque
ess \es\ bless, cess, chess, cress, dress, ess, fess, guess, Hesse, jess, less, loess, mess, ness, press, s, stress, tress, yes, abscess, access, address, aggress, assess, caress, clothespress, coatdress, compress, confess, CS, depress, digress, distress, duress, egress, excess, express, finesse, handpress, headdress, housedress, impress, ingress, largess, Meknes, nightdress, noblesse, obsess, oppress, outguess, pantdress, possess, precess, prestress, princess, process, profess, progress, re-press, recess, redress, regress, repress, shirtdress, sidedress, SS, success, sundress, suppress, top-dress, transgress, undress, unless, winepress, ABS, acquiesce, baroness, coalesce, convalesce, DES, decompress, deliquesce, derepress, dispossess, effervesce, effloresce, evanesce, gentilesse, GR-S, IHS, in-process, incandesce, intumesce, inverness, Inverness, letterpress, luminesce, Lyonnesse, minidress, nonetheless, obsolesce, otherguess, overdress, pennycress, phosphoresce, politesse, prepossess, preprocess, recrudesce, repossess,

reprocess, retrogress, second-guess, SOS, sweaterdress, unsuccess, watercress, window-dress, another-guess, nevertheless
essa \es-ə\ see [3]ESSE
essable \es-ə-bəl\ see ESSIBLE
essage \es-ij\ message, presage, expressage
essaly \es-ə-lē\ Cecily, Thessaly
essamine \es-mən\ see ESSMAN
essan \es-ᵊn\ see ESSEN
essancy \es-ᵊn-sē\ see ESCENCY
essant \es-ᵊnt\ see ESCENT
[1]**esse** \es\ see ESS
[2]**esse** \es-ē\ see ESSY
[3]**esse** \es-ə\ Hesse, Odessa, Vanessa
essed \est\ see EST
essedly \es-əd-lē\ blessedly, confessedly, professedly, possessedly, self-possessedly
essel \es-əl\ see [1]ESTLE
essen \es-ᵊn\ Essen, lessen, lesson, messan, delicatessen
essence \es-ᵊns\ see ESCENCE
esser \es-ər\ see ESSOR
essex \es-iks\ Essex, Wessex
essful \es-fəl\ stressful, distressful, successful, unsuccessful
essian \esh-ən\ see ESSION
essible \es-ə-bəl\ decibel, accessible, addressable, compressible, confessable, depressible, expressible, impressible, processible, putrescible, suppressible, inaccessible, incompressible, inexpressible, insuppressible, irrepressible
essie \es-ē\ see ESSY
essile \es-əl\ see [1]ESTLE
ession \esh-ən\ cession, freshen, hessian, session, accession, aggression, compression, concession, confession, depression, digression, discretion, egression, expression, impression, ingression, obsession, oppression, possession, precession, procession, profession, progression, recession, refreshen, regression, repression, secession, succession, suppression, transgression, decompression, dispossession, indiscretion, intercession, intersession, introgression, misimpression, prepossession, reimpression, repossession, retrogression, self-confession, self-expression, self-possession, supersession
essional \esh-ə-nəl\ sessional, acessional, concessional, congressional, diagressional, expressional, obsessional, possessional, precessional, processional, professional, progressional, recessional, successional, paraprofessional, preprofessional, subprofessional, paraprofessional, semiprofessional
essioner \esh-ə-nər\ freshener, concessioner
essionist \esh-ə-nəst\ expressionist, repressionist, impressionist, secessionist

essity \es-tē\ see ESTY
essive \es-iv\ crescive, aggressive, caressive, compressive, concessive, degressive, depressive, digressive, excessive, expressive, impressive, ingressive, obsessive, oppressive, possessive, progressive, recessive, regressive, successive, suppressive, transgressive, inexpressive, retrogressive, unexpressive, manic-depressive
essly \es-lē\ Leslie, Lesley, Wesley, expressly
essman \es-mən\ chessman, pressman, expressman, jessamine, specimen
essment \es-mənt\ see ESTMENT
esso \es-ō\ gesso, espresso
esson \es-ᵊn\ see ESSEN
essor \es-ər\ dresser, guesser, lesser, pressor, stressor, addresser, aggressor, assessor, caresser, compressor, confessor, depressor, expressor, hairdresser, oppressor, processor, professor, regressor, repressor, successor, suppresssor, transgressor, vinedresser, antecessor, dispossessor, intercessor, predecessor, repossessor, second-guesser, microprocessor, multiprocessor
essory \es-ə-rē\ pessary, accessory, possessory, intercessory
essure \esh-ər\ pressure, impressure, low-pressure, refresher, acupressure, overpressure
essy \es-ē\ Bessie, dressy, Jesse, Jessie, messy
est \est\ best, breast, Brest, chest, crest, gest, geste, guest, hest, jessed, jest, lest, nest, pest, prest, quest, rest, test, tressed, vest, west, West, wrest, zest, abreast, appressed, armrest, arrest, attest, backrest, beau geste, behest, bequest, bird's-nest, celeste, Celeste, compressed, congest, conquest, contest, detest, devest, digest, divest, egest, field-test, flight-test, footrest, gabfest, hard-pressed, headrest, hillcrest, houseguest, imprest, incest, infest, ingest, inquest, interest, invest, low-test, Mae West, Midwest, molest, northwest, posttest, pretest, professed, protest, redbreast, repressed, request, retest, revest, slugfest, southwest, suggest, trapnest, Trieste, t-test, unblessed, undressed, unrest, unstressed, almagest, anapest, Bucharest, Budapest, decongest, disinfest, disinvest, empty-nest, galley-west, manifest, north-northwest, palimpsest, predigest, reinvest, rinderpest, second-best, self-addressed, self-confessed, self-interest, self-possessed, supraprotest, sweatervest, uninterest, unprofessed, autosuggest, disinterest, robin redbreast,

underinvest, thirty-second rest—*also pasts of verbs listed at* ESS

esta \es-tə\ cesta, cuesta, testa, vesta, Vesta, Avesta, celesta, egesta, fiesta, ingesta, siesta, Zend-Avesta

estable \es-tə-bəl\ see ESTIBLE

estae \es-tē\ see ESTY

estal \es-t^{ə}l\ crestal, pestle, vestal

estan \es-tən\ see ESTINE

estant \es-tənt\ arrestant, contestant, infestant, protestant, Protestant, decongestant, disinfestant, manifestant

este \est\ see EST

ested \es-təd\ bested, crested, nested, tested, vested, time-tested, barrel-chested, double-breasted, hairy-chested, indigested, single-breasted—*also pasts of verbs listed at* EST

ester \es-tər\ Chester, ester, Esther, fester, Hester, jester, Leicester, Lester, nester, Nestor, pester, quaestor, quester, questor, nester, tester, wester, yester, zester, ancestor, arrester, contester, detester, digester, infester, investor, Manchester, molester, northwester, Rochester, semester, sequester, southwester, sou'wester, suggester, Sylvester, trimester, Winchester, arbalester, empty-nester, monoester, polyester

esti \es-tē\ seeESTY

estial \es-tē-əl\ celestial, forestial

estible \es-tə-bəl\ testable, comestible, detestable, digestible, ingestible, investable, suggestible, incontestable, indigestible

estic \es-tik\ gestic, domestic. majestic, anapestic, catachrestic

estical \es-ti-kəl\ see ESTICLE

esticle \es-ti-kəl\ testicle, catachrestical

estimate \es-tə-mət\ estimate. guesstimate

estinate \es-tə-nət\ festinate, predestinate

estine \es-tən\ destine, Preston. Avestan, clandestine, intestine, predestine

esting \es-tiŋ\ cresting, vesting, westing, arresting

estion \es-chən\ question, congestion, cross-question, digestion, egestion, ingestion. self-question, suggestion, decongestion, indigestion, self-suggestion, autosuggestion

estis \es-təs\ cestus, testis, Alcestis, asbestos, Hephaestus

estival \es-tə-vəl\ estival, festival

estive \es-tiv\ festive, restive congestive, digestive, egestive, ingestive, suggestive, decongestive

[1]**estle** \es-əl\ Bessel, Cecil, decile, nestle, pestle, sessile, trestle, vessel, wrestle, Indian-wrestle

[2]**estle** \as-əl\ see [2]ASSEL

[3]**estle** \əs-əl\ see USTLE
estless \est-ləs\ crestless, restless
estment \es-mənt\ vestment, arrestment, assessment, divestment, impressment, investment, disinvestment, reinvestment
esto \es-tō\ pesto, presto, manifesto
eston \es-tən\ see ESTINE
estor \es-tər\ see ESTER
estos \es-təs\ see ESTIS
estra \es-trə\ fenestra, orchestra, palaestra, Clytemnestra
estral \es-trəl\ estral, kestrel, ancestral, campestral, fenestral, semestral, orchestral
estrel \es-trəl\ see ESTRAL
estress \es-trəs\ see ESTRUS
estrial \es-trē-əl\ semestrial, terrestrial, extraterrestrial
estrian \es-trē-ən\ equestrian, pedestrian
estrous \es-trəs\ see ESTRUS
estrum \es-trəm\ estrum, sequestrum
estrus \es-trəs\ estrous, estrus, ancestress
estry \es-trē\ vestry, ancestry
estuous \es-chə-wəs\ incestuous, tempestuous
esture \es-chər\ gesture, vesture
estus \es-təs\ see ESTIS
esty \es-tē\ chesty, testae, testy, pesty, zesty, res gestae, necessity, Tibesti
esus \ē-səs\ see ESIS
[1]**et** \et\ bet, Bret, Brett, debt, et, fret, get, jet, let, Lett, met, net, pet, ret, set, stet, sweat, Tet, threat, vet, wet, whet, yet, abet, aigrette, Annette, asset, Babette, backset, baguette, banquette, barbette, Barnet, Barnett, barquette, barrette, beget, beset, blanquette, boneset, brevet, briquette, brochette, brunet, burette, burnet, cadet, cassette, cermet, Claudette, Colette, coquet, coquette, cornet, corselet, corvette, coset, courgette, croquette, curette, curvet, cuvette, daleth, dinette, diskette, dragnet, duet, egret, fan-jet, fishnet, flechette, forget, frisette, gazette, georgette, Georgette, gillnet, godet, grisette, handset, hard-set, headset, ink-jet, inlet, inset, Janette, Jeanette, Jeannette, Juliet, kismet, layette, lorgnette, lunette, Lynette, maquette, Marquette, mind-set, moonset, moquette, motet, musette, Nanette, Nannette, noisette, nonet, nymphet, octet, offset, onset, Osset, outlet, outset, paillette, palet, pallette, palmette, Paulette, pipette, piquet, planchette, poussette, preset, quartet, quickset, quintet, raclette, ramet, regret, reset, revet, rocket, roomette, rosette, roulette, saw-whet, septet, sestet, sextet, sharp-set, soubrette, spinet, stylet, sublet, subset, sunset, Syrette, tacet, thickset, Tibet, toilette, tonette, trijet, twinset, typeset, unset, upset, vedette, vignette,

well-set, Yvette, aiguillette, alphabet, anchoret, andouilette, anisette, Antoinette, avocet, banneret, basinet, bassinet, bayonet, Bernadette, bobbinet, briolette, burgonet, calumet, canzonet, castanet, cellarette, chemisette, cigarette, clarinet, consolette, coronet, corselet, crepe suzette, dragonet, electret, en brochette, epaulet, epithet, etiquette, falconet, farmerette, featurette, flageolet, flannelette, guillemet, heavyset, jaconet, Juliett, kitchenette, Lafayette, landaulet, lanneret, laundcrotte, Leatherette, luncheonette, maisonette, majorette, marmoset, marquisette, martinet, mignonette, minaret, minuet, miquelet, novelette, Olivet, oubliette, parapet, paupiette, photoset, pirouette, quodlibet, rondelet, Samoset, satinet, scilicet, sermonette, serviette, silhouette, sobriquet, solleret, somerset, Somerset, soviet, spinneret, statuette, stockinette, suffragette, superjet, swimmeret, taboret, thermoset, towelette, trebuchet, tricolette, underlet, usherette, vinaigrette, wagonette, analphabet, bachelorette, drum majorette, electrojet, Hospitalet, marionette, microcassette, micropipette, musique concrète, photo-offset, videlicet, audiocassette, cauliflroweret, hail-fellow-well-met, Marie Antoinette, videocassette

[2]**et** \ā\ see [1]AY

[3]**et** \āt\ see [1]ATE

[4]**et** \es\ see ESS

[1]**eta** \āt-ə\ see [2]ATA

[2]**eta** \et-ə\ see ETTA

[3]**eta** \ēt-ə\ see [2]ITA

[1]**etable** \et-ə-bəl\ see ETTABLE

[2]**etable** \ēt-ə-bəl\ see EATABLE

[1]**etal** \ēt-[ə]l\ beetle, betel, fetal, decretal, excretal

[2]**etal** \et-[ə]l\ see ETTLE

[1]**etan** \et-[ə]n\ Breton, threaten, Cape Breton, Tibetan

[2]**etan** \ēt-[ə]n\ see [1]EATEN

etch \ech\ catch, etch, fetch, fletch, ketch, kvetch, lech, letch, retch, sketch, stretch, vetch, wretch, backstretch, homestretch, outstretch

etched \echt\ teched, farfetched—*also pasts of verbs listed at* ETCH

etcher \ech-ər\ etcher, catcher, fetcher, fletcher, Fletcher, lecher, sketcher, stretcher, cowcatcher, dogcatcher, eye-catcher, flycatcher, gnatcatcher

etching \ech-iŋ\ etching, fletching—*also present participles of verbs listed at* ETCH

etchy \ech-ē\ sketchy, stretchy, tetchy

[1]**ete** \āt\ see [1]ATE

[2]**ete** \et\ see [1]ET

[3]**ete** \ēt\ see [1]EAT

[4]**ete** \āt-ē\ see ATY

ête \āt\ see [1]ATE
eted \ād\ see [1]ADE
etel \ēt-ᵊl\ see ETAL
etely \ēt-lē\ see EETLY
eteor \ēt-ē-ər\ meteor, confiteor—*also comparatives of adjectives listed at* EATY
eter \ēt-ər\ see [1]EATER
etera \e-trə\ see ETRA
eterate \et-ə-rət\ see ETERIT
eterit \et-ə-rət\ preterit, inveterate
etes \ēt-əs\ see ETUS
[1]**eth** \eth\ Beth, breath, breadth, death, saith, Seth, snath, daleth, handbreadth, hairbreadth, Macbeth, Ashtoreth, isopleth, megadeath, shibboleth, Elisabeth, Elizabeth
[2]**eth** \ās\ see [1]ACE
[3]**eth** \āt\ see [1]ATE
[4]**eth** \et\ see [1]ET
etha \ē-thə\ Aretha, Ibiza
ethane \e-thān\ ethane, methane, nitromethane, dichloroethane
ethe \ē-thē\ see EATHY
[1]**ether** \eth-ər\ blether, feather, heather, Heather, leather, nether, tether, weather, wether, whether, aweather, bellwether, pinfeather, together, untether, altogether, get-together
[2]**ether** \əth-ər\ see [1]OTHER
ethic \eth-ik\ ethic, erethic
ethral \ē-thrəl\ urethral, bulbourethral
ethyl \eth-əl\ bethel, Ethel, ethyl, methyl, triethyl
[1]**eti** \ēt-ē\ see EATY
[2]**eti** \āt-ē\ see ATY
etia \ē-shə\ see [1]ESIA
etian \ē-shən\ see [1]ETION
[1]**etic** \ēt-ik\ thetic, acetic, docetic
etic \et-ik\ etic, thetic, aesthetic, ascetic, athletic, balletic, bathetic, cosmetic, docetic, eidetic, emetic, frenetic, gametic, genetic, hermetic, kinetic, limnetic, magnetic, mimetic, noetic, Ossetic, paretic, pathetic, phenetic, phonetic, phrenetic, phyletic, poetic, prophetic, prosthetic, pyretic, splenetic, syncretic, syndetic, synthetic, tonetic, Venetic, alphabetic, analgetic, anesthetic, antithetic, apathetic, asyndetic, copacetic, cybernetic, diabetic, dietetic, digenetic, diphyletic, diuretic, empathetic, energetic, epithetic, geodetic, homiletic, Masoretic, nomothetic, parenthetic, sympathetic, synergetic, synesthetic, aeromagnetic, antimagnetic, antipathetic, antipoetic, antipyretic, apologetic, epexigetic, epigenetic, ferrimagnetic, ferromagnetic, geomagnetic, gyromagnetic, homogametic, hydrokinetic, hydromagnetic, hyperkinetic, isomagnetic, monophyletic, morphogenetic, ontogenetic, optokinetic, palingenetic, paramagnetic, pathogenetic, peripatetic, phylogenetic, polyphyletic, psychokinetic,

telekinetic, thermomagnetic, aposiopetic, cyanogenetic, electrokinetic, electromagnetic, heterogametic, parasympathetic, parthenogenetic, psychotomimetic, unapologetic, onomatopoetic

etical \et-i-kəl\ metical, reticle, aesthetical, genetical, heretical, phonetical, antithetical, arithmetical, catechetical, cybernetical, epithetical, exegetical, geodetical, hypothetical, parenthetical, theoretical, atheoretical, epexegetical

eticist \et-ə-səst\ geneticist, kineticist, cyberneticist

etics \et-iks\ aesthetics, athletics, genetics, homiletics, kinetics, phonetics, poetics, tonetics, cybernetics, dietetics, apologetics, cytogenetics, immunogenetics—*also plurals and possessives of nouns listed at* ETIC

etid \et-əd\ fetid, fretted, sweated, indebted, parapeted—*also pasts of verbs listed at* [1]ET

etin \ēt-ᵊn\ see [1]EATEN

[1]**etion** \ē-shən\ Grecian, accretion, Capetian, completion, concretion, deletion, depletion, excretion, Ossetian, Phoenician, repletion, secretion, suppletion, Tahitian, Austronesian, Diocletian, Melanesian, Polynesian, Taracahitian

[2]**etion** \esh-ən\ see ESSION

etious \ē-shəs\ see ECIOUS

[1]**etis** \ēt-əs\ see ETUS

[2]**etis** \et-əs\ see ETTUCE

etist \et-əst\ cornetist, librettist. vignettist, clarinetist, exegetist, operettist—*also superlatives of adjectives listed at* [1]ET

etitive \et-ət-iv\ competitive. repetitive, uncompetitive, anticompetitive

etium \ē-shē-əm\ see ECIUM

etius \ē-shəs\ see ECIOUS

etive \ēt-iv\ accretive, completive, decretive, depletive, secretive, suppletive

[1]**etl** \āt-ᵊl\ see ATAL

[2]**etl** \et-ᵊl\ see ETTLE

etland \et-lənd\ Shetland, wetland

etment \et-mənt\ abetment, besetment, curettement, revetment

[1]**eto** \āt-ō\ see [2]ATO

[2]**eto** \ēt-ō\ see [1]ITO

eton \ēt-ᵊn\ see [1]EATEN

[1]**etor** \et-ər\ see ETTER

[2]**etor** \ēt-ər\ see [1]EATER

etory \ēt-ə-rē\ eatery, decretory secretory, suppletory

etous \ēt-əs\ see ETUS

[1]**etra** \e-trə\ Petra, tetra, etcetera

[2]**etra** \ē-trə\ Petra, Kenitra

[1]**etral** \ē-trəl\ petrel, retral

[2]**etral** \e-trəl\ see [1]ETREL

être \etrᵊ\ fête champêtre, raison d'être

[1]etrel \e-trəl\ petrel, petrol, retral

[2]etrel \ē-trəl\ see [1]ETRAL

etric \e-trik\ metric, obstetric, symmetric, asymmetric, barometric, decametric, dekametric, diametric, dissymmetric, geometric, hypsometric, isometric, optometric, psychometric, telemetric, volumetric, acidometric, amperometric, sociometric

etrical \e-tri-kəl\ metrical, obstetrical, symmetrical, asymmetrical, barometrical, diametrical, geometrical, unsymmetrical

etrics \e-triks\ obstetrics, geometrics, isometrics, sabermetrics

etrist \e-trəst\ metrist, belletrist

etrol \e-trəl\ see [1]ETREL

ets \ets\ let's, Donets, rillettes, Steinmetz, pantalets, solonetz, Sosnowiec—*also plurals and possessives of nouns and third person singular presents of verbs listed at* [1]ET

etsk \etsk\ Donetsk, Kuznetsk, Lipetsk, Novokuznetsk

ett \et\ see [1]ET

etta \et-ə\ betta, Etta, feta, geta, Greta, Quetta, biretta, cabretta, galleta, Loretta, mozzetta, pancetta, poinsettia, Rosetta, Valletta, vendetta, anchoveta, arietta, cabaletta, Henrietta, Marietta, operetta, sinfonietta

ettable \et-ə-bəl\ retable, wettable, forgettable, regrettable, unforgettable

ette \et\ see [1]ET

etter \et-ər\ better, bettor, debtor, fetter, getter, letter, netter, rhetor, setter, sweater, tetter, wetter, whetter, abettor. begetter, bonesetter, enfetter, gill-netter, go-getter, jet-setter. newsletter, pacesetter, pinsetter, red-letter, regretter. trendsetter, typesetter, unfetter, vignetter, carburetter—*also comparatives of adjectives listed at* [1]ET

ettered \et-ərd\ fettered, lettered, unfettered, unlettered

ettes \ets\ see ETS

ettia \et-ə\ see ETTA

ettie \et-ē\ see [1]ETTY

ettier \it-ē-ər\ see ITTIER

ettiness \it-ē-nəs\ see ITTINESS

etting \et-iŋ\ netting, setting, bed-wetting, bloodletting, go-getting, onsetting, typesetting. thermosetting, phototypesetting

ettish \et-ish\ fetish, Lettish, pettish, wettish, coquettish. novelettish

ettle \et-[ə]l\ fettle, kettle, metal. mettle, nettle, petal, settle, shtetl, bimetal, gunmetal, nonmetal, teakettle, unsettle. Citialtepetl, Popocatepetl

ettlesome \et-[ə]l-səm\ mettlesome, nettlesome

ettling \et-liŋ\ fettling, settling. unsettling

etto \et-ō\ ghetto, stretto, cavetto, falsetto, in petto.

larghetto, libretto, palmetto, stiletto, zucchetto, allegretto, amaretto, amoretto, fianchetto, Kazan Retto, lazaretto, Tintoretto, vaporetto

ettor \et-ər\ see ETTER

ettuce \et-əs\ lettuce, Thetis, Hymettus

ettus \et-əs\ see ETTUCE

[1]**etty** \et-ē\ Betty, jetty, Nettie, netty, petit, petty, sweaty, yeti, brown Betty, cavetti, confetti, libretti, machete, Rossetti, spaghetti, amoretti, Donizetti, Serengeti, spermacetti, cappelletti, cavalletti, vaporetti

[2]**etty** \it-ē\ see ITTY

etum \ēt-əm\ pinetum, arboretum, equisetum

etus \ēt-əs\ Cetus, fetus, Thetis, treatise, acetous, Admetus, boletus, coitus, quietus, diabetes

etzsche \ē-chē\ see EACHY

euben \ü-bən\ Cuban, Reuben, Ruben, von Steuben

euce \üs\ see [1]USE

euced \ü-səd\ see UCID

eucey \ü-sē\ see UICY

euch \ük\ see UKE

euchre \ü-kər\ see UCRE

eucid \ü-səd\ see UCID

[1]**eud** \üd\ see UDE

[2]**eud** \òid\ see [1]OID

eudal \üd-^{ə}l\ see OODLE

eudist \üd-əst\ see [1]UDIST

eudo \üd-ō\ see UDO

eue \ü\ see [1]EW

euer \ü-ər\ see [1]EWER

euil \āl\ see AIL

euille \ē\ see [1]EE

euk \ük\ see UKE

eukin \ü-kən\ see UCAN

[1]**eul** \əl\ see [1]ULL

[2]**eul** \ərl\ see [1]IRL

eulah \ü-lə\ see ULA

eulean \ü-lē-ən\ see ULEAN

[1]**eum** \ē-əm\ geum, lyceum, museum, no-see-um, odeum, per diem, Te Deum, athenaeum, coliseum, colosseum, hypogeum, mausoleum

[2]**eum** \ā-əm\ see AHUM

[3]**eum** \üm\ see [1]OOM

euma \ü-mə\ see UMA

eume \üm\ see [1]OOM

eumon \ü-mən\ see UMAN

eumy \ü-mē\ see OOMY

eunice \ü-nəs\ see EWNESS

eunt \ùnt\ see [1]UNT

eunuch \ü-nik\ see UNIC

[1]**eur** \ər\ birr, blur, buhr, burr, Burr, chirr, churr, cur, curr, err, fir, for, fur, her, knur, murre, myrrh, per, purr, shirr, sir, skirr, slur, spur, stir, thir, 'twere, were, whir, your, you're, à deux, as per, astir, auteur, aver, bestir, chasseur, chauffeur, claqueur, coiffeur, concur, confer, danseur, defer, demur, deter, douceur, du jour, farceur, flaneur, friseur, frondeur, hauteur, him/her, his/her, incur, infer, inter, jongleur, larkspur, liqueur, longspur, masseur, Malmö, millefleur, occur, Pasteur, poseur, prefer, recur, refer, sandbur, sandspur, seigneur, transfer, voyeur, accoucheur, amateur, cocklebur,

colporteur, connoisseur, cri de coeur, cross-refer, cubature, curvature, de rigueur, disinter, force majeure, franc-tireur, monseigneur, nonconcur, pasticheur, prosateur, raconteur, rapporteur, regisseur, saboteur, secateur, underfur, voyageur, arbitrageur, carillonneur, conglomerateur, entrepreneur, litterateur, provacateur, restaurateur, agent provocateur

[2]**eur** \u̇r\ see [1]URE

eure \ər\ see [1]EUR

eurial \u̇r-ē-əl\ see [1]URIAL

eurish \ər-ish\ see OURISH

eurs \ərz\ see [1]ERS

eury \u̇r-ē\ see [1]URY

[1]**eus** \ē-əs\ Aeneas, Aggeus, Alpheus, Arius, Chryseis, Linnaeus, Micheas, Piraeus, uraeus, coryphaeus, epigeous, scarabaeus, prelate nullius, Duque de Caxias, Judas Maccabaeus

[2]**eus** \üs\ see [1]USE

[1]**euse** \əz\ buzz, 'cause, coz, does, fuzz, 'twas, was, abuzz, because, outdoes, undoes, overdoes

[2]**euse** \üs\ see [1]USE

[3]**euse** \üz\ see [2]USE

[1]**eusel** \ü-səl\ see [1]USAL

[2]**eusel** \ü-zəl\ see [2]USAL

eut \üt\ see UTE

euter \üt-ər\ see UTER

euth \üth\ see [2]OOTH

eutian \ü-shən\ see UTION

eutic \üt-ik\ see UTIC

eutical \üt-i-kəl\ see UTICAL

eutics \üt-iks\ toreutics, hermeneutics, therapeutics

eutist \üt-əst\ see UTIST

euton \üt-ᵊn\ see UTAN

eutonist \üt-ᵊn-əst\ see UTENIST

euve \əv\ see [1]OVE

euver \ü-vər\ see [3]OVER

[1]**eux** \ü\ see [1]EW

[2]**eux** \ər\ see [1]EUR

[1]**ev** \ef\ see [1]EF

[2]**ev** \ȯf\ see [2]OFF

eva \ē-və\ see [2]IVA

eval \ē-vəl\ see IEVAL

evalent \ev-ə-lənt\ see EVOLENT

[1]**evan** \ē-vən\ see EVEN

[2]**evan** \ev-ən\ see EAVEN

[1]**eve** \ev\ breve, rev, Sevres, Negev, alla breve

[2]**eve** \ēv\ see [1]EAVE

evel \ev-əl\ bevel, devil, level, Neville, revel, baselevel, bedevil, bi-level, daredevil, dishevel, go-devil, split-level, entry-level

eveler \ev-lər\ leveler, reveler

evelly \ev-ə-lē\ heavily, levelly, reveille

evement \ēv-mənt\ achievement, aggrievement, bereavement, underachievement

even \ē-vən\ even, Stephen, Steven, breakeven, break-even, Genevan, Kesteven, uneven

eventh \ev-ənth\ seventh, eleventh

[1]**ever** \ev-ər\ clever, ever, lever, never, sever, Trevor, dissever, endeavor, forever, however, soever, whatever, whenever, wherever, whichever,

whoever, whomever, cantilever, howsoever, live-forever, whatsoever, whencesoever, whensoever, wheresoever, whichsoever, whomsoever, whosesoever, whosoever, whithersoever

[2]**ever** \ē-vər\ see [1]EVER

everage \ev-rij\ beverage, leverage

everence \ev-rəns\ reverence, severance, disseverance, irreverence

every \ev-rē\ every, reverie

eves \ēvz\ see EAVES

eviate \ē-vē-ət\ deviate, qiviut

evice \ev-əs\ clevis, crevice, Ben Nevis

evil \ē-vəl\ see IEVAL

eville \ev-əl\ see EVEL

evilry \ev-əl-rē\ devilry, revelry

evin \ev-ən\ see EAVEN

evious \ē-vē-əs\ devious, previous

[1]**evis** \ev-əs\ see EVICE

[2]**evis** \ē-vəs\ see EVUS

evity \ev-ət-ē\ brevity, levity, longevity

evo \ē-vō\ in vivo, relievo, ring-a-lievo, alto-relievo, basso-relievo, mezzo-relievo, recitativo, Antananavivo

evocable \ev-ə-kə-bəl\ evocable, revocable, irrevocable

evolence \ev-ə-ləns\ prevalence, benevolence, malevolence

evolent \ev-ə-lənt\ prevalent, benevolent, malevolent

evor \ev-ər\ see [1]EVER

evous \ē-vəs\ grievous, Nevis, nevus, longevous, redivivus, Saint Kitts and Nevis

evsk \efsk\ see EFSK

evus \ē-vəs\ see EVOUS

evy \ev-ē\ bevy, heavy, levee, levy, replevy, top-heavy

[1]**ew** \ü\ blue, boo, brew, chew, clew, clue, coo, coup, crew, cue, dew, do, doux, drew, due, ewe, few, flew, flu, flue, fou, glue, gnu, goo, hew, hue. Hugh, Jew, knew, lieu, loo, Lou, mew, moo, moue, mu, new, nu, ooh, pew, phew, piu. pooh, prau, q, queue, roux, rue, screw, shoe, shoo, shrew. Sioux, skew, slew, slough, slue, smew, sou, sous, spew, sprue, stew, strew, sue, Sue, thew, threw, thro, through, to. too, true, two, u, view, whew, who, woo, Wu, xu, yew, you. zoo, accrue, adieu, ado, aircrew, airscrew, anew, Anjou, askew, au jus, Baku, bamboo, battu, battue, bedew. beshrew, bestrew, bijou, boubou, brand-new, breakthrough, burgoo, cachou, can-do, canoe, caoutchouc, Cebu, Cheng-du, Chongju, Chonju, construe, Corfu, corkscrew, coypu, CQ, debut, ecu, endue, ensue, eschew, floor-through, fondue, fordo. foreknew, Gansu, Gentoo, Gifu, gansun, gumshoe, guru. hairdo, hereto, Honshu, horseshoe, how-to, HQ, Hutu. imbrue, imbue, IQ, jackscrew K2, Kansu, karoo, Karoo, kazoo, Khufu, kung fu,

Kwangju, leadscrew, lean-to, make-do, Matthew, me-too, mildew, milieu, miscue, misdo, misknew, muumuu, Nehru, non-U, old-shoe, one-two, outdo, outgrew, perdu, Peru, poilu, preview, pursue, purview, ragout, redo, renew, Ren Crew, review, revue, rough-hew, run-through, sandshoe, see-through, set-to, setscrew, shampoo, Shih Tzu, skiddoo, snafu, snowshoe, soft-shoe, span-new, subdue, surtout, taboo, Taegu, tattoo, thank-you, thereto, thumbscrew, to-do, too-too, undo, undue, unglue, unscrew, untrue, vatu, vendue, venue, vertu, virtu, wahoo, walk-through, wherethrough, whereto, who's who, withdrew, worldview, aperçu, avenue, babassu, ballyhoo, barbecue, barley-broo, billet-doux, black-and-blue, buckaroo, bugaboo, callaloo, caribou, catechu, clerihew, cockapoo, cockatoo, Cotonou, counterview, déjà vu, derring-do, detinue, feverfew, follow-through, gardyloo, hitherto, honeydew, Ignaçu, ingenue, interview, IOU, jabiru, Jiangsu, kangaroo, Kathmandu, kinkajou, loup-garou, Makalu, manitou, marabou, Masaru, Montague, Montesquieu, ormolu, overdo, overdue, overflew, overgrew, overshoe, overstrew, overthrough, overview, parvenu, parvenue, pas de deux, passe-partout, PDQ, peekaboo, Port Salut, rendezvous, residue, retinue, revenue, Richelieu, Ryukyu, seppuku, Shikoku, succès fou, switcheroo, talking-to, teleview, Telugu, thereunto, thirty-two, thitherto, Timbuktu, tinamou, trou-de-loup, twenty-two, view halloo, vindaloo, wallaroo, waterloo, well-to-do, whoop-de-do, Xanadu, Aracaju, Brian Boru, didgeridoo, hullabaloo, Kota Bharu, Nova Iguaçu, Ouagadougou, pirarucu, Port du Salut, tu-whit tu-whoo, Vanuatu, Daman and Diu, Guangxi Zhuangzu, Ningxia Huizu, Havant and Waterloo

[2]**ew** \ō\ see [1]OW

[1]**ewable** \ō-ə-bəl\ see [1]OWABLE

[2]**ewable** \ü-ə-bəl\ see UABLE

ewage \ü-ij\ brewage, sewage

ewal \ü-əl\ see [1]UEL

ewar \ü-ər\ see [1]EWER

[1]**eward** \ürd\ see [1]URED

[2]**eward** \ü-ərd\ Seward, steward

ewd \üd\ see UDE

ewdness \üd-nəs\ see UDINOUS

[1]**ewe** \ō\ see [1]OW

[2]**ewe** \ü\ see [1]EW

ewed \üd\ see UDE

ewee \ē-wē\ see EEWEE

ewel \ü-əl\ see [1]UEL

eweled \üld\ see OOLED

ewell \ü-əl\ see [1]UEL

[1]**ewer** \ü-ər\ brewer, chewer. dewar, doer, ewer, fewer, hewer, queuer, screwer,

sewer, skewer, spewer, suer, viewer, wooer, you're, horseshoer, me-tooer, misdoer, previewer, renewer, reviewer, shampooer, snowshoer, tattooer, undoer, wrongdoer, barbecuer, evildoer, interviewer, revenuer, televiewer—*also comparatives of adjectives listed at* [1]EW

[2]**ewer** \u̇r\ see [1]URE

[3]**ewer** \ō-ər\ see [4]OER

ewerage \u̇r-ij\ see [1]OORAGE

ewery \u̇r-ē\ see [1]URY

ewess \ü-əs\ Jewess, lewis, Lewis, Louis, Luis, Port Louis, Saint Louis

ewey \ü-ē\ see EWY

ewie \ü-ē\ see EWY

[1]**ewing** \ō-iŋ\ see [1]OING

[2]**ewing** \ü-iŋ\ see [2]OING

ewis \ü-əs\ see EWESS

ewish \ü-ish\ bluish, Jewish, newish, shrewish, aguish

ewl \ül\ see [1]OOL

ewless \ü-ləs\ clueless, crewless, dewless, shoeless, viewless

ewly \ü-lē\ see ULY

ewman \ü-mən\ see UMAN

ewment \ü-mənt\ strewment, accruement

ewn \ün\ see [1]OON

ewness \ü-nəs\ blueness, dueness, Eunice, newness, skewness, Tunis, askewness

ewpie \ü-pē\ see OOPY

ewry \u̇r-ē\ see [1]URY

ews \üz\ see [2]USE

ewsman \üz-mən\ bluesman, newsman

ewsy \ü-zē\ see OOZY

ewt \üt\ see UTE

ewter \üt-ər\ see UTER

ewterer \üt-ər-ər\ see UITERER

ewton \üt-ᵊn\ see UTAN

ewy \ü-ē\ bluey, buoy, chewy, Dewey, dewy, flooey, gluey, gooey, hooey, Louie, Louis, newie, phooey, rouille, screwy, sloughy, viewy, chop suey, mildewy, Port Louis, ratatouille, waterzooi

ex \eks\ dex, ex, flex, hex, lex, rex, Rex, sex, specs, vex, x, annex, apex, carex, codex, complex, convex, cortex, culex, desex, duplex, DX, fourplex, ibex, ilex, index, Kleenex, Lastex, latex, mirex, murex, MX, narthex, perplex, Perspex, pollex, Pyrex, reflex, remex, Rx, scolex, silex, silvex, simplex, spandex, telex, Tex-Mex, triplex, unsex, vertex, videotex, vortex, analects, belowdecks, biconvex, circumflex, cross-index, googolplex, haruspex, intersex, Malcolm X, Middlesex, multiplex, PBX, pontifex, retroflex, spinifex, subindex, unisex—*also plurals and possessives of nouns and third person singular presents of verbs listed at* ECK

exas \ek-səs\ see EXUS

exed \ekst\ see EXT

exedly \ek-səd-lē\ vexedly, perplexedly

exer \ek-sər\ flexor, hexer,

duplexer, indexer, multiplexer, demultiplexer
exia \ek-sē-ə\ dyslexia, anorexia
exic \ek-sik\ dyslexic, anorexic
exical \ek-si-kəl\ lexical, indexical, nonlexical
exion \ek-shən\ see ECTION
exis \ek-səs\ see EXUS
exity \ek-sət-ē\ complexity, convexity, perplexity
exor \ek-sər\ see EXER
ext \ekst\ next, sexed, sext, text, vexed, context, deflexed, inflexed, perplexed, plaintext, pretext, reflexed, subtext, urtext, ciphertext, oversexed, teletext, undersexed—*also pasts of verbs listed at* EX
extant \ek-stənt\ extant, sextant
exterous \ek-strəs\ dexterous, ambidextrous
extrous \ek-strəs\ see EXTEROUS
extual \eks-chəl\ textual, contextual, subtextual
exual \eksh-wəl\ sexual, asexual, bisexual, effectual, pansexual, transsexual, ambisexual, homosexual, hypersexual, intersexual, parasexual, psychosexual, unisexual, heterosexual, sociosexual, anti-intellectual
exural \ek-shrəl\ see [2]ECTURAL
exus \ek-səs\ lexis, nexus, plexus, texas, Texas, Alexis
exy \ek-sē\ prexy, sexy, apoplexy
[1]**ey** \ā\ see [1]AY
[2]**ey** \ē\ see [1]EE
[3]**ey** \ī\ see [1]Y
[1]**eya** \ā-ə\ see [1]AIA
[2]**eya** \ē-ə\ see [1]IA
eyance \ā-əns\ abeyance, conveyance, purveyance, surveillance, reconveyance
eyant \ā-ənt\ mayn't, abeyant, surveillant
eyas \ī-əs\ see IAS
ey'd \ād\ see [1]ADE
eye \ī\ see [1]Y
[1]**eyed** \ēd\ see EED
[2]**eyed** \īd\ see [1]IDE
eyedness \īd-nəs\ eyedness. snideness, cockeyedness
eyeless \ī-ləs\ see ILUS
eyelet \ī-lət\ see ILOT
eyen \īn\ see [1]INE
[1]**eyer** \ā-ər\ see [1]AYER
[2]**eyer** \īr\ see [1]IRE
eyes \īz\ see IZE
eying \ā-iŋ\ see AYING
[1]**ey'll** \āl\ see AIL
[2]**ey'll** \el\ see [1]EL
eyn \in\ see [1]IN
eynes \ānz\ see AINS
eyness \ā-nəs\ see AYNESS
eyor \ā-ər\ see [1]AYER
ey're \er\ see [4]ARE
eyre \er\ see [4]ARE
eyrie \īr-ē\ see [1]IRY
eys \ēz\ see EZE
eyser \ī-zər\ see IZER
eyte \ā-tē\ see ATY
ey've \āv\ see [2]AVE
[1]**ez** \ez\ see [1]AYS
[2]**ez** \ā\ see [1]AY
[3]**ez** \ās\ see [1]ACE
eza \ē-zə\ Giza, Lisa, Pisa, visa mestiza, lespedeza
eze \ēz\ bise, breeze, cheese, ease, feaze, feeze, freeze, frieze, he's, jeez, lees, please res, seize, she's, sleaze,

sneeze, squeeze, tease, tweeze, wheeze, Andes, appease, Aries, Belize, betise, Burmese, camise, Castries, cerise, chemise, Chinese, deep-freeze, Deep-freeze, degrease, Denise, disease, displease, disseise, d.t.'s, Elise, fasces, fauces, Ganges, headcheese, heartsease, Hermes, Kirghiz, Louise, Maltese, marquise, menses, nates, Pisces, quick-freeze, Ramses, reprise, sharp-freeze, soubise, striptease, Tabriz, Thales, trapeze, unease, unfreeze, Xerxes, Amboinese, Androcles, Annamese, antifreeze, Assamese, Balinese, Brooklynese, Cantonese, Cervantes, Chersonese, Congolese, Cyclades. Damocles, diocese, Eloise, Erinyes, expertise, Faeroese, federalese, genovese, gourmandise, Hebrides, Heracles, Hercules, Hunanese, Hyades, Japanese, Javanese, Johnsonese, journalese, Kanarese, Lake Louise, legalese, litotes, manganese, Nipponese, overseas, Pekinese, Pekingese, Pericles, Pleiades, Portuguese, Pyrenees, Siamese, Silures, Sinhalese, Socrates, Sophocles, Sporades, Albigenses, antipodes, Aragonese, archdiocese, Averroës, bona fides, bureaucratese, cheval-de-frise, computerese, Diogenes, Dodecanese, Eumenides, Euripides, Florida Keys, Gaucher's disease, governmentese, Great Pyrenees, Hesperides, Hippocrates, Hippomenes, Hodgkin's disease, Indo-Chinese, nephritides, officialese, pentagonese, Philoctetes, Sammarinese, superficies, telegraphese, Themistocles, Thucydides, Vietnamese, Alcibiades, Aristophanes, educationese, ferromanganese, Lou Gehrig's disease, Mephistopheles, sociologese, sword of Damocles, muscae volitantes. Pillars of Hercules—*also plurals and possessives of nouns and third person singular presents of verbs listed at* [1]EE

ezel \ē-zəl\ see EASEL

ezi \ē-zē\ see [1]EASY

ezium \ē-zē-əm\ cesium, magnesium, trapezium

ezzle \ez-əl\ bezel, embezzle

i

[1]i \ē\ see [1]EE

[2]i \ī\ see [1]Y

[3]i \ā\ see [1]AY

[1]ia \ē-ə\ Gaea, kea, Leah, Mia, rhea, Rhea, rya, via, Achaea, Crimea, althaea, Apia, Bahia, buddleia, cabrilla, cattleya, Chaldea, Euboea, Hygeia, idea, Judea, Kaffiyeh, Korea, mantilla, Maria, Medea, mens rea, Morea, Nicaea, ohia, Omiya, Oriya, ouguiya, rupiah, sangria, Sofia, Sophia, spirea, tortilla, Baile Atha Cliath, Banranquilla, barathea, bougainvillea, camarilla, Caesarea, cascarilla, Cytherea, dulcinea, Eritrea, fantasia, Galatea, gonorrhea, granadilla, hamartia, Hialeah, Idumea, Ikaria, Jicarilla, Kampuchea, latakia, Latakia, logorrhea, Manzanilla, mausolea, mythopoeia, Nabatea, Nicosia, panacea, Parousia, pizzeria, ratafia, sabadilla, Santeria, sapodilla, seguidilla, sinfonia, Tanzania, trattoria, alfilaria, Andalucia, Andalusia, Ave Maria, Cassiopeia, Diego Garcia, echeveria, Ismailia, peripeteia, pharmacopoeia, prosopopoeia, onomatopoeia, Joseph of Arimathea

[2]ia \ī-ə\ see [1]IAH

[3]ia \ä\ see [1]A

[1]iable \ī-ə-bəl\ dryable, dyeable, flyable, friable, liable, pliable, triable, viable, deniable, inviable, reliable, certifiable, classifiable, justifiable, liquefiable, notifiable, pacifiable, qualifiable, quantifiable, rectifiable, satisfiable, specifiable, undeniable, unifiable, verifiable, emulsifiable, identifiable, unfalsifiable

[2]iable \ē-ə-bəl\ see EEABLE

iacal \ī-ə-kəl\ dandiacal, heliacal, maniacal, theriacal, zodiacal, ammoniacal, elegiacal, simoniacal, dipsomaniacal, egomaniacal, hypochondriacal, monomaniacal, nympomaniacal, pyromaniacal, paradisiacal, bibliomaniacal, megalomaniacal

iad \ī-əd\ see YAD

[1]iah \ī-ə\ ayah, maya, Maya, playa, Praia, stria, via, Aglaia, Mariah, messiah, papaya, pariah, Thalia, Hezekiah, jambalaya, Jeremiah, Nehemiah, Obadiah, Surabaja, Zechariah, Zephaniah, Atchafalaya, Iphigenia, peripeteia

[2]**iah** \ē-ə\ see [1]IA
[1]**ial** \ī-əl\ dial, diel, pial, redial
[2]**ial** \īl\ see [1]ILE
ialer \ī-lər\ see ILAR
ially \ē-ə-lē\ see [1]EALLY
iam \ī-əm\ Priam, per diem
[1]**ian** \ē-ən\ see [1]EAN
[2]**ian** \ī-ən\ see [1]ION
iance \ī-əns\ science, affiance, alliance, appliance, compliance, defiance, nonscience, reliance, mesalliance, misalliance
iancy \ī-ən-sē\ pliancy, compliancy
ianist \ē-t-nist\ pianist, Indo-Europeanist
iant \ī-ənt\ Bryant, client, giant, pliant, riant, affiant, compliant, defiant, reliant, incompliant, self-reliant, supergiant
iao \au̇\ see [2]OW
iaour \au̇r\ see [2]OWER
iaper \ī-pər\ see IPER
iar \īr\ see [1]IRE
[1]**iary** \ī-ə-rē\ diary, fiery, miry, priory
[2]**iary** \īr-ē\ see [1]IRY
[1]**ias** \ī-əs\ Aias, bias, dais, eyas, Laius, Lias, pious, Pius, Abdias, Elias, Messias, Nehemias, Tobias, Ananias, Jeremias, Malachias, Roncesvalles, Sophonias, Zacharias, Mount Saint Elias
[2]**ias** \ē-əs\ see [1]EUS
[3]**ias** \äsh\ see [1]ASH
iasis \ī-ə-səs\ diesis, diocese, archdiocese, psoriasis, acariasis, amebiasis, ascariasis, bilharziasis, helminthiasis, leishmaniasis, satyriasis, elephantiasis, hypochondriasis, schistosomiasis
[1]**iat** \ē-ət\ see [1]EIT
[2]**iat** \ī-ət\ see IET
iate \ī-ət\ see IET
[1]**iath** \ī-əth\ Wyeth, Goliath
[2]**iath** \ē-ə\ see [1]IA
iatry \ī-ə-trē\ podiatry, psychiatry
iaus \au̇s\ see [2]OUSE
iaz \äsh\ see [1]ASH
[1]**ib** \ib\ bib, bibb, crib, drib, fib. gib, glib, jib, lib, nib, rib, sib, squib, ad-lib, corncrib, midrib, sahib, memsahib
[2]**ib** \ēb\ see [2]EBE
[3]**ib** \ēv\ see [1]EAVE
iba \ē-bə\ see EBA
ibable \ī-bə-bəl\ bribable, ascribable, describable, indescribable
ibal \ī-bəl\ bible, Bible, libel, scribal, tribal
ibb \ib\ see [1]IB
ibband \ib-ən\ see IBBON
ibbed \ibd\ bibbed, rock-ribbed—*also pasts of verbs listed at* [1]IB
ibber \ib-ər\ bibber, cribber, dibber, fibber, gibber, glibber, jibber, libber, ribber
ibbet \ib-ət\ gibbet, exhibit, inhibit, prohibit, flibbertigibbet
ibbing \ib-iŋ\ cribbing, ribbing
ibble \ib-əl\ dibble, dribble, fribble, gribble, kibble, nibble, quibble, scribble, sibyl, Sibyl
ibbler \ib-lər\ dribbler, nibbler, quibbler, scribbler

ibbly \ib-lē\ dribbly, ghibli, glibly
ibbon \ib-ən\ gibbon, Gibbon, ribbon, inhibin
ibby \ib-ē\ Libby, ribby
1ibe \īb\ bribe, gibe, gybe, jibe, kibe, scribe, tribe, vibe, ascribe, conscribe, describe, imbibe, inscribe, prescribe, proscribe, subscribe, transcribe, circumscribe, diatribe, redescribe, superscribe, oversubscribe
2ibe \ē-bē\ see 1EBE
ibel \ī-bəl\ see IBAL
iber \ī-bər\ briber, fiber, giber, Khyber, scriber, Tiber, describer, inscriber, prescriber, proscriber, subscriber, transcriber
ibi \ē-bē\ see 1EBE
ibia \i-bē-ə\ Lybia, tibia, Namibia
ibin \ib-ən\ see IBBON
ibit \ib-ət\ see IBBET
ibitive \ib-ət-iv\ exhibitive, prohibitive
ibitor \ib-ət-ər\ exhibitor, inhibitor, ACE inhibitor
ible \ī-bəl\ see IBAL
iblet \ib-lət\ driblet, giblet, riblet
ibli \ib-lē\ see IBBLY
ibly \ib-lē\ see IBBLY
ibo \ē-bō\ Ibo, Kibo, gazebo
iboly \i-ə-lē\ see YBELE
ibrous \ī-brəs\ fibrous, hybris
ibs \ibz\ dibs, nibs, spareribs—*also plurals and possessives of nouns and third person singular presents of verbs listed at* 1IB
ibular \ib-yə-lər\ fibular, mandibular, vestibular, infundibular
1ibute \ib-yət\ tribute, attribute, contribute, distribute, redistribute
2ibute \ib-ət\ see IBBET
ibutive \ib-yət-iv\ attributive, contributive, distributive, retributive, redistributive
ibutor \ib-ət-ər\ see IBITOR
ibyl \ib-əl\ see IBBLE
1ic \ik\ see ICK
2ic \ēk\ see 1EAK
1ica \ī-kə\ mica, Micah, pica, pika, plica, spica, Spica, Formica, lorica, balalaika
2ica \ē-kə\ see 1IKA
icable \ik-ə-bəl\ despicable, explicable, extricable, inexplicable, inextricable
icah \ī-kə\ see 1ICA
ical \ik-əl\ see ICKLE
icament \ik-ə-mənt\ medicament, predicament
ican \ē-kən\ see EACON
icar \ik-ər\ see 1ICKER
icative \ik-ət-iv\ fricative, siccative, affricative, explicative, indicative, vindicative, multiplicative
iccative \ik-ət-iv\ see ICATIVE
iccio \ē-chō\ capriccio, pasticcio
1ice \īs\ Bryce, dice, fice, fyce, gneiss, ice, lice, lyse, mice, nice, pice, price, rice, rise, slice, spice, splice, syce, thrice, trice, twice, vice, vise, advice, allspice, Brandeis, bride-price, concise, cut-price, deice, device, entice, excise, precise, suffice, beggars-lice, cockatrice, edelweiss,

imprecise, merchandise, overprice, paradise, point-device, sacrifice, underprice, imparadise, self-sacrifice
[2]**ice** \ē-chā\ see [1]ICHE
[3]**ice** \ēs\ see IECE
[4]**ice** \ī-sē\ see ICY
[5]**ice** \īz\ see IZE
[6]**ice** \ēt-zə\ see [1]ITZA
iceless \ī-sləs\ iceless, priceless
icely \is-lē\ see ISTLY
iceous \ish-əs\ see [1]ICIOUS
icer \ī-sər\ dicer, Dreiser, nicer, pricer, ricer, slicer, splicer, deicer, sufficer, sacrificer, self-sacrificer
ices \ī-sēz\ Pisces, Anchises, Polynices, Coma Berenices
icety \ī-stē\ see EISTY
icey \ī-sē\ see ICY
[1]**ich** \ich\ see ITCH
[2]**ich** \ik\ see ICK
ichael \ī-kəl\ see [1]YCLE
[1]**iche** \ē-chā\ ceviche, seviche, Beatrice, cantatrice
[2]**iche** \ēsh\ fiche, leash, quiche, sneesh, baksheesh, corniche, hashish, maxixe, pastiche, schottische, unleash, microfiche, nouveau riche
[3]**iche** \ish\ see [1]ISH
[4]**iche** \ich\ see ITCH
[5]**iche** \ē-chē\ see EACHY
[1]**ichen** \ī-kən\ lichen, liken, proteoglycan
[2]**ichen** \ich-ən\ see ITCHEN
ichener \ich-nər\ see ITCHENER
icher \ich-ər\ see ITCHER
iches \ich-əz\ see ITCHES
[1]**ichi** \ē-chē\ see EACHY
[2]**ichi** \ē-shē\ see ISHI
ichment \ich-mənt\ see ITCHMENT
ichore \ik-rē\ see ICKERY
ichu \ish-ü\ see [1]ISSUE
[1]**icia** \ish-ə\ see ITIA
[2]**icia** \ēsh-ə\ see [1]ESIA
icial \ish-əl\ altricial, comitial, initial, judicial, official, simplicial, solstitial, surficial, artificial, beneficial, cicatricial, interstitial, prejudicial, sacrificial, superficial
ician \ē-shən\ see [1]ETION
icience \ish-əns\ omniscience, insufficience
iciency \ish-ən-sē\ deficiency, efficiency, proficiency, sufficiency, inefficiency, immunodeficiency
icient \ish-ənt\ deficient, efficient, omniscient, proficient, sufficient, coefficient, cost-efficient, inefficient, insufficient, self-sufficient
icinable \is-nə-bəl\ see ISTENABLE
icinal \is-[ə]n-əl\ vicinal, medicinal, officinal, vaticinal
[1]**icing** \ī-siŋ\ icing, splicing, self-sufficing
[2]**icing** \ī-ziŋ\ see IZING
[1]**icious** \ish-əs\ vicious, ambitious, auspicious, capricious, delicious, factitious, fictitious, flagitious, judicious, lubricious, malicious, Mauritius, nutritious, officious, pernicious, propitious, pumiceous, seditious,

sericeous, suspicious, adscititious, adventitious, avaricious, expeditious, inauspicious, injudicious, meretricious, prejudicious, subreptitious, superstitious, suppositious, surreptitious, excrementitious, supposititious

²icious \ē-shəs\ see ECIOUS

icipal \is-ə-bəl\ see ISSIBLE

icipant \is-ə-pənt\ anticipant, participant

icit \is-ət\ licit, complicit, elicit, explicit, illicit, implicit, solicit, inexplicit

¹icitor \is-ət-ər\ elicitor, solicitor

²icitor \is-tər\ see ISTER

icitous \is-ət-əs\ complicitous, duplicitous, felicitous, solicitous, infelicitous

¹icity \is-ət-ē\ basicity, causticity, centricity, chronicity, complicity, conicity, cyclicity, duplicity, ethnicity, felicity, lubricity, mendicity, plasticity, publicity, rhythmicity, seismicity, simplicity, spasticity, sphericity, tonicity, toxicity, triplicity, atomicity, authenticity, canonicity, catholicity, concentricity, domesticity, eccentricity, elasticity, electricity, ellipticity, endemicity, ergodicity, historicity, iconicity, impudicity, infelicity, multiplicity, organicity, pneumaticity, quadruplicity, specificity, synchronicity, volcanicity, aperiodicity, aromaticity, automaticity, ecumenicity, egocentricity, epidemicity, ethnocentricity, hydrophilicity, hydrophobicity, inauthenticity, inelasticity, pathogenicity, periodicity, theocentricity, aeroelasticity, anthropocentricity, carcinogenicity, homoscedasticity, quasiperiodicity

²icity \is-tē\ christie, Christie, misty, twisty, wristy, Corpus Christi, sacahuiste

ick \ik\ brick, chick, click, crick, creek, Dick, flick, hick, kick, KWIC, lick, mick, nick, Nick, pic, pick, prick, quick, rick, shtick, sic, sick, slick, snick, spick, stick, strick, thick, tic, tick, trick, wick, airsick, alsike, bluetick, bootlick, boychick, brainsick, broomstick, carsick, chopstick, cowlick, crabstick, dabchick, dead-stick, detick, dik-dik, dipstick, drop-kick, drumstick, firebrick, flagstick, goldbrick, greensick, handpick, hayrick, heartsick, homesick, joystick, lipstick, lovesick, matchstick, moujik, muzhik, nightstick, nitpick, nonstick, nutpick, outslick, peacenik, pigstick, pinprick, placekick, redbrick, rubric, seasick, self-stick, shashlik, sidekick, slapstick, slipstick, Tajik, toothpick, topkick, unpick, unstick, uptick, yardstick, bailiwick, biopic, Bolshevik, candlestick, candlewick, Dominic, dominick, Dominick, double-quick, EBCDIC, fiddlestick, hemistich, heretic, lunatic, Menshevik, meterstick, overtrick, politic, politick, polyptych, Reykjavik, singlestick, taperstick, undertrick, Watson-Crick, arithmetic, carrot-and-stick, computernik, impolitic, kinnikinnick

icka \ē-kə\ see [1]IKA

[1]**icked** \ik-əd\ picked, wicked

[2]**icked** \ikt\ see [1]ICT

ickel \ik-əl\ see ICKLE

icken \ik-ən\ chicken, quicken, sicken, stricken, thicken, awestricken, panic-stricken, planet-stricken, poverty-stricken

ickens \ik-ənz\ dickens, Dickens, pickings—*also plurals and possessives of nouns and third person singular presents of verbs listed at* ICKEN

[1]**icker** \ik-ər\ bicker, dicker, flicker, icker, licker, liquor, nicker, picker, pricker, sicker, slicker, snicker, sticker, ticker, tricker, vicar, whicker, wicker, billsticker, bootlicker, dropkicker, flea-flicker, nitpicker, pigsticker, placekicker, pot likker, ragpicker, dominicker, politicker—*also comparatives of adjectives listed at* ICK

[2]**icker** \ek-ər\ see ECKER

ickery \ik-rē\ chicory, flickery, hickory, snickery, trickery, Terpsichore

icket \ik-ət\ cricket, picket, Pickett, pricket, spigot, stickit, thicket, ticket, wicket, Big Thicket, big-ticket

ickett \ik-ət\ see ICKET

ickety \ik-ət-ē\ rickety, thickety, pernickety, persnickety

ickey \ik-ē\ see ICKY

icki \ik-ē\ see ICKY

ickie \ik-ē\ see ICKY

icking \ik-iŋ\ ticking, wicking, brain-picking, flat-picking, high-sticking, nit-picking, cotton-picking, finger-picking

ickings \ik-ənz\ see ICKENS

ickish \ik-ish\ hickish, sickish, trickish

ickit \ik-ət\ see ICKET

ickle \ik-əl\ brickle, chicle, fickle, mickle, nickel, pickle, picul, prickle, sickle, stickle, strickle, tical, tickle, trickle, bicycle, icicle, obstacle, Popsicle, spectacle, tricycle, vehicle, pumpernickel

ickler \ik-lər\ stickler, tickler, bicycler, particular

ickly \ik-lē\ fickly, prickly, quickly, sickly, slickly, impoliticly

ickness \ik-nəs\ lychnis, quickness, sickness, slickness, thickness, airsickness, heartsickness, homesickness, lovesickness, seasickness

icksy \ik-sē\ see IXIE

icky \ik-ē\ dickey, hickey, icky,

kicky, Mickey, picky, quickie, rickey, sickie, sticky, tricky, Vicki, Vickie, Vicky, doohickey

icle \ik-əl\ see ICKLE

[1]icly \ik-lē\ see ICKLY

[2]icly \ē-klē\ see EEKLY

ico \ē-kō\ see ICOT

icope \ik-ə-pē\ see ICOPY

icopy \ik-ə-pē\ wicopy, pericope

icory \ik-rē\ see ICKERY

icot \ē-kō\ fico, pekoe, picot, tricot, Tampico, Puerto Rico

ics \iks\ see [1]IX

[1]ict \ikt\ picked, Pict, strict, ticked, addict, afflict, conflict, constrict, convict, delict, depict, edict, evict, inflict, lipsticked, predict, restrict, unlicked, benedict, Benedict, contradict, derelict, interdict, maledict, retrodict, eggs Benedict—*also pasts of verbs listed at* ICK

[2]ict \īt\ see [1]ITE

ictable \īt-ə-bəl\ see [1]ITABLE

ictal \ik-tᵊl\ fictile, rictal, edictal

icted \ik-təd\ conflicted, evicted, restricted—*also pasts of verbs listed at* ICT

icter \ik-tər\ see ICTOR

ictic \ik-tik\ deictic, panmictic, amphimictic, apodictic

ictile \ik-tᵊl\ see ICTAL

ictim \ik-təm\ see ICTUM

iction \ik-shən\ diction, fiction, friction, stiction, addiction, affliction, confliction, constriction, conviction, depiction, eviction, indiction, infliction, nonfiction, prediction, reliction, restriction, transfixion, benediction, contradiction, crucifixion, dereliction, jurisdiction, malediction, metafiction, valediction

ictional \ik-shnəl\ fictional, frictional, nonfictional, jurisdictional

ictionist \ik-shnəst\ fictionist, restrictionist

ictive \ik-tiv\ fictive, addictive, afflictive, conflictive, constrictive, inflictive, restrictive, vindictive, nonrestrictive

ictment \īt-mənt\ see ITEMENT

ictor \ik-tər\ lictor, stricter, victor, constrictor, depicter, evictor, inflicter, contradictor, vasoconstrictor

ictory \ik-tə-rē\ victory, benedictory, contradictory, maledictory, valedictory

ictual \it-ᵊl\ see ITTLE

ictualler \it-ᵊl-ər\ see ITALER

ictum \ik-təm\ dictum, victim, obiter dictum

icture \ik-chər\ picture, stricture

icul \ik-əl\ see ICKLE

icula \ik-yə-lə\ auricula, Canicula

iculant \ik-yə-lənt\ gesticulant, matriculant

[1]icular \ik-yə-lər\ spicular, acicular, articular, auricular, canicular, clavicular, curricular, cuticular, fascicular, follicular, funicular, lenticular, navicular, orbicular, ossicular, particular, radicular, reticular, testicular, vehicular, ventricular, vermicular, versicular, vesicular, appendicular, perpendicular, extracurricular, extravehicular, intra-articular, supraventricular

[2]icular \ik-lər\ see ICKLER

icularly \ik-lē\ see ICKLY

iculate \ik-yə-lət\ articulate, denticulate, geniculate, particulate, reticulate, straticulate, vermiculate, inarticulate

iculous \ik-yə-ləs\ meticulous, pediculous, ridiculous

iculum \ik-yə-ləm\ curriculum, reticulum, diverticulum

icuous \ik-yə-wəs\ conspicuous, perspicuous, transpicuous, inconspicuous

icy \ī-sē\ dicey, icy, pricey, spicy

[1]id \id\ bid, chid, Cid, did, fid, gid, grid, hid, id, kid, Kidd, lid, mid, quid, rid, skid, slid, squid, SQUID, whid, Yid, amid, backslid, bifid, El Cid, equid, eyelid, forbid, grandkid, Madrid, nonskid, outdid, resid, schoolkid, trifid, undid, katydid, ootid, overbid, overdid, pyramid, underbid, tertium quid, Valadolid

[2]id \ēd\ see EED

I'd \īd\ see [1]IDE

[1]ida \ēd-ə\ see [1]EDA

[2]ida \ī-də\ Haida, Ida, Vida

[1]idable \īd-ə-bəl\ guidable, decidable, dividable, subdividable

[2]idable \id-ə-bəl\ see IDDABLE

idal \īd-ᵊl\ bridal, bridle, idle, idol, idyll, seidel, sidle, tidal, unbridle, Barmecidal, fratricidal, fungicidal, genocidal, germicidal, herbicidal, homicidal, intertidal, lunitidal, matricidal, parricidal, patricidal, septicidal, spermicidal, suicidal, viricidal, virucidal, bactericidal, infanticidal, insecticidal

idance \īd-ᵊns\ guidance, stridence, abidance, misguidance

idas \īd-əs\ Midas, nidus

iday \īd-ē\ Friday, Heidi, tidy, vide, alcaide, man Friday, untidy, mala fide

idays \īd-ēz\ see [1]IDES

idd \id\ see [1]ID

iddable \id-ə-bəl\ biddable, formidable

iddance \id-ᵊns\ riddance, forbiddance

idden \id-ᵊn\ bidden, chiden, hidden, midden, ridden, stridden, swidden, backslidden, bedridden, bestridden, forbidden, outbidden, unbidden, overridden

idder \id-ər\ bidder, gridder, kidder, siddur, skidder, consider, forbidder, reconsider, underbidder

iddie \id-ē\ see IDDY

iddish \id-ish\ kiddish, Yiddish

iddity \id-ət-ē\ see IDITY

iddle \id-ᵊl\ diddle, fiddle, griddle, middle, piddle, riddle, twiddle, unriddle, paradiddle, taradiddle

iddler \id-lər\ diddler, fiddler, middler, riddler, tiddler,

iddling \id-liŋ\ fiddling, middling, piddling, riddling

iddly \id-le\ diddly, ridley, tiddly

iddock \id-ik\ see IDIC

iddur \id-ər\ see IDDER

iddy \id-ē\ biddy, giddy, kiddie, middy, midi, skiddy, widdy

¹ide \īd\ bide, bride, chide, Clyde, eyed, fried, glide, guide, hide, I'd, pied, plied, pride, ride, side, slide, snide, stride, thighed, tide, tried, wide, abide, allied, applied, aside, astride, backside, backslide, bankside, beachside, bedside, beside, bestride, betide, blear-eyed, blindside, blowdried, blue-eyed, broadside, bromide, bug-eyed, Burnside, clear-eyed, cockeyed, cold-eyed, collide, confide, courtside, cowhide, cross-eyed, curbside, dayside, decide, deride, divide, dockside, doe-eyed, downside, dry-eyed, elide, fireside, foreside, four-eyed, freeze-dried, glass-eyed, graveside, green-eyed, hagride, hawkeyed, hayride, hillside, horsehide, inside, ironside, joyride, kingside, lakeside, landslide, lynx-eyed, misguide, moon-eyed, nearside, nightside, noontide, offside, onside, outride, outside, pie-eyed, poolside, pop-eyed, preside, provide, quayside, queenside, rawhide, reside, ringside, riptide, roadside, seaside, sharp-eyed, shipside, shoreside, Shrovetide, sloe-eyed, snowslide, springtide, squint-eyed, stateside, statewide, storewide, Strathclyde, streamside, subside, tailslide, Tayside, tongue-tied, topside, trackside, trailside, untried, upside, vat-dyed, walleyed, waveguide, wayside, wide-eyed, wild-eyed, worldwide, yuletide, alkoxide, almond-eyed, alongside, Argus-eyed, Barmecide, bleary-eyed, bona fide, chicken-fried, Christmastide, citified, citywide, classified, coincide, countrified, countryside, countrywide, cut-and-dried, cyanide, deicide, demand-side, dewy-eyed, dignified, double-wide, downslide, Eastertide, eventide, feticide, fluoride, formamide, fratricide, fungicide, genocide, germicide, gimlet-eyed, glassy-eyed, goggle-eyed, googly-eyed, harbor-side, herbicide, homicide, Humberside, humified, matricide, Merseyside, misty-eyed, miticide, monoxide, mountainside, nationwide, Naugahyde, open-eyed, override, overstride, parricide,

Passiontide, patricide, pesticide, planetwide, qualified, rarefied, raticide, regicide, riverside, Riverside, set-aside, silverside, sissified, slickenside, spermicide, starry-eyed, subdivide, suicide, supply-side, trisulfide, underside, verbicide, vermicide, viricide, waterside, Whitsuntide, wintertide, acrylamide, antimonide, borohydride, dissatisfied, formaldehyde, infanticide, insecticide, interallied, Jekyll and Hyde, preoccupied, rodenticide, self-satisfied, thalidomide, Trinitytide, tyrannicide, uxoricide, monoglyceride, overqualified, parasiticide—*also pasts of verbs listed at* [1]Y

[2]**ide** \ēd\ see EED

idean \id-ē-ən\ see IDIAN

ided \īd-əd\ sided, lopsided, misguided, one-sided, slab-sided, two-sided, many-sided, sobersided—*also pasts of verbs listed at* [1]IDE

ideless \īd-ləs\ idlesse, tideless

iden \īd-ᵊn\ guidon, Hayden, widen, Poseidon

idence \īd-ᵊns\ see IDANCE

ideness \īd-nəs\ see EYEDNESS

ident \īd-ᵊnt\ strident, trident

ideon \id-ē-ən\ see IDIAN

ideous \id-ē-əs\ see IDIOUS

[1]**ider** \īd-ər\ bider, cider, eider, glider, guider, hider, rider, slider, spider, strider, stridor, abider, backslider, confider, decider, derider, divider, insider, joyrider, misguider, outrider, outsider, presider, provider, resider, rough rider, Top-Sider, subdivider, supply-sider, supercollider—*also comparatives of adjectives listed at* [1]IDE

[2]**ider** \id-ər\ see IDDER

[1]**ides** \īd-ēz\ Fridays, Aristides—*also plurals and possessives of nouns and third person singular presents of verbs listed at* IDAY

[2]**ides** \īdz\ ides, besides, burnsides, silversides, sobersides—*also plurals and possessives of nouns and third person singular presents of verbs listed at* [1]IDE

idge \ij\ bridge, fidge, fridge, midge, ridge, abridge, Blue Ridge, browridge, drawbridge, footbridge, Oxbridge, teethridge

idged \ijd\ ridged, unabridged—*also pasts of verbs listed at* IDGE

idgen \ij-ən\ see YGIAN

idget \ij-ət\ Brigitte, digit, fidget, midget, widget, double-digit

idgin \ij-ən\ see YGIAN

idi \id-ē\ see IDDY

idia \i-dē-ə\ Lydia, basidia, chlamydia, clostridia, coccidia, conidia, glochidia, nephridia, Numidia, oidia, peridia, Pisidia, presidia, pycnidia, pygidia, antheridia, enchiridia, hesperidia, miricidia, ommatidia

idian \id-ē-ən\ Gideon, Lydian, Midian, ascidian, Dravidian, euclidean, Floridian, meridian, obsidian, ophidian, quotidian, viridian, enchiridion, non-euclidean
idic \id-ik\ piddock, acidic, bromidic, Davidic, druidic, fatidic, fluidic, Hasidic, nuclidic
idical \id-i-kəl\ druidical, fatidical, juridical, veridical, pyramidical
idice \id-ə-sē\ Chalcidice, Eurydice
idiem \id-ē-əm\ idiom, iridium, presidium, rubidium, post meridiem, ante meridiem
iding \īd-iŋ\ riding, Riding, siding, tiding, abiding, confiding, East Riding, joyriding, West Riding, law-abiding, nondividing
idiom \id-ē-əm\ see IDIEM
idious \id-ē-əs\ hideous, fastidious, insidious, invidious, perfidious
idity \id-ət-ē\ quiddity, acidity, aridity, avidity, cupidity, fluidity, flaccidity, floridity, frigidity, gelidity, gravidity, hispidity, humidity, hybridity, limpidity, liquidity, lividity, lucidity, morbidity, rabidity, rapidity, rigidity, sapidity, solidity, stupidity, tepidity, timidity, torridity, turbidity, turgidity, validity, vapidity, viridity, viscidity, illiquidity, insipidity, intrepidity, invalidity
idium \id-ē-əm\ see IDIEM
idle \īd-ᵊl\ see IDAL
idlesse \īd-ləs\ see IDELESS
idley \id-lē\ see IDDLY
idney \id-nē\ kidney, Sidney, Sydney
[1]**ido** \īd-ō\ dido, Dido, fido, Hokkaido
[2]**ido** \ēd-ō\ see [1]EDO
idol \īd-ᵊl\ see IDAL
[1]**idz** \idz\ Beskids, rapids, Grand Rapids—*also plurals of nouns listed at* [1]ID
[2]**ids** \ēdz\ see EEDS
idst \idst\ didst, midst, amidst
[1]**idual** \ij-wəl\ residual, individual
[2]**idual** \ij-əl\ see IGIL
idulent \ij-ə-lənt\ see IGILANT
idulous \ij-ə-ləs\ stridulous, acidulous
idus \īd-əs\ see IDAS
iduum \ij-ə-wəm\ triduum, residuum
idy \īd-ē\ see IDAY
idyll \īd-ᵊl\ see IDAL
[1]**ie** \ā\ see [1]AY
[2]**ie** \ē\ see [1]EE
[3]**ie** \ī\ see [1]Y
iece \ēs\ cease, crease, fleece, grease, Greece, kris, lease, Nice, niece, peace, piece, apiece, Bernice, Burmese, camise, caprice, cassis, cerise, chemise, Chinese, Clarice, Cochise, codpiece, coulisse, crosspiece, decease, decrease, degrease, Denise, Dumfries, earpiece, Elise, eyepiece, Felice, fieldpiece, grandniece, hairpiece, headpiece, heelpiece, increase, Janice, lend-lease, Matisse, Maurice,

mouthpiece, nosepiece, obese, patsis, pelisse, police, re-lease, release, seapiece, shankpiece, showpiece, sidepiece, stringpiece, sublease, surcease, tailpiece, Therese, timepiece, toepiece, two-piece, valise, workpiece, afterpiece, altarpiece, Amboinese, Annamese, Assamese, Balinese, Brooklynese, Cantonese, centerpiece, Chersonese, chimneypiece, diocese, directrice, ex libris, expertise, Faeroese, frontispiece, mantelpiece, masterpiece, Nipponese, Pekinese, Pekingese, Portugese, predecease, rerelease, São Luis, Siamese, Sinhalese, timed-release, verdigris, archdiocese, computerese, Dodecanese, officialese, telegraphese, Vietnamese, educationese

iecer \ē-sər\ see [1]EASER

[1]**ied** \ēd\ see EED

[2]**ied** \ēt\ see [1]EAT

[3]**ied** \īd\ see [1]IDE

ieda \ēd-ə\ see [1]EDA

[1]**ief** \ēf\ beef, brief, chief, fief, grief, kef, leaf, lief, reef, sheaf, thief, belief, debrief, endleaf, enfeoff, flyleaf, loose-leaf, massif, motif, naif, O'Keefe, relief, sharif, sherif, shinleaf, bas-relief, cloverleaf, disbelief, handkerchief, leatherleaf, neckerchief, leitmotiv, misbelief, overleaf, unbelief, waterleaf, aperitif, Capitol Reef, Vinson Massif, Great Berrier Reef, Santa Cruz de Tenerife

[2]**ief** \ēv\ see [1]EAVE

iefless \ē-fləs\ briefless, leafless

iefly \ē-flē\ briefly, chiefly

[1]**ieg** \ēg\ see IGUE

[2]**ieg** \ig\ see IG

[1]**iege** \ēj\ liege, siege, besiege, prestige

[2]**iege** \ēzh\ see [1]IGE

ieger \ē-jər\ see EDURE

iek \ēk\ see [1]EAK

[1]**iel** \ēl\ see [2]EAL

[2]**iel** \ī-əl\ see [1]IAL

iela \el-ə\ see ELLA

ield \ēld\ bield, field, keeled, shield, weald, wheeled, wield, yield, afield, airfield, backfield, brickfield, coalfield, cornfield, downfield, Enfield, four-wheeled, Garfield, goldfield, grainfield, infield, Masefield, midfield, minefield, outfield, playfield, Sheffield, Smithfield, snowfield, Springfield, subfield, unsealed, upfield, well-heeled, windshield, Winfield, battlefield, broken-field, chesterfield, Chesterfield, color-field, Huddersfield, track-and-field, unaneled—*also pasts of verbs listed at* [2]EAL

ielder \ēl-dər\ fielder, shielder, wielder, yielder, infielder, outfielder

ields \ēldz\ South Shields—*also possessives and plurals of nouns and third person*

singular presents of verbs listed at IELD
ieler \ē-lər\ see EALER
ieless \ī-ləs\ see ILUS
[1]ieling \ē-lən\ see ELIN
[2]ieling \ē-liŋ\ see EELING
[1]iem \ē-əm\ see [1]EUM
[2]iem \ī-əm\ see IAM
ien \ēn\ see [3]INE
ience \ī-əns\ see IANCE
iend \end\ see END
iendless \en-ləs\ see ENDLESS
iendliness \en-lē-nəs\ see ENDLINESS
iendly \en-lē\ see ENDLY
iene \ēn\ see [3]INE
[1]iener \ē-nər\ see EANER
[2]iener \ē-nē\ see [1]INI
ienic \en-ik\ see [2]ENIC
ienics \en-iks\ see ENICS
ienie \ē-nē\ see [1]INI
ienist \ē-nəst\ see [2]INIST
iennes \en\ see [1]EN
ient \ī-ənt\ see IANT
ieper \ē-pər\ see EEPER
[1]ier \ir\ see [2]EER
[2]ier \ē-ər\ see [1]EER
[3]ier \īr\ see [1]IRE
ierate \ir-ət\ see IRIT
ierce \irs\ Bierce, birse, fierce, pierce, Pierce, tierce, transpierce
[1]iere \er\ see [4]ARE
[2]iere \ir\ see [2]EER
iered \ird\ see [1]EARD
ieria \ir-ē-ə\ see [1]ERIA
ierial \ir-ē-əl\ see ERIAL
ierian \ir-ē-ən\ see [1]ERIAN
ierly \ir-lē\ see [1]EARLY
[1]ierre \ir\ see [2]EER
[2]ierre \er\ see [4]ARE
iers \irz\ Algiers, Pamirs—*also plurals and possessives of nouns and third person singular presents of verbs listed at* EER
iersman \irz-mən\ see EERSMAN
iery \ī-rē\ see [1]IARY
[1]ies \ēz\ see EZE
[2]ies \ē\ see [1]EE
[3]ies \ēs\ see IECE
[1]iesel \ē-zəl\ see EASEL
[2]iesel \ē-sᵊl\ see [1]ECIL
ieseling \ēz-liŋ\ see ESLING
iesian \ē-zhən\ see [1]ESIAN
iesis \ī-ə-səs\ see IASIS
iesling \ēz-liŋ\ see ESLING
iest \ēst\ see [1]EAST
iester \ē-stər\ see EASTER
iestley \ēst-lē\ see EASTLY
iestly \ēst-lē\ see EASTLY
iet \ī-ət\ diet, fiat, quiet, riot, striate, Wyatt, disquiet, unquiet
ietal \ī-ət-ᵊl\ parietal, societal, varietal
ieter \ī-ət-ər\ dieter, quieter, rioter, proprietor
ietor \ī-ət-ər\ see IETER
ietzsche \ē-chē\ see EACHY
iety \ī-ət-ē\ piety, anxiety, dubiety, impiety, nimiety, propriety, satiety, sobriety, society, Society, variety, contrariety, impropriety, inebriety, insobriety, notoriety
ieu \ü\ see [1]EW
ieur \ir\ see [2]EER
iev \ef\ see [1]EF
ievable \ē-və-bəl\ see EIVABLE
ieval \ē-vəl\ evil, shrieval, weevil, coeval, khedival, medieval, primeval, reprieval, retrieval, upheaval

[1]**ieve** \iv\ see [2]IVE
[2]**ieve** \ēv\ see [1]EAVE
ieved \ēvd\ see EAVED
ievement \ēv-mənt\ see EVEMENT
iever \ē-vər\ beaver, cleaver, fever, griever, leaver, reaver, reiver, weaver, achiever, believer, conceiver, deceiver, enfever, perceiver, receiver, reliever, retriever, upheaver, school-leaver, transceiver, cantilever, disbeliever, misbeliever, misconceiver, unbeliever, overachiever, underachiever
ievish \ē-vish\ see EEVISH
ievo \ē-vō\ see EVO
ievous \ē-vəs\ see EVOUS
ieze \ēz\ see EZE
[1]**if** \if\ see IFF
[2]**if** \ēf\ see [1]IEF
[1]**ife** \īf\ fife, Fife, knife, life, rife, strife, wife, alewife, drawknife, fishwife, flick-knife, goodwife, half-life, housewife, jackknife, loosestrife, lowlife, mid-life, nightlife, oldwife, penknife, pro-life, true-life, wakerife, whole-life, wildlife, afterlife, antilife, Duncan Phyfe, nurse-midwife, pocketknife, Yellowknife, right-to-life
[2]**ife** \ē-fə\ see EPHA
[3]**ife** \ēf\ see [1]IEF
ifeless \ī-fləs\ lifeless, strifeless, wifeless
ifer \ī-fər\ see IPHER
iferous \if-ər-əs\ coniferous, floriferous, lactiferous, luciferous, pestiferous, somniferous, splendiferous, vociferous, carboniferous, luminiferous, odoriferous, salutiferous, seminiferous, soporiferous, sudoriferous
iff \if\ biff, cliff, glyph, if, iff, jiff, kif, miff, quiff, riff, Riff, skiff, sniff, spiff, spliff, stiff, syph, tiff, whiff, Er Rif, midriff, Plovdiv, triglyph, what-if, Wycliffe, anaglyph, bindle stiff, hieroglyph, hippogriff, logogriph, petroglyph
iffany \if-ə-nē\ see IPHONY
iffe \if\ see IFF
iffed \ift\ see IFT
iffen \if-ən\ see IFFIN
iffey \if-ē\ see IFFY
iffian \if-ē-ən\ Riffian, Pecksniffian
iffin \if-ən\ griffin, griffon, stiffen, tiffin
iffish \if-ish\ sniffish, stiffish
iffle \if-əl\ piffle, riffle, skiffle, sniffle, whiffle, Wiffle
iffler \if-lər\ riffler, sniffler, whiffler
iffness \if-nəs\ stiffness, swiftness
iffon \if-ən\ see IFFIN
iffy \if-ē\ iffy, cliffy, jiffy, Liffey, sniffy, spiffy
ific \if-ik\ glyphic, calcific, febrific, horrific, magnific, pacific, Pacific, prolific, salvific, specific, terrific, vivific, anaglyphic, beatific, calorific, colorific, felicific, frigorific, hieroglyphic, honorific, scientific, soporific,

sudorific, tenebrific, prescientific
ifical \if-i-kəl\ magnifical, pontifical
ificate \if-i-kət\ certificate, pontificate
ificent \if-ə-sənt\ magnificent, omnificent
ifle \ī-fəl\ rifle, stifle, trifle
ifling \ī-fliŋ\ rifling, stifling, trifling
ift \ift\ drift, gift, grift, lift, rift, shift, shrift, sift, squiffed, swift, Swift, thrift, adrift, airlift, blueshift, downshift, face-lift, festschrift, forklift, frameshift, gearshift, Great Rift, makeshift, redshift, shoplift, snowdrift, spendthrift, spindrift, spoondrift, unshift, uplift, upshift—*also pasts of verbs listed at* IFF
ifter \if-tər\ drifter, snifter, swifter, sceneshifter, shape-shifter, shoplifter
ifth \ith\ see [2]ITH
iftness \if-nəs\ see IFFNESS
ifty \if-tē\ drifty, fifty, nifty, shifty, thrifty, wifty, fifty-fifty, LD50
ig \ig\ big, brig, dig, fig, frig, gig, Grieg, grig, jig, pig, prig, rig, sprig, swig, trig, twig, vig, Whig, wig, zig, bagwig, bigwig, bushpig, earwig, hedgepig, lime-twig, renege, shindig, unrig, caprifig, infra dig, jury-rig, periwig, thimblerig, whirligig, WYSIWYG, Zagazig, thingamajig
[1]iga \ē-gə\ Riga, Vega, viga, Antigua, omega, quadriga
[2]iga \ī-gə\ see AIGA
igamous \ig-ə-məs\ bigamous, polygamous
igamy \ig-ə-mē\ bigamy, digamy, polygamy
[1]igan \ī-gən\ ligan, tigon
[2]igan \ig-ən\ see IGGIN
igand \ig-ənd\ brigand, ligand
igas \ī-gəs\ see YGOUS
igate \ig-ət\ see [1]IGOT
[1]ige \ēzh\ siege, prestige, noblesse oblige
[2]ige \ēj\ see [1]IEGE
igel \ij-əl\ see IGIL
igenous \ij-ə-nəs\ see IGINOUS
igeon \ij-ən\ see YGIAN
iger \ī-gər\ tiger, braunschweiger
igerent \ij-rənt\ belligerent, refrigerant, cobelligerent
iggan \ig-ən\ see IGGIN
iggard \ig-ərd\ niggard, triggered—*also pasts of verbs listed at* IGGER
igged \igd\ twigged, wigged, bewigged, cat-rigged, square-rigged, periwigged—*also pasts of verbs listed at* IG
igger \ig-ər\ bigger, chigger, digger, jigger, nigger, rigger, rigor, snigger, swigger, trigger, vigor, vigour, ditchdigger, outrigger, rejigger, reneger, square-rigger, thimblerigger
iggered \ig-ərd\ see IGGARD
iggery \ig-ə-rē\ piggery, priggery, Whiggery
iggie \ig-ē\ see IGGY

iggin \ig-ən\ biggin, piggin, wigan, balbriggan
iggish \ig-ish\ biggish, piggish, priggish, Whiggish
iggle \ig-əl\ giggle, higgle, jiggle, niggle, sniggle, squiggle, wiggle, wriggle
iggler \ig-lər\ giggler, higgler, niggler, wiggler, wriggler
iggy \ig-ē\ biggie, piggy, twiggy
igh \ī\ see [1]Y
ighed \īd\ see [1]IDE
ighland \ī-lənd\ highland, Highland, island, Thailand, Long Island, Rhode Island, Staten Island, Prince Edward Island
ighlander \ī-lən-dər\ highlander, islander
ighlands \ī-lənz\ Highlands, Virgin Islands
ighly \ī-lē\ see YLY
ighness \ī-nəs\ see [1]INUS
ight \īt\ see [1]ITE
ightable \īt-ə-bəl\ see [1]ITABLE
ighted \īt-əd\ blighted, sighted, whited, attrited, benighted, clear-sighted, farsighted, foresighted, longsighted, nearsighted, sharp-sighted, shortsighted, skylighted, united, unrequited—*also pasts of verbs listed at* [1]ITE
ighten \īt-ᵊn\ brighten, Brighton, chitin, chiton, frighten, heighten, lighten, tighten, titan, Titan, triton, Triton, whiten, enlighten
ightener \īt-nər\ brightener, lightener, tightener, whitener
ightening \īt-niŋ\ see IGHTNING
ighter \īt-ər\ see [1]ITER
ightful \īt-fəl\ frightful, rightful, spiteful, sprightful, delightful, despiteful, foresightful, insightful
ightie \īt-ē\ see [2]ITE
ightily \īt-ᵊl-ē\ flightily, mightily
ightiness \īt-ē-nəs\ flightiness, mightiness, almightiness
ighting \īt-iŋ\ see ITING
ightless \īt-ləs\ flightless, lightless, sightless
ightly \īt-lē\ knightly, lightly, nightly, rightly, sightly, sprightly, whitely, fortnightly, midnightly, unsightly—*also adverbs formed by adding* -ly *to adjectives listed at* [1]ITE
ightment \īt-mənt\ see ITEMENT
ightning \īt-niŋ\ lightning, tightening, belt-tightening
ightn't \īt-ᵊnt\ see ITANT
ighton \īt-ən\ see IGHTEN
ights \īts\ lights, nights, tights, footlights, houselights, weeknights, Dolomites, Golan Heights—*also plurals and possessives of nouns and third person singular presents of verbs listed at* [1]ITE
ightsome \īt-səm\ lightsome, delightsome
ighty \īt-ē\ see [2]ITE
igian \ij-ən\ see YGIAN
igid \ij-əd\ Brigid, frigid, rigid
igil \ij-əl\ Rigel, sigil, strigil, vigil, residual
igilant \ij-ə-lənt\ vigilant, acidulent
igine \ij-ə-nē\ polygyny, aborigine

iginous \ij-ə-nəs\ caliginous, fuliginous, indigenous, polygynous, vertiginous
igion \ij-ən\ see YGIAN
igious \ij-əs\ litigious, prestigious, prodigious, religious, irreligious
igit \ij-ət\ see IDGET
igitte \ij-ət\ see IDGET
iglet \ig-lət\ piglet, wiglet
[1]**igm** \im\ see [1]IM
[2]**igm** \īm\ see [1]IME
igma \ig-mə\ sigma, stigma, enigma, kerygma
igment \ig-mənt\ figment, pigment
ign \īn\ see [1]INE
ignable \ī-nə-bəl\ see INABLE
ignancy \ig-nən-sē\ benignancy, malignancy
ignant \ig-nənt\ benignant, indignant, malignant
igned \īnd\ see [1]IND
igneous \ig-nē-əs\ igneous, ligneous
igner \ī-nər\ see [1]INER
igness \ig-nəs\ bigness, Cygnus
ignet \ig-nət\ see YGNET
igning \ī-niŋ\ see INING
ignity \ig-nət-ē\ dignity, indignity, malignity
ignly \īn-lē\ see [1]INELY
ignment \īn-mənt\ alignment, assignment, confinement, consignment, enshrinement, refinement, nonalignment, realignment
ignon \in-yən\ see INION
ignor \ē-nyər\ see ENIOR
[1]**igo** \ī-gō\ Sligo, prurigo, vitiligo
[2]**igo** \ē-gō\ see EGO
igoe \ē-gō\ see EGO
igon \ī-gən\ see [1]IGAN
igor \ig-ər\ see IGGER
igorous \ig-rəs\ rigorous, vigorous
[1]**igot** \ig-ət\ bigot, frigate, gigot, spigot
[2]**igot** \ik-ət\ see ICKET
igour \ig-ər\ see IGGER
igrapher \ig-rə-fər\ calligrapher, epigrapher, polygrapher, serigrapher
igraphist \ig-rə-fəst\ calligraphist, epigraphist, polygraphist
igraphy \ig-rə-fē\ calligraphy, epigraphy, pseudepigraphy
igua \ē-gə\ see [1]IGA
igue \ēg\ gigue, Grieg, league, blitzkrieg, colleague, fatigue, garigue, intrigue, sitzkrieg, squeteague, wampumpeag
iguer \ē-gər\ see EAGER
iguous \ig-yə-wəs\ ambiguous, contiguous, exiguous, unambiguous
igured \ig-ərd\ see IGGARD
ii \ī\ see [1]Y
iing \ē-iŋ\ see EEING
ija \ē-jə\ see EGIA
ijah \ī-jə\ Elijah, steatopygia
iji \ē-jē\ Fiji, squeegee
ijl \īl\ see [1]ILE
ijn \īn\ see [1]INE
ijssel \ī-sə\ see ISAL
[1]**ik** \ik\ see ICK
[2]**ik** \ēk\ see [1]EAK
[1]**ika** \ē-kə\ pika, theca, areca, eureka, Frederica, Fredericka, paprika, Costa Rica, Dominica, oiticica, Topeka, Tanganyika, bibliotheca

[2]**ika** \ī-kə\ see [1]ICA
[1]**ike** \ī-kē\ Nike, Psyche, crikey, spiky
[2]**ike** \īk\ bike, caique, dike, dyke, fyke, haik, hike, kike, like, mike, Mike, pike, psych, shrike, sike, spike, strike, trike, tyke, alike, belike, catlike, childlike, clocklike, dislike, fly-strike, garpike, godlike, handspike, hitchhike, homelike, Klondike, lifelike, mislike, pealike, prooflike, push-bike, rampike, restrike, scalelike, sheaflike, shunpike, suchlike, ten-strike, turnpike, unlike, Updike, Vandyke, warlike, wifelike, winglike, berrylike, businesslike, fatherlike, ladylike, look-alike, machinelike, marlinespike, marlinspike, minibike, motorbike, rubberlike, Scafell Pike, soundalike, thunderstrike, womanlike, workmanlike, unsportsmanlike
[3]**ike** \ik\ see ICK
[1]**iked** \īkt\ liked, piked, spiked, vandyked—*also pasts of verbs listed at* [2]IKE
[2]**iked** \ī-kəd\ see YCAD
iken \ī-kən\ see [1]ICHEN
iker \ī-kər\ biker, diker, duiker, hiker, piker, spiker, striker, disliker, hitchhiker, shunpiker, minibiker
ikes \īks\ yikes—*also possessives and plurals of nouns and third person singular presents of verbs listed at* IKE
ikey \ī-kē\ see [1]IKE
ikh \ēk\ see [1]EAK
[1]**iki** \ik-ē\ see ICKY
[2]**iki** \ē-kē\ see EAKY
iking \ī-kiŋ\ liking, striking, Viking, shunpiking
ikker \ik-ər\ see [1]ICKER
iky \ī-kē\ see [1]IKE
[1]**il** \il\ see ILL
[2]**il** \ēl\ see [2]EAL
[1]**ila** \il-ə\ see [2]ILLA
[2]**ila** \ē-lə\ see [1]ELA
[3]**ila** \ī-lə\ Lila, Delilah
ilae \ī-le\ see YLY
ilage \ī-lij\ mileage, silage
ilah \ī-lə\ see [3]ILA
ilament \il-ə-mənt\ filament, habiliment, monofilament
ilar \ī-lər\ dialer, filar, flier, hilar, miler, smiler, stylar, styler, tiler, Tyler, beguiler, bifilar, compiler, defiler, freestyler, profiler, rottweiler, stockpiler, unifilar
ilary \il-ə-rē\ see ILLARY
ilate \ī-lət\ see ILOT
ilbe \il-be\ see ILBY
ilbert \il-bərt\ filbert, gilbert, Gilbert
ilby \il-bē\ trilby, astilbe
[1]**ilch** \ilk\ see ILK
[2]**ilch** \ilch\ filch, milch, zilch
[1]**ild** \īld\ mild, piled, wild, Wilde, brainchild, godchild, grandchild, hog-wild, man-child, pantiled, Rothschild, schoolchild, self-styled, stepchild—*also pasts of verbs listed at* [1]ILE
[2]**ild** \il\ see ILL
[3]**ild** \ilt\ see ILT
[4]**ild** \ild\ see ILLED

ilda \il-də\ Hilda, tilde, Wilda
[1]ilde \il-də\ see ILDA
[2]ilde \īld\ see [1]ILD
[1]ilding \il-dər\ builder, gilder, guilder, wilder, bewilder, boatbuilder, shipbuilder, upbuilder, bodybuilder, jerry-builder
[2]ilder \īl-dər\ milder, wilder, Wilder
ilding \il-diŋ\ building, gilding, hilding, abuilding, outbuilding, shipbuilding, bodybuilding—*also present participles of verbs listed at* ILLED
ildish \īl-dish\ childish, wildish
ildly \īld-lē\ childly, mildly, wildly
[1]ile \īl\ aisle, bile, dial, faille, file, guile, I'll, isle, Kyle, lisle, Lyle, mile, Nile, phial, pile, rile, roil, smile, spile, stile, style, tile, trial, vial, vile, viol, while, wile, abseil, aedile, agile, anile, argyle, Argyll, audile, awhile, axile, beguile, Blue Nile, Carlyle, compile, condyle, cross-file, de Stijl, decile, defile, denial, docile, ductile, enisle, ensile, erewhile, erstwhile, espial, exile, febrile, fictile, fissile, flexile, fragile, freestyle, futile, genial, gentile, gracile, habile, hairstyle, Kabyle, labile, life-style, meanwhile, mistrial, mobile, motile, nubile, pantile, penile, pensile, profile, puerile, quartile, quintile, redial, reptile, resile, retrial, revile, sandpile, scissile, sectile, senile, servile, sessile, stabile, stockpile, sundial, tactile, tensile, textile, turnstile, typestyle, unpile, utile, vagile, virile, woodpile, worthwhile, afebrile, airmobile, Anglophile, chamomile, contractile, crocodile, discophile, domicile, endostyle, epistyle, erectile, extensile, Francophile, Gallophile, halophile, homophile, hypostyle, infantile, interfile, juvenile, low-profile, mercantile, negrophile, oenophile, otherwhile, pedophile, percentile, peristyle, prehensile, projectile, protractile, pulsatile, reconcile, refractile, retractile, self-denial, Slavophile, spermophile, technopile, thermopile, turophile, urostyle, versatile, vibratile, xenophile, ailurophile, amphiprostyle, audiophile, bibliophile, electrophile, fluviatile, Germanophile, heterophile, Italophile, nucleophile
[2]ile \il\ see ILL
[3]ile \ē-lē\ see EELY
[4]ile \ēl\ see [2]EAL
[5]ile \il-ē\ see [1]ILLY
ilead \il-ē-əd\ see ILIAD
ileage \ī-lij\ see ILAGE
ileal \il-ē-əl\ see [1]ILIAL
ileless \īl-ləs\ guileless, pileless, smileless
[1]iler \ē-lər\ see EALER

[2]iler \ī-lər\ see ILAR
iles \īlz\ Giles, Miles, Niles, Wade-Giles, British Isles, Western Isles
ileum \il-ē-əm\ see ILIUM
iley \ī-lē\ see YLY
ilford \il-fərd\ Milford, Wilford
[1]ili \il-ē\ see [1]ILLY
[2]ili \ē-lē\ see EELY
[1]ilia \il-ē-ə\ Celia, cilia, Cecelia, Cecilia, Massilia, Anglophilia, basophilia, coprophilia, hemophilia, juvenilia, necrophilia, neophilia, pedophilia, sensibilia, memorabilia
[2]ilia \il-yə\ Brasilia, sedilia, bougainvillea, sensibilia, memorabilia
[3]ilia \ēl-yə\ see ELIA
iliad \il-ē-əd\ Gilead, Iliad, balm of Gilead
ilial \il-ē-əl\ filial, ileal, familial, unfilial
[1]ilian \il-ē-ən\ Gillian, Ilian, Lillian, Basilian, reptilian, Abbevillian, crocodilian, preexilian, vespertilian
[2]ilian \il-yən\ see ILLION
ilias \il-ē-əs\ see [1]ILIOUS
iliate \il-ē-ət\ ciliate, affiliate
ilic \il-ik\ killick, acrylic, allylic, Cyrillic, dactylic, exilic, idyllic, sibylic, amphiphilic, Anglophilic, hemophilic, necrophilic, pedophilic, postexilic, zoophilic, bibliophilic
ilica \il-i-kə\ silica, basilica
ilican \il-i-kən\ see ILICON
ilicon \il-i-kən\ Millikan, silicon, spillikin, basilican, ferrosilicon
ilience \il-yəns\ see ILLIANCE
iliency \il-yən-sē\ see ILLIANCY
ilient \il-yənt\ brilliant, resilient
iliment \il-ə-mənt\ see ILAMENT
[1]iling \ī-liŋ\ filing, piling, spiling, styling, tiling, hairstyling
[2]iling \ē-liŋ\ see EELING
[1]ilion \il-yən\ see ILLION
[2]ilion \il-ē-ən\ see [1]ILIAN
[1]ilious \il-ē-əs\ punctilious, supercilious, materfamilias, paterfamilias
[2]ilious \il-yəs\ bilious, atrabilious, supercilious
ilip \il-əp\ see ILLIP
ilitant \il-ə-tənt\ militant, rehabilitant
ility \il-ət-ē\ ability, agility, anility, civility, debility, docility, ductility, facility, fertility, fragility, futility, gentility, gracility, hostility, humility, lability, mobility, motility, nobility, nubility, scurrility, sectility, senility, stability, sterility, suability, tactility, tranquility, utility, vagility, virility, actability, affability, arability, audibility, bearability, biddability, breathability, brushability, capability, changeability, coilability, contractility, countability, credibility, crossability, culpability, curability, cutability, disability, disutility, drapability, drillability, drinkability, durability,

dyeability, edibility, equability, erectility, fallibility, feasibility, fishability, flammability, flexibility, forgeability, formability, frangibility, friability, gullibility, imbecility, immobility, inability, incivility, indocility, infantility, infertility, instability, inutility, juvenility, laudability, leachability, legibility, liability, likability, livability, mailability, meltability, miscibility, movability, mutability, notability, packability, placability, plausibility, playability, portability, possibility, potability, pregnability, prehensility, printability, probability, puerility, readability, risibility, roadability, salability, sensibility, sewability, shareability, sociability, solubility, solvability, spreadability, squeezability, stainability, stretchability, tenability, testability, traceability, treatability, tunability, usability, vendability, versatility, viability, visibility, volatility, washability, wearability, wettability, workability, absorbability, acceptability, accessibility, accountability, adaptability, adjustability, admirability, admissibility, adoptability, adorability, advisability, affectability, agreeability, alterability, amenability, amiability, amicability, appealability, applicability, approachability, assumability, attainability, automobility, availability, believability, collapsibility, combustability, comparability, compatibility, compensability, compressability, computability, conceivability, conductability, confirmability, contemptibility, contractibility, controllability, convertibility, corrigibility, corruptibility, cultivability, damageability, decidability, deductibility, defeasibility, defensibility, delectability, demonstrability, deniability, dependability, desirability, destructibility, detachability, detectability, deterrability, detonability, digestibility, dilatability, dispensability, disposability, dissociability, dissolubility, distensibility, distractibility, divisibility, educability, electability, eligibility, employability, enforceability, equitability, erasability, erodability, exchangeability, excitability, excludability, exhaustibility, expansibility, expendability, explosibility, exportability, extensibility, extractibility, extrudability, fashionability, fatigability, filterability, fissionability, formidability, habitability, heritability, illegibility, immiscibility, immovability, immutability, impalpability, impassability, impassibility, impeccability, implacability, implausibility, impossibility, impregnability, impressibility, improbability, improvability, inaudibility, incapability, incredibility, indelibility, inductibility, ineffability, infallibility, infeasibility, inflammability, inflexibility, infrangibility, infusibility, insensibility, insolubility, insurability, intangibility, invincibility, invisibility, irascibility, irritability, knowledgeability, machinability, maintainability, manageability, marketability, merchantability, measurability, modulability, navigability, negligibility, nonflammability, openability, operability, opposability, palatability, penetrability, perceptibility, perdurability, perfectibility, performability, perishability, permeability, permissibility, pleasurability, practicability, preferability, presentability, preservability, preventability, processibility, programmability, punishability, reasonability, refundability, reliability, renewability, repeatability, reputability, resistibility, respectability, responsibility, retrievability, reusability, reversability, salvageability, separability, severability, serviceability, suggestability, supportability, suppressibility, survivability, susceptibility, sustainability, tolerability, trafficability, transferability, translatability, transmissibility, transplantability, transportability, unflappability, unthinkability, untouchability, variability, violability, vulnerability, weatherability, alienability, analyzability, assimilability, codifiability, commensurability, communicability, comprehensibility, decomposability, deliverability, discriminability, disrespectability, distinguishability, enumerability, exceptionability, hypnotizability, illimitability, impenetrability, imperishability, impermeability, impermissibility, imponderability, impracticability, impressionability, inaccessibility, inadmissibility, inadvisability inalterability, inapplicability, incalculability, incombustibility, incomparability, incompatibility, incompressibility, inconceivability, incontestability, inconvertibility, incorrigibility, incorruptibility, indefeasibility, indefensibility, indefinability, indestructibility, indigestibility, indispensability, indissolubility, indivisibility, indomitability, indubitability, ineducability, ineffaceability, ineligibility, ineluctability, inevitability, inexhaustibility, inexplicability, inexpressibility, inextricability, inheritability, insatiability, inseparability, insociability, insusceptibility, intelligibility, interchangeability, intolerability, invariability, invulnerability, irreducibility, irreformability, irrefutability, irremovability, irrepealability, irreplaceability, irrepressibility, irreproachability, irresistibility, irresponsibility, irretrievability, irreversibility, irrevocability, maneuverability, manipulability, negotiability, polarizability, recognizability, recoverability, rectifiability, reprehensibility, reproducibility, substitutability, unacceptability, unaccountability, understandability, undesirability, verifiability, biocompatability, biodegradability, differentiability, inalienability, incommensurability, incommunicability, incomprehensibility, indefatigability, indistinguishability, ineradicability, incontrovertibility, irreconcilability, irreproducibility, interoperability

ilium \il-ē-əm\ cilium, ileum, ilium, Ilium, milium, trillium, beryllium, penicillium

ilk \ilk\ bilk, ilk, milch, milk, silk, buttermilk, liebfraumilch

ilker \il-kər\ bilker, milker

ilky \il-kē\ milky, silky

ill \il\ bill, Bill, brill, chill, dill, drill, fill, frill, gill, grill, grille, hill, ill, Jill, kill, krill, mil, mill, mille, Milne, nil, nill, Phil, pill, prill, quill, rill, shill, shrill, sild, sill, skill, spill, squill, still, swill, thill, thrill, til, till, trill, twill, vill, will, Will, anthill, backfill, bluegill, Brazil, Catskill, Churchill, cranesbill, crossbill, de Mille, dentil, deskill, distill, doorsill, downhill, duckbill, dullsville, dunghill, fiberfill, foothill, freewill, fulfill, goodwill, Granville, gristmill, handbill, hawksbill, hornbill, Huntsville, instill, Knoxville, lambkill, landfill, limekiln, manille, Melville, molehill, mudsill, Nashville, no-till, playbill, quadrille, refill, roadkill, sawmill, self-will, Seville, sheathbill, shoebill, sidehill, sigil, spadille, spoonbill, stabile, standstill, stockstill, storksbill, T-bill, treadmill, unreal, until, uphill, vaudeville, waxbill, waybill, windchill, windmill, Brazzaville, chlorophyll, daffodil, deshabille, de Toqueville, dishabille, escadrille, espadrille, Evansville, Francophil, Hooverville, Jacksonville, Libreville, Louisville, minimill, overfill, overkill, overspill, razorbill, rototill, tormentil, verticil, windowsill, whippoorwill, winter-kill, Yggdrasil, acidophil, ivorybill, minoxydil, Nizhni Togil, run-of-the-mill

I'll \īl\ see [1]ILE

[1]**illa** \ē-yə\ barilla, cuadrilla, banderilla, quesadilla

[2]**illa** \il-ə\ scilla, Scylla, squilla, villa, Willa, ancilla, Aquila, Attila, axilla, Camilla, cedilla, chinchilla, flotilla, gorilla, guerrilla, manila, Manila, megillah, papilla, perilla, Priscilla, scintilla, vanilla, camarilla, cascarilla, granadilla, potentilla, sabadilla, sapodilla, sarsaparilla

[3]**illa** \ē-ə\ see [1]IA

[4]**illa** \ēl-yə\ see ELIA

[5]**illa** \ē-lə\ see [1]ELA

illable \il-ə-bəl\ billable, drillable, fillable, spillable, syllable, tillable, disyllable, refillable, trisyllable, decasyllable, monosyllable, octosyllable, polysyllable, hendecasyllable

illage \il-ij\ grillage, millage, pillage, spillage, tillage, village, no-tillage, permillage, Greenwich Village

illah \il-ə\ see [2]ILLA

illain \il-ən\ see ILLON

illar \il-ər\ see ILLER

illary \il-ə-rē\ Hilary, Hillary, phyllary, codicillary

illate \il-ət\ see ILLET

[1]**ille** \il\ see ILL

[2]**ille** \ē\ see [1]EE

[3]**ille** \ēl\ see [2]EAL

illea \il-yə\ see [2]ILIA

illed \ild\ build, dilled, drilled, gild, gilled, guild, skilled, twilled, willed, Brynhild, engild, gold-filled, goodwilled, rebuild, self-willed, spoonbilled, unbuild, unskilled, upbuild, wergild, jerry-build, overbuild, semiskilled—*also pasts of verbs listed at* ILL

illedness \il-nəs\ see ILLNESS

illein \il-ən\ see ILLON

iller \il-ər\ biller, chiller, driller, filler, giller, griller, hiller, killer, miller, Miller, pillar, schiller, spiller, swiller, thriller, tiller, triller, axillar, distiller, fulfiller, painkiller, pralltriller, von Schiller, caterpillar, lady-killer, Rototiller—*also comparatives of adjectives listed at* ILL

illery \il-rē\ pillory, artillery, distillery
illes \il-ēz\ see ILLIES
illet \il-ət\ billet, fillet, millet, rillet, skillet, willet, distillate
illful \il-fəl\ skillful, willful, unskillful
[1]illi \il-ē\ see [1]ILLY
[2]illi \ē-lē\ see EELY
[1]illian \il-ē-ən\ see [1]ILIAN
[2]illian \il-yən\ see ILLION
illiance \il-yəns\ brilliance, resilience
illiancy \il-yən-sē\ brilliancy, resiliency
illiant \il-yənt\ see ILIENT
illick \il-ik\ see ILIC
illie \il-ē\ see [1]ILLY
illies \il-ēz\ willies, Achilles, Antilles, Greater Antilles, Lesser Antilles, Netherlands Antilles—*also plurals and possessives of nouns listed at* [1]ILLY
illikan \il-i-kən\ see ILICON
illikin \il-i-kən\ see ILICON
[1]illin \il-əm\ see ILLUM
[2]illin \il-ən\ see ILLON
illing \il-iŋ\ billing, drilling, filling, killing, milling, schilling, shilling, skilling, twilling, willing, fulfilling, spine-chilling, unwilling
illion \il-yən\ billion, jillion, Lillian, million, pillion, trillion, zillion, caecilian, Castilian, centillion, civilian, cotillion, decillion, modillion, nonillion, octillion, pavilion, postilion, quadrillion, Quintilian, quintillion, reptilian, septillion, sextillion, toubillion, vaudevillian, vermilion, crocodilian, Maximilian, preexilian, quindecillion, sexdecillion, tredecillion, undecillion, vespertilian, vigintillion, duodecillion, novemdecillion, octodecillion, septendecillion. quattuordecillion
illip \il-əp\ fillip, Philip
illis \il-əs\ see ILLUS
illium \il-ē-əm\ see ILIUM
illness \il-nəs\ chillness, illness, shrillness, stillness
[1]illo \il-ō\ billow, pillow, willow, Negrillo, tornillo, Amarillo, armadillo, cigarillo, coyotillo, peccadillo. tamarillo
[2]illo \ē-ō\ see [2]IO
illon \il-ən\ billon, Dylan, Uilleann, villain, villein, tefillin, penicillin, amoxycillin
illory \il-rē\ see ILLERY
illous \il-əs\ see ILLUS
[1]illow \il-ə\ see [2]ILLA
[2]illow \il-ō\ see [1]ILLO
illowy \il-ə-wē\ billowy, pillowy, willowy
ills \ilz\ Black Hills, no-frills, Alban Hills—*also plurals and possessives of nouns, third person singular presents of verbs at* ILL
illum \il-əm\ chillum, vexillum
illus \il-əs\ Phyllis, villous, Willis, bacillus, lapillus, amaryllis, toga virilis
[1]illy \il-ē\ Billie, billy, Chile, chili, chilly, dilly, filly, frilly, gillie, hilly, illy, Lillie, lily, Lily, Millie, really, Scilly,

silly, stilly, Willie, Willy, bacilli, Caerphilly, daylily, fusilli, guidwillie, hillbilly, piccalilli, rockabilly, willy-nilly

²illy \il-lē\ shrilly, stilly

¹iln \il\ see ILL

²iln \iln\ kiln, Milne

¹ilne \iln\ see ²ILN

²ilne \il\ see ILL

¹ilo \ī-lō\ milo, Milo, phyllo, silo

²ilo \ē-lō\ helo, kilo, phyllo, Iloilo

ilom \ī-ləm\ see ILUM

iloquence \il-ə-kwəns\ grandiloquence, magniloquence

iloquent \il-ə-kwənt\ grandiloquent, magniloquent

iloquist \il-ə-kwəst\ soliloquist, ventriloquist

iloquy \il-ə-kwē\ soliloquy, ventriloquy

ilot \ī-lət\ eyelet, islet, Pilate, pilot, stylet, copilot, autopilot, Pontius Pilate

ils \ils\ fils, grilse, Nils

ilse \ils\ see ILS

ilt \ilt\ built, gilt, guilt, hilt, jilt, kilt, lilt, milt, quilt, silt, stilt, tilt, wilt, atilt, bloodguilt, Brunhild, homebuilt, inbuilt, rebuilt, unbuilt, uptilt, carvel-built, clinker-built, custom-built, purpose-built

ilter \il-tər\ filter, kilter, milter, philter, off-kilter

ilth \ilth\ filth, spilth, tilth

iltie \il-tē\ see ILTY

ilton \ilt-ᵊn\ Hilton, Milton, Stilton, Wilton

ilty \il-tē\ guilty, kiltie, milty, silty, bloodguilty

ilum \ī-ləm\ filum, hilum, phylum, whilom, xylem, asylum

ilus \ī-ləs\ eyeless, pilus, stylus, tieless

¹ily \ī-lē\ see YLY

²ily \il-ē\ see ¹ILLY

¹im \im\ bream, brim, dim, glim, grim, Grimm, gym, him, hymn, Jim, Kim, limb, limn, mim, nim, prim, rim, scrim, shim, skim, slim, swim, Tim, trim, vim, whim, bedim, dislimn, forelimb, passim, prelim, Purim, Sikkim, slim-jim, snap-brim, acronym, anonym, antonym, eponym, homonym, metonym, paradigm, paronym, pseudonym, seraphim, synonym, tautonym, toponym, underbrim, ad interim, heteronym

²im \ēm\ see ¹EAM

I'm \īm\ see ¹IME

ima \ē-mə\ see EMA

imable \ī-mə-bəl\ climable, sublimable, unclimbable

imace \im-əs\ grimace, tzimmes

image \im-ij\ image, scrimmage, self-image, afterimage

iman \ē-mən\ see ¹EMON

imate \ī-mət\ climate, primate, acclimate

¹imb \im\ see ¹IM

²imb \īm\ see ¹IME

imba \im-bə\ limba, kalimba, marimba

imbable \ī-mə-bəl\ see IMABLE
imbal \im-bəl\ see IMBLE
imbale \im-bəl\ see IMBLE
imbed \imd\ limbed, rimmed, clean-limbed—*also pasts of verbs listed at* [1]IM
[1]**imber** \im-bər\ limber, timber, sawtimber, unlimber
[2]**imber** \ī-mər\ see [1]IMER
imble \im-bəl\ cymbal, gimbal, nimble, symbol, thimble, timbal, timbale, wimble
imbo \im-bō\ bimbo, limbo, akimbo, gumbo-limbo
imbral \am-brəl\ see AMBREL
imbre \am-bər\ see [2]AMBAR
imbrel \im-brəl\ timbrel, whimbrel
imbus \im-bəs\ limbus, nimbus
[1]**ime** \īm\ chime, climb, clime, crime, dime, disme, grime, I'm, lime, mime, prime, rhyme, rime, slime, stime, thyme, time, airtime, all-time, bedtime, begrime, big time, birdlime, daytime, downtime, dreamtime, enzyme, flextime, foretime, halftime, lifetime, longtime, lunchtime, Mannheim, Maytime, mealtime, meantime, nighttime, noontime, old-time, onetime, part-time, pastime, peacetime, playtime, quicklime, ragtime, schooltime, seedtime, small-time, sometime, space-time, springtime, sublime, teatime, two-time, uptime, wartime, aftertime, Anaheim, anytime, beforetime, Christmastime, dinnertime, double-time, harvesttime, Jotunheim, lysozyme, maritime, monorhyme, overtime, pantomime, paradigm, summertime, wintertime, nickel-and-dime
[2]**ime** \ēm\ see [1]EAM
imel \im-əl\ gimel, gimmal, kümmel
imeless \īm-ləs\ rhymeless, timeless
imely \īm-lē\ primely, timely, untimely
imen \ī-mən\ flyman, hymen, Hymen, limen, Lyman, Simon
imeon \im-ē-ən\ see IMIAN
imeous \ī-məs\ see IMIS
[1]**imer** \ī-mər\ chimer, climber, dimer, mimer, primer, rhymer, timer, trimer, full-timer, old-timer, small-timer, sublimer, two-timer, wisenheimer
[2]**imer** \im-ər\ see IMMER
imerick \im-rik\ see YMRIC
[1]**imes** \īmz\ times, betimes, daytimes, sometimes, betweentimes, oftentimes—*also plurals and possessives of nouns and third person singular presents of verbs listed at* [1]IME
[2]**imes** \ēm\ see [1]EAM
imeter \im-ət-ər\ dimeter, limiter, scimitar, trimeter, altimeter, delimiter, perimeter, tachymeter
imetry \im-ə-trē\ symmetry, gravimetry, polarimetry, sypersymmetry
imian \im-ē-ən\ Simeon, simian, Endymion, prosimian

imic \im-ik\ see ²YMIC
imical \im-i-kəl\ inimical, metonymical, synonymical, toponymical
imicry \im-i-krē\ gimmickry, mimicry
imilar \im-ə-lər\ similar, dissimilar
imile \im-ə-lē\ simile, swimmily, facsimile
¹iminal \im-ən-ᵊl\ criminal, liminal, subliminal, supraliminal
²iminal \im-nəl\ see YMNAL
iminy \im-ə-nē\ see IMONY
imis \ī-məs\ primus, thymus, timeous, imprimis, untimeous
imitable \im-ət-ə-bəl\ imitable, illimitable, inimitable
imitar \im-ət-ər\ see IMETER
imiter \im-ət-ər\ see IMETER
imits \im-its\ limits, Nimitz
imity \im-ət-ē\ dimity, proximity, sublimity, anonymity, equanimity, longanimity, magnanimity, pseudonymity, synonymity, unanimity, pusillanimity
imitz \im-its\ see IMITS
imm \im\ see ¹IM
immable \im-ə-bəl\ dimmable, swimmable
immage \im-ij\ see IMAGE
immal \im-əl\ see IMEL
imme \i-mē\ see IMMY
immed \imd\ see IMBED
immer \im-ər\ brimmer, dimmer, glimmer, krimmer, limmer, limner, primer, shimmer, simmer, skimmer, slimmer, swimmer, trimmer—*also comparatives of adjectives listed at* ¹IM
immes \im-əs\ see IMACE
immick \im-ik\ see ²YMIC
immickry \im-i-krē\ see IMICRY
immily \im-ə-lē\ see IMILE
immy \im-ē\ gimme, jimmy, limby, shimmy, swimmy
imn \im\ see ¹IM
imner \im-ər\ see IMMER
imo \ē-mō\ primo, sentimo
imon \ī-mən\ see IMEN
imony \im-ə-nē\ simony, niminy-piminy
imothy \im-ə-thē\ timothy, Timothy, polymathy
imp \imp\ blimp, chimp, crimp, gimp, guimpe, imp, limp, pimp, primp, scrimp, shrimp, simp, skimp, wimp, comsymp
impe \imp\ see IMP
imper \im-pər\ limper, shrimper, simper, whimper
imping \im-pən\ see YMPAN
impish \im-pish\ blimpish, impish
imple \im-pəl\ dimple, pimple, simple, wimple, oversimple
imply \im-plē\ dimply, limply, pimply, simply
impy \im-pē\ crimpy, gimpy, scrimpy, shrimpy, skimpy, wimpy
imsy \im-zē\ flimsy, slimsy, whimsy
imulus \im-yə-ləs\ limulus, stimulus
imus \ī-məs\ see IMIS
imy \ī-mē\ grimy, limey, limy, rimy, slimy, stymie, thymy, old-timey
¹in \in\ been, bin, blin, chin,

din, fin, Finn, gin, grin, Gwyn, hin, in, inn, kin, linn, Lynn, Lynne, pin, shin, Shin, sin, skin, spin, thin, tin, twin, whin, win, wyn, yin, zin, again, agin, akin, all-in, backspin, bearskin, begin, Benin, Berlin, Boleyn, bowfin, break-in, buckskin, built-in, burn-in, calfskin, capeskin, cave-in, chagrin, check-in, Chongjin, close-in, clothespin, coonskin, Corinne, crankpin, cut-in, deerskin, doeskin, drive-in, drop-in, duckpin, dustbin, fade-in, fill-in, foreskin, goatskin, Guilin, hairpin, Harbin, has-been, headpin, herein, Jilin, Kerin, kidskin, kingpin, lambskin, lead-in, lie-in, linchpin, live-in, lived-in, lobe-fin, locked-in, look-in, love-in, moleskin, munchkin, Nankin, ninepin, no-win, oilskin, Pekin, phone-in, pigskin, pinyin, plug-in, pushpin, redskin, ruin, run-in, saimin, scarfpin, scarfskin, sealskin, set-in, sharkskin, sheepskin, shoo-in, shut-in, sidespin, sit-in, sleep-in, snakeskin, stand-in, step-in, stickpin, swanskin, tailspin, take-in, tap-in, teach-in, tenpin, therein, tholepin, threadfin, throw-in, tie-in, tiepin, tip-in, toe-in, trade-in, tuned-in, turn-in, unpin, walk-in, weigh-in, wherein, wineskin, within, woolskin, write-in, candlepin, catechin, Ha-erh-pin, Ho Chi Minh, Lohengrin, lying-in, mandolin, maximin, Mickey Finn, onionskin, palanquin, Tianjin, underpin, underspin, Vietminh, violin, whipper-in, canthaxanthin

[2]**in** \ēn\ see [3]INE

[3]**in** \an\ see [5]AN

[4]**in** \a^{n}\ Chopin, doyen, Gauguin, moulin, Petain, Rodin, serin, coq au vin, coup de main, fleur de coin, Mazarin

[5]**in** \ən\ see [1]UN

[1]**ina** \ī-nə\ china, China, Dina, Dinah, Heine, Ina, mina, mynah, Aegina, angina, Lucina, nandina, piscina, Regina, salina, shechinah, vagina, Cochin China, Carolina, Indochina, kamaaina, Poland China, North Carolina, South Carolina

[2]**ina** \ē-nə\ Deena, Dena, kina, Lena, Nina, plena, Shina, Tina, vena, vina, arena, Athena, cantina, catena, Christina, coquina, corbina, corvina, czarina, Edwina, euglena, farina, fontina, Georgina, hyena, kachina, Kristina, marina, Marina, medina, Medina, Messina, nandina, novena, patina, piscina, platina, Regina, retsina, Rowena, salina, sestina, Shechinah, subpoena, verbena, Agrippina, amberina, Angelina, Argentina, ballerina, casuarina, Carolina, Catalina, catilena, cavatina,

Chianina, concertina, Filipina, javelina, Katerina, ocarina, Palestrina, palomino, Pasadena, Saint Helena, semolina, signorina, sonatina, Taormina, Teresina, Wilhelminia, Herzegovina, Pallas Athena, Strait of Messina

inable \ī-nə-bəl\ minable, consignable, declinable, definable, inclinable, indeclinable, indefinable

inach \in-ich\ Greenwich, spinach

[1]inah \ē-nə\ see [2]INA

[2]inah \ī-nə\ see [1]INA

[1]inal \īn-ᵊl\ clinal, final, rhinal, spinal, trinal, vinyl, matutinal, officinal, quarterfinal, semifinal, serotinal

[2]inal \ēn-ᵊl\ see ENAL

inally \īn-ᵊl-ē\ clinally, finally, spinally, matutinally

inary \ī-nə-rē\ binary, trinary

[1]inas \ī-nəs\ see [1]INUS

[2]inas \ē-nəs\ see [1]ENUS

inative \in-ət-iv\ see INITIVE

inc \iŋk\ see INK

inca \iŋ-kə\ Dinka, Inca, vinca, Mandinka

incal \iŋ-kəl\ see INKLE

incan \iŋ-kən\ Incan, Lincoln

[1]ince \ins\ blintz, chintz, mince, prince, quince, rinse, since, wince, convince, evince, shinsplints, Port-au-Prince

[2]ince \ans\ see [3]ANCE

incely \in-slē\ princely, tinselly

incer \in-chər\ see INCHER

inch \inch\ chinch, cinch, clinch, finch, flinch, grinch, inch, lynch, pinch, squinch, winch, bullfinch, goldfinch, greenfinch, hawfinch, unclinch

incher \in-chər\ clincher, flincher, lyncher, pincer, pincher, wincher, affenpinscher, penny-pincher, Doberman pinscher

inching \in-chiŋ\ unflinching, penny-pinching

incible \in-sə-bəl\ principal, principle, vincible, evincible, invincible, inconvincible

incing \in-siŋ\ ginseng, mincing, convincing, unconvincing

incipal \in-sə-bəl\ see INCIBLE

inciple \in-sə-bəl\ see INCIBLE

inck \iŋk\ see INK

incky \iŋ-kē\ see INKY

incoln \iŋ-kən\ see INCAN

inct \iŋt\ linked, kinked, tinct, distinct, extinct, instinct, precinct, succinct, unlinked, indistinct

inction \iŋ-shən\ distinction, extinction, contradistinction

inctive \iŋ-tiv\ distinctive, extinctive, instinctive, indistinctive

incture \iŋ-chər\ cincture, tincture

[1]ind \īnd\ bind, blind, find, grind, hind, kind, mind, rind, signed, spined, tined, wind, wynd, affined, behind, confined, inclined, in-kind, night-blind, purblind, refined, remind, rewind, sand-blind, snow-blind, spellbind, stone-blind, streamlined, unbind, unkind, unwind, color-blind, double-blind, gavelkind, gravel-blind, hoodman-blind, humankind, mastermind, nonaligned, single-blind, unaligned, undersigned, well-defined, womankind—*also pasts of verbs listed at* [1]INE

[2]**ind** \ind\ finned, Ind, Sind, skinned, wind, buckskinned, crosswind, downwind, exscind, prescind, rescind, soft-finned, thick-skinned, thin-skinned, upwind, whirlwind, woodwind, Amerind, spiny-finned, tamarind—*also pasts of verbs listed at* [1]IN

[3]**ind** \int\ see INT

inda \in-də\ Linda, Lucinda, Melinda, Samarinda

indar \in-dər\ see [2]INDER

[1]**inded** \īn-dəd\ minded, rinded, broad-minded, fair-minded, high-minded, large-minded, like-minded, low-minded, right-minded, small-minded, strong-minded, tough-minded, weak-minded, absentminded, bloody-minded, civic-minded, evil-minded, feebleminded, narrow-minded, open-minded, simpleminded, single-minded, social-minded, tender-minded—*also regular pasts of verbs listed at* [1]IND

[2]**inded** \in-dəd\ brinded, long-winded, short-winded, broken-winded—*also pasts of verbs listed at* [2]IND

[1]**inder** \īn-dər\ binder, blinder, finder, grinder, hinder, minder, winder, bookbinder, faultfinder, highbinder, netminder, pathfinder, ring binder, self-binder, sidewinder, spellbinder, stem-winder, viewfinder, organ-grinder—*also comparatives of adjectives listed at* [1]IND

[2]**inder** \in-dər\ cinder, hinder, Pindar, tinder

indful \īn-fəl\ mindful, remindful, unmindful

indhi \in-dē\ see INDY

indi \in-dē\ see INDY

indic \in-dik\ Indic, syndic

indie \in-dē\ see INDY

inding \īn-diŋ\ binding, finding, winding, bookbinding, fact-finding, faultfinding, pathfinding, self-winding, spellbinding, stem-winding

indlass \in-ləs\ see INLESS

indle \in-dᵊl\ brindle, dwindle, kindle, spindle, swindle, enkindle

indless \īn-ləs\ kindless, mindless, spineless

[1]**indling** \in-lən\ pindling, spindling

[2]**indling** \ind-liŋ\ dwindling, kindling, pindling, spindling

[1]**indly** \in-lē\ see INLY

[2]**indly** \īn-lē\ see [1]INELY

indness \īn-nəs\ blindness, fineness, kindness, purblindness, unkindness, loving-kindness

indowed \in-dəd\ see [2]INDED

indus \in-dəs\ Indus, Pindus

indy \in-dē\ Cindy, Hindi, indie, lindy, shindy, Sindhi, windy, Rawalpindi

[1]**ine** \īn\ bine, brine, chine,

cline, dine, dyne, eyen, fine, Jain, kine, line, Line, Main, mine, nine, pine, Rhein, Rhine, rind, shine, shrine, sign, spine, spline, stein, Stein, swine, syne, thine, tine, trine, twine, vine, whine, wine, A-line, affine, airline, align, alkyne, alpine, assign, balkline, baseline, beeline, benign, Bernstein, bloodline, bovine, bowline, branchline, breadline, buntline, bustline, byline, canine, caprine, carbine, carmine, cervine, clothesline, coastline, combine, compline, condign, confine, consign, corvine, cutline, dateline, deadline, decline, define, design, divine, dragline, driveline, earthshine, Einstein, eiswein, enshrine, ensign, entwine, equine, ethyne, feline, ferine, fraulein, frontline, gantline, grapevine, guideline, hairline, hard-line, headline, hemline, hipline, Holbein, Holstein, incline, indign, in-line, jawline, landline, lang syne, lifeline, longline, lupine, mainline, malign, midline, moline, moonshine, off-line, old-line, opine, outline, outshine, ovine, Pauline, Pennine, Petrine, pipeline, piscine, plotline, pontine, Pontine, porcine, potline, propine, quinine, rapine, recline, redline, refine, reline, repine, resign, ridgeline, roofline, Sabine, saline, setline, shoreline, sideline, Sixtine, skyline, soft-line, straight-line, strandline, streamline, strychnine, subline, sunshine, supine, syncline, taurine, tie-line, time-line, topline, touchline, towline, tramline, trapline, trephine, trotline, truckline, tumpline, turbine, untwine, ursine, vespine, vulpine, waistline, woodbine, zayin, zebrine, aerodyne, alkaline, androgyne, Angeline, anodyne, anserine, anticline, aquiline, argentine, asinine, auld lang syne, borderline, bottom-line, Byzantine, calamine, calcimine, Caroline, catarrhine, Catiline, celandine, centerline, cisalpine, Cisalpine, clandestine, colubrine, columbine, Columbine, concubine, Constantine, countermine, countersign, crystalline, cytokine, disincline, eglantine, endocrine, exocrine, falconine, fescennine, Frankenstein, gregarine, infantine, interline, intertwine, iodine, Johannine, leonine, Liechtenstein, monkeyshine, muscadine, opaline, palatine, Palestine, passerine, porcupine, psittacine, realign, redefine, redesign, riverine, Rubenstein, saccharine, sapphirine, saturnine, serpentine, sibylline, sixty-nine, subalpine, Theatine, timberline, turnverein, turpentine, underline, undermine, Ursuline, uterine, valentine, vespertine, viperine, vulturine, waterline, zibeline, accipitrine, adamantine, adulterine, alexandrine, amaranthine, Capitoline, elephantine, Evangeline, Frankfurt am Main, Rembrandt van Rijn, Scheswig-Holstein, nonoxynol-9, Newcastle-upon Tyne

[2]**ine** \ē-nā\ fine, wahine

[3]**ine** \ēn\ bean, clean, dean, Dean, Deane, dene, e'en, gene, Gene, glean, green, Green, greene, jean, Jean, Jeanne, keen, lean, lien, mean, mesne, mien, peen, preen, quean, queen, scene, screen, seen, sheen, shin, sin, skean, skene, spean, spleen, teen, tween, wean, ween, wheen, yean, Aileen, Arlene, baleen, beguine, Beguine, Benin, Bernstein, between, boreen, bovine, buckbean, caffeine, canteen, carbine, careen, Carlene, Cathleen, Charlene, chlorine, chopine, chorine, Christine, citrine, Claudine, codeine, colleen, Colleen, convene, Coreen, cotquean, cuisine, Darlene, dasheen, dauphine, demean, demesne, dentine, Doreen, dry-clean, dudeen, eighteen, Eileen, Essene, Eugene, fanzine, fascine, fifteen, fourteen, Francine, gamine, gangrene, glassine, gyrene, Helene, Hellene, Hermine, hoatzin, holstein, Holstein, horsebean, houseclean, hygiene, Ilene, Irene, Jacqueline, Jeanine, Jeannine, Jolene, Justine, Kathleen, khamsin, Kristine, Ladin, lateen, latrine, Lorene, Lublin, machine, malines, marine, Marlene, Maureen, Maxine, moline, moreen, morphine, Nadine, nankeen, naphthene, Nicene, nineteen, nongreen, Noreen, obscene, offscreen, on-screen, patine, Pauline, piscine, Pontine, poteen, praline, preteen, pristine, propine, protein, quinine, Rabin, Racine, ratteen, ravine, routine, saline, saltine, Salween, sardine, sateen, scalene, serene, shagreen, Sharlene, shebeen, siren, Sistine, sixteen, Slovene, soybean, spalpeen, strychnine, subteen, sunscreen, Szczecin, takin, taurine, terrene, terrine, thirteen, Tolkien, tontine, tureen, umpteen, unclean, undine, unseen, vaccine, vitrine, windscreen, yestreen, Yibin, zechin, Aberdeen, almandine, Angeline, argentine, Argentine, Augustine, barkentine, bengaline, Bernadine, bombazine, Borodin, brigandine, brigantine, brilliantine, Byzantine, carotene, carrageen, celandine, clandestine, columbine, Constantine,

contravene, crepe de chine, crystalline, damascene, Dexedrine, Dramamine, duvetyn, eglantine, endocrine, Eocene, epicene, Ernestine, estaurine, evergreen, fescennine, figurine, Florentine, fluorine, fukerene, gabardine, gaberdine, gadarene, galantine, gasoline, Geraldine, Ghibelline, go-between, grenadine, Gretna Green, guillotine, Halloween, haute cuisine, Hippocrene, histamine, Holocene, Imogene, in-between, indigene, intervene, Jeraldine, Josephine, Kalinin, kerosene, langoustine, legatine, libertine, limousine, M16, magazine, mangosteen, margravine, Medellìn, melamine, messaline, Methedrine, mezzanine, Miocene, mousseline, Nazarene, nectarine, nicotine, overseen, opaline, organzine, palanquin, palatine, pelerine, percaline, peregrine, philhellene, Philistine, plasticene, plasticine, Pleistocene, Pliocene, riverine, quarantine, reserpine, saccharine, Sakhalin, Saladin, San Joaquin, San Martin, sapphirine, schizophrene, serpentine, seventeen, silkaline, Stelazine, submarine, subroutine, supervene, tambourine, tangerine, Theatine, tourmaline, trampoline, transmarine, travertine, Tridentine, Vaseline, velveteen, wintergreen, wolverine, Ursuline, adamantine, alexandrine, amphetamine, aquamarine, Benedictine, bromocriptine, carbon 13, doxycycline, elephantine, Evangeline, internecine, leukotirene, methylxanthene, mujahideen, niphedipine, nouvelle cuisine, Oligocene, Paleocene, pentamedine, tricothecene, ultramarine, antihistamine, benzoapyrene, diphenhydramine, Mary Magdalene, NC-17, polybutadiene, alpha-fetaprotein, apolipoprotein, buckminsterfullerene, General San Martin, oleomargarine

[4]**ine** \in-ē\ see INNY

[5]**ine** \ē-nē\ see [1]INI

[6]**ine** \ən\ see UN

inea \in-ē\ see INNY

ineal \in-ē-əl\ finial, lineal, matrilineal, patrilineal, unilineal

ined \īnd\ see [1]IND

inee \ī-nē\ see [1]INY

ineless \īn-ləs\ see INDLESS

[1]**inely** \īn-lē\ blindly, finely, kindly, affinely, condignly, equinely, felinely, purblindly, unkindly

[2]**inely** \ēn-lē\ see [1]EANLY

inement \īn-mənt\ see IGNMENT

ineness \īn-nəs\ see INDNESS

ineous \in-ē-əs\ gramineous, sanguineous, consanguineous, ignominious

[1]**iner** \ī-nər\ briner, diner, finer, liner, miner, minor, shiner, Shriner, signer, twiner, whiner, airliner, aligner, baseliner, byliner, combiner, confiner, cosigner, definer, designer, diviner, eyeliner, hardliner, headliner, incliner, jetliner, long-liner, moonshiner, one-liner, recliner, refiner, repiner, sideliner, soft-liner, streamliner, Asia Minor, Canis Minor, forty-niner, party-liner, Ursa Minor, superliner

[2]**iner** \ē-nər\ see EANER

[1]**inery** \īn-rē\ finery, pinery, vinery, winery, refinery

[2]**inery** \ēn-rē\ see EANERY

[1]**ines** \ēn\ see [3]INE

[2]**ines** \ēnz\ see EENS

[3]**ines** \īnz\ Mainz, Appenines—*also plurals and possessives of nouns and third person singular presents of verbs listed at* [1]INE

inest \ī-nəst\ see [1]INIST

inet \in-ət\ see INNET

inew \in-yü\ see INUE

infield \in-fēld\ infield, Winfield

ing \iŋ\ bring, Ching, cling, ding, fling, king, King, ling, Ming, ping, ring, sing, sling, spring, sting, string, swing, thing, wing, wring, zing, backswing, Baoding, bedspring, Beijing, bi-swing, bitewing, bowstring, bullring, Chongqing, clearwing, downswing, drawstring, D ring, earring, first-string, forewing, G-string, greenwing, hairspring, hamstring, handspring, headspring, heartstring, Kunming, lacewing, lapwing, latchstring, mainspring, Nanjing, Nanning, O-ring, offspring, Paoting, plaything, redwing, shoestring, showring, unsling, unstring, upspring, upswing, wellspring, whitewing, windwing, wingding, Xining, à la king, anything, buck-and-wing, ding-a-ling, double-ring, everything, innerspring, Liaoning, pigeonwing, superstring, underwing

inga \iŋ-gə\ anhinga, syringa

inge \inj\ binge, cringe, dinge, fringe, hinge, singe, springe, swinge, tinge, twinge, whinge, impinge, infringe, syringe, unhinge

inged \iŋd\ ringed, stringed, winged, net-winged—*also regular pasts of verbs listed at* ING

ingement \inj-mənt\ impingement, infringement

ingency \in-jən-sē\ stringency, astringency, contingency

ingent \in-jənt\ stringent, astringent, constringent, contingent, refringent

[1]**inger** \iŋ-ər\ bringer, clinger, dinger, flinger, pinger, ringer, singer, springer, stinger, stringer, swinger, winger, wringer, zinger, folksinger, gunslinger, humdinger, left-winger, mudslinger, right-

winger, mastersinger, Meistersinger, minnesinger

[2]**inger** \iŋ-gər\ finger, linger, five-finger, forefinger, malinger, ladyfinger

[3]**inger** \in-jər\ ginger, Ginger, injure, singer, swinger

ingery \inj-rē\ gingery, injury

inghy \iŋ-ē\ see [1]INGY

ingi \iŋ-ē\ see [1]INGY

ingian \in-jən\ Thuringian, Carlovingian, Carolingian, Merovingian

inging \iŋ-iŋ\ ringing, springing, stringing, swinging, folksinging, free-swinging, gunslinging, handwringing, mudslinging, upbringing

ingit \iŋ-kət\ see INKET

ingle \iŋ-gəl\ cringle, dingle, jingle, mingle, shingle, single, tingle, atingle, commingle, immingle, Kriss Kringle, surcingle, intermingle

ingler \iŋ-glər\ jingler, shingler

inglet \iŋ-lət\ kinglet, ringlet, winglet

ingletree \iŋ-gəl-trē\ singletree, swingletree

ingli \ing-lē\ see INGLY

inglish \iŋ-glish\ see ENGLISH

ingly \iŋ-glē\ jingly, shingly, singly, tingly, Zwingli

ingo \iŋ-gō\ bingo, dingo, gringo, jingo, lingo, pingo, flamingo, Mandingo, Santo Domingo

ings \iŋz\ Kings, springs, eyestrings, Hot Springs, Colorado Springs—*also plurals and possessives of nouns and third person singular presents of verbs listed at* ING

ingue \aŋ\ see [2]ANG

inguish \iŋ-wish\ distinguish, extinguish

[1]**ingy** \iŋ-ē\ clingy, dinghy, springy, stringy, swingy, zingy, shilingi

[2]**ingy** \in-jē\ dingy, mingy, stingy

inh \in\ see [1]IN

[1]**ini** \ē-nē\ beanie, djinni, genie, greeny, Jeanie, Jeannie, meanie, meany, jinni, Meany, sheeny, spleeny, teeny, weanie, weeny, wienie, Alcmene, Athene, Bellini, Bernini, bikini, Bikini, Cabrini, Cellini, Eugenie, linguine, martini, Mazzini, Mbini, Mycenae, Puccini, rappini, Rossini, Selene, tahini, wahine, zucchini, fantoccini, fettucine, kundalini, malihini, Mussolini, Mytilene, nota bene, scaloppine, spaghettini, teeny-weeny, tetrazzini, tortellini

[2]**ini** \in-ē\ see INNY

inia \in-ē-ə\ zinnia, Bithynia, Gdynia, gloxinia, Lavinia, Sardinia, Virginia, Abyssinia, West Virginia

inial \in-ē-əl\ see INEAL

[1]**inian** \in-ē-ən\ dynein, Arminian, Darwinian, Latinian, Sardinian, Socinian, Apollinian, Argentinian, Augustinian, Carolinian

[2]**inian** \in-yən\ see INION

[1]**inic** \ē-nik\ Enoch, nicotinic

[2]**inic** \in-ik\ clinic, cynic, Finnic, platinic, rabbinic, Jacobinic, mandarinic, misogynic, muscarinic, nicotinic, parafinic
inical \in-i-kəl\ binnacle, clinical, cynical, finical pinnacle, dominical, Jacobinical
inican \in-i-kən\ see INIKIN
inikin \in-i-kən\ minikin, Dominican
inim \in-əm\ minim, Houyhnhnm
ining \ī-niŋ\ lining, mining, shining, declining, designing, inclining, long-lining, interlining, undesigning
inion \in-yən\ minion, minyan, pinion, piñon, champignon, dominion, Justinian, opinion, Sardinian, Abyssinian
[1]**inis** \in-əs\ finis, pinnace, Erinys
[2]**inis** \ī-nəs\ see [1]INUS
inish \in-ish\ finish, Finnish, thinnish, diminish, refinish
[1]**inist** \ī-nəst\ dynast, finest
[2]**inist** \ē-nəst\ hygienist, machinist, Orleanist, Byzantinist, magazinist, trampolinist
initive \in-ət-iv\ carminative, definitive, infinitive
inity \in-ət-ē\ trinity, Trinity, affinity, bovinity, concinnity, divinity, felinity, feminity, infinity, latinity, salinity, sanguinity, vicinity, virginity, alkalinity, aquitinity, clandestinity, consanguinity, crystallinity, femininity, inconcinnity, masculinity, saccharinity
inium \in-ē-əm\ delphinium, triclinium, condominium
injure \in-jər\ see [3]INGER
injury \inj-rē\ see INGERY
ink \iŋk\ blink, brink, chink, Chink, clink, dink, drink, fink, gink, ink, jink, kink, link, mink, pink, plink, prink, rink, shrink, sink, skink, slink, stink, swink, sync, think, wink, zinc, bethink, chewink, cross-link, eyewink, groupthink, hoodwink, iceblink, lip-synch, misthink, outthink, preshrink, rethink, snowblink, unkink, bobolink, countersink, distelfink, doublethink, interlink, kitchen-sink, Maeterlinck, rinky-dink
inka \iŋ-kə\ see INCA
inkable \iŋ-kə-bəl\ drinkable, sinkable, thinkable, undrinkable, unsinkable, unthinkable
inkage \iŋ-kij\ linkage, shrinkage, sinkage
inke \iŋ-kē\ see INKY
inked \iŋt\ see INCT
inker \iŋ-kər\ blinker, clinker, drinker, pinker, sinker, skinker, stinker, tinker, winker, diesinker, freethinker, headshrinker
inket \iŋ-kət\ Tlingit, trinket
inkey \iŋ-kē\ see INKY
inkgo \iŋ-kō\ see INKO
inki \iŋ-kē\ see INKY
inkie \iŋ-kē\ see INKY

inking \iŋ-kiŋ\ freethinking, unblinking, unthinking
inkle \iŋ-kəl\ crinkle, inkle, sprinkle, tinkle, twinkle, winkle, wrinkle, besprinkle, periwinkle, Rip van Winkle
inkling \iŋ-kliŋ\ inkling, sprinkling, twinkling
inkly \iŋ-klē\ crinkly, pinkly, tinkly, twinkly, wrinkly
inko \iŋ-kō\ ginkgo, pinko
inks \iŋs\ see INX
inky \iŋ-kē\ dinkey, dinky, inky, kinky, pinkie, pinky, slinky, stinky, zincky, Helsinki, Malinke
inland \in-lənd\ Finland, inland, Vinland
inless \in-ləs\ chinless, sinless, skinless, spinless, windlass
inley \in-lē\ see INLY
inly \in-lē\ inly, spindly, thinly, McKinley, Mount McKinley
inn \in\ see [1]IN
innace \in-əs\ see [1]INIS
innacle \in-i-kəl\ see INICAL
inned \ind\ see [2]IND
inner \in-ər\ dinner, ginner, grinner, inner, pinner, sinner, skinner, spinner, spinor, thinner, tinner, winner, beginner, breadwinner, prizewinner, money-spinner
innet \in-ət\ linnet, minute, spinet
inney \in-ē\ see INNY
inni \ē-nē\ see [1]INI
innia \in-ē-ə\ see INIA
innic \in-ik\ see [2]INIC
innie \in-ē\ see INNY
inning \in-iŋ\ ginning, inning, spinning, winning, beginning, breadwinning, prizewinning, underpinning
innish \in-ish\ see INISH
innity \in-ət-ē\ see INITY
innow \in-ō\ minnow, winnow, topminnow
inny \in-ē\ cine, finny, ginny, guinea, Guinea, hinny, mini, Minnie, ninny, pinny, Pliny, shinny, skinny, spinney, squinny, tinny, whinny, Winnie, ignominy, micromini, pickaninny, Papua New Guinea, Equatorial Guinea
[1]**ino** \ī-nō\ lino, rhino, Taino, wino, albino
[2]**ino** \ē-nō\ beano, chino, fino, keno, leno, Pinot, vino, Zeno, bambino, casino, cioppino, ladino, merino, sordino, zecchino, andantino, Angeleno, Bardolino, campesino, cappuccino, concertino, Filipino, maraschino, palomino, Philipino, San Marino, pecorino, sopranino, Cape Mendocino, San Bernardino
[3]**ino** \ē-nə\ see [2]INA
iñon \in-yən\ see INION
[1]**inor** \in-ər\ see INNER
[2]**inor** \ī-nər\ see [1]INER
inos \ī-nəs\ see INNS
inot \ē-nō\ see [2]INO
inous \ī-nəs\ see [1]INUS
inscher \in-chər\ see INCHER
inse \ins\ see INCE
inselly \in-slē\ see INCELY
inseng \in-siŋ\ see INCING
insk \insk\ Minsk, Dzerzhinsk, Semipalatinsk

insky \in-skē\ buttinsky, kolinsky, Nijinsky, Stravinsky
inster \in-stər\ minster, spinster, Axminster, Westminster, Kidderminster
int \int\ bint, Clint, dint, flint, Flint, glint, hint, lint, mint, print, quint, skint, splint, sprint, squint, stint, suint, tint, blueprint, catmint, footprint, forint, gunflint, handprint, hoofprint, horsemint, imprint, in-print, large-print, newsprint, offprint, preprint, remint, reprint, skinflint, spearmint, thumbprint, voiceprint, aquatint, calamint, cuckoopint, fingerprint, mezzotint, monotint, overprint, peppermint, photoprint, wunderkind, Septuagint
intage \int-ij\ mintage, vintage
intager \int-i-jər\ see INTEGER
intain \int-ᵊn\ see INTON
[1]**intal** \int-ᵊl\ lintel, pintle, quintal, Septuagintal
[2]**intal** \ant-ᵊl\ see ANTLE
integer \int-i-jər\ integer, vintager
intel \int-ᵊl\ see [1]INTAL
inter \int-ər\ hinter, linter, minter, printer, sinter, splinter, sprinter, squinter, tinter, winter, imprinter, midwinter, reprinter, overwinter, teleprinter
intery \int-ə-rē\ printery, splintery
inth \inth\ plinth, synth, helminth, colocynth, labyrinth, terebinth
inthia \in-thē-ə\ Cynthia, Carinthia
inthian \in-thē-ən\ Corinthian, labyrinthian
inthine \in-thən\ hyacinthine, labyrinthine
inting \int-iŋ\ imprinting, unstinting—*also present participles of verbs listed at* INT
intle \int-ᵊl\ see [1]INTAL
[1]**into** \in-tō\ pinto, Shinto, spinto
[2]**into** \in-tü\ thereinto, whereinto
inton \int-ᵊn\ Clinton, quintain, Winton, badminton
ints \ins\ see INCE
inty \int-ē\ flinty, linty, minty, squinty, pepperminty
intz \ins\ see INCE
inue \in-yü\ sinew, continue, discontinue
inuous \in-yə-wəs\ sinuous, continuous, discontinuous
[1]**inus** \ī-nəs\ dryness, finis, highness, Minas, Minos, minus, shyness, sinus, slyness, spinous, vinous, wryness, Aquinas, Delphinus, echinus, Quirinus, Antoninus, Pontus Euxinus
[2]**inus** \ē-nəs\ see [1]ENUS
inute \in-ət\ see INNET
inx \iŋs\ jinx, links, lynx, minx, sphinx, hijinks, methinks, tiddledywinks
[1]**iny** \ī-nē\ briny, heinie, liny, piny, shiny, spiny, tiny, twiny, viny, whiny, winy, enshrinee, sunshiny
[2]**iny** \in-ē\ see INNY
inya \ē-nyə\ see [2]ENIA

inyan \in-yən\ see INION
inyl \īn-ᵊl\ see ¹INAL
inys \in-əs\ see ¹INIS
¹io \ī-ō\ bayou, bio, Clio, Io, Lucayo, Ohio
²io \ē-ō\ brio, Cleo, clio, guyot, Krio, Leo, Rio, trio, caudillo, con brio, Negrillo, tornillo, Trujillo, cigarillo, Hermosillo, Manzanillo, ocotillo
iocese \ī-ə-səs\ see IASIS
iolate \ī-ə-lət\ see ¹IOLET
¹iolet \ī-ə-lət\ triolet, violate, violet, Violet, inviolate, ultraviolet, near-ultraviolet
²iolet \ē-ə-lət\ see EOLATE
¹ion \ī-ən\ ayin, Brian, Bryan, cyan, ion, lion, Lyon, Mayan, Ryan, scion, Sion, Zion, Amphion, anion, Bisayan, Ixion, Orion, Visayan, counterion, dandelion, zwitterion
²ion \ē-ən\ see ¹EAN
³ion \ē-än\ see ²EON
ior \īr\ see ¹IRE
iory \ī-rē\ see ¹IARY
iot \ī-ət\ see IET
ioter \ī-ət-ər\ see IETER
iouan \ü-ən\ see UAN
ious \ī-əs\ see IAS
ioux \ü\ see ¹EW
ip \ip\ blip, chip, clip, dip, drip, flip, grip, grippe, gyp, hip, kip, lip, nip, pip, quip, rip, scrip, ship, sip, skip, slip, snip, strip, tip, trip, whip, yip, zip, airship, airstrip, atrip, bullwhip, catnip, chiefship, clerkship, courtship, cowslip, deanship, equip, fieldstrip, filmstrip, flagship, friendship, guildship, gunship, half-slip, handgrip, hardship, harelip, headship, horsewhip, inclip, judgeship, kingship, kinship, landslip, lightship, lordship, nonslip, outstrip, oxlip, pip-pip, princeship, Q-ship, queenship, reship, round-trip, saintship, sheep-dip, sideslip, spaceship, steamship, thaneship, township, transship, troopship, unship, unzip, wardship, warship, airmanship, authorship, battleship, biochip, brinkmanship, censorship, chairmanship, chaplainship, chieftainship, churchmanship, coverslip, dealership, draftsmanship, ego-trip, externship, fellowship, fingertip, gamesmanship, Gaza Strip, grantsmanship, helmsmanship, horsemanship, internship, ladyship, leadership, lectureship, listenership, marksmanship, membership, microchip, oarsmanship, overslip, ownership, partnership, penmanship, pogonip, premiership, readership, ridership, rulership, salesmanship, scholarship, seamanship, showmanship, skinny-dip, speakership, sponsorship, sportsmanship, statesmanship, stewardship, studentship, swordsmanship, trusteeship, underlip, upmanship, viewership,

workmanship, assistantship, attorneyship, championship, chancellorship, citizenship, companionship, containership, cross-ownership, dictatorship, directorship, good-fellowship, guardianship, instructorship, landownership, laureateship, governorship, musicianship, one-upmanship, outdoorsmanship, professorship, protectorship, receivership, relationship, survivorship, treasurership, ambassadorship, associateship, bipartisanship, entrepreneurship, librarianship, nonpartisanship, proprietorship, secretaryship, solicitorship, interrelationship

ipal \ē-pəl\ see EOPLE

ipari \ip-rē\ see IPPERY

ipatus \ip-ət-əs\ see IPITOUS

ipe \īp\ Cuyp, gripe, hype, pipe, ripe, slype, snipe, stipe, stripe, swipe, tripe, type, wipe, bagpipe, blowpipe, downpipe, drainpipe, hornpipe, hosepipe, lead-pipe, n-type, p-type, panpipe, pinstripe, rareripe, sideswipe, standpipe, stovepipe, tintype, touch-type, unripe, windpipe, archetype, calotype, Dutchman's-pipe, guttersnipe, haplotype, Linotype, liripipe, logotype, monotype, overripe, prototype, stenotype, Teletype, electrotype, stereotype, daguerreotype, anti-idiotype

[1]**iped** \ī-ped\ biped, parallelepiped

[2]**iped** \īpt\ stiped, striped, pinstriped—*also pasts of verbs listed at* IPE

ipend \ī-pənd\ ripened, stipend

iper \ī-pər\ diaper, griper, hyper, piper, riper, sniper, striper, viper, wiper, bagpiper, sandpiper, candy-striper, stereotyper

iperous \ī-prəs\ see YPRESS

ipetal \ip-ət-ᵊl\ basipetal, bicipital, centripetal, occipital

ipety \ip-ət-ē\ snippety, peripety, serendipity

iph \if\ see IFF

iphany \if-ə-nē\ see IPHONY

ipher \ī-fər\ cipher, lifer, rifer, decipher, encipher, pro-lifer, right-to-lifer

iphery \if-rē\ see IFERY

iphon \ī-fən\ see YPHEN

iphony \if-ə-nē\ tiffany, Tiffany, antiphony, epiphany, polyphony

ipi \ē-pē\ see EEPY

ipid \ip-əd\ lipid, insipid

ipience \ip-ē-əns\ incipience, percipience, impercipience

ipient \ip-ē-ənt\ excipient, incipient, percipient, recipient, impercipient

iping \ī-piŋ\ piping, striping, blood-typing

ipit \ip-ət\ see IPPET

ipital \ip-ət-əl\ see IPETAL

ipitance \ip-ət-əns\ see IPOTENCE

ipitant \ip-ət-ənt\ see IPOTENT

ipitous \ip-ət-əs\ peripatus, precipitous, serendipitous

ipity \ip-ət-ē\ see IPETY
[1]**iple** \ip-əl\ see IPPLE
[2]**iple** \ī-pəl\ see YPAL
ipless \ip-ləs\ dripless, lipless, zipless
ipling \ip-liŋ\ Kipling, stripling
ipment \ip-mənt\ shipment, equipment, transshipment
ipo \ēp-ō\ see EPOT
ipoli \ip-ə-lē\ see IPPILY
ipotence \ip-ət-əns\ omnipotence, precipitance
ipotent \ip-ət-ənt\ omnipotent, plenipotent, pluripotent, precipitant
[1]**ippe** \ip\ see IP
[2]**ippe** \ip-ē\ see IPPY
[3]**ippe** \ēp\ see EEP
ipped \ipt\ see IPT
ippee \ip-ē\ see IPPY
ippen \ip-ən\ lippen, pippin
ipper \ip-ər\ chipper, clipper, dipper, dripper, flipper, gripper, hipper, kipper, nipper, ripper, shipper, sipper skipper, slipper, snipper, stripper, tipper, tripper, whipper, zipper, blue-chipper, day-tripper, mudskipper, Yom-Kippur, double-dipper, gallinipper, lady's slipper, skinny-dipper
ippery \ip-rē\ frippery, Lipari, slippery
ippet \ip-ət\ pipit, sippet, snippet, tippet, trippet, whippet
ippety \ip-ət-ē\ see IPETY
ippi \ip-ē\ see IPPY
ippie \ip-ē\ see IPPY
ippily \ip-ə-lē\ nippily, tripoli, Tripoli, Gallipoli
ippin \ip-ən\ see IPPEN
ipping \ip-iŋ\ chipping, clipping, dripping, lipping, nipping, ripping, shipping, double-dipping, skinny-dipping
ippingly \ip-iŋ-lē\ grippingly, nippingly, trippingly
ipple \ip-əl\ cripple, nipple, ripple, stipple, tipple, triple, participle
ippur \ip-ər\ see IPPER
ippy \ip-ē\ chippy, dippy, drippy, flippy, grippy, hippie, hippy, Lippi, lippy, nippy, slippy, snippy, tippy, trippy, whippy, yippee, yippie, zippy, Xanthippe, Mississippi
ips \ips\ snips, thrips, yips, eclipse, ellipse, midships, amidships, athwartships, fish-and-chips, tidytips, apocalypse—*also plurals and possessives of nouns and third person singular presents of verbs listed at* IP
ipse \ips\ see IPS
ipso \ip-sō\ dipso, calypso, Calypso
ipster \ip-stər\ hipster, quipster, tipster
ipsy \ip-sē\ see YPSY
ipt \ipt\ crypt, hipped, lipped, ripped, script, tipped, conscript, decrypt, encrypt, harelipped, postscript, prescript, rescript, subscript, tight-lipped, transcript, typescript, eucalypt, filter-tipped, manuscript, nondescript, superscript,

swivel-hipped—*also pasts of verbs listed at* IP
ipter \ip-tər\ scripter, lithotripter
iptic \ip-tik\ see YPTIC
iption \ip-shən\ ascription, conniption, conscription, decryption, description, Egyptian, encryption, inscription, prescription, proscription, subscription, transcription, circumscription, nonprescription
iptive \ip-tiv\ ascriptive, descriptive, inscriptive, prescriptive, proscriptive
iptych \ip-tik\ see YPTIC
ipular \ip-yə-lər\ stipular, manipular
ipy \ī-pē\ stripy, typey, stenotypy, daguerrotypy, stereotypy
iquant \ē-kənt\ see ECANT
ique \ēk\ see [1]EAK
iquey \ē-kē\ see EAKY
iquish \ē-kish\ see EAKISH
iquitous \ik-wət-əs\ iniquitous, ubiquitous
iquity \ik-wət-ē\ antiquity, iniquity, obliquity, ubiquity
iquor \ik-ər\ see [1]ICKER
[1]ir \ir\ see [2]EER
[2]ir \ər\ see [1]EUR
[1]ira \ir-ə\ see [2]ERA
[2]ira \ī-rə\ see YRA
irable \ī-rə-bəl\ wirable, acquirable, desirable, respirable, undesirable
iracle \ir-i-kəl\ see [2]ERICAL
irae \īr-ē\ see [1]IRY
iral \ī-rəl\ chiral, gyral, spiral, viral
irant \ī-rənt\ spirant, tyrant, aspirant, retirant
irate \ir-ət\ see IRIT
irby \ər-bē\ see ERBY
irca \ər-kə\ see [1]URKA
irce \ər-sē\ see ERCY
irch \ərch\ see URCH
[1]irchen \ər-chən\ see URCHIN
[2]irchen \ər-kən\ see IRKIN
ircher \ər-chər\ Bircher, lurcher, nurture
irchist \ər-chəst\ Birchist, researchist
ircon \ər-kən\ see IRKIN
ircuit \ər-kət\ circuit, trifurcate, microcircuit
ircular \ər-kyə-lər\ circular, opercular, tubercular, semicircular
ird \ərd\ bird, burred, curd, furred, gird, heard, herd, nerd, spurred, surd, third, turd, word, absurd, begird, bellbird, blackbird, bluebird, buzzword, byword, Cape Verde, catbird, catchword, cowbird, cowherd, crossword, cussword, engird, goatherd, headword, jailbird, jaybird, kingbird, loanword, lovebird, lyrebird, oilbird, password, potsherd, railbird, rainbird, redbird, reword, ricebird, seabird, Sigurd, shorebird, snakebird, snowbird, songbird, sunbird, surfbird, swearword, swineherd, textured, ungird, unheard, watchword, yardbird, afterword, bowerbird, butcher-bird, cedarbird, dollybird, hummingbird,

ladybird, mockingbird, ovenbird, overheard, riflebird, tailorbird, thunderbird, undergird, wattlebird, weaverbird, wirlybird—*also pasts of verbs listed at* [1]EUR

irder \ərd-ər\ see ERDER

irdie \ərd-ē\ see URDY

irdle \ərd-ᵊl\ see URDLE

irdum \ərd-əm\ dirdum, reductio ad absurdum

[1]**ire** \īr\ briar, brier, byre, choir, dire, drier, fire, flier, friar, fryer, gyre, hire, ire, liar, lyre, mire, prier, prior, pyre, quire, shire, sire, Speyer, spier, spire, squire, tier, tire, trier, tyer, Tyre, wire, zaire, acquire, admire, afire, Altair, aspire, attire, backfire, balefire, barbed wire, barbwire, bemire, Blantyre, blow-dryer, bonfire, brushfire, bushfire, catbrier, cease-fire, complier, conspire, defier, denier, desire, drumfire, empire, Empire, entire, esquire, expire, flytier, grandsire, greenbrier, gunfire, haywire, hellfire, highflier, hot-wire, inquire, inspire, misfire, outlier, perspire, pismire, prior, quagmire, require, respire, retire, rimfire, samphire, sapphire, satire, Shropshire, spitfire, surefire, suspire, sweetbrier, tightwire, transpire, umpire, vampire, wildfire, amplifier, Biedermeier, butterflyer, classifier, fly-by-wire, fortifier, lammergeier, magnifier, modifier, multiplier, nitrifier, nullifier, pacifier, qualifier, quantifier, rapid-fire, rectifier, retrofire, sanctifier, signifier, testifier, versifier, identifier, intensifier, Second Empire, down-to-the-wire—*also nouns formed by adding* -er *to verbs listed at* [1]Y

[2]**ire** \ir\ see [2]EER

[3]**ire** \ī-rē\ see [1]IARY

[4]**ire** \īr-ē\ see [1]IRY

[5]**ire** \ər\ see EUR

ired \īrd\ fired, spired, tired, wired, hardwired, retired—*also pasts of verbs listed at* [1]IRE

ireless \īr-ləs\ tireless, wireless

ireman \īr-mən\ fireman, wireman

irement \īr-mənt\ environment, requirement, retirement

iren \ī-rən\ Byron, gyron, Myron, siren, environ, ribavirin

irge \ərj\ see URGE

irgin \ər-jən\ see URGEON

irgo \ər-gō\ see ERGO

iri \ir-ē\ see EARY

iriam \ir-ē-əm\ see ERIUM

iric \ir-ik\ see [2]ERIC

irin \i-rən\ see IREN

irine \ī-rən\ see IREN

iring \īr-iŋ\ firing, wiring, retiring

irious \ir-ē-əs\ see ERIOUS

iris \ī-rəs\ see IRUS

irish \īr-ish\ Irish, squirish

irit \ir-ət\ Meerut, spirit,

dispirit, emirate, inspirit, vizierate
irium \ir-ē-əm\ see ERIUM
irius \ir-ē-əs\ see ERIOUS
[1]irk \irk\ birk, dirk, Dirk, kirk
[2]irk \ərk\ see [1]ORK
irker \ər-kər\ see [1]ORKER
irkie \ər-kē\ see ERKY
irkin \ər-kən\ firkin, gherkin, jerkin, zircon, Gelsenkirchen
irky \ər-kē\ see ERKY
[1]irl \ərl\ birl, burl, churl, curl, dirl, earl, Earl, Earle, furl, girl, hurl, knurl, merle, Merle, pearl, Pearl, purl, skirl, squirrel, swirl, thirl, thurl, tirl, twirl, virl, whirl, whorl, aswirl, awhirl, cowgirl, impearl, pas seul, playgirl, salesgirl, schoolgirl, showgirl, uncurl, unfurl, mother-of-pearl
[2]irl \irl\ dirl, skirl
irler \ər-lər\ birler, curler, pearler, twirler, whirler
irley \ər-lē\ see URLY
irlie \ər-lē\ see URLY
irling \ər-liŋ\ see URLING
irlish \ər-lish\ see URLISH
irly \ər-lē\ see URLY
irm \ərm\ see [1]ORM
irma \ər-mə\ see ERMA
irmary \ərm-rē\ spermary, infirmary
irmess \ər-məs\ see ERMIS
irmity \ər-mət-ē\ furmity, infirmity
irmy \ər-mē\ see ERMY
[1]irn \irn\ firn, girn, pirn
[2]irn \ərn\ see URN
[1]iro \ir-ō\ see [3]ERO
[2]iro \ē-rō\ see [1]ERO
[3]iro \ī-rō\ see [1]YRO
[1]iron \īrn\ iron, andiron, environ, flatiron, gridiron
[2]iron \ī-rən\ see IREN
ironment \īr-mənt\ see IREMENT
irp \ərp\ see URP
irps \ərps\ stirps, turps—*also plurals and possessives of nouns and third person singular presents of verbs listed at* URP
irpy \ər-pē\ chirpy, Euterpe
irque \ərk\ see [1]ORK
[1]irr \ir\ see [2]EER
[2]irr \ər\ see [1]EUR
irra \ir-ə\ see [2]ERA
irrah \ir-ə\ see [2]ERA
[1]irrel \ərl\ see [1]IRL
[2]irrel \ər-əl\ see ERRAL
irrely \ər-lē\ see URLY
irrer \ər-ər\ see ERRER
irrhous \ir-əs\ see EROUS
irrhus \ir-əs\ see EROUS
irring \ər-iŋ\ see URRING
irror \ir-ər\ see [2]EARER
irrous \ir-əs\ see EROUS
irrup \ər-əp\ chirrup, stirrup, syrup
irrupy \ər-ə-pē\ chirrupy, syrupy
irrus \ir-əs\ see EROUS
irry \ər-ē\ see URRY
irs \irz\ see IERS
irsch \irsh\ see IRSH
[1]irse \irs\ see IERCE
[2]irse \ərs\ see ERSE
irsh \irsh\ girsh, kirsch
irst \ərst\ see URST
irsty \ər-stē\ thirsty, bloodthirsty

irt \ərt\ see [1]ERT

irted \ərt-əd\ see ERTED

irter \ərt-ər\ see ERTER

irth \ərth\ berth, birth, dearth, earth, firth, girth, mirth, Perth, worth, childbirth, Fort Worth, rebirth, self-worth, stillbirth, unearth, Wordsworth, afterbirth, down-to-earth, pennyworth

irthful \ərth-fəl\ mirthful, worthful

irthless \ərth-ləs\ mirthless, worthless

irtinent \ərt-nənt\ pertinent, appurtenant, impertinent

irting \ərt-iŋ\ see ERTING

irtle \ərt-ᵊl\ see ERTILE

irtually \ərch-lē\ see URCHLY

irtue \ər-chə\ see ERCHA

irty \ərt-ē\ dirty, QWERTY, shirty, thirty

irus \ī-rəs\ Cyrus, iris, Iris, Skyros, virus, desirous, Epirus, Osiris, papyrus, lentivirus, parvovirus, rotavirus, papillomavirus

irv \ərv\ see ERVE

irving \ər-viŋ\ see ERVING

irwin \ər-wən\ see ERWIN

[1]**iry** \īr-ē\ eyrie, friary, miry, spiry, wiry, expiry, inquiry, venire, praemunire, anno hegirae

[2]**iry** \ī-rē\ see [1]IARY

i's \īz\ see IZE

[1]**is** \is\ see [1]ISS

[2]**is** \iz\ see [1]IZ

[3]**is** \ē\ see [1]EE

[4]**is** \ēs\ see IECE

[5]**is** \ish\ see [1]ISH

[1]**isa** \ē-zə\ see EZA

[2]**isa** \ī-zə\ Lisa, Liza, Elisa, Eliza

isabeth \iz-ə-bəth\ see IZABETH

isable \ī-zə-bəl\ see IZABLE

[1]**isal** \ī-səl\ Faisal, Ijssel, sisal, skysail, trysail, radisal

[2]**isal** \ī-zəl\ Geisel, incisal, reprisal, revisal, surprisal, paradisal

isan \is-ᵊn\ see ISTEN

isbane \iz-bən\ see ISBON

isbe \iz-bē\ Frisbee, Thisbe

isbee \iz-bē\ see ISBE

isbon \iz-bən\ Brisbane, Lisbon

isc \isk\ see ISK

iscable \is-kə-bəl\ confiscable, episcopal

iscan \is-kən\ see ISKIN

iscate \is-kət\ see ISKET

isce \is\ see [1]ISS

[1]**iscean** \ī-sē-ən\ Piscean, Dionysian

[2]**iscean** \is-kē-ən\ Piscean, saurischian, ornithischian

[3]**iscean** \is-ē-ən\ see [1]YSIAN

iscence \is-ᵊns\ puissance, dehiscence, impuissance, indehiscence, reminiscence, reviviscence

iscent \is-ᵊnt\ puissant, dehiscent, impuissant, indehiscent, reminiscent, reviviscent

isces \ī-sēz\ see ICES

ische \ēsh\ see [2]ICHE

ischian \is-kē-ən\ see [2]ISCEAN

iscia \ish-ə\ see ITIA

iscible \is-ə-bəl\ see ISSIBLE

iscience \ish-əns\ see ICIENCE

iscient \ish-ənt\ see ICIENT

isco \is-kō\ cisco, disco,

Francisco, Jalisco, Morisco, San Francisco
iscopal \is-kə-bəl\ see ISCABLE
iscous \is-kəs\ see ISCUS
iscuit \is-kət\ see ISKET
iscus \is-kəs\ discus, viscous, viscus, hibiscus, meniscus
[1]**ise** \ēs\ see IECE
[2]**ise** \ēz\ see EZE
[3]**ise** \īs\ see [1]ICE
[4]**ise** \īz\ see IZE
[1]**ised** \īst\ see [1]IST
[2]**ised** \īzd\ see IZED
isel \iz-əl\ see IZZLE
iseled \iz-əld\ see IZZLED
iseler \iz-lər\ see IZZLER
isement \īz-mənt\ advisement, chastisement, despisement, disguisement, advertisement, disfranchisement, enfranchisement, disenfranchisement
iser \ī-zər\ see IZER
ises \ī-sēz\ see ICES
[1]**ish** \ish\ dish, fiche, fish, flysch, Nis, pish, squish, swish, whish, wish, blackfish, blowfish, bluefish, bonefish, catfish, codfish, crawfish, crayfish, dogfish, filefish, finfish, flatfish, garfish, globefish, goldfish, goosefish, Irtysh, kingfish, knish, lungfish, lumpfish, monkfish, pigfish, pipefish, ratfish, redfish, rockfish, sailfish, sawfish, shellfish, spearfish, starfish, stonefish, sunfish, swordfish, tilefish, unwish, weakfish, whitefish, angelfish, anglerfish, archerfish, butterfish, candlefish, cuttlefish, damselfish, devilfish, jellyfish, John Bullish, ladyfish, lionfish, microfiche, muttonfish, needlefish, overfish, paddlefish, ribbonfish, silverfish, surgeonfish, triggerfish
[2]**ish** \ēsh\ see [2]ICHE
isha \ish-ə\ see ITIA
ishable \ish-ə-bəl\ fishable, justiciable
ished \isht\ dished, whisht—*also pasts of verbs listed at* [1]ISH
isher \ish-ər\ fisher, fissure, swisher, ill-wisher, kingfisher, well-wisher
ishery \ish-rē\ fishery, Tishri, shellfishery
ishi \ē-shē\ chichi, specie, maharishi
ishing \ish-iŋ\ bonefishing, fly-fishing, sportfishing, well-wishing
ishioner \ish-nər\ see ITIONER
ishna \ish-nə\ Krishna, Mishnah
ishnah \ish-nə\ see ISHNA
isht \isht\ see ISHED
ishu \ish-ü\ see [1]ISSUE
ishy \ish-ē\ dishy, fishy, squishy, swishy
[1]**isi** \ē-zē\ see [1]EASY
[2]**isi** \ē-sē\ see EECY
[1]**isia** \izh-ə\ baptisia, Dionysia, artemisia
[2]**isia** \ē-zhə\ see [2]ESIA
[1]**isian** \izh-ən\ see ISION
[2]**isian** \ē-zhən\ see [1]ESIAN
isible \iz-ə-bəl\ risible, visible, divisible, invisible, indivisible

isin \i-zən\ see [2]ISON
ising \ī-ziŋ\ see IZING
ision \izh-ən\ fission, Frisian, scission, vision, abscission, collision, concision, decision, derision, division, elision, elysian, envision, excision, incision, misprision, precisian, precision, prevision, provision, recision, rescission, revision, circumcision, Dionysian, imprecision, indecision, subdivision, supervision, television
isional \izh-ə-nəl\ visional, collisional, decisional, divisional, excisional, previsional, provisional
isis \ī-səs\ crisis, Isis, lysis, nisus, Dionysus, stare decisis
isit \iz-ət\ visit, exquisite, revisit
isite \iz-ət\ see ISIT
isitive \iz-ət-iv\ acquisitive, inquisitive
isitor \iz-ət-ər\ visitor, acquisitor, inquisitor
[1]**isive** \ī-siv\ visive, decisive, derisive, divisive, incisive, indecisive
[2]**isive** \iz-iv\ visive, derisive, divisive
isk \isk\ bisque, brisk, disc, disk, fisc, frisk, risk, whisk, lutefisk, asterisk, basilisk, blastodisc, compact disc, laserdisc, obelisk, odalisque, tamarisk, videodisc
isker \is-kər\ brisker, frisker, risker, whisker
isket \is-kət\ biscuit, brisket, frisket
iskey \is-kē\ see ISKY
iskie \is-kē\ see ISKY
iskin \is-kən\ siskin, Franciscan
isky \is-kē\ frisky, pliskie, risky, whiskey
island \ī-lənd\ see IGHLAND
islander \ī-lən-dər\ see IGHLANDER
islands \ī-lənz\ see IGHLANDS
isle \īl\ see [1]ILE
isles \īlz\ see ILES
islet \ī-lət\ see ILOT
isling \iz-liŋ\ brisling, quisling
isly \iz-lē\ see IZZLY
ism \iz-əm\ chrism, chrisom, ism, prism, schism, abysm, autism, baalism, baptism, Birchism, bossism, Buddhism, casteism, centrism, charism, Chartism, chemism, classism, cubism, cultism, czarism, deism, dwarfism, faddism, fascism, fauvism, Gaullism, Grecism, Hobbism, holism, Jainism, Klanism, leftism, lyrism, Mahdism, Maoism, Marxism, monism, mutism, Nazism, nudism, Orphism, priggism, purism, racism, Ramism, rightism, sadism, Saivism, sapphism, Scotism, sexism, Shaktism, Shiism, Sikhism, simplism, snobbism, sophism, statism, Sufism, tachism, Tantrism, Taoism, theism, Thomism, tourism, tropism, truism, Turkism, verism, Whiggism, Yahwism, absurdism, activism, Adventism, alarmism, albinism, alpinism, altruism, amorphism,

anarchism, aneurysm, anglicism, animism, aphorism, Arabism, archaism, asterism, atavism, atheism, atomism, atticism, Bahaism, barbarism, Benthamism, biblicism, blackguardism, bolshevism, boosterism, botulism, bourbonism, Brahmanism, Briticism, Byronism, cabalism, Caesarism, Calvinism, careerism, Castroism, cataclysm, catechism, Catharism, centralism, chauvinism, chimerism, classicism, colorism, communism, concretism, conformism, cretinism, criticism, cronyism, cynicism, dadaism, dandyism, Darwinism, defeatism, de Gaullism, despotism, die-hardism, dimorphism, dirigisme, Docetism, do-goodism, dogmatism, Donatism, Don Juanism, druidism, dualism, dynamism, egoism, egotism, elitism, embolism, endemism, erethism, ergotism, erotism, escapism, Essenism, etatism, eunuchism, euphemism, euphuism, exorcism, expertism, extremism, fairyism, familism, fatalism, feminism, feudalism, fideism, Fidelism, fogyism, foreignism, formalism, futurism, Galenism, gallicism, galvanism, gangsterism, genteelism, Germanism, giantism, gigantism, globalism, gnosticism, Gongorism, Gothicism, gourmandism, gradualism, grangerism, greenbackism, Hasidism, heathenism, Hebraism, hedonism, Hellenism, helotism, hermetism, hermitism, heroism, highbrowism, Hinduism, hipsterism, hirsutism, hispanism, Hitlerism, hoodlumism, hoodooism, hucksterism, humanism, Hussitism, hybridism, hypnotism, Ibsenism, idealism, imagism, Irishism, Islamism, Jansenism, jingoism, journalism, John Bullism, Judaism, Junkerism, kaiserism, Krishnaism, Ku Kluxism, laconism, laicism, Lamaism, Lamarckism, landlordism, Latinism, legalism, Leninism, lobbyism, localism, locoism, Lollardism, luminism, lyricism, magnetism, mammonism, mannerism, Marcionism, masochism, mechanism, melanism, meliorism, Menshevism, Mendelism, mentalism, mesmerism, methodism, me-tooism, modernism, Mohockism, monachism, monadism, monarchism, mongolism, Montanism, moralism, Mormonism, morphinism, mullahism, mysticism, narcissism, nationalism,

nativism, nepotism,
neutralism, new dealism,
nihilism, nomadism,
occultism, onanism,
optimism, oralism,
Orangeism, organism,
ostracism, pacifism,
paganism, Pan-Slavism,
pantheism, paroxysm,
Parsiism, passivism,
pauperism, pessimism,
phallicism, pianism, pietism,
plagiarism, Platonism,
pleinairism, Plotinism,
pluralism, pointillism,
populism, pragmatism,
presentism, privatism,
prosaism, Prussianism,
puerilism, pugilism,
Puseyism, Pyrrhonism,
Quakerism, quietism,
rabbinism, racialism,
rationalism, realism,
reformism, rheumatism,
rigorism, robotism,
Romanism, Rousseauism,
rowdyism, royalism, satanism,
savagism, scapegoatism,
schematism, scientism,
sciolism, Scotticism,
Semitism, Shakerism,
Shamanism, Shintoism,
skepticism, socialism,
solecism, solipsism,
Southernism, specialism,
speciesism, Spartanism,
Spinozism, spiritism,
spoonerism, Stalinism,
standpattism, stoicism,
syllogism, symbolism,
synchronism, syncretism,
synergism, talmudism,
tarantism, tectonism,
tenebrism, terrorism,
Teutonism, titanism, Titoism,
tokenism, Toryism, totalism,
totemism, transvestism,
traumatism, tribalism,
tritheism, Trotskyism,
ultraism, unionism, urbanism,
utopism, Vaishnavism,
vampirism, vandalism,
vanguardism, Vedantism,
veganism, verbalism, virilism,
vitalism, vocalism, volcanism,
voodooism, vorticism,
voyeurism, vulcanism,
vulgarism, Wahhabism,
warlordism, welfarism,
Wellerism, witticism,
yahooism, Yankeeism,
Yiddishism, Zionism,
zombiism, absenteeism,
absolutism, abstractionism,
adoptionism, adventurism,
aestheticism, Africanism,
agnosticism, alcoholism,
alienism, amateurism,
amoralism, anabaptism,
anachronism, Anglicanism,
animalism, antagonism,
Arianism, astigmatism,
athleticism, asynchronism,
Atlanticism, atonalism,
Australianism, automatism,
avant-gardism, behaviorism,
Big Brotherism, bilingualism,
biologism, bipedalism,
biracialism, Bonapartism,
bureaucratism, cannibalism,
capitalism, Cartesianism,
catastrophism, Catholicism,
cavalierism, charlatanism,
clericalism, collectivism,

Colonel Blimpism, commensalism, commercialism, communalism, Confucianism, conservatism, constructivism, consumerism, corporatism, creationism, credentialism, determinism, diabolism, didacticism, diffusionism, dilettantism, doctrinairism, do-nothingism, eclecticism, ecumenism, egocentrism, Eleatism, empiricism, epicenism, epicurism, epigonism, eremitism, eroticism, erraticism, essentialism, ethnocentrism, eudaemonism, euhemerism, evangelism, exceptionalism, exclusivism, exoticism, expansionism, expressionism, externalism, Fabianism, factionalism, factualism, fanaticism, favoritism, federalism, Fenianism, feuilletonism, fifth columnism, flagellantism, Fourierism, fraternalism, freneticism, Freudianism, funambulism, functionalism, gallicanism, gutturalism, henotheism, hermeticism, Hispanicism, historicism, hooliganism, Hugenotism, hypocorism, idiotism, illiberalism, illuminism, illusionism, immanentism, immobilism, impressionism, indifferentism, Indianism, infantilism, inflationism, initialism, insularism, invalidism, iotacism, irredentism, Ishmaelitism, Italianism, Jacobinism, Jacobitism, jesuitism, Keynesianism, know-nothingism, legitimism, lesbianism, liberalism, libertinism, literalism, Lutheranism, Lysenkoism, Magianism, malapropism, mandarinism, McCarthyism, medievalism, mercantilism, messianism, metabolism, metamorphism, militarism, minimalism, misoneism, monasticism, monetarism, monotheism, mosaicism, mutualism, naturalism, Naziritism, necrophilism, negativism, neologism, neo-Nazism, neuroticism, nice-nellyism, nominalism, nonconformism, objectivism, obscurantism, obstructionism, officialism, opportunism, organicism, pacificism, Pantagruelism, parallelism, parasitism, pastoralism, paternalism, patriotism, Peeping Tomism, perfectionism, personalism, pharisaism, physicalism, plebeianism, poeticism, polyglotism, polytheism, positivism, postmodernism, pragmaticism, primitivism, probabilism, progressivism, proselytism, protectionism, Protestantism, provincialism, pseudomorphism, psychologism, puritanism, radicalism, rationalism, recidivism, reductionism, refugeeism, regionalism, relativism, restrictionism, revisionism, revivalism, ritualism, romanticism, ruffianism, Sadduceeism, salvationism, sansculottism, sardonicism, scholasticism, secessionism, sectarianism, sectionalism, secularism, sensualism, separatism, serialism, Slavophilism, solidarism, somnambulism, sovietism, Stakhanovism, structuralism, subjectivism, suprematism, surrealism, Sybaritism, sycophantism, systematism, Tammanyism, teetotalism, theocentrism, triumphalism, Uncle Tomism, vagabondism, ventriloquism, vigilantism, voluntarism, volunteerism, Wesleyanism, workaholism, Zwinglianism, abolitionism, academicism, agrarianism, Americanism, analphabetism, anthropomorphism, anthropopathism, anti-Semitism, Arminianism, autoerotism, barbarianism, bibliophilism, bicameralism, biculturalism, biloquialism, bipartisanism, bohemianism, colloquialism, colonialism, conceptualism, confessionalism, constitutionalism, conventionalism, corporativism, cosmopolitism, deviationism, ecumenicism, emotionalism, esotericism, Europocentrism, evolutionism, exhibitionism, existentialism, expatriatism, fundamentalism, governmentalism, Hegelianism, hermaphroditism, hypercriticism, hyperrealism, hyperurbanism, imperialism, incendiarism, incrementalism, indeterminism, industrialism, instrumentalism, interventionism, introspectionism, irrationalism, isolationism, Malthusianism, Manichaeanism, manorialism, materialism, millennialism, Monarchianism, mongolianism, Monophysitism, Muhammadanism, multilingualism, neoclassicism, Neoplatonism, neorealism, Nestorianism, Occidentalism, operationism, orientalism, Palladianism, parajournalism, parochialism, particularism, pedestrianism, Pelagianism, Pentecostalism, phenomenalism, photojournalism, pictorialism, pococurantism, Postimpressionism, professionalism, pseudoclassicism, reconstructionism, republicanism, Rosicrucianism, sacerdotalism, sacramentalism, self-determinism, sadomasochism, sectarianism, sensationalism, sentimentalism, socinianism, spiritualism, theatricalism, Tractarianism, traditionalism, transcendentalism, transsexualism, trilateralism, ultramontanism, universalism, utopianism, vernacularism, Victorianism, vocationalism, voluntaryism, Albigensianism, anticlericalism, antiquarianism, apocalypticism, assimilationism, associationism, Augustinianism, autoeroticism, ceremonialism, collaborationism, congregationalism, cosmopolitanism, ecclesiasticism, ecumenicalism, environmentalism, Evangelicalism, Hamiltonianism, homoeroticism, epicureanism, experimentalism, immaterialism, individualism, institutionalism, intellectualism, internationalism, libertarianism, middle-of-the-roadism, millenarianism, neo-conservatism, neo-impressionism, operationalism, Pan-Americanism, Peripateticism, photoperiodism, Pre-Raphaelitism, Presbyterianism, Pythegoreanism, Rastafarianism, reactionaryism, Sabbatarianism, supernaturalism, Swedenborgianism, territorialism, Trinitarianism, unitarianism, vegetarianism, Zoroastrianism, Aristotelianism, authoritarianism, egalitarianism, Episcopalianism, humanitarianism, Machiavellianism, neocolonialism, neo-Expressionism, predestinarianism, representationalism, utilitarianism, establishmentarianism, latitudinarianism

isma \iz-mə\ charisma, melisma

ismal \iz-məl\ see YSMAL

[1]isme \īm\ see [1]IME

[2]isme \izᵊm\ see ISM

ismo \ēz-mō\ machismo, verismo, caudillismo

iso \ē-sō\ miso, piso

isom \iz-əm\ see ISM

[1]ison \īs-ᵊn\ bison, hyson, Meissen, streptomycin, Aureomycin, erythromycin

[2]ison \iz-ᵊn\ dizen, mizzen, prison, risen, weasand, wizen, arisen, imprison, Tok Pisin, uprisen

isor \ī-zər\ see IZER

isored \ī-zərd\ guisard, visored

isory \īz-rē\ advisory, provisory, revisory, supervisory

isp \isp\ crisp, lisp, LISP, wisp, will-o-the-wisp

isper \is-pər\ crisper, lisper, whisper
ispy \is-pē\ crispy, wispy
isque \isk\ see ISK
iss \is\ bis, bliss, cis, Chris, cuisse, Dis, hiss, kiss, miss, sis, Swiss, this, vis, wis, abyss, amiss, coulisse, dehisce, dismiss, iwis, koumiss, remiss, submiss, ambergris, hit-and-miss, hit-or-miss, reminisce, verdigris
issa \is-ə\ abscissa, mantissa, Melissa, Orissa, vibrissa
issable \is-ə-bəl\ see ISSIBLE
issal \is-əl\ see ISTLE
issance \is-ᵊns\ see ISCENCE
issant \is-ᵊnt\ see ISCENT
[1]**isse** \is\ see ISS
[2]**isse** \ēs\ see IECE
issed \ist\ see [2]IST
issel \is-əl\ see ISTLE
isser \is-ər\ hisser, kisser
issible \is-ə-bəl\ kissable, miscible, admissible, immiscible, municipal, omissible, permissible, remissible, transmissible, impermissible, inadmissible
issile \is-əl\ see ISTLE
[1]**ission** \ish-ən\ see ITION
[2]**ission** \izh-ən\ see ISION
issionable \ish-nə-bəl\ fissionable, conditionable
issioner \ish-nər\ see ITIONER
issive \is-iv\ missive, admissive, derisive, dismissive, emissive, permissive, submissive, transmissive
issome \is-əm\ lissome, alyssum
issor \iz-ər\ scissor, whizzer
[1]**issue** \ish-ü\ fichu, issue, tissue, reissue, Mogadishu, overissue
[2]**issue** \ish-ə\ see ITIA
issure \ish-ər\ see ISHER
issus \is-əs\ byssus, missus, Mrs., narcissus, Narcissus
issy \is-ē\ hissy, missy, prissy, sissy
[1]**ist** \īst\ Christ, feist, heist, hist, tryst, zeitgeist, Antichrist, black-a-vised, poltergeist—*also pasts of verbs listed at* [1]ICE
[2]**ist** \ist\ cist, cyst, fist, gist, grist, kist, list, Liszt, mist, schist, tryst, twist, whist, wist, wrist, assist, backlist, blacklist, checklist, consist, delist, desist, encyst, enlist, entwist, exist, handlist, insist, persist, playlist, protist, Rehnquist, resist, shortlist, subsist, untwist, catechist, coexist, dadaist, exorcist, intertwist, preexist, love-in-a-mist—*also pasts of verbs listed at* ISS
[3]**ist** \ēst\ see [1]EAST
[1]**ista** \ē-stə\ turista, camorrista, Fidelista
[2]**ista** \is-tə\ crista, vista, arista, ballista, sacahuiste
istaed \is-təd\ see ISTED
istal \is-tᵊl\ Bristol, crystal, Crystal, distal, listel, pistil, pistol
istan \is-tən\ see ISTON
istance \is-təns\ see ISTENCE
istant \is-tənt\ see ISTENT
[1]**iste** \is-tē\ see [2]ICITY
[2]**iste** \ēst\ see [1]EAST

[3]iste \is-tə\ see [2]ISTA
isted \is-təd\ twisted, vistaed, closefisted, enlisted, hamfisted, hardfisted, limpwristed, tightfisted, two-fisted, unlisted, untwisted, whitelisted, ironfisted, unassisted—*also pasts of verbs listed at* [2]IST
istel \is-tᵊl\ see ISTAL
isten \is-ᵊn\ christen, glisten, listen, Nisan
istenable \is-nə-bəl\ listenable, medicinable
istence \is-təns\ distance, assistance, consistence, existence, insistence, outdistance, persistence, resistance, subsistence, coexistence, inconsistence, inexistence, nonexistence, nonresistance, preexistence
istency \is-tən-sē\ consistency, insistency, persistency, inconsistency
istent \is-tənt\ distant, assistant, consistent, existent, insistent, persistent, resistant, subsistent, coexistent, equidistant, inconsistent, inexistent, nonexistent, nonpersistent, nonresistant, preexistent
ister \is-tər\ bister, blister, clyster, glister, klister, lister, Lister, mister, sister, twister, resister, resistor, solicitor, stepsister, transistor
istery \is-trē\ see ISTORY
istful \ist-fəl\ tristful, wistful
isthmus \is-məs\ see ISTMAS
isti \is-tē\ see [2]ICITY
istic \is-tik\ cystic, distich, fistic, mystic, artistic, autistic, ballistic, cladistic, cubistic, eristic, fascistic, faunistic, floristic, heuristic, holistic, hubristic, juristic, linguistic, logistic, meristic, monistic, patristic, phlogistic, puristic, sadistic, simplistic, sophistic, statistic, stylistic, Taoistic, theistic, Thomistic, touristic, truistic, veristic, wholistic, Yahwistic, activistic, agonistic, alchemistic, altruistic, amoristic, anarchistic, animistic, aphoristic, archaistic, atavistic, atheistic, atomistic, belletristic, cabalistic, Calvinistic, casuistic, catechistic, Catharistic, centralistic, chauvinistic, communistic, crosslinguistic, dadaistic, dualistic, dyslogistic, egoistic, egotistic, essayistic, eucharistic, eulogistic, euphemistic, euphuistic, exorcistic, fabulistic, familistic, fatalistic, feministic, fetishistic, feudalistic, fideistic, formalistic, futuristic, gongoristic, haggadistic, Hebraistic, hedonistic, Hellenistic, humanistic, humoristic, idealistic, imagistic, inartistic, Jansenistic, jingoistic, journalistic, Judaistic, Lamaistic, legalistic, masochistic, mechanistic, melanistic, mentalistic,

methodistic, modernistic, moralistic, narcissistic, nationalistic, nativistic, nepotistic, nihilistic, novelistic, onanistic, optimistic, pantheistic, pessimistic, pianistic, pietistic, plagiaristic, Platonistic, pluralistic, pointillistic, populistic, pugilistic, quietistic, realistic, Romanistic, sciolistic, shamanistic, shintoistic, socialistic, solecistic, solipsistic, specialistic, surrealistic, syllogistic, symbolistic, synchronistic, syncretistic, synergistic, terroristic, totalistic, totemistic, ultraistic, unrealistic, urbanistic, utopistic, vandalistic, verbalistic, vitalistic, voodooistic, voyeuristic, Zionistic, absolutistic, adventuristic, anachronistic, animalistic, anomalistic, antagonistic, behavioristic, cannibalistic, capitalistic, characteristic, collectivistic, contortionistic, deterministic, evangelistic, eudaemonistic, euhemeristic, expansionistic, expressionistic, extralinguistic, functionalistic, Hinayanistic, hypocoristic, immanentistic, impressionistic, liberalistic, literalistic, Mahayanistic, melioristic, mercantilistic, militaristic, mediumistic, metalinguistic, misogynistic, monopolistic, monotheistic, naturalistic, negativistic, neologistic, opportunistic, paternalistic, physicalistic, polytheistic, probabilistic, propagandistic, psycholinguistic, rationalistic, recidivistic, reductionistic, relativistic, revivalistic, ritualistic, secularistic, sensualistic, separatistic, sociolinguistic, somnambulistic, ventriloquistic, violinistic, voluntaristic, colonialistic, commercialistic, Deuteronomistic, emotionalistic, exhibitionistic, fundamentalistic, existentalistic, imperialistic, indeterministic, introspectionistic, irrationalistic, materialistic, oligopolistic, Postimpressionistic, sadomasochistic, sensationalistic, sociolinguistic, spiritualistic, traditionalistic, individualistic

istical \is-ti-kəl\ mystical, deistical, eristical, linguistical, logistical, monistical, patristical, sophistical, statistical, theistical, alchemistical, atheistical, casuistical, egoistical, egotistical, exorcistical, pantheistical, anomalistical, hypocoristical, monotheistical, polytheistical

istich \is-tik\ see ISTIC

istics \is-tiks\ ballistics, ekistics,

linguistics, logistics, patristics, statistics, stylistics, futuristics, criminalistics—*also plurals and possessives of nouns listed at* ISTIC

istie \is-tē\ see [2]ICITY

istil \is-tᵊl\ see ISTAL

istin \is-tən\ see ISTON

istine \is-tən\ see ISTON

istle \is-əl\ bristle, fissile, gristle, missal, missile, scissile, thistle, whistle, abyssal, dickcissel, dismissal, epistle, pennywhistle

istler \is-lər\ whistler, Whistler, epistler

istless \ist-ləs\ listless, resistless

istly \is-lē\ bristly, gristly, thistly, sweet cicely

istmas \is-məs\ Christmas, isthmus, Kiritimati

isto \is-tō\ aristo, Callisto

istol \is-tᵊl\ see ISTAL

iston \is-tən\ Kristin, piston, Tristan, Philistine, phlogiston, amethystine

istor \is-tər\ see ISTER

istory \is-trē\ blistery, history, mystery, consistory, prehistory

istral \is-trəl\ mistral, sinistral

istress \is-trəs\ mistress, headmistress, postmistress, schoolmistress, sinistrous, taskmistress, toastmistress

istrophe \is-trə-fē\ antistrophe, epistrophe

istrous \is-trəs\ see ISTRESS

isty \is-tē\ see [2]ICITY

isus \ī-səs\ see ISIS

iszt \ist\ see [2]IST

[1]it \it\ bit, bitt, brit, Brit, chit, dit, fit, flit, frit, git, grit, hit, it, kit, knit, lit, mitt, nit, pit, Pitt, quit, sit, skit, slit, snit, spit, split, Split, sprit, teat, tit, twit, whit, wit, writ, zit, acquit, admit, armpit, backbit, backfit, befit, bowsprit, Brigitte, bushtit, cesspit, close-knit, cockpit, commit, culprit, demit, Dewitt, dimwit, emit, fleapit, gaslit, godwit, half-wit, henbit, house-sit, legit, lit crit, misfit, mishit, moonlit, nitwit, obit, omit, outfit, outwit, peewit, permit, pinch-hit, Prakrit, pulpit, refit, remit, sandpit, Sanskrit, snakebit, starlit, submit, sunlit, switch-hit, tidbit, tight-knit, titbit, tomtit, transmit, turnspit,twilit, two-bit, unfit, unknit,well-knit, baby-sit, benefit,candlelit, counterfeit, hypocrite, intermit, intromit, manumit, megahit, recommit, retrofit, cost-benefit, lickety-split, overcommit, jack-in-the-pulpit

[2]it \ē\ see [1]EE

[3]it \ēt\ see [1]EAT

[1]ita \īt-ə\ vita, baryta, amanita

[2]ita \ēt-ə\ cheetah, eta, Greta, Nita, pita, Rita, theta, vita, zeta, Akita, Anita, Bonita, bonito, casita, excreta, Granita, Juanita, Lolita, mosquito, partita, Suita, amanita, arboreta, feterita, incognita, manzanita, margarita, senhorita, senorita, Bhagavad Gita

[1]itable \īt-ə-bəl\ citable,

writable, excitable, indictable, copyrightable, extraditable

²itable \it-ə-bəl\ see ITTABLE

itae \īt-ē\ see ²ITE

itain \it-n\ see ITTEN

¹ital \īt-ᵊl\ title, vital, detrital, entitle, nontitle, recital, requital, subtitle, disentitle, intravital, supravital

²ital \it-ᵊl\ see ITTLE

italer \it-ᵊl-ər\ whittler, victualler, belittler, Hospitaler

italist \īt-ᵊl-əst\ titlist, vitalist, recitalist

itan \īt-ᵊn\ see IGHTEN

itant \īt-ᵊnt\ mightn't, excitant, incitant, renitent

itany \it-ᵊn-ē\ Brittany, dittany, litany

itch \ich\ ditch, fitch, flitch, glitch, hitch, itch, kitsch, niche, pitch, quitch, rich, snitch, stitch, such, switch, twitch, which, witch, backstitch, bewitch, cross-stitch, enrich, fast-twitch, hemstitch, lockstitch, slow-pitch, slow-twitch, topstitch, unhitch, whipstitch, czarevitch, featherstitch, microswitch

itchen \ich-ən\ kitchen, richen

itchener \ich-nər\ Kitchener, Michener

itcher \ich-ər\ hitcher, pitcher, richer, snitcher, stitcher, switcher, enricher, hemstitcher, Lubavitcher, water witcher

itchery \ich-ə-rē\ bitchery, obituary, stitchery, witchery, bewitchery

itches \ich-əz\ britches, riches, Dutchman's-breeches—*also plurals and possessives of nouns and third person singular presents of verbs listed at* ITCH

itchman \ich-mən\ pitchman, switchman

itchment \ich-mənt\ bewitchment, enrichment

itchy \ich-ē\ bitchy, itchy, kitschy, pitchy, twitchy, witchy

it'd \it-əd\ see ITTED

¹ite \īt\ bight, bite, blight, bright, byte, cite, dight, dite, Dwight, fight, flight, fright, height, hight, kite, knight, krait, kyte, light, lite, might, mite, night, plight, quite, right, rite, sight, site, sleight, slight, smite, spite, sprite, tight, trite, white, White, wight, Wight, wite, wright, Wright, write, affright, airtight, albite, alight, all right, all-night, aright, backbite, backlight, bedight, Birchite, birthright, bobwhite, bombsight, bullfight, campsite, cockfight, contrite, Cushite, daylight, deadlight, delight, despite, dogfight, downright, droplight, earthlight, excite, eyebright, eyesight, fanlight, finite, firefight, firelight, fistfight, flashlight, fleabite, floodlight, foresight, forthright, fortnight, frostbite, Gadite, gaslight, gastight, ghostwrite, graphite, gunfight, Gunite, half-light, Hamite, handwrite, headlight, highlight, hindsight, Hittite, homesite, hoplite, Hussite, ignite, illite, infight, in-flight, incite, indict, indite, insight, invite, jacklight, jadeite, lamplight, Levite, lighttight, lignite, limelight, lintwhite, lowlight, Lucite, Luddite, lyddite, Melchite, midnight, millwright, miswrite, moonlight, night-light, off-site, off-white, on-site, outright, outsight, partite, penlight, playwright, polite, prizefight, pyrite, recite, requite, respite, rushlight, safelight, searchlight, Semite, Servite, Shemite, Shiite, shipwright, sidelight, skintight, skylight, skywrite, smectite, snakebite, snow-white, spaceflight, speedlight, spotlight, starlight, sticktight, stoplight, streetlight, sunlight, Sunnite, taillight, termite, tonight, torchlight, trothplight, twilight, twi-night, typewrite, unite, unsight, upright, uptight, wainwright, weeknight, wheelwright, acolyte, aconite, Ammonite, Amorite, amosite, anchorite, anthracite, antiwhite, apartheid, appetite, Bakelite, Benthamite, bipartite, black-and-white, blatherskite, bleacherite, chalcocite, Canaanite, Carmelite, castroite, catamite, cellulite, copyright, disinvite, disunite, dynamite, erudite, expedite, extradite, Fahrenheit, featherlight, fly-by-night, gelignite, gesundheit, gigabyte, Hashemite, Hepplewhite, Himyarite, Hitlerite, hug-me-tight, impolite, Ishmaelite, Israelite, Jacobite, Josephite, Kimberlite, laborite, Leninite, leukocyte, lily-white, localite, malachite, manganite, Marcionite, Masonite, Mennonite, Minorite, Moabite, muscovite, Nazirite, out-of-sight, overbite, overflight, overnight, oversight, overwrite, parasite, perovskite, plebiscite, proselyte, Puseyite, pyrrhotite, recondite, reunite, satellite, shergottite, socialite, sodalite, sodomite, Stagirite, stalactite, stalagmite, Sybarite, time-of-flight, transfinite, transvestite, tripartite, troglodyte, Trotskyite, ultralight, underwrite, urbanite, Wahhabite, watertight, Wycliffite, yesternight, adipocyte, anthophyllite, cosmopolite, exurbanite, gemütlichkeit, hermaphrodite, Indo-Hittite, McCarthyite, multipartite, quadripartite, suburbanite, theodolite, Areopagite, Pre-Raphaelite, Great Australian Bight

[2]**ite** \īt-ē\ flighty, mighty, nightie, righty, whitey, whity, almighty, Almighty, Venite, Aphrodite, aqua vitae, arborvitae, lignum vitae

[3]**ite** \it\ see [1]IT

[4]ite \ēt\ see [1]EAT
ited \īt-əd\ see IGHTED
iteful \īt-fəl\ see IGHTFUL
itely \īt-lē\ see IGHTLY
item \īt-əm\ item, ad infinitum
itement \īt-mənt\ alightment, excitement, incitement, indictment
iten \īt-ᵊn\ see IGHTEN
itener \īt-nər\ see IGHTENER
itent \īt-ᵊnt\ see ITANT
iteor \ēt-ē-ər\ see ETEOR
[1]iter \īt-ər\ blighter, fighter, lighter, miter, niter, titer, writer, all-nighter, braillewriter, exciter, first-nighter, lamplighter, nail-biter, one-nighter, prizefighter, screenwriter, scriptwriter, songwriter, speechwriter, sportswriter, states righter, typewriter, copywriter, expediter, fly-by-nighter, Gastarbeiter, underwriter, teletypewriter—*also nouns and comparatives of adjectives formed by adding* -er *to verbs listed at* [1]ITE
[2]iter \it-ər\ see ITTER
[3]iter \ēt-ər\ see [1]EATER
iteral \it-ə-rəl\ clitoral, literal, littoral, sublittoral, triliteral
iterally \it-ər-lē\ see ITTERLY
iterate \it-ə-rət\ literate, illiterate, nonliterate, postliterate, preliterate, presbyterate, subliterate, semiliterate
[1]ites \īt-ēz\ barytes, sorites, Thersites—*also plurals and possessives of nouns listed at* [2]ITE
[2]ites \īts\ see IGHTS
itey \īt-ē\ see [2]ITE
ith \ith\ fifth, frith, grith, kith, myth, pith, sith, smith, Smith, swith, with, withe, blacksmith, forthwith, goldsmith, Goldsmith, gunsmith, herewith, locksmith, songsmith, therewith, tinsmith, tunesmith, wherewith, whitesmith, wordsmith, coppersmith, eolith, Granny Smith, Hammersmith, megalith, metalsmith, microlith, monolith, neolith, silversmith, paleolith
[3]ith \ēt\ see [1]EAT
[4]ith \ēth\ see [1]EATH
[1]ithe \īth\ blithe, kithe, lithe, scythe, tithe, withe, writhe
[2]ithe \ith\ see [2]ITH
[3]ithe \ith\ see [1]ITH
[1]ithee \ith-ē\ see [2]ITHY
[2]ithee \ith-ē\ see [1]ITHY
ither \ith-ər\ blither, cither, dither, hither, slither, swither, thither, whither, wither, zither, come-hither, nowhither, somewhither
itherward \ith-ər-wərd\ thitherward, whitherward
ithesome \īth-səm\ blithesome, lithesome
ithia \ith-ē-ə\ see YTHIA
ithic \ith-ik\ lithic, ornithic, batholithic, Eolithic, granolithic, megalithic, Mesolithic, monolithic, neolithic, Paleolithic

ithing \ī-t͟hiŋ\ tithing, trithing
ithmic \it͟h-mik\ see YTHMIC
[1]ithy \it͟h-ē\ prithee, withy
[2]ithy \ith-ē\ mythy, pithy, prithee, smithy, withy
iti \ēt-ē\ see EATY
[1]itia \ish-ə\ Lycia, Mysia, wisha, Alicia, Cilicia, comitia, episcia, Galicia, indicia, Letitia, militia, Patricia, Phoenicia, Dionysia
[2]itia \ē-shə\ see [1]ESIA
itial \ish-əl\ see ICIAL
[1]itian \ish-ən\ see ITION
[2]itian \ē-shən\ see [1]ETION
itiate \ish-ət\ initiate, novitiate, uninitiate
itic \it-ik\ clitic, critic, arthritic, bronchitic, dendritic, enclitic, granitic, graphitic, Hamitic, jaditic, mephitic, proclitic, pruritic, rachitic, Sanskritic, Semitic, Shemitic, Sinitic, anaclitic, analytic, anchoritic, catalytic, cenobitic, copralitic, crystallitic, diacritic, dialytic, dynamitic, eremitic, Himyaritic, hypercritic, jesuitic, paralytic, parasitic, sodomitic, stalactitic, stalagmitic, sybaritic, thallophytic, thrombolytic, troglodytic, cryptanalytic, electrolytic, hermaphroditic, meteoritic, Monophysitic, psychoanalytic
itical \it-i-kəl\ critical, Levitical, political, analytical, apolitical, cenobitical, diacritical, eremitical, hypercritical, hypocritical, impolitical, Jacobitical, jesuitical, parasitical, sodomitical, supercritical, geopolitical, meteoritical, sociopolitical
itics \it-iks\ Semitics, analytics, meteoritics—*also plurals and possessives of nouns listed at* ITIC
itid \it-əd\ see ITTED
itimati \is-məs\ see ISTMAS
itin \īt-ᵊn\ see IGHTEN
iting \īt-iŋ\ biting, flyting, lighting, whiting, writing, backbiting, bullfighting, cockfighting, daylighting, exciting, freewriting, frostbiting, handwriting, infighting, inviting, newswriting, prewriting, prizefighting, skywriting, songwriting, sportswriting, typewriting
ition \ish-ən\ fission, hycian, mission, titian, Titian, addition, admission, ambition, attrition, audition, beautician, clinician, cognition, coition, commission, condition, contrition, demission, dentition, dismission, Domitian, edition, emission, ethician, fruition, ignition, lenition, logician, magician, monition, mortician, munition, musician, nutrition, omission, optician, partition, patrician, perdition, permission, petition, Phoenician, physician, position, punition, remission, rendition, sedition, submission, suspicion, tactician, technician, tradition,

transition, transmission, tuition, volition, abolition, acquisition, admonition, aesthetician, air-condition, ammunition, apparition, apposition, coalition, competition, composition, cosmetician, decommission, decondition, definition, demolition, deposition, dietitian, Dionysian, disposition, disquisition, electrician, erudition, exhibition, expedition, exposition, extradition, imposition, inhibition, inquisition, intermission, intromission, intuition, linguistician, logistician, malnutrition, malposition, manumission, mathematician, mechanician, micturition, obstetrician, opposition, Ordovician, parturition, phonetician, politician, precognition, precondition, premonition, preposition, prohibition, proposition, recognition, recondition, repetition, requisition, rhetorician, statistician, submunition, superstition, supposition, transposition, academician, arithmetician, decomposition, diagnostician, dialectician, disinhibition, geometrician, geriatrician, indisposition, interposition, juxtaposition, metaphysician, onomastician, pediatrician, presupposition, redefinition, semiotician, theoretician, superimposition

itionable \ish-nə-bəl\ see ISSIONABLE

itional \ish-ə-nəl\ additional, attritional, cognitional, coitional, conditional, nutritional, positional, traditional, transitional, tuitional, volitional, apparitional, appositional, compositional, definitional, depositional, expositional, inquisitional, oppositional, prepositional, propositional, repetitional, suppositional, transpositional, unconditional, juxtapositional, presuppositional

itioner \i-shə-nər\ missioner, commissioner, conditioner, parishioner, partitioner, petitioner, practitioner, exhibitioner, malpractitioner, nurse-practitioner

itionist \i-shə-nəst\ nutritionist, partitionist, abolitionist, coalitionist, demolitionist, exhibitionist, intuitionist, oppositionist, prohibitionist

itious \ish-əs\ see [1]ICIOUS

itis \īt-əs\ situs, Titus, arthritis, botrytis, bronchitis, bursitis, colitis, cystitis, detritus, gastritis, iritis, mastitis, nephritis, neuritis, phlebitis, dermatitis, enteritis, gingivitis, hepatitis, Heracleitus, ileitis, laryngitis, meningitis, pharyngitis, pneumonitis, prostatitis, retinitis, sinusitis, tonsillitis, spondylitis, tendinitis, urethritis, vaginitis, appendicitis, conjunctivitis, encephalitis, endocarditis, endometritus, folliculitis, Hermaphroditus, peritonitis, analysis situs, diverticulitis, gastroenteritis, poliomyelitis

itish \it-ish\ British, skittish

itius \ish-əs\ see ICIOUS

itle \īt-ᵊl\ see [1]ITAL

it'll \it-ᵊl\ see ITTLE

itment \it-mənt\ fitment, commitment, remitment, recommitment, overcommitment

itness \it-nəs\ fitness, witness, earwitness, eyewitness, unfitness

itney \it-nē\ jitney, Whitney, Mount Whitney

[1]**ito** \ēt-ō\ keto, Leto, Quito, Tito, veto, bonito, burrito, graffito, magneto, Miskito, mosquito, Negrito, Hirohito, incognito, sanbenito

[2]**ito** \ēt-ə\ see [2]ITA

[1]**iton** \it-ᵊn\ see ITTEN

[2]**iton** \īt-ᵊn\ see IGHTEN

itoral \it-ə-rəl\ see ITERAL

itra \ē-trə\ see [2]ETRA

itral \ī-trəl\ mitral, nitrile

itrile \ī-trəl\ see ITRAL

it's \its\ see ITS

its \its\ blitz, ditz, Fritz, glitz, grits, it's, its, quits, spitz, Chemnitz, Saint Kitts, slivovitz—*also plurals and possessives of nouns and third person singular presents of verbs listed at* [1]IT

itsail \it-səl\ see ITZEL

itsch \ich\ see ITCH

itschy \ich-ē\ see ITCHY

itsy \it-sē\ see ITZY

itt \it\ see [1]IT

itta \it-ə\ shittah, vitta

ittable \it-ə-bəl\ committable, habitable, hospitable, remittable, transmittable, inhospitable

ittah \it-ə\ see ITTA

ittal \it-ᵊl\ see ITTLE

ittance \it-ᵊns\ pittance, quittance, acquittance, admittance, emittance, immittance, remittance, transmittance, intermittence

ittany \it-ᵊn-ē\ see ITANY

itte \it\ see [1]IT

itted \it-əd\ fitted, it'd, nitid, pitted, teated, witted, committed, dim-witted, half-witted, quick-witted, sharp-witted, slow-witted, thick-witted, unbitted, unfitted, uncommitted—*also pasts of verbs listed at* [1]IT

ittee \it-ē\ see ITTY

itten \it-ᵊn\ bitten, Britain, Briton, Britten, kitten, litten, Lytton, mitten, smitten, witting, written, backbitten, flea-bitten, Great Britain, hard-bitten, New Britain, rewritten, snakebitten, unwritten

ittence \it-ᵊns\ see ITTANCE

ittent \it-ᵊnt\ remittent, intermittent, intromittent

itter \it-ər\ bitter, chitter, critter, fitter, flitter, fritter, glitter, hitter, jitter, knitter, litter, quitter, quittor, sitter, skitter, slitter, spitter, titter, twitter, aglitter, atwitter, bed-sitter, embitter, emitter, hairsplitter, no-hitter, outfitter, rail-splitter, remitter, shipfitter, steamfitter, switch-hitter, transmitter, benefiter, counterfeiter, intromitter

itterer \it-ər-ər\ fritterer, litterer, twitterer

itterly \it-ər-lē\ bitterly, literally

ittern \it-ərn\ bittern, cittern, gittern

ittery \it-ə-rē\ glittery, jittery, littery, skittery, twittery

ittie \it-ē\ see ITTY

ittier \it-ē-ər\ grittier, prettier, Whittier, wittier

ittiness \it-ē-nəs\ grittiness, prettiness, wittiness

[1]itting \it-iŋ\ fitting, sitting, splitting, witting, befitting, earsplitting, fence-sitting, formfitting, hairsplitting, hard-hitting, house-sitting, resitting, sidesplitting, unfitting, unwitting, unremitting

[2]itting \it-ᵊn\ see ITTEN

ittish \it-ish\ see ITISH

ittle \it-ᵊl\ brittle, it'll, kittle, little, skittle, spital, spittle, tittle, victual, whittle, wittol, acquittal, belittle, committal, embrittle, hospital, lickspittle, remittal, transmittal, noncommittal, recommittal

ittler \it-ᵊl-ər\ see ITALER

ittol \it-ᵊl\ see ITTLE

ittor \it-ər\ see ITTER

ittoral \it-ə-rəl\ see ITERAL

itts \its\ see ITS

itty \it-ē\ bitty, city, ditty, gritty, kitty, Kitty, pity, pretty, tittie, witty, committee, self-pity, itty-bitty, Kansas City, megacity, nitty-gritty, Salt Lake City, subcommittee, supercity, Walter Mitty, Ho Chi Minh City

itual \ich-ə-wəl\ ritual, habitual

ituary \ich-ə-rē\ see [1]ITCHERY

itum \īt-əm\ see ITEM

itus \īt-əs\ see ITIS

[1]ity \it-ē\ see ITTY

[2]ity \īt-ē\ see [2]ITE

itz \its\ see ITS

[1]itza \ēt-sə\ pizza, czaritza, Chichén Itza, Katowice

[2]itza \it-sə\ czaritza, tamburitza

itzel \it-səl\ schnitzel, spritsail, Wiener schnitzel

itzi \it-sē\ see ITZY

itzy \it-sē\ bitsy, glitzy, Mitzi, ritzy, schizy

iu \ü\ see [1]EW

[1]ius \ē-əs\ see [1]EUS

[2]ius \ī-əs\ see [1]IAS

[1]iv \iv\ see [2]IVE

[2]iv \ēf\ see [1]IEF

[3]iv \if\ see IFF

[4]iv \ēv\ see EAVE

[1]iva \ī-və\ Saiva, gingiva, Godiva, saliva

[2]iva \ē-və\ diva, Eva, kiva, Shiva, siva, Siva, viva, geneva, Geneva, yeshiva

[3]iva \iv-ə\ Shiva, Siva

[1]ivable \ī-və-bəl\ drivable, derivable, revivable, survivable

[2]ivable \iv-ə-bəl\ livable, forgivable

ival \ī-vəl\ rival, archival, arrival, revival, survival,

adjectival, conjunctival, genitival, substantival, infinitival
ivalent \iv-ə-lənt\ ambivalent, equivalent, unambivalent
ivan \iv-ən\ see IVEN
ivance \ī-vəns\ connivance, contrivance, survivance
ivative \iv-ət-iv\ privative, derivative
[1]**ive** \īv\ chive, dive, drive, five, gyve, hive, I've, jive, live, rive, shrive, skive, strive, thrive, wive, alive, archive, Argive, arrive, beehive, connive, contrive, deprive, derive, endive, nosedive, ogive, revive, self-drive, skin-dive, survive, test-drive, forty-five, overdrive, power-dive
[2]**ive** \iv\ give, live, sheave, shiv, sieve, spiv, forgive, misgive, outlive, relive, unlive, underactive
[3]**ive** \ēv\ see [1]EAVE
ivel \iv-əl\ civil, drivel, frivol, shrivel, snivel, swivel
iven \iv-ən\ driven, given, riven, Sivan, striven, thriven, forgiven, menu-driven
[1]**iver** \ī-vər\ diver, driver, fiver, arriver, cabdriver, conniver, contriver, deriver, reviver, screwdriver, survivor
[2]**iver** \iv-ər\ flivver, giver, liver, quiver, river, shiver, sliver, almsgiver, aquiver, deliver, downriver, forgiver, lawgiver, quicksilver, upriver, Guadalquivir
[1]**ivers** \ī-vərz\ divers, vivers—*also plurals and possessives of nouns listed at* [1]IVER
[2]**ivers** \ē-vərz\ see EAVERS
ivery \iv-rē\ livery, shivery, delivery
ives \īvz\ fives, hives, Ives—*also plurals and possessives of nouns and third person singular presents of verbs listed at* [1]IVE
ivet \iv-ət\ civet, divot, pivot, privet, rivet, swivet, trivet
[1]**ivi** \iv-ē\ see IVVY
[2]**ivi** \ē-vē\ see EAVEY
ivia \iv-ē-ə\ Bolivia, Olivia
ivial \iv-ē-əl\ trivial, convivial, quadrivial
ivid \iv-əd\ livid, vivid
ivil \iv-əl\ see IVEL
ivilly \iv-ə-lē\ civilly, privily, uncivilly
ivily \iv-ə-lē\ see IVILLY
iving \iv-iŋ\ giving, living, almsgiving, forgiving, free-living, misgiving, thanksgiving
ivion \iv-ē-ən\ Vivian, oblivion
ivious \iv-ē-əs\ lascivious, oblivious
ivir \iv-ər\ see [2]IVER
ivity \iv-ət-ē\ privity, acclivity, activity, captivity, declivity, festivity, motivity, nativity, proclivity, absorptivity, adaptivity, additivity, affectivity, aggressivity, coercivity, cognitivity, collectivity, compulsivity, conductivity, connectivity, creativity, destructivity, diffusivity, directivity, effectivity, emissivity,

emotivity, exclusivity, exhaustivity, expansivity, expressivity, impassivity, inactivity, infectivity, negativity, perceptivity, perfectivity, permittivity, positivity, primitivity, productivity, progressivity, reactivity, receptivity, reflexivity, relativity, resistivity, retentivity, selectivity, sensitivity, subjectivity, susceptivity, transitivity, distributivity, hyperactivity, insensitivity, overactivity, retroactivity, radioactivity, hypersensitivity

ivium \iv-ē-əm\ trivium, quadrivium

iviut \ē-vē-ət\ see EVIATE

ivo \ē-vō\ see EVO

ivocal \iv-ə-kəl\ equivocal, univocal, unequivocal

ivol \iv-əl\ see IVEL

ivor \ī-vər\ see [1]IVER

ivorous \iv-rəs\ carnivorous, granivorous, omnivorous, insectivorous

ivot \iv-ət\ see IVET

ivus \ē-vəs\ see EVOUS

ivver \iv-ər\ see [2]IVER

ivvy \iv-ē\ chivy, civvy, divvy, Livy, privy, skivvy, tantivy, divi-divi

ivy \iv-ē\ see IVVY

iw \ef\ see [1]EF

iwi \ē-wē\ see EEWEE

[1]ix \iks\ Brix, Dix, fix, mix, nix, pyx, six, Styx, admix, affix, blanc fixe, commix, deep-six, immix, infix, postfix, prefix, premix, prix fixe, prolix, subfix, suffix, transfix, unfix, antefix, cicatrix, crucifix, eighty-six, intermix, politics, six-o-six, superfix, geopolitics, RU 486—*also plurals and possessives of nouns and third person singular presents of verbs listed at* ICK

[2]ix \ē\ see [1]EE

ixal \ik-səl\ pixel, affixal, prefixal, suffixal

[1]ixe \ēks\ breeks, prix fixe, idée fixe, Macgillicuddy's Reeks—*also plurals and possessives of nouns and third person singular presents of verbs listed at* [1]EAK

[2]ixe \iks\ see [1]IX

[3]ixe \ēsh\ see [2]ICHE

ixed \ikst\ fixed, mixed, twixt, betwixt, well-fixed—*also pasts of verbs listed at* [1]IX

ixel \ik-səl\ see IXAL

ixen \ik-sən\ vixen, Nixon, Mason-Dixon

ixer \ik-sər\ fixer, mixer, elixir

ixia \ik-sē-ə\ asphyxia, panmixia

ixie \ik-sē\ Dixie, nixie, Nixie, pixie, pyxie, tricksy

ixion \ik-shən\ see ICTION

ixir \ik-sər\ see IXER

ixit \ik-sət\ quixote, ipse dixit

ixon \ik-sən\ see IXEN

ixote \ik-sət\ see IXIT

ixt \ikst\ see IXED

ixture \iks-chər\ fixture, mixture, admixture, commixture, intermixture

iya \ē-ə\ see [1]IA

iyeh \ē-ə\ see [1]IA

¹iz \iz\ biz, fizz, frizz, his, is, Ms., phiz, quiz, 'tis, whiz, wiz, gee-whiz, show biz

²iz \ēz\ see EZE

¹iza \ē-zə\ see EZA

²iza \ē-thə\ see ETHA

izabeth \iz-ə-bəth\ Elisabeth, Elizabeth, Port Elizabeth

izable \ī-zə-bəl\ sizable, advisable, cognizable, devisable, excisable, amortizable, analyzable, criticizable, dramatizable, exercisable, fertilizable, hypnotizable, inadvisable, localizable, magnetizable, mechanizable, memorizable, pulverizable, recognizable, vaporizable, computerizable, generalizable, uncompromisable

izar \ī-zər\ see IZER

izard \iz-ərd\ blizzard, gizzard, izzard, lizard, vizard, wizard

¹ize \īz\ guise, prise, prize, rise, size, wise, abscise, advise, apprise, apprize, arise, assize, baptize, breadthwise, capsize, chastise, clockwise, cognize, comprise, crabwise, crosswise, demise, despise, devise, disguise, disprize, downsize, earthrise, edgewise, emprise, endwise, excise, fanwise, franchise, full-size, grecize, high-rise, incise, king-size, leastwise, lengthwise, Levi's, life-size, likewise, low-rise, man-size, midsize, misprize, moonrise, nowise, outsize, piecewise, pint-size, premise, quantize, remise, reprise, revise, slantwise, streetwise, stylize, suffice, sunrise, surmise, surprise, twin-size, uprise, advertise, aggrandize, agonize, alchemize, amortize, analyze, anglicize, anywise, aphorize, arabize, atomize, authorize, autolyze, balkanize, barbarize, bastardize, bestialize, bolshevize, botanize, bowdlerize, brutalize, burglarize, canalize, canonize, capsulize, caramelize, carbonize, cartelize, catalyze, catechize, cauterize, centralize, channelize, Christianize, cicatrize, circumcise, civilize, classicize, colonize, communize, compromise, concertize, concretize, creolize, criticize, crystalize, customize, demonize, deputize, dialyze, digitize, disfranchise, dogmatize, dramatize, elegize, empathize, emphasize, energize, enfranchise, enterprise, equalize, erotize, eternize, etherize, eulogize, euphemize, exercise, exorcise, factorize, fantasize, fascistize, feminize, fertilize, feudalize, fictionize, finalize, formalize, formulize, fossilize, fragmentize, fraternize, gallicize, galvanize, germanize, ghettoize, glamorize, globalize, gormandize, gothicize, gourmandize, grecianize, harmonize, heathenize, hebraize, hellenize, hierarchize, humanize, hybridize, hypnotize, idolize, immunize, improvise, ionize, ironize, Islamize, itemize, jeopardize, journalize, Judaize, laicize, latinize, legalize, lionize, liquidize, localize, magnetize, marbleize, martyrize, maximize, mechanize, melanize, melodize, memorize, merchandise, mesmerize, methodize, metricize, minimize, mobilize, modernize, moisturize, monetize, mongrelize, moralize, motorize, mythicize, narcotize, nasalize, neutralize, normalize, notarize, novelize, obelize, odorize, optimize, organize, ostracize, otherwise, oversize, oxidize, paganize, paradise, paralyze, pasteurize, patronize, pauperize, penalize, penny-wise, pidginize, plagiarize, plasticize, Platonize, pluralize, pocket-size, poetize, polarize, polemize, pressurize, privatize, prussianize, publicize, pulverize, randomize, realize, recognize, rhapsodize, robotize, romanize, rubberize, sanitize, satirize, scandalize, schematize, schismatize, scrutinize, sensitize, sermonize, signalize, simonize, sinicize, slenderize, sloganize, socialize, sodomize, solarize, sonnetize, specialize, stabilize, Stalinize, standardize, sterilize, stigmatize, strategize, subsidize, summarize, supervise, syllogize, symbolize, sympathize, synchronize, syncretize, synopsize, synthesize, systemize, tantalize, televise, temporize, tenderize, terrorize, tetanize, teutonize, texturize, theorize, thermalize, totalize, tranquilize, traumatize, tyrannize, unionize, unitize, urbanize, utilize, valorize, vandalize, vaporize, verbalize, vernalize, victimize, vitalize, vocalize, vulcanize, vulgarize, weather-wise, weatherize, westernize, winterize, womanize, worldly-wise, accessorize, acclimatize, actualize, allegorize, alphabetize, analogize, anatomize, anesthetize, animalize, annualize, antagonize, anthologize, anticlockwise, apologize, apostatize, apostrophize, arabicize, aromatize, baby blue-eyes, bureaucratize, cannibalize, capitalize, categorize, catholicize, characterize, commercialize, communalize, computerize, conservatize, containerize, contrariwise, conveyorize, cosmeticize, counterclockwise, criminalize, cryptanalize, decentralize, decolonize, de-emphasize, de-energize, dehumanize, deionize, demagnetize, demobilize, democratize, demoralize, deodorize, depersonalize, depolarize, desalinize, desensitize, destabilize, digitalize, disenfranchise, disorganize, economize, emotionalize, epitomize, epoxidize, eroticize, eternalize, euthanatize, evangelize, extemporize, externalize, familiarize, fanaticize, federalize, fictionalize, formularize, gelatinize, generalize, geologize, Hispanicize, homogenize, hospitalize, hypothesize, idealize, illegalize, immobilize, immortalize, impersonalize, Indianize, indigenize, initialize, internalize, italicize, legitimize, liberalize, literalize, lobotomize, lysogenize, macadamize, metabolize, metastasize, militarize, mineralize, monopolize, mythologize, nationalize, naturalize, parenthesize, philosophize, politicize, popularize, proselytize, regularize, reorganize, revitalize, romanticize, secularize, sexualize, sovietize, subjectivize, suburbanize, subvocalize, systematize, temporalize, theologize, traditionalize, transistorize, trivialize, ventriloquize, visualize, Americanize, apotheosize, colonialize, compartmentalize, conceptualize, contextualize, decriminalize, demilitarize, denaturalize, departmentalize, depoliticize, desexualize, Europeanize, exteriorize, ideologize, immaterialize, individualize, industrialize, internationalize, legitimatize, materialize, miniaturize, particularize, politicalize, phychoanalyze, self-actualize, sentimentalize, spiritualize, underutilize, universalize, constitutionalize, dematerialize, editorialize, intellectualize, deinstitutionalize—*also plurals and possessives of nouns and third person singular presents of verbs listed at* [1]Y

[2]**ize** \ēz\ see EZE

ized \īzd\ sized, advised, outsized, ergotized, ill-advised, pearlized, Sanforized, unadvised, undersized, varisized, well-advised, elasticized, modularized, unexercised, immunocompromised—*also pasts of verbs listed at* IZE

[1]**izen** \īz-ᵊn\ bison, dizen, greisen, bedizen, horizon, spiegeleisen

[2]**izen** \iz-ᵊn\ see [2]ISON

izer \ī-zər\ Dreiser, geyser, kaiser, miser, prizer, riser, sizar, visor, wiser, adviser, divisor, incisor, appetizer, atomizer, energizer, enterpriser, equalizer, exerciser, fertilizer, organizer, oxidizer, stabilizer, supervisor, synthesizer, totalizer, tranquilizer, tyrannizer, vaporizer, complementizer, deodorizer—*also nouns formed by adding* -er *to verbs listed at* IZE

izing \ī-ziŋ\ rising, sizing, uprising, appetizing, enterprising, merchandising, self-sufficing, unsurprising, self-sacrificing, uncompromising

[1]izo \ē-zō\ sleazo, chorizo, mestizo

[2]izo \ē-sō\ see ISO

izon \īz-ᵊn\ see [1]IZEN

izy \it-sē\ see ITZY

izz \iz\ see [1]IZ

izza \ēt-sə\ see [1]ITZA

izzard \iz-ərd\ see IZARD

izzen \iz-ᵊn\ see [2]ISON

izzer \iz-ər\ see ISSOR

izzical \iz-i-kəl\ see YSICAL

izzie \i-zē\ see IZZY

izzle \iz-əl\ chisel, drizzle, fizzle, frizzle, grizzle, mizzle, pizzle, sizzle, swizzle

izzled \iz-əld\ chiseled, grizzled—*also pasts of verbs listed at* IZZLE

izzler \iz-lər\ chiseler, sizzler, swizzler

izzly \iz-lē\ drizzly, grisly, grizzly, mizzly

izzy \iz-ē\ busy, dizzy, fizzy, frizzy, tizzy, tin lizzie

O

[1]**o** \ü\ see [1]EW

[2]**o** \ō\ see [1]OW

[3]**o** \ər\ see [1]EUR

[1]**oa** \ō-ə\ boa, Goa, koa, moa, Noah, proa, stoa, aloha, balboa, Balboa, jerboa, Samoa, Krakatoa, Mauna Loa, Shenandoah, Sinaloa, Guanabacoa, João Pessoa

[2]**oa** \ō\ see [1]OW

oable \ü-ə-bəl\ see UABLE

oach \ōch\ broach, brooch, coach, loach, poach, roach, abroach, approach, caroche, cockroach, encroach, reproach, stagecoach

oachable \ō-chə-bəl\ coachable, approachable, inapproachable, irreproachable, unapproachable

oacher \ō-chər\ broacher, coacher, cloture, poacher, encroacher

[1]**oad** \ōd\ see ODE

[2]**oad** \ȯd\ see [1]AUD

oader \ōd-ər\ see ODER

oadie \ōd-ē\ see [2]ODY

oady \ōd-ē\ see [2]ODY

oaf \ōf\ loaf, oaf, qoph, meatloaf, witloof, sugarloaf

oafer \ō-fər\ see OFER

oagie \ō-gē\ see OGIE

oah \ō-ə\ see [1]OA

oak \ōk\ see OKE

oaken \ō-kən\ see OKEN

oaker \ō-kər\ see OKER

oakum \ō-kəm\ see OKUM

oaky \ō-kē\ see OKY

oal \ōl\ see [1]OLE

oalie \ō-lē\ see [1]OLY

[1]**oam** \ō-əm\ see [1]OEM

[2]**oam** \ōm\ see [1]OME

oamer \ō-mər\ see [1]OMER

oaming \ō-miŋ\ coaming, combing, gloaming, Wyoming—*also present participles of verbs listed at* [1]OME

oamy \ō-mē\ foamy, homey, loamy, show-me, Suomi, Dahomey, Naomi, Salome

[1]**oan** \ō-ən\ Owen, roan, rowan, Minoan, Samoan, waygoing, Eskimoan, protozoan

[2]**oan** \ōn\ see [1]ONE

oaner \ō-nər\ see [1]ONER

oaning \ō-niŋ\ see [2]ONING

oap \ōp\ see OPE

oaper \ō-pər\ see OPER

oapy \ō-pē\ see OPI

oar \ōr\ see [1]OR

oard \ōrd\ board, bored, chord, cord, cored, floored, ford, Ford, gourd, hoard, horde, lord, Lord, oared, pored, poured, sward, sword, toward, ward, Ward, aboard, accord, afford, award, backboard, backsword, baseboard, billboard, blackboard, breadboard, broadsword, buckboard, cardboard, chalkboard, chessboard, chipboard, clapboard, clipboard, concord, corkboard, dashboard, discord, duckboard, fjord, flashboard, floorboard, footboard, freeboard, garbord, Gaylord, greensward, hardboard, headboard, inboard, keyboard, kickboard, landlord, lapboard, leeboard, longsword, matchboard, moldboard, onboard, outboard, packboard, pasteboard, patchboard, pegboard, pressboard, punchboard, rearward, record, reward, sailboard, scoreboard, seaboard, shipboard, sideboard, signboard, skateboard, slumlord, smallsword, snowboard, soundboard, splashboard, springboard, surfboard, switchboard, tailboard, untoward, wallboard, washboard, word-hoard, warlord, whipcord, aboveboard, bungee cord, centerboard, checkerboard, clavichord, disaccord, fiberboard, fingerboard, harpsichord, mortarbord, motherboard, overboard, overlord, paddleboard, paperboard, pinafored, plasterboard, pompadoured, shuffleboard, smorgasbord, storyboard, teeterboard, tetrachord, untoward, weatherboard, misericord, particleboard—*also pasts of verbs listed at* [1]OR

oarder \ōrd-ər\ boarder, hoarder, keyboarder, skateboarder, surfboarder

oarding \ōrd-iŋ\ boarding, hoarding, skateboarding, weatherboarding

oared \ōrd\ see OARD

[1]**oarer** \ōr-ər\ see [1]ORER

[2]**oarer** \ȯr-ər\ see [1]ORRER

oaring \ōr-iŋ\ see ORING

oarious \ȯr-ē-əs\ see ORIOUS

oarish \ȯr-ish\ see [1]ORISH

[1]**oarse** \ōrs\ see [1]OURSE

[2]**oarse** \ȯrs\ see [1]ORSE

oarsen \ōrs-^{ə}n\ coarsen, hoarsen, whoreson

oarsman \ōrz-mən\ oarsman, outdoorsman

oart \ȯrt\ see [1]ORT

oary \ōr-ē\ see ORY

oast \ōst\ see [2]OST

oastal \ōs-t^{ə}l\ see [1]OSTAL

oaster \ō-stər\ coaster, poster, roaster, throwster, toaster, billposter, four-poster, roller-coaster, roller coaster

oasty \ō-stē\ see OSTY

oat \ōt\ bloat, boat, coat, cote, dote, float, gloat, goat, groat, haute, moat, mote, note, oat, phot, quote, rote, shoat, smote, stoat, throat, tote, vote, wrote, afloat, airboat, bareboat, bluecoat, bumboat, capote, catboat, compote, connote, coyote, cutthroat, demote, denote, devote, dovecote, eighth note, emote, endnote, fireboat, fistnote, flatboat, footnote, greatcoat, gunboat, half note, headnote, Hohhot, houseboat, housecoat, iceboat, keelboat, keynote, lifeboat, longboat, one-note, pigboat, promote, Q-boat, quarter note, raincoat, Rajkot, redcoat, remote, rewrote, rowboat, sailboat, scapegoat, sheepcote, showboat, speedboat, steamboat, stoneboat, Sukkot, Sukkoth, surfboat, tailcoat, topcoat, towboat, tugboat, turncoat, U-boat, unquote, wainscot, whaleboat, whitethroat, whole note, woodnote, workboat, anecdote, antidote, asymptote, creosote, entrecote, ferryboat, Huhehot, motorboat, overcoat, paddleboat, papillote, petticoat, powerboat, redingote, riverboat, rubythroat, Shabuoth, Sialkot, sugarcoat, symbiote, table d'hôte, sixteenth note, undercoat, yellowthroat, thirty-second note

oate \ō-ət\ see [1]OET

oated \ōt-əd\ coated, noted, throated, devoted, tailcoated, petticoated—*also pasts of verbs listed at* OAT

oaten \ōt-^{ə}n\ see OTON

oater \ōt-ər\ bloater, boater, coater, doter, floater, gloater, motor, noter, oater, rotor, scoter, toter, voter, houseboater, iceboater, keynoter, promoter, pulmotor, sailboater, tilt-rotor, trimotor, locomotor, motorboater

oath \ōth\ see OWTH

oathe \ōth\ see OTHE

oathing \ō-thiŋ\ see OTHING

oating \ōt-iŋ\ boating, coating, floating, free floating, sailboating, scapegoating, speedboating, wainscoting, motorboating, undercoating—*also present participles of verbs listed at* OAT

oatswain \ōs-^{ə}n\ see OSIN

oaty \ōt-ē\ see [1]OTE

oax \ōks\ coax, hoax—*also plurals and possessives of nouns and third person singular presents of verbs listed at* OKE

[1]ob \äb\ Ab, blob, bob, Bob, cob, daub, fob, glob, gob, hob, job, knob, lob, mob, nob, Ob, rob, slob, snob, sob, squab, stob, swab, throb, yob, bedaub, corncob, demob, doorknob, heartthrob, hobnob, kabob, macabre, nabob, nawab, Punjab, skibob, memsahib, shish kebab, thingamabob

[2]ob \ōb\ see [1]OBE

oba \ō-bə\ arroba, jojoba, algaroba, Manitoba

obably \äb-lē\ see OBBLY

obal \ō-bəl\ see OBLE

obally \ō-bə-lē\ globally, primum mobile

obar \ō-bər\ see OBER

obber \äb-ər\ bobber, caber, clobber, cobber, jobber, robber, slobber, swabber, throbber, hobnobber, Micawber, Skibobber, stockjobber

obbery \äb-rē\ bobbery, jobbery, robbery, slobbery, snobbery, corroboree
obbes \äbz\ Hobbes—*also possessives and plurals of nouns and third person singular presents of verbs listed at* OB
obbet \äb-ət\ gobbet, probit
obbie \äb-ē\ see OBBY
obbin \äb-ən\ see OBIN
obbish \äb-ish\ slobbish, snobbish
obble \äb-əl\ see [1]ABBLE
obbler \äb-lər\ cobbler, gobbler, hobbler, nobbler, squabbler, wobbler
obbly \äb-lē\ knobbly, probably, wobbly, Wobbly
obby \äb-ē\ Bobbie, bobby, Bobby, cobby, dobby, globby, hobby, knobby, lobby, nobby, snobby, swabbie, Mesabi, Punjabi, Wahhabi, Abu Dhabi, Hammurabi
[1]**obe** \ōb\ daube, globe, Job, lobe, probe, robe, strobe, bathrobe, conglobe, disrobe, earlobe, enrobe, microbe, wardrobe, Anglophobe, claustrophobe, Francophobe, homophobe, negrophobe, xenophobe, ailurophobe, computerphobe
[2]**obe** \ō-bē\ see OBY
obeah \ō-bē-ə\ see OBIA
obee \ō-bē\ see OBY
obelus \äb-ə-ləs\ see ABILIS
ober \ō-bər\ lobar, sober, October
obi \ō-bē\ see OBY
obia \ō-bē-ə\ cobia, obeah, phobia, acrophobia, algophobia, Anglophobia, claustrophobia, homophobia, hydrophobia, negrophobia, photophobia, technophobia, xenophobia, agoraphobia, triskaidekaphobia
obic \ō-bik\ phobic, aerobic, anaerobic, claustrophobic, homophobic, hydrophobic, photophobic, xenophobic
[1]**obile** \ō-bə-lē\ see OBALLY
[2]**obile** \ō-bəl\ see OBLE
obin \äb-ən\ bobbin, dobbin, graben, robin, Robin, Robyn, round-robin
[1]**obit** \ō-bət\ obit, Tobit, post-obit
[2]**obit** \äb-ət\ see OBBET
oble \ō-bəl\ coble, global, mobile, noble, airmobile, ennoble, Grenoble, ignoble, immobile, San Cristóbal
obo \ō-bō\ gobo, hobo, kobo, lobo, oboe, adobo
oboe \ō-bō\ see OBO
obol \äb-əl\ see [1]ABBLE
oboree \äb-ə-rē\ see OBBERY
obot \ō-bət\ see [1]OBIT
obra \ō-brə\ cobra, dobra
obster \äb-stər\ lobster, mobster
obular \äb-yə-lər\ globular, lobular
obule \äb-yül\ globule, lobule
oby \ō-bē\ Gobi, goby, Kobe, obi, Obie, toby, Toby, adobe, Nairobi, Okeechobee
obyn \äb-ən\ see OBIN
[1]**oc** \ōk\ see OKE
[2]**oc** \äk\ see [1]OCK
[3]**oc** \ȯk\ see ALK
oca \ō-kə\ coca, mocha, oca,

Asoka, carioca, Fukuoka, mandioca, Shizuoka, tapioca
ocable \ō-kə-bəl\ smokable, vocable, evocable
ocage \äk-ij\ see OCKAGE
ocal \ō-kəl\ focal, local, socle, vocal, yokel, bifocal, subvocal, trifocal, unvocal
ocally \ō-kə-lē\ locally, vocally
ocative \äk-ət-iv\ locative, vocative, evocative, provocative
occa \äk-ə\ see [1]AKA
occer \äk-ər\ see OCKER
occie \äch-ē\ see OTCHY
occhi \ȯ-kē\ see ALKIE
occo \äk-ō\ socko, taco, cheechako, guanaco, morocco, Morocco, scirocco, sirocco
occule \äk-yül\ floccule, locule
occulent \äk-yə-lənt\ flocculent, inoculant
occulus \äk-yə-ləs\ flocculus, loculus, oculus
oce \ō-chē\ see [1]OCHE
ocean \ō-shən\ see OTION
ocent \ōs-ᵊnt\ docent, nocent
ocess \äs-əs\ Knossos, process, colossus, proboscis
[1]**och** \ōk\ see OKE
[2]**och** \äk\ see [1]OCK
[3]**och** \ȯsh\ see [2]ASH
[4]**och** \ȯk\ see ALK
ocha \ō-kə\ see OCA
ochal \äk-əl\ see OCKLE
ochan \ä-k̲ən\ see ACHEN
[1]**oche** \ō-chē\ Kochi, Sochi, penoche, sotto voce, veloce, mezza voce
[2]**oche** \ōsh\ cloche, gauche, skosh, brioche, caroche, guilloche
[3]**oche** \ō-kē\ see OKY
[4]**oche** \ōch\ see OACH
[5]**oche** \ȯsh\ see [2]ASH
ochee \ō-kē\ see OKY
ocher \ō-kər\ see OKER
ochi \ō-chē\ see [1]OCHE
ochle \ək-əl\ see UCKLE
ochs \äks\ see OX
ochum \ō-kəm\ see OKUM
ocia \ō-shə\ see [1]OTIA
ociable \ō-shə-bəl\ sociable, associable, dissociable, insociable, negotiable, unsociable, indissociable, renegotiable
ocial \ō-shəl\ social, asocial, dissocial, precocial, unsocial, antisocial
ocile \äs-əl\ see OSSAL
ocious \ō-shəs\ atrocious, ferocious, precocious, Theodosius
[1]**ock** \äk\ Bach, bloc, block, bock, brock, chock, clock, cock, croc, crock, doc, dock, floc, flock, frock, hock, Jacque, Jacques, jock, knock, lakh, loch, lock, Locke, lough, Mach, moc, mock, nock, pock, roc, rock, schlock, shock, smock, sock, stock, wok, yak, yock, acock, ad hoc, aftershock, amok, Arak, backblock, Balzac, bangkok, Bangkok, baroque, Bartok, bawcock, bedrock, bemock, bibcock, bitstock, blackcock, blesbok, bloodstock, bois d'arc, Brecknock, breechblock,

burdock, buttstock, caprock, coldcock, Comstock, deadlock, debacle, defrock, dry dock, duroc, Dvořák, earlock, en bloc, epoch, fatstock, feedstock, fetlock, firelock, flintlock, forelock, foreshock, gamecock, gemsbok, gridlock, gunlock, Hancock, havelock, haycock, headlock, headstock, hemlock, Hickock, Iraq, jazz-rock, Kanak, Kazak, Kazakh, kapok, kneesock, Langnedoc, livestock, lovelock, matchlock, Mohock, Nisroch, nostoc, o'clock, oarlock, padlock, peacock, penstock, petcock, pibroch, picklock, pinchcock, Polack, post doc, post hoc, rhebok, rimrock, roadblock, rootstock, Rorschach, Rostock, rowlock, shamrock, Sheetrock, sherlock, shylock, Sirach, slick rock, Slovak, springbok, steenbok, stopcock, Tarlak, tarok, ticktock, traprock, van Gogh, warlock, wedlock, woodcock, wristlock, zwieback, alpenstock, Anahuac, antiknock, antilock, Antioch, Arawak, Ayers Rock, billycock, chockablock, hammerlock, hollyhock, interlock, John Hancock, lady's-smock, laughingstock, Little Rock, manioc, mantlerock, monadnock, Offenbach, Otomac, poppycock, Ragnarok, Sarawak, shuttlecock, spatterdock, turkey-cock, weathercock, Czechoslovak, Bialystok, electroshock, Inupiaq, Pontianak, Vladivostok

[2]ock \ȯk\ see ALK

ockage \äk-ij\ blockage, brockage, dockage, lockage, socage

ocke \äk\ see [1]OCK

ocked \äkt\ blocked, crocked, concoct, decoct, entr'acte, half-cocked, landlocked, periproct, entoproct—*also pasts of verbs listed at* [1]OCK

ocker \äk-ər\ blocker, clocker, cocker, docker, hocker, knocker, locker, makar, mocker, rocker, shocker, soccer, stocker, footlocker, appleknocker, beta-blocker, knickerbocker

ockery \äk-rē\ crockery, mockery, rockery

ocket \äk-ət\ brocket, crocket, Crockett, docket, locket, pocket, rocket, socket, sprocket, pickpocket, skyrocket, out-of-pocket, retro-rocket

ockett \äk-ət\ see OCKET

ockey \äk-ē\ see OCKY

ockian \äk-ē-ən\ Comstockian, Slovakian, Czechoslovakian

ockiness \äk-ē-nəs\ cockiness, rockiness, stockiness

ocking \äk-iŋ\ flocking, shocking, smocking, stocking, bluestocking, silk-stocking

ockish \äk-ish\ blockish, stockish

ockle \äk-əl\ coccal, cockle, socle, debacle, epochal
ockney \äk-nē\ cockney, Procne
ocko \äk-ō\ see OCCO
ocks \äks\ see OX
ocky \äk-ē\ blocky, cocky, hockey, jockey, pocky, rocky, Rocky, sake, schlocky, stocky, Yaqui, Abnaki, Iraqi, Ontake, pea cocky, rumaki, jabberwocky, Kawasaki, Miyazaki, Nagasaki, Okazaki, sukiyaki, teriyaki, Amagasaki, enokidake
ocle \ō-kəl\ see OCAL
ocne \äk-nē\ see OCKNEY
oco \ō-kō\ coco, cocoa, loco, poco, Bioko, iroko, rococo, crème de cacao, locofoco, Orinoco, poco a poco
ocoa \ō-kō\ see OCO
ocracy \äk-rə-sē\ autocracy, bureaucracy, democracy, hypocrisy, mobocracy, plutocracy, slavocracy, technocracy, theocracy, aristocracy, gerontocracy, gynecocracy, meritocracy, thalassocracy
ocre \ō-kər\ see OKER
ocrisy \äk-rə-sē\ see OCRACY
ocsin \äk-sən\ see OXIN
oct \äkt\ see OCKED
oction \äk-shən\ concoction, decoction
octor \äk-tər\ doctor, proctor, concocter
oculant \äk-yə-lənt\ see OCCULENT
ocular \äk-yə-lər\ jocular, locular, ocular, binocular, monocular, intraocular
ocule \äk-yül\ see OCCULE
oculus \äk-yə-ləs\ see OCCULUS
ocum \ō-kəm\ see OKUM
ocus \ō-kəs\ crocus, focus, hocus, locus, prefocus, refocus, soft-focus, hocus-pocus
ocused \ō-kəst\ see OCUST
ocust \ō-kəst\ locust, unfocused
ocutor \äk-yət-ər\ prolocutor, interlocutor
[1]**od** \äd\ bod, clod, cod, fade, Fahd, gaud, god, hod, mod, nod, od, odd, plod, pod, prod, quad, quod, rod, scrod, shod, sod, squad, tod, trod, wad, Akkad, amphipod, Arad, aubade, ballade, Belgrade, Beograde, bipod, Cape Cod, couvade, croustade, dry-shod, ephod, facade, fantod, glissade, hot-rod, jihad, lingcod, Nimrod, oeillade, pomade, peasecod, ramrod, Riyadh, roughshod, roulade, saccade, scalade, seedpod, slipshod, synod, tie-rod, tightwad, tomcod, torsade, tripod, accolade, arthropod, Ashkhabad, Bacolod, bigarade, carbonnade, chiffonade, defilade, demigod, enfilade, esculade, esplanade, fulsillade, gallopade, gastropod, goldenrod, hexapod, lycopod, monkeypod, Novgorod, Novi Sad, octopod, promenade, pseudopod, Ahmadabad, Allahabad, cephalopod, Faisalabad, Islamabad, ornithopod, prosauropod,

rodomontade, dégringolade, fanfaronade, Upanishad, Scheherazade, Nizhni Novgorod

[2]od \ō\ see [1]OW

[3]od \ōd\ see ODE

[4]od \u̇d\ see [1]OOD

[5]od \ȯd\ see [1]AUD

o'd \üd\ see UDE

oda \ōd-ə\ coda, Rhoda, soda, Baroda, pagoda, sal soda

odal \ōd-ᵊl\ Godel, modal, nodal, yodel, cathodal, intermodal

odden \äd-ᵊn\ sodden, trodden, downtrodden, Ibadan

odder \äd-ər\ dodder, fodder, khaddar, modder, nodder, odder, plodder, prodder, solder, wadder, glissader, hot-rodder—*also comparatives of adjectives listed at* [1]OD

oddery \äd-rē\ see AWDRY

oddess \äd-əs\ bodice, goddess, demigoddess

oddish \äd-ish\ cloddish, kaddish

oddle \äd-ᵊl\ coddle, model, noddle, swaddle, toddle, twaddle, waddle, remodel, mollycoddle

oddler \äd-lər\ coddler, modeler, toddler, twaddler, waddler, mollycoddler

oddly \äd-lē\ see ODLY

oddy \äd-ē\ see [1]ODY

ode \ōd\ bode, bowed, code, goad, load, lode, mode, node, ode, road, rode, Spode, strode, toad, toed, woad, wood, abode, bestrode, boatload, busload, byroad, carload, cartload, caseload, commode, corrode, crossroad, decode, displode, embowed, encode, epode, erode, explode, forebode, freeload, geode, highroad, implode, inroad, no-load, off-load, outmode, payload, planeload, postcode, railroad, rhapsode, sarod, shipload, square-toed, threnode, trainload, truckload, two-toed, unload, upload, à la mode, antipode, Comstock Lode, discommode, eigenmode, electrode, episode, impastoed, incommode, Kozhikode, Nesselrode, overrode, palinode, pigeon-toed—*also pasts of verbs listed at* [1]OW

odeine \ōd-ē-ən\ see ODIAN

odel \ōd-ᵊl\ see ODAL

odeler \äd-lər\ see ODDLER

oden \ōd-ᵊn\ loden, Odin, Woden

odeon \ōd-ē-ən\ see ODIAN

oder \ōd-ər\ coder, loader, Oder, odor, breechloader, decoder, freeloader, malodor, railroader, unloader, middle-of-the-roader

oderate \äd-rət\ quadrate, moderate, immoderate

odes \ōdz\ Rhodes—*possessives and plurals of nouns and third person singular presents of verbs listed at* ODE

odest \äd-əst\ Mahdist, modest, haggadist, immodest—*also superlatives of adjectives listed at* [1]OD

odesy \äd-ə-sē\ odyssey, geodesy, theodicy
odeum \ōd-ē-əm\ see ODIUM
odge \äj\ see [1]AGE
odger \äj-ər\ codger, dodger, lodger, roger, Roger, Jolly Roger, stinking roger
odgy \äj-ē\ dodgy, podgy, stodgy, mistagogy, pedagogy
odian \ōd-ē-ən\ Cambodian, custodian, melodeon, nickelodeon
odic \äd-ik\ zaddik, cathodic, ergodic, melodic, methodic, monodic, periodic, prosodic, rhapsodic, spasmodic, synodic, threnodic, episodic, periodic, antismasmodic, aperiodic, upanishadic, quasiperiodic
odical \äd-i-kəl\ methodical, monodical, prosodical, synodical, episodical, immethodical, periodical
odice \äd-əs\ see ODDESS
odicy \äd-ə-sē\ see ODESY
odie \ō-dē\ see [2]ODY
odin \ōd-ᵊn\ see ODEN
odious \ōd-ē-əs\ odious, commodious, melodious, Methodius, incommodious
odity \äd-ət-ē\ oddity, commodity, incommodity
odium \ōd-ē-əm\ odeum, odium, podium, rhodium, sodium
odius \ō-dē-əs\ see ODIOUS
odless \äd-ləs\ godless, rodless
odling \äd-liŋ\ codling, godling
odly \äd-lē\ godly, oddly, ungodly
odo \ōd-ō\ dodo, Komodo, Quasimodo
odom \äd-əm\ shahdom, Sodom
odor \ōd-ər\ see ODER
odsk \ätsk\ see ATSK
odular \äj-ə-lər\ modular, nodular
odule \äj-ül\ module, nodule
[1]**ody** \äd-ē\ body, cloddy, gaudy, Mahdi, noddy, sadhe, shoddy, toddy, waddy, wadi, anybody, blackbody, dogsbody, embody, homebody, nobody, somebody, wide-body, antibody, busybody, disembody, everybody, Irrawaddy, underbody
[2]**ody** \ōd-ē\ Cody, Jodie, Jody, roadie, toady, polypody
odyssey \äd-ə-sē\ see ODESY
odz \üj\ see [1]UGE
[1]**oe** \ō\ see [1]OW
[2]**oe** \ō-ē\ see OWY
[3]**oe** \ē\ see [1]EE
[4]**oe** \ȯï\ see OY
[1]**oea** \ȯi-ə\ see OIA
[2]**oea** \ē-ə\ see [1]IA
oeba \ē-bə\ see EBA
oebe \ē-bē\ see [1]EBE
oebel \ā-bəl\ see ABLE
oebus \ē-bəs\ see EBUS
oed \ōd\ see ODE
oehn \ən\ see UN
oeia \ē-ə\ see [1]IA
oeic \ē-ik\ see EIC
oek \u̇k\ see [1]OOK
oel \ō-əl\ Joel, Lowell, Noel, bestowal, Baden-Powell, protozoal
[1]**oeless** \ō-ləs\ see OLUS
[2]**oeless** \ü-ləs\ see EWLESS

[1]**oem** \ō-əm\ poem, proem, jeroboam
[2]**oem** \ōm\ see [1]OME
[3]**oem** \ȯm\ see [1]AUM
oeman \ō-mən\ see OMAN
oena \ē-nə\ see [2]INA
[1]**oentgen** \en-chən\ see ENSION
[2]**oentgen** \ən-chən\ see UNCHEON
oepha \ē-fə\ see EPHA
[1]**o'er** \ōr\ see [1]ORE
[2]**o'er** \ȯr\ see [1]OR
[1]**oer** \ōr\ see [1]OR
[2]**oer** \ü-ər\ see [1]EWER
[3]**oer** \u̇r\ see [1]URE
[4]**oer** \ō-ər\ blower, knower, lower, mower, sewer, shower, sower, beachgoer, churchgoer, flamethrower, filmgoer, foregoer, forgoer, mindblower, snowblower, snowthrower, winegrower, concertgoer, moviegoer, cinemagoer, operagoer, theatergoer, whistleblower
[1]**oes** \əz\ see [1]EUSE
[2]**oes** \ōz\ see [2]OSE
[3]**oes** \üz\ see [2]USE
oesia \ē-shə\ see [1]ESIA
oesn't \əz-ᵊnt\ see ASN'T
oest \ü-əst\ see OOIST
oesus \ē-səs\ see ESIS
[1]**oet** \ō-ət\ poet, inchoate, introit
[2]**oet** \ȯit\ see [1]OIT
oetess \ō-ət-əs\ coitus, poetess
oeuf \əf\ see UFF
oeur \ər\ see [1]EUR
oeuvre \ərv\ see ERVE
oey \ō-ē\ see OWY
[1]**of** \äv\ see [2]OLVE
[2]**of** \əv\ see [1]OVE
[3]**of** \ȯf\ see [2]OFF
ofar \ō-fər\ see OFER
ofer \ō-fər\ chauffeur, gofer, gopher, loafer, Ophir, shofar
[1]**off** \äf\ boff, coif, doff, goif, kaph, prof, quaff, scoff, shroff, taw, toff, carafe, cook-off, pilaf, Romanov
[2]**off** \ȯf\ cough, doff, off, scoff, taw, trough, Azov, beg off, blast-off, brush-off, cast-off, castoff, checkoff, Chekhov, cook-off, cutoff, die-off, drop-off, face-off, falloff, far-off, goof-off, hands-off, jump-off, Khartov, kickoff, Kirov, knockoff, Khruschev, layoff, leadoff, lift-off, Lvov, one-off, Pavlov, payoff, pick-off, pickoff, play-off, rake-off, rip-off, roll-off, runoff, Salchow, sawed-off, sell-off, send-off, setoff, show-off, shutoff, spin-off, standoff, takeoff, Tambov, tap-off, tip-off, trade-off, turnoff, well-off, Wolof, write-off, Wroclaw, better-off, cooling-off, damping-off, Gorbachev, Molotov, Nabokov, philosophe, Pribilof, Rostov, beef Stroganoff, Rachmaninoff, Rimsky-Korsakov
[1]**offal** \äf-əl\ see AFEL
[2]**offal** \ȯ-fəl\ see AWFUL
offaly \ȯf-ə-lē\ see AWFULLY
offee \ȯ-fē\ coffee, toffee
[1]**offer** \äf-ər\ coffer, gauffer, goffer, offer, proffer, quaffer, scoffer, troffer, reoffer
[2]**offer** \ȯf-ər\ goffer, offer, troffer, reoffer

offin \ȯ-fən\ coffin, dauphin, soften, uncoffin
offit \äf-ət\ see OFIT
offle \ȯ-fəl\ see AWFUL
ofit \äf-ət\ profit, prophet, soffit, nonprofit, not-for-profit
ofle \ü-fəl\ see UEFUL
[1]**oft** \ȯft\ croft, loft, oft, soft, toft, aloft, hayloft, undercroft—*also pasts of verbs listed at* [2]OFF
[2]**oft** \äft\ see [1]AFT
often \ȯ-fən\ see OFFIN
ofty \ȯf-tē\ lofty, softy, toplofty
[1]**og** \äg\ bog, clog, cog, flog, fog, frog, grog, hog, jog, log, nog, Prague, prog, quag, shog, slog, smog, tog, wog, agog, backlog, bullfrog, defog, eclogue, eggnog, footslog, groundhog, gulag, photog, prologue, putlog, quahog, Rolvaag, sandhog, stalag, warthog, analog, analogue, antilog, apalogue, catalog, decalogue, demagogue, dialogue, golliwog, monologue, mummichog, mystagogue, nouvelle vague, pedagogue, pollywog, semilog, sinologue, synagogue, Taganrog, theologue, waterlog
[2]**og** \ȯg\ bog, clog, dog, fog, frog, hog, jog, log, smog, wog, backlog, bandog, befog, bird-dog, bulldog, bullfrog, coydog, defog, eclogue, firedog, groundhog, hangdog, hedgehog, hotdog, lapdog, leapfrog, prologue, quahog, sandhog, seadog, sheepdog, warthog, watchdog, analog, analogue, apologue, catalog, decalogue, dialogue, dog-eat-dog, duologue, epilogue, homologue, monologue, mummichog, overdog, pettifog, pollywog, sinologue, theologue, Tagalog, travelogue, underdog, waterlog, yellow-dog, ideologue
[3]**og** \ōg\ see [1]OGUE
oga \ō-gə\ toga, yoga, Conestoga
ogamous \äg-ə-məs\ endogamous, exogamous, monogamous, heterogamous
ogamy \äg-ə-mē\ endogamy, exogamy, homogamy, misogamy, monogamy
ogan \ō-gən\ brogan, Mount Logan, shogun, slogan
ogany \äg-ə-nē\ see OGONY
ogative \äg-ət-iv\ derogative, prerogative, interrogative
[1]**oge** \ōj\ doge, gamboge, horologe
[2]**oge** \ōzh\ loge, Limoges
[3]**oge** \ō-jē\ see OJI
[4]**oge** \üzh\ see [2]UGE
ogel \ō-gəl\ see [1]OGLE
ogenous \äj-ə-nəs\ androgynous, erogenous, homogenous, monogynous, heterogenous
ogeny \äj-ə-nē\ progeny, androgeny, autogeny, homogeny, misogyny, monogyny, ontogeny, phylogeny, heterogeny
[1]**oger** \äj-ər\ see ODGER
[2]**oger** \ȯg-ər\ see [2]OGGER

oges \ōzh\ see [2]OGE
[1]ogey \ō-gē\ see OGIE
[2]ogey \u̇g-ē\ see OOGIE
oggan \äg-ən\ see OGGIN
oggar \äg-ər\ see [1]OGGER
[1]ogger \äg-ər\ agar, clogger, flogger, Hoggar, jogger, laager, lager, logger, slogger, Ahaggar, defogger, footslogger, agar-agar, cataloger, pettifogger
[2]ogger \ȯg-ər\ auger, augur, clogger, jogger, logger, maugre, sauger, defogger, hotdogger, cataloger, pettifogger
[1]oggery \äg-rē\ toggery, demagoguery
[2]oggery \ȯ-gə-rē\ augury, doggery
oggin \äg-ən\ noggin, toboggan, Copenhagen
oggle \äg-əl\ boggle, goggle, joggle, ogle, toggle, boondoggle, hornswoggle, synagogal
[1]oggy \äg-ē\ boggy, foggy, groggy, moggy, quaggy, smoggy, soggy, yagi, demagogy
[2]oggy \ȯg-ē\ foggy, soggy
[1]ogh \ōg\ see [1]OGUE
[2]ogh \ōk\ see OKE
[3]ogh \äk\ see [1]OCK
[4]ogh \ō\ see OW
ogi \ō-gē\ see OGIE
ogian \ō-jən\ see OJAN
ogic \äj-ik\ logic, choplogic, illogic, anagogic, analogic, biologic, chronologic, cryptologic, cytologic, demagogic, dendrologic, dialogic, ecologic, ethnologic, geologic, histologic, horologic, hydrologic, mythologic, neurologic, nosologic, oncologic, pathologic, pedagogic, pedologic, petrologic, phonologic, proctologic, psychologic, serologic, technologic, theologic, virologic, zoologic, dermatologic, etiologic, gerontologic, gynecologic, hagiologic, hematologic, ideologic, immunologic, ophthalmologic, ornithologic, pharmacologic, physiologic, roentgenologic, sociologic, teleologic, teratologic, toxicologic, volcanologic, bacteriologic, endocrinologic, meteorologic, paleontologic, parasitologic, sedimentologic, symptomologic, epidemiologic
ogical \äj-i-kəl\ logical, alogical, illogical, anagogical, analogical, biological, Christological, chronological, cosmological, cryptological, cytological, dendrological, ecological, enological, ethnological, ethological, extralogical, gemological, geological, graphological, histological, horological, hydrological, limnological, morphological, mycological, mythological, necrological, neurological, nomological, oncological, pathological, pedagogical, pedological,

penological, petrological, philological, phonological, phrenological, phycological, proctological, psephological, psychological, scatological, seismological, serological, sinological, tautological, technological, theological, topological, typological, ufological, virological, zoological, abiological, anthropological, archaeological, cardiological, climatological, criminological, demonological, dermatological, embryological, entomological, eschatological, etiological, etymological, futurological, genealogical, gerontological, gynecological, hagiological, hematological, herpetological, ichthyological, iconological, ideological, immunological, Mariological, methodological, mineralogical, musicological, numerological, ophthalmological, ornithological, pharmacological, phraseological, physiological, primatological, roentgenological, selenological, semiological, sociological, teleological, teratological, terminological, thanatological, toxicological, volcanological, bacteriological, characterological, dialectological, ecclesiological, endocrinological, epistemological, geomorphological, meteorological, paleontological, parasitological, phenomenological, sedimentological, symptomatological, epidemiological, gastroenterological

ogie \ō-gē\ bogey, bogie, dogie, fogy, hoagie, logy, pogy, stogie, vogie, yogi, pirogi

[1]ogle \ō-gəl\ Gogel, ogle

[2]ogle \äg-əl\ see OGGLE

oglio \ōl-yō\ see [1]OLLO

[1]ogna \ō-nə\ see ONA

[2]ogna \ō-nē\ see [1]ONY

[3]ogna \ōn-yə\ see [2]ONIA

ogne \ōn\ see [1]ONE

ogned \ōnd\ see [1]ONED

ogo \ō-gō\ go-go, logo, Logo, Togo, a-go-go

ogony \äg-ə-nē\ cosmogony, mahogany, theogony

ographer \äg-rə-fər\ biographer, cartographer, chorographer, cryptographer, demographer, discographer, ethnographer, geographer, lithographer, mythographer, phonographer, photographer, pornographer, stenographer, typographer, bibliographer, choreographer, hagiographer, heliographer, iconographer, lexicographer, oceanographer, paleographer, autobiographer, biogeographer, chromatographer, cinematographer, historiographer

ography \äg-rə-fē\ aerography, autography, biography, cacography, cartography, chorography, chronography, cosmography, cryptography, demography, discography, ethnography, filmography, geography, holography, hydrography, hypsography, lithography, lymphography, mammography, mythography, nomography, orthography, phonography, photography, pictography, planography, pornography, reprography, sonography, stenography, thermography, tomography, topography, typography, venography, xerography, xylography, angiography, aortography, bibliography, cardiography, choreography, chromatography, crystallography, hagiography, heliography, iconography, lexicography, metallography, oceanography, paleography, physiography, radiography, roentgenography, videography, arteriography, autobiography, cinematography, encephalography, historiography, psychobiography, electroencephalography

ogress \ō-grəs\ ogress, progress

ogrom \äg-rəm\ grogram, pogrom

[1]ogue \ōg\ brogue, drogue, rogue, togue, vogue, yogh, collogue, crannog, pirogue, prorogue, Krivoy Rog, disembogue

[2]ogue \äg\ see [1]OG

[3]ogue \ȯg\ see [2]OG

oguery \äg-rē\ see [1]OGGERY

oguish \ō-gish\ roguish, voguish

ogun \ō-gən\ see OGAN

ogynous \äj-ə-nəs\ see OGENOUS

ogyny \äj-ə-nē\ see OGENY

oh \ō\ see [1]OW

oha \ō-ə\ see [1]OA

ohl \ōl\ see [1]OLE

ohm \ōm\ see [1]OME

ohn \än\ see [1]ON

ohns \änz\ see ONZE

ohn's \onz\ see ONZE

ohnson \än-sən\ Johnson, Jonson, Wisconsin

ohr \ōr\ see [1]OR

[1]oi \ä\ see [1]A

[2]oi \ȯi\ see OY

oia \ȯi-ə\ cholla, Goya, Hoya, olla, toea, Nagoya, sequoia, Sequoya, atemoya, cherimoya, paranoia

oian \ȯi-ən\ see OYEN

oic \ō-ik\ stoic, azoic, bistroic, echoic, heroic, anechoic, Cenozoic, Mesozoic, mock-heroic, vetinoic, antiheroic, Paleozoic

oice \ȯis\ choice, Joyce, Royce, voice, devoice, Du Bois, invoice, pro-choice, rejoice, unvoice, sailor's-choice

oiced \ȯist\ see OIST

oicer \ȯi-sər\ choicer, voicer, pro-choicer, rejoicer

[1]oid \ȯid\ Boyd, Floyd, Freud, void, android, avoid, chancroid, colloid, conoid, cuboid, cycloid, deltoid, dendroid, devoid, discoid, factoid, fungoid, globoid, hydroid, hypnoid, keloid, mucoid, Negroid, ovoid, percoid, prismoid, pygmoid, rhizoid, rhomboid, schizoid, scombroid, sigmoid, spheroid, steroid, styloid, tabloid, thalloid, thyroid, toroid, toxoid, trochoid, typhoid, Veddoid, viroid, adenoid, alkaloid, amoeboid, aneroid, anthropoid, arachnoid, asteroid, Australoid, carcinoid, Caucasoid, celluloid, crystalloid, ellipsoid, embryoid, eunuchoid, helicoid, hemorrhoid, hominoid, humanoid, hysteroid, metalloid, Mongoloid, myeloid, nautiloid, nucleoid, obovoid, opioid, osteoid, overjoyed, paranoid, philanthropoid, planetoid, Polaroid, retinoid, rheumatoid, solenoid, Stalinoid, trapezoid, unalloyed, unemployed, cannabinoid, carotenoid, eicosanoid, meteoroid, tuberculoid, underemployed, Neanderthaloid—*also pasts of verbs listed at* OY

[2]oid \ä\ see [1]A

oidal \ȯid-ᵊl\ chancroidal, choroidal, colloidal, conchoidal, cuboidal, cycloidal, discoidal, spheroidal, toroidal, adenoidal, asteroidal, ellipsoidal, emulsoidal, hemorrhoidal, metalloidal, planetoidal, saccharoidal, trapezoidal, paraboloidal

oider \ȯid-ər\ broider, voider, avoider, embroider, reembroider

oie \ä\ see [1]A

oif \äf\ see [1]OFF

oign \ȯin\ see [1]OIN

oil \ȯil\ boil, Boyle, broil, coil, Doyle, foil, hoyle, moil, loyal, noil, oil, roil, royal, Royal, soil, spoil, toil, voile, aboil, airfoil, assoil, charbroil, cinquefoil, despoil, embroil, entoil, garboil, gargoyle, gumboil, hard-boil, Isle Royal, langue d'oïl, milfoil, non-oil, parboil, recoil, subsoil, supercoil, tinfoil, topsoil, trefoil, turmoil, counterfoil, disloyal, hydrofoil, quatrefoil, rhyme royal, surroyal, pennyroyal

oilage \ȯi-lij\ soilage, spoilage

[1]oile \äl\ see [1]AL

[2]oile \ȯil\ see OIL

oiled \ȯild\ foiled, oiled, hard-boiled, soft-boiled, uncoiled, well-oiled—*also pasts of verbs listed at* OIL

oiler \ȯi-lər\ boiler, broiler, moiler, oiler, spoiler, toiler, charbroiler, despoiler, Free-Soiler, subsoiler, potboiler

oiling \ȯi-liŋ\ boiling, moiling

oilless \ȯil-ləs\ soilless, recoilless

oilsman \óilz-mən\ foilsman, spoilsman
oilus \ói-ləs\ see OYLESS
oily \ói-lē\ doily, oily, roily
[1]oin \óin\ coin, foin, groin, groyne, join, loin, quoin, adjoin, Burgoyne, conjoin, Des Moines, disjoin, eloign, enjoin, essoin, purloin, recoin, rejoin, sainfoin, sirloin, subjoin, tenderloin, Assiniboin
[2]oin \a^n\ see [4]IN
oine \än\ see [1]ON
oined \óind\ conjoined, uncoined—*also pasts of verbs listed at* [1]OIN
oiner \ói-nər\ coiner, joiner
oines \óin\ see [1]OIN
o-ing \ō-iŋ\ see [1]OING
[1]oing \ō-iŋ\ bowing, going, knowing, rowing, sewing, showing, churchgoing, deep-going, foregoing, free-flowing, glassblowing, ingrowing, mind-blowing, ongoing, outgoing, seagoing, waygoing, concertgoing, easygoing, moviegoing, oceangoing, operagoing, theatergoing, thoroughgoing, whistle-blowing, to-ing and fro-ing—*also present participles of verbs listed at* [1]OW
[2]oing \ü-iŋ\ bluing, doing, Ewing, misdoing, undoing, wrongdoing, evildoing—*also present participles of verbs listed at* [1]EW
[3]oing \ō-ən\ see [1]OAN
oings \ō-iŋz\ outgoings—*also possessives and plurals of nouns and third person singular presents of verbs listed at* [1]OING
[1]oint \óint\ joint, point, adjoint, anoint, appoint, aroint, ballpoint, bluepoint, checkpoint, conjoint, disjoint, drypoint, eyepoint, gunpoint, knifepoint, midpoint, nonpoint, outpoint, pinpoint, pourpoint, standpoint, tuck-point, viewpoint, counterpoint, disappoint, needlepoint, petit point, silverpoint
[2]oint \ant\ see [5]ANT
ointe \ant\ see [5]ANT
ointed \óint-əd\ jointed, pointed, lap-jointed, loose-jointed, double-jointed, well-appointed —*also pasts of verbs listed at* [1]OINT
ointer \óint-ər\ jointer, pointer, anointer
ointing \óin-tiŋ\ finger-pointing—*present participles of verbs listed at* [1]OINT
ointment \óint-mənt\ ointment, anointment, appointment, disappointment
[1]oir \īr\ see [1]IRE
[2]oir \är\ see [3]AR
[3]oir \óir\ see OYER
[4]oir \ór\ see [1]OR
[1]oire \är\ see [3]AR
[2]oire \óir\ see OYER
[3]oire \ór\ see [1]OR
[1]ois \ä\ see [1]A
[2]ois \ói\ see OY
[3]ois \ō-əs\ Lois, Powys
[4]ois \óis\ see OICE

[1]**oise** \äz\ poise, 'twas, vase, was, Ahwaz, bourgeoise, Lamaze, Shiraz, vichyssoise, The Afars and the Isas—*also plurals and possessives of nouns and third person singular presents of verbs listed at* [1]A

[2]**oise** \ȯiz\ hoise, noise, Noyes, poise, turquoise, counterpoise, equipoise, avoirdupois—*also plurals and possessives of nouns and third person singular presents of verbs listed at* OY

[3]**oise** \oi-zē\ see OISY

oison \ȯiz-ᵊn\ foison, poison, empoison

oist \ȯist\ foist, hoist, joist, moist, voiced, unvoiced, semimoist—*also pasts of verbs listed at* OICE

oister \ȯi-stər\ cloister, moister, oyster, roister

oisterous \ȯi-strəs\ see OISTRESS

oistral \ȯi-strəl\ cloistral, coistrel

oistrel \ȯi-strəl\ see OISTRAL

oistress \ȯi-strəs\ cloistress, boisterous, roisterous

oisy \ȯi-zē\ Boise, noisy, cramoisie

[1]**oit** \ȯit\ doit, droit, poet, quoit, adroit, Detroit, exploit, maladroit, Massasoit

[2]**oit** \āt\ see [1]ATE

[3]**oit** \ō-ət\ see [1]OET

[4]**oit** \ä\ see [1]A

oite \ät\ see [1]OT

oiter \ȯit-ər\ goiter, loiter, exploiter, reconnoiter

oitus \ō-ət-əs\ see OETESS

oivre \äv\ see [1]OLVE

[1]**oix** \ä\ see [1]A

[2]**oix** \ȯi\ see OY

oiz \ȯis\ see [2]OISE

ojan \ō-jən\ Trojan, theologian

oje \ō-jē\ see OJI

oji \ō-jē\ Moji, shoji, anagoge, Hachioje

[1]**ok** \äk\ see [1]OCK

[2]**ok** \ək\ see UCK

[3]**ok** \ȯk\ see ALK

oka \ō-kə\ see OCA

okable \ō-kə-bəl\ see OCABLE

[1]**oke** \ōk\ bloke, broke, choke, cloak, coke, Coke, croak, folk, hoke, joke, moke, oak, oke, poke, Polk, roque, smoke, soak, soke, spoke, stoke, stroke, toke, toque, woke, yogh, yoke, yolk, ad hoc, awoke, backstroke, baroque, bespoke, breaststroke, chain-smoke, convoke, cowpoke, downstroke, evoke, heatstroke, housebroke, in-joke, invoke, keystroke, kinfolk, kinsfolk, menfolk, Nisroch, outspoke, presoak, provoke, revoke, she-oak, sidestroke, slowpoke, sunchoke, sunstroke, townsfolk, uncloak, unyoke, upstroke, workfolk, artichoke, equivoque, fisherfolk, gentlefolk, herrenvolk, masterstroke, okeydoke, Roanoke, thunderstroke, womenfolk, Mount Revelstoke

[2]**oke** \ō-kē\ see OKY

[3]**oke** \ō\ see [1]OW
[4]**oke** \u̇k\ see [1]OOK
oked \ōkt\ stoked, yolked
okee \ō-kē\ see OKY
okel \ō-kəl\ see OCAL
oken \ō-kən\ broken, oaken, spoken, token, woken, awoken, bespoken, betoken, fair-spoken, foretoken, free-spoken, heartbroken, housebroken, outspoken, plainspoken, short-spoken, soft-spoken, unbroken, well-spoken, wind-broken
oker \ō-kər\ broker, choker, croaker, joker, ocher, poker, soaker, smoker, stoker, stroker, chain-smoker, invoker, pawnbroker, provoker, revoker, stockbroker, mediocre
okey \ō-kē\ see OKY
oki \ō-kē\ see OKY
okie \ō-kē\ see OKY
oking \ō-kiŋ\ broking, choking
oko \ō-kō\ see OCO
okum \ō-kəm\ Bochum, hokum, locum, oakum
oky \ō-kē\ choky, croaky, folkie, hokey, Loki, Okie, pokey, poky, smoky, troche, trochee, yolky, enoki, Great Smoky, hokeypokey, karaoke, Okefenokee
[1]**ol** \ōl\ see [1]OLE
[2]**ol** \äl\ see [1]AL
[3]**ol** \ȯl\ see ALL
ola \ō-lə\ bola, cola, Kola, Lola, tola, Zola, Angola, boffola, Canola, gondola, granola, mandola, payola, pergola, plugola, scagliola, Savanarola, viola, Viola, acerola, ayatollah, braciola, Española, gladiola, Gorgonzola, hemiola, Hispaniola, moviola, Osceola, roseola, Victrola
olable \ō-lə-bəl\ see OLLABLE
olace \äl-əs\ see OLIS
olan \ō-lən\ see OLON
oland \ō-lənd\ see OWLAND
olander \əl-ən-dər\ colander, Julunder
[1]**olar** \ō-lər\ see OLLER
[2]**olar** \äl-ər\ see OLLAR
olas \ō-ləs\ see OLUS
olater \äl-ət-ər\ bardolater, idolater, bibliolater, Mariolater
olatrous \äl-ə-trəs\ idolatrous, bibliolatrous, heliolatrous
olatry \äl-ə-trē\ bardolatry, idolatry, statolatry, zoolatry, bibliolatry, heliolatry, iconolatry, Mariolatry
[1]**old** \ōld\ bold, bowled, cold, fold, gold, hold, mold, mould, old, polled, scold, sold, soled, souled, told, wold, acold, age-old, ahold, behold, billfold, blindfold, controlled, Cotswold, cuckold, enfold, fanfold, foothold, foretold, freehold, gatefold, handhold, household, ice-cold, infold, leasehold, pinfold, potholed, roothold, scaffold, sheepfold, stone-cold, stronghold, threshold, toehold, twice-told, unfold, unmold, untold, uphold, whole-souled, withhold, centerfold, copyhold, fingerhold, manifold, manyfold,

marigold, multifold, oversold, petioled, severalfold, stranglehold, throttlehold—*also pasts of verbs listed at* [1]OLE

[2]**old** \ȯld\ see ALD

oldan \ōl-dən\ see OLDEN

olden \ōl-dən\ golden, holden, olden, soldan, beholden, embolden

[1]**older** \ōl-dər\ boulder, folder, holder, molder, polder, shoulder, smolder, bondholder, cardholder, householder, jobholder, landholder, placeholder, shareholder, slaveholder, stadtholder, stakeholder, stallholder, stockholder, toolholder, officeholder, titleholder, policyholder—*also comparatives of adjectives listed at* [1]OLD

[2]**older** \äd-ər\ see ODDER

oldi \ȯl-dē\ see ALDI

oldie \ōl-dē\ see OLDY

olding \ōl-diŋ\ folding, holding, molding, hand-holding, inholding, landholding, slaveholding

oldster \ōl-stər\ see OLSTER

oldt \ōlt\ [1]OLT

oldy \ōl-dē\ moldy, oldie

[1]**ole** \ōl\ bole, boll, bowl, coal, cole, Cole, dhole, dole, droll, foal, goal, hole, knoll, kohl, Kohl, mole, ole, pole, Pole, poll, prole, role, roll, scroll, Seoul, shoal, skoal, sol, sole, soul, stole, stroll, thole, tole, toll, troll, vole, whole, armhole, atoll, bankroll, beanpole, bedroll, blowhole, bolthole, borehole, bunghole, cajole, catchpole, charcoal, chuckhole, condole, console, control, creole, Creole, drumroll, enroll, ensoul, extol, eyehole, fishbowl, flagpole, foxhole, frijol, hellhole, Huichol, inscroll, insole, keyhole, kneehole, knothole, logroll, loophole, manhole, maypole, midsole, Mongol, Nicole, outsole, parole, patrol, payroll, peephole, pesthole, pinhole, pistole, pitchpole, porthole, posthole, pothole, redpoll, resole, ridgepole, Sheol, sinkhole, sotol, stokehole, tadpole, taphole, thumbhole, top-hole, touchhole, turnsole, unroll, Walpole, washbowl, wormhole, amatol, aureole, banderole, bannerol, barcarole, buttonhole, cabriole, camisole, capriole, caracole, carmagnole, casserole, croquignole, cubbyhole, decontrol, Demerol, escarole, farandole, fumarole, girandole, grand guignol, innersole, methanol, oriole, oversoul, petiole, pick-and-roll, pigeonhole, protocol, rigmarole, Seminole, cholesterol, Costa del Sol

[2]**ole** \ō-lē\ see [1]OLY

[3]**ole** \ȯl\ see ALL

olean \ō-lē-ən\ see [1]OLIAN

oled \ōld\ see [1]OLD

oleful \ōl-fəl\ doleful, soulful

olely \ō-lē\ see [1]OLY

[1]**olem** \ō-ləm\ golem, solum
[2]**olem** \ā-ləm\ see ALAAM
olemn \äl-əm\ see OLUMN
[1]**oleon** \ō-lē-ən\ see [1]OLIAN
[2]**oleon** \ōl-yən\ see [2]OLIAN
[1]**oler** \ō-lər\ see OLLER
[2]**oler** \äl-ər\ see OLLAR
olery \ōl-rē\ see OLLERY
olesome \ōl-səm\ dolesome, Folsom, wholesome
oless \ō-ləs\ see OLUS
oleum \ō-lē-əm\ see OLIUM
oleus \ō-lē-əs\ coleus, soleus
oley \ō-lē\ see [1]OLY
[1]**olf** \älf\ golf, Rolf, Adolph, Randolph, Rudolph, Lake Rudolf
[2]**olf** \əlf\ see ULF
olfing \ȯf-iŋ\ see OFFING
olga \äl-gə\ Olga, Volga
oli \ō-lē\ see [1]OLY
olia \ō-lē-ə\ Mongolia, pignolia, Anatolia, melancholia, Inner Mongolia, Outer Mongolia
olian \ō-lē-ən\ aeolian, Aeolian, eolian, Mongolian, napoleon, Napoleon, simoleon, Tyrolean, Anatolian
[1]**olic** \äl-ik\ colic, frolic, Gaelic, rollick, Aeolic, bucolic, carbolic, embolic, Mongolic, symbolic, systolic, alcoholic, anabolic, apostolic, catabolic, diabolic, hyperbolic, melancholic, metabolic, parabolic, vitriolic, workaholic
[2]**olic** \ō-lik\ colic, fumarolic, bibliopolic
olicking \ä-lik-iŋ\ frolicking, rollicking
olicy \äl-ə-sē\ policy, Wallasey
olid \äl-əd\ solid, squalid, stolid—*also pasts of verbs listed at* [2]ALA
[1]**olin** \äl-ən\ see [5]OLLEN
[2]**olin** \ō-lən\ see OLON
olis \äl-əs\ braless, Hollis, polis, solace, tallith, Wallace, Wallis, Cornwallis, Manizales, torticollis
olish \äl-ish\ polish, abolish, demolish, apple-polish
olitan \äl-ət-ᵊn\ cosmopolitan, megapolitan, metropolitan, Neapolitan, megalopolitan
olity \äl-ət-ē\ see [1]ALITY
olium \ō-lē-əm\ scholium, linoleum, petroleum, trifolium
olivar \äl-ə-vər\ see OLIVER
[1]**olk** \elk\ see [1]ELK
[2]**olk** \ōk\ see OKE
[3]**olk** \əlk\ see ULK
[4]**olk** \ȯk\ see ALK
olked \ōkt\ see OKED
olkie \ō-kē\ see OKY
olky \ō-kē\ see OKY
[1]**oll** \ōl\ see [1]OLE
[2]**oll** \äl\ see [1]AL
[3]**oll** \ȯl\ see ALL
[1]**olla** \äl-ə\ see [2]ALA
[2]**olla** \ȯi-ə\ see OIA
ollable \ō-lə-bəl\ controllable, inconsolable, uncontrollable
ollack \äl-ək\ see OLOCH
[1]**ollah** \ō-lə\ see OLA
[2]**ollah** \äl-ə\ see [2]ALA
[3]**ollah** \əl-ə\ see [1]ULLAH
ollands \äl-ənz\ see OLLINS
ollar \äl-ər\ choler, collar, dollar, dolor, haler, holler, Mahler, scholar, squalor, taler, thaler, blue-collar, brass-collar, half-dollar,

white-collar, Emmentaler, Eurodollar, petrodollar
ollard \äl-ərd\ bollard, collard, collered, hollered, Lollard, pollard
olled \ōld\ see [1]OLD
ollee \ō-lē\ see [1]OLY
ollege \äl-ij\ see OWLEDGE
[1]**ollen** \ō-lən\ see OLON
[2]**ollen** \əl-ə\ see [1]ULLAH
[3]**ollen** \əl-ən\ see ULLEN
[4]**ollen** \ȯ-lən\ see ALLEN
[5]**ollen** \äl-ən\ Colin, pollen, Rollin, Nordrhein-Westfalen
oller \ō-lər\ bowler, choler, dolor, droller, molar, polar, poler, poller, roller, solar, stroller, troller, bankroller, cajoler, comptroller, controller, extoller, patroller, premolar, steamroller, antisolar, buttonholer, logroller, Maryknoller, pigeonholer
ollery \ōl-rē\ drollery, cajolery
ollet \äl-ət\ collet, Smollett, tallith, wallet, whatchamacallit
ollett \äl-ət\ see OLLET
olley \äl-ē\ see [1]OLLY
ollick \äl-ik\ see [1]OLIC
ollicking \ä-lik-iŋ\ see OLICKING
ollie \äl-ē\ see [1]OLLY
ollin \äl-ən\ see [5]OLLEN
olling \ō-liŋ\ bowling, logrolling—*also present participles of verbs listed at* [1]OLE
ollins \äl-ənz\ collins, Hollands, Tom Collins
ollis \äl-əs\ see OLIS
ollity \äl-ət-ē\ see [1]ALITY
[1]**ollo** \ōl-yō\ imbroglio, arroz con pollo
[2]**ollo** \ō-yō\ yo-yo, criollo
[3]**ollo** \äl-ō\ see [1]OLLOW
ollop \äl-əp\ collop, dollop, lollop, polyp, scallop, scollop, trollop, wallop, codswallop, escallop
[1]**ollow** \äl-ō\ follow, hollo, hollow, swallow, wallow, Apollo, robalo, Leoncavallo
[2]**ollow** \äl-ə\ see [2]ALA
ollower \äl-ə-wər\ follower, swallower, wallower
ollster \ōl-stər\ see OLSTER
[1]**olly** \äl-ē\ Bali, Cali, brolly, collie, colly, dolly, folly, golly, Halle, holly, Holly, jolly, Lally, lolly, Mali, Mollie, molly, Molly, Ollie, Pali, poly, Polly, quale, Raleigh, trolley, volley, Denali, finale, Kigali, loblolly, Nepali, petrale, Somali, Svengali, tamale, melancholy, pastorale, teocalli
[2]**olly** \ȯ-lē\ see AWLY
olm \ōm\ see [1]OME
olman \ōl-mən\ dolman, dolmen, patrolman
olmen \ōl-mən\ see OLMAN
olmes \ōmz\ Holmes—*also possessives and plurals of nouns and third person singular presents of verbs listed at* [1]OME
olo \ō-lō\ bolo, kolo, nolo, polo, solo, Barolo, Marco Polo
oloch \äl-ək\ Moloch, pollack, rowlock
ologer \äl-ə-jər\ astrologer,

chronologer, horologer, mythologer

ologist \äl-ə-jəst\ anthologist, biologist, cetologist, conchologist, cosmologist, cryptologist, cytologist, dendrologist, ecologist, enologist, ethnologist, ethologist, fetologist, gemologist, geologist, graphologist, histologist, horologist, hydrologist, Indologist, limnologist, mixologist, morphologist, mycologist, mythologist, necrologist, nephrologist, neurologist, oncologist, ontologist, oologist, pathologist, pedologist, penologist, petrologist, philologist, phonologist, phrenologist, phycologist, psychologist, seismologist, serologist, sexologist, sinologist, technologist, topologist, typologist, ufologist, virologist, zoologist, anthropologist, archaeologist, audiologist, cardiologist, climatologist, cosmetologist, criminologist, dermatologist, Egyptologist, embryologist, entomologist, enzymologist, escapologist, etymologist, futurologist, genealogist, gerontologist, gynecologist, hematologist, herpetologist, ichthyologist, ideologist, immunologist, kremlinologist, lexicologist, martyrologist, methodologist, mineralogist, musicologist, nematalogist, numerologist, oceanologist, ophthalmologist, ornithologist, osteologist, papyrologist, pharmacologist, phraseologist, physiologist, planetologist, primatologist, rheumatologist, roentgenologist, semiologist, sociologist, speleologist, teleologist, teratologist, thanatologist, toxicologist, urbanologist, volcanologist, bacteriologist, diabetologist, dialectologist, endocrinologist, epistemologist, liturgiologist, meteorologist, neonatologist, paleontologist, parasitologist, phenomenologist, sedimentologist, anesthesiologist, epidemiologist, gastroenterologist, otolaryngologist

ologous \äl-ə-gəs\ heterologous, homologous, tautologous

ology \äl-ə-jē\ anthology, apology, astrology, biology, bryology, cetology, Christology, chronology, conchology, cosmology, cryptology, cytology, dendrology, doxology, ecology, enology, ethnology, ethology, fetology, gemology, geology, graphology, haplology, histology, homology, horology, hydrology, hymnology, Indology, limnology, lithology, mixology, morphology, mycology, myology, mythology, necrology, nephrology, neurology, nosology, oncology, ontology, oology, pathology, pedology, penology, petrology, philology, phlebology, phonology, phrenology, phycology, proctology, psychology, scatology, seismology, serology, sexology, sinology, symbology, tautology, technology, tetralogy, theology, topology, trichology, typology, ufology, urology, virology, zoology, angelology, anthropology, archaeology, audiology, axiology, cardiology, climatology, codicology, cohomology, cosmetology, craniology, criminology, dactylology, demonology, deontology, dermatology, Egyptology, embryology, entomology, enzymology, escapology, eschatology, etiology, etymology, futurology, genealogy, gerontology, gynecology, hematology, herpetology, ichthyology, iconology, ideology, immunology, kremlinology, laryngology, lexicology, lichenology, Mariology, martyrology, methodology, mineralogy, museology, musicology, narratology, nematology, numerology, oceanology, opthalmology, ornithology, osteology, pharmacology, phraseology, physiology, planetology, primatology, radiology, reflexology, rheumatology, roentgenology, semiology, sociology, speleology, sumerology, teleology, teratology, terminology, thanatology, toxicology, urbanology, volcanology, vulcanology, bacteriology, chronobiology, cryptozoology, dialectology, ecclesiology, endocrinology, epistemology, liturgiology, metapsychology, meteorology, microbiology, micromorphology, neonatology, onomatology, paleontology, parapsychology, parasitology, phenomenology, sedimentology, symptomatology, anesthesiology, epidemiology, ethnomusicology, gastroenterology, otolaryngology, paleobiology, paleopathology, periodontology, otorhinolaryngology

olon \ō-lən\ bowline, Colin, colon, Nolan, solon, stolen, stollen, stolon, swollen, eidolon, semicolon

olonel \ərn-ᵊl\ see ERNAL

olonist \äl-ə-nəst\ colonist, Stalinist

¹olor \əl-ər\ color, cruller, culler, muller, sculler, bicolor, discolor, off-color, three-color, tricolor, Technicolor, watercolor

[2]**olor** \ō-lər\ see OLLER
[3]**olor** \äl-ər\ see OLLAR
olored \əl-ərd\ colored, dullard, bicolored, rose-colored, varicolored
olp \ōp\ see OPE
olpen \ō-pən\ see OPEN
olph \älf\ see OLF
ols \älz\ hols, Casals
olsom \ōl-səm\ see OLESOME
olster \ōl-stər\ bolster, holster, oldster, pollster, upholster
[1]**olt** \ōlt\ bolt, colt, dolt, holt, jolt, molt, poult, smolt, volt, eyebolt, Humboldt, kingbolt, revolt, ringbolt, unbolt, thunderbolt
[2]**olt** \ölt\ see ALT
olta \äl-tə\ see ALTA
olter \ōl-tər\ bolter, coulter
oltish \ōl-tish\ coltish, doltish
oluble \äl-yə-bəl\ soluble, voluble, dissoluble, insoluble, irresoluble, resoluble, indissoluble
olum \ō-ləm\ see OLEM
olumn \äl-əm\ column, slalom, solemn, Malayalam
olus \ō-ləs\ bolas, bolus, solus, snowless, toeless, Coriolus, electroless, gladiolus, holus-bolus
olvable \äl-və-bəl\ solvable, dissolvable, evolvable, insolvable, resolvable, revolvable, irresolvable
[1]**olve** \älv\ salve, solve, absolve, au poivre, convolve, devolve, dissolve, evolve, involve, resolve, revolve, coevolve
[2]**olve** \äv\ grave, of, salve, Slav, suave, taw, waw, moshav, thereof, whereof, Zouave, Tishah-b'Ab, unheard-of, well-thought-of
olvement \älv-mənt\ evolvement, involvement, noninvolvement
olvent \äl-vənt\ solvent, dissolvent
olver \äl-vər\ solver, absolver, dissolver, involver, revolver
[1]**oly** \ō-lē\ goalie, holey, holy, lowly, mole, moly, pollee, slowly, solely, aioli, amole, anole, cannoli, frijole, pinole, unholy, guacamole, ravioli, roly-poly
[2]**oly** \äl-ē\ see [1]OLLY
olyp \äl-əp\ see OLLOP
[1]**om** \äm\ balm, bomb, bombe, calm, from, gaum, Guam, glom, malm, mom, palm, Pom, pram, prom, psalm, qualm, rhomb, ROM, tom, A-bomb, aplomb, ashram, becalm, Ceram, cheongsam, coulomb, Coulomb, dive-bomb, embalm, EPROM, firebomb, grande dame, H-bomb, imam, Islam, Long Tom, napalm, nizam, noncom, phenom, pogrom, pom-pom, reclame, rhabdom, salaam, seram, sitcom, Songnam, tam-tam, therefrom, tom-tom, wherefrom, wigwam, cardamom, diatom, intercom, Peeping Tom, Uncle Tom, Vietnam, Dar es Salaam, Omar Kayyam
[2]**om** \ōm\ see [1]OME
[3]**om** \üm\ see [1]OOM

[4]om \əm\ see [1]UM
[5]om \u̇m\ see [2]UM
[6]om \ȯm\ see [1]AUM
oma \ō-mə\ chroma, coma, Roma, soma, aroma, diploma, glaucoma, sarcoma, Tacoma, carcinoma, granuloma, melanoma, Oklahoma, glioblastoma, neurofibroma
omac \ō-mik\ see [2]OMIC
[1]omace \äm-əs\ see OMISE
[2]omace \əm-əs\ see UMMOUS
omach \əm-ək\ see UMMOCK
omache \äm-ə-kē\ see OMACHY
omachy \äm-ə-kē\ Andromache, logomachy
omal \ō-məl\ domal, stomal, prodromal, chromosomal
omaly \äm-ə-lē\ balmily, homily, anomaly
oman \ō-mən\ bowman, foeman, gnomon, nomen, omen, Roman, showman, snowman, yeoman, agnomen, cognomen, crossbowman, longbowman, praenomen, Sertoman
omany \äm-ə-nē\ see OMINY
omas \äm-əs\ see OMISE
omathy \äm-ə-thē\ chrestomathy, stichomythy
[1]omb \ōm\ see [1]OME
[2]omb \üm\ see [1]OOM
[3]omb \äm\ see [1]OM
[4]omb \əm\ see [1]UM
omba \äm-bə\ see AMBA
[1]ombe \ōm\ see [1]OME
[2]ombe \üm\ see [1]OOM
[3]ombe \äm\ see [1]OM
ombed \ümd\ see OOMED
[1]omber \äm-ər\ bomber, calmer, palmar, palmer, Palmer, dive-bomber, embalmer, fighter-bomber
[2]omber \äm-bər\ ombre, sambar, somber
[3]omber \ō-mər\ see [1]OMER
ombic \ō-mik\ see [2]OMIC
ombical \ō-mi-kəl\ see [2]OMICAL
ombie \äm-bē\ zombie, Abercrombie
ombing \ō-miŋ\ see OAMING
[1]ombo \äm-bō\ combo, mambo, sambo
[2]ombo \əm-bō\ see UMBO
[1]ombre \äm-brē\ hombre, ombre
[2]ombre \äm-bər\ see [2]OMBER
[3]ombre \əm-brē\ see UMBERY
ombus \äm-bəs\ rhombus, thrombus
[1]ome \ōm\ brougham, chrome, comb, combe, dome, foam, gloam, gnome, holm, home, loam, mome, nome, ohm, om, poem, pome, roam, Rom, Rome, tome, airdrome, at-home, bichrome, cockscomb, coulomb, coxcomb, defoam, down-home, Jerome, Nichrome, ogham, seadrome, shalom, sholom, Stockholm, syndrome, aerodrome, astrodome, catacomb, chromosome, currycomb, double-dome, gastronome, halidrome, hecatomb, hippodrome, honeycomb, metronome, monochrome, motordrome, palindrome, ribosome, stay-at-home, Styrofoam
[2]ome \ō-mē\ see OAMY
[3]ome \əm\ see [1]UM

omedy \äm-əd-ē\ comedy, psalmody, tragicomedy
omely \əm-lē\ see ²UMBLY
omen \ō-mən\ see OMAN
omenal \äm-ən-ᵊl\ see OMINAL
omene \äm-ə-nē\ see OMINY
¹omer \ō-mər\ comber, foamer, homer, Homer, omer, roamer, vomer, beachcomber, Reaumur, Lag b'Omer, misnomer
²omer \əm-ər\ see UMMER
omery \əm-ə-rē\ see UMMERY
omet \äm-ət\ comet, grommet, vomit
ometer \äm-ət-ər\ barometer, chronometer, cyclometer, drunkometer, ergometer, gasometer, geometer, hydrometer, hygrometer, kilometer, manometer, micrometer, odometer, pedometer, photometer, pulsometer, pyrometer, rheometer, seismometer, spectrometer, speedometer, tachometer, thermometer, anemometer, audiometer, diffractometer, electrometer, magnetometer, alcoholometer
ometry \äm-ə-trē\ astrometry, barometry, chronometry, cytometry, geometry, isometry, micrometry, optometry, photometry, psychometry, seismometry, thermometry, craniometry, sociometry, trigonometry
omey \ō-mē\ see OAMY
omi \ō-mē\ see OAMY
omia \ō-mē-ä\ peperomia, Utsunomia
¹omic \äm-ik\ comic, anomic, atomic, coelomic, Islamic, tsunamic, agronomic, anatomic, antinomic, autonomic, economic, ergonomic, gastronomic, metronomic, subatomic, taxonomic, tragicomic, Deuteronomic, heroicomic, physiognomic, polyatomic, seriocomic, macroeconomic, microeconomic, socioeconomic
²omic \ō-mik\ gnomic, oghamic, Potomac, rhizomic, catacombic, monochromic, palindromic
¹omical \äm-i-kəl\ comical, domical, agronomical, anatomical, astronomical, economical, gastronomical, metronomical, tragicomical, heroicomical, physiognomical
²omical \ō-mi-kəl\ domical, coxcombical
omics \äm-iks\ atomics, Islamics, tectonics, bionomics, economics, ergonomics, macroeconomics, microeconomics—*also plurals and possessives of nouns listed at* ¹OMIC
omily \äm-ə-lē\ see OMALY
ominal \äm-ən-ᵊl\ nominal, abdominal, cognominal, phenomenal, epiphenomenal
ominance \äm-nəns\ dominance, prominence, predominance
ominant \äm-nənt\ dominant, prominent, predominant,

semidominant, subdominant, superdominant
ominate \äm-ə-nət\ innominate, prenominate
omine \äm-ə-nē\ see OMINY
ominence \äm-nəns\ see OMINANCE
ominent \äm-nənt\ see OMINANT
[1]oming \əm-iŋ\ coming, plumbing, becoming, forthcoming, homecoming, incoming, oncoming, shortcoming, upcoming, unbecoming, up-and-coming—*also present participles of verbs listed at* [1]UM
[2]oming \ō-miŋ\ see OAMING
omini \äm-ə-nē\ see OMINY
ominous \äm-ə-nəs\ ominous, prolegomenous
ominy \äm-ə-nē\ hominy, Romany, Melpomene, anno Domini, eo nomine
omise \äm-əs\ pomace, promise, shammes, shamus, Thomas, Saint Thomas, doubting Thomas
omish \ō-mish\ gnomish, Romish
omit \äm-ət\ see OMET
omium \ō-mē-əm\ chromium, holmium, encomium, prostomium
[1]omma \äm-ə\ see [2]AMA
[2]omma \əm-ə\ see UMMA
[1]ommel \äm-əl\ pommel, Jamil, Rommel, trommel
[2]ommel \əm-əl\ pommel, pummel, Beau Brummell
ommet \äm-ət\ see OMET
ommie \äm-ē\ see [1]AMI
ommon \äm-ən\ Amon, Brahman, common, shaman, yamen, Roscommon, Tutankhamen
ommoner \äm-ə-nər\ almoner, commoner, gewürztraminer
[1]ommy \äm-ē\ see [1]AMI
[2]ommy \əm-ē\ see UMMY
omo \ō-mō\ bromo, Como, homo, Pomo, promo, Oromo, majordomo
omon \ō-mən\ see OMAN
[1]omp \ämp\ champ, chomp, clomp, comp, pomp, romp, stamp, stomp, swamp, tramp, tromp, whomp
[2]omp \əmp\ see UMP
ompany \əmp-nē\ company, accompany, intracompany
ompass \əm-pəs\ compass, rumpus, encompass, gyrocompass
omper \äm-pər\ romper, stamper, stomper, swamper, wafflestomper
ompers \äm-pərz\ Gompers—*also possessives and plurals of nouns listed at* OMPER
ompey \äm-pē\ see OMPY
omplement \äm-plə-mənt\ complement, compliment
ompliment \äm-plə-mənt\ see OMPLEMENT
ompo \äm-pō\ campo, compo
ompous \äm-pəs\ see [1]OMPASS
ompson \äm-sən\ see AMSUN
ompt \aủnt\ see [2]OUNT
ompy \äm-pē\ Pompey, swampy
omythy \äm-ə-thē\ see OMATHY
[1]on \än\ ban, Bonn, chon, con,

conn, dawn, don, Don, Donn, drawn, Fan, faun, fawn, gone, guan, Han, John, Jon, khan, maun, mon, on, pan, pawn, phon, prawn, Ron, Shan, spawn, swan, Vaughn, wan, yawn, yon, yuan, aeon, add-on, agon, agone, Akan, alençon, Amman, ancon, anon, Anshan, Anton, archon, argon, Argonne, Aswan, atman, Avon, axon, barchan, baton, blouson, bon ton, bonbon, boron, boson, bouillon, Brython, bygone, caisson, Calgon, canton, capon, Ceylon, chaconne, chiffon, chignon, Chiron, chiton, chrismon, cistron, clip-on, codon, come-on, cordon, coupon, crampon, crayon, crepon, cretonne, crouton, Dacron, dead-on, Dear John, dewan, doggone, doggoned, Dogon, Don Juan, eon, exon, far-gone, flacon, foregone, Freon, fronton, Fujian, Garonne, Gibran, gluon, gnomon, Golan, Gosplan, guidon, hadron, Hainan, hazan, Henan, hogan, Huainan, Hunan, icon, Inchon, intron, Ivan, Jinan, Kanban, kaon, Kashan, Kazan, Kerman, Khoisan, Kirman, koan, krypton, kurgan, Kurgan, lauan, Leon, lepton, liman, log on, Luzon, macron, Massan, Medan, Memnon, meson, micron, Milan, mod con, moron, mouton, Multan, muon, natron, neon, nephron, neuron, neutron, ninon, nylon, odds-on, Oman, Oran, Orlon, outgone, pacon, parton, Pathan, pavane, pecan, peon, Phaethon, photon, phyton, pion, pinon, piton, plankton, pluton, pompon, prion, proton, Pusan, put-on, pylon, python, Qur'an, radon, rayon, recon, rhyton, run-on, Saint John, Saipan, salon, San Juan, Schumann, Shaban, shaman, shaitan, Shingon, Simplon, Sjoelland, slip-on, snap-on, solon, soupçon, soutane, Stefan, stolon, Suwon, Szechuan, Szechwan, Tainan, Taiwan, talpan, tampon, taxon, Teflon, teston, Tétouan, Tetuán, thereon, tisane, torchon, toucan, toyon, trigon, Tristan, triton, trogon, Tucson, Typhon, tzigane, uhlan, Ulsan, upon, walk-on, witan, whereon, Wonsan, wonton, Wuhan, xenon, Xi'an, yaupon, Yukon, Yunnan, Yvonne, zircon, Abadan, Abijan, Acheron, Ahriman, aileron, amazon, Amazon, amnion, Aragon, autobahn, Avalon, Babylon, Bakhtaran, Balaton, balmacaan, Bantustan, Barbizon, baryon, Basilan, betatron, biathlon, cabochon, calutron, carillon, carryon, celadon, chorion, colophon, Culiacàn, cyclotron, decagon, decathlon, demijohn, deuteron, dipteron, echelon, electron, elevon, epsilon, etymon, fermion, follow-on, Fujisan, Genghis Khan, goings-on, gonfalon, Grand Teton, graviton, harijan, helicon, heptagon, hexagon, hopping John, Huascaràn, Ilion, Irian, Isfahan, Kazakhstan, Kublai Khan, Kyrgyzstan, Lake Huron, Lebanon, leprechaun, lexicon, liaison, Lipizzan, logion, macédoine, marathon, Marathon, marzipan, mastodon, Mazatlàn, Mbabane, Mellotron, Miquelon, morion, myrmidon, negatron, nonagon, noumenon, nucleon, Oberon, octagon, omicron, Oregon, organon, ostracon, Pakistan, Palawan, pantheon, paragon, Parmesan, parmigiana, Parthenon, pentagon, Percheron, Phaethon, Phlegethon, polygon, positron, Procyon, put-upon, Rajasthan, Ramadan, Rubicon, silicon, Suleiman, tachyon, Taiyuan, talkathon, Teheran, telamon, telethon, thereupon, Tian Shan, Tucuman, undergone, upsilon, virion, walkathon, whereupon, woebegone, Yerevan, Zahedan, abutilon, Agamemnon, archenteron, arrière-ban, asyndeton, automaton, Azerbaijan, Bellerophon, bildungsroman, carrying-on, Diazenon, dimetrodon, dodecagon, encephalon, ephemeron, himation, interferon, kakiemon, Laocoön, mesenteron, Michoacàn, millimicron, oxymoron, phenomenon, protozoon, Saskatchewan, septentrion, sine qua non, t'ai chi ch'uan, Taklimakan, Vientiane, West Irian, Xiangtan, anacoluthon, diencephalon, ferrosilicon, mesencephalon, metencephalon, prolegomenon, prothalamion, prosencephalon, pteranodon, spermatozoon, telencephalon, ultramarathon, epiphenomenon, myelencephalon, kyrie eleison, San Miguel de Tucumàn

[2]**on** \ō^{n}\ fond, ton, ballon, baton, bouillon, Dijon, flacon, fourgon, frisson, Gabon, garçon, lorgnon, Lyons, maçon, marron, Marron, mouflon, soupçon, Toulon, Villon, Aubusson, bourguignon, feuilleton, Ganelon, gueridon, limaçon, papillon, filet mignon, Saint Emilion

[3]**on** \ȯn\ awn, Bonn, bonne, brawn, dawn, Dawn, drawn, faun, fawn, gone, lawn, maun, on, pawn, prawn, Sean, spawn, Vaughn, won, yawn, add-on, agon, agone, begone, bygone, chaconne, clip-on, come-on, dead-on, doggone, far-gone, foregone, hands-on, hard-on, head-on, hereon,

impawn, indrawn, Kherson, odds-on, outgone, Puchon, put-on, Quezon, run-on, slip-on, snap-on, Taejon, thereon, turned-on, upon, walk-on, whereon, wiredrawn, withdrawn, bourguignonne, carryon, follow-on, goings-on, hanger-on, hereupon, looker-on, put-upon, thereupon, undergone, whereupon, woebegone, carrying-on

[4]on \ōn\ see [1]ONE

[5]on \ən\ see UN

[1]ona \ō-nə\ dona, Dona, Jonah, krone, Mona, Nona, Rhona, Rona, Shona, trona, Ancona, Bellona, bologna, Bologna, cinchona, corona, kimono, Leona, madrona, Pamplona, persona, Ramona, Verona, Arizona, Barcelona, Desdemona, in propria persona

[2]ona \än-ə\ see [1]ANA

oña \ōn-yə\ see [3]ONIA

onachal \än-i-kəl\ see ONICAL

onae \ō-nē\ see [1]ONY

onah \ō-nə\ see ONA

[1]onal \ōn-^{ə}l\ clonal, tonal, zonal, atonal, coronal, hormonal, baritonal, microtonal, polyclonal, polytonal, semitonal

[2]onal \än-^{ə}l\ Donal, Ronal

onald \än-^{ə}ld\ Donald, Ronald, MacDonald

onant \ō-nənt\ see ONENT

onas \ō-nəs\ see [2]ONUS

onative \ō-nət-iv\ conative, donative

onc \äŋk\ see [1]ONK

[1]once \äns\ see [2]ANCE

[2]once \əns\ see UNCE

[1]onch \äŋk\ see [1]ONK

[2]onch \änch\ see [1]AUNCH

oncha \äŋ-kə\ see ANKA

oncho \än-chō\ honcho, poncho, rancho

onchus \äŋ-kəs\ bronchus, rhonchus

onco \äŋ-kō\ bronco, Franco

[1]ond \änd\ blond, bond, fond, frond, Gond, pond, rand, sonde, wand, yond, abscond, Armand, beau monde, beyond, despond, fishpond, Gironde, gourmand, haut monde, millpond, neoned, pair-bond, respond, allemande, towmond, correspond, demimonde, Eurobond, Trebizond, Trobriand, vagabond, radiosonde, slough of despond—*also pasts of verbs listed at* [1]ON

[2]ond \ō^{n}\ see [2]ON

[3]ond \ȯnt\ see [1]AUNT

onda \än-də\ Lahnda, Rhonda, Rhondda, Ronda, Wanda, Golconda, Luganda, Ruanda, Rwanda, Uganda, anaconda, Campo Grande

ondam \än-dəm\ see [1]ONDOM

ondant \än-dənt\ see ONDENT

onday \ən-dē\ see UNDI

ondays \ən-dēz\ see UNDAYS

ondda \än-də\ see ONDA

onde \änd\ see [1]OND

ondeau \än-dō\ see ONDO

ondel \än-d^{ə}l\ condyle, fondle, rondel

ondence \än-dəns\ correspondence, despondence
ondency \än-dən-sē\ despondency, correspondency
ondent \än-dənt\ fondant, despondent, respondent, corespondent, correspondent
[1]**onder** \än-dər\ bonder, condor, maunder, ponder, squander, wander, yonder, zander, absconder, responder, transponder—*also comparatives of adjectives listed at* [1]OND
[2]**onder** \ən-dər\ see UNDER
ondly \än-lē\ see [1]ANLY
ondness \än-nəs\ see ANNESS
ondo \än-dō\ condo, Hondo, rondeau, rondo, secondo, tondo, forzando, glissando, lentando, parlando, scherzando, sforzando, allargando, rallentando, ritardando, accelerando
[1]**ondom** \än-dəm\ condom, quondam
[2]**ondom** \ən-dəm\ see UNDUM
ondor \än-dər\ see [1]ONDER
ondrous \ən-drəs\ see UNDEROUS
ondyle \än-dᵊl\ see ONDEL
[1]**one** \ōn\ blown, bone, clone, cone, crone, drone, flown, groan, grown, hone, Joan, known, loan, lone, moan, Mon, mown, none, own, phone, pone, prone, Rhone, roan, Saône, scone, sewn, shone, shoon, shown, sone, sown, stone, throne, thrown, tone, trone, won, zone, agon, aitchbone, alone, atone, backbone, bemoan, birthstone, Blackstone, breastbone, brimstone, brownstone, capstone, cheekbone, chinbone, cogon, cologne, Cologne, colon, Coloón, condone, curbstone, cyclone, daimon, debone, depone, dethrone, disown, drystone, earphone, enthrone, fieldstone, flagstone, flyblown, freestone, full-blown, gallstone, gemstone, Gijón, Gladstone, gravestone, grindstone, hailstone, halftone, handblown, headphone, headstone, high-flown, hipbone, homegrown, hormone, impone, ingrown, inkstone, intone, jawbone, keystone, León, leone, limestone, lodestone, Mount Mayon, milestone, millstone, misknown, moonstone, oilstone, outgrown, outshown, ozone, peon, pinbone, pinecone, pinon, pinyon, postpone, propone, Ramon, rezone, rhinestone, sandstone, shade-grown, shinbone, Shoshone, soapstone, T-bone, tailbone, thighbone, tombstone, touchstone, Touch-Tone, tritone, trombone, turnstone, twelve-tone, two-tone, Tyrone, unknown, unthrone, well-known, whalebone, wheel-thrown, whetstone, windblown, wishbone, Yangon, allophone, anglophone, anklebone,

barbitone, Barbizon, barytone, Bayamon, bombardon, Canal Zone, chaperon, cherrystone, cobblestone, collarbone, cornerstone, cortisone, cuttlebone, diaphone, Dictaphone, epigone, francophone, free-fire zone, Gaborone, gramophone, herringbone, homophone, ironstone, knucklebone, marrowbone, megaphone, mellophone, methadone, microphone, microtone, minestrone, monotone, overblown, overflown, overgrown, overthrown, overtone, Picturephone, polyphone, rottenstone, sacaton, saxophone, semitone, shacklebone, silicone, sousaphone, speakerphone, stepping-stone, telephone, Toreón, undertone, vibraphone, xylophone, Yellowstone, anticyclone, Asunción, bred-in-the-bone, Concepción, eau de cologne, mesocyclone, norethindrone, Nuevo Leon, radiophone, sine qua non, testosterone, videophone, Darby and Joan, Ponce de Leon, Sierra Leone, radiotelephone

[2]**one** \ō-nē\ see [1]ONY

[3]**one** \än\ see [1]ON

[4]**one** \ən\ see UN

[5]**one** \ȯn\ see [3]ON

onean \ō-nē-ən\ see [1]ONIAN

[1]**oned** \ōnd\ boned, stoned, toned, cologned, high-toned, pre-owned, rawboned, rhinestoned, two-toned, cobblestoned—*also pasts of verbs listed at* [1]ONE

[2]**oned** \än\ see [1]ON

oneless \ōn-ləs\ boneless, toneless

onely \ōn-lē\ lonely, only, pronely

onement \ōn-mənt\ atonement, cantonment, dethronement, disownment, enthronement

oneness \ən-nəs\ dunness, doneness, oneness, rotundness

onent \ō-nənt\ sonant, component, deponent, exponent, opponent, proponent, bicomponent

oneous \ō-nē-əs\ see ONIOUS

[1]**oner** \ō-nər\ boner, donor, droner, groaner, honer, loaner, loner, stoner, toner, zoner, condoner, dethroner, intoner, landowner, shipowner, telephoner

[2]**oner** \ȯn-ər\ see [1]AWNER

onerous \än-ə-rəs\ onerous, sonorous

ones \ōnz\ Jones, nones, sawbones, Davy Jones, lazybones, skull and crossbones—*also plurals and possessives of nouns and third person singular presents of verbs listed at* [1]ONE

onest \än-əst\ honest, dishonest, Hinayanist, Mahayanist

[1]**oney** \ō-nē\ see [1]ONY

[2]**oney** \ən-ē\ see UNNY

[3]**oney** \ü-nē\ see OONY

[1]**ong** \äŋ\ Chang, Fang, gong, hong, Huang, prong, Shang, Tang, tong, yang, Anyang,

barong, biltong, Da Nang, dugong, Guiyang, Hanyang, Heng-yang, Hong Kong, kiang, liang, Mah-Jongg, Malang, Padang, satang, Wuchang, Zhejiang, Zhenjiang, billabong, Chittagong, Liaoyang, Pyongyang, Semarang, scuppernong, Shenyang, Sturm und Drang, Vietcong, Shijiazhuang, Ujung Pandang, Wollongong, ylang-ylang, Heilongjiang

[2]**ong** \ȯŋ\ bong, dong, gong, long, prong, song, strong, thong, throng, tong, wrong, agelong, along, Armstrong, barong, belong, biltong, birdsong, chaise longue, daylong, dingdong, diphthong, dugong, endlong, erelong, furlong, Geelong, Haiphong, headlong, headstrong, Kaesong, kampong, lifelong, livelong, Mekong, monthlong, Nanchang, nightlong, oblong, oolong, part-song, ping-pong, Ping-Pong, plainsong, prolong, sarong, Shandong, sidelong, singsong, so long, souchong, weeklong, yardlong, yearlong, billabong, Chittagong, cradlesong, evensong, Palembang, scuppernong, sing-along, summerlong, tagalong, Vietcong

[3]**ong** \əŋ\ see [1]UNG

[4]**ong** \u̇ng\ see [2]UNG

onga \äŋ-gə\ conga, panga, tonga, Tonga, Kananga, mridanga, Alba Longa, Zamboanga, Bucaramanga

onge \ənj\ see UNGE

onged \ȯŋd\ pronged, thonged, multipronged—*also pasts of verbs listed at* [2]ONG

[1]**onger** \əŋ-gər\ hunger, monger, younger, fellmonger, fishmonger, ironmonger, newsmonger, phrasemonger, scaremonger, warmonger, whoremonger, wordmonger, costermonger, fashionmonger, gossipmonger, rumormonger, scandalmonger

[2]**onger** \ən-jər\ see [1]UNGER

ongery \əŋ-grē\ hungry, fellmongery, ironmongery

ongful \ȯŋ-fəl\ wrongful, songful

ongin \ən-jən\ see UNGEON

ongish \ȯŋ-ish\ longish, strongish

ongo \äŋ-gō\ bongo, Congo, congou, Kongo, mongo, Niger-Congo, Pago Pago

ongous \əŋ-gəs\ see UNGOUS

[1]**ongue** \əŋ\ see [1]UNG

[2]**ongue** \ȯŋ\ see [2]ONG

ongued \əŋd\ lunged, tongued

ongy \ən-jē\ see UNGY

onhomous \än-ə-məs\ see ONYMOUS

oni \ō-nē\ see [1]ONY

[1]**onia** \ō-nē-ə\ bignonia, clintonia, Estonia, Laconia, Livonia, mahonia, paulownia, Polonia, Slavonia, Snowdonia, tithonia, valonia, zirconia, Amazonia,

Caledonia, Catalonia, Macedonia
[2]onia \ō-nyə\ Konya, Sonia, Sonja, Sonya, ammonia, Bologna, pneumonia, Polonia, tithonia, valonia, anhedonia, Caledonia, Macedonia, New Caledonia, Patagonia
[3]onia \ōn-yə\ doña, begonia
onial \ō-nē-əl\ baronial, colonial, ceremonial, matrimonial, testimonial
[1]onian \ō-nē-ən\ chthonian, aeonian, Antonian, Baconian, Clactonian, demonian, Devonian, draconian, Estonian, Etonian, favonian, gorgonian, Ionian, Jacksonian, Oxonian, plutonian, Samsonian, Shoshonean, Slavonian, Amazonian, Apollonian, Arizonian, Babylonian, calypsonian, Chalcedonian, Hamiltonian, parkinsonian
[2]onian \ō-nyən\ Zonian, Amazonian, Babylonian, Estonian, Macedonian
onic \än-ik\ chronic, chthonic, conic, dornick, phonic, sonic, tonic, Aaronic, agonic, atonic, benthonic, bionic, Brittonic, Brythonic, bubonic, Byronic, canonic, carbonic, cryonic, cyclonic, daimonic, demonic, draconic, euphonic, gnomonic, harmonic, hedonic, ionic, Ionic, ironic, laconic, Masonic, mnemonic, planktonic, platonic, plutonic, pneumonic, Puranic, Pythonic, sardonic, Saronic, sermonic, Slavonic, symphonic, synchronic, tectonic, Teutonic, ultrasonic, zirconic, catatonic, diachronic, diatonic, disharmonic, electronic, embryonic, hegemonic, histrionic, homophonic, hydroponic, inharmonic, isotonic, macaronic, megaphonic, microphonic, monophonic, monotonic, nonionic, pharaonic, Philharmonic, polyphonic, quadraphonic, semitonic, Solomonic, supersonic, supertonic, telephonic, thermionic, architectonic, chameleonic, cardiotonic, electrotonic, geotectonic, Neoplatonic, stereophonic, extraembryonic
onica \än-i-kə\ Monica, harmonica, japonica, Salonika, veronica, Veronica, Thessalonica
onical \än-i-kəl\ chronicle, conical, monachal, monocle, canonical, demonical, ironical, deuterocanonical
onicals \än-i-kəlz\ Chronicles, canonicals
onicker \ä-ni-kər\ see ONNICKER
onicle \än-i-kəl\ see ONICAL
onicles \än-i-kəlz\ see ONICALS
onics \än-iks\ onyx, phonics, bionics, cryonics, mnemonics, Ovonics, photonics, sardonyx, tectonics, avionics, electronics, histrionics, hydroponics, microphonics,

nucleonics, quadriphonics, radionics, supersonics, thermionics, architectonics—*also plurals and possessives of nouns listed at* ONIC
onika \än-i-kə\ see ONICA
oniker \ä-ni-kər\ see ONNICKER
[1]**oning** \än-iŋ\ awning, couponing
[2]**oning** \ō-niŋ\ loaning, jawboning, landowning
onion \ən-yən\ see UNION
onious \ō-nē-əs\ erroneous, euphonious, felonious, harmonious, Polonius, Suetonius, symphonious, acrimonious, ceremonious, disharmonious, inharmonious, parsimonious, sanctimonious, Marcus Antonius, unceremonious
[1]**onis** \ō-nəs\ see [2]ONUS
[2]**onis** \än-əs\ see [1]ONUS
onish \än-ish\ donnish, monish, admonish, astonish, premonish, leprechaunish
onishment \än-ish-mənt\ admonishment, astonishment
onium \ō-nē-əm\ euphonium, harmonium, plutonium, pandemonium, Pandemonium
onius \ō-nē-əs\ see ONIOUS
onja \ō-nyə\ see [2]ONIA
onjon \ən-jən\ see UNGEON
onjure \än-jər\ conjure, rondure
[1]**onk** \äŋk\ ankh, bronc, clonk, conch, conk, Franck, honk, Planck, plonk, zonk, honkytonk
[2]**onk** \əŋk\ see UNK
onker \äŋ-kər\ conker, conquer, honker
[1]**onkey** \äŋ-kē\ see ONKY
[2]**onkey** \əŋ-kē\ see UNKY
onkian \äŋ-kē-ən\ conquian, Algonkian
onky \äŋ-kē\ conkey, donkey, honkie, wonky, yanqui
onless \ən-ləs\ see UNLESS
only \ōn-lē\ see ONELY
onment \ōn-mənt\ see ONEMENT
[1]**onn** \än\ see [1]ON
[2]**onn** \ȯn\ see [3]ON
[1]**onna** \ȯn-ə\ donna, Donna, fauna, prima donna, megafauna
[2]**onna** \än-ə\ see [1]ANA
onnage \ən-ij\ see UNNAGE
[1]**onne** \än\ see [1]ON
[2]**onne** \ən\ see UN
[3]**onne** \ȯn\ see [3]ON
onner \än-ər\ see [1]ONOR
onnet \än-ət\ bonnet, sonnet, bluebonnet, sunbonnet, warbonnet
onnicker \ä-ni-kər\ donnicker, doniker, monicker, moniker
onnie \än-ē\ see [1]ANI
onnish \än-ish\ see ONISH
onnor \än-ər\ see [1]ONOR
[1]**onny** \än-ē\ see [1]ANI
[2]**onny** \ən-ē\ see UNNY
[1]**ono** \ō-nō\ phono, cui bono, kimono, pro bono, kakemono, makimono
[2]**ono** \ō-nə\ see ONA
[3]**ono** \än-ō\ see [1]ANO
onocle \än-i-kəl\ see ONICAL
onomer \än-ə-mər\ monomer, astronomer, comonomer
onomist \än-ə-məst\ agronomist, autonomist, economist, ergonomist,

gastronomist, synonymist, taxonomist, Deuteronomist
onomous \än-ə-məs\ see ONYMOUS
onomy \än-ə-mē\ agronomy, antonymy, astronomy, autonomy, economy, eponymy, gastronomy, homonomy, metonymy, synonymy, taphonomy, taxonomy, toponymy, Deuteronomy, diseconomy, heteronomy, teleonomy
[1]onor \än-ər\ Bonner, fawner, goner, honor, dishonor, O'Connor, Lipizzaner, marathoner, Afrikaner, weimaraner
[2]onor \ō-nər\ see [1]ONER
onorous \än-ə-rəs\ see ONEROUS
onquer \äŋ-kər\ see ONKER
onquian \äŋ-kē-ən\ see ONKIAN
[1]ons \änz\ see ONZE
[2]ons \ōn\ see [2]ON
onsil \än-səl\ see ONSUL
onsin \än-sən\ see OHNSON
onson \än-sən\ see OHNSON
onsor \än-sər\ panzer, sponsor
onsul \än-səl\ consul, tonsil
on't \ōnt\ don't, won't
[1]ont \ənt\ blunt, brunt, bunt, front, grunt, hunt, lunt, punt, runt, shunt, strunt, stunt, want, wont, affront, beachfront, bowfront, breakfront, confront, forefront, housefront, lakefront, manhunt, out-front, seafront, shirtfront, shorefront, storefront, swell-front, up-front, witch-hunt, battlefront, oceanfront, riverfront, waterfront
[2]ont \änt\ see [2]ANT
[3]ont \ȯnt\ see [1]AUNT
[1]ontal \änt-əl\ pontil, fontal, quantal, horizontal, periodontal
[2]ontal \ənt-əl\ see UNTLE
ontan \ änt-ən\ see ONTON
ontas \änt-əs\ see ONTUS
[1]onte \änt-ē\ see [1]ANTI
[2]onte \än-tā\ see [1]ANTE
onted \ȯnt-əd\ vaunted, wonted, undaunted—*also pasts of verbs listed at* [1]AUNT
onter \ənt-ər\ see UNTER
onth \ənth\ month, billionth, millionth, trillionth, twelvemonth
ontian \änt-ē-ən\ Zontian, post-Kantian
ontic \änt-ik\ ontic, deontic, Vedantic, orthodontic, anacreontic
ontil \änt-əl\ see [1]ONTAL
ontinent \änt-ən-ənt\ continent, incontinent, subcontinent, supercontinent
ontis \än-təs\ see [2]ANTOS
ontist \änt-əst\ Vedantist, orthodontist, prosthodontist
onto \än-tō\ see [1]ANTO
onton \änt-ən\ ponton, wanton, Lahontan
ontra \än-trə\ contra, mantra, tantra, per contra
ontre \änt-ər\ see [1]AUNTER
ontus \änt-əs\ Pontus, Pocahontas
onty \änt-ē\ see [1]ANTI
[1]onus \än-əs\ Cronus, Faunus, Adonis

[2]onus \ō-nəs\ bonus, Cronus, Jonas, onus, slowness, Adonis, colonus

[1]ony \ō-nē\ bony, coney, crony, phony, pony, stony, Toni, tony, Tony, yoni, baloney, Benoni, bologna, canzone, Marconi, Moroni, Oenone, padrone, spumoni, tortoni, abalone, acrimony, agrimony, alimony, antimony, cannelloni, ceremony, chalcedony, colophony, macaroni, mascarpone, matrimony, minestrone, palimony, parsimony, patrimony, pepperoni, provolone, rigatoni, sanctimony, telephony, testimony, zabaglione, con espressione, conversazione, dramatis personae

[2]ony \än-ē\ see [1]ANI

onya \ō-nyə\ see [2]ONIA

onymist \än-ə-məst\ see ONOMIST

onymous \än-ə-məs\ bonhomous, anonymous, antonymous, autonomous, eponymous, homonymous, pseudonymous, synonymous, heteronomous

onymy \än-ə-mē\ see ONOMY

[1]onyon \än-yən\ ronyon, wanion

[2]onyon \ən-yən\ see UNION

onyx \än-iks\ see ONICS

onze \änz\ bonze, bronze, pons, long johns, Saint John's, Afrikaans, solitons, islet of Langerhans—*also plurals and possessives of nouns and third person singular presents of verbs listed at* [1]ON

onzi \än-zē\ see ONZY

onzy \än-zē\ bronzy, Ponzi

[1]oo \ü\ see [1]EW

[2]oo \ō\ see [1]OW

oob \üb\ see UBE

oober \ü-bər\ see UBER

ooby \ü-bē\ booby, looby, ruby, Ruby

[1]ooch \üch\ brooch, hooch, mooch, pooch, smooch, capuche, scaramouch

[2]ooch \ōch\ see OACH

oocher \ü-chər\ see UTURE

oochy \ü-chē\ smoochy, Baluchi, penuche, Vespucci, Kawaguchi

[1]ood \u̇d\ good, hood, pud, rudd, should, stood, wood, would, yod, basswood, bentwood, blackwood, boxwood, brushwood, childhood, cordwood, deadwood, do-good, dogwood, driftwood, Ellwood, Elwood, falsehood, fatwood, feel-good, firewood, fruitwood, girlhood, godhood, greasewood, greenwood, groundwood, gumwood, hardwood, ironwood, kingwood, knighthood, maidhood, manhood, monkhood, monkshood, Mount Hood, no-good, pinewood, plywood, priesthood, pulpwood, redwood, rosewood, sainthood, selfhood, Sherwood, softwood, sonhood, statehood, stinkwood, Talmud, teakwood, unhood, Wedgwood, wifehood, withstood, wormwood, arrowwood, bachelorhood, brotherhood, buttonwood, candlewood, cedarwood, cottonwood, fatherhood, hardihood, Hollywood, likelihood, livelihood, maidenhood, motherhood, nationhood, neighborhood, parenthood, peckerwood, personhood, Robin Hood, sandalwood, scattergood, servanthood, sisterhood, spinsterhood, toddlerhood, tulipwood, understood, widowhood, womanhood, misunderstood, unlikelihood, widowerhood

[2]**ood** \ōd\ see ODE

[3]**ood** \üd\ see UDE

[4]**ood** \əd\ see [1]UD

[1]**ooded** \əd-əd\ blooded, cold-blooded, full-blooded, half-blooded, hot-blooded, pure-blooded, red-blooded, star-studded, warm-blooded—*also pasts of verbs listed at* [1]UD

[2]**ooded** \u̇d-əd\ hooded, wooded, hard-wooded, soft-wooded

[1]**ooder** \üd-ər\ see UDER

[2]**ooder** \əd-ər\ see UDDER

ooding \u̇d-iŋ\ pudding, do-gooding

oodle \üd-ᵊl\ boodle, doodle, feudal, noodle, poodle, strudel, caboodle, flapdoodle, paludal, Yankee-Doodle

oodman \u̇d-mən\ goodman, woodman

oodoo \üd-ü\ doo-doo, hoodoo, kudu, voodoo

oods \u̇dz\ backwoods, dry goods, piney woods—*also plurals and possessives of nouns and third person singular presents of verbs listed at* [1]OOD

oodsman \u̇dz-mən\ woodsman, backwoodsman, ombudsman

[1]**oody** \üd-ē\ broody, Judi, Judie, Judy, moody, Rudy, Trudy

[2]**oody** \u̇d-ē\ cuddy, goody, hoody, woody, goody-goody

[3]**oody** \əd-ē\ see [1]UDDY

ooer \ü-ər\ see [1]EWER

ooey \ü-ē\ see EWY

[1]**oof** \üf\ goof, kloof, poof, pouf, proof, roof, spoof, woof, aloof, behoof, disproof, fireproof, foolproof, forehoof, rustproof, shadoof, soundproof, sunroof, Tartuffe, unroof, bulletproof, opera bouffe, shatterproof, waterproof, weatherproof

[2]**oof** \u̇f\ hoof, poof, roof, woof, forehoof, Tartuffe

[3]**oof** \ōf\ see OAF

[4]**oof** \üv\ see [3]OVE

oofah \ü-fə\ see UFA

[1]**oofer** \ü-fər\ proofer, roofer, twofer, waterproofer

[2]**oofer** \u̇f-ər\ hoofer, woofer

oofy \ü-fē\ goofy, spoofy, Sufi

ooga \ü-gə\ see UGA

ooge \üj\ see [1]UGE

ooger \u̇g-ər\ see UGUR

oogie \u̇g-ē\ bogey, boogie, boogie-woogie

oo-goo \ü-gü\ see UGU

ooh \ü\ see [1]EW

ooh-pooh \ü-pü\ hoopoe, pooh-pooh

ooi \ü-ē\ see EWY

ooist \ü-əst\ doest, tattooist, voodooist—*also superlatives of adjectives listed at* [1]EW

[1]**ook** \u̇k\ book, brook, Brooke, chook, cook, Cook, crook, gook, hook, look, nook, rook, schnook, shook, snook, stook, took, bankbook, betook, billhook, caoutchouc, chapbook, checkbook, Chinook, cookbook, forsook, fishhook, guidebook, handbook, hornbook, hymnbook, Insbruck, Kobuk, logbook, matchbook, mistook, Mount Cook, notebook, outlook, partook, passbook, Pembroke, playbook, pothook, promptbook, psalmbook, retook, schoolbook, scrapbook, sketchbook, skyhook, songbook, studbook, textbook, unhook, Windhoek, workbook, yearbook, buttonhook, copybook, donnybrook, gerenuk, inglenook, Leeuwenhoek, overbook, overlook, overtook, pocketbook, storybook, tenterhook, undertook, Volapuk, gobbledygook

[2]**ook** \ük\ see UKE

ooka \ü-kə\ yuca, bazooka, felucca, palooka, Toluca, verruca, Juan de Fuca

ookah \u̇k-ə\ hookah, sukkah

ooke \u̇k\ see [1]OOK

ooker \u̇k-ər\ booker, cooker, hooker, Hooker, looker, snooker, good-looker, onlooker

ookery \u̇k-ə-rē\ crookery, rookery

ookie \u̇k-ē\ bookie, brookie, cookie, cooky, hooky, nooky, rookie, rooky, Takatsuki, walkie-lookie

ooking \u̇k-iŋ\ booking, cooking, good-looking, onlooking

ooklet \u̇k-lət\ booklet, brooklet, hooklet

[1]**ooks** \üks\ deluxe, gadzooks—*also plurals and possessives of nouns and third person singular presents of verbs listed at* UKE

[2]**ooks** \u̇ks\ Brooks, crux, luxe, zooks, deluxe, gadzooks—*also plurals and possessives of nouns and third person singular presents of verbs listed at* [1]OOK

[1]**ooky** \ü-kē\ kooky, spooky, bouzouki, Kabuki, saluki, tanuki

[2]**ooky** \u̇k-ē\ see OOKIE

[1]**ool** \ül\ boule, boulle, buhl, cool, drool, fool, fuel, ghoul, gul, joule, mewl, mule, pool, Poole, pul, pule, rule, school, spool, stool, tool, tulle, you'll, yule, air-cool, ampoule, babul, Banjul, befool, Blackpool, carpool, cesspool,

curule, Elul, faldstool, footstool, hangul, Kabul, Kurnool, misrule, Mosul, preschool, retool, self-rule, synfuel, toadstool, tomfool, uncool, vanpool, whirlpool, Barnaul, fascicule, gallinule, graticule, groupuscule, Hartlepool, Istanbul, lenticule, Liverpool, majuscule, minuscule, molecule, monticule, overrule, reticule, ridicule, vestibule, water-cool, biomolecule

[2]ool \ůl\ see [1]UL

oola \ü-lə\ see ULA

oole \ül\ see [1]OOL

oolean \ü-lē-ən\ see ULEAN

ooled \üld\ bejeweled, unschooled, vestibuled—*also pasts of verbs listed at* [1]OOL

ooler \ü-lər\ cooler, gular, puler, ruler, carpooler, grade-schooler, high schooler, preschooler, ridiculer, watercooler

oolie \ü-lē\ see ULY

oolish \ü-lish\ coolish, foolish, ghoulish, mulish, pound-foolish

[1]oolly \ü-lē\ see ULY

[2]oolly \ůl-ē\ see [2]ULLY

[1]oom \üm\ bloom, boom, broom, brougham, brume, combe, cwm, doom, flume, fume, gloom, glume, groom, Hume, khoum, loom, neume, plume, rheum, room, spume, tomb, toom, vroom, whom, womb, zoom, abloom, assume, backroom, ballroom, barroom, bathroom, bedroom, boardroom, bridegroom, broadloom, checkroom, classroom, cloakroom, coatroom, consume, costume, courtroom, darkroom, dayroom, entomb, enwomb, exhume, foredoom, greenroom, guardroom, headroom, heirloom, homeroom, houseroom, illume, inhume, jibboom, Khartoum, legroom, legume, lunchroom, mudroom, mushroom, newsroom, perfume, playroom, poolroom, pressroom, presume, proofroom, relume, resume, salesroom, schoolroom, showroom, sickroom, simoom, stateroom, stockroom, storeroom, subsume, taproom, Targum, tearoom, toolroom, wardroom, washroom, workroom, anteroom, checkerbloom, dyer's broom, elbowroom, impostume, locker-room, miniboom, nom de plume, smoke-filled room, witches'-broom

[2]oom \ům\ see [2]UM

oomed \ümd\ groomed, plumed, wombed, well-groomed—*also pasts of verbs listed at* [1]OOM

oomer \ü-mər\ see UMER

oomily \ü-mə-lē\ gloomily, contumely

[1]ooming \ü-mən\ see UMAN

[2]ooming \ü-miŋ\ see UMING

oomlet \üm-lət\ boomlet, plumelet

oomy \ü-mē\ bloomy, boomy,

doomy, fumy, gloomy, plumy, rheumy, roomy, spumy, costumey

[1]oon \ün\ boon, Boone, coon, croon, dune, goon, hewn, June, loon, lune, moon, noon, prune, rune, shoon, soon, spoon, swoon, strewn, toon, tune, aswoon, attune, baboon, balloon, bassoon, buffoon, Calhoun, cardoon, cartoon, cocoon, commune, doubloon, dragoon, festoon, fine-tune, forenoon, gaboon, gadroon, galloon, Gudrun, half-moon, harpoon, immune, impugn, jargoon, jejune, Kowloon, Kunlun, lagoon, lampoon, lardoon, maroon, monsoon, Neptune, oppugn, Pashtun, patroon, platoon, poltroon, pontoon, premune, puccoon, quadroon, raccoon, ratoon, repugn, rockoon, rough-hewn, saloon, shalloon, soupspoon, spittoon, spontoon, teaspoon, Torun, tribune, triune, tuchun, tycoon, typhoon, untune, Walloon, afternoon, barracoon, Brigadoon, Cameroon, demilune, dessertspoon, honeymoon, importune, macaroon, octoroon, opportune, pantaloon, picaroon, picayune, rigadoon, saskatoon, Saskatoon, tablespoon, contrabassoon, inopportune

[2]oon \ōn\ see [1]ONE

oona \ü-nə\ see UNA

oonal \ün-ᵊl\ see UNAL

oone \ün\ see [1]OON

ooner \ü-nər\ crooner, crowner, lunar, pruner, schooner, sooner, swooner, tuner, harpooner, lacunar, lampooner, oppugner, honeymooner, semilunar

[1]oonery \ün-rē\ buffoonery, lampoonery, poltroonery

[2]oonery \ü-nə-rē\ see UNARY

ooney \ü-nē\ see OONY

oonie \ü-nē\ see OONY

ooning \ü-niŋ\ nooning, ballooning, cartooning, gadrooning

oonish \ü-nish\ moonish, buffoonish, cartoonish, picayunish

oonless \ün-ləs\ moonless, tuneless, woundless

oons \ünz\ lunes, zounds, eftsoons, afternoons—*also plurals and possessives of nouns and third person singular presents of verbs listed at* [1]OON

oony \ü-nē\ gooney, loony, luny, Moonie, moony, muni, puisne, puny, spoony, Zuni, Mulroney

o-op \üp\ see [1]OOP

oop \üp\ bloop, coop, croup, droop, drupe, dupe, goop, group, hoop, loop, loupe, poop, roup, scoop, sloop, snoop, soup, stoop, stoup, stupe, swoop, troop, troupe, whoop, age-group, in-group, out-group, recoup, regroup, subgroup, T-group, alley-oop, cock-a-hoop, Guadalupe,

Guadeloupe, nincompoop, paratroop, supergroup
ooped \üpd\ looped—*pasts of verbs listed at* OOP
oopee \ü-pē\ see OOPY
ooper \ü-pər\ blooper, cooper, Cooper, Cowper, duper, grouper, looper, scooper, snooper, stupor, swooper, super, trooper, trouper, party pooper, paratrooper, pooper-scooper, super-duper
ooping \ü-piŋ\ grouping, trooping, trouping
oopoe \ü-pü\ see OOH-POOH
oops \u̇ps\ hoops, oops, whoops, woops
oopy \ü-pē\ croupy, droopy, groupie, Kewpie, loopy, snoopy, soupy, Tupi, whoopee
[1]**oor** \ōr\ see [1]OR
[2]**oor** \u̇r\ see [1]URE
[1]**oorage** \u̇r-ij\ moorage, sewerage
[2]**oorage** \ōr-ij\ see [2]ORAGE
[3]**oorage** \ȯr-ij\ see [3]ORAGE
[1]**oore** \ōr\ see [1]ORE
[2]**oore** \u̇r\ see [1]URE
oored \ōrd\ see OARD
oorer \ōr-ər\ see [1]ORER
oori \u̇r-ē\ see [1]URY
[1]**ooring** \ōr-iŋ\ see [1]ORING
[2]**ooring** \u̇r-iŋ\ see URING
[1]**oorish** \u̇r-ish\ boorish, Moorish, poorish
[2]**oorish** \ȯr-ish\ see [1]ORISH
oorly \u̇r-lē\ see URELY
oorman \ōr-mən\ see OREMAN
oors \ōrz\ Bors, yours, drawers, indoors, outdoors, underdrawers, withindoors, withoutdoors, Louis Quatorze—*also plurals and possessives of nouns and third person singular presents of verbs listed at* [1]ORE
oorsman \ōrz-mən\ see OARSMAN
oort \ȯrt\ see [1]ORT
oosa \ü-sə\ see [1]USA
[1]**oose** \üs\ see [1]USE
[2]**oose** \üz\ see [2]USE
[1]**ooser** \ü-sər\ see UCER
[2]**ooser** \ü-zər\ see USER
oosey \ü-sē\ see UICY
[1]**oosh** \üsh\ see OUCHE
[2]**oosh** \u̇sh\ see [2]USH
oost \üst\ boost, juiced, Proust, roost, langouste, produced, self-induced, Zlatoust—*also pasts of verbs listed at* [1]USE
oosy \ü-zē\ see OOZY
[1]**oot** \u̇t\ foot, put, root, Root, soot, afoot, barefoot, bigfoot, bird's-foot, Blackfoot, clubfoot, crow's-foot, enroot, flatfoot, forefoot, hotfoot, input, kaput, outfoot, output, Rajput, snakeroot, splayfoot, taproot, throughput, uproot, acre-foot, arrowroot, bitterroot, cajeput, candle-foot, gingerroot, orrisroot, pussyfoot, tenderfoot, underfoot
[2]**oot** \üt\ see UTE
[3]**oot** \ət\ see [1]UT
[1]**ootage** \üt-ij\ fruitage, rootage, scutage
[2]**ootage** \u̇t-ij\ footage, rootage
[1]**ooted** \üt-əd\ booted, fruited, muted, suited, abluted, deep-rooted, jackbooted,

pantsuited, voluted—*also pasts of verbs listed at* UTE

[2]**ooted** \u̇t-əd\ footed, barefooted, clubfooted, deep-rooted, duckfooted, fleet-footed, four-footed, light-footed, slow-footed, splayfooted, surefooted, web-footed, wing-footed, cloven-footed—*also pasts of verbs listed at* [1]OOT

[1]**ooter** \u̇t-ər\ footer, putter, shot-putter, pussyfooter

[2]**ooter** \üt-ər\ see UTER

[1]**ooth** \üt͟h\ smooth, soothe, tooth

[2]**ooth** \üth\ booth, Booth, couth, crwth, routh, ruth, Ruth, scouth, sleuth, sooth, tooth, truth, Truth, youth, bucktooth, Duluth, eyetooth, forsooth, half-truth, sawtooth, selcouth, tollbooth, uncouth, untruth, vermouth, snaggletooth

oothe \üt͟h\ see [1]OOTH

oothed \ütht\ toothed, gap-toothed, snaggletoothed

oothless \üth-ləs\ see UTHLESS

oothly \üth-lē\ soothly, uncouthly

oothy \ü-thē\ couthie, toothy

ootie \üt-ē\ see [1]OOTY

[1]**ooting** \u̇t-iŋ\ footing, off-putting

[2]**ooting** \üt-iŋ\ see UTING

ootle \üt-ᵊl\ see UTILE

ootless \üt-ləs\ bootless, fruitless

ootlet \üt-lət\ fruitlet, rootlet

oots \üts\ boots, firstfruits, grassroots, slyboots, Vaduz, shoot-the-chutes—*also plurals and possessives of nouns and third person singular presents of verbs listed at* UTE

ootsie \u̇t-sē\ footsie, tootsie

[1]**ooty** \üt-ē\ beauty, booty, Clootie, cootie, cutie, duty, footy, fluty, fruity, hooty, rooty, snooty, sooty, tutti, zooty, agouti, Djibouti, Funafuti, heavy-duty, persecutee, tutti-frutti

[2]**ooty** \u̇t-ē\ rooty, sooty, tutti

[3]**ooty** \ət-ē\ see UTTY

oove \üv\ see [3]OVE

oover \ü-vər\ see [3]OVER

oovy \ü-vē\ groovy, movie

ooze \üz\ see [2]USE

oozer \ü-zər\ see USER

oozle \ü-zəl\ see [2]USAL

oozy \ü-zē\ bluesy, boozy, choosy, floozy, newsy, oozy, Susie, woozy, Jacuzzi

[1]**op** \äp\ bop, chap, chop, clop, cop, crop, drop, flop, fop, glop, hop, knop, lop, mop, op, plop, pop, prop, scop, shop, slop, sop, stop, strop, swap, top, whop, wop, Aesop, airdrop, atop, backdrop, backstop, bakeshop, barhop, bebop, bellhop, blacktop, bookshop, carhop, cartop, chop-chop, clip-clop, clop-clop, coin-op, cooktop, co-op, desktop, dewdrop, doorstop, dramshop, Dunlop, eardrop, eavesdrop, ESOP, estop, f-stop, fire-stop, flattop, flip-flop, foretop, grogshop, gumdrop, hardtop, hedgehop, high-top, hilltop, hip-hop,

hockshop, housetop, joypop, maintop, milksop, nonstop, one-stop, outcrop, pawnshop, pop-top, ragtop, raindrop, redtop, ripstop, rooftop, sharecrop, shortstop, skin-pop, slipslop, snowdrop, soursop, stonecrop, sweatshop, sweetshop, teardrop, tip-top, treetop, unstop, workshop, agitprop, barbershop, carrottop, countertop, double-crop, double-stop, Ethiop, island-hop, lollipop, malaprop, mom-and-pop, mountaintop, overtop, table-hop, tabletop, techno-pop, teenybop, turboprop, whistle-stop, window-shop, Babelthuap

[2]op \ō\ see [1]OW

opa \ō-pə\ opa, opah, Europa

opah \ō-pə\ see OPA

opal \ō-pəl\ copal, nopal, opal, Opal, Simferopol, Constantinople

ope \ōp\ cope, coup, dope, grope, holp, hope, Hope, lope, mope, nope, ope, pope, Pope, rope, scop, scope, slope, soap, stope, taupe, tope, trope, aslope, borescope, downslope, elope, gantlope, gantelope, Good Hope, myope, nightscope, pyrope, sandsoap, soft-soap, tightrope, towrope, antelope, antipope, calliope, cantaloupe, chronoscope, envelope, epitope, Ethiope, gyroscope, horoscope, interlope, isotope, kinescope, microscope, misanthrope, periscope, phalarope, radarscope, sniperscope, snooperscope, stethoscope, telescope, heliotrope, kaleidoscope, stereoscope

opean \ō-pē-ən\ see OPIAN

opee \ō-pē\ see OPI

open \ō-pən\ holpen, open, reopen, wide-open

opence \əp-əns\ see UPPANCE

openny \əp-nē\ threepenny, twopenny

oper \ō-pər\ coper, doper, groper, loper, moper, roper, soaper, toper, eloper, no-hoper, soft-soaper, interloper

opera \äp-rə\ see OPRA

opery \ō-prē\ popery, ropery

opey \ō-pē\ see OPI

oph \ōf\ see OAF

ophagous \äf-ə-gəs\ coprophagous, esophagus, necrophagous, sarcophagus, zoophagous, anthropophagous

ophagy \äf-ə-jē\ geophagy, coprophagy, anthropophagy

[1]ophe \ō-fē\ see OPHY

[2]ophe \ȯf\ see [2]OFF

opher \ō-fər\ see OFER

ophet \äf-ət\ see OFIT

[1]ophic \äf-ik\ strophic, antistrophic, apostrophic, catastrophic

[2]ophic \ō-fik\ strophic, trophic, atrophic

ophical \äf-i-kəl\ philosophical, theosophical

ophie \ō-fē\ see OPHY

ophir \ō-fər\ see OFER

ophonous \äf-ə-nəs\ cacophonous, homophonous

ophony \äf-ə-nē\ cacophony,

colophony, homophony, monophony, theophany, heterophony, stereophony
ophy \ō-fē\ Sophie, sophy, strophe, trophy
opi \ō-pē\ dopey, Hopi, mopey, ropy, soapy, topee, topi
opia \ō-pē-ə\ dystopia, myopia, sinopia, utopia, cornucopia, Ethiopia
opian \ō-pē-ən\ Aesopian, cyclopean, dystopian, utopian, Ethiopian, cornucopian
[1]opic \äp-ik\ topic, tropic, Aesopic, anthropic, ectopic, Ethiopic, subtropic, gyroscopic, hygroscopic, macroscopic, microscopic, misanthropic, periscopic, philanthropic, semitropic, stethoscopic, telescopic, kaleidoscopic, stereoscopic
[2]opic \ō-pik\ tropic, myopic, Ethiopic, psychotropic
opical \äp-i-kəl\ topical, tropical, anthropical, subtropical, microscopical, philanthropical, semitropical, Neotropical
oplar \äp-lər\ see OPPLER
ople \ō-pəl\ see OPAL
opol \ō-pəl\ see OPAL
[1]opolis \äp-ə-ləs\ propolis, acropolis, cosmopolis, necropolis, Heliopolis, megalopolis, metropolis, Florianopolis
[2]opolis \äp-ləs\ see OPLESS
opolist \äp-ə-ləst\ monopolist, bibliopolist
opoly \äp-ə-lē\ choppily, floppily, sloppily, duopoly, monopoly, vox populi, oligopoly, Tiruchchirappalli
oppa \äp-ə\ see [1]APA
opped \äpt\ see OPT
oppel \äp-əl\ see OPPLE
opper \äp-ər\ bopper, chopper, copper, cropper, dropper, flopper, hopper, lopper, mopper, popper, proper, shopper, stopper, swapper, topper, whopper, yapper, clodhopper, eavesdropper, eyedropper, eyepopper, grasshopper, hedgehopper, improper, job-hopper, joypopper, leafhopper, namedropper, rockhopper, sharecropper, showstopper, skin-popper, table-hopper, teenybopper, treehopper, woodchopper, window-shopper
oppery \äp-rē\ coppery, foppery
oppet \äp-ət\ moppet, poppet
oppily \äp-ə-lē\ see OPOLY
oppiness \äp-ē-nəs\ choppiness, floppiness, sloppiness
opping \äp-iŋ\ hopping, sopping, topping, whopping, clodhopping, eye-popping, job-hopping, name-dropping, outcropping
opple \äp-əl\ popple, stopple, topple, estoppel
oppler \äp-lər\ Doppler, poplar
oppy \äp-ē\ choppy, copy, crappie, floppy, gloppy, hoppy, kopje, poppy, sloppy, soppy, stroppy, jalopy, okapi, serape, microcopy, Nahuel Huapi, photocopy
opra \äp-rə\ copra, opera

ops \äps\ chops, copse, Ops, tops, beechdrops, cyclops, eyedrops, Pelops, pinedrops, sundrops, muttonchops, triceratops—*also plurals and possessives of nouns and third person singular presents of verbs listed at* [1]OP

opse \äps\ see OPS

opsy \äp-sē\ dropsy, autopsy, biopsy, necropsy

opt \äpt\ Copt, knopped, opt, topped, adopt, close-cropped, co-opt, end-stopped—*also pasts of verbs listed at* [1]OP

opter \äp-tər\ copter, adopter, helicopter, ornithopter

optic \äp-tik\ Coptic, optic, panoptic, synoptic, electro-optic

optimist \äp-tə-məst\ optimist, Optimist, Soroptimist

option \äp-shən\ option, adoption, co-option

optric \äp-trik\ catoptric, dioptric

opula \äp-yə-lə\ copula, scopula

opulace \äp-yə-ləs\ populace, populous

opulate \äp-yə-lāt\ copulate, populate, over-populate

opuli \äp-ə-lē\ see OPOLY

opulous \äp-yə-ləs\ see OPULACE

opus \ō-pəs\ opus, Canopus, magnum opus, pithecanthropus

[1]opy \ō-pē\ see OPI

[2]opy \äp-ē\ see OPPY

[1]oque \ōk\ see OKE

[2]oque \äk\ see [1]OCK

[3]oque \ȯk\ see ALK

oquial \ō-kwē-əl\ colloquial, ventriloquial

[1]or \ōr\ boar, Boer, Bohr, bore, chore, core, corps, crore, door, drawer, floor, for, fore, four, frore, gore, Gore, hoar, hoer, kor, lore, Moore, mor, more, More, nor, o'er, oar, or, ore, poor, pore, pour, roar, score, shore, snore, soar, sore, splore, spoor, spore, store, swore, Thor, tor, tore, torr, war, whore, wore, yore, your, you're, abhor, actor, adore, afore, and/or, ashore, backdoor, bailor, bandore, Beardmore, bedsore, before, bezoar, bookstore, candor, captor, centaur, claymore, closed-door, condor, decor, deplore, dime-store, donor, downpour, drugstore, encore, ephor, explore, Exmoor, eyesore, feoffor, fetor, Fillmore, folklore, footsore, forebore, forswore, forscore, galore, hardcore, ichor, ignore, implore, Indore, indoor, inpour, inshore, Lahore, lakeshore, Lenore, lessor, memoir, mentor, Mysore, nearshore, Nestor, offshore, onshore, outdoor, outpour, outsoar, outwore, pastor, psywar, rancor, rapport, raptor, Realtor, restore, rhetor, savior, seafloor, seashore, sector, seignior, senhor, señor, sensor, settlor, Seymour, signor, smoothbore, sophomore, stentor, stertor, stressor, stridor, subfloor, temblor, tensor, therefor, therefore, threescore, Timor, trapdoor, turgor, uproar, vendor, wherefore, woodlore, albacore, alongshore, anaphor, anymore, archosaur, Baltimore, Bangalore, Barrymore, brontosaur, carnivore, CD4, Coimbatore, commodore, comprador, confessor, consignor, corridor, cuspidor, devisor, dinosaur, door-to-door, Ecuador, either-or, Eleanor, Eleanore, elector, Elinor, en rapport, evermore, franchisor, furthermore, guarantor, Gwalior, hackamore, hadrosaur, hellebore, herbivore, heretofore, humidor, Labrador, louis d'or, man-of-war, manticore, matador, metaphor, meteor, millepore, Minotaur, mirador, Mount Rushmore, nevermore, omnivore, out-of-door, petit four, picador, pinafore, pompadour, predator, promisor, pterosaur, reservoir, sagamore, Salvador, Salvatore, semaphore, Singapore, stegosaur, stevedore, superstore, sycamore, Theodore, theretofore, troubador, tug-of-war, two-by-four, uncalled-for, underscore, vavasor, warrantor, alienor, ambassador, ankylosaur, conquistador, conservator, Corregidor, de Pompadour, El Salvador, esprit de corps, forevermore, hereinbefore, ichthyosaur, insectivore, legislator, plesiosaur, San Salvadore, toreador, tyrannosaur, Ulan Bator, administrator, lobster thermidor, Talleyrand-Perigord

²or \ər\ see ¹EUR

ora \ōr-ə\ aura, bora, Cora, Dora, flora, Flora, hora, Laura, Lora, mora, Nora, sora, Torah, Andorra, angora, aurora, Aurora, begorra, camorra, fedora, gemara, Gomorrah, Lenora, Masora, menorah, pandora, Pandora, remora, senhora, señora, signora, Sonora, grandiflora, Juiz de Fora, Leonora, Simchas Torah, Tuscarora, Lomas de Zamora

orable \ōr-ə-bəl\ horrible, pourable, storable, adorable, deplorable, restorable

orace \ȯr-əs\ see AURUS

oracle \ȯr-ə-kəl\ coracle, oracle

orage \ōr-ij\ borage, floorage, forage, porridge, storage

orah \ōr-ə\ see ORA

¹oral \ōr-əl\ aural, choral, coral, Coral, floral, laurel, Laurel, moral, oral, quarrel, sorrel, aboral, amoral, auroral, balmoral, binaural, immoral, monaural, peroral, restoral, sororal

²oral \ȯrl\ schorl, whorl, ceorl

oram \ōr-əm\ see ORUM

orate \ōr-ət\ see ORET

orative \ōr-ət-iv\ explorative, pejorative, restorative
oray \ə-rē\ see URRY
orb \ȯrb\ forb, orb, sorb, Sorb, absorb, adsorb, desorb, resorb
orbate \ȯr-bət\ see ORBIT
orbeil \ȯr-bəl\ see ORBEL
orbel \ȯr-bəl\ corbeil, corbel, warble
orbent \ȯr-bənt\ absorbent, immunosorbent
orbet \ȯr-bət\ see ORBIT
orbit \ȯr-bət\ orbit, sorbet, adsorbate
orc \ȯrk\ see [2]ORK
orca \ȯr-kə\ orca, Majorca, Minorca, Palma de Mallorca
orcas \ȯr-kəs\ Dorcas, orchis
orce \ōrs\ see [1]OURSE
orced \ȯrst\ see [1]ORST
[1]**orceful** \ōrs-fəl\ forceful, resourceful
[2]**orceful** \ȯrs-fəl\ see ORSEFUL
[1]**orcement** \ōr-smənt\ deforcement, divorcement, enforcement, reinforcement
[2]**orcement** \ȯr-smənt\ see ORSEMENT
orcer \ōr-sər\ courser, enforcer, reinforcer—*also comparatives of adjectives listed at* [1]OURSE
orch \ȯrch\ porch, scorch, torch, blowtorch, sunporch
orcher \ȯr-chər\ scorcher, torture
orchid \ȯr-kəd\ forked, orchid, cryptorchid, monorchid
orchis \ȯr-kəs\ see ORCAS
[1]**ord** \ōrd\ see OARD
[2]**ord** \ərd\ see IRD
[3]**ord** \ȯr\ see [1]OR
ordan \ȯrd-ᵊn\ see [2]ARDEN
ordancy \ȯrd-ᵊn-sē\ mordancy, discordancy
ordant \ȯrd-ᵊnt\ mordant, mordent, accordant, concordant, discordant
orde \ōrd\ see OARD
orded \ȯrd-əd\ see [2]ARDED
ordent \ȯrd-ᵊnt\ see ORDANT
order \ȯrd-ər\ boarder, border, corder, order, warder, awarder, disorder, recorder, reorder, rewarder, made-to-order
ordered \ȯrd-ərd\ bordered, ordered—*also pasts of verbs listed at* ORDER
orders \ȯrd-ərz\ Borders—*also possessives and plurals of nouns and third person singular presents of verbs listed at* ORDER
ordial \ȯrd-ē-əl\ exordial, primordial
ordid \ȯrd-əd\ see [2]ARDED
[1]**ording** \ȯrd-iŋ\ lording, recording, rewarding—*also present participles of verbs listed at* [2]OARD
[2]**ording** \ərd-iŋ\ see ERDING
ordingly \ȯrd-iŋ-lē\ accordingly, rewardingly
ordion \ȯrd-ē-ən\ accordion, Edwardian
ordist \ȯrd-əst\ recordist, clavichordist, harpsichordist
ordon \ȯrd-ᵊn\ see [2]ARDEN
ordure \ȯr-jər\ see ORGER
[1]**ordy** \ȯrd-ē\ Geordie, Lordy, awardee
[2]**ordy** \ərd-ē\ see URDY
[1]**ore** \ȯr-ē\ see ORY
[2]**ore** \u̇r\ see [1]URE

[3]ore \ər-ə\ see [1]OROUGH
[4]ore \ōr\ see [1]OR
oreal \ōr-ē-əl\ see ORIAL
orean \ȯr-ē-ən\ see ORIAN
oreas \ȯr-ē-əs\ see ORIOUS
ored \ōrd\ see OARD
oredom \ōrd-əm\ boredom, whoredom
orehead \ȯr-əd\ see ORRID
[1]oreign \är-ən\ see [1]ORIN
[2]oreign \ȯr-ən\ see [2]ORIN
oreigner \ȯr-ə-nər\ see ORONER
orem \ōr-əm\ see ORUM
oreman \ōr-mən\ corpsman, doorman, foreman, longshoreman
orence \ȯr-ən(t)s\ see AWRENCE
oreous \ȯr-ē-əs\ see ORIOUS
orer \ōr-ər\ borer, corer, floorer, pourer, roarer, scorer, schnorrer, snorer, soarer, adorer, deplorer, explorer—*also comparatives of adjectives listed at* [1]ORE
[1]ores \ōr-əs\ see [1]ORUS
[2]ores \ōrz\ Azores, indoors, outdoors—*also possessives and plurals of nouns and third person singular presents of verbs listed at* [1]ORE
[3]ores \ȯr-əs\ see AURUS
oreson \ōrs-ᵊn\ see OARSEN
orest \ȯr-əst\ see [1]ORIST
orester \ȯr-ə-stər\ see ORISTER
oret \ōr-ət\ floret, sororate
oreum \ōr-ē-əm\ see ORIUM
oreward \ōr-wərd\ see OREWORD
oreword \ōr-wərd\ foreword, shoreward
orey \ȯr-ē\ see ORY
orf \ȯrf\ see ORPH
[1]org \ȯrg\ morgue, cyborg
[2]org \ȯr-ē\ see ORY
organ \ȯr-gən\ gorgon, morgan, Morgan, organ, Glamorgan, Demogorgon, Mid Glamorgan, South Glamorgan, West Glamorgan
orge \ȯrj\ forge, George, gorge, scourge, disgorge, drop-forge, engorge, Lloyd George, reforge, Olduvai Gorge
orger \ȯr-jər\ bordure, forger, gorger, ordure
orgi \ȯr-gē\ see ORGY
orgia \ȯr-jə\ Borgia, Georgia, Strait of Georgia
orgian \ȯr-jən\ Georgian, Swedenborgian
orgon \ȯr-gən\ see ORGAN
orgue \ȯrg\ see ORG
orgy \ȯr-gē\ corgi, porgy
ori \ȯr-ē\ see ORY
oria \ȯr-ē-ə\ gloria, Gloria, noria, scoria, centaurea, euphoria, Peoria, Pretoria, victoria, Victoria, Vitoria, phantasmagoria
orial \ōr-ē-əl\ boreal, oriel, oriole, arboreal, armorial, auctorial, authorial, cantorial, censorial, corporeal, cursorial, factorial, fossorial, manorial, marmoreal, memorial, pictorial, praetorial, proctorial, raptorial, rectorial, sartorial, seignorial, sensorial, sponsorial, tonsorial, tutorial, uxorial, vectorial, conductorial, consistorial, curatorial, dictatorial, directorial, editorial, equatorial, immemorial,

incorporeal, janitorial, monitorial, monsignorial, natatorial, piscatorial, preceptorial, professorial, purgatorial, reportorial, senatorial, territorial, ambassadorial, conservatorial, combinatorial, conspiratorial, extracorporeal, gladiatorial, gubernatorial, imperatorial, inquisitorial, legislatorial, procuratorial, propriatorial, prosecutorial, extraterritorial, improvisatorial

oriam \ōr-ē-əm\ see ORIUM

orian \ór-ē-ən\ Dorian, saurian, Taurean, aurorean, Gregorian, historian, Nestorian, praetorian, stentorian, victorian, dinosaurian, hyperborean, Oratorian, prehistorian, senatorian, terpsichorean, salutatorian, valedictorian

oriant \ōr-ē-ənt\ see ORIENT

oriat \ór-ē-ət\ see [2]AUREATE

oric \ór-ik\ auric, choric, Doric, toric, Armoric, caloric, clitoric, dysphoric, euphoric, folkloric, historic, phosphoric, plethoric, pyloric, anaphoric, cataphoric, metaphoric, meteoric, paregoric, prehistoric, sophomoric, aleatoric, phantasmagoric

orical \ór-i-kəl\ auricle, historical, rhetorical, ahistorical, allegorical, categorical, metaphorical, oratorical, transhistorical, sociohistorical

orics \ór-iks\ see ORYX

orid \ór-əd\ see ORRID

oriel \ōr-ē-əl\ see ORIAL

orient \ōr-ē-ənt\ orient, Orient, euphoriant

[1]**orin** \ór-ən\ florin, foreign, Lauren, Orrin, sarin, sporran, warren, Warren, Gagarin, cyclosporine

[2]**orin** \ōr-ən\ see [1]ORINE

[1]**orine** \ōr-ən\ chlorine, florin, cephalosporin

[2]**orine** \ór-ən\ see [1]ORIN

oring \ōr-iŋ\ boring, flooring, roaring, shoring, inpouring, longshoring, outpouring, rip-roaring—*also present participles of verbs listed at* [1]OR

öring \ər-iŋ\ see URRING

oriole \ōr-ē-əl\ see ORIAL

orious \ór-ē-əs\ aureus, Boreas, glorious, arboreous, censorious, inglorious, laborious, notorious, sartorius, uproarious, uxorious, vainglorious, victorious, meritorious

[1]**oris** \ōr-əs\ see [1]ORUS

[2]**oris** \ór-əs\ see AURUS

[1]**orish** \ór-ish\ boarish, poorish, whorish, folklorish

[2]**orish** \ůr-ish\ see [1]OORISH

orist \ór-əst\ florist, forest, Forrest, sorest, afforest, Black Forest, deforest, folklorist, reforest, allegorist, Petrified Forest—*also superlatives of adjectives listed at* [1]OR

orister \ór-ə-stər\ chorister, forester

ority \ór-ət-ē\ authority, majority, minority, priority, seniority, sonority, apriority, exteriority, inferiority, interiority, posteriority, superiority

orium \ōr-ē-əm\ castoreum, ciborium, emporium, pastorium, scriptorium, sensorium, auditorium, crematorium, in memoriam, moratorium, natatorium, sanitorium, sudatorium

[1]ork \ərk\ burke, Burke, chirk, cirque, clerk, dirk, Dirk, irk, jerk, kirk, Kirk, lurk, murk, perk, quirk, shirk, smirk, stirk, Turk, work, yerk, zerk, artwork, berserk, breastwork, brickwork, bridgework, brightwork, brushwork, capework, casework, clockwork, coachwork, de Klerk, ductwork, Dunkirk, earthwork, falsework, fieldwork, firework, flatwork, footwork, formwork, framework, goldwork, groundwork, guesswork, hackwork, handwork, headwork, homework, housework, ironwork, knee-jerk, legwork, lifework, make-work, meshwork, millwork, network, outwork, paintwork, patchwork, piecework, presswork, quillwork, rework, roadwork, salesclerk, schoolwork, Selkirk, Southwark, spadework, steelwork, stickwork, stonework, teamwork, timework, topwork, waxwork, webwork, woodwork, basketwork, busywork, crewelwork, donkeywork, fancywork, handiwork, journeywork, laquerwork, masterwork, needlework, openwork, overwork, paperwork, plasterwork, soda jerk, wonderwork, cabinetwork

[2]ork \ȯrk\ cork, Cork, dork, fork, pork, quark, stork, torque, York, bulwark, Cape York, futhorc, hayfork, New York, North York, pitchfork, uncork

[1]orked \ȯrkt\ corked, forked, uncorked

[2]orked \ȯr-kəd\ see ORCHID

[1]orker \ər-kər\ jerker, lurker, shirker, worker, berserker, caseworker, dockworker, fieldworker, handworker, ironworker, outworker, pieceworker, steelworker, tearjerker, wageworker, woodworker, autoworker, metalworker, needleworker, wonderworker

[2]orker \ȯr-kər\ corker,forker, porker, torquer

orkie \ȯr-kē\ see ORKY

orking \ər-kiŋ\ hardworking, tear-jerking, woodworking, wonder-working

orky \ȯr-kē\ corky, dorky, forky, Gorky, porky, Yorkie

[1]orl \ərl\ see [1]IRL

[2]orl \ȯrl\ see [3]ORAL

orld \ərld\ burled, knurled, whorled, world, dreamworld, New World, old-world, demiworld, microworld, netherworld, otherworld, underworld—*also pasts of verbs listed at* [1]IRL

orled \ərld\ see ORLD

[1]**orm** \ərm\ berm, firm, germ, herm, perm, Perm, sperm, squirm, term, therm, worm, affirm, bookworm, budworm, confirm, cutworm, deperm, deworm, earthworm, flatworm, glowworm, heartworm, hookworm, hornworm, inchworm, infirm, long-term, lugworm, lungworm, midterm, pinworm, ringworm, roundworm, sandworm, screwworm, short-term, silkworm, tapeworm, woodworm, angleworm, armyworm, caddis worm, disaffirm, disconfirm, gymnosperm, pachyderm, reconfirm, angiosperm, echinoderm

[2]**orm** \ȯrm\ corm, dorm, form, norm, storm, swarm, warm, aswarm, barnstorm, brainstorm, conform, deform, Delorme, firestorm, free-form, hailstorm, inform, L-form, landform, life-form, lukewarm, perform, planform, platform, postform, preform, rainstorm, re-form, reform, sandstorm, snowstorm, transform, triform, windstorm, chloroform, cruciform, dendriform, dentiform, disciform, fungiform, funnelform, fusiform, letterform, microform, multiform, nonconform, thunderstorm, uniform, vermiform

ormable \ȯr-mə-bəl\ formable, conformable, performable, transformable

ormal \ȯr-məl\ formal, normal, abnormal, conformal, informal, subnormal, paranormal, semiformal, supernormal

ormally \ȯr-mə-lē\ formally, formerly, normally, stormily, abnormally, informally, subnormally, paranormally, supernormally

orman \ȯr-mən\ corpsman, Mormon, Norman, Anglo-Norman

ormance \ȯr-məns\ conformance, performance, nonconformance

ormant \ȯr-mənt\ dormant, formant, informant

ormative \ȯr-mət-iv\ formative, normative, informative, performative, reformative, transformative

orme \ȯrm\ see [2]ORM

ormed \ȯrmd\ formed, normed, informed, malformed, unformed—*also pasts of verbs listed at* [2]ORM

[1]**ormer** \ȯr-mər\ dormer, former, swarmer, warmer, barnstormer, benchwarmer, brainstormer, conformer, heart-warmer, informer, performer, reformer, transformer

[2]**ormer** \ər-mər\ see URMUR

ormerly \ȯr-mə-lē\ see ORMALLY
ormie \ȯr-mē\ see [1]ORMY
ormily \ȯr-mə-lē\ see ORMALLY
orming \ȯr-miŋ\ brainstorming, heartwarming, housewarming, habit-forming, nonperforming
ormist \ȯr-məst\ warmest, conformist, reformist, nonconformist
ormity \ȯr-mət-ē\ conformity, deformity, enormity, nonconformity, uniformity
ormless \ȯrm-ləs\ formless, gormless
ormon \ȯr-mən\ see ORMAN
[1]**ormy** \ȯr-mē\ stormy, dormie
[2]**ormy** \ər-mē\ see ERMY
[1]**orn** \ōrn\ born, borne, bourn, corn, horn, lorn, morn, mourn, Norn, porn, scorn, shorn, sworn, thorn, torn, warn, worn, acorn, adorn, airborne, alphorn, althorn, baseborn, bicorne, bighorn, blackthorn, boxthorn, broomcorn, buckthorn, bullhorn, Cape Horn, careworn, Christ's-thorn, Dearborn, dehorn, earthborn, einkorn, firethorn, firstborn, foghorn, foreborn, foresworn, forewarn, forlorn, forworn, freeborn, greenhorn, hartshorn, hawthorn, Hawthorne, highborn, inborn, inkhorn, krummhorn, leghorn, longhorn, lovelorn, lowborn, newborn, outworn, popcorn, pronghorn, reborn, seaborne, shipborne, shoehorn, shopworn, shorthorn, skyborne, soilborne, staghorn, stillborn, stinkhorn, suborn, timeworn, tinhorn, tricorne, trueborn, twice-born, unborn, unworn, wayworn, wellborn, well-worn, wind-borne, alpenhorn, barleycorn, Capricorn, flügelhorn, foreign-born, Golden Horn, Matterhorn, peppercorn, unicorn, waterborne, waterworn, weatherworn winterbourne
[2]**orn** \ərn\ see URN
ornament \ȯr-nə-mənt\ ornament, tournament
[1]**orne** \ōrn\ see [1]ORN
[2]**orne** \ȯrn\ see [2]ORN
orned \ȯrnd\ horned, thorned, unadorned—*also pasts of verbs listed at* [2]ORN
orner \ȯr-nər\ warner, Warner, Cape Horner, dehorner, suborner
ornery \än-rē\ see [1]ANNERY
orney \ər-nē\ see [1]OURNEY
ornful \ȯrn-fəl\ mournful, scornful
ornice \ȯr-nəs\ cornice, ornice, notornis
orning \ȯr-niŋ\ morning, mourning, warning, aborning
ornis \ȯr-nəs\ see ORNICE
ornment \ərn-mənt\ see ERNMENT
orny \ȯr-nē\ corny, norny, porny, thorny, tourney
[1]**oro**\ ər-ə\ see [1]OROUGH
[2]**oro** \ō-rō\ Chamorro, Mindoro, Rio de Oro
oroner \ȯr-ə-nər\ coroner, foreigner, warrener

[1]**orough** \ər-ə\ borough, burgh, burro, burrow, curragh, furrow, ore, thorough, Gainsborough, Greensboro, Roxborough, Scarborough, Yarborough, Edinburgh, kookaburra, Peterborough, Soke of Peterborough, Huntingdon and Peterborough
[2]**orough** \ər-ō\ see [1]URROW
[1]**orous** \ōr-əs\ see [1]ORUS
[2]**orous** \ȯr-əs\ see AURUS
orp \ȯrp\ dorp, gorp, thorp, warp, Australorp, Krugersdorp, octothorp, Oglethorpe
orpe \ȯrp\ see ORP
orper \ȯr-pər\ dorper, torpor
orph \ȯrf\ corf, dwarf, morph, Düsseldorf, anthropomorph
orphan \ȯr-fən\ orphan, endorphin, beta-endorphin
orpheus \ȯr-fē-əs\ Morpheus, Orpheus
orphic \ȯr-fik\ orphic, ectomorphic, endomorphic, mesomorphic, pseudomorphic, metamorphic, anthropomorphic
orphin \ȯr-fən\ see ORPHAN
orphous \ȯr-fəs\ amorphous, isomorphous
orphrey \ȯr-frē\ orphrey, porphyry
orphyrin \ȯr-fə-rən\ see ARFARIN
orphyry \ȯr-frē\ see ORPHREY
orpoise \ȯr-pəs\ see ORPUS
orpor \ȯr-pər\ see ORPER
orps \ōr\ see [1]OR
[1]**orpsman** \ōr-mən\ see OREMAN
[2]**orpsman** \ȯr-mən\ see ORMAN
orpus \ȯr-pəs\ corpus, porpoise, habeas corpus
orque \ȯrk\ see [2]ORK
orquer \ȯr-kər\ see [2]ORKER
[1]**orra** \är-ə\ see [1]ARA
[2]**orra** \ȯr-ə\ see [2]ORA
[3]**orra** \ō-rə\ see [1]ORA
orrader \är-əd-ər\ see ORRIDOR
[1]**orrah** \ōr-ə\ see ORA
[2]**orrah** \är-ə\ see [1]ARA
[1]**orran** \är-ən\ see [1]ORIN
[2]**orran** \ȯr-ən\ see [2]ORIN
orrence \ȯr-əns\ see AWRENCE
orrel \ȯr-əl\ see [2]ORAL
orrent \ȯr-ənt\ horrent, torrent, warrant, abhorrent
[1]**orrer** \ȯr-ər\ borer, horror, roarer, schnorrer, sorer, abhorrer, explorer
[2]**orrer** \ōr-ər\ see [1]ORER
orres \ȯr-əs\ see AURUS
orrest \ȯr-əst\ see [1]ORIST
orrible \ȯr-ə-bəl\ see [2]ORABLE
orrid \ȯr-əd\ florid, horrid, torrid
[1]**orridge** \är-ij\ see [1]ORAGE
[2]**orridge** \ȯr-ij\ see [3]ORAGE
orridor \är-əd-ər\ corridor, forrader
[1]**orrie** \är-ē\ see [1]ARI
[2]**orrie** \ȯr-ē\ see ORY
orrier \ȯr-ē-ər\ see ARRIOR
orrin \ȯr-ən\ see [2]ORIN
[1]**orris** \är-əs\ charas, Juárez, Maurice, morris, Morris, Norris, orris, Banaras, Benares, Polaris, Ciudad Juárez
[2]**orris** \ōr-əs\ see [1]ORUS
[3]**orris** \ȯr-əs\ see AURUS
orro \ō-rō\ see [2]ORO

orror \ȯr-ər\ see [1]ORRER
[1]**orrow** \är-ō\ borrow, claro, morrow, sorrow, taro, Pizarro, saguaro, tomorrow, Catanzaro, Kilimanjaro, Mohenjo-Daro
[2]**orrow** \är-ə\ see [1]ARA
[1]**orry** \är-ē\ see [1]ARI
[2]**orry** \ər-ē\ see URRY
ors \ōrz\ see OORS
orsal \ȯr-səl\ see ORSEL
[1]**orse** \ȯrs\ coarse, corse, course, force, gorse, hoarse, horse, Morse, Norse, source, clotheshorse, concourse, deforce, discourse, divorce, endorse, enforce, extrorse, introrse, midcourse, packhorse, perforce, posthorse, racecourse, racehorse, recourse, remorse, retrorse, sawhorse, stringcourse, unhorse, war-horse, Whitehorse, workhorse, charley horse, Crazy Horse, hobbyhorse, nonrecourse, stalking-horse, reinforce, watercourse
[2]**orse** \ərs\ see ERSE
orseful \ȯrs-fəl\ forceful, remorseful, resourceful
orsel \ȯr-səl\ dorsal, morsel
orseman \ȯr-smən\ horseman, Norseman
orsement \ȯr-smənt\ endorsement, reinforcement
orsen \ərs-ᵊn\ see ERSON
orser \ər-sər\ see URSOR
orset \ȯr-sət\ corset, Dorset
orsey \ȯr-sē\ see ORSY
orsion \ȯr-shən\ see [2]ORTION
[1]**orst** \ȯrst\ forced, horst—*also pasts of verbs listed at* [1]ORSE
[2]**orst** \ərst\ see URST
orsted \ər-stəd\ see ERSTED
orsum \ȯr-səm\ dorsum, foursome
orsy \ȯr-sē\ gorsy, horsey
[1]**ort** \ȯrt\ boart, bort, court, fort, forte, mort, Oort, ort, port, Porte, quart, short, snort, sort, sport, swart, thwart, tort, torte, wart, wort, abort, airport, amort, aport, assort, athwart, backcourt, bellwort, birthwort, bistort, Bridgeport, cavort, cohort, colewort, comport, consort, contort, crosscourt, deport, disport, distort, downcourt, effort, escort, exhort, export, extort, forecourt, frontcourt, glasswort, gosport, half-court, homeport, milkwort, Newport, outport, passport, presort, purport, ragwort, report, resort, resort, retort, seaport, Shreveport, spaceport, spoilsport, Stockport, support, transport, bladderwort, davenport, life-support, nonsupport, pennywort, Saint-John's wort, teleport, ultrashort, worrywart, pianoforte, underreport
[2]**ort** \ōr\ see [1]OR
[3]**ort** \ərt\ see [1]ERT
ortable \ōrt-ə-bəl\ portable, deportable, exportable, importable, reportable, supportable, transportable, insupportable

ortage \ȯrt-ij\ portage, shortage, colportage
ortal \ȯrt-ᵊl\ chortle, mortal, portal, quartile, immortal
ortar \ȯrt-ər\ see ORTER
ortative \ȯrt-ət-iv\ hortative, portative, assortative, exhortative
[1]**orte** \ȯrt\ see [1]ORT
[2]**orte** \ȯrt-ē\ see ORTY
orted \ȯrt-əd\ warted, assorted, ill-sorted—*also pasts of verbs listed at* [1]ORT
ortedly \ōrt-əd-lē\ purportedly, reportedly
orten \ȯrt-ᵊn\ quartan, shorten, foreshorten
orter \ȯrt-ər\ mortar, porter, Porter, quarter, snorter, sorter, colporteur, distorter, exhorter, exporter, extorter, headquarter, importer, lambs-quarter, reporter, resorter, ripsnorter, transporter—*also comparatives of adjectives listed at* [1]ORT
orteur \ȯrt-ər\ see ORTER
[1]**orth** \ȯrth\ forth, Forth, fourth, north, North, thenceforth, Firth of Forth
[2]**orth** \ərth\ see IRTH
orthful \ərth-fəl\ see IRTHFUL
orthless \ərth-ləs\ see IRTHLESS
orthy \ər-t͟hē\ earthy, worthy, airworthy, blameworthy, Galsworthy, newsworthy, noteworthy, praiseworthy, seaworthy, trustworthy, creditworthy
ortic \ȯrt-ik\ see [2]ARTIC
ortical \ȯrt-i-kəl\ cortical, vortical
ortie \ȯrt-ē\ see ORTY
orting \ōrt-iŋ\ sporting, self-supporting
ortion \ōr-shən\ portion, torsion, abortion, apportion, contortion, distortion, extorsion, extortion, proportion, retortion, disproportion, proabortion, reapportion, antiabortion
ortionate \ȯr-shnət\ extortionate, proportionate, disproportionate
ortionist \ȯr-shnəst\ abortionist, contortionist, extortionist
ortis \ȯrt-əs\ fortis, mortise, tortoise, aquafortis, rigor mortis
ortise \ȯrt-əs\ see ORTIS
ortive \ȯrt-iv\ sportive, abortive, contortive, extortive
ortle \ȯrt-ᵊl\ see ORTAL
ortly \ōrt-lē\ courtly, portly, shortly, thwartly
ortment \ȯrt-mənt\ assortment, comportment, deportment, disportment
ortoise \ȯrt-əs\ see ORTIS
orton \ȯrt-ᵊn\ Morton, Norton, Wharton
orts \ȯrts\ quartz, shorts, sports, undershorts—*also plurals and possessives of nouns and third person singular presents of verbs listed at* [1]ORT
ortunate \ȯrch-nət\ fortunate, importunate, unfortunate
orture \ȯr-chər\ see ORCHER
orty \ȯrt-ē\ forty, shorty, sortie, sporty, warty, mezzo forte, pianoforte
orum \ōr-əm\ foram, forum,

jorum, quorum, decorum, Mizoram, ad valorem, cockalorum, indecorum, Karakoram, variorum, pons asinorum, sanctum sanctorum, schola cantorum

[1]**orus** \ōr-əs\ Boris, chorus, Doris, Horus, loris, porous, sorus, torus, canorous, decorous, Delores, Dolores, pelorus, phosphorus, sonorous, deoch an doris, doch-an-dorris

[2]**orus** \ȯr-əs\ see AURUS

orward \ȯr-wərd\ forward, shoreward, flash-forward, henceforward, carryforward

ory \ȯr-ē\ Corey, corrie, dory, glory, gory, hoary, Laurie, Lori, lorry, lory, nori, quarry, saury, sorry, story, Tory, zori, centaury, clerestory, John Dory, outlawry, satori, vainglory, a priori, allegory, amatory, auditory, cacciatore, castratory, category, con amore, crematory, damnatory, decretory, desultory, dilatory, dormitory, expletory, feudatory, fumitory, Goteborg, gustatory, gyratory, hortatory, hunky-dory, inventory, laudatory, lavatory, mandatory, migratory, minatory, monitory, Montessori, nugatory, offertory, oratory, overstory, predatory, prefatory, probatory, promissory, promontory, purgatory, repertory, Ruwenzori, signatory, statutory, sudatory, territory, transitory, understory, vibratory, vomitory, yakitori, accusatory, admonitory, adulatory, a fortiori, aleatory, ambulatory, amendatory, applicatory, approbatory, celebratory, circulatory, combinatory, commendatory, compensatory, condemnatory, confirmatory, confiscatory, conservatory, consolatory, contributory, copulatory, cosignatory, declamatory, declaratory, dedicatory, defamatory, denigratory, depilatory, depository, derogatory, designatory, dispensatory, divinatory, escalatory, excitatory, exclamatory, exculpatory, excusatory, exhibitory, exhortatory, expiatory, expiratory, explanatory, explicatory, exploratory, expository, expurgatory, incantatory, incubatory, indicatory, inflammatory, informatory, innovatory, inspiratory, inundatory, invitatory, judicatory, laboratory, Lake Maggiore, masticatory, masturbatory, memento mori, millefiori, modulatory, obfuscatory, obligatory, observatory, performatory, persecutory, predicatory, premonitory, preparatory, prohibitory, reformatory, regulatory, repository, retributory, revelatory, respiratory, salutatory, stipulatory, supplicatory, transmigratory, undulatory, adjudicatory, a posteriori, annihilatory, annunciatory, anticipatory, appreciatory, assimilatory, circumlocutory, classificatory, concilliatory, confabulatory, congratulatory, de-escalatory, denunciatory, depreciatory, discriminatory, ejaculatory, hallucinatory, improvisatore, improvisatory, interrogatory, intimidatory, investigatory, participatory, propitiatory, recommendatory, recriminatory, renunciatory, reverberatory, viola d'amore, amelioratory, overcompensatory, reconciliatory, supererogatory, immunoregulatory

oryx \ȯr-iks\ oryx, Armorics, combinatorics

orze \ōrz\ see OORS

[1]os \äs\ boss, doss, dross, floss, fosse, gloss, joss, Maas, os, pross, stoss, toss, Argos, bathos, benthos, bugloss, chaos, Chios, cosmos, Delos, demos, Ellás, emboss, Eos, epos, Eros, ethos, Hyksos, kaross, kudos, kvass, Lagos, Laplace, Lemnos, Lesbos, Logos, Madras, Melos, mythos, nol-pros, nonpros, Paros, pathos, peplos, pharos, ringtoss, Samos, telos, topos, tripos, coup de grace, demitasse, extrados, gravitas, intrados, isogloss, omphalos, reredos, semigloss, Thanatos. underboss, volte-face

[2]os \ō\ see [1]OW

[3]os \ōs\ see [1]OSE

[4]os \ȯs\ see [1]OSS

[1]osa \ō-sə\ Xhosa, Formosa, mimosa, Reynosa, curiosa, virtuosa, anorexia nervosa

[2]osa \ō-zə\ mimosa, mucosa, serosa, Spinoza, sub rosa, curiosa, virtuosa, Zaragoza

[1]osable \ō-zə-bəl\ closable, disposable, erosible, explosible, opposable, reclosable, supposable, decomposable, superposable. indecomposable, superimposable

[2]osable \ü-zə-bəl\ see USABLE

osal \ō-zəl\ hosel, losel, deposal, disposal, proposal, reposal, supposal

osan \ōs-ᵊn\ see OSIN

osch \äsh\ see [2]ASH

[1]oschen \ō-shən\ see OTION

[2]oschen \ȯ-shən\ see AUTION

oscible \äs-ə-bəl\ see OSSIBLE

osco \äs-kō\ see OSCOE

oscoe \äs-kō\ Bosco, roscoe, Roscoe, fiasco

oscopy \äs-kə-pē\ arthroscopy. microscopy, spectroscopy, sigmoidoscopy

[1]ose \ōs\ close, dose, gross, os. arkose, Carlos, cosmos, crustose, cymose, dextrose, engross, erose, fructose, globose, glucose, jocose, lactose, maltose, mannose, megadose, morose, mythos, nodose, pappose, pathos, pentose, pilose, plumose, ramose, rhamnose, ribose, rugose, scapose, schistose, setose, spinose, strigose, sucrose, Sukkoth, triose, vadose, ventricose, verbose, viscose, adios, adipose, bellicose, calvados, cellulose, comatose, diagnose, grandiose, granulose, Helios, lachrymose, otiose, overdose, racemose, Shabuoth, tuberose, varicose, inter alios, inter vivos, metamorphose, religiose

²ose \ōz\ brose, Broz, chose, close, clothes, cloze, doze, froze, gloze, hose, nose, pose, prose, rose, Rose, Ambrose, appose, aros, bedclothes, bluenose, brownnose, bulldoze, Burroughs, compose, depose, dextrose, disclose, dispose, enclose, expose, foreclose, fructose, glucose, hardnose, impose, nightclothes, oppose, plainclothes, primrose, propose, quickfroze, repose, rockrose, suppose, transpose, tuberose, unclose, uprose, viscose, wind rose, Berlioz, counterpose, decompose, diagnose, discompose, indispose, interpose, juxtapose, letters close, pettitoes, predispose, presuppose, pussytoes, recompose, shovelnose, superpose, underclothes, anastomose, metamorphose, overexpose, superimpose, underexpose—*also plurals and possessives of nouns and third person singular presents of verbs listed at* ¹OW

³ose \üz\ see ²USE

osed \ōzd\ closed, nosed, composed, exposed, hard-nosed, opposed, pug-nosed, snub-nosed, stenosed, supposed, unclosed, indisposed, shovel-nosed, toffee-nosed, well-disposed—*also pasts of verbs listed at* ²OSE

osee \ō-zē\ see OSY

osel \ō-zəl\ see OSAL

osen \ōz-ᵊn\ chosen, frozen, quickfrozen, lederhosen

¹oser \ō-zər\ closer, dozer, poser, proser, brownnoser, bulldozer, composer, discloser, disposer, exposer, imposer, opposer, proposer, decomposer, interposer, photocomposer

²oser \ü-zər\ see USER

¹oset \ō-zət\ see ²OSIT

²oset \äz-ət\ see ¹OSIT

³oset \äs-ət\ see OSSET

osey \ō-zē\ see OSY

¹osh \ȯsh\ see ²ASH

²osh \ōsh\ see ²OCHE

¹oshed \äsht\ sloshed, galoshed—*also pasts of verbs listed at* ¹ASH

²oshed \ȯsht\ see ¹ASHED

oshen \ō-shən\ see OTION

osher \äsh-ər\ see ¹ASHER

osia \ō-shə\ see ¹OTIA

osible \ō-zə-bəl\ see ¹OSABLE

osier \ō-zhər\ see OSURE

osily \ō-zə-lē\ cozily, nosily, rosily

osin \ōs-ᵊn\ boatswain, Mosan, pocosin
osing \ō-ziŋ\ closing, nosing, disclosing, imposing, supposing
osion \ō-zhən\ plosion, corrosion, displosion, erosion, explosion, implosion
osis \ō-səs\ gnosis, hypnosis, narcosis, necrosis, neurosis, orthosis, osmosis, prognosis, psychosis, sclerosis, thrombosis, brucellosis, cyanosis, dermatosis, diagnosis, halitosis, heterosis, psittacosis, scoliosis, silicosis, symbiosis, anaplasmosis, autohypnosis, coccidiosis, hyperhidrosis, pediculosis, psychoneurosis, tuberculosis, mononucleosis, immunodiagnosis, neurofibromatosis
[1]**osit** \äz-ət\ closet, posit, composite, deposit, exposit
[2]**osit** \ō-zət\ prosit, roset
osite \äz-ət\ see [1]OSIT
ositive \äz-ət-iv\ positive, appositive, seropositive
ositor \äz-ət-ər\ compositor, depositor, expositor
osius \ō-shəs\ see OCIOUS
osive \ō-siv\ plosive, corrosive, erosive, explosive, implosive, purposive
osk \äsk\ mosque, kiosk, abelmosk
[1]**oso** \ō-sō\ proso, maestoso, rebozo, arioso, furioso, gracioso, grandioso, mafioso, Mato Grosso, oloroso, spiritoso, vigoroso, virtuoso, concerto grosso
[2]**oso** \ō-zō\ bozo, rebozo, furioso, gracioso, grandioso, spiritoso, vigoroso
[3]**oso** \ü-sō\ see USOE
osophy \äs-ə-fē\ philosophy, theosophy, anthroposophy
osque \äsk\ see OSK
[1]**oss** \ȯs\ boss, cross, crosse, floss, gloss, loss, moss, Ross, sauce, toss, across, bugloss, crisscross, emboss, Kinross, kouros, lacrosse, outcross, pathos, ringtoss, topcross, uncross, albatross, applesauce, autocross, double-cross, intercross, motocross, semigloss
[2]**oss** \ōs\ see [1]OSE
[3]**oss** \äs\ see [1]OS
ossa \äs-ə\ see [1]ASA
ossable \äs-ə-bəl\ see OSSIBLE
ossal \äs-əl\ docile, dossal, fossil, glossal, jostle, tassel, throstle, warsle, wassail, apostle, colossal, indocile, isoglossal
[1]**osse** \äs\ see [1]OS
[2]**osse** \äs-ē\ see [1]OSSY
[3]**osse** \ȯs\ see [1]OSS
ossed \ȯst\ see [3]OST
osser \ȯ-sər\ Chaucer, crosser, saucer, double-crosser
osset \äs-ət\ cosset, faucet, Osset, posset, Samoset
ossible \äs-ə-bəl\ possible, cognoscible, embossable, impossible
ossic \äs-ik\ see OSSICK
ossick \äs-ik\ fossick, isoglossic
ossil \äs-əl\ see OSSAL

ossity \äs-ət-ē\ adiposity, atrocity, callosity, ferocity, gibbosity, monstrosity, pomposity, porosity, precocity, velocity, viscosity, zygosity, animosity, bellicosity, curiosity, generosity, grandiosity, hideosity, luminosity, nebulosity, preciosity, reciprocity, scrupulosity, sensuosity, sinuosity, strenuosity, tortuosity, tuberosity, varicosity, virtuosity, impetuosity, religiosity, voluminosity, impecuniosity

ossly \ȯs-lē\ costly, crossly

osso \ō-sō\ see [1]OSO

ossos \äs-əs\ see OCESS

ossular \äs-ə-lər\ grossular, wassailer

ossum \äs-əm\ blossom, passim, possum, opossum

ossus \äs-əs\ see OCESS

[1]ossy \äs-ē\ Aussie, bossy, dassie, drossy, flossy, glossy, posse, quasi, dalasi, Kumasi, Likasi, sannyasi

[2]ossy \ȯ-sē\ Aussie, bossy, lossy, mossy

[1]ost \äst\ sol-faist, Pentecost, teleost—*also pasts of verbs listed at* [1]OS

[2]ost \ōst\ boast, coast, ghost, host, most, oast, post, roast, toast, almost, bedpost, compost, doorpost, endmost, foremost, gatepost, goalpost, Gold Coast, guidepost, headmost, hindmost, impost, inmost, midmost, milepost, Milquetoast, outmost, outpost, provost, rearmost, riposte, seacoast, signpost, sternmost, sternpost, topmost, upcoast, upmost, utmost, aftermost, ante-post, bottommost, coast-to-coast, easternmost, farthermost, fingerpost, furthermost, headforemost, hithermost, innermost, Ivory Coast, lowermost, nethermost, northernmost, outermost, rudderpost, southernmost, sternforemost, undermost, uppermost, uttermost, westernmost

[3]ost \ȯst\ cost, frost, lost, accost, defrost, exhaust, hoarfrost, star-crossed, holocaust, Pentecost, permafrost—*also pasts of verbs listed at* [1]OSS

[4]ost \əst\ see [1]UST

osta \äs-tə\ costa, pasta

[1]ostal \ōs-tᵊl\ coastal, postal, bicoastal, intercostal

[2]ostal \äs-tᵊl\ see OSTEL

ostasy \äs-tə-sē\ apostasy, isostasy

oste \ōst\ see [2]OST

ostel \äs-tᵊl\ hostel, hostile, Pentecostal

[1]oster \äs-tər\ coster, foster, Foster, roster, impostor, piaster, Double Gloucester, paternoster, snollygoster

[2]oster \ȯs-tər\ foster, Foster, roster, Double Gloucester

[3]oster \ō-stər\ see OASTER

ostic \äs-tik\ Gnostic, acrostic, agnostic, prognostic, diagnostic

ostile \äs-tᵊl\ see OSTEL
ostle \äs-əl\ see OSSAL
[1]**ostly** \ōst-lē\ ghostly, hostly, mostly
[2]**ostly** \ȯs-lē\ see OSSLY
ostomy \äs-tə-mē\ ostomy, colostomy, enterostomy
oston \ȯs-tən\ Austin, Boston, Godwin Austen
ostor \äs-tər\ see [1]OSTER
[1]**ostral** \ȯs-trəl\ austral, rostral
[2]**ostral** \äs-trəl\ see OSTREL
ostrel \äs-trəl\ austral, costrel, nostril, rostral, wastrel, colostral
ostril \äs-trəl\ see OSTREL
ostrum \äs-trəm\ nostrum, rostrum, colostrum
osty \ō-stē\ ghosty, toasty
osure \ō-zhər\ closure, crosier, osier, composure, disclosure, disposure, enclosure, exclosure, exposure, foreclosure, discomposure, overexposure, underexposure
osy \ō-zē\ cozy, dozy, mosey, nosy, Osee, posy, prosy, rosy, ring-around-a-rosy
osyne \äs-ᵊn-ē\ Euphrosyne, Mnemosyne
osz \ȯsh\ see [2]ASH
oszcz \ȯsh\ see [2]ASH
[1]**ot** \ät\ aught, baht, blot, boite, bot, chott, clot, cot, dot, ghat, got, grot, hot, jat, jot, khat, knot, kyat, lot, Lot, lotte, motte, naught, not, plot, pot, rot, scot, Scot, Scott, shot, skat, slot, snot, sot, spot, squat, swat, swot, tot, trot, watt, Watt, what, wot, yacht, allot, ascot, begot, besot, big shot, bloodshot, bowknot, boycott, buckshot, bullshot, cachepot, calotte, cannot, Connacht, crackpot, Crockpot, culotte, dashpot, despot, dreadnought, earshot, ergot, escot, eyeshot, eyespot, feedlot, fiat, firepot, fleshpot, forgot, fox-trot, fusspot, fylfot, garrote, gavotte, grapeshot, gunshot, half-knot, have-not, highspot, hotchpot, hotshot, ikat, jackpot, Korat, kumquat, long shot, loquat, marplot, mascot, motmot, nightspot, one-shot, Pequot, potshot, Rabat, red-hot, robot, Sadat, sandlot, sexpot, Shabbat, shallot, Shebat, sheepcote, slingshot, slipknot, slungshot, snapshot, somewhat, stinkpot, stockpot, subplot, sunspot, teapot, tin-pot, topknot, tosspot, try-pot, upshot, wainscot, whatnot, white-hot, woodlot, aeronaut, aliquot, apparat, apricot, aquanaut, argonaut, astronaut, bergamot, cachalot, Camelot, caveat, carry-cot, coffeepot, cosmonaut, counterplot, diddley-squat, doodley-squat, flowerpot, gallipot, guillemot, Gujarat, Hottentot, Huguenot, kilowatt, Lancelot, megawatt, microdot, Nouakchott, ocelot, overshot, paraquat, patriot, Penobscot, peridot, polka dot, polyglot, samizdat, sansculotte, scattershot, terawatt, tommyrot, touch-me-not, underplot, undershot,

Willemstadt, Wyandot, wyandotte, compatriot, forget-me-not, immunoblot, Inupiat, requiescat, Johnny-on-the-spot

[2]ot \ō\ see [1]OW

[3]ot \ōt\ see OAT

[4]ot \ȯt\ see [1]OUGHT

ôt \ō\ see [1]OW

ota \ōt-ə\ bota, flota, lota, quota, rota, biota, Dakota, iota, Lakota, pelota, Toyota, Minnesota, North Dakota, South Dakota

otable \ōt-ə-bəl\ notable, potable, quotable

otage \ōt-ij\ dotage, flotage, anecdotage

otal \ōt-ᵊl\ dotal, motile, scrotal, total, immotile, subtotal, teetotal, anecdotal, antidotal, sacerdotal

otalist \ōt-ᵊl-əst\ teetotalist, anecdotalist, sacerdotalist

otamus \ät-ə-məs\ see OTOMOUS

otany \ät-ᵊn-ē\ botany, cottony, monotony

otarist \ōt-ə-rəst\ motorist, votarist

otary \ōt-ə-rē\ coterie, rotary, votary, locomotory, prothonotary

otas \ō-təs\ see OTUS

otch \äch\ blotch, botch, crotch, hotch, notch, scotch, Scotch, splotch, swatch, watch, bird-watch, deathwatch, debauch, dogwatch, hopscotch, hotchpotch, Sasquatch, stopwatch, top-notch, wristwatch, butterscotch

otchet \äch-ət\ crotchet, rochet

otchman \äch-mən\ Scotchman, watchman

otchy \äch-ē\ blotchy, boccie, botchy, splotchy, hibachi, huarache, huisache, Karachi, vivace, mariachi

[1]ote \ōt-ē\ dhoti, floaty, loti, roti, throaty, cenote, coyote, chayote, peyote, quixote

[2]ote \ōt\ see OAT

[3]ote \ät\ see [1]OT

otea \ōt-ē-ə\ protea, scotia

oted \ōt-əd\ see OATED

otem \ōt-əm\ see OTUM

oten \ōt-ᵊn\ see OTON

oter \ōt-ər\ see OATER

oterie \ōt-ə-rē\ see OTARY

[1]oth \äth\ broth, cloth, froth, Goth, moth, sloth, swath, troth, wroth, betroth, breechcloth, broadcloth, cheesecloth, dishcloth, facecloth, floorcloth, loincloth, Naboth, oilcloth, sackcloth, sailcloth, washcloth, Alioth, behemoth, tablecloth, Ustrogoth, Visigoth

[2]oth \ōs\ see [1]OSE

[3]oth \ōt\ see OAT

[4]oth \ōth\ see OWTH

othal \ȯth-əl\ see OTHEL

othe \ō<u>th</u>\ clothe, loathe, betroth, unclothe

othel \ȯth-əl\ brothel, betrothal

[1]other \ə<u>th</u>-ər\ brother, mother, nother, other, rather, smother, tother, another, foremother, godmother, grandmother, housemother, stepbrother, stepmother

[2]other \ä<u>th</u>-ər\ see [1]ATHER

otherly \əth-ər-lē\ brotherly, motherly, southerly, grandmotherly

othes \ōz\ see [2]OSE

othesis \äth-ə-səs\ prothesis, hypothesis

othic \äth-ik\ gothic, neo-Gothic, Ostrogothic, Visigothic

othing \ō-thiŋ\ clothing, loathing, underclothing

otho \ō-tō\ see [1]OTO

[1]oti \ōt-ē\ see [1]OTE

[2]oti \ȯt-ē\ see AUGHTY

[1]otia \ō-shə\ scotia, Scotia, agnosia, dystocia, Cappadocia, Nova Scotia

[2]otia \ōt-ē-ə\ see OTEA

otiable \ō-shə-bəl\ see OCIABLE

otiant \ō-shənt\ see OTIENT

[1]otic \ät-ik\ Scotic, aquatic, biotic, chaotic, demotic, despotic, erotic, exotic, hypnotic, narcotic, necrotic, neurotic, Nilotic, osmotic, psychotic, quixotic, robotic, sclerotic, semiotic, abiotic, anecdotic, asymptotic, bibliotic, embryotic, epiglottic, homeotic, Huguenotic, idiotic, macrobiotic, melanotic, patriotic, posthypnotic, sansculottic, symbiotic, antibiotic, autoerotic, compatriotic, homoerotic

[2]otic \ōt-ik\ lotic, photic, aphotic, aprotic, dichotic, robotic

[3]otic \ȯt-ik\ see AUTIC

otica \ät-i-kə\ erotica, exotica

otice \ōt-əs\ see OTUS

otics \ät-iks\ robotics, astronautics, bibliotics—*also plurals and possessives of nouns listed at* [1]OTIC

otid \ät-əd\ see OTTED

otient \ō-shənt\ quotient, negotiant

otile \ōt-ᵊl\ see OTAL

[1]oting \ōt-iŋ\ see OATING

[2]oting \ät-iŋ\ see OTTING

[1]otinous \ät-nəs\ see OTNESS

[2]otinous \ät-ᵊn-əs\ see [1]OTONOUS

otion \ō-shən\ Goshen, groschen, lotion, motion, notion, ocean, potion, commotion, demotion, devotion, emotion, Laotian, promotion, slow-motion, locomotion

otional \ō-shnəl\ motional, notional, devotional, emotional, promotional, unemotional

otis \ōt-əs\ see OTUS

otist \ōt-əst\ protist, Scotist, anecdotist

otive \ōt-iv\ motive, votive, emotive, promotive, automotive, locomotive

otl \ät-ᵊl\ see OTTLE

otle \ät-ᵊl\ see OTTLE

otley \ät-lē\ see OTLY

otly \ät-lē\ Atli, hotly, motley

otment \ät-mənt\ allotment, ballottement

otness \ät-nəs\ hotness, squatness

oto \ō-tō\ koto, photo, roto, Sotho, Basotho, con moto, de Soto, ex-voto, in toto, Kyoto,

Lesotho, Mosotho, Sesotho, Kumamoto, telephoto
otomous \ät-ə-məs\ dichotomous, hippopotamus
otomy \ät-ə-mē\ dichotomy, lobotomy, tracheotomy, episiotomy
oton \ōt-ᵊn\ croton, Jotun, oaten, Lofoten, verboten
¹otonous \ät-ᵊn-əs\ rottenness, monotonous, serotinous
²otonous \ät-nəs\ see OTNESS
otor \ōt-ər\ see OATER
otorist \ōt-ə-rəst\ see OTARIST
otory \ōt-ə-rē\ see OTARY
ots \äts\ Graz, hots, lots, Scots, Spaatz, swats, ersatz, Galati—*also plurals and possessives of nouns and third person singular presents of verbs listed at* ¹OT
otsk \ätsk\ see ATSK
otsman \ät-smən\ Scotsman, yachtsman
ott \ät\ see ¹OT
otta \ät-ə\ see ¹ATA
ottage \ät-ij\ cottage, plottage, pottage, wattage
ottal \ät-ᵊl\ see OTTLE
¹otte \ät\ see ¹OT
²otte \ȯt\ see ¹OUGHT
otted \ät-əd\ knotted, potted, spotted, carotid, proglottid, polka-dotted—*also pasts of verbs listed at* ¹OT
ottement \ät-mənt\ see OTMENT
otten \ät-ᵊn\ cotton, gotten, gratin, ratton, rotten, shotten, au gratin, begotten, forgotten, guncotton, ill-gotten, misbegotten, sauerbraten
ottenness \ät-ᵊn-əs\ see ¹OTONOUS
otter \ät-ər\ blotter, cotter, dotter, knotter, otter, plotter, potter, Potter, Qatar, rotter, spotter, squatter, swatter, Tatar, totter, trotter, water, alotter, boycotter, flyswatter, garroter, globe-trotter, pinspotter, sandlotter, alma mater, imperator, teeter-totter—*also comparatives of adjectives listed at* ¹OT *and words ending in* -water *listed at* ¹ATER
ottery \ät-ə-rē\ lottery, pottery, Tatary, tottery, watery
ottic \ät-ik\ see ¹OTIC
ottid \ät-əd\ see OTTED
ottie \ät-ē\ see ATI
otting \ät-iŋ\ jotting, wainscoting
ottis \ät-əs\ glottis, clematis, epiglottis, literatus
ottische \ät-ish\ see OTTISH
ottish \ät-ish\ hottish, schottische, Scottish, sottish, sanculottish
ottle \ät-ᵊl\ bottle, dottle, glottal, mottle, pottle, ratel, rotl, throttle, wattle, atlatl, bluebottle, Aristotle, monocotyl, Nahuatl, epiglottal, Quetzalcoatl
¹otto \ät-ō\ see ¹ATO
²otto \ȯt-ō\ see ¹AUTO
ottom \ät-əm\ see ¹ATUM
otty \ät-ē\ see ATI
otum \ōt-əm\ notum, scrotum, totem, factotum, teetotum
otun \ōt-ᵊn\ see OTON
oture \ō-chər\ see OACHER

otus \ōt-əs\ lotus, notice, Otis, denotice, Pelotas
oty \ȯt-ē\ see [1]AUGHTY
otyl \ät-əl\ see OTTLE
[1]**ou** \ō\ see [1]OW
[2]**ou** \ü\ see [1]EW
[3]**ou** \au̇\ see [2]OW
oubled \ə-bəld\ see UBBLED
ouble \əb-əl\ see UBBLE
oubler \əb-lər\ doubler, bubbler, troubler
oubly \əb-lē\ see UBBLY
oubt \au̇t\ see [3]OUT
oubted \au̇t-əd\ see OUTED
oubter \au̇t-ər\ see [2]OUTER
[1]**ouc** \ü\ see [1]EW
[2]**ouc** \ük\ see UKE
[3]**ouc** \u̇k\ see [1]OOK
ouce \üs\ see [1]USE
[1]**oucester** \äs-tər\ see [1]OSTER
[2]**oucester** \ȯs-tər\ see [2]OSTER
[1]**ouch** \üch\ see [1]OOCH
[2]**ouch** \üsh\ see OUCHE
[3]**ouch** \əch\ see [1]UTCH
[4]**ouch** \au̇ch\ couch, crouch, grouch, ouch, pouch, slouch, vouch, avouch, debouch, scaramouch, retort pouch
ouche \üsh\ douche, louche, ruche, squoosh, swoosh, whoosh, barouche, capuche, cartouche, debouch, farouche, kurus, tarboosh, scaramouch
[1]**ouchy** \əch-ē\ see UCHY
[2]**ouchy** \au̇-chē\ grouchy, pouchy, slouchy
ou'd \üd\ see UDE
[1]**oud** \üd\ see UDE
[2]**oud** \au̇d\ boughed, bowed, cloud, crowd, loud, proud, shroud, stroud, aloud, becloud, enshroud, highbrowed, house-proud, purse-proud, Red Cloud, unbowed, overcrowd, thundercloud—*also pasts of verbs listed at* [2]OW
ouda \üd-ə\ see UDA
oudy \au̇d-ē\ see OWDY
oue \ü\ see [1]EW
ouf \üf\ see [1]OOF
ouffe \üf\ see [1]OOF
oug \əg\ see UG
[1]**ouge** \üj\ see [1]UGE
[2]**ouge** \üzh\ see [2]UGE
[3]**ouge** \au̇j\ gouge, scrouge
[1]**ough** \ō\ see [1]OW
[2]**ough** \ü\ see [1]EW
[3]**ough** \au̇\ see [2]OW
[4]**ough** \äk\ see [1]OCK
[5]**ough** \əf\ see UFF
[6]**ough** \ȯf\ see [2]OFF
[1]**ougham** \ōm\ see [1]OME
[2]**ougham** \üm\ see [1]OOM
oughed \au̇d\ see [2]OUD
oughen \əf-ən\ see UFFIN
ougher \əf-ər\ see UFFER
oughie \əf-ē\ see UFFY
oughish \əf-ish\ see UFFISH
oughly \əf-lē\ see UFFLY
oughs \ōz\ see [2]OSE
[1]**ought** \ȯt\ aught, bought, brought, caught, dot, fought, fraught, ghat, lotte, naught, nought, ought, sought, taught, taut, thought, wrought, besought, distraught, dreadnought, forethought, handwrought, high-wrought, onslaught, self-taught, store-bought, unthought, aeronaut, aforethought, afterthought, aquanaut, argonaut, astronaut,

cosmonaut, juggernaut, overbought, overwrought
[2]**ought** \aůt\ see [3]OUT
oughten \ȯt-[ə]n\ see AUTEN
oughty \aůt-ē\ doughty, droughty, gouty, pouty, snouty, trouty
[1]**oughy** \ō-ē\ see OWY
[2]**oughy** \ü-ē\ see EWY
ouie \ü-ē\ see EWY
ouille \ü-ē\ see EWY
[1]**ouis** \ü-ē\ see EWY
[2]**ouis** \ü-əs\ see EWESS
ouk \ük\ see UKE
ouki \ü-kē\ see [1]OOKY
[1]**oul** \ōl\ see [1]OLE
[2]**oul** \ül\ see [1]OOL
[3]**oul** \aůl\ see [2]OWL
[1]**ould** \ōld\ see [1]OLD
[2]**ould** \ůd\ see [1]OOD
oulder \ōl-dər\ see [1]OLDER
ouldered \ōl-dərd\ bouldered, shouldered, round-shouldered, square-shouldered—*also pasts of verbs listed at* [1]OLDER
ouldest \ůd-əst\ couldest, shouldest, wouldest, Talmudist
ouldn't \ůd-[ə]nt\ shouldn't, wouldn't
[1]**oule** \ü-lē\ see ULY
[2]**oule** \ül\ see [1]OOL
ouled \ōld\ see [1]OLD
oulee \ü-lē\ see ULY
[1]**ouleh** \ü-lə\ see ULA
[2]**ouleh** \ü-lē\ see ULY
ouli \ü-lē\ see ULY
oulie \ü-lē\ see ULY
ouling \aů-liŋ\ see [2]OWLING
oulish \ü-lish\ see OOLISH
[1]**ou'll** \ül\ see [1]OOL
[2]**ou'll** \ůl\ see [1]UL
oulle \ül\ see [1]OOL
oulli \ü-lē\ see ULY
oully \aů-lē\ see [2]OWLY
oult \ōlt\ see [1]OLT
oulter \ōl-tər\ see OLTER
oum \üm\ see [1]OOM
oumenal \ü-mən-[ə]l\ see UMINAL
[1]**oun** \aůn\ see [2]OWN
[2]**oun** \ün\ see [1]OON
ounce \aůns\ bounce, flounce, jounce, ounce, pounce, trounce, announce, denounce, enounce, pronounce, renounce, mispronounce
ouncement \aůn-smənt\ announcement, denouncement, pronouncement
ouncer \aůn-sər\ bouncer, announcer
ouncil \aůn-səl\ see OUNSEL
ouncy \aůn-sē\ bouncy, flouncy, jouncy, viscountcy
[1]**ound** \ünd\ stound, swound, wound—*also pasts of verbs listed at* [1]OON
[2]**ound** \aůnd\ bound, crowned, found, ground, hound, mound, pound, Pound, round, sound, stound, swound, wound, abound, aground, all-round, around, astound, background, black-crowned, bloodhound, campground, chowhound, compound, confound, coonhound, dachshund, deerhound, deskbound, earthbound, eastbound, elkhound, expound, fairground, fogbound, foot-pound, foreground, foxhound, go-round, greyhound,

hardbound, hellhound, hidebound, homebound, horehound, housebound, icebound, impound, inbound, newfound, newshound, northbound, outbound, playground, pot-bound, profound, propound, rebound, redound, resound, rockbound, snowbound, softbound, southbound, spellbound, stone-ground, stormbound, strikebound, surround, unbound, well-found, westbound, white-crowned, wolfhound, year-round, aboveground, all-around, belowground, battleground, decompound, go-around, muscle-bound, outward-bound, paperbound, Puget Sound, runaround, turnaround, ultrasound, underground, weather-bound, wraparound, merry-go-round, superabound—*also pasts of verbs listed at* [2]OWN

oundal \au̇n-dᵊl\ poundal, roundel

oundary \au̇n-drē\ see OUNDRY

ounded \au̇n-dəd\ drownded, rounded, confounded, unbounded, unfounded, well-founded, well-grounded

oundel \au̇n-dᵊl\ see OUNDAL

ounder \au̇n-dər\ bounder, flounder, founder, grounder, pounder, rounder, sounder, all-rounder, backgrounder, dumbfounder, tenpounder

ounding \au̇n-diŋ\ drownding, grounding, sounding, astounding, high-sounding, rockhounding

[1]**oundless** \ün-ləs\ see OONLESS

[2]**oundless** \au̇n-ləs\ groundless, soundless

oundlet \au̇n-lət\ see OWNLET

oundling \au̇n-liŋ\ foundling, groundling

oundly \au̇nd-lē\ roundly, soundly

oundness \au̇n-nəs\ roundness, unsoundness

oundry \au̇n-drē\ boundary, foundry

[1]**ounds** \ünz\ see OONS

[2]**ounds** \au̇nz\ hounds, zounds, inbounds, Barren Grounds, out-of-bounds—*also plurals and possessives of nouns and third person singular presents of verbs listed at* [2]OUND

oundsel \au̇n-səl\ see OUNSEL

oundsman \au̇nz-mən\ see OWNSMAN

ounge \au̇nj\ lounge, scrounge, chaise lounge

[1]**ounger** \au̇n-jər\ lounger, scrounger

[2]**ounger** \əŋ-gər\ see [1]ONGER

ounker \əŋ-kər\ see UNKER

ounsel \au̇n-səl\ council, counsel, groundsel

[1]**ount** \änt\ see [2]ANT

[2]**ount** \au̇nt\ count, fount, mount, account, amount, demount, discount, dismount, high-count, miscount, recount, remount, seamount, surmount, viscount, catamount, paramount, rediscount, tantamount, undercount

ountable \au̇nt-ə-bəl\

countable, accountable, demountable, discountable, surmountable, insurmountable, unaccountable

ountain \aůnt-ᵊn\ fountain, mountain, transmountain, cat-a-mountain, Riding Mountain

ountcy \aůn-sē\ see OUNCY

ounter \aůnt-ər\ counter, discounter, encounter, recounter, rencounter

ountess \aůnt-əs\ countess, viscountess

ountie \aůnt-ē\ see OUNTY

ounting \aůnt-iŋ\ mounting, accounting

ounty \aůnt-ē\ bounty, county, Mountie, viscounty

[1]**oup** \ōp\ see OPE

[2]**oup** \ü\ see [1]EW

[3]**oup** \üp\ see [1]OOP

[1]**oupe** \ōp\ see OPE

[2]**oupe** \üp\ see [1]OOP

ouper \ü-pər\ see OOPER

oupie \ü-pē\ see OOPY

ouping \ü-piŋ\ see OOPING

ouple \əp-əl\ see [1]UPLE

ouplet \əp-lət\ see [1]UPLET

oupous \ü-pəs\ see UPUS

oupy \ü-pē\ see OOPY

[1]**our** \ōr\ see [1]OR

[2]**our** \ůr\ see [1]URE

[3]**our** \aůr\ see [2]OWER

[4]**our** \är\ see [3]AR

[5]**our** \ər\ see [1]EUR

oura \ůr-ə\ see URA

ourable \ōr-ə-bəl\ see [1]ORABLE

ourage \ər-ij\ courage, demurrage, discourage, encourage

[1]**ourbon** \ər-bən\ see [1]URBAN

[2]**ourbon** \ůr-bən\ see [2]URBAN

[1]**ource** \ōrs\ see [1]OURSE

[2]**ource** \ȯrs\ see [1]ORSE

[1]**ourceful** \ōrs-fəl\ see [1]ORCEFUL

[2]**ourceful** \ȯrs-fəl\ see ORSEFUL

ourcing \ōr-siŋ\ outsourcing—*also present participles of verbs listed at* [1]OURSE

ourd \ōrd\ see OARD

ourde \ůrd\ see [1]URED

[1]**ou're** \ōr\ see [1]OR

[2]**ou're** \ü-ər\ see [1]EWER

[3]**ou're** \ůr\ see [1]URE

[4]**ou're** \ər\ see [1]EUR

oured \ōrd\ see OARD

[1]**ourer** \ōr-ər\ see [1]ORER

[2]**ourer** \ůr-ər\ see [1]URER

[3]**ourer** \aůr-ər\ flowerer, scourer, deflowerer, devourer—*also comparatives of adjectives listed at* [2]OWER

[1]**ourg** \ůr\ see [1]URE

[2]**ourg** \ərg\ see ERG

[1]**ourge** \ərj\ see URGE

[2]**ourge** \ȯrj\ see ORGE

ourger \ər-jər\ see ERGER

ouri \ůr-ē\ see [1]URY

[1]**ourier** \ůr-ē-ər\ courier, couturier, couturiere, vaunt-courier

[2]**ourier** \ər-ē-ər\ see URRIER

[1]**ouring** \ōr-iŋ\ see ORING

[2]**ouring** \ůr-iŋ\ see URING

ourish \ər-ish\ currish, flourish, nourish, amateurish

ourist \ůr-əst\ see URIST

ourly \aůr-lē\ dourly, hourly, sourly

[1]**ourn** \ōrn\ see [1]ORN

[2]**ourn** \ərn\ see URN

[3]**ourn** \ȯrn\ see [2]ORN

ournal \ərn-ᵊl\ see ERNAL
ournament \ȯr-nə-mənt\ see ORNAMENT
ourne \ōrn\ see [1]ORN
[1]ourney \ər-nē\ Bernie, Ernie, ferny, gurney, journey, tourney, attorney
[2]ourney \ȯr-nē\ see ORNY
ourneyer \ər-nē-ər\ journeyer, vernier
ournful \ȯrn-fəl\ see ORNFUL
ourning \ȯr-niŋ\ see ORNING
ournment \ərn-mənt\ see ERNMENT
[1]ours \ōrz\ see [1]OORS
[2]ours \ärz\ see ARS
[3]ours \ȯrz\ see [2]OORS
[4]ours \au̇rz\ ours, after-hours—*also plurals and possessives of nouns and third singular presents of verbs listed at* [2]OWER
[5]ours \u̇r\ see [1]URE
[1]ourse \ōrs\ coarse, course, force, hoarse, source, concourse, deforce, discourse, divorce, enforce, perforce, racecourse, recourse, resource, intercourse, reinforce, telecourse, tour de force, watercourse
[2]ourse \ȯrs\ see [1]ORSE
oursome \ȯr-səm\ see ORSUM
[1]ourt \ȯrt\ see [1]ORT
[2]ourt \u̇rt\ see [1]URT
ourtesy \ərt-ə-sē\ courtesy, curtesy, discourtesy
ourth \ȯrth\ see [1]ORTH
ourtier \ȯr-chər\ see ORCHER
[1]ourtly \ōrt-lē\ see [1]ORTLY
[2]ourtly \ȯrt-lē\ see [2]ORTLY
oury \au̇r-ē\ see OWERY
[1]ous \ü\ see [1]EW
[2]ous \üs\ see [1]USE
[1]ousa \ü-sə\ see [1]USA
[2]ousa \ü-zə\ see [2]USA
ousal \au̇-zəl\ housel, spousal, tousle, arousal, carousal
ousand \au̇z-ᵊn\ see OWSON
[1]ouse \üs\ see [1]USE
[2]ouse \au̇s\ blouse, chiaus, chouse, douse, Gauss, grouse, house, Klaus, Laos, louse, mouse, scouse, souse, spouse, Strauss, baghouse, bathhouse, Bauhaus, birdhouse, blockhouse, bughouse, bunkhouse, cathouse, chophouse, clubhouse, cookhouse, courthouse, deckhouse, degauss, delouse, doghouse, dollhouse, dormouse, espouse, farmhouse, firehouse, flophouse, gashouse, gatehouse, glasshouse, greenhouse, guardhouse, henhouse, hothouse, icehouse, in-house, jailhouse, lighthouse, lobscouse, longhouse, madhouse, Manaus, nuthouse, outhouse, penthouse, playhouse, poorhouse, roadhouse, roughhouse, roundhouse, schoolhouse, smokehouse, springhouse, statehouse, storehouse, teahouse, titmouse, tollhouse, warehouse, washhouse, wheelhouse, White House, whorehouse, workhouse, boardinghouse, clearinghouse, coffeehouse, countinghouse,

customhouse, house-to-house, meetinghouse, Mickey Mouse, overblouse, pilothouse, porterhouse, powerhouse, slaughterhouse, sugarhouse, summerhouse, treasure-house, Westinghouse
[3]**ouse** \au̇z\ blouse, bouse, bowse, browse, douse, dowse, drowse, house, mouse, rouse, spouse, touse, arouse, carouse, delouse, doss-house, espouse, rehouse, roughhouse, warehouse—*also plurals and possessives of nouns and third person singular presents of verbs listed at* [2]OW
[4]**ouse** \üz\ see [2]USE
ousel \au̇-zəl\ see OUSAL
ouser \au̇-zər\ dowser, houser, mouser, schnauzer, trouser, wowser, warehouser, rabble-rouser
ousin \əz-ᵊn\ see [1]OZEN
ousinage \əz-ᵊn-ij\ cousinage, cozenage
ousing \au̇-ziŋ\ housing, rousing, rabble-rousing
[1]**ousle** \ü-zəl\ see [2]USAL
[2]**ousle** \au̇-zəl\ see OUSAL
ousse \üs\ see [1]USE
ousseau \ü-sō\ see USOE
[1]**oust** \au̇st\ Faust, joust, oust, roust—*also pasts of verbs listed at* [2]OUSE
[2]**oust** \üst\ see OOST
ouste \üst\ see OOST
[1]**ousy** \au̇-zē\ see OWSY
[2]**ousy** \au̇-sē\ mousy, Firdawsi
[1]**out** \ü\ see [1]EW
[2]**out** \üt\ see UTE
[3]**out** \au̇t\ bout, clout, doubt, drought, flout, glout, gout, grout, knout, kraut, lout, out, pout, rout, route, scout, shout, snout, spout, sprout, stout, tout, trout, ablaut, about, all-out, bailout, blackout, blissed-out, blowout, breakout, breechclout, brownout, burned-out, burnout, checkout, clapped-out, closeout, cookout, cop-out, cutout, devout, dishclout, downspout, dropout, dugout, eelpout, fade-out, fallout, far-out, flameout, flat-out, foldout, force-out, freak-out, freeze out, full-out, gross-out, groundout, handout, hangout, hideout, holdout, ice-out, knockout, layout, lights-out, lockout, lookout, misdoubt, payout, phaseout, pitchout, printout, psych-out, pullout, punch-out, putout, rainspout, readout, redoubt, rollout, sellout, setout, shakeout, shoot-out, shutout, sick-out, sold-out, spaced-out, speak-out, spinout, stakeout, standout, straight-out, stressed-out, stretch-out, strikeout, takeout, thought-out, throughout, throw out, time-out, tryout, turnout, umlaut, veg out, walkout, washed-out, washout, way-out, whacked-out, whiteout, wigged-out, wipeout, without, workout, worn-out, zonked-out, all get-out, carryout, diner-out, down-and-out, falling-out, gadabout,

hereabout, knockabout, layabout, out-and-out, roundabout, rouseabout, roustabout, runabout, sauerkraut, stirabout, thereabout, turnabout, walkabout, waterspout
[1]**oute** \üt\ see UTE
[2]**oute** \au̇t\ see [3]OUT
outed \au̇t-əd\ snouted, spouted, undoubted—*also pasts of verbs listed at* [3]OUT
[1]**outer** \üt-ər\ see UTER
[2]**outer** \au̇t-ər\ doubter, flouter, grouter, outer, pouter, router, scouter, shouter, spouter, touter, come-outer, down-and-outer, out-and-outer
[1]**outh** \üth\ see [2]OOTH
[2]**outh** \au̇th\ mouth, routh, scouth, south, bad-mouth, goalmouth, loudmouth, poor-mouth, blabbermouth, cottonmouth, hand-to-mouth, motormouth, word-of-mouth
outherly \əth-ər-lē\ see OTHERLY
outhey \au̇-thē\ see OUTHY
outhful \üth-fəl\ see UTHFUL
outhie \ü-thē\ see OOTHY
outhly \üth-lē\ see OOTHLY
outhy \au̇-thē\ mouthy, Southey
outi \üt-ē\ see [1]OOTY
outing \au̇t-iŋ\ outing, scouting
outish \au̇t-ish\ loutish, snoutish
outre \üt-ər\ see UTER
outrement \ü-trə-mənt\ see UTRIMENT
outs \au̇ts\ hereabouts, ins and outs, thereabouts, whereabouts
outy \au̇t-ē\ see OUGHTY
ou've \üv\ see [3]OVE
ouver \ü-vər\ see [3]OVER
oux \ü\ see [1]EW
ouy \ē\ see [1]EE
ouyhnhnm \in-əm\ see INIM
ouzel \ü-zəl\ see [2]USAL
[1]**ov** \äf\ see [1]OFF
[2]**ov** \ȯf\ see [2]OFF
ova \ō-və\ nova, Cralova, Jehovah, Moldova, bossa nova, Casanova, Czestochowa, Kemerovo, supernova
ovable \ü-və-bəl\ movable, provable, approvable, disprovable, immovable, improvable, removable, irremovable
ovah \ō-və\ see OVA
oval \ü-vəl\ approval, removal, disapproval
ovat \əv-ət\ see OVET
[1]**ove** \əv\ dove, glove, love, of, shove, above, foxglove, hereof, kid-glove, ringdove, thereof, truelove, whereof, ladylove, light-o'-love, roman-fleuve, turtledove, unheard of, well-thought-of, hereinabove
[2]**ove** \ōv\ clove, cove, dove, drove, fauve, grove, hove, Jove, mauve, rove, stove, strove, throve, trove, wove, alcove, behove, cookstove, mangrove, woodstove, Garden Grove, interwove, treasure trove
[3]**ove** \üv\ groove, move, poof, poove, prove, you've, approve, behoove, commove,

disprove, improve, remove, reprove, disapprove

[1]ovel \äv-əl\ grovel, novel, antinovel, Yaroslavl

[2]ovel \əv-əl\ grovel, hovel, shovel

ovement \üv-mənt\ movement, improvement

[1]oven \əv-ən\ coven, oven, sloven

[2]oven \ō-vən\ cloven, coven, woven, Beethoven, handwoven, interwoven

[1]over \əv-ər\ cover, glover, hover, lover, plover, bedcover, discover, dustcover, hardcover, re-cover, recover, slipcover, softcover, uncover, windhover, undercover

[2]over \ō-vər\ clover, Dover, drover, Grover, over, plover, rover, stover, trover, allover, changeover, crossover, cutover, flashover, flopover, flyover, hangover, Hannover, Hanover, holdover, layover, leftover, makeover, moreover, once-over, Passover, popover, pullover, pushover, rollover, runover, slipover, spillover, stopover, strikeover, takeover, turnover, voice-over, walkover, warmed-over, carryover, crossing-over, going-over, Strait of Dover

[3]over \ü-vər\ groover, Hoover, louver, mover, prover, earthmover, improver, maneuver, remover, reprover, Vancouver, disapprover

[4]over \äv-ər\ see [1]AVER

overable \əv-rə-bəl\ discoverable, recoverable, irrecoverable

overly \əv-ər-lē\ loverly, Sir Roger de Coverley

overt \ō-vərt\ covert, overt

overy \əv-rē\ discovery, recovery

ovet \əv-ət\ covet, lovat

ovey \ə-vē\ covey, lovey-dovey

ovian \ō-vē-ən\ Jovian, Markovian, Pavlovian, Varsovian

ovie \ü-vē\ see OOVY

ovo \ō-vō\ Provo, ab ovo, de novo, Porto Novo

ovost \äv-əst\ see AVIST

ovsk \ȯfsk\ Dnepropetrovsk, Petropavlovsk

[1]ow \ō\ beau, blow, bow, bro, Chou, crow, do, doe, dough, ewe, floe, flow, foe, fro, froe, frow, glow, go, grow, ho, hoe, jo, Jo, joe, Joe, know, lo, low, mho, mot, mow, no, No, O, oh, owe, Po, Poe, pow, pro, rho, roe, row, schmo, sew, shew, show, sloe, slow, snow, so, sow, stow, Stowe, strow, though, throe, throw, toe, tow, trow, whoa, woe, yo, aglow, ago, airflow, airglow, alow, although, backflow, backhoe, bandeau, Baotou, barlow, bateau, below, bestow, bon mot, Bordeaux, bravo, by-blow, cachepot, caló, Carlow, chapeau, chateau, Ch[illegible] cockcrow, cornrow[illegible] Day-Glo, daygl[illegible] trop, deathbl[illegible] bow, elbo[illegible] fencerow, flambeau, flyblow, fogbow, forego, foreknow, forgo, Fuzhou, galop, Gateau, genro, gigot, go-slow, Gounod, Guangzhou, gung ho, hallo, Hangzhou, Hankow, heave-ho, hedgerow, heigh-ho, hello, hollo, hullo, inflow, jabot, Jane Doe, jim crow, Jinzhou, John Doe, Hounslow, kayo, KO, Kwangchow, Lanzhou, longbow, low-low, macho, mahoe, maillot, manteau, Marlowe, matelot, merlot, Meursault, Miró, misknow, Moho, mojo, Monroe, morceau, Moscow, mucro, mudflow, nightglow, no-no, no-show, nouveau, outflow, outgo, outgrow, oxbow, Paot'ou, Pernod, picot, Pinot, plateau, pronto, Quanzhou, rainbow, reflow, regrow, repo, reseau, rondeau, rondo, Roseau, rouleau, Rousseau, sabot, salchow, scarecrow, self-sow, serow, shadblow, Shantou, sideshow, skid row, Soho, so-so, sourdough, sunbow, Suzhou, tableau, Taizhou, tiptoe, Thoreau, tonneau, trousseau, Trudeau, uh-oh, unsew, up-bow, upthrow, van Gogh, Watteau, windrow, windthrow, Xuzhou, Zhangzhou, Zhengzhou, Zhuzhon, Zibo, afterglow, aikido, alpenglow, [illegible]ngelo, apropos, art deco, art [illegible]au, audio, Baguio, [illegible]barrio, Bergamo, bibelot, Bilbao, bordereau, Borneo, buffalo, Buffalo, bungalow, Bushido, buteo, calico, cameo, cachalot, cembalo, centimo, CEO, chassepot, cheerio, Cicero, Clemenceau, cogito, comedo, comme il faut, Comoro, counterflow, curaçao, Curaçao, curassow, curio, daimyo, danio, dataflow, Delano, Diderot, do-si-do, domino, dynamo, embryo, entrepôt, Erato, escargot, Eskimo, extrados, fabliau, folio, fricandeau, furbelow, gigolo, go-no-go, guacharo, hammertoe, haricot, heel-and toe, hetero, HMO, Holy Joe, Idaho, indigo, Jericho, kakapo, Kosciuszko, latigo, long-ago, Maceió, Manchukuo, Mario, massicot, medico, Mexico, mistletoe, modulo, Monaco, Navaho, Navajo, NCO, nuncio, oleo, olio, overflow, overgrow, overthrow, ovolo, Pamlico, Papago, patio, peridot, picaro, piccolo, Pierrot, polio, pomelo, pompano, portico, PPO, Prospero, proximo, quid pro quo, radio, raree-show, ratio, Richard Roe, Rochambeau, rococo, rodeo, Romeo, saddlebow, Sapporo, sapsago, Scorpio, semipro, sloppy joe, so-and-so, SRO, standing O, status quo, stereo, stop-and-go, studio, subito, tallyho, tangelo, Taranto, ticktacktoe, tic-tac-toe, tit-tat-toe, TKO, to-and-fro, Tokyo, tombolo, touch-and-go, touraco, tournedos, tremolo, tuckahoe, tupelo, UFO, ultimo, undergo, undertow, Veneto, vertigo, vibrio, virago, vireo, zydeco, Antonio, Arapaho, centesimo, con spirito, continuo, DMSO, Etobicoke, ex nihilo, fantastico, fellatio, Fernando Póo, fortissimo, Geronimo, get-up-and-go, Guantanamo, hereinbelow, in utero, in vacuo, La Rochfoucauld, lentissimo, lothario, magnifico, malapropos, milesimo, New Mexico, oregano, politico, portfolio, presidio, prestissimo, punctilio, Querétaro, Quintana Roo, Rosario, quo warranto, Sarajevo, scenario, simpatico, Zhangjiakou, ab initio, archipelago, braggadocio, duodecimo, ex officio, generalissimo, impresario, internuncio, oratorio, Paramaribo, pianissimo, rose of Jericho

[2]**ow** \aů\ bough, bow, brow, chiao, chow, ciao, cow, dhow, Dou, dow, Dow, Frau, hao, how, howe, Howe, jow, Lao, mow, now, ow, plow, pow, prau, prow, row, scow, slough, sough, sow, Tao, tau, thou, vow, wow, Yao, allow, avow, Belau, Bissau, bowwow, cacao, cahow, Callao, Davao, chowchow, chow chow, Cracow, Donau, endow, enow, erenow, eyebrow, gangplow, Haikou, Hankow, hausfrau, haymow, highbrow, hoosegow, Jungfrau, know-how, kowtow, Krakow, landau, lowbrow, luau, Lucknow, Macao, meow, miaow, Moscow, Niihau, nohow, Pelau, powwow, Qing-dao, snowplow, somehow, Zwickau, anyhow, curaçao, Curaçao, disallow, disavow, disendow, middlebrow, Guinea-Bissau, Marianao, Mindanao, holier-than-thou

[3]**ow** \ȯv\ see [2]OFF

owa \ō-vᵊ\ see OVA

[1]**owable** \ō-ə-bəl\ knowable, sewable, unknowable

[2]**owable** \aů-ə-bəl\ plowable, allowable, disavowable

owage \ō-ij\ flowage, stowage, towage

[1]**owal** \ō-əl\ see OEL

[2]**owal** \aůl\ see [2]OWL

[1]**owan** \ō-ən\ see [1]OAN

[2]**owan** \aů-ən\ Gawain, gowan, rowan, rowen, Bandar Seri Begawan

[1]**oward** \ōrd\ see OARD

[2]**oward** \aůrd\ see OWERED

[1]**owd** \üd\ see UDE

[2]**owd** \aůd\ see [2]OUD

owdah \aůd-ə\ see [3]AUDE

owder \aůd-ər\ chowder, powder, gunpowder, five-spice powder—*also comparatives of adjectives listed at* [2]OUD

owdown \ō-daůn\ blowdown,

lowdown, showdown, slowdown

owdy \aủd-ē\ cloudy, dowdy, howdy, rowdy, cum laude, pandowdy, magna cum laude, summa cum laude

owe \ō\ see [1]OW

[1]owed \ōd\ see ODE

[2]owed \aủd\ see [2]OUD

owedly \aủ-əd-lē\ allowedly, avowedly

owel \aủl\ see [2]OWL

oweling \aủ-liŋ\ see [2]OWLING

[1]owell \aủl\ see [2]OWL

[2]owell \ō-əl\ see OEL

[1]owen \aủ-ən\ see [2]OWAN

[2]owen \ō-ən\ see [1]OAN

[1]ower \ōr\ see [1]OR

[2]ower \aủr\ bower, cower, dour, dower, flour, flower, gaur, giaour, glower, hour, lower, our, plower, power, scour, shower, sour, tour, tower, vower, avower, cornflower, deflower, devour, embower, empower, firepower, high-power, man-hour, mayflower, moonflower, off-hour, pasqueflower, Peshawar, repower, safflower, sunflower, wallflower, watchtower, wildflower, willpower, candlepower, cauliflower, disendower, Eisenhower, overpower, passionflower, person-hour, Schopenhauer, superpower, sweet-and-sour, thundershower, waterpower, womanpower

[3]ower \ō-ər\ see [5]OER

owered \aủrd\ coward, flowered, powered, towered, high-powered, ivory-towered, superpowered, underpowered—*also pasts of verbs listed at* [2]OWER

owerer \aủr-ər\ see [3]OURER

owerful \aủr-fəl\ flowerful, powerful

owering \aủ-riŋ\ lowering, nonflowering

owery \aủr-ē\ bowery, cauri, dowry, floury, flowery, kauri, Maori, showery

owff \aủf\ howff, langlauf

owhee \ō-ē\ see OWY

owie \aủ-ē\ Maui, zowie

owing \ō-iŋ\ see [1]OING

[1]owl \ōl\ see [1]OLE

[2]owl \aủl\ bowel, cowl, dowel, foul, fowl, growl, Howell, howl, jowl, owl, prowl, rowel, scowl, towel, trowel, vowel, yowl, avowal, batfowl, befoul, embowel, peafowl, seafowl, wildfowl, disavowal, disembowel, waterfowl

owland \ō-lənd\ lowland, Poland, Roland

owledge \äl-ij\ college, knowledge, acknowledge, foreknowledge

[1]owler \ō-lər\ see OLLER

[2]owler \aủ-lər\ growler, howler, waterfowler

owless \ō-ləs\ see OLUS

owline \ō-lən\ see OLON

[1]owling \ō-liŋ\ see OLLING

[2]owling \aủ-liŋ\ cowling, growling, howling, toweling, antifouling, biofouling, waterfowling

owlock \äl-ək\ see OLOCH

[1]owly \ō-lē\ see [1]OLY

[2]**owly** \au̇-lē\ foully, growly, haole, jowly
[1]**owman** \ō-mən\ see OMAN
[2]**owman** \au̇-mən\ bowman, cowman, plowman
ow-me \ō-mē\ see OAMY
[1]**own** \ōn\ see [1]ONE
[2]**own** \au̇n\ brown, Brown, clown, crown, down, Down, drown, frown, gown, lown, noun, town, blowdown, boomtown, breakdown, Bridgetown, bringdown, Capetown, clampdown, closedown, comedown, cooldown, countdown, crackdown, crosstown, downtown, drawdown, embrown, facedown, Freetown, Georgetown, George Town, godown, hoedown, hometown, Jamestown, knockdown, letdown, lockdown, lookdown, lowdown, markdown, meltdown, nightgown, pastedown, phasedown, pronoun, pushdown, put-down, renown, rubdown, rundown, scale-down, shakedown, showdown, shutdown, sit-down, slowdown, Southdown, splashdown, stand-down, step-down, stripped-down, sundown, thumbs-down, tie-down, top-down, touchdown, turndown, uncrown, uptown, Von Braun, write-down, Youngstown, Allentown, broken-down, buttondown, Charlottetown, Chinatown, dressing-down, eiderdown, Germantown, hand-me-down, reach-me-down, shantytown, tumbledown, upside down, watered-down, man-about-town
ownded \au̇n-dəd\ see OUNDED
ownding \au̇n-diŋ\ see OUNDING
[1]**owned** \ōnd\ see [1]ONED
[2]**owned** \au̇nd\ see [2]OUND
[1]**owner** \ō-nər\ see [1]ONER
[2]**owner** \ü-nər\ see OONER
[3]**owner** \au̇-nər\ browner, crowner, downer, sundowner
owness \ō-nəs\ see [2]ONUS
ownia \ō-nē-ə\ see [1]ONIA
ownie \au̇-nē\ see OWNY
[1]**owning** \ō-niŋ\ see [2]ONING
[2]**owning** \au̇-ning\ Browning—*also present participles of verbs listed at* [2]OWN
ownish \au̇-nish\ brownish, clownish
ownlet \au̇n-lət\ roundlet, townlet
ownsman \au̇nz-mən\ gownsman, groundsman, roundsman, townsman
owny \au̇-nē\ brownie, browny, downy, townie
owper \ü-pər\ see OOPER
owry \au̇r-ē\ see OWERY
owse \au̇z\ see [2]OUSE
owser \au̇-zər\ see OUSER
owson \au̇z-ᵊn\ thousand, advowson
owster \ō-stər\ see OASTER
owsy \au̇-zē\ blousy, blowsy, drowsy, lousy
owth \ōth\ both, growth, loath, loth, oath, quoth, sloth, troth,

wroth, betroth, outgrowth, upgrowth, Alioth, intergrowth, overgrowth, undergrowth

owy \ō-ē\ blowy, Chloe, doughy, joey, Joey, showy, snowy, towhee, echoey, kalanchoe

owys \ō-əs\ see [3]OIS

ox \äks\ box, cox, fox, Fox, gox, Knox, lox, ox, pax, phlox, pox, aurochs, bandbox, boondocks, cowpox, detox, dreadlocks, firebox, Fort Knox, gearbox, gravlax, hatbox, hotbox, icebox, jukebox, lockbox, mailbox, matchbox, musk-ox, outfox, pillbox, postbox, redox, saltbox, sandbox, skybox, smallpox, snuffbox, soapbox, strongbox, sweatbox, toolbox, unbox, volvox, witness-box, workbox, Xerox, chatterbox, equinox, orthodox, Orthodox, paradox, pillar-box, shadowbox, Skinner box, tinderbox, econobox, Greek Orthodox, heterodox, homeobox, jack-in-the-box, unorthodox, neoorthodox, dementia praecox—*also plurals and possessives of nouns and third person singular presents of verbs listed at* [1]OCK

oxen \äk-sən\ oxen, Niedersachsen

oxer \äk-sər\ boxer, Boxer, bobby-soxer

oxie \äk-sē\ see OXY

oxin \äk-sən\ coxswain, tocsin, toxin, dioxin, aflatoxin, mycotoxin

oxswain \äk-sən\ see OXIN

oxy \äk-sē\ boxy, doxy, foxy, moxie, oxy, proxy, epoxy, orthodoxy, Orthodoxy, heterodoxy, neoorthodoxy

oy \ȯi\ boy, buoy, cloy, coy, foy, goy, hoy, joy, Joy, koi, ploy, poi, Roy, soy, strawy, toy, troy, Troy, ahoy, alloy, Amoy, annoy, batboy, bellboy, bok choy, borzoi, busboy, callboy, carboy, charpoy, choirboy, convoy, cowboy, decoy, deploy, destroy, doughboy, employ, enjoy, envoy, fly-boy, footboy, Hanoi, hautbois, highboy, houseboy, killjoy, Khoikhoi, Leroy, linkboy, lowboy, McCoy, newsboy, pak choi, playboy,plowboy, po'boy, postboy, potboy, Quemoy, Rob Roy, Saint Croix, Savoy, schoolboy, sepoy, tallboy, teapoy, Tolstoy, tomboy, travois, viceroy, Adonai, attaboy, bullyboy, copyboy, corduroy, hoi polloi, Illinois, Iroquois, Kawagoe, maccaboy, Niterói, overjoy, paperboy, redeploy, reemploy, Tinkertoy, Helen of Troy

oya \ȯi-ə\ see OIA

oyable \ȯi-ə-bəl\ deployable, employable

[1]**oyal** \īl\ see [1]ILE

[2]**oyal** \ȯil\ see OIL

oyalist \ȯi-ə-ləst\ loyalist, royalist

oyalty \ȯil-tē\ loyalty, royalty, disloyalty, viceroyalty
oyance \ȯi-əns\ buoyance, joyance, annoyance, chatoyance, clairvoyance, flamboyance
oyancy \ȯi-ən-sē\ buoyancy, chatoyancy, flamboyancy
oyant \ȯi-ənt\ buoyant, chatoyant, clairvoyant, flamboyant
oyce \ois\ see OICE
oyd \ȯid\ see [1]OID
oyden \ȯi-d^{ə}n\ Croydon, hoyden
oydon \ȯi-d^{ə}n\ see OYDEN
oyed \ȯid\ see [1]OID
oyen \ȯi-ən\ doyen, Goyen, Iroquoian
oyer \ȯir\ coir, foyer, moire, caloyer, destroyer
oyes \oiz\ see [2]OISE
oying \ȯiŋ\ see AWING
oyle \ȯil\ see OIL
oyless \ȯi-ləs\ joyless, Troilus
oyment \ȯi-mənt\ deployment, employment, enjoyment, unemployment
oyne \ȯin\ see [1]OIN
[1]**oyo** \ȯi-ō\ boyo, arroyo
[2]**oyo** \ȯi-ə\ see OIA
o-yo \ō-yō\ see [2]OLLO
oyster \ȯi-stər\ see OISTER
[1]**oz** \əz\ see [1]EUSE
[2]**oz** \ȯz\ see [1]AUSE
[3]**oz** \ōz\ see [2]OSE
oza \ō-zə\ see [2]OSA
oze \ōz\ see [2]OSE
[1]**ozen** \əz-^{ə}n\ cousin, cozen, dozen, cater-cousin
[2]**ozen** \ōz-^{ə}n\ see OSEN
ozenage \əz-^{ə}n-ij\ see OUSINAGE
ozer \ō-zər\ see [1]OSER
ozily \ō-zə-lē\ see OSILY
[1]**ozo** \ō-sō\ see [1]OSO
[2]**ozo** \ō-zō\ see [2]OSO
ozy \ō-zē\ see OSY
ozzer \äz-ər\ rozzer, alcazar
ozzle \äz-əl\ Basel, Basil, nozzle, schnozzle

u

[1]u \ü\ see [1]EW
[2]u \ə\ Chang-de, hao-tzu
[1]ua \ü-ə\ skua, Karlsruhe, lehua, Quechua, Timucua
[2]ua \ä\ see [1]A
uable \ü-ə-bəl\ chewable, doable, suable, viewable, accruable, construable, renewable
ual \ü-əl\ see [1]UEL
uan \ü-ən\ bruin, ruin, Siouan, yuan
uancy \ü-ən-sē\ see UENCY
uant \ü-ənt\ see UENT
uart \u̇rt\ see [1]URT
ub \əb\ blub, chub, club, cub, drub, dub, flub, grub, hub, nub, pub, rub, scrub, shrub, slub, snub, stub, sub, tub, bathtub, flubdub, hubbub, nightclub, washtub, overdub, Beelzebub
uba \ü-bə\ Cuba, juba, scuba, tuba, Aruba, Santiago de Cuba
ubal \ü-bəl\ Jubal, nubile, ruble, tubal
uban \ü-bən\ see EUBEN
ubbard \əb-ərd\ cupboard, Mother Hubbard
ubber \əb-ər\ blubber, clubber, drubber, dubber, grubber, lubber, rubber, scrubber, slubber, snubber, tubber, landlubber, nightclubber, money-grubber
ubbery \əb-rē\ blubbery, rubbery, shrubbery
ubbily \əb-ə-lē\ bubbly, chubbily, grubbily
ubbin \əb-ən\ dubbin, nubbin
ubbing \əb-iŋ\ drubbing, rubbing, slubbing, landlubbing
ubble \əb-əl\ bubble, double, nubble, rubble, stubble, trouble, abubble, redouble, undouble, hubble-bubble
ubbled \ə-bəld\ bubbled, doubled, troubled, redoubled
ubbler \əb-lər\ see OUBLER
[1]ubbly \əb-lē\ bubbly, doubly, nubbly, stubbly
[2]ubbly \əb-ə-lē\ see UBBILY
ubby \əb-ē\ chubby, clubby, cubby, grubby, hubby, nubby, Rabi, scrubby, shrubby, snubby, stubby, tubby
ube \üb\ boob, cube, lube, rube, tube, blowtube, Danube, flashcube, haboob, jujube, hypercube
uben \ü-bən\ see EUBEN
ubens \ü-bənz\ Rubens—*also possessives and plurals of nouns listed at* EUBEN
uber \ü-bər\ Buber, cuber, goober, tuber
uberance \ü-brəns\ exuberance, protuberance
uberant \ü-brənt\ exuberant, protuberant

uberous \ü-brəs\ see UBRIS
ubic \ü-bik\ cubic, pubic, cherubic
ubile \ü-bəl\ see UBAL
ubious \ü-bē-əs\ dubious, rubious
ubis \ü-bəs\ pubis, rubus, Anubis
uble \ü-bəl\ see UBAL
ublic \əb-lik\ public, republic
ublican \əb-li-kən\ publican, republican
ubman \əb-mən\ clubman, Tubman
ubric \ü-brik\ lubric, rubric
ubrious \ü-brē-əs\ lugubrious, salubrious, insalubrious
ubris \ü-brəs\ hubris, tuberous
ubtile \ət-ᵊl\ see UTTLE
ubus \ü-bəs\ see UBIS
uby \ü-bē\ see OOBY
uca \ü-kə\ see OOKA
ucal \ü-kəl\ ducal, nuchal, archducal
ucan \ü-kən\ glucan, kuchen, Lucan, interleukin
ucat \ək-ət\ see UCKET
[1]ucca \ü-kə\ see OOKA
[2]ucca \ək-ə\ see UKKA
uccal \ək-əl\ see UCKLE
ucci \ü-chē\ see OOCHY
ucco \ək-ō\ see UCKO
uccor \ək-ər\ see UCKER
uccory \ək-rē\ see UCKERY
ucculence \ək-yə-ləns\ see UCULENCE
uce \üs\ see [1]USE
uced \üst\ see OOST
ucement \ü-smənt\ inducement, seducement
ucence \üs-ᵊns\ nuisance, translucence
ucer \ü-sər\ juicer, looser, adducer, Bull Mooser, inducer, lime-juicer, producer, transducer, introducer, reproducer
[1]uch \ich\ see ITCH
[2]uch \ük\ see UKE
[3]uch \əch\ see [1]UTCH
uchal \ü-kəl\ see UCAL
[1]uche \ü-chē\ see OOCHY
[2]uche \üch\ see [1]OOCH
[3]uche \üsh\ see OUCHE
uchen \ü-kən\ see UCAN
ucher \ü-chər\ see UTURE
uchin \ü-shən\ see UTION
uchsia \ü-shə\ see UTIA
uchy \əch-ē\ duchy, smutchy, touchy, archduchy
ucia \ü-shə\ see UTIA
ucial \ü-shəl\ crucial, fiducial
ucian \ü-shən\ see UTION
ucible \ü-sə-bəl\ crucible, deducible, educible, inducible, producible, protrusible, irreducible, reproducible, irreproducible
ucid \ü-səd\ deuced, lucid, pellucid, Seleucid
ucifer \ü-sə-fər\ crucifer, Lucifer
ucity \ü-sət-ē\ abstrusity, caducity
ucive \ü-siv\ see USIVE
[1]uck \ək\ buck, Buck, chuck, cluck, cruck, duck, guck, huck, luck, muck, pluck, puck, Puck, ruck, schmuck, shuck, snuck, struck, stuck, suck, truck, Truk, tuck, yech, yuck, amok, awestruck, bushbuck, Canuck, dumbstruck, Kalmuck, lame-

duck, light-struck, moonstruck, mukluk, muktuk, potluck, reedbuck, roebuck, sawbuck, shelduck, stagestruck, starstruck, sunstruck, unstuck, upchuck, woodchuck, geoduck, Keokuk, Habakkuk, megabuck, muckamuck, nip and tuck, high-muck-a-muck

[2]uck \u̇k\ see [1]OOK

ukar \ək-ər\ see UCKER

ucker \ək-ər\ bucker, chukar, chukker, ducker, mucker, plucker, pucker, shucker, succor, sucker, trucker, tucker, bloodsucker, sapsucker, seersucker

uckery \ək-rē\ puckery, succory

ucket \ək-ət\ bucket, ducat, tucket, gutbucket, Nantucket

uckle \ək-əl\ buccal, buckle, chuckle, knuckle, suckle, truckle, Arbuckle, bare-knuckle, parbuckle, pinochle, swashbuckle, turnbuckle, unbuckle, honeysuckle

uckled \ək-əld\ cuckold, knuckled, bare-knuckled—*also pasts of verbs listed at* UCKLE

uckler \ək-lər\ buckler, knuckler, swashbuckler

uckling \ək-liŋ\ duckling, suckling, swashbuckling

ucko \ək-ō\ bucko, stucco

uckold \ək-əld\ see UCKLED

uckoo \ü-kü\ cuckoo, Maluku

ucks \əks\ see [1]UX

uckus \u̇k-əs\ ruckus, Sukkoth

ucky \ək-ē\ ducky, lucky, mucky, plucky, yucky, Kentucky, unlucky, happy-go-lucky

uco \ü-kō\ pachuco, osso buco

ucre \ü-kər\ euchre, lucre

uct \əkt\ duct, abduct, adduct, conduct, construct, deduct, destruct, eruct, induct, instruct, obstruct, aqueduct, deconstruct, reconstruct, usufruct, viaduct—*also pasts of verbs listed at* UCK

uctable \ək-tə-bəl\ see UCTIBLE

uctal \ək-t^{ə}l\ ductal, ductile

uctance \ək-təns\ conductance, inductance, reluctance

uctible \ək-tə-bəl\ conductible, constructible, deductible, destructible, indestructible, ineluctable, reconstructible

uctile \ək-t^{ə}l\ see UCTAL

ucting \ək-tiŋ\ ducting, semiconducting

uction \ək-shən\ fluxion, ruction, suction, abduction, adduction, conduction, construction, deduction, destruction, eduction, effluxion, induction, instruction, obstruction, production, reduction, seduction, deconstruction, introduction, reconstruction, reproduction, photoreproduction

uctive \ək-tiv\ adductive, conductive, constructive, deductive, destructive, inductive, instructive, productive, reductive, seductive, reconstructive, reproductive, self-destructive, counterproductive

uctor \ək-tər\ abductor, adductor, conductor, constructor, destructor, eductor, inductor, instructor, reconstructor, semiconductor

uctress \ək-trəs\ conductress, instructress, seductress

uculence \ək-yə-ləns\ succulence, truculence

ucy \ü-sē\ see UICY

[1]ud \əd\ blood, bud, crud, cud, dud, flood, fud, Judd, mud, rudd, scud, spud, stud, sudd, thud, coldblood, disbud, full-blood, half-blood, hotblood, lifeblood, oxblood, redbud, rosebud, warmblood, stick-in-the-mud

[2]ud \üd\ see UDE

[3]ud \u̇d\ see [1]OOD

uda \üd-ə\ Buddha, Gouda, Judah, Barbuda, Bermuda, remuda, barracuda, Buxtehude, Gautama Buddha

udable \üd-ə-bəl\ excludable, extrudable, includable, ineludible

udah \üd-ə\ see UDA

udal \üd-ᵊl\ see OODLE

udas \üd-əs\ Judas, Santa Gertrudis

[1]udd \u̇d\ see [1]OOD

[2]udd \əd\ see [1]UD

udded \əd-əd\ see [1]OODED

udder \əd-ər\ budder, flooder, judder, rudder, shudder, udder

uddha \üd-ə\ see UDA

uddhist \üd-əst\ see [1]UDIST

uddie \əd-ē\ see [1]UDDY

[1]udding \əd-iŋ\ budding, studding

[2]udding \u̇d-iŋ\ see OODING

uddle \əd-ᵊl\ buddle, cuddle, fuddle, huddle, muddle, puddle, ruddle, befuddle

uddly \əd-lē\ cuddly, Dudley, muddly, studly

[1]uddy \əd-ē\ bloody, buddy, Buddy, cruddy, cuddy, duddie, muddy, ruddy, study, fuddy-duddy, understudy

[2]uddy \u̇d-ē\ see [2]OODY

[1]ude \üd\ brood, crowd, crude, dude, feud, food, hued, Jude, lewd, mood, nude, oud, pood, prude, pseud, rood, rude, shrewd, snood, stewed, who'd, wood, wud, you'd, allude, collude, conclude, delude, denude, elude, etude, exclude, èxtrude, exude, fast-food, Gertrude, include, intrude, obtrude, occlude, postlude, preclude, prelude, protrude, quaalude, Quaalude, seafood, seclude, subdued, transude, unglued, altitude, amplitude, aptitude, attitude, certitude, consuetude, crassitude, desuetude, finitude, fortitude, gratitude, habitude, hebetude, interlude, lassitude, latitude, longitude, magnitude, mansuetude, multitude, negritude, platitude, plenitude, plentitude, promptitude, pulchritude, quietude, rectitude, seminude, servitude, solitude, turpitude, vastitude, beatitude, correctitude, decrepitude, exactitude, inaptitude, incertitude, ineptitude, infinitude,

ingratitude, inquietude, similitude, solicitude, vicissitude, dissimilitude, inexactitude, verisimilitude
[2]**ude** \üd-ə\ see UDA
udel \üd-ᵊl\ see OODLE
udence \ü-dᵊn(t)s\ Prudence, students, imprudence, jurisprudence
udeness \üd-nəs\ see UDINOUS
udent \üd-ᵊnt\ prudent, imprudent, student, jurisprudent
udents \ü-dᵊn(t)s\ see UDENCE
uder \üd-ər\ brooder, Tudor, concluder, deluder, excluder, extruder, intruder, obtruder, preluder—*also comparatives of adjectives listed at* UDE
[1]**udge** \əj\ budge, drudge, fudge, grudge, judge, nudge, sludge, smudge, trudge, adjudge, begrudge, forejudge, misjudge, prejudge
[2]**udge** \üj\ see [1]UGE
udgeon \əj-ən\ bludgeon, dudgeon, gudgeon, curmudgeon
udget \əj-ət\ budget, fussbudget
udgie \əj-ē\ see UDGY
udging \əj-iŋ\ drudging, grudging
udgy \əj-ē\ budgie, pudgy, sludgy, smudgy
udible \üd-ə-bəl\ see UDABLE
udi \ü-dē\ see [1]OODY
udie \ü-dē\ see [1]OODY
udinal \üd-nəl\ altitudinal, aptitudinal, attitudinal, latitudinal, longitudinal, platitudinal
udinous \üd-nəs\ crudeness, lewdness, rudeness, shrewdness, altitudinous, multitudinous, platitudinous, plenitudinous, pulchritudinous
udis \üd-əs\ see UDAS
udish \üd-ish\ dudish, prudish
[1]**udist** \üd-əst\ Buddhist, feudist, nudist—*also superlatives of adjectives listed at* UDE
[2]**udist** \ůd-əst\ see OULDEST
udity \üd-ət-ē\ crudity, nudity
udley \əd-lē\ see UDDLY
udly \əd-lē\ see UDDLY
udo \üd-ō\ judo, kudo, pseudo, scudo, escudo, Matsudo, testudo
udor \üd-ər\ see UDER
udsman \ůdz-mən\ see OODSMAN
udson \əd-sən\ Hudson, Judson
udu \üd-ü\ see OODOO
[1]**udy** \ü-dē\ see [1]OODY
[2]**udy** \əd-ē\ see [1]UDDY
[1]**ue** \ü\ see [1]EW
[2]**ue** \ā\ see [1]AY
ued \üd\ see UDE
ueful \ü-fəl\ rueful, pantofle
ueghel \ü-gəl\ see UGAL
ueil \əi\ Arauil, Argentueil
[1]**uel** \ü-əl\ crewel, cruel, dual, duel, gruel, jewel, Jewel, Jewell, newel, Newell, accrual, eschewal, refuel, renewal, Pantagruel
[2]**uel** \ül\ see [1]OOL
uely \ü-lē\ see ULY
uement \ü-mənt\ see EWMENT
uence \ü-əns\ affluence, confluence, congruence,

effluence, influence, pursuance, refluence, incongruence
uency \ü-ən-sē\ fluency, truancy, affluency, congruency, nonfluency
ueness \ü-nəs\ see EWNESS
uenster \ən-stər\ see UNSTER
uent \ü-ənt\ fluent, suint, truant, affluent, confluent, congruent, effluent, influent, incongruent
uer \ü-ər\ see [1]EWER
uerdon \ərd-ᵊn\ see URDEN
uerile \u̇r-əl\ see URAL
ues \üz\ see [2]USE
uesman \üz-mən\ see EWSMAN
uesome \ü-səm\ gruesome, twosome
uesy \ü-zē\ see OOZY
uet \ü-ət\ bluet, cruet, peewit, suet, conduit, intuit
uette \et\ see [1]ET
uey \ü-ē\ see EWY
ufa \ü-fə\ loofah, tufa, opera buffa
uff \əf\ bluff, buff, chough, chuff, cuff, duff, fluff, gruff, guff, huff, luff, muff, puff, rough, ruff, scruff, scuff, slough, snuff, sough, stuff, tough, tuff, dyestuff, earmuff, enough, foodstuff, handcuff, rebuff, oeil-de-boeuf, overstuff
uffa \ü-fə\ see UFA
[1]uffe \üf\ see [1]OOF
[2]uffe \u̇f\ see [2]OOF
uffed \əft\ chuffed, ruffed, tuft, candytuft—*also pasts of verbs listed at* UFF
uffel \əf-əl\ see [1]UFFLE
uffer \əf-ər\ bluffer, buffer, duffer, puffer, rougher, snuffer, stuffer, suffer, candlesnuffer—*also comparatives of adjectives listed at* UFF
uffet \əf-ət\ buffet, tuffet
uffin \əf-ən\ muffin, puffin, roughen, toughen, ragamuffin
uffish \əf-ish\ huffish, roughish
[1]uffle \əf-əl\ duffel, muffle, ruffle, scuffle, shuffle, snuffle, truffle, kerfuffle, reshuffle, unmuffle
[2]uffle \ü-fəl\ see UEFUL
uffled \əf-əld\ truffled, unruffled—*also pasts of verbs listed at* UFFLE
uffler \əf-lər\ muffler, shuffler, snuffler
uffly \əf-lē\ bluffly, gruffly, roughly, ruffly
uffy \əf-ē\ chuffy, fluffy, huffy, puffy, scruffy, snuffy, stuffy, toughie
ufi \ü-fē\ see OOFY
ufous \ü-fəs\ rufous, Rufus
uft \əft\ see UFFED
ufti \əf-tē\ mufti, tufty
ufty \əf-tē\ see UFTI
ufus \ü-fəs\ see UFOUS
ug \əg\ bug, chug, Doug, drug, dug, fug, hug, jug, lug, mug, plug, pug, rug, shrug, slug, smug, snug, thug, trug, tug, ugh, vug, bedbug, billbug, debug, earplug, firebug, fireplug, goldbug, humbug, lovebug, stinkbug, unplug, antidrug, chugalug, doodlebug, jitterbug, ladybug,

litterbug, mealybug, shutterbug

uga \ü-gə\ beluga, Cayuga, Kaluga, Sevruga, Tortuga, Chattanooga

ugal \ü-gəl\ Brueghel, bugle, frugal, fugal, fugle, kugel, conjugal

ugar \u̇g-ər\ see UGUR

[1]uge \üj\ huge, kludge, Lodz, scrooge, scrouge, stooge, deluge, centrifuge, subterfuge

[2]uge \üzh\ Bruges, luge, rouge, deluge, gamboge, refuge, Baton Rouge

ugel \ü-gəl\ see UGAL

uges \üzh\ see [2]UGE

uggaree \əg-rē\ see [1]UGGERY

[1]ugger \əg-ər\ bugger, chugger, lugger, mugger, plugger, rugger, slugger, Bavagar, Jamnagar, Srinagar, hugger-mugger, Navanagar

[2]ugger \u̇g-ər\ see UGUR

[1]uggery \əg-rē\ buggery, puggaree, snuggery, thuggery, skulduggery

[2]uggery \u̇g-rē\ see UGARY

ugget \əg-ət\ drugget, nugget

uggie \əg-ē\ see UGGY

uggish \əg-ish\ sluggish, thuggish

uggle \əg-əl\ guggle, juggle, smuggle, snuggle, struggle

uggler \əg-lər\ juggler, smuggler, struggler

uggy \əg-ē\ buggy, druggie, druggy, fuggy, luggie, muggy

[1]ugh \əg\ see UG

[2]ugh \ü\ see [1]EW

ughes \üz\ see [2]USE

ugle \ü-gəl\ see UGAL

ugli \ə-glē\ see UGLY

uglia \u̇l-yə\ see ULIA

ugly \əg-lē\ smugly, Ugli, ugly, plug-ugly

ugn \ün\ see [1]OON

ugner \ü-nər\ see OONER

ugric \ü-grik\ tugrik, Ugric, Finno-Ugric

ugrik \ü-grik\ see UGRIC

ugu \ü-gü\ fugu, goo-goo

ugur \u̇g-ər\ booger, bugger, sugar

uhe \ü-ə\ see UA

uhl \ül\ see [1]OOL

[1]uhr \ər\ see [1]EUR

[2]uhr \u̇r\ see [1]URE

ührer \u̇r-ər\ see [1]URER

[1]ui \ā\ see [1]AY

[2]ui \ē\ see [1]EE

uice \üs\ see [1]USE

uiced \üst\ see OOST

uiceless \ü-sləs\ see USELESS

uicer \ü-sər\ see UCER

uicy \ü-sē\ goosey, juicy, Lucy, sluicy, sprucy, Brancusi, Watsui, acey-deucey, Arginusae, loosey-goosey

uid \ü-id\ Clwyd, druid, fluid

uidable \īd-ə-bəl\ see [1]IDABLE

uidance \īd-ᵊns\ see IDANCE

uide \īd\ see [1]IDE

uided \īd-əd\ see IDED

uider \īd-ər\ see [1]IDER

uidon \īd-ᵊn\ see IDEN

uiker \ī-kər\ see IKER

uild \ild\ see ILLED

uilder \il-dər\ see ILDER

uilding \il-diŋ\ see ILDING

uile \īl\ see [1]ILE

uileless \īl-ləs\ see ILELESS

uiler \ī-lər\ see ILAR

uilleann \i-lən\ see ILLON

uilt \ilt\ see ILT
uimpe \amp\ see [3]AMP
[1]**uin** \ü-ən\ see UAN
[2]**uin** \ən\ see UN
[3]**uin** \aⁿ\ see [4]IN
uing \ü-iŋ\ see [2]OING
uint \ü-ənt\ see UENT
uir \u̇r\ see [1]URE
uirdly \u̇r-lē\ see URELY
uis \ü-əs\ see EWESS
uisance \üs-ᵊns\ see UCENCE
uisard \ī-zərd\ see ISORED
[1]**uise** \üz\ see [2]USE
[2]**uise** \īz\ see IZE
uiser \ü-zər\ see USER
uish \ü-ish\ see EWISH
uisne \ü-nē\ see OONY
uiste \is-tē\ see [2]ICITY
[1]**uit** \ü-ət\ see UET
[2]**uit** \üt\ see UTE
uitable \üt-ə-bəl\ see UTABLE
uitage \üt-ij\ see [1]OOTAGE
uite \üt\ see UTE
uited \üt-əd\ see [1]OOTED
uiter \üt-ər\ see UTER
uiterer \üt-ər-ər\ fruiterer, pewterer
uiting \üt-iŋ\ see UTING
uitless \üt-ləs\ see OOTLESS
uitlet \üt-lət\ see OOTLET
uitor \üt-ər\ see UTER
uitous \ü-ət-əs\ circuitous, fortuitous, gratuitous
uits \üts\ see OOTS
[1]**uittle** \üt-ᵊl\ see UTILE
[2]**uittle** \ət-ᵊl\ see UTTLE
[1]**uity** \ü-ət-ē\ acuity, annuity, circuity, congruity, fatuity, fortuity, gratuity, vacuity, ambiguity, assiduity, conspicuity, contiguity, continuity, incongruity, ingenuity, perpetuity, promiscuity, superfluity, discontinuity
[2]**uity** \üt-ē\ see [1]OOTY
[1]**uk** \ük\ see UKE
[2]**uk** \u̇k\ see [1]OOK
[3]**uk** \ək\ see UCK
ukar \ə-kər\ see UCKER
uke \ük\ cuke, duke, fluke, gook, juke, kook, Luke, nuke, puke, snook, souk, spook, suq, tuque, uke, yeuk, archduke, Baruch, caoutchouc, Chinook, Kirkuk, Mamluk, rebuke, Heptateuch, Hexateuch, Pentateuch
[1]**uki** \ü-kē\ see [1]OOKY
[2]**uki** \u̇-kē\ see OOKIE
ukka \ək-ə\ chukka, pukka, yucca, felucca
ukkah \u̇k-ə\ see OOKAH
ukker \ək-ər\ see UCKER
ukkoth \u̇k-əs\ see UCKUS
uku \ü-kü\ see UCKOO
[1]**ul** \u̇l\ bull, Bull, full, pull, shul, wool, you'll, armful, bagful, bellpull, brimful, bulbul, canful, capful, carful, cheekful, chestful, chock-full, cupful, drawerful, earful, eyeful, fistful, forkful, glassful, handful, houseful, jarful, John Bull, jugful, leg-pull, mouthful, outpull, pailful, panful, pipeful, plateful, potful, push-pull, rackful, roomful, sackful, scoopful, shelfful, skinful, spoonful, stickful, tankful, tinful, topful, trainful, trayful, trunkful, tubful, barrelful, basketful, bellyful,

teaspoonful, dyed-in-the-wool, tablespoonful
[2]**ul** \ül\ see [1]OOL
[3]**ul** \əl\ see [1]ULL
ula \ü-lə\ Beulah, Fula, hula, moola, pula, Tula, ampulla, tabbouleh, Ashtabula, San Pedro Sula
ular \ü-lər\ see OOLER
ulcent \əl-sənt\ see ULSANT
ulcer \əl-sər\ see ULSER
ulch \əlch\ cultch, gulch, mulch
[1]**ule** \ü-lē\ see ULY
[2]**ule** \ül\ see [1]OOL
ulean \ü-lē-ən\ Boolean, Acheulean, cerulean
uled \üld\ see OOLED
ulep \ü-ləp\ see ULIP
uler \ü-lər\ see OOLER
ules \ülz\ Jules—*also possessives and plurals of nouns and third person singular presents of verbs listed at* [1]OOL
ulet \əl-ət\ see [1]ULLET
[1]**uley** \ü-lē\ see ULY
[2]**uley** \u̇l-ē\ see [2]ULLY
ulf \əlf\ golf, gulf, Gulf, engulf, Beowulf, Saronic Gulf
ulgar \əl-gər\ see ULGUR
ulge \əlj\ bulge, divulge, indulge, overindulge
[1]**ulgence** \əl-jəns\ divulgence, indulgence, refulgence
[2]**ulgence** \u̇l-jəns\ effulgence, refulgence
ulgent \əl-jənt\ fulgent, indulgent
ulgur \əl-gər\ bulgur, vulgar
ulhas \əl-əs\ see ULLUS
uli \u̇l-ē\ see [2]ULLY
ulia \ül-yə\ Julia, Puglia, Apulia, Friuli-Venezia Guilia
ulie \ü-lē\ see ULY
ulip \ü-ləp\ julep, tulip
ulish \ü-lish\ see OOLISH
ulity \ü-lət-ē\ credulity, garrulity, sedulity, incredulity
ulk \əlk\ bulk, hulk, skulk, sulk, yolk
ulky \əl-kē\ bulky, sulky
[1]**ull** \əl\ cull, dull, gull, hull, Hull, lull, mull, null, scull, skull, stull, trull, annul, Choiseul, mogul, numskull, pas seul, monohull, multihull, Sitting Bull, Solihull, Kingston upon Hull
[2]**ull** \u̇l\ see [1]UL
[1]**ulla** \u̇l-ə\ bulla, mullah, Sulla, ampulla
[2]**ulla** \ü-lə\ see ULA
[3]**ulla** \əl-ə\ see [1]ULLAH
ullage \əl-ij\ sullage, ullage
[1]**ullah** \əl-ə\ Gullah, mullah, nullah, stollen, medulla, ayatollah
[2]**ullah** \u̇l-ə\ see [1]ULLA
ullan \əl-ən\ see ULLEN
ullard \əl-ərd\ see OLORED
ullate \əl-ət\ see [1]ULLET
ulle \ül\ see [1]OOL
ullein \əl-ən\ see ULLEN
ullen \əl-ən\ mullein, stollen, sullen, Lucullan
[1]**uller** \u̇l-ər\ fuller, puller
[2]**uller** \əl-ər\ see [1]OLOR
ulles \əl-əs\ see ULLUS
[1]**ullet** \əl-ət\ culet, cullet, gullet, mullet, cucullate
[2]**ullet** \u̇l-ət\ bullet, Bullitt, pullet

ulley \u̇l-ē\ see [2]ULLY
ullion \əl-yən\ cullion, mullion, scullion, slumgullion
ullis \əl-əs\ see ULLUS
ullitt \u̇l-ət\ see [2]ULLET
ullman \u̇l-mən\ fulmine, Pullman
ullus \əl-əs\ Dulles, Agulhas, Catullus, portcullis, Cape Agulhas
[1]**ully** \əl-ē\ cully, dully, gully, sully
[2]**ully** \u̇l-ē\ bully, fully, gully, muley, puli, pulley, woolly
ulmine \u̇l-mən\ see ULLMAN
ulp \əlp\ gulp, pulp, insculp
ulsant \əl-sənt\ pulsant, convulsant, demulcent
ulse \əls\ dulse, pulse, avulse, convulse, expulse, impulse, repulse
ulser \əl-sər\ pulser, ulcer
ulsion \əl-shən\ pulsion, avulsion, compulsion, convulsion, emulsion, evulsion, expulsion, impulsion, propulsion, repulsion, revulsion
ulsive \əl-siv\ compulsive, convulsive, emulsive, expulsive, impulsive, propulsive, repulsive
ult \əlt\ cult, adult, consult, exult, incult, indult, insult, occult, penult, result, tumult, catapult, antepenult
ultancy \əlt-ᵊn-sē\ consultancy, exultancy
ultant \əlt-ᵊnt\ consultant, exultant, resultant
ultch \əlch\ see ULCH
ulter \əl-tər\ consultor, insulter, occulter
ultery \əl-trē\ see ULTRY
ultor \əl-tər\ see ULTER
ultry \əl-trē\ sultry, adultery
ulture \əl-chər\ culture, multure, vulture, subculture, agriculture, apiculture, aquaculture, aviculture, counterculture, floriculture, horticulture, mariculture, monoculture, silviculture, viniculture, arboriculture
ulty \əl-tē\ see [1]ALTI
ulu \ü-lü\ lulu, Sulu, Zulu, Bangweulu, Honolulu
ulunder \əl-ən-dər\ see OLANDER
ulva \əl-və\ ulva, vulva
ulvar \əl-vər\ see ULVER
ulver \əl-vər\ culver, vulvar
uly \ü-lē\ bluely, boule, coolie, coolly, coulee, duly, ghoulie, Julie, muley, newly, puli, ruly, stoolie, Thule, truly, tule, Bernoulli, guayule, patchouli, tabbouleh, unduly, unruly, ultima Thule
[1]**um** \əm\ bum, chum, come, crumb, cum, drum, dumb, from, glum, gum, hum, lum, mum, numb, plum, plumb, rhumb, rum, scrum, scum, slum, some, strum, sum, swum, them, thrum, thumb, alum, aplomb, become, benumb, degum, dim sum, dumdum, eardrum, ho-hum, humdrum, income, outcome, subgum, succumb, therefrom, Tom Thumb, tom-tom,

wherefrom, yum-yum, bubblegum, kettledrum, overcome, sugarplum, hop-o'my-thumb
[2]**um** \ùm\ cum, groom, Qom, Targum, mare librum
[3]**um** \üm\ see [1]OOM
uma \ü-mə\ duma, pneuma, puma, satsuma, Ancohuma, Montezuma
umable \ü-mə-bəl\ assumable, consumable, presumable, subsumable, inconsumable
umage \əm-ij\ see UMMAGE
uman \ü-mən\ blooming, crewman, human, lumen, Newman, numen, Truman, Yuman, acumen, albumen, albumin, bitumen, ichneumon, illumine, inhuman, panhuman, subhuman, antihuman, catechumen, protohuman, superhuman
umanist \ü-mə-nəst\ see UMENIST
umanous \ü-mə-nəs\ see UMINOUS
umb \əm\ see [1]UM
umbar \əm-bər\ see [1]UMBER
umbed \əmd\ green-thumbed, unplumbed
umbel \əm-bəl\ see UMBLE
umbency \əm-bən-sē\ incumbency, recumbency
umbent \əm-bənt\ decumbent, incumbent, procumbent, recumbent, superincumbent
[1]**umber** \əm-bər\ cumber, Humber, lumbar, lumber, number, slumber, umber, cucumber, encumber, outnumber, renumber, disencumber, Reynolds number, Avogadro's number
[2]**umber** \əm-ər\ see UMMER
umbered \əm-bərd\ unnumbered, unencumbered—*also pasts of verbs listed at* [1]UMBER
umberland \əm-bər-lənd\ Cumberland, Northumberland
umberous \əm-brəs\ see UMBROUS
umbery \əm-brē\ ombre, slumbery
umbing \əm-iŋ\ see OMING
umble \əm-bəl\ bumble, crumble, fumble, grumble, humble, jumble, mumble, rumble, scumble, stumble, tumble, umbel, rough-and-tumble
umbler \əm-blər\ bumbler, fumbler, grumbler, mumbler, rumbler, stumbler, tumbler
umbling \əm-bliŋ\ rumbling, tumbling
[1]**umbly** \əm-blē\ crumbly, grumbly, humbly, mumbly, rumbly
[2]**umbly** \əm-lē\ comely, dumbly, dumly, numbly
umbness \əm-nəs\ dumbness, glumness, numbness, alumnus
umbo \əm-bō\ gumbo, jumbo, umbo, Colombo, mumbo jumbo
umbra \əm-brə\ umbra, penumbra
umbral \əm-brəl\ see UMBRIL
umbria \əm-brē-ə\ Cumbria, Umbria, Northumbria
umbril \əm-brəl\ tumbril, umbral, penumbral

umbrous \əm-brəs\ cumbrous, slumberous
ume \üm\ see [1]OOM
umed \ümd\ see OOMED
umedly \ü-məd-lē\ consumedly, presumedly
umelet \üm-lət\ see OOMLET
umely \ü-mə-lē\ see OOMILY
umen \ü-mən\ see UMAN
umenist \ü-mə-nəst\ humanist, luminist, ecumenist, illuminist, phillumenist
umer \ü-mər\ bloomer, Bloomer, groomer, humor, roomer, rumor, Sumer, tumor, consumer, costumer, exhumer, perfumer, presumer, schussboomer
umeral \üm-rəl\ humeral, humoral, numeral
umerous \üm-rəs\ see UMOROUS
umerus \üm-rəs\ see UMOROUS
umey \ü-mē\ see OOMY
umf \əmf\ see UMPH
umi \ü-mē\ see OOMY
umice \əm-əs\ see UMMOUS
umid \ü-məd\ humid, tumid
[1]**umin** \əm-ən\ cumin, summon
[2]**umin** \ü-mən\ see UMAN
uminal \ü-mən-əl\ luminal, noumenal
uminate \ü-mə-nət\ acuminate, illuminate
umine \ü-mən\ see UMAN
uming \ü-miŋ\ blooming, consuming, everblooming, time-consuming, unassuming—*also present participles of verbs listed at* [1]OOM
uminist \ü-mə-nəst\ see UMENIST
uminous \ü-mə-nəs\ luminous, numinous, albuminous, aluminous, bituminous, leguminous, quadrumanous, voluminous
umma \əm-ə\ gumma, momma, summa
ummage \əm-ij\ rummage, West Brumage
[1]**ummary** \əm-rē\ see [2]UMMERY
[2]**ummary** \əm-ə-rē\ see [1]UMMERY
ummate \əm-ət\ see UMMET
ummel \əm-əl\ see [2]OMMEL
ummell \əm-əl\ see [2]OMMEL
ummer \əm-ər\ bummer, comer, drummer, gummer, hummer, mummer, plumber, rummer, slummer, strummer, summer, latecomer, midsummer, newcomer, overcomer, up-and-comer—*also comparatives of adjectives listed at* [1]UM
ummery \əm-ə-rē\ flummery, mummery, summary, summery, Montgomery
ummet \əm-ət\ grummet, plummet, summit, consummate
ummie \əm-ē\ see UMMY
ummit \əm-ət\ see UMMET
ummock \əm-ək\ hummock, stomach
ummon \əm-ən\ see [1]UMIN
ummoner \əm-nər\ see UMNAR
ummous \əm-əs\ gummous, hummus, pomace, pumice
ummox \əm-əks\ flummox,

hummocks, lummox, stomachs
ummus \əm-əs\ see UMMOUS
ummy \əm-ē\ chummy, crummie, crummy, dummy, gummy, mommy, mummy, plummy, rummy, scummy, slummy, tummy, yummy
umnar \əm-nər\ summoner, Sumner, columnar
umner \əm-nər\ see UMNAR
umness \əm-nəs\ see UMBNESS
umnus \əm-nəs\ see UMBNESS
umor \ü-mər\ see UMER
umoral \üm-rəl\ see UMERAL
umorous \üm-rəs\ humerus, humorous, numerous, tumorous, innumerous
umous \ü-məs\ brumous, humus, spumous, posthumous
ump \əmp\ bump, chump, clomp, clump, comp, crump, dump, flump, frump, grump, hump, jump, lump, mump, plump, pump, rump, slump, stump, sump, thump, trump, tump, ump, whump, mugwump, no-trump, tub-thump, callithump, overtrump
umper \əm-pər\ bumper, dumper, jumper, lumper, plumper, pumper, stumper, thumper, tub-thumper, Bible-thumper
umph \əmf\ bumf, humph, galumph, harrumph
umpish \əm-pish\ dumpish, frumpish, lumpish, plumpish
umpkin \əŋ-kən\ see UNKEN
umple \əm-pəl\ crumple, rumple
umply \əm-plē\ crumply, plumply, rumply
umps \əms\ dumps, mumps—*also plurals and possessives of nouns and third person singular presents of verbs listed at* UMP
umption \əm-shən\ gumption, assumption, consumption, presumption, resumption, subsumption
umptious \əm-shəs\ bumptious, scrumptious, presumptuous
umptive \əm-tiv\ assumptive, consumptive, presumptive
[1]**umptuous** \əm-chəs\ sumptuous, presumptuous
[2]**umptuous** \əm-shəs\ see UMPTIOUS
umpus \əm-pəs\ see [2]OMPASS
umpy \əm-pē\ bumpy, clumpy, dumpy, frumpy, grumpy, humpy, jumpy, lumpy, stumpy
umulous \ü-myə-ləs\ see UMULUS
umulus \ü-myə-ləs\ cumulous, cumulus, tumulus
umus \ü-məs\ see UMOUS
umy \ü-mē\ see OOMY
[1]**un** \ən\ bun, done, Donne, dun, fen, foehn, fun, gun, hon, Hun, jun, maun, none, nun, one, pun, run, shun, son, spun, stun, sun, sunn, ton, tonne, tun, won, A-1, begun, blowgun, chaconne, Chang-chun, Chaplin, finespun, first-run, flashgun, forerun, godson, grandson, handgun, hard-won, homespun, long

run, outdone, outgun, outrun, popgun, pressrun, rerun, sea-run, shotgun, six-gun, stepson, undone, V-1, well-done, Acheron, Algonquin, allemande, all-or-none, Balzacian, hit-and-run, kiloton, machine-gun, megaton, one-on-one, one-to-one, overdone, overrun, PL/1, Sally Lunn, scattergun, tommy gun, twenty-one, underdone, underrun, Xiamen, alexandrine

[2]**un** \ün\ see [1]OON

[3]**un** \u̇n\ Fushun, Lushun, tabun

una \ü-nə\ Buna, Cunha, Luna, Poona, puna, tuna, Altoona, kahuna, lacuna, laguna, vicuña, Tristan da Cunha

[1]**uña** \ü-nə\ see UNA

[2]**uña** \ün-yə\ see UNIA

unal \ün-ᵊl\ communal, jejunal, lagoonal, monsoonal, tribunal

unar \ü-nər\ see OONER

unary \ü-nə-rē\ unary, festoonery, sublunary, superlunary

unate \ü-nət\ unit, lacunate, tribunate

unc \ənk\ see UNK

uncan \əŋ-kən\ see UNKEN

unce \əns\ dunce, once—*also plurals and possessives of nouns and third person singular presents of verbs listed at* [1]ONT

unch \ənch\ brunch, bunch, Bunche, crunch, hunch, lunch, munch, punch, scrunch, keypunch, ploughman's lunch

unche \ənch\ see UNCH

uncheon \ən-chən\ luncheon, puncheon, truncheon

uncher \ən-chər\ cruncher, luncher, muncher, cowpuncher, keypuncher, counterpuncher

unchy \ən-chē\ bunchy, crunchy, punchy

uncial \ən-sē-əl\ uncial, internuncial

uncle \əŋ-kəl\ nuncle, uncle, carbuncle, caruncle, furuncle, granduncle, peduncle

[1]**unco** \əŋ-kō\ bunco, junco, unco

[2]**unco** \əŋ-kə\ see UNKAH

unct \əŋt\ trunked, adjunct, conjunct, defunct, disjunct—*also pasts of verbs listed at* UNK

unction \əŋ-shən\ function, junction, unction, compunction, conjunction, disjunction, dysfunction, injunction, malfunction, extreme unction

unctional \əŋ-shnəl\ functional, junctional, dysfunctional

unctious \əŋ-shəs\ compunctious, rambunctious

unctory \əŋ-trē\ emunctory, perfunctory

uncture \əŋ-chər\ juncture, puncture, acupuncture, conjuncture, disjuncture

uncular \əŋ-kyə-lər\ avuncular, carbuncular, peduncular

unculus \əŋ-kyə-ləs\ homunculus, ranunculus

[1]**und** \ənd\ bund, fund, gunned,

defund, obtund, refund, rotund, secund, cummerbund, orotund, pudibund, rubicund, underfund—*also pasts of verbs listed at* UN

[2]**und** \ünd\ bund, dachshund

[3]**und** \ünt\ see [1]UNT

[4]**und** \aünd\ see [2]OUND

unda \ən-də\ Munda, Sunda, osmunda, rotunda, barramunda, floribunda

undae \ən-dē\ see UNDI

undant \ən-dənt\ abundant, redundant, superabundant

unday \ən-dē\ see UNDI

undays \ən-dēz\ Mondays, Sundays, undies—*also plurals and possessives of nouns listed at* UNDI

undem \ən-dəm\ see UNDUM

under \ən-dər\ Bandar, blunder, plunder, sunder, thunder, under, wonder, asunder, hereunder, thereunder

underous \ən-drəs\ plunderous, wondrous, thunderous

[1]**undi** \ən-dē\ Monday, sundae, Sunday, Whitmonday, Whitsunday, barramundi, Bay of Fundy, jaguarundi, Mrs. Grundy, salmagundi, coatimundi

[2]**undi** \ün-dē\ Burundi, Ruanda-Urundi

undies \ən-dēz\ see UNDAYS

undity \ən-dət-ē\ fecundity, profundity, rotundity, moribundity, orotundity, rubicundity

undle \ən-dᵊl\ bundle, rundle, trundle, unbundle

undness \ən-nəs\ see ONENESS

undum \ən-dəm\ corundum, ad eundem, Carborundum

undy \ən-dē\ see UNDI

une \ün\ see [1]OON

uneau \ü-nō\ see UNO

uneless \ün-ləs\ see OONLESS

uner \ü-nər\ see OONER

unes \ünz\ see OONS

[1]**ung** \əŋ\ bung, clung, dung, flung, hung, lung, pung, rung, slung, sprung, strung, stung, sung, swung, tongue, tung, wrung, young, Young, among, bee-stung, far-flung, high-strung, Kaifeng, low-slung, unstrung, unsung, well-hung, adder's-tongue, double-hung, double-tongue, triple-tongue, overhung, overstrung, underslung

[2]**ung** \üŋ\ Jung, Kung, Sung, Antung, Bandung, Dandong, Dadong, Hamhung, Tatung, Kaohsiung, Zigong, Nibelung, geländesprung, Götterdämmerung

ungal \əŋ-gəl\ see UNGLE

unge \ənj\ lunge, plunge, sponge, expunge

unged \əŋd\ see ONGUED

ungeon \ən-jən\ donjon, dungeon, spongin

[1]**unger** \ən-jər\ lunger, plunger, sponger, expunger

[2]**unger** \əŋ-gər\ see [1]ONGER

ungible \ən-jə-bəl\ fungible, inexpungible

ungle \əŋ-gəl\ bungle, fungal, jungle, pungle

ungo \əŋ-gō\ fungo, mungo

ungous \əŋ-gəs\ fungous, fungus, humongous

ungry \ən-grē\ see ONGERY
ungus \əŋ-gəs\ see UNGOUS
ungy \ən-jē\ grungy, spongy
unha \ü-nə\ see UNA
uni \ü-nē\ see OONY
unia \ün-yə\ petunia, vicuña
unic \ü-nik\ eunuch, Munich, Punic, runic, tunic
unicate \ü-ni-kət\ tunicate, excommunicate
unich \ü-nik\ see UNIC
union \ən-yən\ bunion, grunion, onion, ronyon, trunnion, Paul Bunyan
unis \ü-nəs\ see EWNESS
[1]**unish** \ən-ish\ Hunnish, punish
[2]**unish** \ü-nish\ see OONISH
unit \ü-nət\ see UNATE
unitive \ü-nət-iv\ punitive, unitive
unity \ü-nət-ē\ unity, community, disunity, immunity, impunity, importunity, opportunity, European Community
unk \əŋk\ bunk, chunk, clunk, drunk, dunk, flunk, funk, gunk, hunk, junk, monk, plunk, punk, shrunk, skunk, slunk, spunk, stunk, sunk, thunk, trunk, bohunk, chipmunk, debunk, Podunk, punch-drunk, quidnunc
unkah \əŋ-kə\ punkah, unco
unkard \əŋ-kərd\ bunkered, drunkard, Dunkard, hunkered
unked \əŋt\ see UNCT
unken \əŋ-kən\ Duncan, drunken, pumpkin, shrunken, sunken
unker \əŋ-kər\ bunker, Bunker, clunker, Dunker, flunker, hunker, junker, lunker, plunker, punker, younker, debunker, spelunker
unkie \əŋ-kē\ see UNKY
unkin \əŋ-kəm\ see UNCAN
unks \əŋs\ hunks, quincunx—*also plurals and possessives of nouns and third singular presents of verbs listed at* UNK
unky \əŋ-kē\ chunky, clunky, donkey, flunky, funky, gunky, hunky, Hunky, junkie, junky, monkey, punkie, punky, spunkie, spunky
unless \ən-ləs\ runless, sonless, sunless
unn \ən\ see UN
unnage \ən-ij\ dunnage, tonnage, megatonnage
unned \ənd\ see [1]UND
unnel \ən-ᵊl\ funnel, gunnel, gunwale, runnel, trunnel, tunnel
unner \ən-ər\ cunner, gunner, runner, scunner, stunner, tonner, forerunner, front-runner, gunrunner, roadrunner, rumrunner
unnery \ən-rē\ gunnery, nunnery
unness \ən-nəs\ see ONENESS
unning \ən-iŋ\ cunning, running, stunning
unnion \ən-yən\ see UNION
unnish \ən-ish\ see [1]UNISH
unny \ən-ē\ bunny, funny, gunny, honey, money, runny, sonny, sunny, tunny, Ballymoney
uno \ü-nō\ Bruno, Juneau, Juno, numero uno

unster \ən-stər\ Meunster, punster
[1]unt \ůnt\ dachshund, Dortmund, exeunt
[2]unt \ənt\ see [1]ONT
untal \ənt-ᵊl\ see UNTLE
unter \ənt-ər\ blunter, bunter, chunter, grunter, hunter, punter, shunter, confronter, foxhunter, headhunter, pothunter, witch-hunter
unting \ənt-iŋ\ bunting, foxhunting, head-hunting, witch-hunting—*also present participles of verbs listed at* [1]ONT
untle \ənt-ᵊl\ frontal, gruntle, confrontal, disgruntle, contrapuntal
unty \ənt-ē\ punty, runty
unwale \ən-ᵊl\ see UNNEL
unx \əŋs\ see UNKS
uny \ü-nē\ see OONY
unyan \ən-yən\ see UNION
uoth \ü-əs\ see EWESS
[1]uoy \ü-ē\ see EWY
[2]uoy \ȯi\ see OY
uoyance \ü-əns\ see OYANCE
uoyancy \ȯi-ən-sē\ see OYANCY
uoyant \ȯi-ənt\ see OYANT
up \əp\ cup, dup, hup, pup, scup, sup, tup, up, yup, backup, balls-up, bang-up, beat-up, blowup, breakup, brush up, buildup, built-up, call-up, catch-up, change-up, checkup, chin-up, cleanup, close-up, cock-up, crack-up, cutup, dried-up, dustup, eggcup, eyecup, faceup, fill-up, flare-up, foul-up, frame-up, fry-up, getup, giddap, grown-up, hang-up, heads-up, hepped up, het up, holdup, hookup, hopped-up, jack-up, jam-up, kickup, kingcup, lash-up, lay-up, lead-up, letup, line up, linkup, lockup, lookup, louse up, made-up, makeup, markup, matchup, mix-up, mixed-up, mock-up, mop-up, mug up, nip-up, one-up, pasteup, pickup, pileup, pinup, pop-up, pull-up, punch-up, push-up, put-up, re-up, roundup, run-up, scaleup, screwup, send-up, setup, shack up, shake-up, shape-up, shook-up, shoot up, sign up, sit-up, slap-up, slipup, smashup, speedup, stand-up, start-up, step up, stepped-up, stickup, stuck-up, sum-up, sunup, take-up, teacup, thumbs-up, tie-up, toss-up, touch-up, trumped-up, tune-up, turnup, walk-up, warm-up, washed-up, washup, windup, wised-up, workup, wrap-up, write-up, belly up, buttercup, button-up, cover-up, dial-up, follow-up, higher-up, hurry-up, pick-me-up, pony up, runner-up, seven-up, shoot-em-up, summing-up, up-and-up, wickiup, winding-up, Johnny-jump-up, sunny-side up
upa \ü-pə\ pupa, stupa
upas \ü-pəs\ see UPUS
upboard \əb-ərd\ see UBBARD
upe \üp\ see [1]OOP
upel \ü-pəl\ see [2]UPLE
upelet \ü-plət\ see [2]UPLET

uper \ü-pər\ see OOPER
upi \ü-pē\ see OOPY
upid \ü-pəd\ Cupid, stupid
upil \ü-pəl\ see ²UPLE
¹uple \əp-əl\ couple, supple, decouple
²uple \ü-pəl\ cupel, duple, pupil, scruple, quadruple, quintuple, sextuple
³uple \üp-ᵊl\ supple, quadruple, quintuple, sextuple
¹uplet \əp-lət\ couplet, gradruplet, quintuplet, sextuplet
²uplet \ü-plət\ drupelet, quadruplet
uplicate \ü-pli-kət\ duplicate, quadruplicate, quintuplicate, sextuplicate
upor \ü-pər\ see OOPER
uppance \əp-əns\ threepence, twopence, comeuppance
upper \əp-ər\ crupper, scupper, supper, upper, stand-upper
uppie \əp-ē\ see UPPY
¹upple \üp-əl\ see ³UPLE
²upple \əp-əl\ see ¹UPLE
uppy \əp-ē\ cuppy, guppy, puppy,yuppie
upt \əpt\ abrupt, corrupt, disrupt, erupt, irrupt, developed, incorrupt, interrupt—*also pasts of verbs listed at* UP
upter \əp-tər\ corrupter, disrupter, interrupter
uptible \əp-tə-bəl\ corruptible, eruptible, irruptible, incorruptible, interruptible
uption \əp-shən\ abruption, corruption, disruption, eruption, irruption, interruption
uptive \əp-tiv\ corruptive, disruptive, eruptive, irruptive, interruptive
upus \ü-pəs\ croupous, lupus, upas
uq \ük\ see UKE
uque \ük\ see UKE
¹ur \ōr\ see ¹ORE
²ur \u̇r\ see ¹URE
³ur \ər\ see ¹EUR
ura \u̇r-ə\ dura, durra, Jura, sura, surah, Agoura, bravura, caesura, datura, Madura, tamboura, tempura, aqua pura, Arafura, Bujumbura, appoggiatura, Bonaventura, coloratura, Telanaipura, Anuradhapura, camera obscura
urable \u̇r-ə-bəl\ curable, durable, thuribleendurable, incurable, insurable, perdurable
uracy \u̇r-ə-sē\ curacy, obduracy
urae \u̇r-ē\ see ¹URY
urah \u̇r-ə\ see URA
ural \u̇r-əl\ crural, jural, mural, neural, plural, puerile, rural, Ural, caesural, commissural, extramural, intramural
uralist \u̇r-ə-ləst\ muralist, pluralist, ruralist
uran \ü-rən\ see ²URIN
urance \ur-əns\ durance, assurance, endurance, insurance, coinsurance, reassurance, reinsurance
urate \u̇r-ət\ curate, turret, obdurate, barbiturate

urative \úr-ə-tiv\ curative, durative
urb \ərb\ see ERB
[1]urban \ər-bən\ bourbon, Durban, rurban, turban, turbine, urban, Urban, exurban, suburban, interurban
[2]urban \úr-bən\ bourbon, Bourbon, rurban
urber \ər-bər\ Berber, Ferber, Thurber, disturber
urbia \ər-bē-ə\ Serbia, exurbia, suburbia
urbid \ər-bəd\ turbid, verbid
urbine \ər-bən\ see [1]URBAN
urbit \ər-bət\ burbot, sherbet, turbit, turbot
urble \ər-bəl\ see ERBAL
urbot \ər-bət\ see URBIT
urcate \ər-kət\ see IRCUIT
urch \ərch\ birch, church, Church, curch, lurch, perch, search, smirch, besmirch, Christchurch, research, unchurch
urchin \ər-chən\ birchen, urchin
urchly \ərch-lē\ churchly, virtually
urcia \ər-shə\ see ERTIA
[1]urd \úrd\ see [1]URED
[2]urd \ərd\ see IRD
urdane \ərd-ᵊn\ see URDEN
urden \ərd-ᵊn\ burden, guerdon, lurdane, verdin, disburden, unburden, overburden
urder \ərd-ər\ see ERDER
urderer \ərd-ər-ər\ murderer, verderer
urdle \ərd-ᵊl\ curdle, girdle, hurdle, engirdle
urdu \ər-dü\ see ERDU
urdum \ərd-əm\ see IRDUM
urdy \ərd-ē\ birdie, sturdy, wordy, hurdy-gurdy, Mesa Verde, Monteverdi
[1]ure \ür\ Boer, boor, bourg, cure, dour, ewer, fewer, lure, moor, Moor, Moore, Muir, poor, pure, Ruhr, sewer, skewer, spoor, stour, sure, tour, Tours, your, you're, abjure, adjure, Adour, allure, amour, Ashur, assure, brochure, ceinture, cocksure, coiffure, conjure, contour, couture, demure, detour, dirt-poor, endure, ensure, Exmoor, faubourg, Fraktur, grandeur, gravure, guipure, hachure, immure, impure, insure, inure, kultur, land-poor, langur, ligure, manure, mature, mohur, obscure, parure, perdure, procure, secure, siddur, tambour, tandoor, tenure, Uighur, unmoor, velour, velure, amateur, aperture, armature, blackamoor, carrefour, carte du jour, coinsure, commissure, confiture, connoisseur, coverture, cubature, curvature, cynosure, debouchure, embouchure, epicure, filature, forfeiture, garniture, geniture, green-manure, haute couture, immature, insecure, ligature, manicure, overture, paramour, pedicure, plat du jour, portraiture, prelature, premature, quadrature, reassure, Reaumur, reinsure,

saboteur, sepulture, sequitur, signature, simon-pure, sinecure, soup du jour, tablature, temperature, troubadour, white amur, vavasour, Yom Kippur, candidature, caricature, discomfiture, distemperature, divestiture, entablature, entrepreneur, expenditure, imprimatur, investiture, literature, miniature, musculature, nomenclature, nonsequitur, primogeniture, ultraminiature

[2]**ure** \u̇r-ē\ see [1]URY

urean \u̇r-ē-ən\ see URIAN

ureau \u̇r-ō\ see URO

[1]**ured** \u̇rd\ gourde, Kurd, urd, assured, steward, underinsured—*also pasts of verbs listed at* [1]URE

[2]**ured** \ərd\ see IRD

urely \u̇r-lē\ buirdly, poorly, purely, surely, cocksurely, demurely, impurely, maturely, obscurely, immaturely, insecurely, prematurely

urement \u̇r-mənt\ allurement, immurement, inurement, procurement, securement

uren \u̇r-ən\ see [2]URIN

ureous \u̇r-ē-əs\ see URIOUS

[1]**urer** \u̇r-ər\ curer, führer, furor, furore, juror, lurer, tourer, abjurer, assurer, insurer, manurer, procurer, tambourer, coinsurer, reinsurer—*also comparatives of adjectives listed at* [1]URE

[2]**urer** \ər-ər\ see ERRER

[1]**urety** \u̇r-ət-ē\ see URITY

[2]**urety** \u̇rt-ē\ see URTI

urey \u̇r-ē\ see [1]URY

urf \ərf\ kerf, scurf, serf, surf, turf, enserf, bodysurf

urfy \ər-fē\ Murphy, scurfy, turfy

urg \ərg\ see ERG

urgative \ər-gə-tiv\ see URGATIVE

urge \ərj\ dirge, merge, purge, scourge, serge, splurge, spurge, surge, urge, verge, converge, deterge, diverge, emerge, immerge, resurge, submerge, upsurge, dramaturge

urgence \ər-jəns\ see ERGENCE

urgency \ər-jən-sē\ see ERGENCY

urgent \ər-jənt\ urgent, assurgent, convergent, detergent, divergent, emergent, insurgent, resurgent, preemergent

urgeon \ər-jən\ burgeon, sturgeon, surgeon, virgin

[1]**urger** \ər-gər\ burgher, turgor, cheeseburger, hamburger, Limburger

[2]**urger** \ər-jər\ see ERGER

urgery \ərj-rē\ see ERJURY

[1]**urgh** \ər-ə\ see [1]OROUGH

[2]**urgh** \ər-ō\ see [1]URROW

[3]**urgh** \ərg\ see ERG

urgher \ər-gər\ see [1]URGER

urgic \ər-jik\ see ERGIC

urgical \ər-ji-kəl\ surgical, liturgical, theurgical, dramaturgical

urgid \ər-jəd\ turgid, synergid

urgle \ər-gəl\ burgle, gurgle

urgor \ər-gər\ see [1]URGER

urgy \ər-jē\ clergy, dramaturgy, metallurgy
uri \u̇r-ē\ see [1]URY
[1]**urial** \u̇r-ē-əl\ curial, urial, Uriel, mercurial, seigneurial, tenurial, entrepreneurial
[2]**urial** \er-ē-əl\ see ARIAL
urian \u̇r-ē-ən\ durian, Hurrian, Arthurian, centurion, epicurean
uriance \u̇r-ē-əns\ see URIENCE
uriant \u̇r-ē-ənt\ see URIENT
[1]**urible** \u̇r-ə-bəl\ see URABLE
[2]**urible** \ər-ə-bəl\ see ERABLE
uric \u̇r-ik\ uric, mercuric, sulfuric
urid \u̇r-əd\ lurid, murid
urie \u̇r-ē\ see [1]URY
uriel \u̇r-ē-əl\ see [1]URIAL
urience \u̇r-ē-əns\ prurience, luxuriance
urient \u̇r-ē-ənt\ esurient, luxuriant, parturient
[1]**urier** \er-ē-ər\ see ERRIER
[2]**urier** \u̇r-ē-ər\ see [1]OURIER
uriere \u̇r-ē-ər\ see [1]OURIER
[1]**urin** \ər-ən\ burin, murrain
[2]**urin** \u̇r-ən\ burin, Huron, urine, Belgian Tervuren
urine \u̇r-ən\ see [2]URIN
uring \u̇r-iŋ\ during, mooring, touring
urion \u̇r-ē-ən\ see URIAN
urious \u̇r-ē-əs\ curious, furious, spurious, incurious, injurious, luxurious, penurious, perjurious, sulfureous, usurious
uris \u̇r-əs\ see URUS
urist \u̇r-əst\ purist, tourist, manicurist, pedicurist, caricaturist, chiaroscurist, miniaturist—*also superlatives of adjectives listed at* [1]URE
urity \u̇r-ət-ē\ purity, surety, futurity, impurity, maturity, obscurity, security, immaturity, insecurity, prematurity
urk \ərk\ see [1]ORK
[1]**urka** \ər-kə\ charka, circa, Gurkha, mazurka
[2]**urka** \u̇r-kə\ Gurkha, mazurka
urke \ərk\ see [1]ORK
urker \ər-kər\ see [1]ORKER
urkey \ər-kē\ see ERKY
[1]**urkha** \u̇r-kə\ see [2]URKA
[2]**urkha** \ər-kə\ see [1]URKA
urki \ər-kē\ see ERKY
urky \ər-kē\ see ERKY
url \ərl\ see [1]IRL
urled \ərld\ see ORLD
urlew \ərl-ü\ curlew, purlieu
urlieu \ərl-ü\ see URLEW
urlin \ər-lən\ see ERLIN
urling \ər-liŋ\ curling, hurling, sterling—*also present participles of verbs listed at* [1]IRL
urlish \ər-lish\ churlish, girlish
urly \ər-lē\ burley, burly, curly, early, girlie, hurly, knurly, pearly, squirrely, surly, swirly, twirly, whirly, hurly-burly
urman \ər-mən\ see ERMAN
urmity \ər-mət-ē\ see IRMITY
urmur \ər-mər\ firmer, infirmer, murmur, termer, wormer
urn \ərn\ burn, churn, curn, earn, erne, fern, kern, learn, pirn, quern, spurn, stern, tern, terne, turn, urn, yearn,

adjourn, astern, attorn, casern, concern, discern, downturn, epergne, eterne, extern, heartburn, intern, lucerne, nocturn, nocturne, outturn, return, sauternes, secern, sojourn, sunburn, unlearn, upturn, U-turn, windburn, Comintern, overturn, taciturn, unconcern

urnable \ər-nə-bəl\ burnable, discernible, returnable, indiscernible

urnal \ərn-ᵊl\ see ERNAL

urne \ərn\ see URN

urned \ərnd\ burned, durned, concerned, unearned, unlearned, well-turned, windburned—*also pasts of verbs listed at* URN

urner \ər-nər\ burner, earner, turner, discerner, returner, afterburner

urnery \ər-nə-rē\ see ERNARY

urney \ər-nē\ see [1]OURNEY

urnian \ər-nē-ən\ see ERNIAN

urnish \ər-nish\ burnish, furnish

urnt \ərnt\ see EARNT

urnum \ər-nəm\ sternum, alburnum, laburnum, viburnum

uro \u̇r-ō\ bureau, duro, euro, enduro, maduro, politburo, chiaroscuro

uron \u̇r-ən\ see [2]URIN

uror \u̇r-ər\ see [1]URER

urore \u̇r-ər\ see [1]URER

urous \u̇r-əs\ see URUS

urp \ərp\ burp, chirp, slurp, stirp, twerp, usurp

urphy \ər-fē\ see URFY

urple \ər-pəl\ purple, empurple

urplice \ər-pləs\ see URPLUS

urplus \ər-pləs\ surplice, surplus

urps \ərps\ see IRPS

urr \ər\ see [1]EUR

[1]**urra** \u̇r-ə\ see URA

[2]**urra** \ər-ə\ see [1]OROUGH

urrage \ər-ij\ see OURAGE

urragh \ər-ə\ see [1]OROUGH

urrain \ər-ən\ see [1]URIN

urral \ər-əl\ see ERRAL

urrant \ər-ənt\ see URRENT

urray \ər-ē\ see URRY

urre \ər\ see [1]EUR

urred \ərd\ see IRD

urrence \ər-əns\ concurrence, conferrence, deterrence, incurrence, occurrence, transference, countertransference

urrent \ər-ənt\ currant, current, weren't, concurrent, crosscurrent, decurrent, deterrent, occurrent, recurrent, susurrant, countercurrent, undercurrent, supercurrent

urrer \ər-ər\ see ERRER

urret \u̇r-ət\ see URATE

urrey \ər-ē\ see URRY

urrian \u̇r-ē-ən\ see URIAN

urrie \ər-ē\ see URRY

urrier \ər-ē-ər\ courier, currier, furrier, hurrier, worrier—*also comparatives of adjectives listed at* URRY

urring \ər-iŋ\ furring, shirring, stirring, skiöring—*also present participles of verbs listed at* [1]EUR

urrish \ər-ish\ see OURISH

[1]**urro** \ər-ə\ see [1]OROUGH

[2]**urro** \ər-ō\ see [1]URROW
[1]**urrow** \ər-ō\ borough, burgh, burro, burrow, furrow, thorough
[2]**urrow** \ər-ə\ see [1]OROUGH
urry \ər-ē\ blurry, burry, curry, flurry, furry, dhurrie, gurry, hurry, Moray, Murray, murrey, scurry, slurry, spurrey, surrey, Surrey, whirry, worry, hurry-scurry
ursa \ər-sə\ see ERSA
ursal \ər-səl\ see [1]ERSAL
ursar \ər-sər\ see URSOR
ursary \ərs-rē\ bursary, cursory, mercery, nursery, anniversary
urse \ərs\ see ERSE
ursed \ərst\ see URST
ursement \ər-smənt\ see ERCEMENT
urser \ər-sər\ see URSOR
ursery \ərs-rē\ see URSARY
ursion \ər-zhən\ see [1]ERSION
ursionist \ərzh-nəst\ see ERSIONIST
ursive \ər-siv\ see ERSIVE
ursor \ər-sər\ bursar, cursor, mercer, nurser, purser, worser, disburser, disperser, precursor, rehearser, reverser, traverser
ursory \ərs-rē\ see URSARY
urst \ərst\ burst, cursed, durst, erst, first, Hearst, thirst, verst, worst, wurst, accursed, airburst, Amherst, athirst, cloudburst, downburst, emersed, feetfirst, groundburst, headfirst, outburst, sunburst, liverwurst, microburst—*also pasts of verbs listed at* ERSE
ursus \ər-səs\ see ERSUS
[1]**ursy** \ər-sē\ see ERCY
[2]**ursy** \əs-ē\ see USSY
[1]**urt** \u̇rt\ yurt, Erfurt, Frankfurt, Betancourt
[2]**urt** \ərt\ see [1]ERT
urtain \ərt-ᵊn\ see ERTAIN
urtal \ərt-ᵊl\ see ERTILE
urtenance \ərt-ᵊn-əns\ see ERTINENCE
urtenant \ərt-nənt\ see IRTINENT
urter \ərt-ər\ see ERTER
urtesy \ərt-ə-sē\ see OURTESY
urthen \ər-t͟hən\ burthen, earthen
urther \ər-t͟hər\ further, murther
urti \u̇rt-ē\ pretty, surety, Trimurti
urtium \ər-shəm\ nasturtium, sestertium
urtive \ərt-iv\ see ERTIVE
urtle \ərt-ᵊl\ see ERTILE
urton \ərt-ᵊn\ see ERTAIN
urture \ər-chər\ see IRCHER
uru \u̇r-ü\ guru, kuru, Nauru
urus \u̇r-əs\ urus, Arcturus, mercurous, sulfurous, Epicurus, sui juris, tinea cruris
urve \ərv\ see ERVE
urved \ərvd\ see ERVED
urviness \ər-vē-nəs\ see ERVINESS
urvy \ər-vē\ curvy, nervy, scurvy, topsy-turvy
[1]**ury** \u̇r-ē\ curie, Curie, fleury, fury, houri, Jewry, jury, Kure, Urey, Bhojpuri, de jure, Missouri, tandoori, lusus naturae
[2]**ury** \er-ē\ see [1]ARY

urze \ərz\ see ERS
urzy \ər-zē\ see ERSEY
[1]us \əs\ bus, buss, crus, cuss, fuss, Gus, Huss, muss, plus, pus, Russ, suss, thus, truss, us, airbus, concuss, cost-plus, discuss, nonplus, percuss, railbus, untruss, autobus, blunderbuss, microbus, minibus
[2]us \ü\ see [1]EW
[3]us \üs\ see [1]USE
[4]us \üsh\ see OUCHE
[5]us \üz\ see [2]USE
[1]usa \ü-sə\ Sousa, Azusa, Medusa, Appaloosa, Gebel Musa, Jebel Musa
[2]usa \ü-zə\ Sousa, Susa, Medusa, Arethusa
usable \ü-zə-bəl\ fusible, losable, usable, abusable, diffusible, excusable, infusible, reusable, transfusible, inexcusable, irrecusable
usae \ü-sē\ see UICY
[1]usal \ü-səl\ streusel, occlusal
[2]usal \ü-zəl\ foozle, fusil, ouzel, snoozle, streusel, accusal, bamboozle, occlusal, perusal, refusal
usc \əsk\ see USK
uscan \əs-kən\ buskin, Ruskin, Tuscan, Etruscan, molluscan
uscat \əs-kət\ see USKET
uscle \əs-əl\ see USTLE
uscular \əs-kyə-lər\ muscular, corpuscular, crepuscular, majuscular
uscule \əs-kyül\ crepuscule, opuscule
[1]use \üs\ Bruce, crouse, crus, cruse, deuce, douce, goose, juice, loose, moose, mousse, noose, nous, puce, rhus, ruse, Russ, schuss, sluice, spruce, truce, use, Zeus, Aarhus, abstruse, abuse, adduce, Arhus, Atreus, burnoose, caboose, Cayuse, Cepheus, ceruse, conduce, couscous, deduce, diffuse, disuse, educe, effuse, excuse, footloose, induce, Lanús, misuse, mongoose, Morpheus, negus, obtuse, Orpheus, papoose, Peleus, Perseus, prepuce, produce, profuse, Proteus, Purus, recluse, reduce, refuse, retuse, reuse, Sanctus, seduce, Tereus, Theseus, traduce, transduce, unloose, vamoose, Belarus, Betelgeuse, calaboose, charlotte russe, introduce, mass-produce, Odysseus, Prometheus, reproduce, self-abuse, Syracuse, Typhoeus, hypotenuse, Sancti Spiritus
[2]use \üz\ blues, booze, bruise, choose, cruise, cruse, Druze, flews, fuse, Hughes, lose, Meuse, muse, news, ooze, roose, ruse, schmooze, snooze, trews, use, whose, abuse, accuse, amuse, Andrews, bemuse, berceuse, chanteuse, chartreuse, coiffeuse, confuse, contuse, danseuse, defuse, diffuse, diseuse, disuse, effuse, Elbrus, enthuse, excuse, ill-use, infuse, masseuse, misuse, perruse, peruse, recluse,

recuse, refuse, reuse, suffuse, Toulouse, transfuse, vendeuse, Betelgeuse, disabuse, interfuse, mitrailleuse, Newport News, p's and q's, Santa Cruz, Vera Cruz, Goody Two-shoes

used \üzd\ used, confused, underused—*also pasts of verbs listed at* ²USE

useless \ü-sləs\ juiceless, useless

user \ü-zər\ boozer, bruiser, chooser, cruiser, doozer, loser, snoozer, user, abuser, accuser, amuser, diffuser, excuser, infuser, peruser, multiuser

¹ush \əsh\ blush, brush, crush, flush, gush, hush, Cush, lush, mush, plush, rush, shush, slush, squush, thrush, tush, airbrush, bulrush, bum's rush, hairbrush, hush-hush, inrush, nailbrush, onrush, paintbrush, sagebrush, toothbrush, uprush, bottlebrush, Hindu Kush, underbrush

²ush \ůsh\ bush, Bush, mush, push, shush, squoosh, swoosh, tush, whoosh, ambush, Hindu Kush, rosebush, thornbush

ushabel \ə-shə-bəl\ crushable, flushable

¹usher \əsh-ər\ blusher, brusher, crusher, gusher, musher, rusher, usher, four-flusher, goldrusher—*also comparatives of adjectives listed at* ¹USH

²usher \ůsh-ər\ pusher, ambusher

ushi \ůsh-ē\ see ²USHY

ushing \əsh-iŋ\ onrushing, toothbrushing, unblushing—*also present participles of verbs listed at* ¹USH

ushu \ü-shü\ Kyushu, Kitakyushu

¹ushy \əsh-ē\ brushy, gushy, mushy, plushy, rushy, slushy

²ushy \ůsh-ē\ bushy, cushy, mushy, pushy, sushi

usi \ü-sē\ see UICY

usian \ü-zhən\ see USION

¹usible \ü-sə-bəl\ see UCIBLE

²usible \ü-zə-bəl\ see USABLE

usic \ü-zik\ music, Tungusic

usie \ü-zē\ see OOZY

usil \ü-zəl\ see ²USAL

using \əs-iŋ\ busing, trussing, antibusing

usion \ü-zhən\ fusion, affusion, allusion, Carthusian, collusion, conclusion, confusion, contusion, delusion, diffusion, effusion, elusion, exclusion, extrusion, illusion, inclusion, infusion, intrusion, Malthusian, obtrusion, occlusion, perfusion, prelusion, profusion, prolusion, protrusion, reclusion, seclusion, transfusion, Venusian, Andalusian, disillusion, malocclusion, autotransfusion

usionist \üzh-nəst\ fusionist, diffusionist, exclusionist, illusionist, perfusionist

usity \ü-sət-ē\ see UCITY

usive \ü-siv\ abusive, allusive, amusive, collusive,

conclusive, conducive, delusive, diffusive, effusive, elusive, exclusive, extrusive, illusive, inclusive, intrusive, obtrusive, occlusive, prelusive, protrusive, reclusive, inconclusive
usk \ əsk\ brusque, cusk, dusk, husk, musk, rusk, tusk, subfusc
usker \ əs-kər\ busker, husker, tusker
usket \ əs-kət\ muscat, musket
uskie \ əs-kē\ see USKY
uskin \ əs-kən\ see USCAN
usky \ əs-kē\ dusky, husky, muskie, musky
usly \ əs-lē\ pussley, thusly
uso \ ü-sō\ see USOE
usoe \ ü-sō\ trousseau, whoso, Caruso, Robinson Crusoe
usory \ üs-ə-rē\ delusory, prolusory, illusory
usque \ əsk\ see USK
[1]**uss** \ u̇s\ puss, Russ, schuss, chartreuse, sea puss, sourpuss, glamour-puss, octopus, platypus
[2]**uss** \ üs\ see [1]USE
[3]**uss** \ əs\ see [1]US
ussant \ əs-ᵊnt\ mustn't, discussant
ussate \ əs-ət\ see USSET
usse \ üs\ see [1]USE
ussel \ əs-əl\ see USTLE
ussell \ əs-əl\ see USTLE
usset \ əs-ət\ gusset, russet, decussate
ussia \ əsh-ə\ Prussia, Russia, Belorussia
ussian \ əsh-ən\ see USSION
ussing \ əs-iŋ\ see USING
ussion \ əsh-ən\ Prussian, Russian, concussion, discussion, percussion, Belorussian, repercussion
ussive \ əs-iv\ jussive, tussive, concussive, percussive, repercussive
ussle \ əs-əl\ see USTLE
ussley \ əs-lē\ see USLY
ussy \ əs-ē\ fussy, hussy, mussy, pursy, pussy
[1]**ust** \ əst\ bust, crust, dost, dust, gust, just, lust, must, musth, rust, thrust, trust, wast, adjust, adust, august, combust, degust, disgust, distrust, encrust, entrust, mistrust, moondust, piecrust, robust, stardust, upthrust, antitrust, dryasdust, unitrust, wanderlust—*also pasts of verbs listed at* [1]US
[2]**ust** \ əs\ see [1]US
[3]**ust** \ üst\ see OOST
ustable \ əs-tə-bəl\ see USTIBLE
ustard \ əs-tərd\ bustard, custard, mustard—*also pasts of verbs listed at* USTER
usted \ əs-təd\ busted, disgusted, maladjusted, well-adjusted—*also pasts of verbs listed at* [1]UST
uster \ əs-tər\ bluster, buster, cluster, Custer, duster, fluster, luster, muster, thruster, adjuster, blockbuster, combustor, deluster, gangbuster, lackluster, sodbuster, trustbuster, antitruster, filibuster
ustful \ əst-fəl\ lustful, thrustful, trustful, distrustful

usth \əst\ see [1]UST
ustian \əs-chən\ see USTION
ustible \əs-tə-bəl\ adjustable, combustible, incombustible
ustin \əs-tən\ Justin, Augustine
ustine \əs-tən\ see USTIN
ustic \əs-tik\ fustic, rustic
ustion \əs-chən\ fustian, combustion
ustious \əs-chəs\ robustious, rumbustious
ustive \əs-tiv\ adjustive, combustive, maladjustive
ustle \əs-əl\ bustle, hustle, muscle, mussel, Russell, rustle, trestle, tussle, corpuscle, crepuscle, Jack Russell
ustn't \əs-[ə]nt\ see USSANT
ustom \əs-təm\ custom, frustum, accustom, disaccustom
ustor \əs-tər\ see USTER
ustrious \əs-trē-əs\ illustrious, industrious
ustrous \əs-trəs\ blustrous, lustrous
ustule \əs-chül\ frustule, pustule
ustum \əs-təm\ see USTOM
ustus \əs-təs\ Justus, Augustus
usty \əs-tē\ busty, crusty, dusty, fusty, gusty, lusty, musty, rusty, trusty
usy \iz-ē\ see IZZY
[1]**ut** \ət\ but, butt, cut, glut, gut, hut, jut, mutt, nut, putt, rut, scut, shut, slut, smut, soot, strut, tut, ut, what, abut, beechnut, catgut, chestnut, clean-cut, clear-cut, cobnut, cockshut, crosscut, groundnut, haircut, locknut, offcut, peanut, pignut, rebut, recut, rotgut, shortcut, somewhat, tut-tut, uncut, walnut, woodcut, butternut, congregate, hazelnut, overcut, scuttlebutt, undercut, uppercut, open-and-shut
[2]**ut** \ü\ see [1]EW
[3]**ut** \üt\ see UTE
[4]**ut** \u̇t\ see [1]OOT
uta \üt-ə\ Baruta, likuta, valuta
utable \üt-ə-bəl\ mutable, scrutable, suitable, commutable, computable, disputable, immutable, inscrutable, permutable, statutable, executable, incommutable, incomputable, indisputable, irrefutable, prosecutable, substitutable
utage \üt-ij\ see [1]OOTAGE
utal \üt-[ə]l\ see UTILE
utan \üt-[ə]n\ cutin, gluten, Luton, mutine, Newton, Teuton, Laputan, rambutan, Rasputin, highfalutin
utant \üt-[ə]nt\ mutant, disputant, pollutant
utative \üt-ət-iv\ putative, commutative, imputative
[1]**utch** \əch\ clutch, crutch, cutch, dutch, Dutch, grutch, hutch, much, scutch, smutch, such, touch, nonesuch, retouch, double-clutch, overmuch
[2]**utch** \u̇ch\ butch, putsch
utcher \əch-ər\ scutcher, retoucher
utchy \əch-ē\ see UCHY

ute \üt\ boot, bruit, brut, brute, bute, Bute, butte, chute, cloot, coot, cute, flute, fruit, glout, hoot, jute, Jute, loot, lute, moot, mute, newt, pood, root, Root, rout, route, scoot, scute, shoot, snoot, soot, suit, suite, toot, tout, ut, Ute, acute, astute, Asyût, beetroot, Beirut, birthroot, bloodroot, breadfruit, butut, cahoot, Canute, cheroot, clubroot, commute, compute, confute, crapshoot, deaf-mute, depute, dilute, dispute, elute, en route, enroot, folkmoot, freeboot, galoot, grapefruit, hardboot, hirsute, imbrute, impute, jackboot, jackfruit, jumpsuit, kashruth, lawsuit, minute, nonsuit, offshoot, outshoot, Paiute, pantsuit, permute, playsuit, pollute, pursuit, recruit, refute, repute, salute, seaboot, snowsuit, solute, sunsuit, swimsuit, taproot, tracksuit, transmute, uproot, volute, absolute, Aleut, arrowroot, Asyût, attribute, autoroute, bandicoot, bitterroot, bodysuit, boilersuit, bumbershoot, constitute, convolute, Denver boot, destitute, disrepute, dissolute, evolute, execute, gingerroot, institute, involute, kiwifruit, malamute, overshoot, parachute, persecute, prosecute, prostitute, qiviut, resolute, restitute, revolute, subacute, substitute, troubleshoot, undershoot, electrocute, Hardecanute, Inuktitut, irresolute, reconstitute

uted \üt-əd\ see ¹OOTED

utee \üt-ē\ see ¹OOTY

utely \üt-lē\ cutely, mutely, accutely, astutely, minutely, absolutely, dissolutely, irresolutely

uten \üt-ᵊn\ see UTAN

uteness \üt-nəs\ cuteness, glutenous, glutinous, muteness, mutinous, acuteness, diluteness, hirsuteness, absoluteness, destituteness, dissoluteness, irresoluteness

utenist \üt-ᵊn-əst\ lutenist, Teutonist

utenous \üt-nəs\ see UTENESS

uteous \üt-ē-əs\ beauteous, duteous, gluteus, luteous

uter \üt-ər\ cooter, neuter, fluter, hooter, looter, pewter, rooter, router, scooter, shooter, souter, suiter, suitor, tooter, tutor, accoutre, commuter, computer, confuter, crapshooter, diluter, disputer, freebooter, peashooter, recruiter, saluter, sharpshooter, six-shooter, trapshooter, two-suiter, zoot-suiter, coadjutor, executor, instituter, persecutor, prosecutor, prostitutor, troubleshooter, microcomputer, minicomputer, superminicomputer—*also*

comparatives of adjectives listed at UTE
utes \üts\ see OOTS
uteus \üt-ē-əs\ see UTEOUS
[1]uth \üt\ see UTE
[2]uth \üth\ see [2]OOTH
[1]uther \ü-thər\ Luther, Uther
[2]uther \ə-t͟her\ see [1]OTHER
uthful \üth-fəl\ ruthful, truthful, youthful, untruthful
uthless \üth-ləs\ ruthless, toothless
uti \üt-ē\ see [1]OOTY
utia \ü-shə\ fuchsia, minutia, Saint Lucia
utian \ü-shən\ see UTION
utic \üt-ik\ maieutic, scorbutic, toreutic, hermeneutic, parachutic, propaedeutic, therapeutic
utical \üt-i-kəl\ cuticle, hermeneutical, pharmaceutical
uticle \üt-i-kəl\ see UTICAL
utie \üt-ē\ see [1]OOTY
utiful \üt-i-fəl\ beautiful, dutiful
utile \üt-ᵊl\ brutal, cuittle, footle, futile, tootle, utile, inutile, Kwakiutl
utin \üt-ᵊn\ see UTAN
utine \üt-ᵊn\ see UTAN
uting \üt-iŋ\ fluting, luting, suiting, hip-shooting, sharpshooting, trapshooting
[1]utinous \üt-ᵊn-əs\ glutinous, mutinous
[2]utinous \üt-nəs\ see UTENESS
utiny \üt-ᵊn-ē\ mutiny, scrutiny
ution \ü-shən\ Lucian, ablution, Aleutian, capuchin, Confucian, dilution, elution, locution, pollution, solution, absolution, allocution, attribution, comminution, consecution, constitution, contribution, convolution, destitution, devolution, diminution, dissolution, distribution, elocution, evolution, execution, exsolution, institution, involution, lilliputian, persecution, prosecution, prostitution, resolution, restitution, retribution, revolution, Rosicrucian, substitution, antipollution, circumlocution, electrocution, irresolution, maldistribution, reconstitution, redistribution
utionary \ü-shə-ner-ē\ illocutionary, revolutionary
utionist \ü-shnəst\ devolutionist, elocutionist, evolutionist, revolutionist, redistributionist
utish \üt-ish\ brutish, Vutish
utist \üt-əst\ chutist, flutist, absolutist, parachutist, therapeutist—*also superlatives of adjectives listed at* UTE
utive \üt-iv\ dilutive, constitutive, persecutive, substitutive
utl \ü-tᵊl\ see UTILE
utland \ət-lənd\ Jutland, Rutland
utlass \ət-ləs\ cutlass, gutless
utler \ət-lər\ butler, Butler, cutler, sutler
utless \ət-ləs\ see UTLASS
utlet \ət-lət\ cutlet, nutlet
utment \ət-mənt\ hutment, abutment

utney \ət-nē\ chutney, gluttony, Ascutney
uto \üt-ō\ Bhutto, Pluto, putto, Basuto, cornuto, Maputo, tenuto, sostenuto
uton \üt-^{n}\ see UTAN
utor \üt-ər\ see UTER
utriment \ü-trə-mənt\ nutriment, accoutrement
uts \əts\ see UTZ
utsch \u̇ch\ see [2]UTCH
utsi \üt-sē\ see [2]UZZI
utsk \ütsk\ Irkutsk, Yakutsk
utsy \ət-sē\ gutsy, klutzy
utt \ət\ see [1]UT
uttack \ət-ək\ see UTTOCK
uttal \ət-ᵊl\ see UTTLE
utte \üt\ see UTE
uttee \ət-ē\ see UTTY
[1]**utter** \ət-ər\ butter, clutter, cutter, flutter, gutter, mutter, nutter, putter, scutter, shutter, splutter, sputter, strutter, stutter, utter, abutter, aflutter, haircutter, price-cutter, rebutter, stonecutter, unclutter, woodcutter
[2]**utter** \u̇t-ər\ see [1]OOTER
uttery \ət-ə-rē\ buttery, fluttery, spluttery
[1]**utti** \üt-ē\ see [1]OOTY
[2]**utti** \u̇t-ē\ see [2]OOTY
utting \u̇t-iŋ\ see [1]OOTING
uttish \ət-ish\ ruttish, sluttish
uttle \ət-ᵊl\ cuittle, scuttle, shuttle, subtile, subtle, rebuttal
utto \üt-ō\ see UTO
uttock \ət-ək\ buttock, Cuttack, futtock
utton \ət-ᵊn\ button, glutton, mutton, Sutton, keybutton, unbutton, leg-of-mutton
uttony \ət-nē\ see UTNEY
utty \ət-ē\ butty, gutty, jutty, nutty, puttee, putty, rutty, smutty
utum \üt-əm\ scutum, sputum
uture \ü-chər\ blucher, future, moocher, suture
uty \üt-ē\ see [1]OOTY
utz \əts\ futz, klutz, lutz, nuts, blood-and-guts—*also plurals and possessives of nouns and third person singular presents of verbs listed at* [1]UT
utzy \ət-sē\ see UTSY
uu \ü\ see [1]EW
uvial \ü-vē-əl\ fluvial, pluvial, alluvial, colluvial, diluvial, eluvial
uvian \ü-vē-ən\ alluvion, diluvian, Peruvian, vesuvian, Vesuvian, postdiluvian, antediluvian
uvion \ü-vē-ən\ see UVIAN
uvium \ü-vē-əm\ alluvium, colluvium, effluvium, eluvium
[1]**ux** \əks\ crux, flux, lux, tux, afflux, aw-shucks, conflux, deluxe, efflux, influx, redux, reflux, Benelux—*also plurals and possessives of nouns and third person singular presents of verbs listed at* UCK
[2]**ux** \u̇ks\ see [2]OOKS
[1]**uxe** \üks\ see [1]OOKS
[2]**uxe** \u̇ks\ see [2]OOKS
[3]**uxe** \əks\ see [1]UX
uxion \ək-shən\ see UCTION
uy \ī\ see [1]Y
uygur \ē-gər\ see EAGER
uyot \ē-ō\ see [2]IO

uyp \īp\ see IPE
[1]uz \üts\ see OOTS
[2]uz \u̇z\ see [2]USE
uze \üz\ see [2]USE
uzz \əz\ see [1]EUSE
[1]uzzi \ü-zē\ see OOZY
[2]uzzi \üt-sē\ Tutsi, Abruzzi
uzzle \əz-əl\ guzzle, muzzle, nuzzle, puzzle
uzzler \əz-lər\ guzzler, puzzler, gas-guzzler
uzzy \əz-ē\ fuzzy, muzzy, scuzzy

y

¹y \ī\ ai, ay, aye, bi, buy, by, bye, chi, cry, die, dry, dye, eye, fie, fly, fry, guy, Guy, hi, hie, high, i, I, lie, lye, my, nigh, phi, pi, pie, ply, pry, psi, rye, scythe, sei, shy, sigh, sky, sly, spry, spy, sty, Tai, Thai, thigh, thy, tie, try, vie, why, wry, wye, xi, Y , aby, agley, air-dry, ally, Altai, anti, apply, assai, awry, aye-aye, Bacchae, Baha'i, banzai, barfly, Belgae, belie, bigeye, birds-eye, blackfly, blow-dry, blowby, blowfly, blue-sky, Bottai, bone-dry, bonsai, botfly, Brunei, buckeye, bugeye, bulls-eye, bye-bye, canaille, catchfly, cat's-eye, cockeye, cockshy, comply, cross-eye, deadeye, decry, deep-fry, deep-sky, deerfly, defy, Delphi, deny, descry, drip-dry, Dubai, elhi, Eli, espy, firefly, fish-eye, flyby, forby, freeze-dry, frogeye, gadfly, gallfly, GI, good-bye, greenfly, grisaille, gun-shy, Haggai, Hawkeye, hereby, hi-fi, hog-tie, horsefly, housefly, imply, jai alai, July, Katmai, Kaui, Kenai, knee-high, lanai, Lanai, lay-by, Levi, magpie, mao-tai, Masai, medfly, Moirai, mooneye, nearby, necktie, nisi, outbye, outcry, oxeye, Panay, panfry, Parcae, piece-dye, pigsty, pinkeye, Po Hai, pop eye, potpie, Qinghai, quasi, rabbi, re-try, red-eye, rely, reply, rocaille, rough-dry, Sakai, sci-fi, semi, Sendai, serai, shanghai, Shanghai, shoofly, shut-eye, Sinai, sky-high, small-fry, sockeye, stand by, standby, stir-fry, supply, swing-by, terai, test-fly, thereby, tie-dye, titi, tongue-tie, two-ply, untie, Versailles, walleye, watcheye, well-nigh, whereby, whitefly, wise guy, worms-eye, Adonai, alibi, alkali, amplify, apple-pie, argufy, basify, beautify, butterfly, by-and-by, calcify, certify, Chou En-lai, citify, clarify, classify, cockneyfy, codify, crucify, cut-and-dry, DIY, damnify, damselfly, dandify, deify, densify, dignify, dobsonfly, do-or-die, dragonfly, edify, falsify, fancify, fortify, frenchify, fructify, gasify, Gemini, gentrify, glorify, goggle-eye, goldeneye, gratify, Haggai, hexerei, horrify, Iceni, justify, lignify, liquefy, lithify, Lorelei, lullaby, Madurai, magnify, Malachi, Maracay, modify, mollify, Molokai, Mordecai, mortify, multi-ply, multiply, mummify, mystify, nazify, nitrify, notify, nullify, occupy, Olduvai, ossify, overbuy, overfly, overlie, pacify, Paraguay, passerby, peccavi, petrify, PPI, preachify, prettify, prophesy, purify, putrefy, qualify, quantify, ramify, rarefy, ratify, RBI, rectify, reify, res gestae, resupply, Russify, samurai, sanctify, satisfy, scarify, semidry, signify, simplify, sine die, specify, speechify, stratify, stultify, stupefy, Tenebrae, terrify, testify, tigereye, typify, uglify, ultrahigh, underlie, unify, Uruguay, Veneti, verify, versify, vilify, vinify, vitrify, vivify, zombify, acetify, acidify, a priori, beatify, decertify, declassify, demystify, denazify, detoxify, Dioscuri, disqualify, dissatisfy, diversify, electrify, exemplify, facetiae, Helvetii, humidify, identify, indemnify, intensify, objectify, personify, preoccupy, reliquiae, reunify, revivify, rigidify, saponify, solemnify, solidify, syllabify, transmogrify, undersupply, vox populi, a fortiori, caravanserai, corpus delicti, deacidify, dehumidify, ex hypothesi, modus vivendi, nolle prosequi, oversimplify, amicus curiae, curriculum vitae, modus operandi

[2]**y** \ē\ see [1]EE

ya \ē-ə\ see [1]IA

yable \ī-ə-bəl\ see [1]IABLE

yad \ī-əd\ dryad, dyad, naiad, sayyid, triad, hamadryad, jeremiad

yan \ī-ən\ see [1]ION

yant \ī-ənt\ see IANT

yatt \ī-ət\ see IET

ybe \īb\ see [1]IBE

ybele \ib-ə-lē\ Cybele, ambiboly

yber \ī-bər\ see IBER

ybia \i-bē-ə\ see IBIA

ybris \ī-brəs\ see IBROUS

ycad \ī-kəd\ cycad, spiked

ycan \ī-kən\ see [1]ICHEN

yean \ī-cən\ see [1]ICHEN

yce \īs\ see [1]ICE

[1]**ych** \ik\ see ICK

[2]**ych** \īk\ see [2]IKE

yche \ī-kē\ see [1]IKE

ychnis \ik-nəs\ see ICKNESS

ycia \ish-ə\ see [1]ITIA

ycian \ish-ən\ see ITION

ycin \īs-ᵊn\ see [1]ISON

[1]**ycle** \ī-kəl\ cycle, Michael, recycle, Calvin cycle, epicycle, Exercycle, hemicycle, kilocycle, motorcycle, unicycle, Wanne-Eickel

[2]**ycle** \ik-əl\ see ICKLE

ycler \ik-lər\ see ICKLER

yd \ü-id\ see UID

yde \īd\ see [1]IDE

ydia \i-dē-ə\ see IDIA

ydian \id-ē-ən\ see IDIAN

ydice \id-ə-sē\ see IDICE

ydney \id-nē\ see IDNEY

ye \ī\ see [1]Y

yeable \ī-ə-bəl\ see [1]IABLE

yed \īd\ see [1]IDE

yer \īr\ see [1]IRE

yeth \ī-əth\ see [1]IATH

yfe \īf\ see IFE

yfed \ər-əd\ see OVED

yg \ig\ see IG

ygamous \ig-ə-məs\ see IGAMOUS

ygamy \ig-ə-mē\ see IGAMY

ygia \ī-jə\ see IJAH

ygian \ij-ən\ Phrygian, pidgin, pigeon, smidgen, stygian, wigeon, religion, Cantabrigian, irreligion, callipygian

ygiene \ī-jēn\ see AIJIN

ygma \ig-mə\ see IGMA

ygnet \ig-nət\ cygnet, signet

ygnus \ig-nəs\ see IGNESS

ygos \ī-gəs\ see YGOUS

ygous \ī-gəs\ gigas, azygos, callipygous, hemizygous, homozygous, steatopygous

ygrapher \ig-rə-fər\ see IGRAPHER

ygraphist \ig-rə-fəst\ see IGRAPHIST

ygyny \ij-ə-nē\ see IGINE

ying \ī-iŋ\ crying, flying, lying, trying, high-flying, low-lying, outlying, undying, nitrifying, terrifying, underlying

yke \īk\ see [2]IKE

yked \īkt\ see [1]IKED

yl \ēl\ see [2]EAL

ylan \il-ən\ see ILLON

ylar \ī-lər\ see ILAR

yle \īl\ see [1]ILE

ylem \ī-ləm\ see ILUM

yler \ī-lər\ see ILAR

ylet \ī-lət\ see ILOT

yley \ī-lē\ see YLY

yli \ē-lē\ see EELY

ylic \il-ik\ see ILIC

ylie \ī-lē\ see YLY

yling \ī-liŋ\ see [1]ILING

yll \īl\ see [1]ILE

ylla \il-ə\ see [2]ILLA

yllable \il-ə-bəl\ see ILLABLE

yllary \il-ə-rē\ see ILLARY

yllic \il-ik\ see ILIC

yllis \il-əs\ see ILLUS

yllium \il-ē-əm\ see ILIUM

[1]**yllo** \ē-lō\ see [2]ILO

[2]**yllo** \ī-lō\ see [1]ILO

ylum \ī-ləm\ see ILUM

ylus \ī-ləs\ see ILUS

yly \ī-lē\ dryly, highly, maile, Philae, riley, shyly, slyly, smiley, Wiley, wily, Wyley, wryly, life of Riley

ym \im\ see [1]IM

yma \ī-mə\ Chaima, cyma

yman \ī-mən\ see IMEN

ymathy \im-ə-thē\ see IMOTHY

ymbal \im-bəl\ see IMBLE

ymbalist \im-bə-ləst\ cymbalist, symbolist

ymbol \im-bəl\ see IMBLE

ymbolist \im-bə-ləst\ see YMBALIST

yme \īm\ see [1]IME

ymeless \īm-ləs\ see IMELESS

ymen \ī-mən\ see IMEN

ymer \ī-mər\ see [1]IMER

[1]**ymic** \ī-mik\ thymic, enzymic

[2]**ymic** \im-ik\ gimmick, mimic, bulimic, acronymic, antonymic, eponymic, homonymic, matronymic, metonymic, patronymic, synonymic, toponymic

ymical \im-i-kəl\ see IMICAL

ymie \ī-mē\ see IMY

ymion \im-ē-ən\ see IMIAN

ymity \im-ət-ē\ see IMITY

ymmetry \im-ə-trē\ see IMETRY
ymn \im\ see [1]IM
ymp \imp\ see IMP
ymph \imf\ lymph, nymph
ymric \im-rik\ Cymric, limerick
ymry \əm-rē\ see [2]UMMERY
ymus \ī-məs\ see IMIS
ymy \ī-mē\ see IMY
yn \in\ see [1]IN
ynah \ī-nə\ see [1]INA
ynast \ī-nəst\ see [1]INIST
[1]**ynch** \inch\ see INCH
[2]**ynch** \iŋk\ see INK
yncher \in-chər\ see INCHER
ynd \īnd\ see [1]IND
yndic \in-dik\ see INDIC
yne \īn\ see [1]INE
ynein \in-ē-ən\ see [1]INIAN
yness \ī-nəs\ see [1]INUS
ynia \in-ē-ə\ see INIA
ynic \in-ik\ see [2]INIC
ynical \in-i-kəl\ see INICAL
ynn \in\ see [1]IN
ynne \in\ see [1]IN
ynth \inth\ see INTH
ynthia \in-thē-ə\ see INTHIA
ynx \iŋs\ see INX
yon \ī-ən\ see [1]ION
yone \ī-ə-nē\ see YONY
yony \ī-ə-nē\ bryony, Alcyone
yp \ip\ see IP
ypal \ī-pəl\ typal, disciple, archetypal, prototypal
ype \īp\ see IPE
yper \ī-pər\ see IPER
ypey \ī-pē\ see IPY
yph \if\ see IFF
yphen \ī-fən\ hyphen, siphon
yphic \if-ik\ see IFIC
yphony \if-ə-nē\ see IPHONY
ypic \ip-ik\ typic, philippic, genotypic, holotypic, stereotypic
yping \ī-piŋ\ see IPING
ypo \ī-pō\ hypo, typo
ypress \ī-prəs\ cypress, Cyprus, viperous
yprus \ī-prəs\ see YPRESS
ypse \ips\ see IPS
ypso \ip-sō\ see IPSO
ypsy \ip-sē\ gypsy, Gypsy, tipsy
ypt \ipt\ see IPT
yptian \ip-shən\ see IPTION
yptic \ip-tik\ cryptic, diptych, styptic, triptych, ecliptic, elliptic, apocalyptic
ypy \ī-pē\ see IPY
yr \ir\ see [2]EER
yra \ī-rə\ Ira, Lyra, Myra, naira, bell-lyra, hegira, hetaira, palmyra, spirogyra
yral \ī-rəl\ see IRAL
yrant \ī-rənt\ see IRANT
yre \īr\ see [1]IRE
yreal \ir-ē-əl\ see ERIAL
yria \ir-ē-ə\ see [1]ERIA
yriad \ir-ē-əd\ see ERIOD
yrian \ir-ē-ən\ see [1]ERIAN
yric \ī-rik\ pyric, oneiric, panegyric, see [2]ERIC
yrical \ir-i-kəl\ see [2]ERICAL
[1]**yrie** \ir-ē\ see EARY
[2]**yrie** \ī-rē\ see [1]IARY
yril \ir-əl\ see [1]ERAL
yrist \ir-əst\ see [1]ERIST
yrium \ir-ē-əm\ see ERIUM
yrna \ər-nə\ see ERNA
[1]**yro** \ī-rō\ biro, Cairo, gyro, Gyro, tyro
[2]**yro** \ir-ō\ see [3]ERO
yron \īr-ən\ see IREN
yros \ī-rəs\ see IRUS

yrrh \ər\ see 1EUR
yrrha \ir-ə\ see 2ERA
yrrhic \ir-ik\ see 2ERIC
yrrhus \ir-əs\ see EROUS
yrse \ərs\ see ERSE
yrsus \ər-səs\ see ERSUS
yrtle \ərt-ᵊl\ see ERTILE
yrup \ər-əp\ see IRRUP
yrupy \ər-ə-pē\ see IRRUPY
yrus \ī-rəs\ see IRUS
ysail \ī-səl\ see 1ISAL
ysch \ish\ see 1ISH
yse \īs\ see 1ICE
ysh \ish\ see 1ISH
1ysia \ish-ə\ see ITIA
2ysia \izh-ə\ see ISIA
1ysian \is-ē-ən\ Piscean, Odyssean, Dionysian
2ysian \ish-ən\ see ITION
3ysian \izh-ən\ see ISION
4ysian \ī-sē-ən\ see 1ISCEAN
ysical \iz-i-kəl\ physical, quizzical, metaphysical
ysis \ī-səs\ see ISIS
ysm \iz-əm\ see ISM
ysmal \iz-məl\ dismal, abysmal, baptismal, cataclysmal, catechismal
yson \īs-ᵊn\ see 1ISON
yss \is\ see 1ISS
yssal \is-əl\ see ISTLE
yssean \is-ē-ən\ see 1YSIAN
ysseus \ish-əs\ see 1ICIOUS
yssum \is-əm\ see ISSOME
yssus \is-əs\ see ISSUS
yst \ist\ see 2IST
ystal \is-tᵊl\ see ISTAL
1yster \is-tər\ see ISTER
2yster \ī-stər\ see 1EISTER
ystery \is-trē\ see ISTORY
ystic \is-tik\ see ISTIC
ystical \is-ti-kəl\ see ISTICAL
ystine \is-tən\ see ISTON
1ysus \ē-səs\ see ESIS
2ysus \ī-səs\ see ISIS
yta \īt-ə\ see 1ITA
yte \īt\ see 1ITE
yterate \it-ə-rət\ see ITERATE
ytes \īt-ēz\ see ITES
1ythe \ī\ see 1Y
2ythe \īth\ see 1ITHE
ythia \ith-ē-ə\ lithia, Scythia, forsythia, stichomythia
ythian \ith-ē-ən\ Pythian, Scythian
ythmic \ith-mik\ rhythmic, arrhythmic, eurythmic, logarithmic
ythy \i-thē\ see ITHY
ytic \it-ik\ see ITIC
ytical \it-i-kəl\ see ITICAL
ytics \it-iks\ see ITICS
yting \īt-iŋ\ see ITING
ytis \ī-təs\ see ITIS
ytton \it-ᵊn\ see ITTEN
yve \īv\ see 1IVE
yx \iks\ see 1IX
yxia \ik-sē-ə\ see IXIA
yxie \ik-sē\ see IXIE
yze \īz\ see IZE